NATIONALISM
AND CULTURE

F. ROCKER

NATIONALISM

AND CULTURE

BY RUDOLF ROCKER

Translated by Ray E. Chase

Montréal/New York
London

Black Rose Books No. AA263
Hardcover ISBN: 978-1-55164-095-3 (bound)
Paperback ISBN: 978-1-55164-094-5 (pbk.)
eBook ISBN: 978-155164-500-1
Library of Congress Catalog Card Number: 97-74153

Canadian Cataloguing in Publication Data

Rocker, Rudolf, 1873-1958
Nationalism and culture

Translated from the German.
Includes bibliographical references and index.
Hardcover ISBN: 1-55164-095-3 (bound)
Paperback ISBN: 1-55164-094-5 (pbk.)

1. Nationalism. 2. Culture. I. Title

JC263.R613 1998   320.54   C97-900728-3

Cover design: Associés libres, Montréal

C.P. 35788 Succ. Léo Pariseau
Montreal, QC H2X 0A4
CANADA
Explore our books and subscribe to our newsletter:
www.blackrosebooks.com

ORDERING INFORMATION:

North America:
University of Toronto Press
1(800) 565-9523 (Toll Free)
or +1 (416) 667-7791
utpbooks@utpress.utoronto.ca

UK & Europe:
Central Books
+44 (0)20 8525 8800
order@centralbooks.co.uk

THIS WORK IS DEDICATED TO

MILLY WITCOP-ROCKER

MY WIFE, MY FRIEND, MY COMRADE
IN ALL THESE YEARS OF STRUGGLE
FOR FREEDOM AND SOCIAL JUSTICE.

R. R.

PREFACE TO THE ENGLISH EDITION

This work was originally intended for a German circle of readers. It was to have appeared in Berlin in the autumn of 1933, but the frightful catastrophe which happened in Germany—and which today threatens ever more and more to grow into a world catastrophe—put an abrupt end there to all free discussion of social problems. That a work like this could not appear in present-day Germany will be understood by everyone who is even superficially acquainted with political and social conditions in the so-called "Third Reich"; for the line of thought which is given expression in these pages is in sharpest opposition to all the theoretical assumptions that underlie the idea of the "totalitarian state."

On the other hand, the developments of the past four years in my native country have given the world a lesson not easily misunderstood, which has confirmed in minutest detail everything that is foretold in the book. The insane attempt to attune every expression of the intellectual and social life of a people to the beat of a political machine and to stretch all human thought and action on the Procrustean bed of a pattern prescribed by the state had inevitably to lead to the internal collapse of all intellectual culture; for this is unthinkable without complete freedom of expression.

The degrading of literature in Hitler's Germany, the basing of science on a dreary race-fatalism which believes it possible to replace all ethical principles by ethnological concepts, the ruin of the theater, the misleading of public opinion, the muzzling of the press and of every other organ for the free display of sentiment among the people, the brutalizing of the public administration of justice under pressure from an unintelligent party fanaticism, the ruthless suppression of the entire labor movement, the medieval "Jew hunt," the meddling of the state in the most intimate relations of the sexes, the total abolition of freedom of conscience both religious and political, the unmentionable cruelty of the concentration camps, the political murders for reasons of state, the expulsion from their native country of its most valuable intellectual elements, the spiritual poisoning of youth by a state-conducted propaganda of hate and intolerance, the constant appeal to the basest instincts of the herd through an unscrupulous demagoguery for which the end sanctifies any means, the

vii

standing threat to the peace of the world of a military system developed
to the extreme peak and of an intrinsically hypocritical policy calculated
for the deception of friend and foe alike, respecting neither the principles
of justice nor confirmed treaties—these are the inevitable results of a
system in which the state is everything and man is nothing.

Let us not deceive ourselves; this latest reaction, which under existing
economic and political conditions is constantly gaining ground, is not just
one of those periodical phenomena which occur occasionally in the history
of every country. It is not reaction directed merely against discontented
sections of the population or against certain social movements and currents
of thought. It is reaction as a principle, reaction against culture in general,
reaction against all the social and intellectual achievements of the past two
hundred years, reaction which threatens to smother all freedom of
thought, reaction to whose leaders the most brutal force has become the
measure of everything. It is relapse into a new barbarism to which all
the presumptions of a higher social culture are alien, and whose representatives do reverence to the fanatical belief that all decisions in national
and international life are to be reached only by means of the sword.

A senseless nationalism which fundamentally ignores all the natural
ties of the communal cultural circle has developed into the political
religion of this latest tyranny in the guise of the totalitarian state. It values
human personality only as it may be of use to the apparatus of political
power. The consequence of this absurd idea is the mechanizing of the
general social life. The individual becomes merely a wheel or a cog in
an all-leveling state machine which has become an end in itself and whose
directors tolerate no private right nor any opinion which is not in unconditional agreement with the principles of the state. The concept of heresy,
a concept derived from the darkest periods of human history, is today
carried over into the political realm and finds expression in the fanatical
persecution of everyone who is unwilling to surrender to the new political
religion and has not lost respect for human dignity and freedom of
thought and action.

It is fatal self-delusion to believe that such phenomena can manifest
themselves only in particular countries which are adapted to them by the
peculiar national characteristics of their population. This superstitious
belief in the collective intellectual and spiritual endowment of peoples,
races and classes has already been productive of much mischief and blocks
for us any deeper insight into the unfolding of social phenomena. Where
a close relationship exists among the different human groups belonging
to the same circle of culture, ideas and movements are not restricted, of
course, within the political boundaries of separate states but come to prevail
wherever they are favored by the economic and social conditions of life.
And these conditions are found today in every country where the influence

of our modern civilization is felt, even if the extent of this influence is not everywhere the same.

The disastrous development of our present economic system, which led to a tremendous piling up of social wealth in the hands of small privileged minorities and to the continued impoverishment of the great masses of the people, smoothed the way for the present day social and political reaction and favored it in every way. It sacrificed the general interest of mankind to the private interest of individuals and thus systematically undermined the natural relations between man and man. Our modern economic system has resolved the social organism into its separate components, dulled the social feeling of the individual and hindered his free development. Internally, it has split society in every country into hostile classes, and externally has divided the common cultural circle into hostile nations which confront one another filled with hate and, by their uninterrupted conflicts, continually shatter the very foundations of social communal life.

It is silly to hold the "doctrine of the class struggle" responsible for this state of affairs so long as no one moves a finger to supplant the economic assumptions which underlie this doctrine and to guide social development into other paths. A system which in every utterance of its life is ready to sacrifice the welfare of large sections of the people or of the entire nation to the selfish economic interests of small minorities must of necessity loosen all social ties and lead to a continuous warfare of each against all.

To him who closes his mind to this view the great problems that our time has set us must remain forever unintelligible. To him there remains merely brute force as a last recourse to keep on its feet a system which was long ago condemned by the course of events.

We have forgotten that industry is not an end in itself but only a means to assure to man his material subsistence and make available to him the blessings of a higher intellectual culture. Where industry is everything and man is nothing, there begins the domain of a ruthless economic despotism which is no less disastrous in its operation than is any political despotism. The two despotisms mutually strengthen each other and are fed from the same source. The economic dictatorship of monopoly and the political dictatorship of the totalitarian state arise from the same asocial endeavors, whose directors audaciously try to subordinate the innumerable expressions of social life to the mechanical tempo of the machine and to force organic life into lifeless forms.

So long as we lack the courage to look this danger in the face and to set ourselves against a development of affairs which is driving us irrevocably toward social catastrophe, the best of constitutions are of no avail and the legally guaranteed rights of citizens lose their original meaning.

It was this which Daniel Webster had in mind when he said: "The freest government cannot long endure when the tendency of the law is to create a rapid accumulation of property in the hands of a few, and to render the masses poor and dependent."

Since then the economic development of society has taken on forms that have far surpassed men's worst fears and that today constitute a danger whose extent is hardly to be measured. This development, and the constantly growing power of an unintelligent political bureaucracy that regiments and supervises the life of man from the cradle to the grave, have systematically suppressed the solidaric collaboration of men and the feeling of personal freedom and have in every way supported the threat to human culture from the tyranny of the totalitarian state.

The recent World War and its frightful consequences (which are themselves only the results of the struggles for economic and political power within the existing social system) have greatly accelerated this process of intellectual disfranchisement and anesthetizing of social feeling. The call for a dictator who shall put an end to all the troubles of the time is merely the result of this spiritual and intellectual degeneration of a humanity that is bleeding from a thousand wounds, a humanity that has lost its confidence in itself and so expects from the strength of another what it cannot attain by the cooperation of its own forces.

That people today contemplate this catastrophic trend of affairs with little understanding merely proves that the forces that once freed Europe from the curse of absolutism and revealed new roads for social progress have become alarmingly weak. The vital deeds of our great predecessors are honored only in tradition. It was the great merit of the liberal line of thought of previous centuries, and the popular movements that grew out of it, that they broke the power of absolute monarchy which for centuries had crippled all intellectual progress and sacrificed the life and the welfare of the nation to its leaders' lust for power. The liberalism of that period was the revolt of man against the yoke of an insupportable overlordship which respected no human rights but treated peoples like herds of cattle that existed only to be milked by the state and the privileged orders. And so the representatives of liberalism strove for a social condition which should limit the power of the state to a minimum and should eliminate its influence from the sphere of intellectual and cultural life—a tendency which found expression in the words of Jefferson: "That government is best which governs least."

Today, however, we stand face to face with a reaction which, going far beyond absolute monarchy in its demands for power, strives to deliver over to the "national state" every field of human activity. Just as, the theology of the various religious systems hold God to be everything and man nothing, so this modern political theology regards the "nation" as everything and the citizen nothing. And just as behind the "Will of God" there always lay hidden the will of privileged minorities, so today there hides always behind the "Will of the Nation" the selfish interests of those who feel themselves called to interpret this Will in their own sense and to impose it by force on the people.

It is the purpose of this work to retrace the intricate paths of this development and to lay bare its origins. In order to work out clearly the development and significance of modern nationalism and its relations to culture, the author was compelled to touch upon many different fields which are intimately interconnected. How far he has succeeded in his task is for the reader himself to judge.

The first ideas for the work came to me some time before the War and first found expression in a series of lectures and in various articles that appeared in a number of periodicals. The completion of the work was repeatedly interrupted, by a four-years' internment and by various literary labors, so that I was finally able to arrange the last chapter and prepare this book for the press only shortly before Hitler's accession to power. Then there swept over Germany the "National Revolution," which compelled me, as it did so many others to seek refuge abroad. When I fled I was able to rescue nothing but the manuscript of this work.

Since I could not longer count upon the publication of a work of such length—to which, moreover the circle of readers in Germany was now barred—I gave up all hope that my work would ever appear at all. I had to reconcile myself to this thought, as to so many others that are bound up with a life in exile. The petty disappointments of a disillusioned writer are so unimportant in comparison with the terrible distress of the time, under the yoke of which millions of men groan today.

Then, suddenly came an unexpected change. On a lecture tour through the United States I came in contact with a host of old and new friends who took a lively interest in my work. I have to thank their unselfish activity that in Chicago, Los Angeles, and later in New York, special groups were organized which took up the task of making possible the translation of my work into English, and later of effecting its publication in this country.

I feel under special obligation to Dr. Charles James, who collaborated in the translation with untiring zeal and unselfishly undertook a task, the fulfillment of which was far from easy.

I feel further impelled at this point to acknowledge my gratitude to Dr. Frederick Roman, Prof. Arthur Briggs, T. H. Bell, Walter E. Holloway, Edward A. Cantrell and Clarence L. Swartz, who interested a larger circle of support by lecturing about my book, and by collaboration in other directions also, furthered the appearance of this work.

I owe an especial debt of gratitude to Mr. Ray E. Chase, who despite the serious difficulties imposed by his physical condition has devoted himself to the translation of my work and the revision of the manuscript, and in this has executed a task that only he can justly appreciate who knows how hard it is to render into a foreign tongue thought processes that run outside the everyday channels.

And, last but not least, I must here remember my friends H. Yaffe; C. V. Cook; Sadie Cook, his wife; Joe Goldman; Jeanne Levey; Aron Halperin; Dr. I. A. Rabins; I. Radinovsky, Adelaide Schulkind, and the Kropotkin Society in Los Angeles, who by their self-sacrificing activity have provided the material means for my work. To them, and to all of those who have given support by their efforts but whose names cannot all be mentioned here, my sincerest thanks for their loyal comradeship.

A foreigner in this country, I have met with so kind a reception that I could hope for nothing better, and to such kindness man in banishment is doubly sensitive. May this work contribute to the awakening of the slumbering consciousness of freedom. May it encourage men to face the danger which today is threatening human culture and which must become a fatal destiny for men if they do not bestir themselves to put an end to the mischief. For the words of the poet hold good also for us:

The man of virtuous soul commands not, nor obeys.
Power, like a desolating pestilence,
Pollutes whate'er it touches;
. . . and obedience,
Bane of all genius, virtue, freedom, truth
Makes slaves of men, and of the human frame
A mechanized automaton.

RUDOLF ROCKER

Croton-on-Hudson, N. Y., September 1936

TRANSLATOR'S PREFACE

At the outset the writer of this preface wishes to make an acknowledgment and an explanation. Both are rather difficult to put briefly and clearly. After the collapse of the first arrangements for the translation of this book (details irrelevant to this discussion) Charles James, with a courage that cannot be over-valued, volunteered for the task. His understanding of the proper attitude toward the translation was the finest possible; the devotion with which he applied himself to the task was without limit. Unfortunately, the technique which for certain personal reasons he felt constrained to employ proved unsatisfactory. The transcription of his rendering from the cylinders of a dictating machine was so faulty as to make necessary an almost complete re-translation of most of the chapters he undertook and drastic revision of all the others. It would therefore be unjust to hold Mr. James responsible for any part of the translation as here presented. It would be outrageous not to make plain that but for the impetus that he gave and the example that he set this translation would probably never have been made. The writer is glad to record his recognition of this fact.

For the faults which remain in this translation the writer is alone responsible.

One who has undertaken a task of this magnitude while practically bound to an armchair must needs have owed much to others—much than can never be acknowledged in detail. Mention must, however, in decency be made of some of the many obligations incurred:

First, to all of the Los Angeles members of the Rocker Publications Committee, whose names are given in the author's preface, and among these more particularly to H. Yaffe and to C. V. Cook and Sadie Cook for painstaking care of the business and financial details; to Edward A. Cantrell for invaluable assistance in verifying quotations from English language sources; to Clarence L. Swartz for formal revision of the manuscript and for useful suggestions as to renderings; to T. H. Bell for critical assistance and—especially—for friendly approval.

Second, and above all, to De De B. Welch for the unceasing loyal encouragement which has kept the writer at his task and for her indispensable help in verifying historical and artistic references.

Nationalism and Culture is the first of the works of Rudolf Rocker to appear in English. Although the author is known as a platform speaker to wide circles both in England and the United States some introduction of him to the wider reading public seems appropriate, the more so as his book is in a rather unusual degree an expression of the man.

Rudolf Rocker was born on March 25, 1873, in the ancient Rhine city of Mainz. He refers with a touch of pride to the fact that the city of his birth was founded by the Romans in 57 B.C., and that it was the birthplace of Johann Gutenberg and the site of his first printing house.

With mingled pride and affection he refers to its record of fruitful cultural activity, of democratic spirit and ready acceptance of advanced social ideas—he specifies the "Declaration of the Rights of Man"—and of resistance to oppression—he specifies its antagonism to the encroachments of the Prussian state. He mentions the friendly attitude of a large part of the population of Mainz to the South German federalist, Constantin Frantz, one of Bismarck's most determined opponents.

It seems clear that the atmosphere and the traditions of his native city profoundly influenced him in his youth.

Rocker's father was a music printer (*Notenstecher,* "music typographer"). His mother came from one of the old burger families of Mainz. Rocker early lost his parents, and his boyhood was passed in a Catholic orphans' home.

During his childhood and youth Rocker was strongly influenced in his intellectual development by his uncle Rudolf Naumann, his mother's brother, whom he described as an extremely intelligent and well-read man. The uncle instilled in young Rudolf a fondness for serious studies and assisted him in every way in the pursuit of them. He initiated the youth into the socialist movement, which at that time in Germany was completely under the intellectual domination of Marx and Lassalle. The Bismarckian anti-socialist law was still being rigorously enforced, so that open activity of any sort was out of the question, and the movement was entirely an underground one. Socialist literature was printed abroad, smuggled into the country and distributed secretly. The influence of this situation on young Rudolf is perhaps best described by a slightly condensed rendering of some extracts from one of his recent letters:

This underground activity had a peculiar attraction for me as a young man and appealed strongly to my romantic imagination. It also early developed in me a profound aversion for the brutal suppression of ideas and personal convictions.

This personal sense of justice was also the reason why the socialist movement of Germany could not hold me long. Its dogmatic narrow-mindedness and especially its outspoken intolerance of any opinion that was not in complete accord with the letter of the program very-soon brought me to the conviction that I had no place there.

It was not the idea of socialism that repelled me but their dogmatic interpretation of it, which assumed that they had found a solution for every social problem, and in particular the total lack of any libertarian concept, which was especially characteristic of the German social democratic movement. Socialism in so far as it opposed the monopolizing of the soil, the instruments of production and social wealth was certainly a sound and serviceable idea, but the permeation of this idea by all sorts of vestigial political theories robbed it of its real significance. It was clear to me that socialism was not a simple question of a full belly, but a question of culture that would have to enlist the sense of personality and the free initiative of the individual; without freedom it would lead only to a dismal state capitalism which would sacrifice all individual thought and feeling to a fictitious collective interest. Allied with the liberal lines of thought of the eighteenth and nineteenth centuries, which aimed at the freeing of personality and the elimination of political power from the life of society, it would lead to the development of a new social culture based upon free agreement among human beings and the principle of cooperative labor. And so I turned logically to libertarian socialism as expressed in the writings of William Godwin, Proudhon, Fourier, Bakunin, Kropotkin, Tolstoi, Reclus, Tucker and others.

When his school years were over Rocker was apprenticed to a book-binder, and he followed that calling until his twenty-fifth year, when he abandoned it to devote himself wholly to his studies and his literary activities. After the German custom he traveled as a young journeyman through several countries. Everywhere he got in touch with the libertarian movement and took an active part in it. A natural gift for oratory and the ability to set down his ideas in writing made him an effective worker.

Later, personal acquaintance, warm friendship and close association with men like Peter Kropotkin, Elisée Reclus, Domela Nieuwenhuis, Errico Malatesta, and others furthered his intellectual development and his literary labors, so that his name became known in the libertarian circles of all countries.

From 1893 to 1895 he lived as a political refugee in Paris. This was for him a fruitful period, as it afforded him an opportunity to acquaint himself thoroughly with the social movements of the day.

From Paris he went to London where he became interested in the

Jews of the East Side. He went to live among them and learned their language. From 1898 until the outbreak of the World War he was editor of the Yiddish *Workers' Friend* and of the monthly journal of social theory, *Germinal*.

As a non-Jew who speaks and writes Yiddish and has a clear understanding of the problems of the Jewish people and a fine sympathy for their difficulties, Rocker has had and still has a large following among the Jews of every land.

At the outbreak of the World War Rocker was arrested in London and interned for the duration of the war as an alien enemy. The story of his experiences in a British concentration camp he has embodied in a book, *Hinter Stacheldraht und Gitter*, which as a picture of a terrible but somewhat neglected aspect of the war is unsurpassed by any factual narrative to which that bloody period has given rise. It is soon to appear in English.

After the end of the war Rocker returned to Germany, where he carried on his work until Hitler's seizure of power made him once more a fugitive. He escaped with the manuscript of this book and practically nothing else. His personal belongings were seized. His private papers and correspondence and the greater part of his library of some five thousand volumes were confiscated and probably burned. For three years now he has been a man without a country.

So much for the personal background of our book.

And here it will perhaps not be out of place to remind the English-speaking public, accustomed to a much narrower meaning, that in general Rocker uses the word "socialism" in the broad sense which it commonly has on the Continent to cover all proposals for a society in which production and distribution are carried on and controlled for the benefit of all. This includes not only Marxist and other socialist programs in which collective ownership and control are administered by a central authority, the state, but also the various anarchist and syndicalist schemes which reject central authority on principle. Either specific qualifying words or the obvious implication of the context will always show when the author is referring to some particular Socialist school or program.

Rudolf Rocker's *Nationalism and Culture* is a work *sui generis*. It is at once a scholarly survey and analysis of human culture and human institutions throughout the range of known history and an eloquent, poetical, often almost passionate expression of the feeling of the writer about all of the content of the realm he surveys.

Rocker is a scholar of very unusual attainments, as all will discern from his book. He is an intellectual of keen insight and tremendous power of logical analysis. He is a competent dialectician. Somewhat unusually for one thus endowed he is also an imaginative, poetic, emotional being, incapable of indifferent attitudes, passionately participant, at least in spirit, in every struggle in which he sees imperiled those human values which he regards as precious. This, too, all will probably discern from his book, because it is this above all which permeates and vivifies the book and sets it apart decisively from all mere works of pedantry, however conscientious and scholarly. That Rocker is also a literary artist of very high rank is not so readily discerned perhaps from this translation, but no translation could entirely conceal it.

In his social thinking Rocker takes off from the teachings of Peter Kropotkin, but on the basis of these teachings he has constructed a philosophy that is essentially his own. In conversation, and for the most part in his lectures, Rocker reveals himself as highly realistic and practical; the slightly exaggerated hopefulness that breathes from his printed pages is not so prominent. When he writes, the poet in him sometimes insists on guiding the pen. But the poet guides it pleasingly and well, and though he may on occasion for a moment forget the realities, he never disputes them.

It is hardly necessary to say that *Nationalism and Culture* is not a handbook of Rocker's philosophy. It is, of course, just his analysis and evaluation of the material treated: an analysis and evaluation, naturally, in the light of his philosophy.

The contrast between Rocker's conception of man, his history, his culture, and his institutions and such conceptions as underlie the economic determinism of Marx, the mystic destiny of Spengler, the almost mathematical patterning of Pareto, and so on, will be recognized, of course, by every reader.

Having recognized that the contrast exists the reader may at first feel impatient to find that it is nowhere explicitly defined in the book and that he is unable to state for himself in just what, on the whole, it consists. A moment's analysis will dispel the impatience: Rocker has made it his guiding principle to take man as given and, taking him as given, he finds him altogether too complex and incalculable to be formulated at all— unless it be a formula to say that he *is* complex and incalculable.

And the standard of value, the test that he applies to cultures, institutions, social forms, is that they shall leave to this incalculable complexity the utmost possible freedom—the utmost opportunity to be complex and incalculable. His indictment of authority is that it seeks always and inevitably to make man simple and calculable, seeks, to make sure that he will always do the expected thing at the expected time; and so must also decree that he may do only certain sorts of things at all.

It will be recognized also that Rocker has not always been completely objective in his conception of man, has not always succeeded in taking man quite as he is given (or at any rate as he seems to the translator and probably to some others to be given) but has sometimes had in mind a man of finer sensibility, of loftier character, of profounder and more sympathetic social feeling than—to employ what Rocker calls a loan-translation from the German—the cross-sectional man of whom any society is chiefly composed. That is, Rocker sometimes projects into the world he is evaluating an ideal he has set for himself and fails to recognize it as a projected thing. When he does this he does only what every writer on man and his ways has done, and must do. And he does it chiefly in some of his more rhapsodic finalés when the scholar has finished with the topic under discussion and the poet for the moment seizes the pen. Moreover, Rocker's project-man is still always the complex, incalculable human being who is for him the man given; he is never the over-simplified, easily formulated semi-robot of thinkers like Marx and Pareto, a construct-man about whom can be built a system. And when this project-man does appear in Rocker's work his presence is never allowed to vitiate the factual accuracy of the description, and he in no way alters the standard of value—the test is still that both he and the *Durchschnittsmensch* shall have a field in which to be as complex and incalculable as they severally are.

And all who have been so unconventional as to read this preface before reading the book, or so conscientiously thorough-going as to read it at all, are reminded that it contains, not Rudolf Rocker's analysis and estimate of his book, but the translator's; and if to any of them the estimate seems incorrect or the analysis inadequate, it may be because they *are* incorrect and inadequate; it may be—the translator believes it more likely to be—because *Nationalism and Culture* is not only a masterpiece of scholarly analysis and an important contribution to social philosophy but also a work of art, and therefore, like every work of art, in great degree plastic to the moods and purposes of the reader.

RAY E. CHASE

Los Angeles, March 1937.

CONTENTS

BOOK ONE

BOOK TWO

BOOK ONE

Chapter 1

THE WILL TO POWER AS A HISTORICAL FACTOR. SCIENCE AND HISTORI-
CAL CONCEPTS. THE INSUFFICIENCY OF ECONOMIC MATERIALISM. THE
LAWS OF PHYSICAL LIFE AND "THE PHYSICS OF SOCIETY." THE SIGNIFI-
CANCE OF CONDITIONS OF PRODUCTION. THE EXPEDITIONS OF ALEXAN-
DER. THE CRUSADES. PAPISM AND HERESY. POWER AS A HINDRANCE AND
OBSTRUCTION TO ECONOMIC EVOLUTION. THE FATALISM OF "HISTORIC
NECESSITIES" AND OF THE "HISTORIC MISSION." ECONOMIC POSITION AND
SOCIAL ACTIVITY OF THE BOURGEOISIE. SOCIALISM AND SOCIALISTS.
PSYCHIC PRESUPPOSITIONS OF ALL CHANGES IN HISTORY. WAR AND
ECONOMY. MONOPOLY AND AUTOCRACY. STATE CAPITALISM.

THE DEEPER we trace the political influences in history, the more are
we convinced that the "will to power" has up to now been one of the
strongest motives in the development of human social forms. The idea
that all political and social events are but the result of given economic
conditions and can be explained by them cannot endure careful consideration. That economic conditions and the special forms of social production
have played a part in the evolution of humanity everyone knows who has
been seriously trying to reach the foundations of social phenomena. This
fact was well known before Marx set out to explain it in his manner. A
whole line of eminent French socialists like Saint-Simon, Considérant,
Louis Blanc, Proudhon and many others had pointed to it in their writings, and it is known that Marx reached socialism by the study of these
very writings. Furthermore, the recognition of the influence and significance of economic conditions on the structure of social life lies in the very
nature of socialism.

It is not the confirmation of this historical and philosophical concept
which is most striking in the Marxist formula, but the positive form in
which the concept is expressed and the kind of thinking on which Marx
based it. One sees distinctly the influence of Hegel, whose disciple Marx
had been. None but the "philosopher of the Absolute," the inventor of
"historical necessities" and "historic missions" could have imparted to
him such self-assurance of judgment. Only Hegel could have inspired in
him the belief that he had reached the foundation of the "laws of social
physics," according to which every social phenomenon must be regarded

as a deterministic manifestation of the naturally necessary course of events. In fact, Marx's successors have compared "economic materialism" with the discoveries of Copernicus and Kepler, and no less a person than Engels himself made the assertion that, with this interpretation of history, socialism had become a science.

It is the fundamental error of this theory that it puts the causes of social phenomena on a par with the causes of mechanistic events in nature. Science concerns itself exclusively with the phenomena which are displayed in the great frame which we call Nature, which are consequently limited by space and time and amenable to the calculations of human thought. For the realm of nature is a world of inner connections and mechanical necessities where every event occurs according to the laws of cause and effect. In this world there is no accident. Any arbitrary act is unthinkable. For this reason science deals only with strict facts; any single fact which runs contrary to previous experiments and does not harmonize with the theory can overthrow the most keenly reasoned doctrine.

In the world of metaphysical thought the practical statement that the exception proves the rule may have validity, but in science never. Although the forms nature produces are of infinite variety, every one of them is subject to the same unalterable laws. Every movement in the cosmos occurs according to strict, inexorable rules, just as does the physical existence of every creature on earth. The laws of our physical existence are not subject to the whims of human will. They are an integral part of our being and our existence would be unthinkable without them. We are born, absorb nourishment, discard the waste material, move, procreate and approach dissolution without being able to change any part of the process. Necessities eventuate here which transcend our will. Man can make the forces of nature subservient to his ends, to a certain extent he can guide their operation into definite courses, but he cannot stop them. It is just as impossible to sidetrack the separate events which condition our physical existence. We can refine the external accompanying phenomena and frequently adjust them to our will, but the events themselves we cannot exclude from our lives. We are not compelled to consume our food in the shape which nature offers it to us or to lie down to rest in the first convenient place, but we cannot keep from eating or sleeping, lest our physical existence should come to a sudden end. In this world of inexorable necessities there is no room for human determination.

It was this very manifestation of an iron law in the eternal course of cosmic and physical events which gave many a keen brain the idea that the events of human social life were subject to the same iron necessity and could consequently be calculated and explained by scientific methods. Most historical theories have root in this erroneous concept, which could find a place in man's mind only because he put the laws of physical being on a par with the aims and ends of men, which can only be regarded as results of their thinking.

We do not deny that in history, also, there are inner connections which, even as in nature, can be traced to cause and effect. But in social events it is always a matter of a causality of human aims and ends, in nature always of a causality of physical necessity. The latter occur without any contribution on our part; the former are but manifestations of our will. Religious ideas, ethical concepts, customs, habits, traditions, legal opinions, political organizations, institutions of property, forms of production, and so on, are not necessary implications of our physical being, but purely results of our desire for the achievement of preconceived ends. Every idea of purpose is a matter of belief which eludes scientific calculation. In the realm of physical events only the *must* counts. In the realm of belief there is only probability: *It may be so, but it does not have to be so.*

Every process which arises from our physical being and is related to it, is an event which lies outside of our volition. Every social process, however, arises from human intentions and human goal-setting and occurs within the limits of our volition. Consequently, it is not subject to the concept of natural necessity.

There is no necessity for a Flathead Indian woman to press the head of her newborn child between two boards to give it the desired form. It is but a custom which finds its explanation in the beliefs of men. Whether men practice polygamy, monogamy or celibacy is a question of human purposiveness and has nothing in common with the laws of physical events and their necessities. Every legal opinion is a matter of belief, not conditioned by any physical necessity whatsoever. Whether a man is a Mohammedan, a Jew, a Christian or a worshiper of Satan has not the slightest connection with his physical existence. Man can live in any economic relationship, can adapt himself to any form of political life, without affecting in the slightest the laws to which his physical being is subject. A sudden cessation of gravitation would be unthinkable in its results. A sudden cessation of our bodily functions is tantamount to death. But the physical existence of man would not have suffered the slightest loss if he had never heard of the Code of Hammurabi, of the Pythagorean theorem or the materialistic interpretation of history.

We are here stating no prejudiced opinion, but merely an established fact. Every result of human purposiveness is of indisputable importance for man's social existence, but we should stop regarding social processes as deterministic manifestations of a necessary course of events. Such a view can only lead to the most erroneous conclusions and contribute to a fatal confusion in our understanding of historical events.

It is doubtless the task of the historian to trace the inner connection of historical events and to make clear their causes and effects, but he must not forget that these connections are of a sort quite different from those of natural physical events and must therefore have quite a different valuation. An astronomer is able to predict a solar eclipse or the appearance of a comet to a second. The existence of the planet Neptune was calculated in this manner before a human eye had seen it. But such precision is only possible when we are dealing with the course of physical events. For the calculation of human motives and end-results there is no counterpart, because these are not amenable to any calculations whatsoever. It is impossible to calculate or predict the destiny of tribes, races, nations, or other social units. It is even impossible to find complete explanations of their past. For history is, after all, nothing but the great arena of human aims and ends, and every theory of history, consequently, a matter of belief founded at best only on probability; it can never claim unshakable certainty.

The assertion that the destiny of social structures is determinable according to the laws of a so-called "social physics" is of no greater significance than the claim of those wise women who pretend to be able to read the destinies of man in tea cups or in the lines of the hands. True, a horoscope can be cast for peoples and nations but the prophecies of political and social astrology are of no higher value than the prognostications of those who claim to be able to read the destiny of a man in the configuration of the stars.

That a theory of history may contain ideas of importance for the explanation of historical events is undeniable. We are only opposed to the assertion that the course of history is subject to the same (or similar) laws as every physical or mechanical occurrence in nature. This false, entirely unwarranted assertion contains another danger. Once we have become used to throwing the causes of natural events and those of social changes into one tub, we are only too inclined to look for a fundamental first cause, which would in a measure embody the law of social gravitation, underlying all historical events. When once we have gone so far, it is easy to overlook all the other causes of social structures and the interactions resulting from them.

Every concept of man which concerns itself with the improvement of the social conditions under which he lives, is primarily a wish concept based only on probability. Where such are in question, science reaches its limits, for all probability is based only on assumptions which cannot be calculated, weighed or measured. While it is true that for the foundation of a world-view like, for instance, socialism, it is possible to call upon the results of scientific investigation, the concept itself does not become science, because the realization of its aim is not dependent upon fixed, deterministic processes, as is every event in physical nature. There is no law in history which shows the course for every social activity of man. Whenever up to now the attempt has been made to prove the existence of such a law, the utter futility of the effort has at once become apparent.

Man is unconditionally subject only to the laws of his physical being. He cannot change his constitution. He cannot suspend the fundamental conditions of his physical being nor alter them according to his wish. He cannot prevent his appearance on earth any more than he can prevent the end of his earthly pilgrimage. He cannot change the orbit of the star on which his life cycle runs its course and must accept all the consequences of the earth's motion in space without being able to change it in the slightest. But the shaping of his social life is not subject to this necessary course because it is merely the result of his willing and doing. He can accept the social conditions under which he lives as foreordained by a divine will or regard them as the result of unalterable laws not subject to his volition. In the latter case, belief will weaken his will and induce him to adjust himself to given conditions. But he can also convince himself that all social forms possess only a conditioned existence and can be changed by human hand and human mind. In this case he will try to replace the social conditions under which he lives with others and by his action prepare the way for a reshaping of social life.

However fully man may recognize cosmic laws he will never be able to change them, because they are not his work. But every form of his social existence, every social institution which the past has bestowed on him as a legacy from remote ancestors, is the work of men and can be changed by human will and action or made to serve new ends. Only such an understanding is truly revolutionary and animated by the spirit of the coming ages. Whoever believes in the necessary sequence of all historical events sacrifices the future to the past. He explains the phenomena of social life, but he does not change them. In this respect all fatalism is alike, whether of a religious, political or economic nature. Whoever is caught in its snare is robbed thereby of life's most precious possession; the impulse to act according to his own needs. It is especially dangerous when fatalism appears in the gown of science, which nowadays so often replaces the cassock of the theologian; therefore we repeat: The causes which underlie the processes of social life have nothing in common with the laws of physical and mechanical natural events, for they are purely the results of human purpose, which is not explicable by scientific methods. To misinterpret this fact is a fatal self-deception from which only a confused notion of reality can result.

This applies to all theories of history based on the necessity of the course of social events. It applies especially to historical materialism, which traces every historical event to the prevailing conditions of production and tries to explain everything from that. No thinking man in this day can fail to recognize that one cannot properly evaluate an historical period without considering economic conditions. But much more one-sided is the view which maintains that all history is merely the result of economic conditions, under whose influence all other life phenomena have received form and imprint.

There are thousands of events in history which cannot be explained by purely economic reasons, or by them alone. It is quite possible to bring everything within the terms of a definite scheme, but the result is usually not worth the effort. There is scarcely an historical event to whose shaping economic causes have not contributed, but economic forces are not the only motive powers which have set everything else in motion. All social phenomena are the result of a series of various causes, in most cases so inwardly related that it is quite impossible clearly to separate one from the other. We are always dealing with the interplay of various causes which, as a rule, can be clearly recognized but cannot be calculated according to scientific methods.

There are historical events of the deepest significance for millions of men which cannot be explained by their purely economic aspects. Who would maintain, for instance, that the invasions of Alexander were caused by the conditions of production of his time? The very fact that the enormous empire Alexander cemented together with the blood of hundreds of thousands fell to ruin soon after his death proves that the military and political achievements of the Macedonian world conqueror were not historically determined by economic necessities. Just as little did they in any way advance the conditions of production of the time. When Alexander planned his wars, lust for power played a far more important part than economic necessity. The desire for world conquest had assumed actually pathological forms in the ambitious despot. His mad power obsession was a leading motive in his whole policy, the driving force of his warlike enterprises, which filled a large part of the then known world with murder and rapine. It was this power obsession which made the Caesaro-Papism of the oriental despot appear so admirable to him and gave him his belief in his demi-godhood.

The will to power which always emanates from individuals or from small minorities in society is in fact a most important driving force in history. The extent of its influence has up to now been regarded far too little, although it has frequently been the determining factor in the shaping of the whole of economic and social life.

The history of the Crusades was doubtless affected by strong economic motives. Visions of the rich lands of the Orient may have been for many a Sir Lackland or Lord Have-Naught a far stronger urge than religious convictions. But economic motives alone would never have been sufficient to set millions of men in all countries in motion if they had not been permeated by the obsession of faith so that they rushed on recklessly when the cry, "God wills it!" was sounded, although they had not the slightest notion of the enormous difficulties which attended this strange adventure. The powerful influence of religious conviction on the people of that time is proved by the so-called Children's Crusade of the year 1212. It was instituted when the failure of the former crusading armies became more and more apparent, and pious zealots proclaimed the tidings that the sacred sepulcher could only be liberated by those of tender age, through whom God would reveal a miracle to the world. It was surely no economic motive which persuaded thousands of parents to send those who were dearest to them to certain death.

But even the Papacy, which had at first only hesitatingly resolved on calling the Christian world to the first Crusade, was moved to it far more by power-political than by economic motives. In their struggle for the hegemony of the church it was very convenient for its leaders to have many a worldly ruler, who might have become obstreperous at home, kept busy a long time in the Orient where he could not disturb the church in the pursuit of its plans. True, there were others, as, for instance, the Venetians, who soon recognized what great economic advantages would accrue to them from the Crusades; they even made use of them to extend their rule over the Dalmatian Coast, the Ionic Isles and Crete. But to deduce from this that the Crusades were inevitably determined by the methods of production of the period would be sheer nonsense.

When the Church determined upon its war of extermination against the Albigenses, which cost the lives of many thousands, made waste the freest, intellectually most advanced land in Europe, destroyed its highly developed culture and industry, maimed its trade and left a decimated and bitterly impoverished population behind, it was led into its fight against heresy by no economic considerations whatsoever. What it fought for was the unification of faith, which was the foundation of its efforts at political power. Likewise, the French kingdom, which later on supported the church in this war, was animated principally by political considerations. It became in this bloody struggle the heir of the Count of Languedoc, whereby the whole southern part of the country came into its hands, naturally greatly strengthening its efforts for centralization of power. It was, therefore, principally because of the political motives of church and state that the economic development of one of the richest lands in Europe was violently interrupted, and the ancient home of a splendid culture was converted into a waste of ruins.

The great conquest by the Arabs, and especially their incursion into Spain which started the Seven Hundred Years' War, cannot be explained by any study, however thorough, of the conditions of production of that time. It would be useless to try to prove that the development of economic conditions was the guiding force of that mighty epoch. The contrary is here most plainly apparent. After the conquest of Granada, the last stronghold of the Moors, there arose in Spain a new politico-religious power under whose baneful influence the whole economic development of the country was set back hundreds of years. So effective was this incubus that the consequences are noticeable to this day over the whole Iberian Peninsula. Even the enormous streams of gold, which after the discovery of America poured into Spain from Mexico and the former Inca Empire, could not stay its economic decline; in fact, only hastened it.

The marriage of Ferdinand of Aragon with Isabella of Castile laid the foundation of a Christian monarchy in Spain whose right hand was the Grand Inquisitor. The ceaseless war against the Moorish power waged under the banner of the church had fundamentally changed the mental and spiritual attitude of the Christian population and had created the cruel religious fanaticism which kept Spain shrouded in darkness for hundreds of years. Only under such pre-conditions could that frightful clerico-political despotism evolve, which after drowning the last liberties of the Spanish cities in blood, lay on the land like a horrible incubus for three hundred years. Under the tyrannical influence of this unique power organization the last remnant of Moorish culture was buried, after the Jews and Arabs had first been expelled from the country. Whole provinces which had formerly resembled flowering gardens were changed to unproductive wastes because the irrigating systems and the roads of the Moors had been permitted to fall into ruin. Industries, which had been among the first in Europe, vanished almost completely from the land and the people reverted to long antiquated methods of production.

According to the data of Fernando Garrido there were at the beginning of the sixteenth century in Seville sixteen hundred silk weavers' looms which employed one hundred and thirty thousand workers. By the end of the seventeenth century there were only three hundred looms n action.

It is not known how many looms there were in Toledo in the sixteenth century but there were woven there four hundred and thirty-five thousand pounds of silk annually, employing 38,484 persons. By the end of the seventeenth century this industry had totally vanished. In Segovia there were at the end of the sixteenth century 6,000 looms for weaving cloth, at that time regarded as the best in Europe. By the beginning of the eighteenth century this industry had so declined that foreign workers were imported to teach the Segovians the weaving and dyeing of cloth. The causes of this decline were the expulsion of the Moors, the discovery and settling of America, and the religious fanaticism which emptied the work rooms and increased the number of the priests and monks. When only three hundred looms remained in Seville the number of monasteries there had increased to sixty-two and the clergy embraced 14,000 persons.[1]

And Zancada writes concerning that period: "In the year 1655 seventeen guilds disappeared from Spain; together with them the workers in iron, steel, copper, lead, sulphur, the alum industry and others." [2]

Even the conquest of America by the Spaniards, which depopulated the Iberian Peninsula and lured millions of men away into the new world, cannot be explained exclusively by "the thirst for gold," however lively the greed of the individual may have been. When we read the history of the celebrated *conquista*, we recognize, with Prescott, that it resembles less a true accounting of actual events than one of the countless romances of knight errantry which, in Spain especially, were so loved and valued.

It was not solely economic reasons which repeatedly enticed companies of daring adventurers into the fabled El Dorado beyond the great waste of waters. Great empires like those of Mexico and the Inca state which contained millions, besides possessing a fairly high degree of culture, were conquered by a handful of desperate adventurers who did not hesitate to use any means, and were not repelled by any danger, because they did not value their own lives any too highly. This fact becomes explicable only when we take a closer view of this unique human material, hardened by danger, which through a seven hundred years' war had been gradually evolved. Only an epoch in which the idea of peace among men must have seemed like a fairy tale out of a long-vanished past and in which the centuries-long wars, waged with every cruelty, appeared as the normal condition of life, could have evolved the wild religious fanaticism characteristic of the Spaniards of that time. Thus becomes explicable that peculiar urge constantly to seek adventure. For a mistaken concept of honor, frequently lacking all real background, a man was instantly ready to risk his life. It is no accident that it was in Spain that the character of Don Quixote was evolved. Perhaps that theory goes too far which seeks to replace all sociology by the discoveries of psychology, but it is undeniable that the psychological condition of men has a strong influence in the shaping of man's social environment.

Hundreds of other examples might be cited from which it is clearly apparent that economics is not the center of gravity of social development in general, even though it has indisputably played an important part in the formative processes in history, a fact which should not be overlooked any

[1] Fernando Garrido, "*La España contemporanea.*" Tome I. Barcelona, 1865. This work contains rich material, as do Garrido's other writings, especially his work, *Historia de las Clases Trabajadores.*

[2] Praxedes Zancada, *El obrero en España: Notas para su historia politica y social.* Barcelona 1902.

more than it should be excessively overestimated. There are epochs when the significance of economic circumstances in the course of social events becomes surprisingly clear, but there are others where religious or political motives obviously interfere arbitrarily with the normal course of economics and for a long time inhibit its natural development or force it into other channels. Historical events like the Reformation, the Thirty Years' War, the great revolutions in Europe, and many others, are not comprehensible at all as purely economic. We may however readily admit that in all these events economic factors played a part and helped to bring them about.

This misapprehension becomes still more serious when we try to identify the various social strata of a definite epoch as merely the typical representations of quite definite economic interests. Such a view not only narrows the general field of view of the scholar, but it makes of history as a whole a distorted picture which can but lead us on to wrong conclusions. Man is not purely the agent of specific economic interests. The bourgeoisie, for instance, has in all countries where it achieved social importance, frequently supported movements which were by no means determined by its economic interests, but often stood in open opposition to them. Its fight against the church, its endeavors for the establishment of lasting peace among the nations, its liberal and democratic views regarding the nature of government, which brought its representatives into sharpest conflict with the traditions of kingship by the grace of God, and many other causes for which it has at some time shown enthusiasm are proofs of this.

It will not do to argue that the bourgeoisie under the steadily growing influence of its economic interests quickly forgot the ideals of its youth or basely betrayed them. When we compare the storm and stress period of the socialistic movement in Europe with the practical politics of the modern labor parties, we are soon convinced that the pretended representatives of the proletariat are in no position to attack the bourgeoisie for its inner changes. None of these parties has, during the worst crisis which the capitalist world has ever passed through, made even the slightest attempt to influence economic conditions in the spirit of socialism. Yet never before were economic conditions riper for a complete transformation of capitalistic society. The whole capitalistic economic system has gotten out of control. The crisis, which formerly was only a periodic phenomenon of the capitalistic world, has for years become the normal condition of social life. Crisis in industry, crisis in agriculture, crisis in commerce, crisis in finance! All have united to prove the inadequacy of the capitalistic system. Nearly thirty million men are condemned for life to miserable beggary in the midst of a world which is being ruined by its surplus. But the spirit is lacking—the socialistic spirit that strives for a fundamental reconstruction of social life and is not content with petty patchwork, which merely prolongs the crisis but can never heal its causes. Never before has it been so clearly proved that economic conditions alone cannot change the social structure, unless there are present in men the spiritual and intellectual prerequisites to give wings to their desires and unite their scattered forces for communal work.

But the socialist parties, and the trade union organizations, which are permeated with their ideas, have not only failed when it became a question of the economic reconstruction of society; they have even shown themselves incapable of guarding the political legacy of the bourgeois democracy; for they have everywhere yielded up long-won rights and liberties without a struggle and have in this manner aided the advance of fascism in Europe, even though against their will.

In Italy, one of the most prominent representatives of the Socialist Party became the perpetrator of the fascist *coup d'état*, and a whole group of the best-known labor leaders, with D'Aragona at their head, marched with flying banners into Mussolini's camp.

In Spain, the Socialist Party was the only one which made peace with the dictator, Primo de Rivera. Likewise today, in the glorious era of the Republic, whose hands are red with the blood of murdered workers, that party proves itself the best guard of the capitalistic system and willingly offers its services for the limitation of political rights.

In England, we witness the peculiar spectacle of the best-known and ablest leaders of the Labor Party suddenly turning into the nationalistic camp, by which action they inflicted on the party, whose advocates they had been for decades, a crushing defeat. On this occasion Philip Snowden charged against his former comrades that "they had the interest of their class more in view than the good of the state," a reproach which unfortunately is not justified but which is very characteristic of "His Lordship," as he is now called.

In Germany, the social democracy as well as the trade unions have supported with all their powers the notorious attempts of the great capitalist industrialists at the "rationalization" of industry, which has reacted so catastrophically upon labor and has given a morally stagnated bourgeoisie the opportunity to recuperate from the shocks which the lost war had given them. Even a pretentiously revolutionary labor party like the Communist Party in Germany appropriated the nationalistic slogans of reaction, by which contemptuous denial of all socialistic principles they hoped to take the wind out of the sails of threatening fascism.

To these examples many more might be added to show that the representatives of the great majority of organized socialistic labor hardly have the right to reproach the bourgeoisie with political unreliability or treason to its former ideals. The representatives of liberalism and bourgeois democracy showed at recent elections at least a desire to preserve appearances, while the pretended defenders of proletarian interests abandoned their former ideals with shameless complacency in order to do the work of their opponents.

A long line of leading political economists, uninfluenced by any socialistic considerations, have expressed their conviction that the capitalistic system has had its day and that in place of an uncontrolled profit economy a production-for-use economy based on new principles must be instituted if Europe is not to be ruined. Nevertheless, it becomes even more apparent that socialism as a movement has in no wise grown to meet the situation. Most of its representatives have never advanced beyond shallow reform, and they waste their forces in factional fights as purposeless as they are dangerous, which in their idiotic intolerance remind us of the behavior of mentally petrified church organizations. Small wonder that hundreds of thousands of socialists fell into despair and let themselves be caught by the rat-catchers of the Third Reich.

It could be objected here that the necessities of life itself, even without the assistance of the socialists, were working toward the alteration of existing economic conditions, because a crisis with no way out becomes at last unendurable. We do not deny this, but we fear that with the present cessation in the socialistic labor movement there may occur an economic reconstruction about which the producers will have absolutely nothing to say. They will be confronted with the accomplished facts which others have created for them, so that in the future, too, they will have to be content with the part of coolies which had been planned for them all the while. Unless all signs deceive us, we are marching with giant strides toward an epoch of state capitalism, which is likely to assume for the workers the shape of a modern system of bondage in which man may be regarded as merely an instrument of production, and all personal freedom will be absolutely extinguished.

Economic conditions can, under certain circumstances, become so acute that a change in the existing social system is a vital necessity. It is only a question in which direction we shall then move. Will it be a road to freedom, or will it result merely in an improved form of slavery which, while it secures for man a meager living, will rob him of all independence of action? This, and this only, is the question. The social constitution of the Inca Empire secured for every one of its subjects the necessary means of subsistence, but the land was subject to an unlimited despotism, which cruelly punished any opposition to its command and degraded the individual to a will-less tool of the state power.

State capitalism might be a way out of the present crisis, but most assuredly it would not be a road to social freedom. On the contrary, it would submerge men in a slough of servitude which would mock at all human dignity. In every prison, in every barrack there is a certain equality of social condition. Everyone has the same food, the same clothes, renders the same service, or performs the same task; but who would affirm that such a condition presents an end worth working for?

It makes a difference whether the members of a social organization are masters of their fate, control their own affairs and have the inalienable right to participate in the administration of their communal interests, or are but the instruments of an external will over which they possess no influence whatsoever. Every soldier has the right to share the common rations, but he is not permitted to have a judgment of his own. He must blindly obey the orders of his superior, silencing, if need be, the voice of his own conscience, for he is but a part of a machine which others set in motion.

No tyranny is more unendurable than that of an all-powerful bureaucracy which interferes with all the activities of men and leaves its stamp on them. The more unlimited the power of the state over the life of the individual, the more it cripples his creative capacities and weakens the force of his personal will. State capitalism, the most dangerous antithesis of real socialism, demands the surrender of all social activities to the state. It is the triumph of the machine over the spirit, the rationalization of all thought, action and feeling according to the fixed norms of authority, and consequently the end of all real intellectual culture. That the full scope of this threatening development has not been grasped up to now, that the idea that it is necessitated by current economic conditions has even been accepted, may well be regarded as one of the most fateful signs of the times.

The dangerous mania which sees in every social phenomenon only the inevitable result of capitalistic methods of production has implanted in men the conviction that all social events arise from definite necessity and are economically unalterable. This fatalistic notion could only result in crippling men's power of resistance, and consequently making them receptive to a compromise with given conditions, no matter how horrible and inhuman they may be.

Every one knows that economic conditions have an influence on the changes in social relations. How men will react in their thoughts and actions to this influence is of great importance, however, in determining what steps they may decide to take to initiate an obviously necessary change in the conditions of life. But it is just the thoughts and actions of men which refuse to accept the imprint of economic motives alone. Who would, for instance, maintain that the Puritanism which has decidedly influenced the spiritual development of Anglo-Saxon people up to the present day was the necessary result of the economic capitalistic order then in its infancy, or who would try to prove that the World War was absolutely conditioned by the capitalistic system and was consequently unavoidable?

Economic interests undoubtedly played an important part in this war as they have in all others, but they alone would not have been able to cause this fatal catastrophe. Merely the sober statement of concrete economic purposes would never have set the great masses in motion. It was therefore necessary to prove to them that the quarrel for which they were to kill others, for which they were to be killed themselves, was "the good and righteous cause." Consequently, one side fought "against the Russian despotism," for the "liberation of Poland"—and, of course, for the "interests of the fatherland," which the Allies had "conspired" to destroy. And the other side fought "for the triumph of Democracy" and the "overthrow of Prussian militarism" and "that this war should be the last war."

It might be urged that behind all the camouflage by which the people were fooled for over four years there stood, after all, the economic interests of the possessing classes. But that is not the point. The decisive factor is that without the continuous appeal to men's ethical feelings, to their sense of justice, no war would have been possible. The slogan, "God punish England!" and the cry, "Death to the Huns!" achieved in the last war far greater miracles than did the bare economic interests of the possessing classes. This is proved by the fact that before men can be driven to war they must be lashed into a certain pitch of passion and by the further fact that this passion can only be aroused by spiritual and moral motives.

Did not the very people who year after year had proclaimed to the working masses that every war in the era of capitalism springs from purely economic motives, at the outbreak of the World War abandon their historic-philosophical theory and raise the affairs of the nation above those of the class? And these were the ones who, with Marxist courage of conviction, supported the statement in *The Communist Manifesto:* "The history of all society up to now has been the history of class struggles."

Lenin and others have attributed the failure of most of the socialist parties at the beginning of the war to the leaders' fear of assuming responsibility, and with bitter words they have flung this lack of courage in their faces. Admitting that there is a great deal of truth in this assertion—although we must beware in this case of generalizing too freely— what is proved by it?

If it was indeed fear of responsibility and the lack of moral courage which induced the majority of the socialist leaders to support the national interests of their respective countries, then this is but a further proof of the correctness of our view. Courage and cowardice are not conditioned by the prevailing forms of production but have their roots in the psychic feelings of men. But if purely psychic motives could have such a compelling influence on the leaders of a movement numbering millions that they abandoned their fundamental principles even before the cock had crowed thrice, and marched with the worst foes of the socialistic labor movement against the so-called hereditary enemy, this only proves that men's actions cannot be explained by conditions of production, with which they often stand in sharpest contrast. Every epoch in history provides superabundant evidence of this.

It is, then, a patent error to explain the late war solely as the necessary result of opposing economic interests. Capitalism would still be conceivable if the so-called "captains of world industry" should agree in an amicable manner concerning the possession of sources of raw materials and the spheres of market and exploitation, just as the owners of the various economic interests within a country come to terms without having to settle their differences on each occasion with the sword. There exist already quite a number of international organizations for production in which the capitalists of certain industries have gotten together to establish a definite quota for the production of their goods in each country. In this manner they have regulated the total production of their branches by mutual agreement on fundamental principles. The International Steel Trust in Europe is an example of it. By such a regulation capitalism loses nothing of its essential character; its privileges remain untouched. In fact, its mastery over the army of its wage slaves is considerably strengthened.

Considered purely economically, the War was therefore by no means inevitable. Capitalism could have survived without it. In fact, one can assume with certainty that if the directors of the capitalistic order could have anticipated the war's results it would never have happened.

It was not solely economic interests which played an important part in the late war, but motives of political power, which in the end did most to let loose the catastrophe. After the decline of Spain and Portugal, the dominant power in Europe had fallen to Holland, France and England, who opposed each other as rivals. Holland quickly lost its leading position, and after the Peace of Breda its influence on the course of European politics grew gradually less. But France also had lost after the Seven Years' War a large part of its former predominance and could never recover it, especially since its financial difficulties became constantly more acute and led to that unexampled oppression of the people from which the Revolution sprang. Napoleon later made enormous efforts to recover for France the position she had lost in Europe, but his gigantic efforts were without result. England remained the implacable enemy of Napoleon, who soon recognized that his plans for world power could never come to fruition as long as the "nation of shopkeepers," as he contemptuously called the English, was unconquered. Napoleon lost the game after England had organized all Europe against him. Since then England has maintained its leading position in Europe, indeed in the whole world.

But the British Empire is not a continuous territory as other empires were before it. Its possessions are scattered over all the five continents, and their security is dependent upon the position of power which Britain occupies in Europe. Every threat to this position is a threat to the continued possession of colonies by England. As long as on the continent the formation of the modern great states, with their gigantic armies and fleets, their bureaucracy, their capitalistic enterprises, their highly developed industries, their foreign trade agreements, their exports and their growing need of expansion could still be overlooked, Britain's position as a world power remained fairly untouched; but the stronger the capitalistic states of the continent became, the more had Britain to fear for its hegemony. Every attempt by a European power to secure new trade, or territory supplying raw materials, to further its export by trade agreements with foreign countries, and to give its plans for expansion the widest possible room, inevitably led sooner or later to a conflict somewhere with British spheres of interest and had always to look for hidden opposition by Britain.

For this reason it necessarily became the chief concern of the British foreign policy to prevent any power from obtaining predominant influence on the continent, or, when this was unavoidable, to use its whole skill to play one power against the other. Therefore, the defeat of Napoleon III by the Prussian army and Bismarck's diplomacy could only be very welcome to Britain, for France's power was thereby crippled for decades. But Germany's development of its military power, the initiation of its colonial policy and, most of all, the building of its fleet and its steadily growing plans for expansion (as its "urge to eastward" became increasingly noticeable and distasteful to the English) conjured up a danger for the British Empire that its representatives could not afford to disregard.

That British diplomacy unhesitatingly used any means to oppose the danger is no proof that its directors were by nature more treacherous or unscrupulous than are the diplomats of other countries. The idle talk about "perfidious Albion" is just as silly as the chatter about "a civilized warfare." If British diplomacy proved superior to that of the Germans, if it was cleverer in its secret intrigues, it was so only because its representatives had had much longer experience and because, fortunately for them, the majority of responsible German statesmen from Bismarck's time were but will-less lackeys of imperial power. None of them had the courage to oppose the dangerous activities of an irresponsible psychopath and his venal camarilla.

However, the foundation of this evil is to be sought not in individual persons but in power politics itself, irrespective of who practices it or what immediate aims it pursues. Power politics is only conceivable as making use of all means, however condemnable these may appear to private conscience, so long as they promise results, conform to reasons of state and further the state's ends.

Machiavelli, who had the courage to collect systematically the methods of procedure of power politics and to justify them in the name of reasons of state, has set this forth already in his "Discorsi" clearly and definitely: "If we are dealing with the welfare of the Fatherland at all, we must not permit ourselves to be influenced by right or wrong, compassion or cruelty, praise or blame. We must cavil at nothing, but we must always grasp at the means which will save the life of the country and preserve its freedom."

For the perfect power politics every crime done in the service of the state is a meritorious deed if it is successful. The state stands beyond good and evil; it is the earthly Providence whose decisions are in their profundity as inexplicable to the ordinary subject as is the fate ordained for the believer by the power of God. Just as, according to the doctrines of theologians and pundits, God in his unfathomable wisdom often uses the most cruel and frightful means to effect his plans, so also the state, according to the doctrines of political theology, is not bound by the rules of ordinary human morality when its rulers are determined to achieve definite ends by a cold-blooded gamble with the lives and fortunes of millions.

When a diplomat falls into a trap another has set for him, it ill becomes him to complain of the wiles and lack of conscientiousness of his opponent, for he himself pursues the same object, from the opposite side, and only suffers defeat because his opponent is better able to play the part of Providence. One who believes that he cannot exist without the organized force which is personified in the state must be ready also to accept all the consequences of this superstitious belief, to sacrifice to this Moloch the most precious thing he owns, his own personality.

It was principally power-political conflict, growing out of the fateful evolution of the great capitalistic states, which contributed importantly to the outbreak of the World War. Since the people, and especially the workers, of the various countries neither understood the seriousness of the situation nor could summon the moral courage to put up a determined resistance to the subterranean machinations of the diplomats, militarists and profiteers, there was no power on earth which could stay the catastrophe. For decades every great state appeared like a gigantic army camp which opposed the others, armed to the teeth, until a spark finally sprung the mine. Not because all happened as it had to happen did the world drive with open eyes toward the abyss, but because the great masses in every country had not the slightest idea what a despicable game was being played behind their backs. They had to thank their incredible carelessness and above all their blind belief in the infallible superiority of their rulers and so-called spiritual leaders, that for over four years they could be led to slaughter like a will-less herd.

But even the small group of high finance and great industry, whose owners so unmistakably contributed to the releasing of the red flood, were not animated in their actions exclusively by the prospect of material gain. The view which sees in every capitalist only a profit-machine may very well meet the demands of propaganda, but it is conceived much too narrowly and does not correspond to reality. Even in modern giant capitalism the power-political interests frequently play a larger part than the purely economic considerations, although it is difficult to separate them from each other. Its leaders have learned to know the delightful sensation of power, and adore it with the same passion as did formerly the great conquerors, whether they find themselves in the camp of the enemies of their government, like Hugo Stinnes and his followers in the time of the Germany money crisis, or interfere decisively in the foreign policy of their own country.

The morbid desire to make millions of men submissive to a definite will and to force whole empires into courses which are useful to the secret purposes of small minorities, is frequently more evident in the typical representatives of modern capitalism than are purely economic considerations or the prospect of greater material profit. The desire to heap up ever increasing profits today no longer satisfies the demands of the great capitalistic oligarchies. Every one of its members knows what enormous power the possession of great wealth places in the hands of the individual and the caste to which he belongs. This knowledge gives a tempting incentive and creates that typical consciousness of mastery whose consequences are frequently more destructive than the facts of monopoly itself. It is this mental attitude of the modern Grand Seigneur of industry and high finance which condemns all opposition and will tolerate no equality.

In the great struggles between capital and labor this brutal spirit of mastery often plays a more decided part than immediate economic interests. The small manufacturers of former times still had certain rather intimate relationships to the masses of the working population and were consequently able to have more or less understanding of their position. Modern moneyed aristocracy, however, has even less relationship with the great masses of the people than did the feudal barons of the eighteenth century with their serfs. It knows the masses solely as collective objects of exploitation for its economic and political interests. It has in general no understanding of the hard conditions of their lives. Hence the conscienceless brutality, the power urge, contemptuous of all human right, and the unfeeling indifference to the misery of others.

Because of his social position there are left no limits to the power lust of the modern capitalist. He can interfere with inconsiderate egoism in the lives of his fellowmen and play the part of Providence for others. Only when we take into consideration this passionate urge for political power over their own people as well as over foreign nations are we able really to understand the character of the typical representatives of modern capitalism. It is just this trait which makes them so dangerous to the social structure of the future.

Not without reason does modern monopolistic capitalism support the National Socialist and fascist reaction. This reaction is to help beat down any resistance of the working masses, in order to set up a realm of industrial serfdom in which productive man is to be regarded merely as an economic automaton without any influence whatsoever on the course and character of economic and social conditions. This Caesarean madness stops at no barrier. Without compunction it rides roughshod over those achievements of the past which have all too often had to be purchased with the heart's blood of the people. It is always ready to smother with brutal violence the last rights and the last liberties which might interfere with its plans for holding all social activities within the rigid forms set by its will. This is the great danger which threatens us today and which immediately confronts us. The success or failure of monopolistic capitalistic power plans will determine the structure of the social life of the near future.

Chapter 2

RELIGION AND POLITICS. THE ROOTS OF THE POWER IDEA. THE ORIGIN
OF RELIGIOUS CONCEPTIONS. ANIMISM AND FETISHISM. THE SACRIFICE.
THE FEELING OF DEPENDENCE. EFFECT OF TERRESTRIAL POWER ON THE
SHAPE OF RELIGIOUS CONSCIOUSNESS. RELIGION AND SLAVERY. THE
RELIGIOUS FOUNDATIONS OF ALL RULERSHIP. TRADITION. MOSES. HAM-
MURABI. THE PHARAOHS. THE LAWS OF MANU. THE PERSIAN DIVINE
KINGDOM. LAMAISM. ALEXANDER AND CAESARO-PAPISM. CAESARISM IN
ROME. THE INCA. GENGHIS KHAN. POWER AND THE PRIESTHOOD.
CHURCH AND STATE. ROUSSEAU. ROBESPIERRE. NAPOLEON. MUSSOLINI
AND THE VATICAN. FASCISM AND RELIGION.

IN ALL epochs of that history which is known to us, two forces are
apparent that are in constant warfare. Their antagonism, open or veiled,
results from the intrinsic difference between the forces themselves and
between the activities in which they find expression. This is clear to anyone
who approaches the study of human social structures without ready-
formulated hypotheses or fixed schemes of interpretation, especially to
anyone who sees that human objectives and purposes are not subject to
mechanical laws, as are cosmic events in general. We are speaking here
of the political and economic elements in history, which could also be
called the governmental and social elements. Strictly speaking, the concepts of the political and the economic are in this case conceived somewhat
too narrowly; for in the last analysis, all politics has its roots in the
religious concepts of men, while everything economic is of a cultural
nature, and is consequently in the most intimate relationship with the
value-creating forces of social life; so that we are plainly compelled to
speak of an inner opposition between religion and culture.

Political and economic, governmental and social, or, in a larger sense,
religious and cultural manifestations, have many points of contact: they
all spring from human nature, and consequently there are between them
inner relations. We are here simply concerned to get a clearer view of
the connection which exists between these manifestations. Every political
form in history has its definite economic foundations which are especially
marked in the later phases of social advancement. On the other hand, it
is undeniable that the forms of politics are subject to the changes in the

NATIONALISM AND CULTURE   43

conditions of economic and general cultural life, and with them assume
new aspects. But the inner character of all politics always remains the
same, just as the inner character of each and every religion never changes,
despite the alteration of its outward form.

Religion and culture have their roots in man's instinct of self-
preservation, which endows them with life and form; but, once come to
life, each follows its own course, since there are no organic ties between
them, so that, like antagonistic stars, they pursue opposite directions. One
who overlooks this antagonism or, for whatever reason, fails to give it
the consideration it deserves, will never be able to see clearly the inner
concatenation of social events.

As to where the realm of religion proper begins, opinions are divided
to this day; but it is fairly agreed that the foundation of man's religious
concepts is not to be found in speculative philosophy. We have come to
recognize that Hegel's notion, that all religion merely demonstrates the
elevation of the spirit to the Absolute, and therefore tries to find the
union of the human with the divine, can only be regarded as an empty
figure of speech which in no way explains the origin of religion. The
"Philosopher of the Absolute," who endows every nation with a special
historical mission, is equally arbitrary when he asserts that every people
in history is the bearer of a typical form of religion: the Chinese of the
religion of moderation, the Chaldeans of the religion of pain, the Greeks
of the religion of beauty, and so on, until at last the line of religious
systems ends in Christianity, "the revealed religion," whose communicants
recognize in the person of Christ the union of the human with the divine.

Science has made men more critical. We realize now that all research
into the origin and gradual shaping of religion must use the same methods
which today serve sociology and psychology in trying to comprehend the
phenomena of social and mental life in their beginnings.

The once widely held view of the English philologist, Max Müller,
who thought he recognized in religion man's innate urge to explain the
Infinite, and who maintained that the impress of the forces of nature
released the first religious feelings in man, and that consequently one could
not go wrong in regarding nature worship as the first form of religion,
hardly finds adherents today. Most of the present leaders of ethnological
religious research are of the opinion that animism, the belief in the ghosts
and souls of the departed, is to be regarded as the first stage of religious
consciousness in man.

The whole mode of life of nomadic primitive man, his relative ignorance, the mental influence of his dream pictures, his lack of understanding
when confronted with death, the compulsory fasts he often had to endure
—all this made him a natural born clairvoyant, with whom the belief in
ghosts lay, so to speak, in his blood. What he felt when confronted with

the ghosts with which his imagination peopled the world, was primarily fear. This fear troubled him all the more as he was here confronted, not with an ordinary enemy, but with unseen forces which could not be met by simple means. From this arose quite spontaneously the desire to secure the good will of those powers, to escape their wiles and earn their favor by whatever means. It is the naked urge for self-preservation of primitive man which here finds expression.

From animism sprang fetishism, the idea that the ghost dwelt in some object or at a certain place, a belief which even today continues to live in the superstitious notions of civilized men, who are firmly convinced that ghosts walk and talk and that there are places which are haunted. The religious ritual of Lamaism and that of the Catholic Church are also in their essence fetishism. As to whether animism and the first crude concepts of fetishism can already be regarded as religion, opinions differ; but that here is to be sought the starting point of all religious concepts can hardly be doubted.

Religion proper begins with the alliance between "ghost" and man which finds expression in ritual. For primitive man, the "ghost" or the "soul" is no abstract idea, but a completely corporeal concept. It is, therefore, quite natural that he should try to impress the spirits by concrete proofs of his veneration and submission. Thus arose in his brain the idea of sacrifice and, as repeated experience proved to him that the life of the slain animal or enemy departed with the streaming blood, he early learned to recognize that blood is indeed "a most peculiar juice." This recognition also gave the idea of sacrifice a specific character. The blood-offering was certainly the first form of the rite of sacrifice and was, moreover, necessitated by the primitive huntsman's life. The idea of the blood offering, which was doubtless among the oldest products of religious consciousness, persists in the great religious systems of the present. The symbolic transmutation of bread and wine in the Christian Eucharist into the "flesh and blood" of Christ is an example of this.

Sacrifice became the central point of all religious usages and festivities, which manifested themselves also in incantation, dance and song, and gradually congealed into specific rituals. It is very likely that the offering of sacrifice was at first a purely personal affair and that each could make the offering suited to his need, but this condition probably did not last long before it was replaced by a professional priesthood of the type of the medicine men, Shamans, Gangas, and so on. The development of fetishism into totemism, by which name, after an Indian word, we call the belief in a tribal deity, usually embodied in the form of an animal from which the tribe derived its origin, has especially favored the evolution of a special magician-priesthood. With that, religion took on a social character which it did not have before.

When we regard religion in the light of its own gradual evolution, we recognize that two phenomena constitute its essence: *Religion is primarily the feeling of man's dependence on higher unknown powers. To seek ways and means to make these powers favorably inclined toward him and to protect himself from their harmful influences, man is impelled by the instinct of self-preservation.* Thus arises ritual, which gives to religion its external character.

That the idea of sacrifice can be traced back to the custom, prevailing in the primitive human institutions and organizations of primeval times, of giving the tribal leaders and chiefs voluntary or compulsory presents, is an assumption which has some possibility. The assertion that primitive man without this institution would never have arrived at the idea of sacrifice seems to us too bold.

Religious concepts could only originate when the question of the why and how of things arose in the brain of man. But this presupposes considerable mental development. It is, therefore, to be assumed that a long period had to pass before this question could engage him. The concept which primeval man forms of the world around him, is primarily of a sensuous nature; just as a child recognizes the objects of his environment primarily sensuously and uses them long before any question concerning their origin arises in him. Furthermore, with many savage people it remains today the custom to let the ghosts of the departed ones participate at meals, just as nearly all of the festivities of primitive tribes are connected with sacrificial rites. Therefore, it is quite possible that the idea of sacrifice could have arisen without any preceding related social custom.

Be that as it may, the fact remains that in every religious system which made its appearance in the course of millenniums there was mirrored the dependency of man upon a higher power which his own imagination had called into being and whose slave he had become. All gods had their time, but religion itself, in the core of its being, has always remained the same despite all changes in its outward form. Always it is the illusion to which the real essence of man is offered as a sacrifice; the creator becomes the slave of his own creature without ever becoming conscious of the tragedy of this. Only because there has never been any change in the inmost essence of all and every religion could the well known German religious teacher, Koenig, begin his book for instruction in the Catholic religion with these words: "Religion in general is the recognition and veneration of God and specifically of the relationship of man to God as his supreme ruler."

Thus was religion even in its poor primitive beginning most intimately intergrown with the idea of might, of supernatural superiority, of power over the faithful, in one word, of rulership. Modern philology has, accordingly, in numerous instances been able to prove that even the names of the various divinities were in their origins expressions of the concepts in which the idea of power was embodied. Not without reason do all advocates of the principle of authority trace its origin back to God. For does not the Godhead appear to them the epitome of all power and strength? In the very earliest myths the heroes, conquerors, lawgivers, tribal ancestors appear as gods or demi-gods; for their greatness and superiority could only have divine origin. Thus we arrive at the foundations of every system of rulership and recognize that all politics is in the last instance religion, and as such tries to hold the spirit of man in the chains of dependence.

Whether religious feeling is already in its earliest beginnings only an abstract reflection of terrestrial institutions of power, as Nordau and others maintained, is a question which is open to discussion. Those who regard the original condition of mankind as one of "war of all against all," as Hobbes and his numerous followers have done, will be readily inclined to see in the malevolent and violent character of the original deities a faithful counterpart of the despotic chieftains and warlike leaders who kept both their own tribesmen and strangers in fear and terror. It is not so long since we saw the present "savages" in a quite similar light, as cunning and cruel fellows ever set on murder and rapine, until the manifold results of modern ethnology in all parts of the world gave us proof of how fundamentally false this concept is.

That primitive man did as a rule picture his spirits and gods as violent and terrible need not necessarily be traced to earthly models. Everything unknown (incomprehensible to the simple mind) affects the spirit as uncanny and fearsome. It is only a step from the uncanny to the gruesome, to the horrible, the frightful. This must have been all the more true in those long-vanished ages when man's imaginative power was uninfluenced by the millenniums of accumulated experience which could fit him for logical counter-argument. But even if we are not compelled to trace every religious concept to some exercise of earthly power, it is a fact that in later epochs of human evolution the outer forms of religion were frequently determined by the power needs of individuals or small minorities in society.

Every instance of rulership of particular human groups over others was preceded by the wish to appropriate the product of labor, the tools, or the weapons of those others or to drive them from some territory which seemed more favorable for the winning of a livelihood. It is very probable that for a long time the victors contented themselves with this simple form of robbery and, when they met resistance, simply massacred their opponents. But gradually it was discovered that it was more profitable to exact tribute from the vanquished or to subject them to a new order of things by ruling over them; thereby laying the foundation for slavery.

This was all the easier as mutual solidarity extended only to members of the same tribe and found its limits there. All systems of rulership were originally foreign rulerships, where the victors formed a special privileged class and subjected the vanquished to their will. As a rule it was nomadic hunter tribes which imposed their rule upon settled and agricultural people. The calling of the hunter, which constantly makes great demands on man's activity and endurance, makes him by nature more warlike and predatory. But the farmer who is tied to his acre, and whose life as a rule runs more peacefully and less dangerously, is in most cases no friend of violent dispute. He is, therefore, seldom equal to the onset of warlike tribes and submits comparatively easily if the foreign rule is not too oppressive.

Once the victor has tasted the sweets of power and learned to value the economic advantages which it gives, he is easily intoxicated by his practice of power. Every success spurs him on to new adventures, for it is in the nature of all power that its possessors constantly strive to widen the sphere of their influence and to impose their yoke on weaker peoples. Thus gradually a separate class evolved whose occupation was war and rulership over others. But no power can in the long run rely on brute force alone. Brutal force may be the immediate means for the subjugation of men, but alone it is incapable of maintaining the rule of the individual or of a special caste over whole groups of humanity. For that more is needed; the belief of man in the inevitability of such power, the belief in its divinely willed mission. Such a belief is rooted deeply in man's religious feelings and gains power with tradition, for above the traditional hovers the radiance of religious concepts and mystical obligation.

This is the reason why the victors frequently imposed their gods upon the vanquished, for they recognized very clearly that a unification of religious rites would further their own power. It usually mattered little to them if the gods of the vanquished continued to be on show so long as this was not dangerous to their leadership, and so long as the old gods were assigned a role subordinate to that of the new ones. But this could only happen when their priests favored the rulership of the victors or themselves participated in the drive for political power, as often happened. Thus it is easy to prove the political influence on the later religious forms of the Babylonians, Chaldeans, Egyptians, Persians, Hindus, and many others. And just as easily can the famous monotheism of the Jews be traced to the struggle for the political unification of the arising monarchy.

All systems of rulership and dynasties of antiquity derived their origin from some godhead, and their possessors soon learned to recognize that the belief of their subjects in the divine origin of the ruler was the one unshakable foundation of every kind of power. Fear of God was always the mental preliminary of voluntary subjection. This alone is necessary; it forms the eternal foundation of every tyranny under whatever mask it may appear. Voluntary subjection cannot be forced; only belief in the divinity of the ruler can create it. It has, therefore, been up to now the foremost aim of all politics to awaken this belief in the people and to make it a mental fixture. Religion is the prevailing principle in history; it binds the spirit of man and forces his thought into definite forms so that habitually he favors the continuation of the traditional and confronts every innovation with misgivings. It is the inner fear of falling into a bottomless abyss which chains man to the old forms of things as they are. That determined champion of the principle of absolute power, Louis de Bonald, understood the connection between religion and politics very well when he wrote the words: "God is the sovereign power over all things; the god-man is the power over all mankind; the head of the state is the power over the subjects; the head of the family is the power in his own house. But as all power is made in the image of God and originates with God, therefore all power is absolute."

All power has its roots in God, all rulership is in its inmost essence divine. Moses received directly from the hand of God the tables of the law, which begin with the words: "I am the Lord, thy God, thou shalt have no other gods before me," and which sealed the covenant of the Lord with his people. The famous stone on which the laws of Hammurabi are recorded, which have carried the name of the Babylonian king through the millenniums, shows us Hammurabi before the face of the sun god Chamasch. The introduction which precedes the statement of the law begins thus:

When Anu, the exalted, the king of the Anunnaki, and Bel, the lord of heaven and earth, who carries the destiny of the world in his hand, partitioned the masses of mankind to Marduk, the first-born of Ea, the divine lord of the law, they made him great among the Igigi. In Babylon they proclaimed his exalted name, which is praised in all lands which they have destined to him for his kingdom, and which is eternal as are heaven and earth. Afterwards Anu and Bel made glad the body of mankind when they called upon me, the glorious ruler and god-fearing Hammurabi, that I may establish justice upon earth, destroy the wicked and the ruthless, ward off the strong and succor the weak, reign like the sun god over the destiny of black-haired men and illumine the land.

In Egypt, where the religious cult under the influence of a powerful priestly caste had shown its power in all social institutions, the deification of the ruler had assumed quite uncanny forms. The Pharaoh, or priest-king, was not alone the representative of God on earth, he was himself a god and received godlike honors. Already in the age of the first six dynasties the kings were regarded as sons of the sun god, Ra. Chufu (Cheops), in whose reign the great pyramids were built, called himself "the incarnate Horus." In a vaulted cave at Ibrim, King Amenhotep III was pictured as a god in a circle of other gods. This same ruler also built a temple at Soleb where religious veneration was offered to his own person. When his successor, Amenhotep IV, later on prohibited in Egypt the veneration of any other god, and raised the cult of the radiant sun god, Aton, who became alive in the person of the king, to the dignity of a state religion, it was doubtless political motives which moved him to it. The unity of faith was to be made to render post-chaise service to the unity of earthly power in the hands of the Pharaohs.

In the old Hindu lawbook of Manu it is written:

> God has made the king that he may protect creation. For this purpose he took parts from Indra, from the winds, from Jama, from the sun, from fire, from the heavens, from the moon and from the lord of creation. Therefore, since the king has been created from parts of these lords of the gods, his glory outshines the splendor of all created beings, and like the sun he blinds the eye and the heart, and no one can look into his face. He is fire and air, sun and moon. He is the god of right, the genius of riches, the ruler of the floods and the commander of the firmament.

In no other country outside of Egypt and Tibet has an organized priestcraft attained to such power as in India. This has left its impress on the whole social evolution of the enormous land, and by the cunning caste division of the whole population, pressed all events into iron forms; which have proved the more enduring because they are anchored in the traditions of faith. Quite early the Brahmans entered into a compact with the warrior caste to share with it the rulership of the people of India, wherein the priest-caste was always careful to see that the real power remained in their hands, that the king remained a tool of their desires. Priests and warriors were both of divine origin, the Brahmans sprang from the head of Brahma, the warriors from Brahma's breast. Both had the same objective and the law commanded: "The two castes must act in unison, for neither can do without the other." In this manner arose the system of Caesaro-Papism, in which the union of religious and political lust for power found its fullest expression.

In ancient Persia, also, the ruler was the living incarnation of divinity. When he entered a town he was received by the Magi in white garments and with the chanting of religious songs. The road along which he was carried was strewn with myrtle branches and roses and on the side stood silver altars on which incense was burned. His power was unlimited, his will the highest law, his command irrevocable, as stated in the *Zendavesta*, the sacred book of the old Persians. Only on rare occasions did he show himself to the people, and when he appeared all had to grovel in the dust and hide their faces.

In Persia, also, there were castes and an organized priestly class, which, while it did not have the omnipotent power of that of India, was, nevertheless, the first caste in the land, whose representatives, as the closest council of the king, always had the opportunity to make their influence felt and definitely to affect the destiny of the realm. Concerning the parts played by the priests in the social order, we are informed by a passage in the *Zendavesta* which reads:

> Though your good works were more numerous than the leaves of the trees, the drops of rain, the stars in heaven, or the sands of the sea, they would not profit you, if they were not pleasing to the Destur (*priest*). To gain the favor of this guide on the way of salvation you must faithfully give to him the tithe of all you possess, of your goods, of your land, and of your money. If you have satisfied the Destur, your soul will have escaped the tortures of hell, and you will find peace in this world and happiness in the one beyond; for the Desturs are teachers of religion, they know all things, and they grant absolution to all mankind.

Fu-hi, whom the Chinese designate as the first ruler of the Celestial Kingdom, and who, according to their chronicles, is said to have lived about twenty-eight centuries before our era, is venerated in Chinese mythology as a supernatural being and usually appears in their pictures as a man with a fish tail, looking like a Triton. Tradition acclaims him as the real awakener of the Chinese people, who, before his coming, lived in the wilderness in separate groups like packs of animals, and were only through him shown the way to a social order which had its foundation in the family and the veneration of ancestors. All dynasties which since that time have succeeded one another in the Middle Kingdom have traced their origin from the gods. The Emperor called himself the "Son of Heaven"; and since China never had an organized priestly class, the practice of the cult, in so far as it concerned the state religion, rested in the hands of the highest imperial official, who, however, influenced only the upper strata of the Chinese social order.

In Japan, the Mikado, the "High Gate," is regarded as a descendant of Amaterasu, the sun goddess, who in that country is worshiped as the highest divinity. She makes known her will through the person of the ruler, and in his name she governs the people. The Mikado is the living incarnation of the godhead, wherefore his palace is called "Miya," that is, shrine of the soul. Even in the time of the Shogunate, when the leaders of the military caste for hundreds of years exercised the real rulership of the land, and the Mikado played only the part of a decorative figure, the sanctity of his person remained inviolate in the eyes of the people.

Likewise, the foundation of the mighty Inca Empire, whose obscure history has presented so many problems to modern research, is ascribed by tradition to the work of the gods. The saga recounts how Manco Capac with his wife, Ocllo Huaco, appeared one day to the natives of the high plateau of Cuzco, presented himself to them as Intipchuri, the son of the sun, and induced them to acknowledge him as their king. He taught them agriculture and brought them much useful knowledge, which enabled them to become the creators of a great culture.

In Tibet there arose under the mighty influence of a power-lustful priest-caste, that strange church-state whose inner organization has such a curious kinship with Roman Papism. Like it, it has oral confession, the rosary, smoking censers, the veneration of relics, and the tonsure of the priest. At the head of the state stands the Dalai-Lama and the Bogdo-Lama, or Pen-tschen-rhin-po-tsche. The former is regarded as the incarnation of Gautama, the sacred founder of the Buddhist religion; the latter as the living personification of Tsongkapa, the great reformer of Lamaism —to him, even as to the Dalai-Lama, divine honors are offered, extending even to his most intimate physical products.

Genghis Khan, the mighty Mongol ruler, whose great wars and conquests once held half the world in terror, quite openly used religion as the chief instrument of his power policy; although he himself apparently belonged in the class of "enlightened despots." His own tribe regarded him as a descendant of the sun, but as in his enormous realm, which extended from the banks of the Dnieper to the Chinese Sea, there lived men of the most varied religious convictions, his clever instinct recognized that his rule over the subjected nations even as over the core people of his realm, could only be confirmed through priestly power. His Sun-papacy no longer sufficed. Nestorian Christians, Mohammedans, Buddhists, Confucianists and Jews inhabited his lands by the million. He had to be the high priest of every religious cult. With his North-Asiastic Shamanists he cultivated magic and inquired of the oracle which manifested itself in the cracks of the shoulder blades of sheep when thrown into fire. Sundays he went to Mass, celebrated communion with wine, held discussions with Christian priests. On the Sabbath he went to the synagogue and showed himself as Chahan, as Cohen. On Fridays he held a sort of Selamik and was just as good a Caliph as, later on, the Turk in Constantinople. But preferably he was a Buddhist; held religious discourses with Lamas, and even summoned the Grand Lama of Ssatya to him; for since he intended to change the center of his realm to Buddhistic territory in Northern Asia, he conceived the grandiose plan of setting up Buddhism as the state religion.[1]

And did not Alexander of Macedonia, whom history calls "The

[1] Alexander Ular, *Die Politik*. Frankfurt a/M. 1906, S. 44.

Great," act with the same calculation, apparently animated by the same motives, as, long after, Genghis Khan? After he had conquered a world and cemented it together with streams of blood, he must have felt that such a work could not be made permanent by brute force alone. He therefore tried to anchor his rule in the religious beliefs of the conquered people. So he, "the Hellene," sacrificed to the Egyptian gods in the temple at Memphis and led his army through the burning deserts of Libya to consult the oracle of Zeus-Ammon in the oasis of Siva. The compliant priests greeted him as the son of the "Great God" and offered him divine honors. Thus Alexander became a god and appeared before the Persians in his second campaign against Darius as a descendant of the mighty Zeus-Ammon. Only thus can we explain the complete subjugation of the enormous empire by the Macedonians, a thing which even the Persian kings had not been able to accomplish to the same degree.

Alexander had used this means only to further his political plans, but gradually he became so intoxicated with the thought of his godlikeness that he demanded divine honors not only from the subjected nations but even from his own countrymen, to whom such a cult must have remained strange, since they knew him only as Philip's son. The slightest opposition could goad him to madness and frequently led him into abominable crimes. His insatiable desire for ever greater extension of power, strengthened by his military successes, set aside all limits to his self-esteem and blinded him to all reality. He introduced at his court the ceremony of the Persian kings which symbolized the complete subjection of all mankind to the potent will of the despot. Indeed, in him, the "Hellene," the megalomania of barbaric tyranny achieved its most genuine expression.

Alexander was the first to transplant Caesarism and the idea of the divinity of the king to Europe, for up to now it had only prospered on Asiatic soil, where the state had developed with the least hindrance and where the relationship between religion and politics had come to earliest maturity. We must not conclude from this, however, that we are here concerned with a special proclivity of a race. The prevalence which Caesarism has since attained in Europe is patent proof that we are here dealing with a special type of the instinct of religious veneration, which, under similar circumstances, may appear among men of all races and nations. It is not to be denied, however, that its outward forms are bound up with the conditions of its social environment.

It was from the Orient, too, that the Romans took over Caesarism and developed it in a manner that can hardly be observed earlier in any other country. When Julius Caesar raised himself to the dictatorship of Rome, he tried to root his power in the religious concepts of the people. He traced the origin of his family from the gods and claimed Venus as an ancestress. His every effort was directed toward making himself the unlimited ruler of the realm and into an actual god, whom no interrelationship connected with ordinary mortals. His statue was set among those of the seven kings of Rome, and his adherents quickly spread the rumor that the Oracle had designated him to be the sole ruler of the realm, in order to conquer the Parthians who thus far had defied the Roman power. His image was placed among those of the immortal gods of the *Pompa Circensis*. A statue of him was erected in the Temple of Quirinus, and on its pedestal the inscription read: "To the unconquerable god." A college was established in his honor at Luperci and special priests were appointed to serve his divinity.

Caesar's murder put a sudden end to his ambitious plans, but his successors completed his work, so that presently there shone about the emperor the aura of the godhead. They erected altars to him and rendered to him religious veneration. Caligula, who had the ambition to raise himself to the highest protective divinity of the Roman state, Capitoline Jupiter, maintained the divinity of the Caesars with these words: "Just as men, who herd sheep and oxen, are not themselves sheep and oxen, but of a nature superior to these, so are those who have been set as rulers above men, not men like the others, but gods."

The Romans, who did not find it objectionable that the leaders of their army had divine honors offered to them in the Orient and Greece, at first protested against the claim that the same should be demanded of Roman citizens, but they got used to it as quickly as did the Greeks in the time of their social decline, and subsided quietly into cowardly self-debasement. Not alone did numbers of poets and artists sound the praise of "the divine Caesar" continuously throughout the land; the people and the Senate, too, outdid themselves in cringing humility and despicable servility. Virgil in his *Aeneid* glorified Caesar Augustus in slavish fashion, and legions of others followed his example. The Roman astrologer, Firmicus Maternus, who lived in the reign of Constantine, declared in his work *De erroribus profanarum religiosum:* "Caesar alone is not dependent on the stars. He is the lord of the whole world, which he guides by the fiat of the highest gods. He, himself, belongs to the circle of the gods, whom the primal godhead has designated for the carrying on and completion of all that occurs."

The divine honors which were offered to the Byzantine emperors are even today embraced in the meaning of the word "Byzantine." In Byzantium the religious honors paid to the emperor culminated in the Kow-Tow, an old Oriental custom which required the ordinary mortal to prostrate himself and to touch the earth with his forehead.

The Roman Empire fell in ruins. The megalomania of its rulers, which in the course of the centuries had led to the extinction of all human dignity in millions of their subjects, the horrible exploitation of all subject peoples, and the increasing corruption in the whole empire, had rotted men morally, killed their social consciousness and robbed them of all power of resistance. Thus in the long run they could not withstand the attack of the so-called "barbarians" who assailed the powerful realm from all sides. But the "Spirit of Rome," as Schlegel called it, lived on, just as the spirit of Caesaro-Papism lived on after the decline of the great Eastern Empire and gradually infected the untamed young forces of the Germanic tribes whose military leaders had taken over the fateful legacy of the Caesars; and Rome lived on in the Church, which developed Caesarism in the shape of Papism to the highest perfection of power, and with persistent energy pursued the aim of converting the whole of mankind into one gigantic herd and forcing it under the scepter of the high priest of Rome.

Animated also by the spirit of Rome were all those later efforts for political unification embodied in the German Kaiser concept: in the mighty empires of the Hapsburgs, Charles V and Philip II; in the Bourbons, the Stuarts, and the dynasties of the Czars. While the person of the ruler is no longer worshiped directly as a god, he is king "by the grace of God" and receives the silent veneration of his subjects, to whom he appears as a being of a superior order. The god concept changes in the course of time, just as the state concept has seen many changes. But the innermost character of all religion remains evermore untouched, just as the kernel of all politics has never undergone a change. It is the principle of power which the possessors of earthly and celestial authority made effective against men, and it is always the religious feeling of dependence which forces the masses to obedience. The head of the state is no longer worshiped as a god in public temples, but he says with Louis XIV, "I am the state!" But the state is the earthly providence which watches over man and directs his steps that he may not depart from the way of the law. The wielder of the force of the state is, therefore, only the high priest of a power which finds its expression in politics just as reverence for God finds it in religion.

Although the priest is the mediator between man and this higher power on which the subject feels himself dependent and which, therefore, becomes fate to him, Volney's contention that religion is the invention of the priest shoots wide of the mark; for there were religious concepts long before there was a priestly caste. It can also be safely assumed that the priest himself was originally convinced of the correctness of his understanding. But gradually there dawned on him the idea of what unlimited power the blind belief and gloomy fear of his fellowmen had put into his hands, and what benefit could accrue to him from this. Thus awoke in the priest the consciousness of power, and with this the lust for power, which grew constantly greater as the priesthood became more and more definitely a separate caste in society. Out of the lust for power there developed the "will to power," and with that there evolved in the priesthood a peculiar need. Impelled by this, they tried to direct the religious feelings of believers into definite courses and so to shape the impulses of their faith as to make them serve the priestly quest for power.

All power was at the outset priestly power and in its inmost essence has remained so till this day. Ancient history knows many instances where the role of the priest fused with that of the ruler and lawgiver in one person. Even the derivation of countless lordly titles from names in which the priestly function of their former bearers is clearly revealed, points with certainty to the common origin of religious and temporal power. Alexander Ular hit the nail on the head when he said in his brilliant essay, "Politics," that the Papacy never engaged in temporal politics, but that every temporal ruler has always tried to play papal politics. This is also the reason why every system of government, without distinction of form, has a certain basic theocratic character.

Every church is constantly striving to extend the limits of its power, and to plant the feeling of dependence deeper in the hearts of men. But every temporal power is animated by the same desire, so in both cases the efforts take the same direction. Just as in religion God is everything and man nothing, so in politics the state is everything, the subject nothing. The two maxims of celestial and earthly authority, "I am the Lord thy God!" and "Be ye subject unto authority!" spring from the same source and are united as are the Siamese twins.

The more man learned to venerate in God the epitome of all perfection, the deeper he sank—he, the real creator of God—into a miserable earthworm, into a living incarnation of all earthly nullity and weakness. The theologian and scribe never tired of assuring him that he was "a sinner conceived in sin," who could only be saved from eternal damnation by a revelation of God's commandments and strict obedience to them. And when the former subject and present citizen endowed the state with all the qualities of perfection, he degraded himself to an impotent and childish puppet on whom the legal pundits and state-theologians never ceased to impress the shameful conviction that in the core of his being he was afflicted with the evil impulses of the born transgressor, who could only be guided on the path of officially defined virtue by the law of the state. The doctrine of original sin is fundamental not only in all the great religious systems, but in every theory of the state. The complete degradation of man, the fateful belief in the worthlessness and sinfulness of his own nature, has ever been the firmest foundation of all spiritual and temporal authority. The divine "Thou shalt!" and the governmental "Thou must!" complement each other perfectly: commandment and law are merely different expressions of the same idea.

This is the reason why no temporal power up to now has been able to dispense with religion, which is in itself the fundamental assumption of power. Where the rulers of the state opposed for political reasons a certain form of religious system, it was always easy to introduce some other systems of belief more favorable to their purposes. Even the so-called "enlightened rulers," who themselves were infidels, were no exception to this rule. When Frederick II of Prussia declared that in his kingdom "everyone could be saved according to his own fashion," he assumed, of course, that such salvation would in no wise conflict with his own powers. The much lauded toleration of the great Frederick would have looked quite different if his subjects, or even a part of them, had conceived the idea that their salvation might be won by lowering the royal dignity, or by disregarding his laws, as the Dukhobors tried to do in Russia.

Napoleon I, who as a young artillery officer had called theology a "cesspool of every superstition and confusion" and had maintained that "the people should be given a handbook of geometry instead of a catechism" radically changed his point of view after he had made himself Emperor of the French. Not only that; according to his own confession, he for a long time flirted with the idea of achieving world rulership with the aid of the pope; he even raised the question whether a state could maintain itself without religion. And he himself gave the answer: "Society cannot exist without inequality of property and the inequality not without religion. A man who is dying of hunger, next to one who has too much, could not possibly reconcile himself to it if it were not for a power which says to him: 'It is the will of God that here on Earth there must be rich and poor, but yonder, in eternity, it will be different.'"

The shameless frankness of this utterance comes all the more convincingly from a man who himself believed in nothing, but who was clever enough to recognize that no power can in the long run maintain itself if it is not capable of taking root in the religious consciousness of mankind.

The close connection between religion and politics is, however, not confined to the fetishist period of the state, when public power still found its highest expression in the person of the absolute monarch. It would be a bitter illusion to assume that in the modern law of the constitutional state this relationship had been fundamentally altered. Just as in later religious systems the god idea became more abstract and impersonal, so has the concept of the state lost most of its concrete character as personified in the single ruler. But even in those countries where the separation of church and state had been publicly accomplished, the interrelation between the temporal power and religion as such has in no way been changed. However, the present possessors of power have frequently tried to concentrate the religious impulses of their citizens exclusively on the state, in order that they might not have to share their power with the church.

It is a fact that the great pioneers of the modern constitutional state have emphasized the necessity of religion for the prosperity of the governmental power just as energetically as did formerly the advocates of princely absolutism. Thus, Rousseau, who in his work, *The Social Contract*, inflicted such incurable wounds on absolute monarchy, declared quite frankly:

> "In order that an evolving people should learn to value the sacred fundamentals of statecraft, and obey the elementary principles of state law, it is necessary that the effect should become cause. The social spirit which would be the result of the constitution would have to play the leading part in the creation of the constitution, and men, even before the establishment of the laws, would have to be that which they would become through these laws. But since the lawgiver can neither compel nor convince, he must needs take refuge in a higher authority which, without external pressure, is able to persuade men and enthuse them without having to convince them. This is the reason why the founding fathers of the nation have at all times felt compelled to take refuge in heaven and to honor the gods for reasons of politics. Thus would men, who are subject to both the laws of the state and those of nature, voluntarily be obedient to the power which has formed both man and the state, and understandingly carry the burden which the fortune of the state imposes on them. It is this higher understanding, transcending the mental vision of ordinary men, whose dictum the legislator puts into the mouth of the godhead, thus carrying along by respect for a higher power those who are not submissive to human wisdom." [2]

Robespierre followed the advice of the master to the letter and sent the Hebertists and the so-called *"Enragés"* to the scaffold because their anti-religious propaganda, which was really anti-church, lowered the regard for the state and undermined its moral foundation. The poor Hebertists! They were just as firm believers as the "Incorruptible" and his Jacobin church congregation, but their veneration-urge moved along different lines, and they would acknowledge no higher power than the state, which to them was the holiest of holies. They were good patriots, and when they spoke of the "Nation," they were enflamed by the same religious ardor as the pious Catholic when he speaks of his God. But they were not the legislators of the country, and consequently they lacked that famous "higher understanding" which, according to Rousseau, transcends the mental grasp of ordinary men and whose decision the legislator is careful to have confirmed from the mouth of the godhead.

Robespierre, of course, possessed this "higher understanding." He felt himself to be the lawgiver of "the Republic, one and indivisible"; consequently he called atheism "an aristocratic affair," and its adherents, hirelings of William Pitt. Just so today, in order to excite the horror of

[2] Jean Jacques Rousseau, *Le contrat social*. Book II, ch. 7.

the faithful, do the partisans of Bolshevism denounce as "counter-revolutionary" every idea which does not suit them. In times of excitement such a designation is deadly dangerous and tantamount to "Strike him dead; he has blasphemed against God!" This the Hebertists, too, had to learn, as so many before and after them. They were believers, but not orthodox believers; consequently the guillotine had to convince them as formerly the stake did the heretics.

In his great speech before the convention in defense of the belief in a higher being Robespierre hardly developed an original thought. He referred to Rousseau's *Social Contract,* on which he commented in his usual long-winded manner. He felt the necessity of a state religion for Republican France, and the cult of the Supreme Being was to serve him by putting the wisdom of his policy in the mouth of the new godhead, and endowing it with the halo of the divine will.

The Convention resolved to publish that speech all over France, to translate it into all languages, thus giving the abominable doctrine of atheism a deadly blow, and to announce to the world the true confession of faith of the French people. The Jacobin Club in Paris made haste to announce its veneration of the Supreme Being in a special memorial declaration. Its content, like that of Robespierre's speech, was rooted completely in Rousseau's ideas. It referred with special gusto to a passage in the Fourth Book of the *Social Contract* which said:

> There exists consequently a purely civic confession of faith and the settling of its Articles is exclusively a matter for the head of the state. It is here a question not so much of religious doctrine as of universal views without whose guidance one can be neither a good citizen nor a faithful subject. Without being able to compel anyone to believe in them, the state can banish anyone who does not believe, not as a godless one, but as one who has violated the Social Contract and is incapable of loving the law and justice with his whole heart, incapable in case of necessity of sacrificing his life to his duty. If anyone, after the public acceptance of these civic articles of faith, announces himself as an infidel, he deserves the death penalty, for he has committed the greatest of all crimes. He has knowingly perjured himself in the face of the law.

The young French Republic was a hardly established power, still without tradition, which had, besides, arisen from the overthrow of an old system of rulership whose deeply rooted institutions were still alive in large sections of the people. It was, therefore, incumbent on her more than on any other state to establish her young power in the religious consciousness of the people. It is true that the wielders of the young power had endowed the state with divine qualities and had raised the cult of the "Nation" to a new religion which had filled France with wild enthusiasm.

But that had happened in the intoxication of the great Revolution, whose fierce tempests were to have shattered the old world. This ecstasy could not last forever, and the time was to be anticipated when increasing sobriety would make a place for critical consideration. For this new religion lacked something—tradition, one of the most important elements in the structure of religious consciousness. It was, therefore, only an act for reasons of state, when Robespierre drove the "Goddess of Reason" from the temple and replaced her by the cult of the "Supreme Being," thus procuring for "the Republic, one and indivisible," the necessary saintly halo.

Recent history, too, shows typical examples of this sort. We need only think of Mussolini's compact with the Catholic Church. Robespierre had never denied the existence of God, neither had Rousseau. Mussolini, however, was a pronounced atheist and a grim opponent of all religious belief; and fascism, true to the anti-clerical traditions of the Italian bourgeoisie, appeared at first as a decided opponent of the church. But as a clever state-theologian, Mussolini soon recognized that his power could only have permanence if he succeeded in rooting it in the feeling of dependence of his subjects, and in giving it an outward religious character. With this motive he shaped the extreme nationalism into a new religion, which in its egotistical exclusiveness, and in its violent separation from all other human groups, recognized no higher ideal than the fascist state and its prophet, *Il Duce*.

Like Robespierre, Mussolini felt that his doctrine lacked tradition, and that his young power was not impressive. This made him cautious. The national tradition in Italy was not favorable to the church. It had not yet been forgotten that the Papacy had once been one of the most dangerous opponents of national unification, which had only been successful after an open conflict with the Vatican. But the men of the Risorgimento, the creators of Italy's national unity, were no anti-religious zealots. Their politics were anti-clerical because the attitude of the Vatican had forced them to it. They were no atheists. Even that grim hater of the clergy, Garibaldi, who in the introduction to his memoirs has written the words: "The priest is the personification of the lie; but the liar is a robber, and the robber a murderer, and I could prove other damnable attributes of the priesthood"—even Garibaldi was not only, as shown by his nationalist endeavors, a deeply religious man, but his whole concept of life was rooted in a belief in God. And so the seventh of his Twelve Articles which in 1867 were submitted to the Congress of the "League for Peace and Freedom" in Geneva, runs as follows: "The Congress adopts the religion of God, and each of its members obligates itself to aid in spreading it over all the earth."

And Mazzini, the leader of Young Italy, and next to Garibaldi the foremost figure in the struggle for national unity, was in the depths of his soul permeated with the deepest religious belief. His whole philosophy was a curious mixture of religious ethics and national-political aspirations which, in spite of their democratic exterior, were of a thoroughly autocratic nature. His slogan, "God and the People," was strikingly characteristic of his aim, for the nation was to him a religious concept which he strove to confine within the frame of a political church.

Mussolini, however, and with him the numerous leaders of Italian fascism, did not find themselves in this enviable position. They had been grim antagonists, not only of the church, but of religion as such. Such a record constitutes a heavy load—especially in a country whose capital has been for hundreds of years the center of a mighty church, with thousands of agencies at its disposal which, on orders from above, were always ready to keep actively alive in the people the memory of the notorious past of the head of the fascist state. It was therefore advisable to come to an understanding with this power. That was not easy, because between the Vatican and the Italian state stood the twentieth of September, 1870, when the troops of Victor Emmanuel marched into Rome and put an end to the temporal power of the Papal States. But Mussolini was ready for any sacrifice. To purchase peace with the Vatican, he recreated, though in diminutive form, the Papal States. He recompensed the Pope financially for the injustice which had once been done to one of his predecessors, he recognized Catholicism as the state religion, and delivered to the priesthood a considerable part of the public educational institutions.

It was surely no religious or moral reason which moved Mussolini to this step, but sober considerations of political power. He needed moral support for his imperialistic plans and could but be especially concerned to remove the suspicion with which the other countries regarded him. Consequently, he sought contact with the power which had up to now weathered all the storms of time and whose mighty world-encircling organization could under certain circumstances prove very dangerous to him. Whether he had the best of the bargain is a question which does not concern us here. But the fact that it had to be exactly the "almighty Duce," who opened again the gates of the Vatican and put an end to the "imprisonment of the Popes," is one of the grotesques of history and will keep the name of Mussolini alive longer than anything else which is associated with it. Even fascism had finally to recognize that on castor oil, assassination and pogroms— however necessary such things may seem for the fascist state in its inner politics—no permanent power can be founded. Consequently, Mussolini forgot for the time being the "fascist miracle," from which the Italian people was said to have been reborn, in order that "Rome might for the third time become the heart of the world." He sought contact with the power which has its secret strength in the millennial tradition, and which, as a result, was so hard to undermine.

In Germany, where the leaders of victorious fascism had neither the adaptability nor the clever insight of Mussolini and, in stupid ignorance of the real facts, believed that the whole life of a people could be changed at the whim of their anemic theories, they had to pay dearly for their mistake. However, Hitler and his intellectual advisers did recognize that the so-called "totalitarian state" must have root in the traditions of the masses in order to attain permanence; but what they called tradition was partly the product of their sickly imagination, and partly concepts which had been dead in the minds of the people for many centuries. Even gods grow old and must die and be replaced by others more suitable to the religious needs of the times. The one-eyed Wotan and the lovely Freia with the golden apples of life are but shadow patterns of long-past ages which no "myth of the twentieth century" can awaken to new life. Consequently, the illusion of a new "German Christianity on a Germanic basis" was infinitely absurd and shamefully stupid.

It was by no means the violent and reactionary character of Hitler's policy that caused hundreds of Catholic and Protestant clergy to oppose the *Gleichschaltung* of the church. It was the certain recognition that this brainless enterprise was irrevocably doomed to suffer a setback, and they were clever enough not to assume responsibility for an adjustment which must prove disastrous to the church. It did not profit the rulers of the Third Reich to drag the obstreperous priests into concentration camps and in the bloody June days shoot down in gangster fashion some of the most prominent representatives of German Catholicism. They could not allay the storm and finally had to yield. Hitler, who had been able to beat down the whole German labor movement, numbering millions, without any opposition worth mentioning, had here bitten upon a nut he could not crack. It was the first defeat which his internal policy suffered, and its consequences cannot yet be estimated; for dictatorships are harder hit by such setbacks than any other form of government.

The leaders of the Russian Revolution found themselves confronted with a church so completely identified, in fact unified, with czarism that compromise with it was impossible; they were compelled to replace it with something else. This they did by making the collectivist state the one omniscient and omnipotent god—and Lenin his prophet. He died at a quite convenient time and was promptly canonized. His picture is replacing the ikon, and millions make pilgrimages to his mausoleum instead of to the shrine of some saint.

Although purely iconoclastic, such work is valuable, for it clears the ground of superstitious rubbish, making it ready for the fine structure which will be demanded when the latent spirituality of man who, as has been truly said, is in his inmost nature incurably religious, asserts itself.

The entire religious policy of the present Soviet Government is in fact only a repetition of the great Hebertist movement of the French Revolution. The activities of the League of Russian Atheists, favored by the government, are directed solely against the old forms of the church faith but by no means against faith itself. In reality the Russian governmental atheism is a religious movement, with this difference—that the authoritarian and religious principles of revealed religion have been transferred to the political field. The famous anti-religious education of the Russian youth, which has aroused the united protest of all church organizations, is in reality a strictly religious education which makes the state the center of all religious activities. It sacrifices the natural religion of men to the abstract dogma of definite political fundamentals established by the state. To disturb these fundamentals is as much taboo in modern Russia as were the efforts of heresy against the authority of the old church. Political heresy finds no warmer welcome from the representative of the Russian State dictatorship than did religious heresy from the papal church. Like every other religion, the political religion of the Bolshevist state has the effect of confirming man's dependence on a higher power, and perpetuating his mental slavery.

Chapter 3

THE FUNDAMENTAL PRINCIPLE OF POWER. CHRISTIANITY AND THE
STATE. PAPISM. AUGUSTINE'S *CITY OF GOD.* THE HOLY CHURCH. THE
STRUGGLE FOR WORLD DOMINION. GREGORY VII. INNOCENT III. THE
EFFECT OF POWER ON ITS POSSESSORS. ROME AND THE GERMANS. GER-
MANIC CAESARISM. THE STRUGGLE FOR ROME. THE FOREIGN DOMINION.
THE SUBMERSION OF OLD SOCIAL INSTITUTIONS. ARISTOCRACY AND
ROYALTY. FEUDALISM AND SERFDOM. THE FRANKISH EMPIRE. CHARLE-
MAGNE AND THE PAPACY. STRUGGLE BETWEEN EMPEROR AND POPE.

EVERY power is animated by the wish to be the only power, because
in the nature of its being it deems itself absolute and consequently opposes
any bar which reminds it of the limits of its influence. Power is active
consciousness of authority. Like God, it cannot endure any other God beside it. This is the reason why a struggle for hegemony immediately
breaks out as soon as different power groups appear together or have to
keep inside of territories adjacent to one another. Once a state has attained
the strength which permits it to make decisive use of its power it will
not rest satisfied until it has achieved dominance over all neighboring
states and has subjected them to its will. While not yet strong enough
for this it is willing to compromise, but as soon as it feels itself powerful
it will not hesitate to use any means to extend its rule, for the will to power
follows its own laws, which it may mask but can never deny.

The desire to bring everything under one rule, to unite mechanically
and to subject to its will every social activity, is fundamental in every
power. It does not matter whether we are dealing with the person of the
absolute monarch of former times, the national unity of a constitutionally
elected representative government, or the centralistic aims of a party which
has made the conquest of power its slogan. The fundamental principle
of basing every social activity upon a definite norm which is not subject
to change is the indispensable preliminary assumption of every will to
power. Hence the urge for outward symbols presenting the illusion of a
palpable unity in the expression of power in whose mystical greatness the
silent reverence of the faithful subject can take root. This was clearly
recognized by de Maistre when he said: "Without the Pope, no sover-

eignty; without sovereignty, no unity; without unity, no authority; without authority, no faith."

Yes, without authority, no faith, no feeling in man of dependence on a higher power; in short, no religion. And faith grows in proportion to the extent of its sphere of influence, to the scope of its authority. The possessors of power are always animated by the desire to extend their influence and, if they are not in a position to do so, to give their faithful subjects at least the illusion of the boundlessness of this influence, and thus to strengthen their faith. The fantastic titles of oriental despots serve as examples.

Where the opportunity offers, the possessors of power are not content with vainglorious titles; they seek rather by every device of diplomatic cunning and brute force to extend their sphere of power at the cost of other power groups. Even in the smallest power units there slumbers like a hidden spark the will to world dominion; even though it can awaken to a devouring flame only under specially favorable circumstances, it always remains alive, if only as a secret wish concept. There is deep meaning in the description which Rabelais gives us in his "Gargantua" of the petty king, Picrochole, whom the mild, yielding disposition of his neighbor, Grandgousier, made so cocky, that, deluded by the crazy advice of his counselors, he already imagined himself a new Alexander. While the possessor of power sees a territory not yet subject to his will, he will never rest content, for the will to power is an insatiable desire which grows and gains strength with every success. The story of the mourning Alexander, who burst into tears because there were no longer any worlds for him to conquer, has a symbolic meaning. It shows us most clearly the real essence of all struggles for power.

The dream of the erection of a world empire is not solely a phenomenon of ancient history. It is the logical result of all power-activity and not confined to any definite period. Since Caesarism penetrated into Europe the vision of world dominion has never disappeared from the political horizon, although it has undergone many changes through the appearance of new social conditions. All the great attempts to achieve universal dominion, like the gradual evolution of the Papacy, the formation of the empire of Charlemagne, the two aims which furnished the basis of the contest between the imperial and papal powers, the creation of the great European dynasties and the contest which later nationalist states waged for the hegemony in the world, have always taken place according to the Roman model. And everywhere the unification of political and social power factors occurred according to the same scheme, characteristic of the manner of genesis of all power.

Christianity had begun as a revolutionary mass movement, and with its doctrine of the equality of men before the sight of God it had undermined the foundation of the Roman state. Hence, the cruel persecution of its followers. It was the opposition to the state which resulted from Christian doctrines that the state strove to suppress. Even after Constantine had elevated Christianity to a state religion, its original aims persisted for a long time among the Chiliasts and Manichaeans, though these were unable to exert a determining influence on the further development of Christianity.

Even as early as the third century Christianity had fully adapted itself to existing conditions. The spirit of theology had been victorious over the vital aspirations of the masses. The movement had come into closer touch with the state which it had once denounced as the "realm of Satan," and under its influence had acquired an ambition for political power. Thus, from the Christian congregation there evolved a church which faithfully guarded the power ideas of the Caesars when the Roman Empire fell to ruin in the storms of the great migration of peoples.

The seat of the Bishop of Rome in the very heart of the world empire gave him from the very beginning a position of dominant power over all other Christian congregations. For Rome remained, even after the decline of the empire, the heart of the world, its center, in which the legacy of ten to fifteen cultures remained alive and held the world under its spell. From here, too, reins were put upon the young, still unused powers of the northern barbarians under whose impetuous assaults the empire of the Caesars had broken down. The teachings of Christianity, even though already degenerated, tamed their savage mood, put fetters on their will and revealed to their leaders new methods, which opened unexpected vistas to their ambitions. With clever calculation the developing Papacy harnessed the still unused energies of the "barbarian" and made them serve its ends. With their help it laid the foundation of a new world power, which was for many centuries to give to the lives of the peoples of Europe a definite direction.

When Augustine was getting ready to set forth his ideas in his *City of God*, Christianity had already undergone a complete inner transformation. From an anti-state movement it had become a state-affirming religion which had absorbed a number of alien elements. But the young church was still decked out in many colors; it lacked the systematic drive toward a great political unity which consciously and with full conviction steers toward the clearly defined goal of a new world dominion. Augustine gave it this goal. He felt the frightful disintegration of his time, saw how thousands of forces strove toward a thousand different goals, how in crazy chaos they whirled about each other and, scarcely born, were scattered by the winds or died fruitless, because they lacked aim and direction. After manifold struggles he came to the conclusion that men lacked a unified power which should put an end to discord and collect the scattered forces for the service of a higher purpose.

Augustine's *City of God* has nothing in common with the original teachings of Christianity. Precisely for this reason his work could become the theoretical foundation of an all-embracing Catholic world concept which made the redemption of humanity dependent upon the aims of a church. Augustine knew that the overlordship of the church had to be deeply rooted in the faith of men if it was to have permanence. He strove to give this faith a basis which could not be shaken by any acuteness of intellect. Hence, he became the real founder of that theological theory of history which attributes every event among the peoples of the earth to the will of God, on which man can have no influence.

During the first century Christianity had declared war against the fundamental ideas of the Roman state and all its institutions, and had consequently brought upon itself all the persecutions of that state. But Augustine maintained that it was not bound to oppose the evils of the world, since "all earthly things are transitory," and "true peace has its abode only in heaven." Consequently, "The true believer must not condemn war but must look upon it as a necessary evil, as a punishment which God has imposed upon men. For war is, like pestilence and famine and all other evils, only a visitation of God for the chastisement of men for their betterment, and to prepare them for salvation."

But to make the divine government comprehensible to men there is needed a visible power, through which God may manifest his holy will and guide sinners on the right road. No temporal power is fitted for this task, for the kingdom of the world is the kingdom of Satan, which must be overcome in order that men may achieve redemption. Only to the *una sancta ecclesia*, "the One Holy Church" is this task reserved and assigned by God himself. The church is the only true representative of the Divine Will on earth, the guiding hand of Providence, which alone does what is right, because illumined by the divine spirit.

According to Augustine all human events take place in six great epochs, the last of which began with the birth of Christ. Consequently, men must recognize that the end of the world is immediately at hand. Hence, the establishment of God's kingdom on earth is most imperatively demanded in order to save souls from damnation and prepare men for the heavenly Jerusalem. But since the church is the sole proclaimer of God's will, her character must needs be intolerant, for man himself cannot know what is good and what is evil. She cannot make the slightest concession to the mind's logic, for all knowledge is vanity and the wisdom of man cannot prevail before God. Thus, faith is not a means to an end, but an end in itself. One must believe for the sake of belief and must not permit oneself to be diverted from the right path by the illusions of reason, for the saying attributed to Tertullian, *"Credo quia absurdum est* ("I believe it because it is absurd"), is correct, and it alone can free man from the talons of Satan.

Augustine's views concerning the world dominated Christianity for centuries. Through the whole of the Middle Ages only Aristotle enjoyed a comparable authority. Augustine bestowed on men the belief in an inevitable fate and welded this belief to the struggle for political unification of the church, which felt itself called upon to restore the lost world dominion of Roman Caesarism and to make it subservient to a far higher purpose.

The bishops of Rome now had a goal which gave their ambition wide scope. But before this goal could be attained and the church converted into a powerful tool for a political purpose, the leaders of the other Christian congregations had to be made amenable to this purpose. Until this could be accomplished the world dominion of the Papacy remained a dream. The church had first to be internally united before she could think to impose her will on the holders of temporal power.

This was no easy task, for the Christian congregations remained for a long time merely loose groups which elected their own priests and leaders and could at any time depose them if they did not prove fit for their office. Furthermore, every congregation had the same right as all the others. It managed its own affairs and was undisputed master in its own house. Questions which transcended the authority of the local groups were adjusted by district synods or church conventions freely elected by the congregations. In matters of faith, however, only the ecumenical council, the general church convention, could make decisions.

The original church organization was therefore fairly democratic, and in this form was much too loose to serve the Papacy as a foundation for its political purposes. The bishops of the larger congregations did, however, gradually achieve greater dignity because of their wider circles of influence. Thus the convention of Nicea granted them a certain monitorship over the smaller congregations by making them metropolitans and archbishops. But the rights of the Metropolitan of Rome extended no further than that of any of his brothers. He had no opportunity to mix in their affairs, and his dignity was sometimes overshadowed by the influence of the Metropolitan of Constantinople.

The tasks of the bishops of Rome were therefore beset with great difficulties, to which not all of them were equal; and centuries had to pass before they could establish their influence over the majority of the clergy. This was all the more difficult as the bishops of the various countries were frequently wholly dependent on the holders of temporal power for their authority and right of maintenance. However, the bishops of Rome pursued their aim with clever calculation and persistent effort; nor were they at all fastidious in their choice of means as long as these promised results.

How unconcernedly the occupants of the Roman chair steered toward their goal is proved by the clever use they knew how to make of the notorious "Isidorian Decretals" which the well-known historian, Ranke, has described as "a quite conscious, very well-conceived, but patent forgery"; a judgment which is hardly disputed anywhere today. However, before the possibility of the forgery of these documents was admitted they had already achieved their purpose. On their authority the pope was confirmed as the viceroy of God on earth, to whom Peter had intrusted the keys of heaven. The whole of the clergy was subjected to his will. He was conceded the right to call general councils whose conclusions he could accept or reject according to his own judgment. Most important of all, these forged "Isidorian Decretals" declared that in all disputes between the temporal states and the clergy the decision was to lie in the last instance with the pope. Thereby the cleric was to be withdrawn entirely from the jurisdiction of the temporal power, so that he might be bound more firmly to the papal chair. Attempts of this kind had already been made. Thus, the Roman bishop, Symachus (498-514), had declared that the bishop of Rome was not responsible to any judge but God; and twenty years before the appearance of the "Isidorian Decretals" the Council of Paris (829) declared that the king was subject to the church and the power of the priest stood above every worldly power. These forged decretals could, therefore, only have the purpose of giving to the claims of the church the stamp of legality.

With Gregory VII (1073-85) begins the real hegemony of the Papacy, the era of the "church triumphant." He was the first who quite publicly and without any limitations asserted the prerogative of the church over every worldly power, and even before his ascent of the papal throne he had worked with iron persistency toward this goal. Above all, he introduced fundamental changes into the church itself to make it a more serviceable tool for his purposes. His implacable severity brought it about that priestly celibacy, which had often been proposed but never carried out, was now imposed effectively. In this manner he created for himself an international army which was not bound by any intimate worldly ties and whose least member felt himself a representative of the papal will. His well-known saying that "the church could never free itself from the servitude to temporal power until the priest was freed from woman" clearly indicates the goal he sought by this reform.

Gregory was a cunning and most astute politician, fully convinced of the justice of his claims. In his letters to Bishop Hermann of Metz he develops his concept with complete clarity, supporting it principally by the *City of God* of Augustine. Starting with the assumption that the church was instituted by God himself, he concludes that in every one of his decisions the will of God is revealed and that the pope, as God's viceroy on earth, is the proclaimer of this divine will. Consequently any disobedience of him is disobedience to God. Every temporal power is but the weak work of men, as is at once apparent from the fact that the state has abolished equality among men and that its origin can be traced only to brutal force and injustice. Any king who does not unconditionally submit himself to the commands of the church is a slave of the devil and an enemy of Christianity. It is the church's task to unite humanity in a great community ruled only by God's laws, revealed to them by the mouth of the pope.

Gregory fought with all the intolerance of his forceful character for a realization of these aims, and although he finally fell a victim to his own policy, he nevertheless succeeded in establishing the hegemony of the church and in making it for centuries the most powerful factor in European history. His immediate successors, however, possessed neither the monkish earnestness nor the boundless energy characteristic of Gregory and therefor suffered many a set-back in their contests with temporal power. But with Innocent III (1198-1216) the papal scepter fell to a man who had not only Gregory's clearness of aim and unbendable will but far excelled him in natural ability.

Innocent III achieved for the church her highest aim and raised her power to a degree it had never before attained. He ruled his cardinals with the despotic will of an autocrat not responsible to anyone and treated the possessors of temporal power with an arrogance no one of his predecessors had dared to assume. To the Patriarch of Constantinople he wrote these proud words: "God did not only lay the dominion of the church in Peter's hands, he also appointed him to be the ruler of the whole world." To the envoy of the French king, Philippe Augustus, he said: "To princes is given power only over earth, but the priest rules also over heaven. The prince has power only over the bodies of his subjects, the priest has power also over the souls of men. Therefore the priesthood is as high above every temporal power as is the soul above the body in which it dwells."

Innocent forced the whole temporal power of Europe under his will. He not only interfered in all dynastic affairs, he even arranged the marriages of the temporal rulers and compelled them to obtain a divorce in case the union did not suit him. Over Sicily, Naples and Sardinia he ruled as actual monarch; Castile, Leon, Navarre, Portugal, and Aragon were tributary to him. His will was obeyed in Hungary, Bosnia, Serbia, Bulgaria, Poland, Bohemia, and in the Scandinavian countries. He interfered in the contest between Philip of Swabia and Otto IV for the German imperial crown and gave it to Otto, only to take it away from him again later and confer it on Frederick II. In his quarrel with the English king,

John Lackland, he proclaimed an interdict over his realm, and not only forced the king to complete submission but even compelled him to accept his own country as a fief from the pope and to pay a tribute for this clemency.

Innocent thought of himself as pope and Caesar in one person and saw in the temporal rulers only vassals of his power, tributary to him. In this sense he wrote to the King of England: "God has founded kingship and priesthood on the church so that the priesthood is thus kingly and kingship priestly; as is apparent from the Epistles of Peter and the laws of Moses. Therefore did the King of Kings set *one above all*, whom he appointed his Viceroy on earth."

By the establishment of oral confession and the organization of mendicant monks, Innocent created for himself a power of tremendous scope. Furthermore, he made free use of his strongest weapon, the ban of the church, which with unyielding resolution he imposed upon whole countries in order to make the temporal rulers submissive to him. In a land hit by the ban all churches remained closed. No bells called the faithful to prayer. There were neither baptisms nor weddings, no confessions were received, no dying were given extreme unction and no dead buried in sanctified ground. One can imagine the terrible effects of such a status on the spirit of men at a time when faith was regarded as supreme.

Just as Innocent tolerated no equal power, he likewise permitted no doctrine which departed in the least from the usage of the church, even though entirely imbued with the spirit of true Christianity. The terrible crusade against heresy in the south of France, which changed one of the most flourishing lands in Europe into a desert, bears bloody witness to this. The dominant ambitious spirit of this fearful man balked at no means to guard the unlimited authority of the church. However, he also was but the slave of a fixed idea which kept his spirit prisoner and estranged it from all human consideration. His power obsession made him lonely and miserable. It became his personal evil genius, as it does with most of those who pursue the same end. Thus he spoke once concerning himself: "I have no leisure to pursue other worldly things; I can scarcely find time to breathe. Truly, so completely must I live for others that I have become a stranger to myself."

It is the secret curse of every power that it becomes fatal, not only to its victims but to its possessors. The bare thought that one must live for the achievement of an end which is opposed to all sound human feeling and is incomprehensible in itself, gradually makes the possessor of power himself into a dead machine, after he has forced all coming under the dominance of his power to a mechanical obedience to his will. There is something puppetlike in the nature of every power, arising from its own illusions, which coerces everything coming into contact with it into fixed form. And all these forms continue to live in tradition even after the last spark of life has died in them, and lie like an incubus on the spirit which submits to their influence.

This, to their sorrow, the Germanic and after them the Slavic tribes —the people who had remained longest immune to the pernicious influence of Roman Caesarism—had to learn. Even after the Romans had subjugated the German lands from the Rhine to the Elbe their influence was confined almost entirely to the western territory. The inhospitality of the country, covered with enormous forests and swamps, never gave them an opportunity to confirm their dominion. When by a confederation of German tribes the Roman army was almost completely annihilated in the Teutoburger Forest and most of the strongholds of the foreign invaders were destroyed, Roman rule over Germany was as good as broken. Even the three campaigns Germanicus waged against the rebellious tribes could not change the situation.

But there had arisen for the Germans, through Roman influence, a much more dangerous enemy in their own camp, to which their leaders especially soon surrendered. The German tribes whose habitat for a long time extended from the Danube to the Baltic and from the Rhine to the Elbe enjoyed a rather far-reaching independence. Most of the tribes were already permanently settled when they came in contact with the Romans; only the eastern part of the country was still semi-nomadic. From Roman records and later sources it is apparent that the social organization of the Germans was still very primitive. The various tribes were formed by families connected with each other by blood relationships; as a rule a hundred of these lived in scattered settlements on the same piece of land, hence the designation "hundred." Ten to twenty such hundreds formed a tribe, whose territory was designated as a county (*Gau*). By the union of related tribes arose a people. The hundreds divided the land among themselves, and in such a manner that periodic repartitions were necessary. From this it is apparent that for a long time private ownership of land did not exist among them, and that private property was limited to weapons and homemade tools and other objects of daily use. The tilling of the soil was done mainly by women and slaves. A part of the men frequently went on war-and-booty raids while the other part took its turn at staying home and maintained justice and right dealing.

All important questions were considered at general assemblies, or Folk-Things, and there decided. At these assemblies all freemen fit to bear arms participated. As a rule they occurred at the time of the new moon and were for a long time the supreme institution of the German people. At the Thing all differences were adjusted. The director of public administration was elected, as well as the commander during war. At these elections the personal character and the experience of the individual were at first the determining factors. Later on, however, especially when the relations with the Romans became more frequent and more intimate, the so-called "foremost ones" or *Fürsten* ("princes") were elected almost exclusively from the ranks of prominent families, which, by reason of real or imagined services to the community, had been the recipients of larger shares of booty, tribute and presents, and thus achieved a state of wealth which permitted them to keep a retinue of tried warriors and thus, quite naturally, to achieve certain prerogatives.

The oftener the Germans came in contact with the Romans the more amenable they became to foreign influence, which could not very well be otherwise, since Roman culture and technique was in all respects superior to the German. Even before the conquest of Germany by the Romans certain tribes had begun to move, had been assigned by the Roman rulers certain districts, and had in return obligated themselves to serve in the Roman army. In fact, German soldiers had already played an important part in the conquest of Gaul by the Romans. Julius Caesar enlisted many German soldiers in his armies and was himself always surrounded by a mounted bodyguard of four hundred Teuton warriors.

Many descendants of Germans who had been in Roman service later returned to their homes and used the booty they had won and the experience they had gained from the Romans to press their own countrymen into their service. Thus one of them, Marbod, succeeded in time in extending his dominion over quite a number of German tribes and subjecting all the land between the Oder and Elbe from Bohemia to the Baltic to his influence. And even Herman, "The Liberator," succumbed to the influence of the Roman will to power, which after his return he tried to impose upon his own people. Not in vain had Herman and Marbod lived in Rome and learned there what enormous attraction power has for the ambitions of man.

Herman's ambitions for political power, which became constantly more apparent after the destruction of the Roman host had led to the liberation of Germany from Roman rule, appear in a somewhat peculiar light. It soon became clear not only that the noble Cheruscan had learned in Rome the art of superior warfare, but also that the statecraft of the Roman Caesars had given his ambitions a mighty impulse which soon developed into a dangerous will to power. Absorbed by his plans he endeavored by every means to make the federation of the Cheruski, Chatti, Marsi, Brukteri and others permanent after they had achieved the destruction of the Roman legions in the Teutoburger Forest. After the final retreat of the Romans he soon engaged in a bloody war with Marbod, the issue of which was solely the rulership in Germany. When Herman's aim to raise himself from the elected leadership of the Cheruski to kingship over this and other tribes became still more clearly apparent, he was treacherously murdered by his own relatives.

But the Germans were by no means united in their struggle against the Romans. There were among them noble families who were quite definitely Roman partisans. Quite a number of them had received Roman honors and distinctions, accepted Roman citizenship, and even after the so-called *"Hermannsschlacht"* ("Herman's battle") still firmly adhered to Rome. Herman's own brother, Flavus, was among these and so was his father-in-law, Segest, who had delivered his own daughter, Herman's wife, Thusnelda, to the Romans. From this side the Roman viceroy, Varus, had been warned of the conspiracy hatched against him, but his confidence in Herman, who because of his reliability had been made a Roman knight, was so unbounded that he spurned all warnings and blindly went into the trap which Herman had set for him. Without this cunning hypocritical breach of faith on Herman's part the celebrated "Battle of Liberation" in the Teutoburger Forest would never have happened. Even a historian so favorable to Germany as Felix Dahn described this event as "one of the most treacherous breaches of the law of nations."

The Germanic tribes who participated in this conspiracy to free themselves from the hated Roman rulership can hardly be reproached for their action. But on Herman personally this despicable breach of faith rests with double weight, for the destruction of the Roman army was to be only a means for the furthering of his political plans, which were to culminate in imposing a new yoke on the liberated peoples.

It is in the nature of all ambitions to political power that those animated by them hesitate at no means which promise success—even though such success must be purchased by treason, lies, mean cunning, and hypocritical intrigue. The maxim that the end justifies the means has always been the first article of faith of all power politics. No Jesuits were needed to invent it. Every power-lustful conqueror, every politician, subscribes to it, Semite and German, Roman and Mongol, for the baseness of method is as closely related to power as decay is to death.

When, later on, the Huns penetrated into Europe, compelling a new migration of the peoples they encountered, ever denser hordes of Germanic tribes moved toward the south and southwest of the continent, always coming into contact with the Romans and enlisting *en masse* in the Roman legions. The Roman armies were thoroughly permeated by Germans, so it was inevitable that finally one of them, the German chieftain, Odoacer, in the year 476 pushed the last Roman emperor from his throne and had himself proclaimed emperor by his soldiers. But he also was, after years of bloody struggle, overcome by Theodoric, the king of the Ostrogoths, who murdered him with his own hands at the feast which was, with all solemnity, to celebrate a treaty of peace.

All state organizations which were in that period created by the power of the sword—the kingdoms of the Vandals, the Ostrogoths and Visigoths, the Lombards, the Huns—were imbued with the idea of Caesarism, and their creators felt themselves to be heirs of Rome. But in the struggle for Rome and Roman possessions the old institutions and tribal habits of the Germans fell into disuse as of no importance in the new conditions. True, some isolated tribes carried their old customs into the Roman world, but they decayed and perished there; for they had left behind the social soil in which alone they could flourish.

This transition took place all the faster, since already a considerable time before the great migrations some rather fundamental changes had occurred in the social life of the Germanic tribes. Thus, Tacitus speaks of a new way of partitioning the land according to the prominence of the various families, a practice of which Caesar makes no mention. And likewise the administration of public affairs presents a different picture. The influence of the so-called "nobles" and army leaders had everywhere increased. All questions of social importance were first discussed at separate sessions of the nobles and then submitted to the Folk-Things, with which, however, the last decision lay. But the followers whom these nobles collected, who frequently lived with them and ate at their tables, must naturally have given them a greater influence at the popular assemblies. How this worked out is clearly apparent from the following words of Tacitus: "He earns lifelong disgrace and shame who in battle does not follow his lord to the death. To defend him, to protect him, even to credit him with his own heroic deeds, is the warrior's supreme duty. *The prince fights for victory; the vassals fight for their lord.*"

The constant contact with the Roman world naturally could but react on the social forms of the Germanic peoples. Especially among the "nobles" it awakened a lust for power which gradually led to readjustments of the conditions of social life. When, later on, the great migration occurred, a considerable part of the German population was already permeated by Roman ideas and institutions. The new state organizations resulting from the great migrations of the tribes and peoples necessarily hastened the internal decay of the old institutions.

All over Europe arose new dominions within which the victors formed a privileged class which imposed their will on the working population and led a parasitic life at their expense. The victorious intruders partitioned large sections of the conquered territory among themselves and made the inhabitants pay tribute, and in this it was inevitable that the chieftains should favor their own followers. Since the relatively small number of the conquerors did not permit them to live together in large families according to custom, but compelled them to spread themselves over the land to maintain their power, the old ties of consanguinity, based on the close association of the families, were loosened more and more. The old customs gradually went out of use to make way for new forms of social life.

The popular assembly, the most important institution of the Germanic tribes, where all public affairs were discussed and decided, gradually lost its old character, a change necessitated by the extent of the occupied territory. Meanwhile the chiefs and army leaders claimed ever greater prerogatives, which logically grew to royal powers. The kings, moreover, intoxicated by Roman influence, were not slow to abolish the last remnants of democratic institutions, which, of course, could only prove a hindrance to the enlargement of their own power.

The aristocracy, likewise, whose first beginnings are early discernible among the Germans, had by the rich booty in lands which fell to them in the newly conquered territory acquired a quite new social importance. Together with the nobles of the subjected peoples, whom the foreign rulers, for weighty reasons, took into their service (their cultural superiority was useful to them), these members of the new aristocracy were at first only vassals of the king, to whom they had to render service in war. For this they were rewarded by rich fiefs at the cost of the conquered.

But the feudal system, which at first bound the nobility to the royal power, already contained the germs which must in time endanger it. The economic power which the feudal system gradually put into the hands of the nobles aroused in them new desires and ambitions, forcing their possessors into a unique position which was not favorable to the centralization of kingly power. It was contrary to the ambition of the nobles to be merely members of the king's retinue. The part of the Grand Seigneur who ruled unhindered on his own possessions without having to obey mandates of a higher power, suited them much better and, most important, it opened for them wider fields for the extension of their own power. For in them also the will to power was active, urging them to throw their economic strength into the balance to check the increasing power of the kings.

As a matter of fact the feudal lords, who in time grew into lesser or greater princes, succeeded for a long time in keeping the king compliant to their will. Thus arose in Europe a new order of parasites who no longer had any close relationship with the people, the foreign intruders being not even connected with the subject peoples by ties of blood. From war and conquest arose a new system of human slavery which for centuries left its imprint on the agrarian sections of the country. By the insatiable greed of the noble landlords the peasants were plunged ever deeper into misery and were robbed of the last liberties they had retained from former times. They were hardly regarded any longer as human beings.

But the dominion over foreign people worked destructively not only on the subject part of the population; it undermined the internal relationship among the conquerors themselves and destroyed their old traditions. The force which had at first only been exerted against the subjugated peoples was gradually extended to the poorer sections of their own tribes until these, too, sank into the quagmire of serfdom. Thus the will to power smothered with implacable consistency the will to freedom and independence which was once so deeply rooted among the German tribes. By the spread of Christianity and the closer connection between the conquerors and the church this baneful development was still further extended; the new religion smothered the last rebellious sparks in men and habituated them to come to terms with the imposed conditions. Just as the will to power under the Roman Caesars had robbed a whole world of its humanity and had plunged it into the hell of slavery, so it later destroyed the free social institutions of the barbarians and thrust them into the misery of serfdom.

Among the newly founded realms which arose in various parts of Europe, that of the Franks achieved the greatest importance. After the Merovingian Clovis, King of the Salic Franks, in the year 486 had inflicted on the Roman viceroy, Sygarius, a decisive defeat, he seized the whole of Gaul without encountering any opposition worth mentioning. As with all others obsessed by the desire for power, Clovis' appetite grew by what it fed on. Not only did he endeavor to secure his internal power, he also embraced every opportunity to extend his frontiers. Ten years after his victory over the Romans he defeated the army of the Allemanni at Zulpich and united their lands with his realm. At that time he also accepted Christianity, not from any inner conviction but simply from political consideration.

In this manner arose in Europe a temporal power of a new kind. The church, which not without reason believed the Frankish ruler could prove serviceable against her many enemies, was soon ready to ally itself with Clovis, all the more as her position was weakened by the defection of the Arians and, even in Rome itself, was threatened by dangerous opponents. Clovis, one of the cruelest and most faithless fellows who ever sat upon a throne, soon realized that such an alliance could not help but further the plan he was ambitiously pursuing with all the guile of his treacherous character. So he had himself baptized at Rheims and was designated by the local bishop as "the most Christian of kings"—which, however, did not prevent him from pursuing his ends by most un-Christian means. The church, moreover, countenanced his bloody crimes, for it could not object to them if it wished to make Clovis useful to its power.

Later however, when the successors of Clovis led in reality but a shadow existence and the rulership of the state was almost completely in the hands of the so-called "Mayors of the Palace" whose tenure became hereditary under Pepin of Herestal, the pope conspired with Pepin's grandson, Pepin the Short, and advised him to make himself king. Pepin then put the last of the Merovingian kings into a cloister and thus became the founder of a new dynasty of the Frankish kingdom. Under his son, Charlemagne, the alliance between the pope and the Frankish royal house reached its highest effectiveness and secured to the Frankish ruler the hegemony of Europe. Thereupon the idea of a universal European monarchy, the achievement of which had been the main object of Charlemagne's life, again assumed definite shape. The church, moreover, which pursued a similar end, could only welcome such an ally. Each had need of the other to complete its plans for political power.

The church needed the sword of the temporal ruler to guard it against its enemies; hence it became the church's highest aim to direct the sword according to its will and by the help of the sword to extend its dominion. Charlemagne, moreover could not dispense with the church, since it gave his rule the needed inner religious cohesion; being the only power which had preserved the spiritual and cultural heritage of the Roman world. In the church was embodied the whole culture of the age. It had in its ranks scholars, philosophers, historians and politicians, and its monasteries were for a long time the only spots where art and industry could flourish and where human wisdom could find an abiding place. Hence the church was a most valuable ally for Charlemagne, creating for him the spiritual atmosphere necessary for the maintenance of his enormous realm. For this reason he tried to bind the clergy to him by economic means—compelling the subjugated people to pay tithes to the church and thus securing to its agents an abundant income. An ally like the pope was all the more welcome to Charlemagne since the prerogative of power still remained firmly in his hands, and the pope was wise enough to play for a time the part of a vassal to the Frankish ruler.

When the pope was hard beset by the Lombard king, Desiderius, Charlemagne hastened to his aid with an army and put an end to the dominion of the Lombards in Northern Italy. For this the Church displayed her gratitude when on Christmas day of the year 800 in St. Peter's Cathedral Leo III placed the imperial crown on the head of the kneeling Charlemagne and proclaimed him "Roman Emperor of the Frankish Nation." This act was meant to demonstrate to humanity that from now on the Christian world of the Occident was to be under the direction of a temporal and a spiritual ruler, designated by God to guard the physical and spiritual welfare of the Christian peoples. Thus pope and Emperor, with separate roles, became symbols of a new concept of world power, which in its practical effects was to prevent peace in Europe for centuries.

While it is readily understandable that the same will, fed by Roman traditions, had to bring the church and monarchy together, it was likewise inevitable that an honorable separation of the parts played by each could not endure. It lies in the nature of every will-to-power that it will tolerate an equally privileged power only so long as it can use it for its purposes, or does not yet feel itself strong enough to engage in a fight for dominance. While church and empire had to establish their power together, and were consequently largely dependent on each other, their union would remain intact, at least outwardly. But it was inevitable that as soon as one or the other of these powers was strong enough to stand on its own feet the struggle for predominance would break out between them and be carried implacably to the end. That the church finally proved victor in this fight was only to be expected in view of the circumstances. Its spiritual superiority, resting on an older and, above all, a much higher culture, to which the barbarians had to be painfully habituated, assured it a mighty advantage. Furthermore, the church was the only power which could unite Christian Europe to resist the onslaught of the Mongolian and oriental hordes. The empire was not equal to this task, for it was bound by a mass of separate political interests and consequently could not give Europe the needed protection by its own power.

While Charlemagne lived, the Papacy, with prudent calculation, was content to play the second part, being almost entirely dependent on the protection of the Frankish ruler. His successor, however, Louis the Pious, a limited and superstitious man, became merely a tool in the hands of the priests. Possessing neither the mental ability nor the reckless activity of his predecessor, he could not maintain the empire which Charlemagne had cemented together with streams of blood and with unscrupulous force. So it soon fell apart, making room for a new partition of Europe.

The Papacy was triumphant over the whole array of temporal power and remained for hundreds of years the dominant institution of the Christian world. But when this world finally became disjointed and everywhere in Europe the national state came more and more into the foreground, then vanished also the dream of a universal world dominion under the scepter of the pope, such as Thomas Aquinas had visioned. Although the church opposed the new development of things with all her power, she could not in the long run prevent the transformation of Europe, and had to be content to make the best possible adjustment with the political ambitions of the arising nationalist states.

Chapter 4

THE CREATION OF CASTES AS A GOVERNMENTAL NECESSITY. PLATO'S
TEACHING CONCERNING THE DIVISION OF THE STATE INTO CLASSES.
EXTERNAL LIMITATIONS OF CLASS DIVISIONS AS AN ASSUMPTION FOR
POLITICAL POWER. ARISTOTLE'S THEORY OF THE STATE AND THE IDEA
OF "INFERIORS." SPIRITUAL BARRENNESS OF POWER. POWER AND CUL-
TURE AS OPPOSITES. STATE AND COMMUNITY. POWER AS A PRIVILEGE
OF A MINORITY. POWER AND LAW. NATURAL LAW AND "POSITIVE LAW."
THE DUAL ROLE OF LAW. FREEDOM AND AUTHORITY. LAW AS BAROM-
ETER OF CULTURE. THE STRUGGLE FOR RIGHTS IN HISTORY.

EVERY POWER presupposes some form of human slavery, for the
division of society into higher and lower classes is one of the first conditions of its existence. The separation of men into castes, orders and classes
occurring in every power structure corresponds to an inner necessity for
the separation of the possessors of privilege from the people. Legend and
tradition provide the means of nourishing and deepening in the concepts
of men the belief in the inevitability of the separation. A young rising
power can end the dominion of old privileged classes, but it can only do
so by immediately creating a new privileged class fitted for the execution
of its plans. Thus, the founders of the so-called "dictatorship of the
Proletariat" in Russia had to call into being the aristocracy of the Com-
missars, which is as distinguishable from the great masses of the working
population as are the privileged classes of the population of any other
country.

Plato already wished, in the interest of the state, to attune the moral
feeling of the individual to an officially established concept of virtue.
Deducing all morality from politics, and thus becoming the first to set
forth the intellectual assumptions of the so-called "reasons of state," he
already saw clearly that class division was an implicit necessity for the
maintenance of the state. For this reason he made membership in one
of the three orders on which his envisioned state was to be founded a
matter of fate, on which the individual had no influence. However, to
imbue men with faith in their "natural destiny," the statesman employs
a "salutary fraud" when he tells them: "The creative god mixed gold in
stuff from which he made those among you who are intended for ruler-

ship; you are therefore of most precious worth. Into your helpers he put silver and into peasants and other laborers, iron and bronze." To the question, how the citizens could be brought to believe this deception he answered: "I think it impossible to convince these themselves, but it is not impossible to make the story seem probable to their sons and descendants during the coming generations." [1]

Here we find man's destiny determined by a mixture of abilities and characteristics received from God, which determines whether he shall be master or servant during his life. To plant deeper in the imagination of men this belief in an inevitable fate and to give it the mystic sanctity of a religious conviction has up to now been the chief aim of every power policy.

Just as the state is always trying within its borders to abolish equality of social position among its subjects and to perpetuate this separation by differences of caste and class, so externally, too, it must take care to keep itself distinct from all other governmental organizations and to instil into its citizens the belief in their national superiority over all other peoples. Plato, the only one among the Greek thinkers in whom the idea of national unity of all Hellenic peoples is at all clearly apparent, felt himself exclusively a Greek and looked down with unconcealed contempt upon the "barbarians." The idea that these could be considered equal to the Hellenes, or could even approximate them, seemed to him as presumptuous as it was incomprehensible. This is the reason why in his ideal state all heavy and degrading work was to be done by foreigners and slaves. He saw in this a benefit not only for the Hellenic master caste but also for the slaves themselves. According to his concept, since they were destined anyhow to perform the lowly services of the slave, it should appear to them a kindly decree of fate that they were to be allowed to serve Greeks.

Aristotle grasped the concept of man's "natural destiny" even more clearly. For him, too, there existed peoples and classes designated by nature to perform the low tasks. To these belonged primarily all non-Greeks and barbarians. It is true, he made a distinction between "slaves according to nature" and "slaves according to law." Among the former he placed those who because of their lack of self-reliance are destined by nature to obey others. Among the latter were those who had lost their freedom by being taken prisoners of war. In both instances, the slave is but "a living machine" and, as such, "a part of his master." According to the principles stated by Aristotle in his *Politics*, slavery is beneficial both to the ruler and the ruled; nature having endowed the one with higher faculties and the other with only the rude strength of the beast, from which fact the roles of master and slave arise quite of themselves.

According to Aristotle man is "a state-forming being," by his whole

[1] Plato, *The Republic*. Third Book.

nature destined to be a citizen under a government. On this ground he condemned suicide, for he denied to the individual the right to withdraw himself from the state. Although Aristotle judged Plato's ideal state rather unfavorably, especially the community of possessions advocated in it, as "running contrary to the laws of nature," the state itself, for all that, was for him the center around which all earthly existence revolved. Like Plato, he believed that the management of the business of the state should always be in the hands of a small minority of selected men destined by nature itself for this calling. Hence, he was logically compelled to justify the prerogative of the elect by the alleged inferiority of the great masses of the people and to trace this condition to the iron rule of the course of nature. In this concept, in the last analysis, every "moral justification" of tyranny has its roots. Once we have agreed to separate our own countrymen into a mentally inferior mass and a minority designed by nature itself for creative activity, the belief in the existence of "inferior" and "select" nationalities or races follows quite self-evidently—especially when the select derive a benefit from the slave labor of the inferior and are relieved by them of care for their own existence.

But the belief in the alleged creative capacity of power rests on a cruel self-deception. Power, as such, is wholly incapable of creating anything, being totally dependent on the creative activity of its subjects, if it is to exist at all. Nothing is more erroneous than the customary view of the state as the real creator of cultural progress. The opposite is true. The state was from the very beginning the hindering force which opposed the development of every higher cultural form with outspoken misgiving. States create no culture; indeed, they are often destroyed by higher forms of culture. Power and culture are, in the deepest sense, irreconcilable opposites, the strength of one always going hand in hand with the weakness of the other. A powerful state machine is the greatest obstacle to every cultural development. Where states are dying or where their power is still limited to a minimum, there culture flourishes best.

This idea will appear daring to most of us because a clearer vision of the real causes of cultural events has been completely obscured by a mendacious education. To conserve the interests of the state our brains have been crowded with a mass of false notions and silly assumptions, so that we are mostly incapable of approaching historical matters without prejudice. We smile at the simplicity of the Chinese chroniclers who record of the legendary ruler, Fu-hi, that he endowed his subjects with the arts of the chase, of fishery and of stock-raising, that he invented the first musical instruments and taught them the use of letters. But we repeat quite thoughtlessly what has been drummed into us concerning the culture of the Pharaohs, the creative activity of the Babylonian kings, the alleged cultural achievements of Alexander of Macedonia or of Frederick the

Great. We do not even suspect that it is all foul witchcraft, lying humbug without a glimmer of truth in it, which has been repeated so often that for most of us it has become a clear certainty.

Culture is not created by command. It creates itself, arising spontaneously from the necessities of men and their social cooperative activity. No ruler could ever command men to fashion the first tools, first use fire, invent the telescope and the steam engine, or compose the *Iliad*. Cultural values do not arise by direction of higher authorities. They cannot be compelled by dictates nor called into life by the resolution of legislative assemblies.

Neither in Egypt nor in Babylon, nor in any other land was culture created by the heads of systems of political power. They merely appropriated an already existing and developed culture and made it subservient to their special political purposes. But thereby they put the ax to the root of all future cultural progress, for in the same degree as political power became confirmed, and subjected all social life to its influence, occurred the inner atrophy of the old forms of culture, until within their former field of action no fresh growth could start.

Political power always strives for uniformity. In its stupid desire to order and control all social events according to a definite principle, it is always eager to reduce all human activity to a single pattern. Thereby it comes into irreconcilable opposition with the creative forces of all higher culture, which is ever on the lookout for new forms and new organizations and consequently as definitely dependent on variety and universality in human undertakings as is political power on fixed forms and patterns. Between the struggles for political and economic power of the privileged minorities in society and the cultural activities of the people there always exists an inner conflict. They are efforts in opposite directions which will never voluntarily unite and can only be given a deceptive appearance of harmony by external compulsion and spiritual oppression. The Chinese sage, Lao-tse, had in mind this opposition when he said:

> Experience teaches that none can guide the community;
> The community is collaboration of forces;
>   as such, thought shows, it cannot be led
>   by the strength of one man.
> To order it is to set it in disorder;
> To fix it is to unsettle it.
> For the conduct of the individual changes:
>   Here goes forward, there draws back;
>   Here shows warmth, there reveals cold;
>   Here exerts strength, there displays weakness;
>   Here stirs passion, there brings peace.

And so:
> The perfected one shuns desire for power,
>   shuns the lure of power,
>   shuns the glamour of power.[2]

Nietzsche also had a profound conception of this truth, although his inner disharmony and his constant oscillation between outlived authoritarian concepts and truly libertarian ideas all his life prevented him from drawing the natural deductions from it. Nevertheless, what he has written about the decline of culture in Germany is of the most impressive significance and finds its confirmation in the decline of culture of every sort.

> No one can finally spend more than he has. That holds good for individuals; it holds good for peoples. If one spends oneself for power, for high politics, for husbandry, for commerce, Parliamentarism, military interests —if one gives away that amount of reason, earnestness, will, self-mastery, which constitutes one's real self, for the one thing, he will not have it for the other. Culture and the state—let no one be deceived about this—are antagonists: The 'Culture State' is merely a modern idea. The one lives on the other, the one prospers at the expense of the other. All great periods of culture are periods of political decline. Whatever is great in a cultural sense is non-political, is even anti-political.[3]

If the state does not succeed in guiding the cultural forces within its sphere of power into courses favorable to its ends, and thus exhibit the growth of higher forms, these very higher forms will sooner or later destroy the political frame which they rightly regard as a hindrance. But if the political machine is strong enough to force the cultural life for any considerable period into definite forms, then it will gradually seek out other channels, not being bound by any political limitations. Every higher form of culture, if it is not too greatly hindered in its natural development by political obstructions, strives constantly to renew its creative urge to construct. Every successful work arouses the need for greater perfection and deeper spirituality. Culture is always creative, always seeks new forms of activity. It is like the trees of the tropical jungle whose branches when they touch the earth always take new root.

Power is never creative. It uses the creative force of a given culture to clothe its nakedness and to increase its dignity. Power is always a negative element in history. It decorates itself in false feathers to give its importance the appearance of creative force. Here also the words in Nietzsche's *Zarathustra* hit the bull's eye :

[2] Lao-tse, *The Course and the Right Way.* Translated from the German of Alexander Ular. Published by the Inselbücherei, Leipzig.

[3] Friedrich Nietzsche, *Götzen-Dämmerung* ("*The Twilight of the Idols*").

Wherever a people still exists, it does not understand the state but hates it like the evil eye and a sin against laws and customs. This sign I give you: Every people speaks its own language of good and evil, which its neighbor does not understand. It invented its own language for laws and customs. But the state lies in all the tongues of good and evil; and whatever it says, it lies. And whatever it has, it has stolen. Everything about it is false. It bites with false teeth, rabidly. Even its guts are false.

Power always acts destructively, for its possessors are ever striving to lace all phenomena of social life into a corset of their laws to give them a definite shape. Its mental expression is dead dogma; its physical manifestation of life, brute force. This lack of intelligence in its endeavors leaves its imprint likewise on the persons of its representatives, gradually making them mentally inferior and brutal, even though they were originally excellently endowed. Nothing dulls the mind and the soul of man as does the eternal monotony of routine, and power is essentially routine.

Since Hobbes gave to the world his work about the citizen, *De Cive*, the ideas expressed there have never quite lost vogue. They have in the course of three centuries in one form or another constantly occupied the minds of men, and today dominate their thoughts more than ever. But although Hobbes, the materialist, did not base his ideas on the dogmas of the church, this did not prevent him from appropriating as his own the fateful dictum: "Man is fundamentally wicked." All his philosophical contemplations are based on this assumption. For him, man was just a born beast guided by selfish instincts, without any consideration for his fellows. The state alone put an end to this condition of "war of all against all" and became a terrestrial Providence whose ordering and punishing hand prevented man from sinking hopelessly into the slough of bestiality. Thus, according to Hobbes, the state became the real creator of culture, forcing man with iron compulsion to rise to a higher level of being, no matter how repugnant this might be to his inner nature. Since then this fable of the cultural creative role of the state has been endlessly repeated, and allegedly confirmed by new facts.

And yet this untenable concept contradicts all historical experience. It is exactly by the state that the remnants of bestiality, man's heritage from ancient ancestors, have been carefully guarded through the centuries and cleverly cultivated. The World War with its abominable methods of mass murder, the conditions in Mussolini's Italy, in Hitler's Third Reich, should convince even the blindest what this so-called "culture state" really is.

All higher understanding, every new phase of intellectual development, every epoch-making thought, giving men new vistas for their cultural activities, has been able to prevail only through constant struggle with the authority of church and state after their supporters had for whole epochs made enormous sacrifices in property, liberty and life for their convictions. When such renewals of spiritual life were finally recognized by church and state, it was always because they had in time become irresistible, and those in authority could not help themselves. But even this recognition, gained only after violent resistance, led in most cases to a planned dogmatizing of the new ideas, which under the spirit-killing guardianship of power gradually became as utterly benumbed as all previous attempts at the construction of a new intellectual outlook.

The very fact that every system of rulership is founded on the will of a privileged minority which has subjugated the common people by cunning or brute force, while each particular phase of culture expresses merely the anonymous force of the community, is indicative of the inner antagonism between them. Power always reverts to individuals or small groups of individuals; culture has its roots in the community. Power is always the sterile element in society, denied all creative force. Culture embodies procreative will, creative urge, formative impulse, all yearning for expression. Power is comparable to hunger, the satisfaction of which keeps the individual alive up to a certain age limit. Culture, in the highest sense, is like the procreative urge, which keeps the species alive. The individual dies, but never society. States perish, cultures only change their scene of action and forms of expression.

The state welcomes only those forms of cultural activity which help it to maintain its power. It persecutes with implacable hatred any activity which oversteps the limits set by it and calls its existence into question. It is, therefore, as senseless as it is mendacious to speak of a "state culture"; for it is precisely the state which lives in constant warfare with all higher forms of intellectual culture and always tries to avoid the creative will of culture.

But although power and culture are opposite poles in history, they nevertheless have a common field of activity in the social collaboration of men, and must necessarily find a *modus vivendi*. The more completely man's cultural activity comes under the control of power, the more clearly we recognize the fixation of its forms, the crippling of its creative imaginative vigor and the gradual atrophy of its productive will. On the other hand, the more vigorously social culture breaks through the limitations set by political power, the less is it hindered in its natural development by religious and political pressure. In this event it grows into an immediate danger to the permanence of power in general.

The cultural forces of society involuntarily rebel against the coercion of institutions of political power on whose sharp corners they bark their shins. Consciously or unconsciously they try to break the rigid forms which obstruct their natural development, constantly erecting new bars before it. The possessors of power, however, must always be on the watch, lest the intellectual culture of the times stray into forbidden paths, and so perhaps disturb or even totally inhibit their political activities. From this continued struggle of two antagonistic aims, the one always representing the caste interests of the privileged minority, the other the interests of the community, a certain legal relationship gradually arises, on the basis of which the limits of influence between state and society, politics and economics—in short, between power and culture—are periodically readjusted and confirmed by constitutions.

What we mean today by "law" and "constitution" is merely the intellectual precipitate of this endless struggle, and inclines in its practical effects more to one side or the other according as power or culture achieves a temporary preponderance in the life of the community. Since a state without society, politics without economics, power without culture, could not exist for a moment and, on the other hand, culture has thus far not been able to eliminate the power principle from the communal social life of men, law becomes the buffer between the two, weakens the shock and guards society against a continuous state of catastrophe.

In law it is primarily necessary to distinguish two forms: "natural law" and so-called "positive law." A natural law exists where society has not yet been politically organized—before the state with its caste and class system has made its appearance. In this instance, law is the result of mutual agreements between men confronting one another as free and equal, motivated by the same interests and enjoying equal dignity as human beings. Positive law first develops within the political framework of the state and concerns men who are separated from one another by reason of different economic interests and who, on the basis of social inequality, belong to various castes and classes.

Positive law becomes effective on the one hand by giving the state (which everywhere in history has its roots in brute force, conquest and enslavement of the conquered) a legal character; on the other hand, by trying to achieve an adjustment between the rights, duties and privileges of the various classes of society. However, this adjustment has permanence only as long as the mass of the conquered submits to the existing condition of the law or does not feel itself strong enough to fight against it. It changes when the demand of the people for a reformation of the laws becomes so urgent and irresistible that the ruling power—obeying necessity and not an inner impulse—has to take account of this desire if they do not wish to run the risk of being completely overthrown by a violent revolution. When this happens, the new government formulates new laws, which will be the more liberal the more vigorously the revolutionary will lives and finds expression among the people.

In the despotic realms of ancient Asia, where all power was embodied in the person of the ruler, whose decisions were uninfluenced by the protest of the community, power was law in the fullest meaning of the word. Since the ruler was revered as the immediate descendant of the godhead, his will prevailed as the highest law of the land, brooking no other pretensions. So, for instance, the famous code of Hammurabi was based wholly on "divine law" revealed to men by sacred command, and in consequence of its origin not subject to human judgment.

However, the legal concepts expressed in the codes of an autocrat are not merely the will of a despot. They are always bound up with ancient morals and traditional customs which have in the course of centuries become habitual in men and are the result of their communal social life. The Code of Hammurabi is no exception to this rule, for all the practical precepts of Babylonian law, springing from the needs of social life, already had validity among the people long before Hammurabi put an end to the rule of the Elamites, and by the conquest of Larsa and Jamutbal laid the foundation of a unified monarchy.

Right here appears the dual character of the law, which cannot be denied even under the most favorable circumstances. On the one hand, law gives ancient custom, which has taken root from antiquity among the people as the so-called "common law," a definite content. On the other hand, it provides for the prerogatives of privileged castes a lawful aspect, which conceals their unholy origin. Only by a careful scrutiny of this patent mystification can we understand the profound belief of men in the sacredness of law: it flatters their sense of justice and at the same time establishes their dependence on a higher power.

This inner discrepancy becomes most clearly apparent when the phase of absolute despotism has been overcome and the community participates more or less in the making of the law. All the great contests in the body politic have been contests about law, for men have always tried to confirm their newly gained rights and liberties by the laws of the state; which naturally led to new difficulties and disappointments. This is the reason why thus far every struggle for right has changed to a struggle for power, why the revolutionary of yesterday has become the reactionary of today; for it is not the form of power but power itself which is the root of the evil. Every power, of whatever kind, has the impulse to reduce the rights of the community to a minimum to make secure its own existence. Society, on the other hand, strives for a constant extension of its rights and liberties, which it seeks to achieve by the limitation of the functions of the state. This is especially apparent in revolutionary periods when men are filled with the longing for new forms of social culture.

The contest between state and society, power and culture, is thus comparable to the motion of a pendulum which proceeds always from one of its two poles—authority—slowly struggling toward the opposite pole—freedom. And just as there was once a time when might and right were one, so we are now apparently moving toward a time when every form of rulership shall vanish, law yield place to justice, liberties to freedom.

Every reconstruction of the law by the incorporation of new rights and liberties or the extension of those already existing emanates from the people, never from the state. The liberties we enjoy today, in a more or less limited degree, the people owe neither to the good will nor the special favor of government. On the contrary, the possessors of public power have left no means untried either to prevent the establishment of new rights or to render them ineffective. Great mass movements, indeed actual revolutions, were necessary to win from the possessors of power every little concession; they would never have yielded one of them voluntarily.

It is, therefore, a complete misconception of historical facts that leads a high-flown radicalism to declare that political rights and liberties as laid down in the constitutions of the various states are without significance because they have been formulated and confirmed by government. It is not because the possessors of power viewed these rights sympathetically that they established them, but because they were compelled by outward pressure. The spiritual culture of the time somewhere burst the bounds of the political frame, and the ruling powers had to submit to forces which for the time being they could not neglect. .

Political rights and liberties were never won in legislative bodies, but compelled from them by external pressure. Moreover, even legal guarantee by no means gives security that such rights will be permanent. Governments are ever ready to curtail existing rights or to abolish them entirely if they believe the country will not resist. It is true that attempts at curtailment have sometimes resulted disastrously for possessors of power who did not rightly estimate the strength of their opponents and did not know how to choose the proper time for action. Charles I had to pay for his attempt with his life; others, with the loss of their power. But this did not prevent constant new attempts from being made in this direction. Even in those countries where certain rights like freedom of the press, of assembly, of organization, and so on, have for centuries been established among the people, the governments seize every favorable opportunity to curtail these rights, or by judicial hair-splitting to give them a narrower interpretation. America and England furnish us in this respect with many examples that constitute food for reflection. Of the famous Weimar constitution of the Germans, put out of commission on almost any rainy day, it is hardly worth while to speak.

Rights and liberties do not persist because written down legally on a scrap of paper. They become permanent only when they have become a vital necessity for the people; have, so to speak, entered their very flesh and blood. They will be given regard only as long as this necessity survives among the people. When this is no longer true, no parliamentary opposition avails, and no appeal, however passionate, to respect the constitution. The recent history of Europe provides striking examples.

Chapter 5

THE REVOLT OF THE COMMUNITIES. THE AGE OF FEDERALISM. PER-
SONAL FREEDOM AND SOCIAL UNION. THE COMMUNITY OF CHRISTEN-
DOM. THE DECLINE OF MEDIEVAL CULTURE. THE DISSOLUTION OF
COMMUNAL INSTITUTIONS. MERCANTILISM. THE GREAT DISCOVERIES.
DECLINE OF THE PAPAL POWER. THE JANUS HEAD OF THE RENAISSANCE.
THE REVOLT OF THE INDIVIDUAL. THE "MASTER MAN." PEOPLE BECOMES
MOB. THE NATIONAL STATE. MACHIAVELLI'S *PRINCIPE*. NATIONAL
UNITY AS A TOOL OF TEMPORAL POWER. THE HIGH PRIESTS OF THE
NEW STATE.

EVERY political power tries to subject all groups in social life to its
supervision and, where it seems advisable, totally to suppress them; for
it is one of its most vital assumptions that all human relations should
be regulated by the agencies of governmental power. This is the reason
why every important phase in the cultural reconstruction of social life
has been able to prevail only when its inner social connections were strong
enough to prevent the encroachments of political power or temporarily
to eliminate them.

After the downfall of the Roman Empire there arose almost everywhere in Europe barbaric states which filled the countries with murder
and rapine and wrecked all the foundations of culture. That European
humanity at that time was not totally submerged in the slough of utter
barbarism, was owing to that powerful revolutionary movement which
spread with astonishing uniformity over all parts of the continent and
is known to history as "the revolt of the communities." Everywhere men
rebelled against the tyranny of the nobles, the bishops, and governmental
authority and fought with armed hands for the local independence of their
communities and a readjustment of the conditions of their social life.

In this manner the victorious communities won their "charters" and
created their city constitutions in which the new legal status found expression. But even where the communities were not strong enough to achieve
full independence they forced the ruling power to far-reaching concessions. Thus evolved from the tenth to the fifteenth century that great
epoch of the free cities and of federalism whereby European culture was
preserved from total submersion and the political influence of the arising

90

royalty was for a long time confined to the non-urban country. The medieval commune was one of those constructive social systems where life in its countless forms flowed from the social periphery toward a common center and, always changing, entered into the most manifold connections, opening for man ever new outlooks for his social being. At such times the individual feels himself an independent member of society; which makes his work fruitful, gives wings to his spirit and prevents his mental stagnation. And this communal spirit, always at work in a thousand places, which by the very fullness of its manifestations in every field of human activity shapes itself into a unified culture, has its own roots in the community and finds expression in every aspect of communal life.

In such a social environment man feels free in his decisions, although intergrown in countless ways with the community. It is this very freedom of associations which gives force and character to his personality and moral content to his will. He carries the "law of the association" in his own breast, and hence any external compulsion appears to him senseless and incomprehensible. He feels, however, the full responsibility arising from his social relations with his fellowmen, and he makes it the basis of his personal conduct.

In that great period of federalism when social life was not yet fixed by abstract theory and everyone did what the necessity of the circumstances demanded of him, all countries were covered by a close net of fraternal associations, trade guilds, church parishes, county associations, city confederations, and countless other alliances arising from free agreement. As dictated by the necessities of the time they were changed or completely reconstructed, or even disappeared, to give place to wholly new leagues without having to await the initiative of a central power which guides and directs everything from above. The medieval community was in all fields of its rich social and vital activities arranged chiefly according to social, not governmental, considerations. This is the reason why the men of today, who from the cradle to the grave are continually subjected to the "ordering hand" of the state, find this epoch frequently quite incomprehensible. In fact, the federalistic arrangement of society of that epoch is distinguished from the later types of organization and the centralizing tendencies arising with the development of the modern state, not only by the form of its purely technical organization, but principally by the mental attitudes of men, which found expression in social union.

The old city was not only an independent political organism, it also constituted a separate economic unit, whose administration was subject to its guilds. Such an organization had necessarily to be founded on a continual adjustment of economic interests. This was in fact one of the most important characteristics of the old city culture. This was the more natural because sharp class distinctions were for a long time absent in the

old cities, and all citizens were therefore equally interested in the stability
of the community. Labor, as such, offered no opportunity for the accumulation of riches so long as the major part of its products were used by the
inhabitants of the city and its nearest environs. The old city knew social
misery as little as deep inner antagonisms. So long as this condition prevailed the inhabitants were easily capable of arranging their affairs
themselves, because no sharp social contrasts existed to disturb the inherent
union of the citizens. Hence federalism, founded on the independence
and the equality of rights of all its members, was the accepted form of
social organization in the medieval communities, with which the state,
insofar as it existed at all, had to come to terms. The church, likewise,
for a long time, did not dare to disturb these forms, since its leaders
recognized clearly that this rich life with its unlimited variety of social
activities was deeply rooted in the general culture of the period.

Precisely because the men of that period were so deeply rooted in
their fraternal associations and local institutions they lacked the modern
concept of the "nation" and "national consciousness" destined to play
such a mischievous role in the coming centuries. The man of the federalistic period doubtless possessed a strong sentiment for the homeland,
because he was much more closely connected with the homeland than
are the men of today. However, no matter how intimately he felt himself
related with the social life of his village or city, there never existed between him and the citizens of another community those rigid, insurmountable barriers which arose with the appearance of the national states in
Europe. Medieval man felt himself to be bound up with a single, uniform
culture, a member of a great community extending over all countries,
in whose bosom all people found their place. It was the community of
Christendom which included all the scattered units of the Christian world
and spiritually unified them.

Church and empire likewise had root in this universal idea, even
though animated by different motives. For pope and emperor Christianity
was the necessary ideological basis for the realization of a new world
dominion. For medieval man it was the symbol of a great spiritual community, wherein were embodied the moral interests of the time. The
Christian idea also was only an abstract concept, like that of the fatherland
and of the nation—with this distinction, however, that while the Christian
idea united them, the idea of the nation separated and organized them
into antagonistic camps. The deeper the concept of Christianity took root
in men, the easier they overcame all barriers between themselves and
others, and the stronger lived in them the consciousness that all belonged
to one great community and strove toward a common goal. But the more
the "national consciousness" found entrance among them, the more dis-
ruptive became the differences between them and the more ruthlessly

was everything which they had had in common pushed into the background to make room for other considerations.

A number of different causes contributed to the decline of the medieval city culture. The incursions of the Mongols and Turks into the East European countries and the Seven Hundred Years' War of the little Christian states at the north of the Iberian peninsula against the Arabs greatly favored the development of strong states in the East and the West of the continent. Principally, however, profound changes had taken place within the cities themselves whereby the federalist communities were undermined and a way made for a reorganization of the conditions of life. The old city was a commune which for a long time could hardly be designated as a state. Its most important task consisted in establishing a fair adjustment of social and economic interests within its borders. Even where more extensive unions were formed, as for instance in the countless leagues of various cities to guard their common security, the principle of fair adjustment and free association played a deciding role; and as every community within the federation enjoyed the same rights as all the others, for a long time no real political power could be maintained.

This condition, however, was thoroughly changed by the gradual increase of the power of commercial capital, due primarily to foreign trade. The creation of a money economy and the development of definite monopolies secured commercial capital an ever growing influence both within and without the city, leading necessarily to far-reaching changes. By this the inner unity of the commune was loosened, giving place to a growing caste system and leading necessarily to a progressive inequality of social interests. The privileged minorities pressed ever more definitely towards a centralization of the political forces of the community and gradually replaced the principles of mutual adjustment and free association by the principle of power.

Every exploitation of public economy by small minorities leads inevitably to political oppression, just as, on the other hand, every sort of political predominance must lead to the creation of new economic monopolies and hence to increased exploitation of the weakest sections of society. The two phenomena always go hand in hand. The will to power is always the will to exploitation of the weakest; and every form of exploitation finds its visible expression in a political structure which is compelled to serve as its tool. Where the will to power makes its appearance, there the administration of public affairs changes into a rulership of man over man; the community assumes the form of the state.

The transformation of the old city in fact took place along this line. Mercantilism in the perishing city republics led logically to a demand for larger economic units; and by this the desire for stronger political forms was greatly strengthened. For the protection of its enterprises commercial capital needed a strong political power with the necessary military forces, which would recognize its interests and protect them against the competition of others. Thus the city gradually became a small state, paving the way for the coming national state. The histories of Venice, Genoa and many other free cities, all show us the separate phases of this evolution and its inevitable accompanying phenomena, a development which was later unexpectedly favored by the discovery of the passage to India and of America. By this the social foundations of the medieval community, already weakened by internal and external struggles, were shaken in their inmost core; and what little remained in them fit for future development was later totally destroyed by victorious absolutism. The further these inner disintegrations progressed the more the old communes lost their original significance, until at last only a waste of dead forms remained, felt by men as an oppressive burden. Thus, later, the Renaissance became a rebellion of men against the social ties of the past, a protest of individualism against the forceful encroachment of the social environment.

With the age of the Renaissance a new epoch commenced in Europe, causing a far-reaching revolution in all traditional views and institutions. The Renaissance was the beginning of that great period of revolutions in Europe which is not yet concluded today. In spite of all social convulsions we have not yet succeeded in finding an inner adjustment of the manifold desires and needs of the individual and the social ties of the community whereby they shall complement each other and grow together. This is the first requisite of every great social culture. Evolutionary possibilities are first set free by such a condition of social life, and can then be brought to full development. The medieval city culture had its roots in this condition before it was infected with the germs of disintegration.

A long line of incidents had contributed to bring about a profound revolution in men's thought. The dogmas of the church, undermined by the shattering criticism of the nominalists, had lost much of their former influence. Likewise, the mysticism of the Middle Ages, already classed as heresy because it proclaimed an immediate relation between God and man, had lost its effectiveness and yielded place to more earthly considerations. The great voyages of discovery of the Spaniards and the Portuguese had greatly widened the outlook of European man and had turned his thoughts to earth again. For the first time since the submersion of the ancient world the scientific spirit revived again, but under the unlimited dominance of the church it found a home only among the Arabs and Jews in Spain. Here it burst the oppressive fetters of a soulless scholasticism and became tolerant of independent thought. As man then turned toward Nature and her laws it was inevitable that his faith in a Divine

Providence should become shaken, for periods of natural scientific knowledge have never been propitious for religious faith in the miraculous.

Furthermore, it became ever clearer that the dream of the *Respublica Christiana,* the union of all Christendom under the pope's shepherd's crook, was at an end. In the struggle against the arising nationalist states the church had been forced into the rear. Furthermore, even in its own camp, the forces of disintegration were becoming constantly stronger, leading in the northern countries to open secession. When in addition to all this we consider the great economic and political changes in the body of the old society we can understand the causes of that great spiritual revolution, the effects of which are perceptible even today.

The Renaissance has been called the starting point for modern man, who at that time first became aware of his personality. It cannot be denied that this assertion is partly based on truth. In fact modern man has by no means exhausted his heritage from the Renaissance. His thought and his feeling in many ways bear the imprint of that period, though he lacks a large part of the characteristics of the man of the Renaissance. It is no accident that Nietzsche, and with him the protagonists of an exaggerated individualism, who unfortunately do not possess Nietzsche's intellect, are so much inclined to revert to that period of "liberated passions" and "the roaming blond beast" in order to give their ideas a historical background.

Jacob Burckhardt cites in his work, *The Culture of the Renaissance in Italy,* a wonderful passage from the speech of Pico della Mirandola about the dignity of man, which is also applicable to the twofold character of the Renaissance. The Creator is speaking to Adam:

"In the middle of the world have I placed thee that thou mayst the more easily look about thee and see all that is therein contained. I created thee as a being neither celestial nor terrestrial, neither mortal nor immortal, only that thou mayst be thine own free creator and master. Thou canst degenerate into the beast or reshape thyself into a godlike being. The beasts bring with them from the mother's womb all they were meant to have; the highest spirits among them are from the beginning, or soon after, what they will remain through all eternity. Thou alone hast the power of development, of growth according to free will. Thou hast the germ of an all-embracing life in thee."

The epoch of the Renaissance wears, in fact, a Janus head, behind whose double brow concepts clash, differences arise. From the one side it declared war against the dead social structure of a vanished period and freed man from the net of social ties which had lost their fitness for him and were felt only as restraints. From the other side it laid the foundation of the present power policies of the so-called "national interests" and developed the ties of the modern state. These have been the more destructive because they have not sprung from free association for the protection of common interests, but have been imposed upon men from above to protect and extend the privileges of small minorities in society.

The Renaissance made an end of the scholasticism of the Middle Ages and freed human thought from the fetters of theological concepts, but at the same time it planted the germs of a new political scholasticism and gave the impulse to our modern state-theology whose dogmatism yields in no way to that of the church and equally with it destroys and enslaves the spirit of man. Along with the old institutions of the community it also destroyed their ethical value without seeming able to provide an effective substitute. Thus the Renaissance developed simply into a revolt of man against society, and sacrificed the soul of the community for an abstract concept of freedom which was itself based on a misconception. The freedom it strove for was but a fateful illusion, for it lacked those social principles by which alone it could survive.

True freedom exists only where it is fostered by the spirit of personal responsibility. Responsibility towards one's fellowmen is an ethical feeling arising from human associations and having justice for each and all as its basis. Only where this principle is present is society a real community, developing in each of its members that precious urge toward solidarity which is the ethical basis of every healthy human grouping. Only when the feeling of solidarity is joined to the inner urge for social justice does freedom become a tie uniting all; only under this condition does the freedom of fellowmen become, not a limitation, but a confirmation and guarantee of individual freedom.

Where this prerequisite is missing, personal freedom leads to unlimited despotism and the oppression of the weak by the strong—whose alleged strength is in most cases founded less on mental superiority than on brutal ruthlessness and open contempt for all social feeling. The revolution of the Renaissance did in fact lead to such a situation. As its chosen leaders shook off all the ethical restraints of the past and contemned every consideration of the welfare of the community as personal weakness, they developed that extreme ego-cult which feels bound by no commandment of social morality and values personal success above any truly human feeling. Thus, from so-called "human freedom" nothing could emerge but the freedom of the Master Man, who welcomed any promising means for gaining power. Contemptuous of all feeling for justice, he was prepared to make his road even over corpses.

The concept of the historical significance of the Great Man, which today is again assuming ominous proportions, was developed by Machiavelli with iron logic. His treatise on the prince is the intellectual precipitate of a time when, on the political horizon, gleamed the gruesome words of the *Assassins;* "Nothing is true; everything is permitted!" The most abominable crime, the most contemptible act, becomes a great deed, becomes a political necessity, as soon as the Master Man puts in appearance. Ethical considerations have validity only for the private use of weaklings; for in politics there is no moral viewpoint, but solely questions of power, for whose solution any means is justifiable which promises success. Machiavelli reduced the amorality of state power to a system and tried to justify it with such cynical frankness that it was frequently assumed, and is still sometimes assumed today, that his *Principe* is only a burning satire on the despots of that time, overlooking the fact that this document was written merely for the private use of one of the Medici, and was not at all intended for the public; for which reason it was not published until after its author's death.

Machiavelli did not just draw his ideas from his inner consciousness. He merely reduced to a system the common practices of the age of Louis XI, Ferdinand the Catholic, Alexander VI, Cesare Borgia, Francesco Sforza and others. These rulers were as handy with poison and dagger as with rosary and scepter and did not permit themselves to be influenced in the least by moral considerations in the pursuit of their plans for political power. *Il Principe* is a true portrait of every one of them. Says Machiavelli:

A prince need not possess all the above-mentioned virtues, but he should have the reputation of possessing them. I even venture to say that it is very harmful to possess them and constantly to observe them; but to appear pious, true, human, God-fearing, Christian, is useful. It is only necessary at once so to shape one's character as to be able when it is necessary to be also the opposite of these. It must, therefore, be understood that a prince, especially a new prince, cannot be expected to observe what is regarded as good by other men, for to maintain his position he must often offend against truth, faith, humanity, mercy, and religion. Therefore he must possess a conscience capable of turning according to the winds of changing fortune and, as we have said, not neglect the good when it is feasible but also do the bad when it is necessary. A prince must therefore be very careful never to utter a word not full of the above-mentioned five virtues. All that one hears of him must exude compassion, truth, humanity, mercy, and piety; and nothing is more necessary than to guard the appearance of these virtues, for men judge in general more by the eye than by the feeling, for all can see, but only few can feel. Everyone sees what you appear to be, few feel what you really are; and these do not dare to oppose the opinion of the mass guarded by the majesty of the State. Of men's acts, especially those of the princes who have no judge over them, we ever regard but the result. Let the prince, therefore, see to it that he maintains his dignity. The means will ever be regarded as honorable and brave by everyone. For the common herd ever regard but the appearance and the result of a matter; and the world is full of the common herd.[1]

What Machiavelli stated here in frank words (bluntly because only meant for the ear of a definite ruler) was only the unadorned profession of faith of the representatives of each and every power policy. It is, therefore, idle to talk of "Machiavellism." What the Florentine statesman set forth so crisply and clearly and so unequivocally has always been practiced and will always be practiced as long as privileged minorities in society have the necessary power to subdue the great majority and to rob them of the fruits of their labor. Or is one to believe that our present secret diplomacy uses other principles? As long as the will to power plays a part in the communal life of men, so long will those means be justified which are best for the winning and the maintenance of power. While the outer form of power policy, now as always, must needs adjust itself to the times and circumstances, the ends it pursues always remain the same and hallow any means serviceable to its purposes; for power is inherently amoral and transgresses against every principle of human justice, which feels that all privilege of individuals or special castes are a disturbance of social equilibrium, and consequently immoral. It would then be senseless to assume that the methods of power are better than the ends they serve.

What Machiavelli reduced to a system was naked, unashamed reasons of state. It was quite clear that brutal power policy was unguided by ethical principles. Therefore he demanded, with the shameless frankness characteristic of him (the trait really does not quite conform to the principles of his own "Machiavellism"), that men who cannot do without the superfluous luxury of private conscience had better leave politics alone. That Machiavelli so completely exposed the inner workings of power politics, that he even despised to gloss over the most inconvenient details with empty phrases and hypocritical words, is his chief merit.

Leonardo da Vinci engraved on the pedestal of his equestrian statue of Francesco Sforza the words: *Ecce Deus!* ("What a God!"). In these words are revealed the fundamental changes everywhere apparent after the disappearance of the medieval social organization. The glamour of the godhead had faded; in its place the Master Man was endowed with new honors, a reversion to the Caesar cult of the Romans. The "hero" became the executor of human destiny, the creator of all things on earth. No one has furthered this hero cult more than Machiavelli. No one has burned more incense to the "strong individual" than he. All devotees of heroism and hero worship have merely drunk from his cup.

The belief in the surpassing genius of the Master Man is always most

[1] Niccolo Machiavelli, *Il Principe*.

noticeable in times of inner dissolution, when the social ties that have bound men become loosened and the interests of the community yield place to the special interests of privileged minorities. The difference of social ambitions and objectives, which always leads to sharper contrasts within the community and to its disintegration into opposing castes and classes, continually undermines the foundations of communal feeling. But where the social instinct is continually disturbed and weakened by alteration of the external conditions of life, there the individual gradually loses his equilibrium and the people becomes the mob. The mob is nothing but the uprooted people driven hither and thither on the stream of events. It must first be collected again into a new community that new forces may arise in it and its social activities be again directed toward a common goal.

Where the people become the mob, the time is favorable for the growth of the "Great Man," of the "recognized Master Man." Only in such periods of social disintegration is it possible for the "hero" to impose his will upon the others and to force the mob under the yoke of his individual desires. The true community permits no rulership to arise because it unites men by the inner bonds of common interests and mutual respect, needing no external compulsion. Rulership and external compulsion always appear where the internal ties of the community fall into decay and communal feeling dies. When the social bond threatens to be broken the rulership of compulsion enters to hold together by force what was once united into a community by free agreement and personal responsibility.

The Renaissance was a time of such dissolution. The people changed to the mob, and from the mob was formed the nation, which was to serve as stepping stone to the new state. This origin is very instructive, for it shows that the whole power apparatus of the national state and the abstract idea of the nation have grown on one tree. It is not by chance that Machiavelli, the theoretician of modern power politics, was also the warmest defender of national unity, which played from then on the same part for the new state as the unity of Christianity had played for the church.

It was not the people who brought about this new condition, for no inner necessity drove them to this division, nor could they derive any benefit from it. The national state is the definite result of the will to temporal power, which in pursuit of its purposes had found a powerful support in commercial capital, which needed its help. The princes imposed their will on the people and resorted to all sorts of tricks to keep them compliant, so that later it appeared as if the division of Christendom into nations had originated with the people themselves, whereas actually they were but the unconscious tools of the special interests of the princes.

The internal disintegration of papal power, and especially the great church schism in the northern countries, gave the temporal rulers the opportunity to turn long-held plans into reality and to give their power a new foundation independent of Rome. But this disrupted the great worldwide unity whereby European humanity had been spiritually and mentally united and wherein the great culture of the federalist period had had its firmest root. It is solely because Protestantism has been regarded, especially in the northern countries, as a great spiritual advance over Catholicism that the fateful result of the Reformation has been almost totally overlooked.[2] And as the political and social reconstruction of Europe had taken the same course also in Catholic lands, and as the national state had there especially achieved its highest perfection in the form of the absolute monarchy, the enormous consequences of this event, resulting in the separation of Europe into nations, were all the more easily overlooked.

It was in furtherance of the political aims of the national state that its princely founders set up differences in principles between their own and foreign peoples and strove to deepen and confirm them, for their whole existence depended upon these artificially created differences. Therefore they attached importance to the development of different languages in the different countries, and they had a love for definite traditions, which they enveloped in a veil of mysticism and tried to keep alive among the people; for the inability to forget is one of the first requisites of "national consciousness." And since among the people only the "holy" took root, it behooved them to give to national institutions the appearance of holiness and in particular to surround the person of the ruler with the glamour of divinity.

In this matter also Machiavelli served as a pioneer, for he understood that a new era had arrived and he could indicate its trend. He was the first decided supporter of the national state against the political ambitions of the church. Because the church stood as the strongest barrier in the way of the national unity of Italy, and therefore of "freeing the land from the Barbarians," he fought it most determinedly and promoted the separation of church and state. At the same time he tried to raise the state on the

---

[2] Novalis had clearly grasped the deeper meaning of this tremendous political change when he wrote:

"Unfortunately the princes had interfered in this schism, and many used it for the confirmation and extension of their temporal power and income. They were glad to be relieved of that high influence, and took the new consistoria under their fatherly protection. They were most eagerly concerned to prevent the complete union of the Protestant churches, and thus religion was most irreligiously enclosed within state boundaries; whereby the ground was laid for the gradual undermining of religious cosmopolitan interests. Thus religion lost its great political peace-making influence, its peculiar role as the unifying individualizing principle of Christianity." (Novalis, *Christianity or Europe*. Fragment written in 1799.)

pedestal of divinity, although he was no Christian and had definitely broken with all belief in the supernatural. But he felt deeply the implicit connection between religion and politics and knew that temporal power could only prosper when it stood close to the source of all authority, so that it might shine with the light of divinity. For reasons of state, then, Machiavelli wished to preserve religion among the people, not as a power outside the state, but as an *instrumentum regni*, as a tool of government by statecraft. Therefore he wrote with cold-blooded realism in the eleventh chapter of the second book of his *Discourses:*

> In reality no one has ever introduced new laws among the people without referring therein to God. The doctrines would otherwise not have been accepted, for a wise man can recognize as good much of whose excellence he cannot convince other men. Therefore do governments take their refuge in divine authority.

The high priests of monarchistic politics continued to work in this direction. They created a new political religious feeling which gradually took shape as "national consciousness" and, fertilized by man's inner urge for a formula, bore, later, the same strange fruit as did formerly the belief in God's eternal providence.

Chapter 6

THE REFORMATION AND THE SOCIAL FOLK MOVEMENTS OF THE MIDDLE
AGES. THE CHURCH AND THE PRINCES IN THE NORTH. LUTHER'S ATTI-
TUDE TOWARD THE STATE. PROTESTANTISM AS A PHASE OF PRINCELY
ABSOLUTISM. NATIONALISM AS INNER ENSLAVEMENT. THE PEASANT RE-
VOLT. WYCLIFFE AND THE REFORMATION IN ENGLAND. THE HUSSITE
MOVEMENT. CALIXTINES AND TABORITES. WAR AS A SOURCE OF DES-
POTISM. CHELCICKY, A REFORMER OF CHURCH AND STATE. PROTES-
TANTISM IN SWEDEN. THE DISESTABLISHMENT OF THE CHURCH. CAL-
VINISM. THE DOCTRINE OF PREDESTINATION. THE REIGN OF TERROR
IN GENEVA. PROTESTANTISM AND SCIENCE.

IN the Reformation of the northern countries, readily distinguishable
by its religious concepts from the Renaissance of the Latin people, where
the concepts were dominantly pagan, two different tendencies must be
carefully distinguished; the mass revolution of the peasants and of the
lower sections of society in the cities, and the so-called Protestantism,
which in Bohemia as well as in England and in Germany and the Scandinavian countries worked toward a separation of the church and state and
strove to concentrate all power in the hands of the state. The memory of
the popular revolution, drowned in blood by the rising Protestantism and
its princely and priestly representatives, was later (as usual) defamed
and belittled by the victors. And as in the writing of current history the
success or failure of a cause are the determining factors, it was inevitable
that in later times the Reformation should be regarded as nothing more
than the movement of Protestantism.

The revolutionary urge of the masses was directed not only against
the Roman Papacy, but was meant to abolish social inequalities and the
prerogatives of the rich and powerful. The leaders of the popular movement felt that these were a mockery of the pure Christian teaching of the
equality of men. Even after the church had achieved its power the spirit
of the early Christian congregations, with their communal mode of life
and the feeling of brotherhood animating them, had never been quite
forgotten among the people. The origin of monasticism was to be traced
to this cause; likewise, the spirit of millennialism, the belief in a thousand

year reign of peace, freedom and common possessions. This found an echo also in the speeches of Joachim of Floris and Almarich of Bena.

These traditions remained alive among the Bogomili in Bulgaria and Servia, and among the Cathari of the Latin countries. They kindled the courage of their faith among the Waldenses and the heretical sects of Languedoc and among the Humiliati and the Apostolic Brethren in Northern Italy, with their inner light. We find them among the Beguines and Beghardes in Flanders, among the Anabaptists of Holland and of Switzerland and the Lollards in England. They lived in the revolutionary popular movements in Bohemia and in the confederacies of the German peasants, who united in the *Bundschuh* and the *Poor Conrad* to break the yoke of serfdom. It was the spirit of these traditions which descended upon the *Enthusiasts of Zwickau* and gave to the revolutionary action of Thomas Münzer so powerful an impulse.

Against some of these movements the church with the help of the temporal powers organized regular crusades, as against the Bogomili and Albigenses, whereby whole countries were for decades filled with murder and rapine and thousands were slaughtered. But these bloody persecutions only contributed to the spread of those movements. Thousands of fugitives roamed through other lands and carried their doctrines to new groups. That between most of the heretical sects of the Middle Ages international relations existed has been fully proved by historical research. Such relationships can be shown between the Bogomili and certain sects in Russia and Northern Italy, between the Waldenses and similar sects in Germany and Bohemia, between the Baptists in Holland, England, Germany and Switzerland.

All the peasant revolts in Northern Italy, Flanders, France, England, Germany, Bohemia, from the thirteenth to the sixteenth century, were inspired by these movements, and give us today a fairly clear picture of the feeling and thinking of large sections of the people of that period. While we cannot speak of a unified movement, we notice a whole series of movements which preceded the great Reformation, and produced it. The well-known derisive song of the English Lollards,

> When Adam delved and Eva span
> Who was then the gentleman?

could well have served most of these movements as a *leitmotif*. The real popular movement of the Reformation period sought no alliance with princes and nobles, for with sure instinct its leaders recognized them as implacable enemies of the people, who would march not with them but against them. And since most of the great reformers, like Wycliffe, Huss, Luther, and others had first taken root among the movements of the people, the rising Protestantism was originally very closely connected with these. This situation changed very rapidly, however, as the social antithesis between the two objectives became ever more sharply accentuated and it was shown that large sections of the people would not be content with merely "away from Rome."

Separation from the Roman church could only be desirable to the princes of the northern countries as long as this separation involved no further consequences, and left their political and economic prerogatives untouched. The break with Rome not only increased their own authority, it also prevented the regular export of great sums of money from the land, for which they had such need at home. Furthermore, it gave them the opportunity to seize the church estates and to put the rich returns into their own treasury. It was these considerations which induced the princes and nobles of the northern countries to lead the Reformation. The petty quarrels of theologians hardly interested them, but the separation from Rome showed them definite advantages in prospect which were not to be despised. Hence it was profitable to follow the "voice of conscience" and to patronize the new prophets. Moreover the theological spokesmen of the Reformation did not make too great religious demands upon the Protestant princes. Instead, they endeavored earnestly to show the rulers the temporal advantages of the matter. Thus Huss spoke to them in the language they best understood: "O ye faithful kings, princes, lords, and knights, awake from the lethargic dreams with which the priests have put a spell on you. Exterminate in your dominions the Simonist heresy—do not permit them in your lands to extort money to your disadvantage." [1]

The spiritual leaders of Protestantism turned from the very beginning to the temporal rulers of their lands, whose assistance seemed to them absolutely necessary to secure victory for their cause. But as they also had to be careful not to break with the enraged people, they strove, although vainly, to reconcile the popular movement with the selfish aims of the princes and nobles. This attempt was doomed to failure, as the social cleft had become too wide to be bridged by a few petty concessions. The more compliant the Reformers showed themselves to the masters, the further they became removed from the revolutionary movement of the people and definitely arrayed against them. This was especially the case with Luther, who possessed the least social feeling of all of them, and whose spiritual vision was so narrow that he actually imagined the great movement could be brought to a close by the foundation of a new church.

Like Huss, Luther quoted Paul to prove that princes are not subject to the guardianship of the church but are called of God to rule over priest and bishop. In his appeal, "To the Christian Nobility of the German

[1] Carl Vogl, *Peter Chelčicky: A Prophet at the Turn of the Time.*

Nation," he tried to prove that according to the doctrines of Holy Writ there was in reality no priestly caste but only a priestly function which anyone could serve who possessed the necessary ability and the confidence of his congregation. From this it followed that the church had no right to exercise temporal power; that belonged to the state. According to Luther's concept all power should be vested in the state, which was appointed by God himself to guard the public order. In effect, in this concept the whole political significance of Protestantism exhausted itself.

Protestantism had freed the conscience of man from the guardianship of the church only to barter it to the state. In this the "Protestant mission" of Martin Luther, who called himself God's servant, but was in reality only the servant of the state and its minion, completely exhausted itself. It was this innate servility which enabled him to betray the German people to the princes, and together with them to lay the foundation stones of a new church which in private agreement sold itself body and soul to the state and proclaimed the will of the princes and nobles as God's commandment. Luther accomplished the unholy union of religion with the interests of the state. He locked the living spirit into the prison of the word and thus became the herald of that dead-letter learning which interprets Christ's revelations to suit the state; which makes of men humble galley slaves, led to the portal of Paradise to compensate them by the life eternal for the slavery of this world.

Medieval man had not yet known the state in the real sense of the word. The concept of a central power which forces every vital activity into definite forms and guides men from the cradle to the grave upon the leading strings of a higher authority was strange to him. His ideas of right were based on custom transmitted to him by tradition. His religious feeling recognized the incompleteness of all human systems and made him inclined to follow his own counsel, and to help himself and to shape his relations with his fellowmen in conformity with the ancient customs of mutual agreement. When the rising state began to undermine these rights and raised its cause to the cause of God, he fought against the injustice which was being done to him. This is the real meaning of the great popular movements of the age of the Reformation, which endeavored to give to the "freedom of the Evangelical Christian man"—as Luther called it—a social significance.

Only after the popular movement had been drowned in seas of blood, while Luther, "the beloved man of God," blessed the butchers of the insurgent German peasants, did victorious Protestantism raise its head and give the state and its legal control of affairs a religious sanction, bloodily purchased with the gruesome slaughter of a hundred and thirty thousand men. Thus was accomplished the "reconciliation between religion and law," as Hegel later chose to call it. The new theology was taught by the lawyers. The dead-letter learning of the law killed conscience or invented a cheap substitute. The throne was transformed into an altar on which man was sacrificed to the new idols. "Positive law" became divine revelation; the state, the representative of God on earth.

In the other countries, too, Protestantism pursued the same ends; everywhere it betrayed the people and made of the Reformation an affair of the princes and the privileged sections of society. The movement started by Wycliffe in England, which spread to other countries, especially to Bohemia, was primarily of political character. Wycliffe fought the pope because the pope had embraced the cause of France, England's mortal enemy, and had demanded of the English government that the kingdom should continue to regard itself as a vassal of the Holy See and pay tribute to it, as John Lackland had done to Innocent III. But those times were passed. When Philip III of France braved the ban of Boniface VIII and compelled his successor to take up his residence at Avignon, the unlimited rulership of the Papacy received a blow from which it never recovered. Consequently, the English parliament could calmly dare to answer the pope's demands with the declaration that no king was ever empowered to surrender the country's independence to the pope.

Wycliffe at first merely defended the complete independence of the temporal power from the church and only advanced to a criticism of churchly dogmas after he had become convinced that the question would never be settled without a bold break with papism. But when the great peasant rebellion in England broke out and the revolting hordes of Wat Tyler and John Ball brought the king and the government into greatest danger, Wycliffe's opponents embraced the opportunity to raise their public accusation against him. Wycliffe declared that he did not sanction the action of the rebellious peasants; but he did it with a gentleness of understanding for the sufferings of the poor which compared most favorably with the Berserker rage wherewith Luther in his notorious screed "against the robbing and murdering peasants" encouraged the German princes to butcher them mercilessly.

When, later on, Henry VIII completed the breach with the papal church and confiscated its estates, he made himself the head of the new state church, which was completely under the dominance of the temporal power. When the same Henry had launched a virulent epistle against Luther, only, soon after, to defend the "national interest" against the Papacy, he did but prove that in England also temporal advantages possessed a greater interest for the tenant of the crown than "the pure word of God" of the new doctrine.

In Bohemia, where the general situation was already very tense, it became accentuated by the national antagonisms between the Czechs and the Germans, in consequence whereof the Reformation assumed there an exceptionally violent expression. The real Hussite movement became prominent in Bohemia only after the death of Huss and Jerome of Prague at the stake. The preachings of Huss had been, on the whole, only the tracts of Wycliffe, which the Czech reformers translated for their countrymen into their own language. Huss, like Wycliffe, urged the complete liberation of the temporal power from the petty guardianship of the church. The church was to concern itself only with the salvation of men's souls and to stand aloof from every temporal governmental office. Of the "two whales," as Peter Chelčicky had called church and state, Huss would concede only to the state the power over temporal things. The church must be poor, must renounce all earthly treasure, and the priests must be amenable to temporal government even as any other subjects. Furthermore, the priestly office was to be open also to laymen, provided they possessed the necessary moral qualities. He condemned the moral degeneracy which had become prevalent among the priesthood, turning with especial severity againts the traffic in indulgences, at that time most shamelessly practiced by the church, especially in Bohemia. Besides the purely political demands, which alone interest us here and which, being understood, appear especially favorable to the nobility, Huss made a number of theological demands directed against the oral confession, the mendicant monks, the doctrine of purgatory and other items. But what principally secured him the support of the Czech population was his teaching that the paying of tithes was no duty and his specially nationalistic position against the Germans, regarded by the Czechs as despoilers of their country.

The Calixtines and Utraquists,[2] to which sects chiefly the nobility and the richer citizens of Prague belonged, had been easily satisfied with the realization of these demands and refused all social reforms, being principally concerned with the acquisition of the rich church estates and, for the rest, with peace and order in the country. But the real popular movement, comprising mainly the peasants and the poorer city population, pushed further and demanded especially the liberation of the peasants from the yoke of serfdom which so heavily oppressed the rural districts. Already Charles V had been compelled to stay the nobles from putting out the eyes and cutting off the hands and feet of their serfs for the slightest transgression. The movement of the so-called Taborites [3] em-

---

[2] "Calixtines," from the Latin *calix*, cup; "Utraquists," from the Latin, *sub utraque specie* ("in both forms"), because they received the Eucharist in two forms, receiving from the priest not only bread but also wine, wherefore the cup became the sign of the Hussites. This custom, however, did not originate with Huss, but with Jacob von Mies, also called Jacobellus.

[3] "Taborites," because they had given to a town which stood on a hill in the neighborhood of Prague, the biblical name of Tabor. Tabor remained, until the suppression of the Taborites, the spiritual center of the movement, and its inhabitants practiced a sort of communal possession which might be called a war communism.

braced especially all democratic elements of the people up to the communists and chiliasts and was inspired with an ardent courage for battle.

It was inevitable that between these two movements of the Hussite agitation violent contentions were sooner or later bound to arise; they were delayed only by the general political condition of the times. When the German Emperor Sigismund, after the sudden death of his brother Wenceslaus, became the wearer of the Bohemian crown, the whole land was seized by a mighty commotion. For by the emperor's dastardly breach of faith Huss had been compelled to mount the pyre, after which Sigismund was regarded in all Bohemia as the sworn enemy of all reform movements. Soon after his ascent of the throne, in March, 1420, Pope Martin V in a special bull called all Christendom to a crusade against the Bohemian heresy, and an army of 150,000 men recruited from all parts of Europe moved against the Hussites. Now revolt arose all over the land to a devouring flame. Calixtines and Taborites, threatened by the same immediate danger, let their inner differences rest for the time being and united quickly for common defense. Under the leadership of the aged Žižka, an experienced warrior, the first crusading army was bloodily and decisively beaten. But that did not end the struggle; pope and emperor continued their attacks against the Bohemian heresies; and thus developed one of the bloodiest of wars, waged on both sides with frightful cruelty. After the Hussites had expelled the enemy from their own country they invaded the neighboring states, wasted cities and villages, and by their irresistible bravery became the terror of their foes.

This brutal warfare lasted for twelve years, until the Hussites put the last army of the crusaders to fight in the battle of Taus. The result of the peace negotiations, concluded at the Council of Basle, was the "compact of Prague," which gave the Hussites far-reaching concessions in matters of faith and, above all, announced the renunciation by the church of its estates which the Czech nobility had appropriated.

This concluded the war against the external enemies, but only to make place for civil war. During the short breathing spells permitted the Hussites in the war against pope and emperor the differences between Calixtines and Taborites had flamed up anew, repeatedly leading to bloody conflicts. As a consequence, the Calixtines had repeatedly started negotiations with the pope and the emperor. And so it was inevitable that after the conclusion of peace, in which outcome they were chiefly instrumental, they should be supported against the Taborites by their former enemies to the best of their ability. In May, 1434, there occurred between the two parties the murderous battle of Lipan, in which thirteen thousand Taborites were killed and their army almost completely annihilated.

With this the popular movement was definitely defeated, and there began hard times for the poor populace of city and village. But thus early it became apparent that the revolutionary popular movement, which by its own or others' fault had come to be involved in a protracted war, was forced by circumstances to abandon its original aims, because military demands exhaust all social forces and thereby nullify all creative activity for the development of new forms of social organization. War not only affects human nature calamitously in general by constant appeal to its most brutal and cruel motives, but the military discipline which it demands at last stifles every libertarian movement among the people and then systematically breeds the degrading brutality of blind obedience, which has always been the father of all reaction.

This the Taborites, too, had to learn. Their opponents, the professors of Prague University, accused them of striving for a condition where "there would be no king nor ruler nor subjects anywhere on earth, all control and guidance would cease, none could compel another to anything, and all would dwell in equality like brothers and sisters." It was soon apparent that the war drove them constantly farther away from this goal, not only because their military leaders suppressed with bloody force all the libertarian tendencies within the movement, but because the nationalist spirit which animated them and which in the course of this terrible war increased to white heat, necessarily estranged them more and more from all truly humanitarian considerations, without which no truly revolutionary movement can ever succeed. Once men have become used to the thought that all problems of social life have to be settled by force, they logically arrive at despotism, even though they give it another name and hide its true character behind some misleading title. And thus it happened in Tabor. The yoke of restriction bore more and more heavily on the citizens and crushed the spirit that had once animated them. Peter Chelčicky, a forerunner of Tolstoi and one of the few innerly free men of that epoch, who opposed both church and state, described, in the following weighty words, the terrible condition into which protracted war had plunged the country:

> . . . and then someone fills vile dens with thieves and commits violence, robbery, and murder and at the same time is a servant of God and does not carry the sword in vain. And truly he does not carry it in vain, but rather to do all sorts of injustice, violence, robbery, oppression of the laboring poor. And thereby have these various lords torn the people asunder and incited them against one another. Everyone drives his people like a herd to battle against others. Thus by these many masters the whole peasantry has been made familiar with murder, for they go about armed, always ready for battle. Thereby all brotherly love is infiltrated with bloodlust and such tension created as easily leads to contest, and murder results.[4]

[4] Peter Chelčicky. *The Net of Faith*, translated into German from the old Czechic by Dr. Carl Vogl. Dachau, Munich, 1925, p. 145.

In Sweden, where the young dynasty founded by Gustavus Vasa imposed Protestantism on the people for purely political motives, the Reformation assumed quite a peculiar character. It was by no means holy zeal for the new divine doctrines that caused Gustavus I to break with Rome, but simply very sober political motives united with highly important economic considerations. Several grave mistakes of the papal power greatly favored the success of his plans.

Soon after the commencement of his reign the king had addressed a most respectful letter to the pope requesting him to appoint new Swedish bishops who would be "concerned to guard the rights of the Church without encroaching upon those of the Crown." More especially Gustavus wished the pope to confirm as Archbishop of Upsala the newly nominated Primus Johannis Magni, whose predecessor, Gustavus Trolle, had been condemned by the Rigsdag as a traitor because he had invited the Danish king, Christian II, into the land to overthrow the regent, Sten Sture. Gustavus had promised the pope to "prove himself a faithful son of the Church" and he assumed that the Vatican would respond to his wishes. But the pope, badly advised by his counselors, believed that Gustavus' reign would not last long, and with unyielding insistence demanded the reinstatement of Gustavus Trolle. With that the die was cast. Gustavus could not have yielded to this demand even if he had intended to avoid an open breach with Rome. Although the great majority of the Swedish people were good Catholics and wanted nothing to do with Luther, a renewal of the Danish dominion appeared even less endurable to the free Swedish peasants. The bloody tyranny of the fatuous despot, Christian II, had given them plenty of cause for fear. Hence the king could risk the breach with papism which, secretly, he doubtless desired. But although Sweden separated from the Holy See, and the king thereafter favored the preaching of Protestantism, the church service remained the same.

What Gustavus principally desired was under some pretext to confiscate the estates of the church, which in Sweden were very rich. After some cautious attempts in this direction, which aroused the opposition of his own bishops, he finally dropped the mask of impartiality and, in order to carry through his political plans, announced himself as an open enemy of the church. In 1526, he suppressed all the Catholic publishing houses in the country and seized two-thirds of the church's income to liquidate the debts of the state. Later, when a serious contention arose between the king and the spiritual dignitaries concerning the further confiscation of church properties, Gustavus Vasa gradually abolished all the prerogatives of the churches and made them subservient to the state.

The king could not, however, take such steps relying solely on his own power, for the peasants were definitely opposed to the so-called "church reforms" and were especially outraged by the theft of church property. How little the people cared for Lutheranism is apparent from the fact that the peasantry frequently threatened to march on Stockholm and destroy that "spiritual Sodom," as they called the capital because of its Protestant tendencies. Their opposition compelled the king and his successors to rely more and more on the nobility; and the nobles granted their assistance to the Crown only for a price. Not only were a great part of the church estates yielded to the nobility to purchase their favor, but the peasants were pressed by royalty ever deeper into servitude to the nobility to retain their good humor.

Naturally, the antagonistic attitude of the peasant population repeatedly brought the young dynasty into a very dangerous position. The Swedish peasants, who had never known serfdom during medieval times, possessed a strong influence in their country. It was they who had elected Gustavus Vasa king to foil the secret machinations of the Danish party. Now, when the king tried to impose upon the country a new faith, and further burdened the peasants with heavy taxes, there arose frequent and serious disagreement between the Crown and the people. From 1526 to 1543 Gustavus had to fight not fewer than six uprisings of the peasants. While these were not at last, it is true, completely successful, they did force the king to curb somewhat his ever growing lust for absolute power.

Gustavus Vasa knew very well that for weal or woe his dynasty was inextricably entwined with Protestantism. By his confiscation of church estates and the public execution at Stockholm of two Catholic bishops he had burned all his bridges behind him and was obliged to pursue the path he had taken. Hence, in his will, he most urgently adjured his successors to remain true to the new faith, for only thus could the dynasty continue to prosper.

Thus Protestantism was in Sweden from the very beginning a purely dynastic affair, systematically imposed on the people. That Gustavus Vasa was converted to Protestantism from inner conviction is just as much a fairy tale as the assertion that his later successor, Gustavus Adolphus, only with a heavy heart and against his will, invaded Germany to aid his hard-pressed fellow religionists. For such a purpose neither "the snow king," as his enemies called him, nor his clever chancellor, Oxenstierna, would have spent a penny. What they were after was unlimited dominion over the Baltic, and for such a purpose any pious lie was acceptable.

Wherever Protestantism attained to any influence it revealed itself as a faithful servant of the rising absolutism and granted the state all the rights it had denied to the Roman Church. That Calvinism fought absolutism in England, France and Holland is not significant, for, with this exception, it was less free than any other phase of Protestantism. That it opposed absolutism in those countries is explained by the special social conditions prevailing in them. At its source it was unendurably despotic, and determined the individual fate of men far more completely than the Roman Church had ever tried to do. No other religion has had such a deep and permanent influence on men's personal lives. Was not the "inner conversion" one of the most important doctrines of Calvin? And he continued to convert till nothing was left of humanity.

Calvin was one of the most terrible personalities in history, a Protestant Torquemada, a narrow-hearted zealot, who tried to prepare men for God's kingdom by the rack and wheel. Crafty and cunning, destitute of all deeper feeling, like a genuine inquisitor he sat in judgment upon the visible weaknesses of his fellowmen and instituted a regular reign of terror in Geneva. No pope ever wielded completer power. The church ordinances regulated the lives of the citizens from the cradle to the grave, reminding them at every step that they were burdened by the curse of original sin, which in the murky light of Calvin's doctrine of predestination assumed an especially somber character. All joy of life was forbidden. The whole land was like a penitent's cell in which there was room only for inner consciousness of guilt and humiliation. Even at weddings music and dancing were forbidden. In the theaters only pieces with religious content were offered. An unendurable censorship took care that no profane writings, especially no novels, were printed. An army of spies infested the land and respected the rights of neither home nor family. Even the walls had ears, for all the faithful were urged to become informers and felt obliged to betray their fellows. In this respect too, political and religious "orthodoxy" always reach the same result.

Calvin's criminal code was a unique monstrosity. The least doubt of the dogmas of the new church, if heard by the watchdogs of the law, was punished by death. Frequently the mere suspicion was enough to bring down the death sentence, especially if the accused for some reason or other was unpopular with his neighbors. A whole series of transgressions which had been formerly punished with short imprisonment, under the rulership of Calvinism led to the executioner. The gallows, the wheel and the stake were busily in use in the "Protestant Rome," as Geneva was frequently called. The chronicles of that time record gruesome abominations, among the most horrible being the execution of a child for striking its mother, and the case of the Geneva executioner, Jean Granjat, who was compelled first to cut off his mother's right hand and then to burn her publicly because, allegedly, she had brought the plague into the land. Best known is the execution of the Spanish physician, Miguel Servetus, who in 1553 was slowly roasted to death over a small fire because he had doubted Calvin's doctrines of the Trinity and predestination. The cowardly and treacherous manner in which Calvin contrived the destruction of the unfortunate scholar throws a gruesome light on the character of that terrible man, whose cruel fanaticism is so uncanny because so frightfully calm and removed from all human feeling.[5]

But as human nature could not, for all that, be exterminated by pious pretense, secret desires continued to glow, and created externally that miserable care for appearances and that revolting hypocrisy characteristic of Protestantism in general and of Calvin's Puritanism in particular. Furthermore, historical research has discovered that under the rule of Calvinism moral degeneration and political corruption flourished to a degree never known before.

Since Calvin is frequently given credit for maintaining democratic principles in political administration, it should be remembered that Geneva was no great monarchic state but a small republic, and that the Reformer was for this reason compelled to accept the democratic tradition. Furthermore, it must not be overlooked that in so fanatical a time, when men had lost all inner balance and were utterly without any reasonable consideration, *it was precisely formal democracy which could best serve Calvin to confirm his power, since he could announce it as the will of the people.* In reality, the democratic appeals in Calvin's policy were but a deceitful camouflage, which could not disguise the theocratic character of his government.

Protestantism did, therefore, by no means unfold the banner of spiritual independence or "the religion of freedom of conscience," as is so often asserted. It was in matters of faith just as intolerant as was Catholicism, and as inclined to the brutal persecution of dissenters. It but assisted the transfer of the principle of authority from the religious to the political field and thereby wakened Caesaro-Papism to new forms and a new life. It was in many respects more narrow-minded and mentally more limited than the heads of the old church, whose rich experience, knowledge of human nature and high intellectual culture were so totally lacking in Protestant leaders. If its rage for persecution found fewer victims than did the consistent intolerance of the papal church it was simply because its activity was confined to a narrower field and cannot be compared with the other.

Toward the rising science, Protestantism was as innately antagonistic as the Catholic church. It frequently manifested its antagonism even more strongly, as the dead-letter beliefs of its representatives barred every freer outlook. The translation of the Bible into the various national languages led to a quite unique result. To the great founders of the Protestant doctrine the Bible was not a book or a collection of books con-

[5] The Genevan historian, J. B. Galiffe, in his two writings, *Some Pages of Exact History*, and *New Pages* collected a mass of material from the old chronicles and file records which gives a positively shocking picture of the conditions prevailing in Geneva at that time.

ceived as written by men, but the very revealed word of God. For this reason "Holy Writ" was for them infallible. They interpreted all events according to the text of the Bible and condemned all knowledge not in harmony with the words of Scripture. Thus, to the adherents of the new church the letter became everything and the spirit nothing. They locked reason within the chains of a dead-letter fetishism and were, for this reason if no other, incapable of scientific thought. Not for nothing had Luther called reason "the whore of the devil." His judgment concerning Copernicus is a masterpiece of Protestant thinking. He called the great scholar a fool and refuted the new cosmic concept by simply stating that it is written in the Bible that Joshua commanded the sun to stand still, and not the earth.

Furthermore, this religious dead-letter faith was the immediate predecessor of the later political belief in miracles, which swears by the letter of the law and is just as disastrous in its results as the blind belief in "God's written Word."

It was the mental bondage, characteristic of all Protestantism, which induced the humanists—who had at first welcomed the Reformation in northern lands most gladly—later to turn away, when it became clear to them how much of theological persecution and how little of spiritual freedom had intrenched itself behind this movement. It was neither irresolution nor over-anxiety which influenced their attitude. It was Protestantism's lack of intellectual culture and obtuseness of feeling which estranged the leaders of humanism. More than this, it was Protestantism's nationalistic limitations, destroying the spiritual and cultural ties which up to then had united the peoples of Europe. But principally, two different modes of thought existed here which could have no genuine point of contact. When Erasmus of Rotterdam publicly asked to have named to him "the men who under Lutherism had made marked progress in science," his question remained for most of his Protestant opponents eternally unintelligible. They sought, not in science, but only in the word of the Bible, to find the unique way to all knowledge. Erasmus's question shows most clearly the width of the gulf which had opened between the two movements.

Chapter 7

THE FABLE OF THE NATIONALIST STATE AS A FURTHERER OF CULTURAL
DEVELOPMENT. THE DECLINE OF INDUSTRY AND DECAY OF ECONOMY.
THE PERIOD OF WARS AND REVERSION TO BARBARISM. COMMERCIAL
CAPITAL AND ABSOLUTISM. MANUFACTURE AND MERCANTILISM. THE
STATE AS CREATOR OF ECONOMIC MONOPOLIES. REGIMENTATION OF
ECONOMICS BY MONARCHIES. COLBERT AND THE ECONOMIC DICTATOR-
SHIP IN FRANCE. THE ENGLISH MONARCHY AND TRAFFIC IN MONOPO-
LIES. THE EAST INDIA COMPANY AND THE HUDSON BAY COMPANY. THE
FRENCH REVOLUTION AS A PIONEER OF NEW ECONOMIC ORGANIZATION.
THE NATIONAL STATE IN SPAIN AND THE DECAY OF ECONOMY AND
CULTURE. THE "MESTA" AND THE EXPLOITATION OF SPANISH PEASANTS.
PHILIP II AND THE INTRODUCTION OF THE "ALCAVALA." WALLENSTEIN
AND GUSTAVUS ADOLPHUS. THE THIRTY YEARS' WAR AND THE DECAY
OF CULTURE IN GERMANY. THE FOUNDING OF MANUFACTURES AS A
SPECULATION BY THE STATE.

IT HAS often been asserted that the development of the social structure
in Europe in the direction of the national state has been along the line
of progress. It is, significantly, the protagonists of "historical materialism"
who have most emphatically defended this concept. They try to prove
that the historic events of the time were caused by economic necessity,
demanding a broadening of the technical conditions of production. In
reality, this fable arises from no serious consideration of historical facts,
but rather from a vain desire to see the social development of Europe
in the light of an advancing evolution. In that important reconstruction
of European society associated with the growth of nationalism, the struggle
of small minorities for political power has frequently played a much
more important part than alleged "economic necessity." Quite apart from
the fact that there is not the least reason to suppose that the evolution
of technical methods of production could not have gone on just as well
without the creation of the national state, it cannot be denied that the
foundation of the national absolutist states of Europe was associated with
a long series of devastating wars by which the economic and cultural

development of many lands was for a long time, yes, even for centuries, completely inhibited.

In Spain the rise of the nationalist state led to a catastrophic decay of once flourishing industries and to a complete disintegration of the whole economic life, which has not been restored to this day. In France the Huguenot wars, waged by the monarchy to fortify the unified state, most seriously injured French industries. Thousands of the best artisans left the country and transplanted their industries to other states. The cities were depopulated and most important lines of industry began to decline. In Germany where the machinations of the princes and nobles did not permit a unified national state to arise as in Spain, France, and England, and where, consequently, a whole set of small national states developed, the Thirty Years' War devastated the whole land; decimated the population, and inhibited every cultural and economic development for the next two hundred years.

But these were not the only obstacles to economic evolution presented by the rising national state. Wherever it arose it tried to inhibit the natural course of economic progress by prohibition of imports and exports, supervision of industry, and bureaucratic ordinances. The guild masters were given orders regarding their methods of production, and whole armies of officials were created to supervise the industries. Thereby all improvements in production were limited, and only by the great revolutions of the seventeenth and eighteenth centuries was industry freed from these burdensome shackles. The rise of the nationalist states not only did not further economic evolution in any way whatever, but the endless wars of that epoch and the senseless interference of despotism in the life of industry created that condition of cultural barbarism in which many of the best achievements of industrial technique were wholly or partly lost and had to be rediscovered later on.[1]

To this must be added the fact that the kings were always suspicious of the citizens and the artisans of the towns, who were the real representatives of industry. They united with them only when they had to break the resistance of the nobles, who were not favorably inclined to the monarchists' efforts at unification. This will appear especially clear in French history. Later, when absolutism had victoriously overcome all

[1] Kropotkin has set forth in very convincing form how by the collapse of the medieval city culture and the forcible suppression of all federalist cooperative arrangements the industrial evolution of Europe received a blow which crippled her best technical forces and put them out of service. How great this set-back was can be measured by the fact that James Watt, the inventor of the steam engine, was for twenty years unable to make use of his invention because he could find in all England no mechanic able to bore a true cylinder for him, though he could have found many such in any of the larger medieval cities. (Peter Kropotkin, *Mutual Aid—a Factor in Evolution.*)

opposition to national unification, by its furthering of mercantilism and economic monopoly it gave the whole social evolution a direction which could only lead to capitalism; and degraded men became galley slaves of industry instead of economic leaders.

In the already existing states, originally founded on ownership of soil, the rising world commerce and the growing influence of commercial capital effected a profound change, for they broke the feudal bars and initiated the gradual transition from feudalism to industrial capitalism. The absolutist national state was dependent upon the help of the new economic forces, and *vice versa*. By the importation of gold from America the development of money economy in Europe was enormously enhanced. Money became, from now on, not only an ever larger factor in industry itself, but it developed into a political instrument of the first order. The boundless profligacy of the courts in the epoch of absolute monarchy, its armies and fleets, and lastly its mighty official apparatus, devoured enormous sums which must be ever newly procured. Furthermore, the endless wars of that period cost a mint of money. These sums could not be raised by the half-starved serf population of the country in spite of all the arts of exploitation of the financial magicians of the courts. Hence, other sources had to be sought. The wars themselves were largely the result of this political-economic evolution and of the struggle of the absolutist states for the hegemony of Europe. Thereby the original character of the old feudal states was thoroughly changed. On the one hand, money made it possible for the king completely to subjugate the nobles, thus establishing firmly the unity of the state; on the other hand, the royal power gave the merchants the protection necessary to escape the confiscations of the robber barons. From this community of interests evolved the real foundation of the so-called nationalist state and the concept of the nation in general.

But this selfsame monarchy, which for weighty reasons sought to further the aims of commercial capital and was, on the other hand, itself aided in its development by capital, grew at last into a crippling obstacle to any further reconstruction of European industry; and by unbridled favoritism it converted entire industrial lines into monopolies and so deprived the people at large of their benefits. Especially disastrous was the senseless regimentation imposed upon industry whereby the development of technical skill was forcibly inhibited and every advance in the field of industrial activity was artificially checked.

The further commerce spread, the more interest its leaders naturally had to have in the development of industry. The absolutist state, whose coffers the expansion of commerce filled by bringing into the country plenty of money, at first furthered the plans of commercial capital. Its armies and fleets, which had reached considerable proportions, contributed to the expansion of industrial production because they demanded a number of things for whose large-scale production the shops of the small trades-man were no longer adapted. Thus gradually arose the so-called manu-factures,[2] the forerunners of the later large industries, which were developed, however, only after the great scientific discoveries of a later period had smoothed the way by their application of new techniques to industry.

Manufactures developed as early as the middle of the sixteenth cen-tury after certain separate branches of production—especially ship-building, mining and ironworks—had opened the way for wider industrial activity. In general, the system of manufactures followed the line of rationalizing the increased productive forces achieved by the division of labor and the improvement of tools, a matter of great importance for the growing commerce.

In France, Prussia, Poland, Austria and other countries, the state had for financial reasons, side by side with private manufacture, itself started large enterprises for the exploitation of important industries. The financiers of the monarchies, indeed the kings themselves, gave the greatest attention to these enterprises and sought to advance them in every way for the enrichment of the state treasury. By prohibition of imports and by high tariffs on foreign goods they tried to protect native industry and keep money in the country. To do this the state sometimes used the most curious means. Thus, in England, an ordinance of Charles I commanded that the dead must be buried in woolen clothes in order to aid the cloth industry. A similar purpose was aimed at by the Austrian "mourning ordinance" of 1716 which, very businesslike, proclaimed that long mourning was prohibited to the citizens, since thereby the demand for colored clothing would be injuriously affected.

To make manufacture as profitable as possible every state sought to attract good workers from other countries, with the result that the emigration of artisans was soon prohibited by strict law; in fact, trans-gressors were even threatened with the death penalty, as in Venice. Furthermore, to the possessors of political power all methods were justifi-able to make labor as cheap and as profitable as possible to the manu-facturers. Thus Colbert, the famous minister of Louis XIV, gave special prizes to parents who sent their children into the factories. In Prussia, an ordinance of Frederick the Great commanded that the children in the Potsdam orphanages should be employed in the royal silk factories. As a result the mortality among the orphans increased fivefold. Similar ordi-nances existed also in Austria and Poland.[3]

[2] The word "manufacture" is derived from *manu facere*, "to make things by hand."

[3] Rich material concerning this epoch is contained in the great work of M. Kowa-

Nevertheless, no matter how the absolutist state strove, in its own interest, to meet the demands of commerce, it still put on industry countless fetters which became gradually more and more oppressive. The organization of industry cannot be pressed into definite forms by bureaucratic dictates without detrimental consequences. This has again been seen recently in Russia. The absolutist state which tried to bring all activities of its subjects under its unlimited guardianship became in time an unbearable burden, an incubus upon the people which paralyzed all economic and social life. The old guild, once the pioneer of handicraft and industry, had been robbed by the arising despotism of its former rights and of its independence. What remained of it was incorporated into the all-powerful state machine and had to serve it in raising taxes. Thus the guild gradually became an element of reaction, bitterly opposed to any change in industry.

Colbert, who is usually exalted as the cleverest statesman of the despotic age, while he sacrificed France's agriculture to trade and industry, yet never really understood the nature of industry. It was for him only the cow which absolutism could milk. Under his régime definite ordinances were instituted for every trade with the alleged purpose of keeping French industry on the height it had attained. Colbert actually imagined that any further perfection of industrial processes was impossible. Only thus can his so-called industrial policy be understood.

By these artificial means the inventive spirit was strangled and every creative impulse smothered at its birth. Work in its every phase became unintelligent imitation of the same old forms, whose constant repetition crippled all inner incentive. Until the outbreak of the great revolution work was done in France by exactly the same methods that had been in vogue at the end of the seventeenth century. During a period of a hundred years not the slightest changes were made. Thus it happened that English industry came gradually to excel the French, even in the production of those goods in which France had formerly held an undisputed leadership. Of the countless ordinances, with their mass of the most senseless details concerning the clothing, dwellings, social activities, and so on, of the members of each calling, we are not going to speak. True, when the intolerable condition had become all too evident, an attempt was made from time to time to obtain some relief by new ordinances, but such decrees were as a rule soon superseded by others. Furthermore, the courts' continual need of money enticed the governments into all kinds of roguish tricks to fill again their empty coffers. Thus a whole series of ordinances was proclaimed purely so that the guilds would get them rescinded again, for an appropriate payment—which always happened.

lewski, *The Economic Development of Europe till the Beginning of the Capitalist Era.* Berlin, 1901-1914.

On the same principle many monopolies were granted to individuals or corporations, seriously affecting the development of industry.

The French Revolution swept away the whole mass of oppressive royal ordinances and freed industry from the fetters that had been imposed on it. It was certainly no nationalistic reason which led to the creation of the modern constitutional state. Social conditions had gradually become so horrible that they could no longer be endured if France was not to be wholly ruined. It was the recognition of this fact which set the French bourgeoisie in motion and forced it into revolutionary paths.

In England also, industry was for a long time supervised by decrees of state and royal ordinances, although there the rage for regimentation never assumed such peculiar forms as in France and in most of the countries of the continent. The decrees of Edward IV, Richard III, Henry VII and Henry VIII burdened industry severely and greatly hindered its natural development; nor were these rulers the only ones who put brakes on industry. Kings and parliaments constantly issued new ordinances by which the economic situation was made increasingly difficult. Even the revolutions of 1642 and 1688 were not able completely to abolish these stacks of senseless rules and bureaucratic regulations, and considerable time had yet to pass before a new spirit became prevalent. For all that, England never had such a governmental supervision of its complete economic life as Colbert achieved in France. On the other hand, countless monopolies greatly hindered the development of industry. To put new money into its coffers the court sold whole branches of industry to natives and foreigners and continued to allot monopolies among its favorites. This had already begun during the Tudor dynasty, and the Stuarts and their successors continued in the same path. The government of Queen Elizabeth was especially profligate in the granting of monopolies, about which Parliament frequently complained.

Whole industries were given over to exploitation by individuals or small companies, and no one else dared to engage in them. Under this system there was no competition, nor any development of forms of production or methods of work. The Crown was concerned purely about the payment. About the inevitable consequences of such an economic policy it cared very little. This went so far that during the reign of Charles I a monopoly for the manufacture of soap was sold to a company of London soap-boilers, and a special royal ordinance forbade any household to make soap for its own consumption. Likewise, the exploitation of the tin deposits and the coal mines in the north of England was for a long time the monopoly of a few persons. The same is true of the glass industry and several other trades of that epoch. The result was that for a long time industry could not develop as a determining factor in national economy, being for a large part in the hands of privileged exploiters who had no interest in its further development. The state was not only the protector but also the creator of monopoly, whereby it received considerable financial advantages, but also burdened industry continually with new fetters.

The worst development of the monopoly system in England occurred after the commencement of its colonial empire. Immense territories then came into the possession of small minorities, who in return for ridiculous payments were given monopolies from which they derived enormous riches in the course of a few years. Thus, during the reign of Queen Elizabeth the well-known East India Company was born, originally consisting of only five hundred shareholders to whom the government granted sole rights of trading in the East Indies and all lands east of the Cape of Good Hope and west of the Strait of Magellan. Every attempt to break this monopoly was severely punished, and citizens who took the risk of trading in such waters on their own account were subject to seizure. That these were not mere paper ordinances the history of those times eloquently testifies.[4]

Charles II gave Virginia to his brother's father-in-law for exploitation. Under the same king the famous Hudson Bay Company was formed, and endowed by the government with incredible powers. By a special royal ordinance this company was given the exclusive and perpetual monopoly of trade and industry in all coastal waters, natural channels, bays, streams and lake territories of Canada in all latitudes up to Hudson Strait. Furthermore, this company was given possession of all lands adjoining these waters so far "as it is not in the possession of one of our subjects or those of some other Christian prince or state." [5]

Even under James II, the successor of Charles II, the barter in overseas' monopolies went merrily on. The king sold whole colonies to individuals or companies. The possessors of these monopolies suppressed the free settlers in the most abominable manner without interference from the Crown so long as it received 20 percent of the profits for its favors. In the same manner, special privileges were granted for ocean transporta-

[4] Very complete information concerning the history of this company, which was to play so important a part .in English foreign commerce, is contained in the books of Beckle Wilson, *Ledger and Sword*, (London, 1903), and W. W. Hunter, *History of British India* (London, 1899).

Commendable books about the development of English industry, monopolies and ordinances of the ancient régime, are T. E. Rogers, *Six Centuries of Work and Wages*, *The Economic Interpretation of History* and *A History of Agriculture and Prices in England*. Much instructive material is contained in Adam Smith's *An Inquiry into the Nature and Causes of the Wealth of Nations*, and the first volume of Marx's *Capital*.

[5] Rich material concerning the history of the Hudson Bay Company is contained in the excellent work, *History of Canadian Wealth*, by Gustavus Myers (Chicago, 1914).

tion, for the exploitation of colonial lands, for the mining of precious metals and much else. Thus it came to pass that for a long time industry could not keep pace with the mighty foreign development commencing for England after the civil war of 1642. Even in 1688 the value of imported products was £7,120,000. while exports amounted to only £4,-310,000—a relationship characteristic of the conditions prevailing at the time. Not until 1689 did the new parliament that resulted from the revolution of the preceding year put a curb on the royal power and take decisive steps to end once and for all the monopoly peddling of the court and the arbitrary restriction of industry and trade. From that time dates the mighty development of English social and economic life, so greatly furthered by a whole line of epoch-making inventions, such as cast-steel, the mechanical loom, the steam engine, and so on. But all this was possible only after the last remnant of absolutism had finally been buried and the fetters it had put on industry had been broken. Just as later in France, so also in England, this development of affairs overshadowed the revolution.

However, such a development was possible only where the rule of the absolute state had not completely crippled the vital forces of the people nor by a senseless policy destroyed every prospect for the further development of industry, as, for instance, had been done in Spain. In a previous chapter it has been shown how ruthless despotism, by the cruel expulsion of the Moors and Jews, had robbed Spain of its best artisans and agriculturalists. By the brutal suppression of communal freedom the economic decline of the country was still more enhanced. Blinded by the golden flood streaming into the land from Peru and Mexico, the monarchs gave no value whatever to the development, or even the maintenance, of industry. True, Charles I had attempted to further Spanish wool and silk industries by prohibition of imports and regulation of production, but his successors had no understanding of such matters. The position which Spain had attained as a world power also gave it first place in world commerce, but it played the part of a middleman who only provided the necessary commercial connections between the industrial countries and the users of their products. Even its own colonies were not permitted to establish trade enterprises without the intervention of the mother country.

Added to this was the fatal agrarian policy of the absolutist state, which had freed the nobility and the clergy of all land taxes, so that the whole burden of the impost had to be borne by the small farmers. The great landed proprietors united into the so-called *"Mesta,"* an association which made a profession of robbing the peasants and compelled incredible concessions from the government. Under the rule of the Arabs there had existed in Andalusia a class of small farmers, and the land was one of the most productive territories in Europe. But now it had actually come to pass that five noble owners held all the land of the whole province, cultivated primitively by the work of landless serfs, and to a large extent used as pasture for sheep. In this manner the cultivation of grains continually declined, and in spite of the importation of precious metals the rural population sank into the deepest poverty.

The continual wars swallowed immense sums, and when, after the revolt of the Netherlands and the destruction of the Armada in 1588 by the English and the Dutch, Spain's sea power was broken and its monopoly of world commerce went over to the victors, the country was so frightfully exhausted that no revival was possible. Its industry was almost completely destroyed, its land laid waste. The great majority of its inhabitants were living in pitiful misery, completely under the dominance of the church, whose representatives in the year 1700 made up nearly one thirtieth of the population, consuming the people's substance. Between 1500 and 1700 the land lost nearly one-half of its previous population. When Philip II assumed his father's heritage, Spain was regarded as the richest land in Europe, although it already contained the germs of its decline. At the end of the long reign of this cruel and fanatical despot it retained merely the shadow of its former greatness. And when Philip, to cover the enormous deficit of the state budget, instituted the notorious *alcavala,* a state tax which compelled every inhabitant to deliver 10 percent of any profits to the government, the realm was wholly given over to destruction. All attempts of later rulers to curb the evil were vain, although here and there they could record a few temporary successes. The consequences of this catastrophic decline are even today everywhere observable in Spain.

In Germany, the creation of a great national state with unified administration, coinage and regulation of finances was inhibited for manifold reasons. The dynasty of the Hapsburgs had with premeditation worked toward the creation of such a state, but it had never been able to subjugate the nobility and the small princes of the land as the monarchy had succeeded in doing in France after a long struggle. In fact, in Germany the princes managed to confirm their territorial powers ever more strongly and to foil successfully all plans for the erection of any centralized power. Nor had they compunctions about betraying emperor and realm at every favorable opportunity to unite themselves with the most dangerous enemies in other countries, when this was useful to their special interests. National limitations were wholly foreign to them, and the internal discord in German industry was very favorable to their ambitions.

Doubtless the Hapsburgs were concerned about safeguarding their special dynastic aims, but most of them lacked greatness and political vision. As a result, they frequently sacrificed their plans for unification to small temporary successes without being clearly aware of what they were doing. This was most clearly apparent when Wallenstein, after four years of war, in the treaty of Lübeck obligated the Danes not to interfere in German affairs. Then was offered the most favorable opportunity, also the last one, for a successful attempt at the erection of a centralized power with the emperor at its head. In fact, the victorious Wallenstein had visions of a goal similar to that which Richelieu at that time strove to obtain for France and gloriously achieved.

But Ferdinand II, influenced by short-sighted counselors, knew of nothing better than to follow the treaty of peace, which had virtually given all North Germany into his hands, with the Edict of Restitution of 1629, which commanded the return of all church and monastic property confiscated since the treaty of Passau. Such an ordinance naturally had an explosive effect. It aroused the whole Protestant population of the country against the emperor and his counselors—most of all, the Protestant princes, who never dreamed of returning their acquired church property. And this happened just at the time when the conquest-hungry king of Sweden, Gustavus Adolphus, had already made all preparations for his incursion into Pomerania.

The Protestant princes were thus concerned about very earthly matters, for whose ideological embellishment Luther's doctrines proved very suitable. After the bloody suppression of the German peasants in the year 1525 the Reformation could no longer be dangerous to them. But even the "religious conviction" of the powerful opponents of Protestantism was no more genuine. For them, too, it was in the first place a question of power and economic interest—for all the rest they cared very little. It caused Richelieu, who was then guiding the interests of the French monarchy, no qualms of conscience to encourage Gustavus Adolphus to fight against the emperor, the Catholic Church and the Catholic League, although he was himself a cardinal, a prince of the Catholic Church. He was simply concerned to prevent the creation of a German national state, thus freeing the French monarchy from an inconvenient neighbor. Quite as little had Gustavus Adolphus the interests of the German Protestants at heart. He had his own dynastic interests and the interests of the Swedish state in view and cared only for these. For the Sultan, as well as for the then-reigning Pope Urban VIII, the Swedish king's Protestantism was no reason for their withdrawal of expressed good will, as long as he was combating the House of Hapsburg, the thorn in the flesh of both of them for political reasons.

After the Thirty Years' War, from whose devastating consequences Germany had hardly recovered after two centuries, every prospect for the foundation of a German unified state completely vanished. For all that, the course of political development there was similar to that in most of the other European states. The separate territorial states, more especially the larger ones, like Austria, Brandenburg-Prussia, Saxony,

Bavaria, strove to imitate the monarchies of the West in their inner structure and to make their economic-political plans effective within their own borders. Of course their rulers could not think of playing the same part as their great neighbors in the west—the economic lag of the German countries and the terrible wounds the long war had inflicted on the whole land did not permit it. So they were frequently compelled to put themselves under the protection of existing great states.

As the disastrous war had robbed Germany of almost two-thirds of its population and laid waste enormous sections of the land, the separate states had to be principally concerned about population; for with the increase of the inhabitants the power of the state grows. So taxes were imposed upon unmarried women, and even polygamy was flirted with, in order to put the country on its feet again. Most of all, they strove to build up agriculture, whereby the home policy of most of the German states received an impulse toward feudalism, which in the absolute states to the west had been more and more forced into the background by increasing mercantilism.

At the same time the larger German states pursued the policy of transforming their lands into self-contained economic territories. To this end the commercial prerogatives of the cities were abrogated, and every trade was subjected to a special ordinance. Thus, above all, they strove for the development of trade and manufactures by commercial treaties, prohibition of imports and exports, protective tariffs, premiums for exports, and so on, to put fresh money into the state treasuries. Thus, William I of Prussia, in his political testament, strongly urged his successor to concern himself about the success of manufactures, assuring him that he would thereby increase his revenues and put his country into a flourishing condition.

But while, on the one hand, the speculations of the smaller rulers for the increase of their revenues helped to further the few manufactures of their countries to a certain degree, on the other hand, the whole flood of senseless ordinances made certain that industry could not really develop, but must for hundreds of years remain fettered by these old legal forms. It is, therefore, a complete misconception of historical fact to maintain that production was furthered by the rising of the nationalist states of Europe and especially that their existence provided the conditions necessary for the development of industry. The very contrary is true. The absolutist national state artificially inhibited and hindered for centuries the development of economic institutions in every country. Its barbarous wars, which wasted many parts of Europe and furthered rapine, caused the best achievements of industrial technique to be forgotten, often to be replaced by antiquated, laborious methods. Senseless ordinances killed the spirit of economy, destroyed all free incentive and all creative activity, without which a development of industry and economic reforms is quite unthinkable.

The present time affords the best possible illustration of such action. Right now, when a crisis of unheard-of extent has smitten the whole capitalist world and is pushing all nations equally toward the abyss, the structure of the nationalist state proves an insurmountable obstacle to relieving this frightful condition or even temporarily suppressing its evils. National selfishness has thus far blocked every earnest attempt at reciprocal understanding and has constantly striven to make capital out of its neighbors' needs. Even the most pronounced advocates of the capitalist order recognize more and more the fatality of this condition. But "national considerations" tie their hands and condemn to sterility in advance every proposal and every attempt at solution from whatever source they may come.

Chapter 8

THE HUMANISTS AND THE DOCTRINE OF THE SOCIAL CONTRACT. MAN
AS THE MEASURE OF THINGS. THE ORIGIN OF THE DOCTRINE OF
NATURAL RIGHTS. THE NATURAL RIGHTS OF THE CYNICS AND STOICS
TILL ZENO. NATURAL RIGHT AND ABSOLUTISM. THE TIME OF THE
SOCIAL UTOPIAS. THOMAS MORE AND FRANÇOIS RABELAIS. THE MONAR-
CHOMACHI. LANGUET'S *VINDICIAE CONTRA TYRANNOS*. THE DUTCH
PROTECTIVE LEAGUE. JESUITISM AND TEMPORAL POWER. FRANCISCO
SUAREZ AND THE "DIVINE RIGHT OF KINGS." JUAN DE MARIANA AND
THE DOCTRINE OF TYRANNICIDE. LA BOÉTIE CONCERNING VOLUNTARY
SERFDOM. GEORGE BUCHANAN AND THE DOCTRINE OF "THE PEOPLE'S
WILL." THOMAS HOBBES' THEORY OF THE STATE. THE *LEVIATHAN*. IN-
DEPENDENTS AND PRESBYTERIANS. JOHN MILTON AND PURITANISM.
THE DOCTRINE OF JOHN LOCKE CONCERNING PEOPLE AND GOVERN-
MENT. INFLUENCE OF THE DOCTRINE OF NATURAL RIGHTS ON THE
DEVELOPMENT OF INTERNATIONAL LAW.

THE Renaissance, with its strong pagan tendency, reawakened men's
interest in earthly affairs and again turned their minds to questions which
had scarcely been discussed since the decline of the ancient civilization.
The great historical significance of the rising humanism lay in the fact
that its leaders broke away from the spiritual bondage and the dead
formalistic rubbish of scholasticism. They again made man and his social
environment the center of their speculation, instead of losing themselves
in the maze of sterile theological concepts, as the leaders of victorious
Protestantism had done in the northern lands. Humanism was no popular
movement, but an intellectual trend, which affected almost all European
countries and furnished the basis of a new concept of life. That later, even
this stream sanded up and became a matter of dry as dust closet-learning,
as it gradually lost its relation to real life, does not negate its original
purpose.

Interest in the natural phenomena of life again directed men's attention to the social groupings of people, and thus the old ideas of natural
rights were revivified. While the ever encroaching absolutism strove to
confirm its power by the doctrine of the divine right of kings, the whole-

hearted and half-hearted opponents of absolute state power appealed to "the natural rights of men," a protection also guaranteed by the so-called "social contract." Thus, quite naturally, they again approached the question which had already occupied the ancient thinkers and which now received new significance by the rediscovery of the ancient civilization. They sought to make clear the position of the individual in society and to discover the origin and significance of the state. However inadequate these attempts may appear today, they nevertheless drew greater attention to the subject, and an attempt was made to understand the relationship of the citizen to the state and to the existing rulership of the people.

As most of the thinkers influenced by humanistic ideals saw in the individual "the measure of all things," they recognized society not as a definite organism obeying its own laws, but as an enduring union of individual men who for one reason or another had associated themselves. From this arose the idea that the social life of men was founded on a definite contractual relationship, supported by ancient and inalienable rights which had validity even before the evolution of organized state power, and served as a natural basis for all communal relationships of men. This idea was the real core of the doctrine of natural rights which again began to flourish at that time.

Under the pressure of the ever encroaching social inequalities within the Greek city-republics there had arisen in the fifth century before our era the doctrine of "the state of nature," sprung from the belief in a traditional "Golden Age" when man was still free and unhindered in the pursuit of happiness before he gradually came under the yoke of political institutions and the concepts of positive law arising therefrom. From this concept there developed quite logically the doctrine of "natural rights" which was later on to play so important a part in the mental history of European peoples.

It was especially the members of the Sophist school who in their criticism of social evils used to refer to a past natural state where man as yet knew not the consequences of social oppression. Thus Hippias of Elis declares that "the law has become man's tyrant, continually urging him to unnatural deeds." On the basis of this doctrine Alkidamas, Lykophron and others advocated the abolition of all social prerogatives, condemning especially the institution of slavery, as not founded upon the nature of man, but as arising from enactments of men who made a virtue of injustice. It was one of the greatest services of the much maligned Sophist school that its members surmounted all national frontiers and consciously allied themselves with the great racial community of mankind. They felt the insufficiency and the spiritual limitations of the patriotic ideal and recognized with Aristippus that "every place is equally far from Hades."

Later, the Cynics, on the basis of the same "natural life" concept, reached similar results. From the little that has been preserved of their doctrines it is clearly apparent that they viewed the institutions of the state very critically and regarded them as being in direct conflict with the natural order of things. The tendency toward world citizenship was especially marked among the Cynics. Since their ideas were opposed to all artificial distinctions between the various classes, castes and social strata, any boast of national superiority could but appear senseless and foolish to them. Antisthenes derided the national pride of the Hellenes and declared the state as well as nationality to be things of no importance. Diogenes of Sinope, the "sage of Corinth" who, lantern in hand, looked in broad daylight for an honest man, likewise had no regard for "the heroic weakness of patriotism" (as Lessing has called it), since he saw in man himself the source of all aspiration.

The loftiest conception of natural law was formulated by the school of the Stoics, whose founder, Zeno of Kittion, rejected all external compulsion and taught men to obey only the voice of the "inner law" which was revealed in nature itself. This led him to a complete rejection of the state and all political institutions, and he took his stand upon complete freedom and equality for everything that bears the human form. The time in which Zeno lived was very favorable to his cosmopolitan thought and feeling, which knew no distinction between Greeks and barbarians. The old Greek society was in full dissolution, the arising Hellenism, which especially furthered the plans for political unification of Alexander of Macedonia, had greatly changed the relationship of the nations and had opened completely new vistas.

Man's social instinct, having its root in communal life and finding in the sense of justice of the individual its completest ethical expression, Zeno combined, by sociological synthesis, with man's need for personal freedom and his sense of responsibility for his own actions. Thus he stood at the opposite pole from Plato, who could conceive a successful communal life of men only on the basis of a moral and intellectual restraint imposed by external compulsion, and who in his views was rooted as deeply in the narrow limits of purely nationalistic concepts as was Zeno in his concept of pure humanity. Zeno was at the spiritual zenith of the tendency which saw in man "the measure of all things," just as William Godwin, two thousand years later, marked the high tide of another mental tendency which strove to "limit the activity of the state to a minimum."

The doctrine of natural rights, rescued from oblivion by the rising humanism, played a decisive part in the great battles against absolutism and gave the struggles against princely power their theoretical foundation. The leaders in these struggles proceeded from the following assumptions: since man possessed from antiquity native and inalienable rights, he could not be deprived of them by the institution of organized government, nor could the individual resign these rights. On the contrary, these rights had to be established by covenant, in agreement with the representatives of the state's power, and openly acknowledged. From this mutual agreement resulted quite self-evidently the relationship between state and people, between ruler and citizen.

This concept, which although it could make no claim to historical foundation,[1] and rested only on assumption, nevertheless dealt the belief in the divine mission of the ruler—which found its highest expression in the "divine right of kings" of victorious absolutism—a powerful blow, which in the course of events proved decisive. If the position of the head of the state was based on a covenant, it followed that the ruler owed responsibility to the people, and that the alleged inviolability of royal power was a fairy tale which had been quietly permitted to pass as truth. But in this event the relation between ruler and people did not rest on the command of a central power with which the people had, *for good or ill*, to be content. The power of the ruler was confronted by the inalienable rights of the individual, which imposed certain limitations on the arbitrary decisions of the head of the state, such that an equalization of the forces in society was made possible.

The destructive consequences resulting from every misuse of power had been recognized; hence the attempt had been made to bridle it by tying it to the natural rights of the people. This idea was doubtless correct, although the means whereby a solution of the inner discord was attempted always proved insufficient, as subsequently became still more clear. Between might and right yawns an abyss which cannot possibly be bridged. While they dwell in the same house this unnatural relationship must always lead to inner friction by which men's peaceful communal life is continually threatened. Every possessor of the state's power must feel the limitation of his power as an uncomfortable fetter on his egotistic ambition; and wherever the opportunity offers, he will attempt to restrict the people's rights, or completely to abolish them if he feels strong enough to do so. History during the last four centuries of struggle for and against the limitation of the state's supreme power speaks an eloquent language; and recent historical events in most of the European countries show with frightful clearness that the struggle is a long way from having reached its end. The uninterrupted attempts to keep the state's power within certain limits have always led logically to the conclusion that the solution

---

[1] The advocates of the idea of natural rights supported them by a long line of historical facts. We recall, for instance, the old coronation formula of the Aragonese: "We, of whom every one of us is as much as thou, and who all of us combined are more than thou, make thee a king. If thou wilt respect our laws and rights, we will obey thee; if not, then not."

of this question is not sought in the limitation of the principle of political power, but in its overthrow. This exhausts the last and highest results of the doctrine of natural rights. This also explains why natural rights have always been the thorn in the flesh of representatives of the unlimited-power idea, even when—like Napoleon I—they owe their rise to this doctrine. Not without reason this revolution-born politician of the highest rank remarked:

> The men of "natural right" are guilty of all. Who else has declared the principle of revolution to be a duty? Who else has flattered the people by endowing it with a sovereignty of which it is not capable? Who else has destroyed respect for the law by making it dependent on an assembly that lacks all understanding of administration and law, instead of adhering to the nature of things?

Prominent representatives of humanism attempted to formulate their ideas of natural rights in fictitious communal systems, and in these descriptions, fantastic as they were, there was mirrored the spirit of the time and the concepts which animated it. One of the most important Humanists was the English statesman, Thomas More; a zealous defender of natural right, whom Henry VIII later beheaded. Animated by Plato's *Politeia* and, more especially, by Amerigo Vespucci's description of newly discovered lands and peoples, More, in his *Utopia*, describes an ideal state whose inhabitants enjoy a community of goods and by wise and simple legislation contrive a harmonious balance between governmental control and the native rights of the citizens. This book became the starting point for a whole literature of social utopias, among which Bacon's *New Atlantis* and the *City of the Sun* of the Italian patriot, Campanella, were especially significant.

A great advance was made by the French Humanist, François Rabelais, who in his novel, *Gargantua*, describes a small community, the famous Abbey of Thélème, of wholly free men who had abolished all compulsion and regulated their lives simply by the principle, "Do what thou wilt."

> . . . because free men, well born, well educated, associating with decent company, have a natural instinct that impels them to virtuous conduct and restrains them from vice which instinct they call honor. Such people when repressed and enslaved by base subjection and constraint forget the noble inclination to virtue that they have felt while free and seek merely to throw off and break the yoke of servitude; for we always try to do what has been forbidden and long for what has been denied.

The idea of natural rights was strongly echoed in the Calvinistic and Catholic literature of that period, although here the political motives of the position became clearly apparent. First, the French Calvinist, Hubert

Languet, in his disquisition, *Vindiciae contra Tyrannos,* the political creed of the Huguenots, develops the thought that after the pope lost dominion over the world, power was not simply transferred to the temporal rulers, but reverted into the hands of the people. According to Languet the relationship between prince and people rests on a reciprocal agreement which obligates the ruler to regard and protect certain inalienable rights of the citizens, among which freedom of belief is the most important; for it is the people who make the king, not the king who makes the people. This covenant between the king and the people need not necessarily be confirmed by an oath nor formulated in a special document; it finds its sanction in the very existence of the people and the ruler and has validity as long as both exist. For this reason the ruler is responsible to the people for his actions and, if he tries to abridge the freedom of conscience of the citizens, he may be judged by the noble representatives of the people, excommunicated and killed by anyone without fear of punishment.

Inspired by the same idea the Netherland provinces of Brabant, Flanders, Holland, Zeeland, Guelderland, and Utrecht convened in 1581 in The Hague and formed an offensive and defensive league. They declared all relationships existing up to that time between them and Philip II of Spain null and void, as the king had broken the covenant, trodden the ancient rights of the inhabitants under foot, and behaved like a tyrant who ruled over the citizens as over slaves. In this sense the famous Act of Abjuration declares:

> Everyone knows that a prince has been designated by God to protect his subjects as a shepherd does his flock. But when a prince no longer fulfills his duty as protector, but oppresses his subjects, destroys their old liberties, and treats them as slaves, he is no longer a prince, but is to be regarded as a tyrant. As such, the estates of the land can according to right and reason dethrone him and elect another in his place.

The monarchomachi of Calvinism were not alone in maintaining this standpoint, so dangerous to temporal power. The counter-Reformation organized by the rising Jesuits reached similar conclusions, although from different premises.

According to the doctrines of the church, monarchy was a God-instituted state form, but the temporal ruler was given his power only to protect the cause of the faith, which found its expression in the doctrines of the church. Hence, Providence had set the pope as ruler over the kings, just as these had been set as rulers over the people. And just as the people owed the prince unqualified obedience, so the commands of the pope were the highest law for the rulers. But now the spreading Protestantism had destroyed the old picture, and veritable heretics sat on princely thrones as representatives of the highest powers of state. Under these circumstances the relationship of the Catholic Church to the temporal power also had to change and take on other forms. Its attempt to adapt its practices to the new social relationships in Europe and to collect its scattered forces into a strong organization ready for action and capable of meeting all demands, had thoroughly revolutionary results. The church's representatives now had no compunctions about flirting temporarily with democratic ideas if their secret aims were thereby furthered.

It was principally the Jesuits who broke ground in this territory. Thus the Spanish Jesuit philosopher, Francisco Suarez, opposed the doctrine of the divine right of kings on fundamental principles and, quite in the sense of the "natural rights" traced the relationship between prince and people to a covenant which imposed on both parties rights and duties. According to Suarez, power cannot naturally remain in the hands of a single individual, but must be partitioned among all, since all men were equal by nature. If the ruler did not conform to the covenant, or even opposed the inalienable rights of the people, the subjects were given the right of rebellion to guard their rights and to prevent tyranny.

It is understandable that James I of England had the principal work of this Spanish Jesuit, written at the instigation of the pope, burned by the hangman, and that he bitterly reproached his colleague on the Spanish throne, Philip II, for having given a home in his land to "such an outspoken enemy of the majesty of kings."

Even further than Suarez went his brother in the "Society of Jesus," Juan de Mariana, who in the sixth chapter of his voluminous work, *Historia de rebus Hispaniae,* not only justified assassination of the covenant-breaking kings as morally right, but even suggested the weapon with which such murder was to be committed. He had in view here, however, only the secret or open adherents of Protestantism, since he, like his predecessor Suarez, was of the opinion that the prince was, in matters of faith at least, subject to the pope. Thus, for him, the king's heresy was tyranny against the people and relieved the subject of all obligation to the head of the state who, as a heretic, had forfeited his rights. That such ideas had not merely a theoretical significance was proved by the murder of Henry III, and his successor Henry IV, of France, both removed by fanatical adherents of papism. Thus, from both Calvinistic and Catholic sources, the limitation of royal power was advocated, although this was by no means done from a libertarian urge, but from well-understood political interests. At all events, the advocacy of natural rights from this source could but draw many more adherents to the idea of the abrogation of power; which at the time of the great struggles in France, the Netherlands and England, was of peculiar importance.

The clearly felt necessity for putting certain limits to the power of the state and the recognition of the right of rebellion against the ruler who abused his power and became a tyrant were then, widespread ideas which only lost currency with the final victory of absolutism, but were never quite forgotten. Under the influence of these and similar trends of thought isolated thinkers of that period were led to pursue these things more deeply and to lay bare the roots of all tyranny. The most notable among them was the youthful Etienne de la Boétie, whose sparkling screed, *Concerning Voluntary Servitude,* was published after his early death by his friend Montaigne. Whether Montaigne did, in fact, make certain alterations in the work, as is often asserted, can probably never be proved. The fact that La Boétie's works played such an important part in the fight against absolutism in France was later almost forgotten, but that in the time of the great revolution it proved its effectiveness anew is the best proof of its intellectual importance.

La Boétie recognized with irresistible clarity that tyranny supports itself less by brutal power than by the deep-rooted feeling of dependency of men, who first endow a hollow puppet with their own inherent forces and then, dazzled by this imaginary power, blindly submit themselves to it. This spirit of "voluntary servitude" is the strongest and most impregnable bulwark of all tyranny, and must be overcome; for tyranny would collapse as helpless as a heap of ashes if men would but recognize what lies hidden behind it, and deny obedience to the idol which they have themselves created. Says La Boétie:

> What a shame and disgrace it is when countless men obey a tyrant willingly, even slavishly! A tyrant who leaves them no rights over property, parents, wife or child, not even over their own lives—what kind of a man is such a tyrant? He is no Hercules, no Samson! Often he is a pygmy, often the most effeminate coward among the whole people—not his own strength makes him powerful, him who is often the slave of the vilest whores. What miserable creatures are his subjects! If two, three or four do not revolt against *one* there is an understandable lack of courage. But when hundreds and thousands do not throw off the shackles of an individual, what remains there of individual will and human dignity? . . . To free oneself it is not necessary to use force against a tyrant. He falls as soon as the country is tired of him. The people who are being degraded and enslaved need but deny him any right. To be free only calls for the earnest will to shake off the yoke. . . . Be firmly resolved no longer to be slaves—and you are free! Deny the tyrant your help and, like a colossus whose pedestal is pulled away, he will collapse and break to pieces.

But those individual thinkers who, like La Boétie, dared to touch the most hidden roots of power were few. In general, the road to libertarian concepts of life ran through the various phases of the concept of natural rights, whose supporters always endeavored to oppose the unlimited power of the head of the state with "the native and inalienable rights of the people," hoping thus to attain to a social balance favorable to the undisturbed development of the conditions of social life. These efforts led later to the well-known demands of liberalism which, no longer satisfied with the limitation of personal power, strove to limit the power of the state to a minimum, on the correct assumption that the continuous guardianship of the state was just as detrimental to the fruitful development of all creative forces in society as the guardianship of the church had been in previous centuries. This idea was by no means the result of idle speculation, it was rather the tacit assumption underlying every cultural development in history; just as the belief in the foreordained dependence of man on a super-terrestrial Providence was always the conscious or unconscious assumption underlying all temporal power.

A prominent pioneer on the long road leading to the limitation of princely power and the formulation of rights of the people was the Scottish humanist, George Buchanan, one of the first to attribute to the question a fundamental importance, independent of the help or harm which the extension or limitation of princely power could do to one creed or another. Buchanan maintained the basic democratic notion that all power comes from the people and is founded in the people. Regarded from this viewpoint the head of the state was under all circumstances subject to the will of the people, and his whole significance exhausted itself in being the first servant of the people. If the head of the state breaks this covenant tacitly agreed upon, he outlaws himself and can be judged and condemned by anyone.

Buchanan gave the relationship between might and right a new and deeper significance. Had he been content merely to assert freedom of conscience in religious matters against the unlimited princely power, the representatives of absolutism might have been willing to accept this limitation. But he dared to declare that all power emanated from the people and that princes were but executors of the people's will; and so doing he turned against himself the irreconcilable enmity of all supporters of hereditary royalty. Thus it was legitimist influences which induced Parliament on two different occasions—1584 and 1664—to suppress Buchanan's work, *De Jure apud Scotos*. Obeying the same influence, Oxford University burnt the work a hundred years after its publication.

But for absolutism also there arose on English soil a powerful defender in the person of Thomas Hobbes. Hobbes was surely one of the most unique figures in the realm of social philosophic thought, an extremely fruitful and original mind; next to Bacon, perhaps the most versatile mind England ever produced. His name lives in history as the decided champion of philosophical materialism and as an outspoken defender of absolute princely power. Hobbes was, in fact, a stern opponent of all religion in the current sense; for although he principally opposes Catholicism, one feels that he is antagonistic to all revealed religion. There is less justification for the assertion that Hobbes was an unqualified advocate of royal absolutism. The very fact that he traces the state's existence to a contractual relation proves that he was no legitimist. Hobbes was an unqualified exponent of the power principle, but had less in view princely absolutism than the absolute power of the state. In general he gave monarchy the preference, but his later attitude toward Cromwell clearly shows that he was chiefly concerned with the inviolability of the power of the state and less with that of its leaders.

The concept that man was by nature a social creature Hobbes opposed most decidedly. According to his conviction there existed in primitive man no trace of social feeling but solely the brutal instinct of the predatory animal, far from any consideration of the welfare of others. Even the distinction between good and evil, he held, was wholly unknown to man in the natural state. This idea was first brought to man by the state, which thus became the founder of all culture. In his original nature man was not amenable to any social feeling whatsoever, but only to fear, the sole power which could influence his reason. It was from fear that the foundation of the state arose, putting an end to the "war of all against all" and binding the human beast with the chain of the law. But although Hobbes traces the origin of the state to contract, he maintains that the first rulers were given the unlimited power to rule over all others. Once agreed upon, the covenant remains binding for all time to come. To rebel against it is the worst of all crimes, for every attempt in this direction brings into question the permanence of all culture, even of society itself.

The materialist Hobbes, who has been maligned in history as a "radical atheist," was in reality a strictly religious man, but his religion had a purely political character; the God whom he served was the unlimited power of the State. Just as in all religion man becomes ever smaller in proportion as the godhead grows beyond him, until at last God is all, and man nothing; so with Hobbes, viewing the state power as limitless, he degrades man's original nature to the lowest stage of bestiality. The result is the same: the state is all, the citizens nothing. Indeed, as F. A. Lange has very correctly remarked: "The name *Leviathan*" (the title Hobbes gave to his principal work) "is only too appropriate for this monster, the state, which guided by no higher consideration, like a terrestrial god orders law and justice, rights and property, according to its pleasure—even arbitrarily defines the concepts of good and evil—and in return guarantees protection of life and property to those who fall on their knees and sacrifice to it." [2]

[2] F. A. Lange, *Geschichte des Materialismus und Kritik seiner Bedeutung in der Gegenwart.* I:242 (10 Aufl.).

According to Hobbes, law and right are concepts which make their appearance only with the formation of political society, meaning the state. Hence the state can never transgress against law, because all law originates with itself. The customary law, which is often referred to as natural right, or the unwritten law, may utterly condemn theft, murder and violence as crimes; but as soon as the state commands men to do these acts, they cease to be crimes. Against the state's law even "divine right" has no power, for only the state is qualified to decide concerning right and wrong. The state is the public conscience, and against it no private conscience nor private conviction can prevail. The will of the state is the highest, is the only, law.

Since Hobbes sees in the state only "Leviathan," the beast of whom the Book of Job says, "upon earth there is not his like," he logically rejects all striving of the church for world dominion and denies to the priests in general, and to the pope in particular, any right to temporal power. For religion also is justified for him only as long as it is recognized and taught by the state. Thus, he says, in an especially significant passage in *Leviathan:* "The fear of unseen powers, whether it be imaginary or whether delivered by tradition, is religion when it is affirmed by the state, and superstition when it is not affirmed by the state."

According to Hobbes the state has not only the right to prescribe for its subjects what they may believe, it also decides whether a belief is religious or only to be regarded as superstitious. The materialist Hobbes, who had no inclination whatever for religion in general, found it quite in order that the government for reasons of state should decide in favor of a certain creed and impose it upon its subjects as the only true religion. It affects one rather curiously, therefore, when Fritz Mauthner opines that Hobbes "goes far beyond the disbelief of the first deists when he demands the submission of the citizens to the state religion, for what he demands is again only obedience to the state, even in religious matters, not to God." [3]

The whole distinction lies here only in the form of the faith. Hobbes endows the state with all the sacred qualities of a godhead, to which man is subject for weal or woe. He gives the devotional need of the faithful another object of veneration, condemns heresy in the political field with the same iron and logical intolerance with which the church used to fight every opposition to its mandates. Belief in the state, to the "atheist" Hobbes, was after all just a religion: man's belief in his dependence on a higher power which decides his personal fate and against which no revolt is possible, since it transcends all human aims and ends.

Hobbes lived at the time when the rise of the nationalist state ended

[3] Fritz Mauthner, *Der Atheismus und seiner Geschichte im Abendlande.* II:535. Stuttgart und Leipzig, 1921.

the struggle of the church for world power as well as the efforts to bring Europe under the domination of a central universal monarchy. Realizing that the course of history cannot be retraced, and that things already belonging to the shadow realm of the past cannot be artificially revivified, he attached himself to this new reality. But since, like all defenders of authority, he started from the inherent bestiality of man and, in spite of his atheism, could not free himself from the misanthropic doctrine of original sin, he had logically to arrive at the same results as his predecessors in the camp of ecclesiastical theology. It profited him little that he had personally freed himself from the fetters of religious faith in miracles; for he enmeshed himself all the more tightly in the net of a political faith in miracles—which in all its consequences was just as hostile to freedom and enslaved the mind of man just as much. This, by the way, is a proof that atheism, in the current sense, need by no means be associated with libertarian ideas. It has a libertarian influence only when it recognizes the inner connections between religion and politics in their utmost profundity, and finds for the possessors of temporal power no greater justification than for the authority of God. The "pagan" Machiavelli and the "atheist" Hobbes are the classical witnesses for this.

All advocates of the power idea, even though, like Machiavelli and Hobbes, they cared nothing for traditional religion, were compelled to assign to the state the part of a terrestrial Providence, surrounded with the same mystical halo that shines about every godhead, and to endow it with all those superhuman qualities without which no power can maintain itself, whether it be of celestial or terrestrial nature. For no power persists by virtue of special characteristics inherent in it; its greatness rests always on borrowed qualities which the faith of man has ascribed to it. Like God, so every temporal power is but "a blank tablet" which gives back only what man has written on it.

The doctrine of the social contract, especially Buchanan's idea that all power emanates from the people, later aroused the Independents in England to a new rebellion, not only against Catholicism, but also against the state religion founded by the Calvinistic Presbyterians, and demanded the complete autonomy of the congregations in all matters of faith. Since the administration of the state church was now acting only as an obedient tool of the princely power, the religious and the political opposition of the ever spreading Puritanism flowed from one and the same source. The well-known English historian, Macaulay, remarks quite correctly regarding the Puritans that they added hatred of the state to their hatred of the church, so that the two emotions mingled and mutually embittered each other.

Animated by this spirit, the poet of *Paradise Lost*, John Milton, was the first to step forward in defense of freedom of the press, in order to safeguard the religious and political freedom of conscience of the citizens. In his tract, *Defensio pro populo Anglicano,* he defended also the unqualified right of the nation to bring a treacherous and faithless tyrant to judgment and to condemn him to death. Like men starving for spiritual food, the best minds of Europe greedily absorbed this book, especially after it had been publicly burned by the hangman at the command of the King of France.

These ideas were most openly advocated among the Levelers, the adherents of John Lilburnes, and found their boldest expression in the scheme of "the people's covenant," presented to the masses by this most radical wing of the revolutionary movement of that time. Almost all of the social-philosophical thinkers of that period, from Gerard Winstanley to P. C. Plockboy and John Bellers, from R. Hooker and A. Sidney to John Locke, were convinced defenders of the doctrine of the social contract.

While on the continent absolutism almost everywhere won unlimited dominion, in England it achieved under the Stuarts only a temporary success, and was soon unhorsed again by the second revolution of 1688. By the Declaration of Rights, in which all of the principles set forth in Magna Charta, were reaffirmed in extended form, the covenantal relationship between crown and people was reëstablished. Owing to this course of historical development, especially in England, the idea of the social contract and the concept of natural rights never lost currency, and had, consequently, a deeper influence on the intellectual attitude of the people than in any other country.

The Continent had become used to surrendering realms and peoples to the unlimited power of princes. The words of Louis XIV, "I am the State," acquired a symbolic significance for the whole epoch of absolutism. In England, however, where the Crown's striving for power was always confronted by the resolute opposition of the citizens—which could be only temporarily silenced, and never for long—there developed quite a different understanding of social issues. Acquired rights were zealously guarded, and despotism was effectively checked by the requirement of parliamentary approval. John Pym, the brilliant leader of the opposition in the House of Commons against the absolutist claims of the crown, gave eloquent expression to this sentiment when he launched these words against the royalist minority:

> That false principle which inspires the princes and makes them believe that the countries over which they rule are their personal property—as if the kingdom existed for the sake of the king and not the king for the sake of the kingdom—is at the root of all the misery of their subjects, the cause of all the attacks on their rights and liberties. According to the recognized laws

of this country not even the crown jewels are the property of the king; they are merely entrusted to him for his adornment and use. And merely entrusted to him are also the cities and fortresses, the treasure-rooms and store-houses, the public offices, in order to safeguard the security, the welfare and the profit of the people and the kingdom. He can, therefore, exercise his power only after invoking the advice of both houses of Parliament.

In these words resounds the echo of all English history; they reveal the eternal struggle between might and right which will end only with the conquest of the power principle. For the principle of representative government had then quite a different meaning than now. That which today only helps to block the way for new forms of social life was then an earnest effort to set definite limits to power, a hopeful beginning toward the complete elimination of all schemes for political power from the life of society.

Furthermore, the doctrine of contractual relationship as the basis of all the political institutions in society had very early in England far-reaching consequences. Thus, the theologian, Richard Hooker, in his work, *Laws of Ecclesiastical Polity*, published in 1593, maintained that it is un-worthy of a man to submit blindly, like a beast, to the compulsion of any kind of authority without consulting his own reason. Hooker bases the doctrine of the social contract on the fact that no man is really able to rule over a large number of his fellowmen unless these have given their consent. According to Hooker's idea such consent could only be obtained by mutual agreement; hence, the contract. In his dissertation concerning the nature of government Hooker declares quite frankly that "in the nature of things it is by no means impossible that men could live in social relations without public government." This work later served John Locke as a foundation for his two celebrated treatises on *Civil Government,* from which the germinating liberalism drew its main nourishment.

Locke likewise based his social-philosophical theories on natural rights. In contra-distinction to Hobbes, he believed, however, that the freedom of the natural man was by no means a state of rude caprice wherein the right of the individual was limited only by the brute force at his disposal. He maintained, rather, that common and binding relationships existed between primitive men, emanating from their social disposition and from considerations of reason. Locke was also of the opinion that in the natural state there existed already a certain form of property. It was true that God had given men all nature for disposal, so that the earth itself belonged to nobody; the harvest, however, which the individual had created by his own labor, did. For this reason there gradually developed certain obligations between men, especially after the separate family groups collected in larger unions. In this manner Locke thought to explain the origin of the state, which in his view existed only as an insurance company on which rested the obligation of guarding the personal security and the property of the citizens.

But if the state has no other task than this, it follows logically that the highest power rests not with the head of the state, but with the people, and finds expression in the elective legislative assemblies. Hence, the holder of the state's power stands not *above* but, like every other member of society, *under* the law, and is responsible to the people for his action. If he misuses the power entrusted to him, he can be recalled by the legislative assembly like any other official who acts contrary to his duty.

These arguments of Locke's are directed against Hobbes and, most of all, against Sir Robert Filmer, the author of *Patriarcha,* one of the most uncompromising defenders of absolute princely power. According to Filmer a king was subject to no human control, nor was he bound in his decisions by the precedents set by his predecessors. The king is chosen by God himself to act as lawgiver for his people, and he only stands *above* the law. All laws under whose protection men have lived up to now have been delivered to them by God's elect; for it is contrary to reason to assume that a common man can make laws for himself. The idea that a people has the right to judge its king and deprive him of the crown seemed positively criminal to Filmer; for in this case the representatives of the people are accuser and judge in one person, which mocks at every principle of justice. Hence, according to his idea, any limitation of the hereditary power is an evil, and must inevitably lead to the dissolution of all social ties.

Locke, who maintained that the king was only the executive organ of the popular will, logically denied him the right to make laws. What he strove for was a triple partition of public power, as the only protection against such misuse of power as must always endanger the public weal if all the agencies of power were united in one person. Hence the law-making power should be entrusted exclusively to the representatives of the people. The executive power, whose agents could at any time be recalled by the legislative assembly and replaced by others, was in all things subject to it and responsible to it.. There remained only the federative power which, according to Locke, had the task of representing the nation abroad, of making treaties and deciding concerning war and peace. This branch of public power also was to be responsible to the representatives of the people and concerned solely with putting their decisions into execution.

For Locke the legislative assembly was the specific instrument for safeguarding the rights of the people against the government; hence he assigned to it such a dominant role. If an irresponsible administration violate its trust, it constitutes a breach of the existing legal relationship and then the people are free to oppose the revolution from above by the revolution from below, in order to protect their inalienable rights.

But though Locke strove to find in advance a solution for all possible or reasonably probable cases, there are deficiencies in his political program which cannot be removed by the separation of the power functions, because they are inherent in power itself, and are further enhanced by the economic inequalities in society. These inequalities constitute the weakness of liberalism itself and of all later constitutional schemes by which in various countries the attempt has been made to limit power and protect the rights of the citizens. This was already recognized by the French Girondist, Louvet, who in the midst of the high tide of enthusiasm for the new constitution spoke these weighty words: "Political equality and the constitution have no more dangerous enemy than the increasing inequality of property."

The stronger this inequality became in the course of time, the more unbridgeable became the social contrasts under victorious capitalism, undermining every communal interest, the faster faded the original significance of the measures which once played so important a part in society and in the struggle against the ambition for political power.

For all that, the idea of natural rights had for centuries the strongest influence of all those social cults in Europe which aimed to set limits to hereditary power and to widen the individual's sphere of independence. This influence persisted even after a line of eminent thinkers in England and France, like Lord Shaftesbury, Bernhard de Mandeville, William Temple, Montesquieu, John Bolingbroke, Voltaire, Buffon, David Hume, Mably, Henry Linguet, A. Ferguson, Adam Smith, and many others, inspired by biological and related science, had abandoned the concept of an original social contract and were seeking other explanations for the social and communal life. In doing so, some of them already recognized the state as the political instrument of privileged minorities in society for the rulership of the great masses.

Likewise, the great founders of international law, like Hugo Grote, Samuel Pufendorf, Christian Thomasius (to mention only the best-known among them) whose great merit it is that in a time when the national separation of the peoples was becoming ever wider they made the first attempts to go beyond the limits of the state and to collect what is common to all men into a foundation for a common law—these also set out from the idea of natural rights. Grote regarded man as a social being and recognized in the social impulse the basis of all social ties. Social communal life developed definite habits, and these formed the first foundations of natural rights. In his work, *Concerning the Law of War and Peace*, published in 1625, he traces the formation of the state to a tacit covenant for the protection of rights and for the benefit of all. Since the state arose by the will of all individuals, the right that appertains to each one of its members can never be abrogated by the state. This natural and inalienable right cannot be changed even by God himself. This legal relationship is likewise the basis of all relations with other peoples and cannot be violated without punishment.

Pufendorf, like Thomasius and Grote, has his roots in the English social philosophers and boldly declares that natural rights exist not only for Christians, but also for Jews and Turks, a point of view very extraordinary in those times. Thomasius traces back all rights to the desire of the individual to live as happily and as long as possible. Since man can find his greatest happiness only in community with others, he should ever strive to make the welfare of all the guiding principle of his actions. For Thomasius this principle exhausts the whole content of natural rights.

All schemes having their roots in natural rights are based on the desire to free man from bondage to social institutions of compulsion in order that he may attain to consciousness of his humanity and no longer bow before any authority which would deprive him of the right to his own thoughts and actions. It is true that most of these schemes still contained a mass of authoritarian elements, and that these frequently grew again into new forms of rulership when they had partly or wholly obtained their ends. But this does not alter the fact that the great popular movements animated by these ideas smoothed the way for the overthrow of power and prepared the field in which the seeds of freedom will some day germinate vigorously.

Thousands of experiences had to be gathered and must still be gathered to make men ready for the thought that it is not the form of power, but power itself, which is the source of all evil, and that it must be abolished to open to man new outlooks for the future. Every slightest achievement along this tedious path was a step forward in the direction of the loosing of all those bonds of political power which have always crippled the free operation of the creative forces of cultural life and hindered their natural development. Only when man shall have overcome the belief in his dependence on a higher power will the chains fall away that up to now have bowed the people beneath the yoke of spiritual and social slavery. Guardianship and authority are the death of all intellectual effort, and for just that reason the greatest hindrance to any close social union, which can arise only from free discussion of matters and can prosper only in a community not hindered in its natural course by external compulsion, belief in a supernatural dogma or economic oppression.

Chapter 9

JEREMY BENTHAM AND UTILITARIANISM. PRIESTLEY AND RICHARD PRICE. THOMAS PAINE CONCERNING STATE AND SOCIETY. WILLIAM GODWIN'S *POLITICAL JUSTICE*. LIBERTARIAN TENDENCIES IN AMERICA. FROM JEFFERSON TO THOREAU. LIBERAL IDEAS IN GERMAN LITERATURE. LESSING ON STATE AND CHURCH. HERDER'S PHILOSOPHY OF HISTORY. SCHILLER'S ESTHETIC OF CULTURE. LICHTENBERG AND SEUME. THE PERSONALITY OF GOETHE. WIELAND'S *GOLDNER SPIEGEL*. JEAN PAUL. HÖLDERLIN'S *HYPERION*. WILHELM VON HUMBOLDT'S *IDEEN ÜBER DIE GRENZEN DER WIRKSAMKEIT DES STAATES*. POLITICAL RADICALISM IN FRANCE. VOLTAIRE. DIDEROT'S CONCEPTION OF FREEDOM. MONTESQUIEU'S *SPIRIT OF THE LAWS*.

IT had become the custom to refer to liberalism as "political individualism," with the consequence that an entirely false concept was set up and the door thrown wide open for all sorts of misunderstandings. Still, the tendency arose from a thoroughly social idea: the principle of utility, which Jeremy Bentham—one of the most distinguished representatives of this school—reduced to the formula: "the greatest possible amount of happiness for the greatest possible number of the members of society." Thus the principle of utility became for him the natural criterion of right and wrong. Says Bentham:

> The interest of the community is one of the most general expressions that can occur in the phraseology of morals: no wonder that the meaning of it is often lost. When it has a meaning, it is this. The community is a fictitious *body*, composed of the individual persons who are considered as constituting, as it were, its *members*. The interest of the community then is, what?—the sum of the interests of the several members who compose it. It is vain to talk of the interest of the community without understanding what is the interest of the individual. A thing is said to promote the interest, or to be *for* the interest, of the individual, when it tends to add to the sum total of his pleasures: or, what comes to the same thing, to diminish the sum total of his pains. . . . A measure of government (which is but a particular kind of action, performed by a particular person or persons) may be said to be conformable to, or dictated by, the principle of utility, when in

144

like manner the tendency which it has to augment the happiness of the community is greater than any which it has to diminish it.[1]

Certainly these words give expression to the sentiment of social justice which in its immediate assumption proceeds, it is true, from the individual, but which nevertheless is to be taken as the result of a clearly marked feeling of solidarity and can in no wise be covered by the common designation "individualism," which may mean anything or nothing.

Although a large number of the celebrated supporters of political radicalism in England, in contrast to Bentham, proceeded from the principle of natural rights, they agreed with him in their final goal. The dissenting preacher, Joseph Priestley, who declared the unlimited perfectibility of man to be a law of God, would concede that government is right only to the extent that its instruments are engaged in furthering this law of the divine will. To assign to government any other purpose is a deadly sin against the right of the people, for the profit and happiness of the individual members of the community is the only standard by which to judge any transaction having to do with the state. Influenced by this line of thought, Priestley defended the right of a people at any time to recall its government as one of the most elementary presuppositions of the state contract and from this arrived logically at the right of revolution which resides in every people when the government abandons the path which is indicated for it by these imperishable principles.

Richard Price, in contrast with Priestley, did not rest his ideas of right and wrong on grounds of pure utility; neither was he in very close agreement with him about the concepts attaching to philosophic materialism, and he believed in the freedom of the human will. He did, however, agree with the views of his friend about the relations of man to government in general; he even went somewhat further, valuing rather more highly the idea of personal freedom.

> In every free state every man is his own legislator. All *taxes* are free gifts for public services. All *laws* are particular provisions or regulations established by COMMON CONSENT for gaining protection and safety. And all *Magistrates* are Trustees or Deputies for carrying these regulations into execution.
>
> Liberty, therefore, is too imperfectly defined, when it is said to be "a Government by Laws, and not by Men." If the laws are made by one man, or a junto of men in a state, and not by COMMON CONSENT, a government by them does not differ from Slavery.[2]

[1] J. Bentham, *Introduction to the Principles of Morals and Legislation*, 1789.
[2] Richard Price, *Observations on the Nature of Civil Liberty and the justice and Policy of the War with America*, 1776.

The pronouncement concerning laws is of especial importance if one recalls what a cult was made of the law in France at the time of the great Revolution. Of course Price recognized that a social status in which the laws arose from the free consent of all was possible only within the frame of a small community, but just for this reason the modern great state appeared to him one of the greatest dangers for the future of Europe.

In advance of all the representatives of political radicalism of that epoch was Thomas Paine, the enthusiastic pioneer fighter for the independence of the English colonies in North America, the man who understood how to give the clearest expression to those aspirations. Deserving of especial note is the manner in which he brought before the eyes of his contemporaries the difference between state and society. He writes:

> Society is produced by our wants and government by our wickedness; the former promotes our happiness *positively* by uniting our affections, the latter *negatively* by restraining our vices. The one encourages intercourse, the other creates distinctions. The first is a patron, the latter is a punisher.
>
> Society is in every state a blessing, but government, even in its best state, is but a necessary evil; in its worst state an intolerable one: for when we suffer, or are exposed to the same miseries *by a government*, which we should expect in a country *without government*, our calamity is heightened by reflecting that we furnish the means by which we suffer. Government, like dress, is the badge of lost innocence.[3]

Like Priestley, Paine believed in a constant upward advance of human culture and deduced from this that "the higher a culture stands, the less is the need for government, because men must in this case look after their own affairs and also those of the government."

In his writings against Edmund Burke, who had himself once belonged among the most enthusiastic representatives of political radicalism but later became the most virulent advocate of modern state reaction, Paine developed again in splendid words his idea of the nature of government, and especially emphasized most incisively that the men of today have no right to prescribe the path for the men of tomorrow. Covenants that have passed into history can never impose on new generations the duty of accepting as legal and binding on themselves limitations set by their forebears. Paine warned his contemporaries against delusive faith in the wisdom of a government in which he saw merely a "national administrative body upon which is imposed the duty of making effective the basic principles prescribed by society."[4] But Paine was also an opponent of that

[3] Thomas Paine, *Common Sense*. Philadelphia, 1776.
[4] Thomas Paine, *The Rights of Man; being an answer to Mr. Burke's Attack on the French Revolution*. London, 1791. The second part of the work, appearing in

formal democracy which sees in the will of the majority the last word of wisdom, and whose supporters strive to prescribe every activity by established law. Thus he gave warning in his fire-breathing series of essays, "The Crisis" (1776-1783), of a tyranny of the majority, a power often more oppressive than the despotism of one individual over all. It was as if he had foreseen intuitively what dangers must arise if men allowed themselves to erect into a fundamental principle of law, a method whose claim to validity is based on the fact that five is more than four.

The ideas of political radicalism were at that time widely disseminated in England and America and left their unmistakable imprint on the intellectual development of both countries. We encounter them again in John Stuart Mill, Thomas Buckle, E. H. Lecky and Herbert Spencer, to mention only four of the best-known names. They found their way into poetical works and inspired men like Byron, Southey, Coleridge, Lamb, Wordsworth, and above all, Shelley, one of the greatest poets of all time, to reach at last their intellectual zenith in Godwin's *Social Justice* a work which powerfully stirred men's minds for a time, but fell later into forgetfulness because his bold conclusions went too far for most.[5]

Godwin clearly recognized that the explanation of the evil was not to be found in the external form of the state, but was grounded in its very essence. For this reason he did not want to see the power of the state reduced to "a minimum"; he wanted to banish from the life of society every institution of force. Thus, the bold thinker arrived at the idea of a stateless society, where man is no longer subjected to the mental and physical compulsion of an earthly Providence, but finds room for the undisturbed development of his natural capacities, and himself manages all his relations with his fellowmen by the method of free agreement to meet existing needs.

But Godwin recognized also that a social development in this direction was not possible without a fundamental revolution in existing economic arrangements; for tyranny and exploitation grow on the same tree and are inseparably bound together. The freedom of the individual is secure only when it rests on the economic and social well-being of all; a fact for which the advocates of purely political radicalism have never had sufficient regard, wherefore they have always been compelled later to make new concessions to the state. The personality of the individual stands

1792, led to an accusation of high treason against Paine. He was able to escape the consequences only by a timely flight to France.

Burke's earlier essay, "A Vindication of Natural Society," which appeared in 1756, is justly regarded as one of the earliest written contributions of modern anarchism; its author anticipated many of Godwin's conclusions.

[5] William Godwin, *An Enquiry Concerning Political Justice and Its Influence Upon General Virtue and Happiness*, London, 1793.

the higher, the more deeply it is rooted in the community, from which arise the richest sources of its moral strength. Only in freedom does there arise in man the consciousness of responsibility for his acts and regard for the rights of others; only in freedom can there unfold in its full strength that most precious social instinct: man's sympathy for the joys and sorrows of his fellow men and the resultant impulse toward mutual aid in which are rooted all social ethics, all ideas of social justice. Thus Godwin's work became at the same time the epilogue of that great intellectual movement which had inscribed on its banner the greatest possible limitation of the power of the state, and the starting point for the development of the ideas of libertarian socialism.

In America the modes of thought of political radicalism for a long time dominated the best minds, and with them public opinion. Even today they are not completely quenched there, although the all-crushing and leveling domination of capitalism and its monopoly economy have so far undermined the old traditions that they can now serve only as watchwords for business undertakings of a totally different sort. But this was not always so. Even so fundamentally conservative a character as George Washington, to whom Paine dedicated the first part of his *Rights of Man* (which did not prevent his later attacking the first President of the United States violently when he thought he saw him turning in a direction that led far from the paths of freedom)—even Washington could declare: "Government is not reason, it is not eloquence—it is force! Like fire it is a dangerous servant and a fearful master; never for a moment should it be left to irresponsible action."

Thomas Jefferson, who was of the opinion that revolt against a government which had sinned against the freedom of the people was not merely the right but the duty of a good citizen, and that a little rebellion from time to time is good for the health of a government, put his idea about all governmental systems into the laconic words: "That government is best which governs least." An irreconcilable opponent of all political restrictions, Jefferson regarded every intrusion of the state into the sphere of the personal life of the citizen as despotism and brutal force.

To the claim that the citizen must surrender to the state an essential part of his freedom as the price of the safety of his person, Benjamin Franklin replied in the incisive words: "They that can give up essential liberty to obtain a little temporary safety deserve neither liberty nor safety."

Wendell Phillips, the mighty champion against negro slavery, expressed the conviction that "government is the fundamental 'ism' of the soldier, bigot and priest"; and he said in one of his speeches: "I think little of the direct influence of governments. I think, with Guizot, that 'it is a gross delusion to believe in the sovereign power of political machinery.' To hear some men talk of government, you would suppose that Congress was the law of gravitation and kept the planets in their place."

Abraham Lincoln warned the Americans against trusting a government to safeguard their human rights: "If there is anything that it is the duty of the whole people never to intrust to any hands but their own, that thing is the preservation and perpetuity of their own liberties and institutions."

From Lincoln come also these significant words: "I have always thought that all men should be free, but if any should be slaves, it should be first those who desire it for themselves, and secondly those who desire it for others."

Ralph Waldo Emerson coined the well-known words: "Every actual state is corrupt. Good men must not obey the laws too well." Emerson, America's poet-philosopher, had in general an outspoken aversion for the fetishism of the law and averred: "Our mutual distrust is very expensive. The money we spend for courts and prisons is very ill laid out. The law of self-preservation is a surer policy than any legislation can be."

This spirit permeates all the political literature of America of that day until the rising capitalism, which led to entirely new conditions of life, by its corrupting intellectual and spiritual influences forced the old traditions more and more into the background or made them over to suit its uses. And as the same currents of thought in England reached their culminating point in the *Political Justice* of William Godwin, so here they ripened to their highest perfection in the work of men like Henry D. Thoreau, Josiah Warren, Stephen Pearl Andrews and many others who courageously dared to take the last step and to say with Thoreau:

> I heartily accept the motto—"That government is best which governs least"; and I should like to see it acted up to more rapidly and systematically. Carried out, it finally amounts to this, which also I believe—That government is best which governs not at all.

But these ideas were not confined to England and America, even though in these countries they penetrated most deeply into the consciousness of the people. Everywhere in Europe where an intellectual life had revealed itself on the eve of the French Revolution, we come upon its traces. A longing for freedom had seized upon men and had brought under its spell many of the best minds of that time. These ambitions received a powerful impulse from the revolutionary occurrences in America and later in France. Into Germany, too, where a select body of outstanding thinkers was at that time striving to lay the foundations of a new intellectual culture, libertarian ideas found their way; and out of the misery and degradation of a reality ruled by a shameful despotism they rose like glittering horizons of a better future. Let one think of Lessing's *Erziehung des Menschengeschlechts,* of *Ernst und Falk,* and of the *Gespräch über die Soldaten und Mönche.* Lessing followed the same paths as, before and after him, the leaders of political radicalism in England and America. He, too, judged the relative perfection of the state according to the amount of happiness which it assured to the individual citizen. But he also recognized that the best state constitution, being a product of the human mind, was of necessity defective and perishable.

> Suppose the best state constitution that can be conceived to be already invented; suppose that all the people in the world have accepted this constitution; do you not think that even from this best constitution there must arise things that will be most detrimental to human happiness and of which man in a state of nature would have known nothing at all?

In support of this view Lessing adduced various examples which reveal the utter futility of the striving after the best form of state. Aroused by his warfare with theology, the bold thinker always returned later to this question, of which apparently he never again for an instant let go. This is proved by the concluding sentences of his *Gespräch über die Soldaten und Mönche,* as brief as it is rich in content:

> *B.* What are soldiers then?
> *A.* Protectors of the state.
> *B.* And monks are props of the church.
> *A.* That for your church!
> *B.* That for your state!
> *A.* Are you dreaming? The state! The state! The happiness which the state guarantees to every individual member in this life!
> *B.* The bliss which the church promises to every man after this life!
> *A.* Promises!
> *B.* Simpleton!

This is a deliberate shaking of the foundations of the old social order. Lessing divined the intimate connection between God and the state, between religion and politics. He divined at least that the inquiry about the best form of the state is just as meaningless as the inquiry about the best religion, since it carries its own contradiction. Lessing touched here on an idea which Proudhon later thought out logically to the end. Perhaps Lessing did so, too. The crystal-clear form of his *Gespräch* indicates this. But he had the misfortune to drag out his days under the yoke of a miserable petty despot and perhaps could not venture to give publicity to his ultimate thoughts. That Lessing was perfectly clear as to the far-reaching importance of these lines of thought is shown by the report of his friend Jacobi in 1781:

Lessing had the liveliest perception of the ridiculous and mischievous in all political machinery. In an interview he once became so excited that he declared that bourgeois society must yet be completely done away with, and as crazy as this sounds, just that close is it to the truth: Men will be well governed only when they no longer need government.

Along similar paths traveled Herder, who especially in his *Ideen zur Philosophie der Geschichte der Menschheit* made the attempt to understand historically the origin of the state. He regarded the state as a product of later times, traceable to quite different assumptions from those giving rise to social combinations in the natural state of humanity. In that condition man knew only a "natural government," which was based neither on overlordship nor on the separation of society into various ranks and castes, and which, therefore, pursued quite different aims from those of the state, with its artificial structure.

As long as a father ruled over his family he was a father and permitted his sons to become fathers, too, and sought to control them by counsel. As long as several families by free deliberation chose judges and leaders for a particular matter, so long were these office-holders just servants of the common purpose, chosen leaders of the assembly; the names lord, king, absolute, arbitrary, hereditary despot, were to the people with this organization a thing unheard of.

But this changed, as Herder thought, when "barbarian hordes" fell upon other peoples, seized upon their dwelling places and enslaved the inhabitants. With this, according to his notion, arose the first state of compulsion, and there developed the beginnings of the present governments in Europe. Principalities, nobility, feudalism and serfdom are the results of this new status and supplant the natural law of past times. For war is the introduction to all later enslavement and tyranny among men.

History proceeds along this kingly path, and facts of history are not to be denied. What brought the world under Rome? Greece and the Orient under Alexander? What set up the great monarchies back to Sesostris and the legendary Semiramis and then overthrew them? War. Conquest by violence thus took the place of right, and later by the lapse of years or, as our state theorists say, by silent contract, became law. The silent contract in this case, however, means nothing more than that the strong takes what he wants, and the weaker gives and endures, because he can do nothing else.

Thus there arose, according to Herder, a new structure of society and with it a new conception of law. The political government of the conqueror supplants the "natural government" of the freely formed alliances; natural law yields to the positive law of the legislator. The era of the state begins, the era of the nations or state-peoples. According to Herder's notion the state is a coercive institution. Its origin can, it is true, be explained historically, but it cannot be justified morally; least of all where an alien ruling caste of conquerors holds an oppressed people under its yoke.

Herder's whole conception shows plainly the influence of Hume, Shaftesbury, Leibnitz, and especially of Diderot, whom Herder respected highly and whose personal acquaintance he had made in Paris. Herder recognized in the state a thing that had arisen historically, but he felt also that by its standardizing of human personality it could but become a cancer on the cultural development of mankind. Therefore the "simple happiness of individual men" seemed to him more desirable than the "expensive state-machines" which made their appearance with the larger societies welded together by conquest and brute force.

Schiller also, despite his being strongly influenced by Kant, in his conception of the state followed the views of the natural rights school, which would acknowledge the propriety of any activity of the state only in so far as it furthered the happiness of the individual. In his *Briefe über die aesthetische Erziehung des Menschengeschlechts* he puts his attitude toward man and the state in these words:

> And I believe that any single human soul developing its powers is more than the great human society, when I regard this as a whole. The state is a matter of chance, but man is a necessary being, and through what else is a state great and venerable except through the strength of its individuals? The state is only a product of human strength, but man is the source of the strength and the creator of the idea.

Also characteristic of Schiller's view is the aphorism, "The Best State" in the votive tablets:

> How do I recognize the best state? Just as you recognize
> The best woman—just, my friend, because no one speaks of either.

In its meaning this is merely a paraphrase of the Jeffersonian idea: "That government is best which governs least." A similar idea underlies also the aphorism, "The Best State Constitution":

> I can recognize as such only that one which each can easily
> Think good, but which never requires that he shall think so.

This innate resistance to the idea of a state which could prescribe for men the manner of their thinking, even when the thoughts could be called good, is characteristic of the intellectual attitude of the best minds of that time. People then would not have understood the patent model citizen of the state advanced today by the supporters of "nationalism" as a patriotic ideal which, they believe, can be artificially created by "genuinely national legislation" or a "strictly national education."

Goethe viewed the political problems of his time with apparent indifference, perhaps because he had recognized that "liberties" do not constitute the essence of liberty, and that liberty cannot be reduced to a political formula. As privy councilor, courtier, minister, Goethe was often shockingly narrow-minded and guilty of shameful meanness. This may be attributed in no small measure to the distressing restraints of the German social life of the day. No one felt the gulf between himself and his people as deeply as did Goethe himself; he never got close to that people, and remains to this very day on the whole a stranger to them. Just because his view of the world was so many-sided and all-embracing he was of necessity all the more painfully aware of the complete repressiveness of the social life in which he was enmeshed. Goethe's roots were not in his people. "Among the German people there prevails a sort of spiritual exaltation that is alien to my nature," he said to the Russian Count Stroganoff. "Art and philosophy stand divorced from life, abstract in character, remote from the natural springs which should feed them."

In these words is reflected the gap that divided Goethe from his German contemporaries; he merely sunk his roots deeper into the first cause of everything human. The silly twaddle about the "inner harmony of soul of the great Olympian" has long been recognized as a conventional lie. A cleft ran through Goethe's whole nature, and the vain effort to master this cleavage was perhaps the most heroic side of this strange life.

But Goethe the poet and seer, who in the far-reaching vision of his genius embraced the culture of centuries, the man who roared at the world in his "Prometheus"—"the greatest revolutionary poem that was ever written," as Brandes justly said—was too great an admirer of human personality to be willing to surrender himself to the dead gearing of an all-leveling machine.

> Folk and conqueror and thrall,
> These in every age we see:
> Best fortune to Earth's child can fall
> Is just his personality.

At the very bottom of his being Goethe was always faithful to this view. In the first part of the *Faust* he had penned the impressive lines:

> All rights and laws are still transmitted
> Like an eternal sickness of the race—
> From generation unto generation fitted
> And shifted round from place to place.

> Reason becomes a sham, beneficence a worry.
> Thou art a grandchild; therefore woe to thee!
> The right born with us, ours in verity,
> This to consult, alas! there is no hurry.

As an old man he still proclaimed:

> Yes, I am altogether of that mind;
> That is wisdom's final view:
> Freedom and life that man alone should find
> Who daily conquers them anew.
> And so, while dangers round them rage,
> They fight through childhood, manhood and old age.
> Such a throng I'd like to see
> Stand on free soil amid a people free.

In hardly any other sense than this can we understand the saying in the *Maximen:* "Which government is the best? That one which teaches us to govern ourselves."

The political radicalism of the English, and the French literature of enlightenment, had a strong influence also upon Wieland, whose conception of the relation of men to the state rested entirely upon natural right. This finds expression especially in his *Der Goldene Spiegel* and *Nachlass des Diogenes von Sinope.* That Wieland chose just this ancient sage of Corinth as the spokesman for his ideas is in itself highly indicative of the school of thought that he followed.

We shall mention here also G. Ch. Lichtenberg, whose intellectual attitude derived from Swift, Fielding, and Sterne, and who was therefore keenly sensitive to the misery of German conditions; likewise, J. G. Seume; and above all, Jean Paul, that firm defender of freedom who, like Herder, traced the origin of the state to conquest and slavery, and whose works had such a compelling influence on the best of his contemporaries. The manly words which he shouted into the ears of the Germans in his *Declaration of War Against War* are, alas, forgotten in Germany today; but are not, for that, the less true.

> No book will conquer the conqueror or persuade him, but one must speak out against the poisonous admiration of him. Schelling speaks of "an almost divine right of the conqueror"; but he has against him the highwaymen, who in this matter may make the same claim for themselves in the face of an Alexander or a Caesar, and who, moreover, have on their side, the Emperor Marcus Aurelius, who had the robbers he conquered in Dalmatia enlisted as soldiers.

And Hölderlin, the unhappy poet who in his *Hyperion* flung such frightful truths into the faces of the Germans, wrote these pregnant words:

You attribute to the state quite too much power. It cannot demand what it cannot compel. What comes as the gift of love or of intellect cannot be compelled. That, it may let alone, or it may take its laws and set it in the pillory! By Heaven! He knows not what a sin he commits who seeks to make the state a school for morals. The state has always made a hell out of that which man wanted it to make into a heaven. The state is the rough husk on the kernel of life, and it is nothing else. It is the wall around the garden of human fruits and flowers. But what is the use of a wall around a garden if the soil lies dry? The only thing that assists vegetation is rain from heaven.

Such ideas were almost universal among the men to whom Germany owes the rebirth of its intellectual life, although, because of the sad disorganization of German affairs and the unrestrained caprice of the typical German petty despotism, it was not always and everywhere set forth with the same vigor and consistency as in England and France. We do find, however, in all these men a strong leaning toward world-citizenship. Their minds were not limited by national ideas, but embraced the whole of mankind. Herder's *Ideen zur Philosophie der Geschichte der Menschheit* and his ingenious *Briefe zur Beförderung der Humanität* ("Letters for the Advancement of Humanity") are splendid evidence of this spirit, which was striking deep into the best minds until it was restricted for a time by the so-called "wars of liberation"; the intellectual precipitate from the ideas of Kant, Fichte, and Hegel; and the Romantics' concept of the state.

Lessing revealed in his letters to Gleim his utter lack of the prescribed patriotic sentiment: "It is true that perhaps even in me the patriot is not completely smothered, although the reputation of a zealous patriot is, according to my way of thinking, the last for which I should be at all greedy; that patriot, that is, who would teach me to forget that I ought to be a citizen of the world." In another place he says: "I have no conception at all of the love of the Fatherland (I am sorry that I must, perhaps to my shame, confess it), and it seems to me at best a heroic weakness which I am right glad to be without."

Schiller also, whom the staunch German of today noisily hails as the great herald of national interests (in support of which he usually cites a quotation from *Wilhelm Tell*, scornfully styled by Friedrich IV as "a piece for Jews and revolutionaries"; and the well-known saying from the *Jungfrau von Orleans:* "The nation is contemptible that will not gladly risk everything for its honor!" which, torn from its context, is made to convey a totally different meaning from that intended)—Schiller also declares, with the assurance of the citizen of the world:

We moderns have at our command an interest that was not known to the Greeks or the Romans and which patriotic interest does not measure up to by far. The latter is important, anyhow, only for immature nations, for the youth of the world. It is a quite different interest to represent forcefully to man every noteworthy event that has happened to men. It is a pitiful, petty ideal to write for one nation; to a man of philosophical mind this limitation is utterly intolerable. He cannot rest content with such a changeable, accidental, and arbitrary form of humanity, with a fragment (and what else is the most important nation?). He can warm himself to enthusiasm for the nation only so far as the nation, or national event, is an important condition for the progress of the race.

Of Goethe, who had asserted of himself: "The sense and significance of my writings and my life is the triumph of the purely human," and whose lack of patriotic sentiment at the time of the "wars of liberation" has not yet been forgotten, nothing more need be said.

The industrious heralds of the Third Reich today proclaim in thunderous tones that liberalism is "an un-German product" and, like Herr Moeller van den Bruck, keep repeating with gramophonic persistence: "Liberalism is the freedom to have no convictions and at the same time to claim that even this is a conviction." One can only reply that this "un-German product" was once the common intellectual property of those who made Germany into a cultural community again after political and social barbarism had smothered the intellectual life of the country for centuries. It was out of that "lack of conviction" that Germany was born anew.

In his essay, *Some Ideas for an Attempt to Determine the Limits of the Effectiveness of the State,* Wilhelm von Humboldt presented a social-philosophical summary of what moved the re-founders of German literature and poesy most deeply. This ingenious work was written in 1792 under the immediate influence of the revolutionary events in France, though only separate extracts appeared in print at that time in various German periodicals; it was not published as a whole until 1851, after the death of the author. Concerning the purpose of his effort Humboldt wrote, in June of 1792, to the intellectually sympathetic Georg Forster: "I have tried to combat the lust to govern and have everywhere drawn more closely the limits of the activity of the state."

Humboldt attacked first of all the baseless idea that the state could give to men anything which it had not first received from men. Especially repugnant to him was the idea that the state was called to uplift the moral qualities of man, a delusion which later, under the influence of Hegel, befogged the best minds in Germany. As a sworn opponent of any uniformity of thought Humboldt rejected fundamentally any standardizing of moral concepts and boldly declared: "The highest and final purpose of every human being is the development of his powers in their personal peculiarity." Freedom, therefore, seems to him the only guarantee of man's cultural and intellectual advance and the unfolding of his best moral and social possibilities. He wished to protect men against the dead gear-work of the political machine into whose unfeeling grasp we have fallen; hence his opposition to everything that is mechanical and forced; that is susceptible of no intellectual vitalizing. For he holds that automatic consistency stifles every breath of life.

> But really, freedom is the necessary condition without which the most soulful undertaking can produce no wholesome effects of this sort. A thing which man has not chosen for himself, a thing in which he is merely constrained and guided can never become a part of his nature; it always remains alien to him; he does not really carry it out with human vigor, merely with mechanical skill.

Therefore Humboldt wanted to see the activity of the state restricted to the actually indispensable and to intrust to it only those fields that were concerned with the personal safety of the individual and of society as a whole. Whatever went beyond this seemed to him evil and a forcible invasion of the rights of the personality, which could only work out injuriously. Prussia gave him in this regard the most instructive example; for in no other country had state guardianship assumed such monstrous forms as there, where under the arbitrary dominion of soulless despots the scepter had become a corporal's baton in civil affairs. This went so far that under Friedrich Wilhelm even the actors in the royal theater in Berlin were subjected to military discipline and a peculiar special order was put in force "according to which the artists, of whatever rank or sex, were to be treated for any violation of the regulations like soldiers or rebels." [6]

The same spirit which saw in the abject debasement of man to a lifeless machine the highest wisdom of all statecraft and lauded the blindest dead obedience as the highest virtue, celebrates in Germany today its shameless resurrection, poisoning the heart of youth, deadening its conscience and throwing to the dogs its humanity.

In France also the great renewers of intellectual life before the revolution were inspired in many ways by the ideas of political radicalism in England. Montesquieu, Voltaire, Helvetius, Holbach, Diderot, Condorcet and many others went to school to the English. Of course, the adopted ideas took on among the Frenchmen a special coloration, which can be in large part attributed to the peculiar social conditions in the country, which differed essentially from those prevailing in England. With the exception of Diderot and Condorcet most of the political innovators in France were closer to a democracy in their line of thought than to genuine liberalism and, despite their sharp attacks on absolutism, contributed materially to

[6] Eduard Vrehse, *Geschichte des preussischen Hofes.* Hamburg, 1851.

strengthen the power of the state by feeding that blind faith in the omnipotence of legislative bodies and written laws which was to be so disastrous in its consequences.

With Voltaire, who was concerned chiefly about the most widely conceived "freedom of thought," the question of the form of government played a rather subordinate part. An enlightened monarch surrounded by the intellectual élite of the country would have satisfied his demands completely. Voltaire was, it is true, a combative spirit, always ready in individual instances to enter the lists against traditional prejudice and perpetrated injustice; but a revolutionary in the proper sense he was not. Nothing lay further from his thought than a social upheaval, although he is counted among the most important of the minds that made the intellectual preparation for the great revolution in France. Least of all was he the supporter of any definite political system; therefore he could not exert the influence of Rousseau or Montesquieu on the social-political structure of the approaching revolution.

The same holds good for Diderot, who was certainly the most comprehensive mind of his time, and just for that reason the least adapted for a political party program. And yet Diderot went much farther than any of his contemporaries in his social-critical conclusions. In him is found the purest embodiment of the liberal mind in France. An enthusiastic adherent of the rising natural science, he revolted against that artificial thinking which, with innate hostility, blocked the way to a natural arrangement of the forms of social life. Consequently, freedom seemed to him the beginning and the end of all things; freedom was, however, for Diderot "the possibility of an action's beginning quite of itself, independent of everything past," as he so cleverly defined it in his "Conversation with d'Alembert." The whole of nature, in his view, existed to demonstrate the occurrence of phenomena of themselves. Without freedom, the history of humanity would have had no meaning at all, for it was freedom that effected every reconstruction of society and cleared the way for every original thought.

With such a conception the French thinker could not fail to arrive at conclusions similar to those reached later by William Godwin. He did not, like Godwin, assemble his ideas in a special work; but strewn all through his writings are clear evidences that his utterance to d'Alembert was not just a chance remark, of the deeper meaning of which he was himself unaware. No. It was the innermost core of his own being that compelled him to speak thus. Whichever of his works we pick up, we find in it the expression of a genuinely free mind that had never committed itself to any dogma and had, therefore, never surrendered its unlimited power of development. Let one read his *Pensées sur l'interpretation de la Nature*, and one feels at once that this wonderful hymn to nature and all life could have been written only by a man who had freed himself from every inner bondage. It was this innermost essential core of Diderot's personality which called forth from the pen of Goethe, to whom Diderot was closely related intellectually, the well-known words in his letter to Zelter: "Diderot is Diderot, a unique individual; whoever carps at him and his concerns is a Philistine, and there are legions of them. But men do not know enough to accept gratefully from God, or from nature, or from their own kind, what is above price."

The libertarian character of Diderot's thought finds most striking expression in his shorter writings, such as *Entretiens d'un père avec ses enfants*, which contains much material from Diderot's own youth; and very particularly the *Supplément au voyage de Bougainville* and the poem, *Les Eleuthéromanes ou abdication d'un roi de la fève*.[7]

Also in numerous articles in the monumental Encyclopedia, which owed its completion entirely to the tenacious energy of Diderot (to it, he alone made over a thousand contributions), the fundamental ideas of his philosophy are often clearly revealed, although the publisher had to employ all his cunning to deceive the watchful eyes of the royal censorship. Thus, in the article, "Authority," which he contributed, he declares that "Nature gave no man the right to rule over others"; and traces every instance of power to forcible subjugation, which endures just so long as the masters are stronger than the slaves and disappears as soon as the situation is reversed. In which case the previously down-trodden have the same right their former masters enjoyed of subjecting them in turn to the arbitrary whim of their tyranny.

Montesquieu, like Voltaire, was strongly influenced by the English constitution and the ideas which had brought it to its existing structure. But, in contrast to Locke and his successors, he did not take as his basis the principle of natural right, the weak points of which did not escape him; rather he tried to explain the origin of the state historically. In this

---

[7] This poem owes its origin to a happy event. In a little company of men and women Diderot was chosen as so-called "Twelfth Night King," and, as chance would have it, for three successive years the baked-in bean turned up in his piece of the cake. The first time, following Rabelais, he laid down for his subjects the single law: "Each of you be happy in his own way!" In the third year, however, he sets forth in the poem, "Les Eleuthéromanes," how he had grown tired of his kingship and resigned the crown and, in doing so expresses most beautifully his love of freedom. The following verses best show this:

> Jamais au public avantage
> L'homme n'a franchement sacrifié ses droits!
> La nature n'a fait ni serviteur ni maître.
> Je ne veux ni donner ni recevoir de lois!
> Et ses mains coudraient les entrailles du prêtre,
> Au défaut d'un cordon, pour étrangler les rois.

attempt he took the standpoint that the search for an ideal form of state which should be equally valid for all peoples was an illusion, because every political structure grows out of definite natural conditions and must, in every country, assume the forms determined by the local environment. Thus he argues very cleverly in his principal work, *L'esprit des lois*, that the residents of a fruitful district which is much exposed to the danger of conquest by military attack from without, will as a rule value their freedom less highly than the inhabitants of an infertile region surrounded by mountains, and will more readily submit to a despot who will guarantee them protection against invasion. And he supports his view by various interesting examples from history.

Montesquieu's own political ideal was a constitutional monarchy after the English pattern, based on the representative system, and with separation of powers, so that the rights of the citizens and the stability of the state should not be endangered by the concentration of all the instruments of power in the same hands. The French thinker distinguished between despotisms, where every activity of the state is determined by the arbitrary decision of the ruler; and true monarchies, or even republics, where all questions of public life are settled by laws. Laws are for Montesquieu not products of arbitrary will, but adjustments of things to one another and to man. Although he himself argued that the importance of the law is to be sought not in its external compulsory power, but in man's belief in its usefulness, it must still be recognized that his ideas, which had great influence on the thought of his time, contributed greatly to develop that blind faith in law which was so characteristic of the time of the great revolution and of the struggles for democracy in the nineteenth century. Montesquieu presented, so to say, the transition from liberalism to democracy, which was to find its most influential advocate in the person of Rousseau.

Chapter 10

THE RELATION OF LIBERALISM TO DEMOCRACY. ROUSSEAU'S IDEA OF THE COMMUNAL WILL. ROUSSEAU AND HOBBES. ROUSSEAU AS CREATOR OF THE MODERN STATE REACTION. THE SOCIAL CONTRACT AND EQUALITY BEFORE THE LAW. ROUSSEAU'S CONCEPTION OF RIGHT. DEMOCRACY AND DICTATORSHIP. ROUSSEAU'S INFLUENCE ON THE FRENCH REVOLUTION. THE JACOBINS AS WILL-EXECUTORS OF THE MONARCHY. CENTRALISM. THE "SUN KING" AND THE "SUN NATION." NATIONALISM AND DEMOCRACY. THE NATION AS THE BEARER OF "THE COMMUNAL WILL." THE NEW SOVEREIGN. NATIONALISM AND THE CULT OF THE NEW STATE. THE "NATIONAL WILL." NAPOLEON AS HEIR OF THE NEW STATE IDEA. THE DREAM OF THE NATIONAL OMNIPOTENCE OF THE STATE. THE CHANGING OF SOCIETY. THE CITIZEN AS SOLDIER. THE NEW DREAM OF POWER.

THERE is an essential difference between liberalism and democracy, based on two different conceptions of the relationship between man and society. Indeed, we have stated in advance that we have in view here solely the social and political trends of liberal and democratic thought, not the endeavors of the liberal and democratic parties, which frequently bear a relationship to their original ideals similar to that which the practical political efforts of the socialistic labor parties bear to socialism. Most of all, one must here beware of throwing liberalism into the same pot with the so-called "Manchester doctrines," as is frequently done.

The ancient wisdom of Protagoras, that man is the measure of all things, has weight for liberalism, also. On the basis of this doctrine it judges the social environment according as it furthers the natural development of the individual or is a hindrance to his personal freedom and independence. Its conceptions of society are those of an organic process resulting from man's natural necessities and leading to free associations, which exist as long as they fulfill their purpose, and dissolve again when this purpose has become meaningless. The less this natural course of things is affected by forceful interference and mechanical regulation from the outside, the freer and more frictionless will be all social procedure and the more fully can man enjoy the happiness of his personal freedom and independence.

From this point of view liberalism judged also the state and all forms of government. Its advocates believed, however, that government in certain matters cannot be entirely dispensed with. Yet they saw clearly that every form of government menaces man's freedom; hence, they always endeavored to guard the individual from the encroachments of governmental power and strove to confine this to the smallest possible field of activity. The administration of *things* always meant more to them than the government of men; hence, the state, for them, had a right to exist only as long as its functionaries strove merely to protect the personal safety of its citizens against forcible attacks. The state constitution of liberalism was, therefore, predominantly of a *negative* nature; the focal point of all the social-political thought of its advocates was the largest possible degree of freedom for the individual.

In contradistinction to liberalism, the starting point of democracy was a collective concept—the people, the community. But although this abstract concept on which the democratic ideal is founded could only lead to results disastrous to the independence of human personality, it was surrounded by the aureole of a fictitious concept of freedom, whose worth or unworth was yet to be proved. Rousseau, the real prophet of the modern democratic state-idea, in his *Contrat social,* had opposed "the sovereignty of the king" with "the sovereignty of the people." Thus the dominance of the people was for him the watchword of freedom against the tyranny of the old régime. This alone necessarily gave the democratic idea a great prestige; for no power is stronger than that which pretends to be founded on the principles of freedom.

Rousseau proceeded in his social-philosophical speculations from the doctrine of the social contract, which he had taken over from the advocates of political radicalism in England; and it was this doctrine which gave his work the power to inflict such terrible wounds on royal absolutism in France. This is also the reason why there came to be current so many contradictory opinions concerning Rousseau and his teachings. Everyone knows to what a degree his ideas contributed to the overthrow of the old system and how strongly the men of the great revolution were influenced by his doctrines. But just because of that it is all too frequently overlooked that Rousseau was at the same time the apostle of a new political religion, whose consequences had just as disastrous effects on the freedom of men as had formerly the belief in the divine right of kings. In fact, Rousseau was one of the inventors of that new abstract state idea arising in Europe after the fetish worship of the state which found its expression in the personal and absolute monarch had reached its end.

Not unjustly Bakunin called Rousseau "the true creator of modern reaction." For was he not one of the spiritual fathers of that monstrous idea of an all-ruling, all-inclusive, political providence which never loses sight of man and mercilessly stamps upon him the mark of its superior will? Rousseau and Hegel are—each in his own way—the two gate-keepers of modern state reaction, which is today, in fascism, preparing to climb to the highest pinnacle of its dominance. But the influence of the "citizen of Geneva" on the course of this development was by far the greater, for his works stirred public opinion in Europe more deeply than did Hegel's obscure symbolism.

Rousseau's ideal state is an artificial structure. Although he had learned from Montesquieu to explain the various state systems from the climatic environment of each people, he nevertheless followed in the footsteps of the alchemists of his time, who made every conceivable experiment with "the ignoble constituents of human nature" in the constant hope of some day pouring out from the crucible of their idle speculation the pure gold of the state founded on absolute reason. He was most positively convinced that it depended only on the right form of government or the best form of legislation to develop men into perfected beings. Thus he declares in his *Confessions:*

> I found that politics was the first means for furthering morals; that, approach the matter as one may, the character of a people will always evolve according to the kind of government it has. In this respect, it seemed to me that the great question concerning the best form of the state can be reduced to this: how must the government be constituted to form a people into the most virtuous, the most enlightened, the wisest, in one word, the best, people in the fullest sense.

This idea is a characteristic starting point for democratic lines of thought in general, and is peculiarly indicative of Rousseau's mentality. Since democracy starts from a collective concept and values the individual accordingly, "man" became for its advocates an abstract being with whom they could continue to experiment until he should take on the desired mental norm and, as model citizen, be fitted to the forms of the state. Not without reason, Rousseau called the legislator "the mechanic who invents the machine." In fact there is about democracy something mechanical, behind whose gear-wheels man vanishes. But as democracy, even in Rousseau's sense, cannot function without man, it first stretches him on the bed of Procrustes that he may assume the mental pattern the state requires.

Just as Hobbes gave the absolute state a power embodied in the person of the monarch, against whom no right of the individual could exist, so Rousseau invented a phantom on which he conferred the same absolute rights. The "Leviathan" which he envisioned derived its fullness of power from a collective concept, the so-called "common will"—the *volonté général*. But Rousseau's common will was by no means that will of all which is formed by adding each individual will to the will of all others, by this means reaching an abstract concept of the social will. No. Rousseau's common will is the immediate result of the "social contract" from which, according to his concept of political society, the state has emerged. Hence, the common will is always right, is always infallible, since its activity in all instances has the general good as a presumption.

Rousseau's idea springs from a religious fancy having its root in the concept of a political providence which, being endowed with the gifts of all-wisdom and complete perfection, can consequently never depart from the right way. Every personal protest against the rule of such a providence amounts to political blasphemy. Men may err in the interpretation of the common will; for, according to Rousseau, "the people can never be bribed, but may often be misled!" The common will itself, however, remains unaffected by any false interpretations; it floats like the spirit of God over the waters of public opinion; and while this may stray from time to time into strange paths, it will always find its way back again to the center of social equilibrium, as the misguided Jews to Jehovah. Starting from this speculative concept, Rousseau rejects every separate association within the state, because by such association the clear recognition of the common will is blurred.

The Jacobins, following in his footsteps, therefore threatened with death the first attempts of the French workers to associate themselves into trade guilds, and declared that the National Convention could tolerate no "state within the state" because by such associations the pure expression of the common will would be disturbed. Today Bolshevism in Russia, fascism in Germany and Italy, enforce the same doctrine and suppress all inconvenient separate associations, transforming those which they permit to exist into organs of the state.

Thus there grew from the idea of the common will a new tyranny, whose chains were more enduring because they were decorated with the false gold of an imaginary freedom, the freedom of Rousseau, which was just as meaningless and shadowy as was the famous concept of the common will. Rousseau became the creator of new idols to which man sacrificed liberty and life with the same devotion as once to the fallen gods of a vanished time. In view of the unlimited completeness of the power of a fictitious common will, any independence of thought became a crime; all reason, as with Luther, "the whore of the devil." For Rousseau, the state became also the creator and preserver of all morality, against which no other ethical concept could maintain itself. It was but a repetition of the same age-old bloody tragedy: God everything, man nothing!

There is much insincerity and glamorous sham-fight in Rousseau's doctrine for which the explanation is perhaps found only in the man's shocking narrowness of mind and morbid mistrust. How much mischievous sophistication and hypocrisy is concealed in the words: "In order that the social contract may be no empty formula it tacitly implies that obligation which alone can give force to all the others: namely, that anyone who refuses obedience to the general will is to be forced to it by the whole body. This merely means that he is to be compelled to be free." [1]

"That he is to be compelled to be free!"—the freedom of the state power's strait-jacket! Could there be a worse parody of libertarian feeling than this? And the man whose sick brain bred such a monstrosity is even today praised as an apostle of freedom! But after all, Rousseau's concept is only the result of thoroughly doctrinaire thinking, which sacrifices every living thing to the mechanics of a theory, and whose representatives, with the obsessed determination of madmen, ride rough-shod over human destinies as unconcernedly as if they were bursting bubbles. For real man, Rousseau had as little understanding as Hegel. *His* man was the artificial product of the retort, the homunculus of a political alchemist, responsive to all the demands the common will had prepared for him. He was master neither of his own life nor of his own thought. He felt, thought, acted, with the mechanical precision of a machine put in motion by a set of fixed ideas. If he lived at all, it was only by the grace of a political providence, so long as it found no offense in his personal existence. For—

> . . . the social contract served the purposes of the contractors. Who wills the end wills also the means, and these means are inseparable from some danger, indeed, even from some loss. He who wishes to preserve his life at the expense of others must also be willing to sacrifice it for them when that becomes necessary. The citizen of a state is therefore no longer the judge concerning the danger to which he must expose himself at the demand of the law, and when the prince (state) says to him, "Thy death is necessary for the state," he must die, since it is only upon this condition that he has thus far lived in security, and his life is no longer merely a gift of nature, but is a conditional grant from the state.[2]

What Rousseau calls freedom is the freedom to do that which the state, the guardian of the common will, prescribes for the citizen. It is the tuning of all human feeling to one note, the rejection of the rich diversity of life, the mechanical fitting of all effort to a designated pattern. To achieve this is the high task of the legislator, who with Rousseau plays the part of a political high priest, a part vouchsafed to him by the sanctity of his calling. It is his duty to correct nature, to trans-

---

[1] Jean Jacques Rousseau, *The Social Contract*, or, *The Principles of State Right*. Bk. I, Chap. VII.
[2] *The Social Contract*. Bk. II, Chap. V.

form man into a peculiar political creature no longer having anything in common with his original status.

He who possesses the courage to give a people institutions must be ready, as it were, to change human nature, to transform every individual, who by himself is a complete and separate whole, into a part of a greater whole from which this individual in a certain sense receives his life and character; to change the constitution of man in order to strengthen it, and to substitute for the corporeal and independent existence which we all have received from nature a merely partial and moral existence. In short, he must take from man his native individual powers and equip him with others foreign to his nature, which he cannot understand or use without the assistance of others. The more completely these natural powers are annihilated and destroyed and the greater and more enduring are the ones acquired, the more secure and the more perfect is also the constitution.[3]

These words not only reveal the whole misanthropic character of this doctrine, but bring out more sharply the unbridgeable antithesis between the original doctrines of liberalism and the democracy of Rousseau and his successors. Liberalism, which emanates from the individual and sees in the organic development of all man's natural capacities and powers the essence of freedom, strives for a condition that does not hinder this natural course but leaves to the individual in greatest possible measure his individual life. To this thought Rousseau opposed the equality principle of democracy, which proclaims the equality of all citizens before the law. And since he quite correctly saw in the manifold and diverse factors in human nature a danger to the smooth functioning of his political machine, he strove to supplant man's natural being by an artificial substitute which was to endow the citizen with the capacity of functioning in rhythm with the machine.

This uncanny idea, aiming not merely at the complete destruction of the personality but really including also the complete abjuration of all true humanity, became the first assumption of a new reason of state, which found its moral justification in the concept of the communal will. Everything living congeals into a dead scheme; all organic function is replaced by the routine of the machine; political technique devours all individual life—just as the technique of modern economics devours the soul of the producer. The most frightful fact is that we are not here dealing with the unforeseen results of a doctrine whose effects the inventor himself could not anticipate. With Rousseau everything happened consciously and with inherent logical sequence. He speaks about these things with the assurance of a mathematician. The natural man existed for him only until the conclusion of the social contract. With that his time was

[3] *The Social Contract.* Book II, Chap. VII.

fulfilled. What has developed since then is but the product of society become the state—the political man. "The natural man is a whole in himself; he is the numerical unit, the absolute whole, which has relationship only to itself and to its equals. Man, the citizen, is only a partial unit, whose worth lies in its relation to the whole which constitutes the social body." [4]

It is one of the most curious phenomena that the same man who professed to despise culture and preached the "return to nature," the man who for reasons of sentiment declined to accept the thought-structure of the Encyclopaedists and whose writings released among his contemporaries such a deep longing for the simple natural life—it is curious that this same man, as a state theoretician, violated human nature far more cruelly than the cruelest despot and staked everything on making it yield itself to the technique of the law.

It might be objected that liberalism likewise rests on a fictitious assumption, since it is difficult to reconcile personal freedom with the existing economic system. Without doubt the present inequality of economic interests and the resulting class conflicts in society are a continued danger to the freedom of the individual and lead inevitably to a steadily increasing enslavement of the working masses. However, the same is also true for the famous "equality before the law," on which democracy is based. Quite apart from the fact that the possessing classes have always found ways and means to corrupt the administration of justice and make it subservient to their ends, it is the rich and the privileged who make the laws today in all lands. But this is not the point: if liberalism fails to function practically in an economic system based on monopoly and class distinction, it is not because it has been mistaken in the correctness of its fundamental point of view, but because the undisturbed natural development of human personality is impossible in a system which has its root in the shameless exploitation of the great mass of the members of society. One cannot be free either politically or personally so long as one is in the economic servitude of another and cannot escape from this condition. This was recognized long ago by men like Godwin, Warren, Proudhon, Bakunin, and many others who subsequently reached the conviction that the dominion of man over man will not disappear until there is an end of the exploitation of man by man.

An "ideal state," however, such as Rousseau strove to achieve, would never make men free, even if they enjoyed the largest possible degree of equality of economic conditions. One creates no freedom by seeking to take from man his natural characteristics and to replace these by foreign ones in order that he may function as the automaton of the common will.

[4] Rousseau, *Emile*. First Book.

From the equality of the barracks no breath of freedom will ever blow. Rousseau's error—if one can, indeed, speak of error—lies in the starting point of his social theory. His idea of a fictitious common will was the Moloch which swallowed men.

While the political liberalism of Locke and Montesquieu strove for a separation of the functions of the state in order to limit the power of government and to protect the citizen from encroachment, Rousseau, on principle, rejected this idea and scoffed at philosophers who, considering the sovereignty of the state, "cannot divide it in principle, but wish to divide it in relation to its object." The Jacobins, consequently, acted quite in accordance with his views when they abolished the partition of powers laid down in the constitution and transferred to the Convention, besides the legislative, also the judicial function, thus facilitating the transition to the dictatorship of Robespierre and his adherents.

Likewise, the attitude of liberalism toward "the native and inalienable rights of men," as Locke states them and as they later on found expression in "the declaration of human rights," differs fundamentally from Rousseau's democratic concept. To the advocates of liberalism these rights constituted a separate sphere which no government could invade; it was the realm of man, which was to be protected from any regimentation by the state. Thus, they emphasized that there existed something apart from the state, and that this other was the most valuable and permanent part of life.

Quite different was Rousseau's position and that of the democratic movement in Europe founded on his doctrine, except as it was softened by ideal liberal views—especially in Spain and among the South German democrats of 1848-49. Even Rousseau spoke of "man's natural rights"; but in his view these rights had their root entirely in the state, and were prescribed for man by government. "One admits that by the social contract one gives up only that part of his power, his fortune and his freedom which the community needs, but one must also admit that only the sovereign can determine the necessity of the part to be yielded." [5]

Hence, according to Rousseau, natural right is by no means a domain of man which lies outside the state's sphere of function; but rather this right exists only in the measure that the state finds it unobjectionable, and its limits are at all times subject to revision by the head of the state. Consequently, a personal right does not really exist. Whatever of private freedom the individual possesses he has, so to speak, as a loan from the state, which can at any time be renounced as void and withdrawn. It does not mean much when Rousseau tries to sweeten this bitter pill for the good citizen by stating:

[5] *The Social Contract.* Bk. II, Chap. IV.

All services which the citizen can render to the state he owes to it as soon as the state demands them. On the other hand, the sovereign cannot load the citizen with chains useless to the community. Indeed, the sovereign cannot even desire this, for according to the laws of reason, just as according to the laws of nature, nothing happens without a cause.

A worse sophistry—inherently insincere, as is apparent at the first glance—designed to endow self-evident despotism with the halo of freedom can hardly be conceived. That according to the law of reason nothing happens without a cause is very comforting; but it is most unfortunate that it is not the citizen, but the head of the state, who determines this cause. When Robespierre delivered crowds of victims to the executioner for treatment he surely did not do so to give the good patriots practical instruction concerning the invention of Dr. Guillotine. Another cause animated him. He had as the goal of all statecraft the ideal structure of "the citizen of Geneva" in view. And since republican virtue did not spring up of itself among the light-hearted Parisians, he tried to help it on with Master Sanson's knife. If virtue will not appear voluntarily, one must hasten it by terror. The lawyer of Arras, therefore, had a motive worthy of his goal, and to reach this goal he took from man, in obedience to the mandate of the common will, the first and most important right, which includes all others—the right to live.

Rousseau, who revered Calvin as a great statesman and who retained so much of his doctrinaire spirit, in the construction of his "social contract" undoubtedly had in view his native city, Geneva. Only in a small community of the type of the Swiss canton was it possible for the people to vote for all the laws in original assemblies and to regard the administration merely as the executive organ of the state. Rousseau recognized very clearly that a form of government such as he desired was not practical for larger states. He even intended to follow *The Social Contract* with another work which was to deal with this question, but he never got to it. In his work, *Considérations sur le gouvernement de Pologne*, he therefore admits delegates as representatives of the popular will, but he assigns to them only the role of functionaries in purely technical matters. Apart from the common will they can make effective no separate expression of their own will. Besides, he strove to mitigate the evils of representation by frequent changes of the representative body.

When Rousseau, in his discussions of the representative system, which contained many good ideas, mentions with approval the republican communities of antiquity, one must by no means infer from this that the ancient democracy was related to his own views. Even the civil law of the Romans recognized a whole series of personal liberties untouched by the guardianship of the state. In the Greek city-republics, moreover, such a monstrous idea as the theory of the communal will could not possibly have been understood. The doctrine that it is the task of the lawgiver to deprive man of his natural characteristics and replace them by alien ones would have appeared to them as the monstrous offspring of a disordered brain. The extraordinary diversity of their culture is principally traceable to the fact that the individual was offered the widest opportunity to develop his natural powers and to make them creatively effective. No. This monstrous thought, which later found its way to other lands through the influence of French Jacobinism, is the entirely original creation of "the citizen of Geneva." In this sense modern democracy is—in contrast to liberalism—a positive force supporting the state.

This is also the reason why from democracy a number of roads lead to dictatorship; from liberalism, none. Hence Rousseau has advocated dictatorship under certain conditions and approved of it in the interest of the common will. Hence, also, his warning against the too unbending power of the law, which under certain circumstances could prove disastrous to the state. He who declares the common will to be the absolute sovereign and yields to it unlimited power over all members of the community, sees in freedom nothing more than the duty to obey the law and to submit to the common will. For him the thought of dictatorship has lost its terror. He has long ago in his own mind sacrificed man to a phantom that has no understanding whatever of individual freedom. Where this condition exists, the fruits of tyranny flourish.

But the eager students took the master at his word. Dry pedants like Robespierre and narrow-minded fanatics like Saint-Just, Couthon and their like, set themselves at the task of "remodeling" men according to their pattern and creating the powerful state machine which smothered every feeling of independence at its birth, and in the name of freedom bent men under a new yoke. In fact, the Jacobin idea of freedom was never anything else but a mechanical enrollment of the individual in the abstract concept of the nation, the unqualified subjection of all personal will to the mandate of the new state. Never before had there existed in France such a law-loving time as the epoch of the great revolution. The law became the holy icon of the nation, became a fetish which held the spirit prisoner, became a miraculous agency by which every wish concept was to be fulfilled. The "spirit of the law" had actually overcome the nation. The men of the Convention felt themselves utterly intoxicated by their role as the lawgivers of the land. "The lawgiver commands the future"—thus Saint-Just once orated in the Convention, in accordance with Rousseau's idea: "his affair it is to will the good, his task it is so to transform men that they are fitted to that will."

They believed that all the failings of mankind could be cured by law, and thus they laid the foundation of a new miraculous faith in the infallibility of authority, which proved even more disastrous in its consequences than the reactionary dogmatism of Bonald, Chateaubriand, and de Maistre. These tried in vain to breathe new life into a dead phantom, to awaken to a new existence a past that lay irrevocably buried in the dust of the ages. The men of the Convention, however, prepared the way for a new reaction; and they did it, not in the name of legitimist succession, but under the sign of Liberty, Equality and Fraternity. The uncanny belief in the omnipotence of the law and the almost superhuman wisdom of the lawmaker run through all the speeches and public utterances of the Jacobin statesmen and makes them indigestible for anyone who is capable of libertarian feeling. And with the belief in the miraculous power of the law there developed a desire to make every expression of individual and social life subject to the nation. Everything was centralized: government, legislation, public administration, religion, language—and legal murder in the form of the "revolutionary terror."

It is true that the revolutionary forces of the people in the city and, more especially, in the country, opposed this universal leveling with great energy; and the contest of the central power with the communities often assumed a violent character, especially in Paris where the communal administration had a strong influence on the course of revolutionary events. We have to thank this resistance of the communal corporations to the national administration that the revolution did not stop halfway, and that the old regime was utterly destroyed. But with the growing influence of Jacobinism all resistance against the centralized state was gradually overcome. The Convention interfered more and more in all the affairs of local administration and subjected the course of all social events to its control. All local independence was systematically inhibited, or even abolished, according to a definite plan. All provincial and communal life had to disappear or be reduced to a definite uniformity. The old communal administrations were replaced by the state prefecture, which directed everything from Paris, crippling all local initiative.

Thus the weal and woe of millions was entrusted to the higher wisdom of a central body whose members felt themselves to be the "mechanics of the machine"—to use Rousseau's term—and quite forgot that it was living men whom they used as guinea pigs in their experiments to prove the political wisdom of the "citizen of Geneva." The actual deeds and purposes of these elect always remain hidden from the simple mind of the average citizen, and it is precisely this hidden activity which becomes the unquenchable source of a blind belief in the unalterability of a political providence—a belief which grows correspondingly more powerful as man's confidence in his own power diminishes. The purely human pales before the radiant halo of political institutions. Just as the devout believer fails to recognize the man in the priest and sees him illumined with the splendor of divinity, so also the lawgiver appears to the simple citizen in the aureole of a terrestrial providence which presides over the fate of all.

This belief is fatal not only to the common man of the people, but also to the chosen herald of the "common will." The very part which he has been given to play causes him to become constantly more estranged from actual life. As his whole thought and action are set on unison in all social matters, the dead gear-work of the machine, obedient to every pressure of the lever, gradually becomes for him the symbol of all perfection, behind which real life with its endless variety completely disappears. For this reason he feels every independent movement, every impulse emanating from the people themselves, as an antagonistic force dangerous to his artificially drawn circle. When this uncontrollable power which transcends all calculations of the statesman will not listen to reason, or even refuses to yield due obedience to the lawgiver, it must be silenced by force. This is done in the name of the "higher interests," which are always in question when something happens outside the range of bureaucratic habits. One feels oneself the chosen guardian of these higher interests, the living incarnation of that metaphysical common will, which has its uncanny existence in Rousseau's brain. In trying to harmonize all manifestations of social life with the tune of the machine, the lawgiver gradually becomes a machine. The *man* Robespierre once spoke great words against the institution of capital punishment; the *dictator* Robespierre made the guillotine "the altar of the fatherland," made it a means of purification of patriot virtue.

In reality the men of the Convention were not the inventors of political centralization. They only continued after their fashion what the monarchy had left to them as an heirloom and developed to the utmost the tendency toward national unification. The French monarchy had since the time of Philip the Fair left no means untried for removing opposing forces in order to establish the political unity of the country under the banner of absolute monarchy. In doing this the supporters of royal power were not particular as to ways and means; treason, murder, forgery of documents, and other crimes were quite acceptable for them, if they promised success. The reigns of Charles V, Charles VII, Louis XI, Francis I, Henry II, are the most prominent milestones in the development of unlimited monarchy, which, after the preliminary labors of Mazarin and Richelieu, shone in fullest glory under Louis XIV.

This splendor of the "Sun King" filled all lands. An army of venal sycophants, poetasters, artists, living by the favor of the court, had as their special task to cause the fame of the megalomaniac despot to glow with brightest colors. French was spoken in all courts. All strove to be intellectually brilliant according to Parisian fashion and imitated French court manners and ceremonies. The most unimportant little despot in Europe was consumed by the sole aim of imitating Versailles, at least in miniature. Small wonder that a ruler entirely unaffected by any inferiority complex considered himself a demi-god and was intoxicated by his own magnificence. But this blind devotion to the king's person gradually intoxicated the whole "nation," which venerated itself in the person of the king. As Gobineau significantly remarks:

> France became in its own eyes the Sun Nation. The universe became a planetary system in which France, at least in its own opinion, had the first place. With other peoples it could have nothing in common except to shed light on them at its pleasure, for it was quite convinced that all were groping in the fog of densest darkness. France, however, was France, and as, in its view, all the rest of the world daily sank into a joyless distance, it gradually satisfied itself more and more with veritable Chinese ideas. Its vanity became a Chinese Great Wall.[6]

The men of the Convention, therefore, not only took over the idea of political centralization from the monarchy, but the cult which they carried on by means of the nation likewise had there its beginning. It is true, however, that in the age of Louis XIV the nation was considered to consist only of the privileged classes, the nobility, the clergy, the prosperous citizens; the great masses of the peasants and the city workers did not count.

It is related that Bonaparte, a few days before the *coup d'etat* had a talk with the Abbé Sieyès—then one of the five members of the Directory —and on this occasion flung these words at the clever theologian who had weathered successfully all the storms of the revolution: "*I* have created the Great Nation!" Whereupon Sieyès smilingly replied: "*Yes*, because *we* had first created the *Nation*." The clever Abbé was right, and spoke with greater authority than Bonaparte. The nation had first to be born, or, as Sieyès so significantly said, to be *created*, before it could become great.

It is significant that it was Sieyès who at the beginning of the revolution gave the concept of the nation its modern meaning. In his essay, *What Is the Third Estate?* he raised and answered three questions of paramount importance: "What is the third estate?—Everything. What has it been up to now in the political order of things?—Nothing. What will it become?—Something." But in order that the third estate might become something entirely new, suitable political conditions had first to be created in France. The bourgeoisie could become dominant only if the so-called "Estates General" was replaced by a national assembly based

---

[6] From a manuscript uncompleted at his death. German translation by Rudolf Schlösser in "Frankreichs Schicksal im Jahre 1870." S. 34 Reclam-Verlag.

on a constitution. Hence the political unification of the nation was the first demand of the beginning revolution looking toward the dissolution of the Estates. The third estate felt itself ready, and Laclos declared in the *Deliberations*, to which the Duke of Orleans had only lent his name: "The Third Estate; that *is* the nation!"

In his essay Sieyès has described the nation as a "community of united individuals subject to the same law and represented by the same legislative body." But, influenced by the ideas of Rousseau, he extended the meaning of this purely technical definition and made the nation the original basis of all political and social institutions. Thus the nation became the actual embodiment of the common will in Rousseau's sense: "Her will is always lawful, for she is herself the embodiment of the law."

From this concept all other conclusions followed quite obviously. If the nation was the embodiment of the common will, then it had to be in its very nature one and indivisible. In this case, however, the national representative assembly had also to be one and indivisible, for it alone had the sacred task of interpreting the nation's will and making it intelligible to the citizens. Against the nation all separate efforts of the estates were futile; nothing could endure beside it, not even the separate organization of the church. Thus Mirabeau declared in the Assembly a few days after the memorable night of August 4th:

> No national law has instituted the clergy as a permanent body in the state. No law has deprived the nation of the right to investigate whether the servants of religion should form a political corporation existing of itself and capable of acquiring and possessing. Could simple citizens by giving their possessions to the clergy and the clergy by receiving them give them the right to constitute themselves a separate order within the state? Could they rob the nation of the right to dissolve it? *All the members of the clergy are merely officials of the state. The service of the clergy is a public function; just as the official and the soldier, so also the priest, is a servant of the nation.*

Not without reason had the king's brother, the Comte d'Artois, with the rest of the royal princes, in his *Mémoirs présentés au Roi, etc.,* protested against the new role which had been assigned to the nation and warned the king that his approval of such ideas would inevitably lead to the destruction of the monarchy and the church, and of all privileges. Indeed, the practical consequences of this new concept were too plain to be misunderstood. If the nation as representative of the communal will stood above all and everything, then the king was nothing more than the highest official of the national state and the time was past, once and for all, when a "most Christian king" could say with Louis XIV: "The nation constitutes in France no corporation; it exists exclusively in the person of the king."

The court recognized very clearly the danger that hung over it and aroused itself to make some threatening gestures; but it was already too late. On the 16th of June, 1789, the representatives of the third estate, who had been joined by the lower clergy, on the motion of Abbé Sieyès declared themselves to be the National Assembly, with the argument that they constituted 96 percent of the nation anyhow, and that the other 4 percent were at any time free to join them. The storming of the Bastille and the march to Versailles soon gave this declaration the necessary revolutionary emphasis. With that the die was cast. An old faith was buried, giving place to a new. The "sovereignty of the king" had to strike its flag before the "sovereignty of the nation." The modern state was lifted from the baptismal font and anointed with the democratic oil—fitted to achieve the importance assigned to it in the history of the modern era in Europe.

The situation was still not fully clarified, however, for in the National Assembly itself there was an influential section which recognized Mirabeau as its leader and with him advocated a so-called "kingdom of the people." These sought to rescue as much of the royal sovereignty as was possible under the circumstances. This became especially noticeable in the discussions concerning the formulation of "human and civil rights," where the disciples of Montesquieu and Rousseau stood often in sharp opposition. If the former could record a success when a majority of the Assembly declared for the representative system and the partition of powers, then the adherents of Rousseau had their success when the third article in the *Declaration* announced: "The principle of all sovereignty rests by its very nature in the nation. No corporation and no individual can exercise an authority which does not openly emanate from it."

It was true that the great masses of the people had little understanding of these differences of opinion in the bosom of the National Assembly; just as they have always been indifferent to the details of political theories and programs. In this instance as in most, events themselves, especially the ever more apparent treachery of the court, contributed much more to the final solution of the question than the dry dogmatism of Rousseau's disciples. Anyway, the slogan, "the sovereignty of the nation" was short and impressive. Particularly, it brought the contrast between the new order of things and the old into the foreground of all discussions—in revolutionary times a matter of great importance. After the royal family's unsuccessful attempt at flight, the internal situation became increasingly acute, until finally the storming of the Tuileries put an end to all half-measures, and the people's representatives entered seriously upon the discussion of the abolition of royalty. Manuel stated the whole problem in one sentence: "It is not enough to have declared the dominance of the one and only true sovereign, the nation. We must also free it from the rivalry of the false sovereign, the king." And the Abbé Grégoire supported him, describing the dynasty as "generations living on human flesh," and declaring: "The friends of freedom must finally be given full security. We must destroy this talisman whose magic power can still darken the minds of many men. I demand the abolition of royalty by a solemn law."

The grim Abbé was not wrong; as a theologian he knew how intimately religion and politics are united. Of course the old talisman had to be broken in order that the simple-minded should no longer be led into temptation. But this could be done only by transferring its magic influence to another idol better fitted to man's need of faith and likely in its practical effects to prove stronger than the dying "divine right" of kings.

In the fight against absolutism the doctrine of the "common will" which found its expression in the "sovereignty of the people" proved a weapon of powerful revolutionary import. For that very reason we all too often forget that the great revolution introduced a new phase of religio-political dependence whose spiritual roots have by no means dried up. By surrounding the abstract concepts of the "Fatherland" and the "Nation" with a mystical aureole it created a new faith which could again work wonders. The old regime was no longer capable of miracles, for the atmosphere of the divine will which once surrounded it had lost its attraction and could no longer set the heart aglow with religious fervor.

The politically organized nation, however, was a new god whose magic powers were still unspent. Over his temple shone the promise-filled words, "Liberty, Equality, Fraternity," arousing in men the belief that the coming order was to bring them salvation. To this divinity France sacrificed the blood of her sons, her economic interests, her all. This new faith resounding in the souls of her citizens filled them with an enthusiasm which worked greater wonders than the best strategy of her generals.

The religious character of this powerful movement, under whose onset the old Europe fell in ruins, showed its full force only when royalty was totally abolished and the "sovereignty of the nation" no longer had a rival which looked back to the old traditions. The French historian, Mathiez, has demonstrated the details of this new cult impressively and has shown how in many of its manifestations it leans on Catholicism.[7]

In an address of one of the Jacobin clubs to the mother society in Paris occurs the statement: "The Frenchman has no other divinity but the nation, the fatherland!" The fatherland, however, was "the new king with seven hundred and forty-nine heads," as Proudhon called it—the new state, which served the nation as makeshift. For Jacobinism the state became the new national Providence, hence its fanatical zeal for the "one and indivisible Republic." For it would not do for others to dabble in the

[7] A. Mathiez; "Les Origines des Cultes Révolutionaires," Paris, 1904.

trade of the new Providence. Declared Danton, in September, 1793, from the rostrum of the Convention:

> They say that there are persons among us who are striving to dismember France. Let us eliminate these inharmonious ideas by proclaiming the death penalty for their originators. France must be an indivisible whole. There must be unity of representation. The citizens of Marseilles wish to grasp the hands of the citizens of Dunkirk. I demand the death penalty for those who would destroy the unity of France, and I move the Convention that we declare as the foundation of government unity of representation and administration.

Legislation, army, public education, press, clubs, assemblies—all must serve to perfect the spiritual drill of the citizens, to make every brain conform to the new political religion. No exception was made of any movement, not even that of the Girondists, who had been reviled as federalists simply because their opponents knew such an accusation would arouse the patriots most violently against them. The Girondists had contributed to the deification of the nation no less than the men of the Mountain; had not one of their best-known leaders, Isnard, given expression to this sentiment?—"The French have become the elect people of the earth. Let us be concerned that their attitude shall justify their new destiny!" There was already in the minds of the representatives of "la grande nation" a premonition of Napoleon's victories.

A new priesthood had put in its appearance—the modern popular assembly. To it had been assigned the task of transmitting the "will of the nation" to the people, just as the earlier priests had transmitted to them "the will of God." Undoubtedly the revolution had swept away a rotten social order with an iron broom and given the people of Europe many glimpses of light for the future; but in the political field its results were, in spite of all revolutionary phraseology, entirely reactionary. It had strengthened the power idea anew, infused new life into prostrate authority, and chained man's will to freedom to a new religious dogma, against which it was sure to break its young wings.

The absolutism of royalty had fallen; but only to give place to a new absolutism even more implacable than the "divine right" of monarchy. The absolute principle of monarchy lay outside the citizen's sphere of activity, and was supported solely by the "grace of God," to whose will it allegedly gave expression. The absolute principle of the nation, however, made the least of mortals a co-bearer of the common will, even while it denied him the right to interpret this according to his own understanding. Imbued by this thought every citizen from now on forged his own link in the chain of dependence which formerly some other had forged for him. The sovereignty of the nation steered everyone into the same path, absorbed every individual consideration, and replaced personal freedom by equality before the law.

Not without reason were Moses' tables of the law set up in the Convention as a symbol of the national will. Not without reason there hung upon the walls of the Assembly the fasces and ax of the lictors as the emblem of the One and Indivisible Republic. Thus was the man sacrificed to the citizen, individual reason to the alleged will of the nation. When the leading men of the revolution, animated by Rousseau's spirit, strove to destroy all natural associations in which the needs and impulses of men sought expression, they destroyed the root of all true association, transformed the people into the mob, and introduced that fateful process of social uprooting which was later speeded up and sharpened by the growing development of capitalistic economy.

Just as the "will of God" has always been the will of the priests who transmitted it and interpreted it to the people, so the "will of the nation" could be only the will of those who happened to have the reigns of public power in their hands and were, consequently, in a position to transmit and interpret the "common will" in their own way. This phenomenon need not necessarily be traced to inherent hypocrisy. Much more reasonably can we in this instance speak of "deceived deceivers"; for the more deeply the enunciators of the national will are convinced of the sacredness of their mission, the more disastrous are the results springing from their inherent honesty. There is deep significance in Sorel's remark: "Robespierre took his part seriously, but his part was an artificial one."

In the name of the nation the Convention outlawed the Girondists and sent their leaders to the scaffold; in the name of the nation Robespierre with Danton's help removed the Hébertists and the so-called "enragés"; in the name of the nation Robespierre and Saint-Just made the Dantonists "sneeze into the sack"; in the name of the nation the men of Thermidor removed Robespierre and his adherents; in the name of the nation Bonaparte made himself Emperor of the French.

Vergniaud maintained that the revolution was "a Saturn who swallowed his own children." This could be said with much more reason of the mystical principle of the sovereignty of the nation, whose priests constantly brought new sacrifices to it. In fact, the nation became a Moloch which could never be satisfied. Just as with all gods, here, too, religious veneration led to its inevitable result: the nation all, man nothing!

Everything appertaining to the nation took on a sacred character. In the smallest villages altars were erected to the fatherland and sacrifices were offered. The holidays of the patriots came to have the character of religious feasts. There were hymns, prayers, sacred symbols, solemn processions, patriotic relics, shrines of pilgrimage—all to proclaim the glory of the fatherland. From now on the "glory of the nation" was spoken of as formerly the "glory of God." One deputy solemnly called the *Declaration of the Rights of Man* the "catechism of the nation." The *Contrat Social* of Rousseau became the "Bible of Liberty." Enthusiastic believers compared the Mountain of the Convention with Mount Sinai, on which Moses received the sacred tablets of the law. The Marseillaise became the *Te Deum* of the new religion. An intoxication of belief had overspread the land. Every critical consideration was submerged in the flood of feeling.

On November 5, 1793, Marie Joseph Chénier, brother of the unhappy poet, André Chénier, said to the assembled Convention:

> If you have freed yourselves from all prejudices to prove yourselves the more worthy of the French nation, whose representatives you are, then you know how on the ruins of the dethroned superstitions can be founded the one natural religion, having neither sects nor mysteries. Her preachers are our legislators, her priests our executive officers of the state. In the temple of this religion humanity will offer incense only on the altar of our country, the mother of us all and our divinity.

In the sultry atmosphere of this new faith modern nationalism was born, and became the religion of the democratic state. And the more deeply the citizen venerated his own nation, the wider became the abyss which separated it from all other nations, the more contemptuously he looked upon all who were not so fortunate as to be of the elect. It is only a step from the "nation" to the "Great Nation"—and that not alone in France.

The new religion had not only its own ritual, its inviolable dogmas, its holy mission, but also the terrible orthodoxy characteristic of all dogmatism, which will permit no opinion but the *one* opinion to find voice; for the will of the nation is the revelation of God, intolerant of all doubt. He who dares to doubt for all that, and to pursue considerations contrary to the expression of the national will, is a social leper and must be weeded out from the communion of the faithful. Saint-Just proclaimed gloomily before the Convention:

> One dare not hope that things will improve so long as one foe of Freedom breathes. Not only the traitors, but also the lukewarm and the indifferent, everyone who takes no part in the republic and moves no finger for it. After the French people has announced its will everything which is contrary to its will stands outside the sovereignty of the nation; and who stands outside the sovereign is his enemy.

The young fanatic who had such a strong influence on Robespierre did not leave open to doubt what he meant by this enmity—"One must rule those with iron whom one cannot rule with justice." But one could not rule with justice over men who could see the nation's will otherwise than as Robespierre and the Jacobins explained it. Hence, one must needs resort to iron. The sharp logic of the guillotine could hardly be justified more explicitly.

This fanatic logic of Saint-Just was but the inevitable result of his absolute faith in his point of view. Every absolutism is based on fixed norms, and must for that reason act as the sworn enemy of any social development which opens new outlooks on life and calls new forms of the community into being. Behind every absolutist idea grins the mask of the inquisitor and the judge of heretics.

The sovereignty of the nation means tyranny as surely as does the sovereignty of God or that of the king. If formerly opposition to the sacred person of the monarch was the most abominable of all crimes, so now any opposition to the sacred majesty of the nation became the sin against the Holy Ghost of the common will. In both instances, the hangman was the executive instrument of a despotic power which felt called upon to guard the dead dogma. Before its soulless cruelty every creative thought had to founder, every human feeling bleed to death.

Robespierre, of whom Condorcet maintains that he had "neither a thought in his brain nor a feeling in his heart," was the man of the dead formula. In place of a soul he had his "principles." Preferably, he would have founded the whole republic on the single formula of virtue. But this virtue did not have root in the personal righteousness of the people; it was a bloodless phantom hovering over men like the spirit of God hovering over creation. Nothing is more cruel and heartless than virtue, and most cruel and heartless is that abstract virtue which is not founded upon a living need, but has its roots in "principles" and must be continually protected by chemical means from becoming moth-eaten.

Although Jacobinism had overthrown monarchy, it became fanatically enamored of the monarchic idea, which it strengthened greatly by anchoring it to the political theology of Rousseau. Rousseau's doctrine culminated in the complete merging of man in "the higher necessity" of a metaphysical idea. Jacobinism had undertaken the task of transmuting this monstrous doctrine into life and quite logically had reached the dictatorship of the guillotine; which in turn smoothed the way for the saber dictatorship of General Bonaparte who, on his part, risked everything in order to develop this new state idea to its highest perfection. Man a machine—not in the sense of La Mettrie, but as the end product of a political religion which undertook to shape everything human according to the same pattern, and in the name of equality raised conformity to a principle.

Napoleon, the laughing heir of the great revolution, who had taken over from the Jacobins the man-devouring machine of the centralized state and the doctrine of the will of the nation, attempted to develop the state institutions into a flawless system in which accident should have no place. What he needed was not men, but chessmen, who would obey every turn of his whim and unconditionally submit to that "higher necessity" whose executive instruments they felt themselves to be. Men in the ordinary sense were not usable for this; only citizens, parts of the machine, members of the state. "Thought is the ruler's chief enemy," Napoleon once said, and this was no chance figure of speech; he understood the truth of the words in their deepest meaning. What he needed was not men who think, but men who have their thinking done for them, men who offer themselves up when "destiny" speaks.

Napoleon dreamed of a state in which, above all, there existed no distinction between the civil and the military power: the whole nation an army, every citizen a soldier. Industry, agriculture, administration, were only conceived as parts of this mighty state body which, divided into regiments and commanded by officers, would obey the slightest pressure of the imperial will without friction, without resistance. The transmutation of the "Great Nation" into a gigantic unit in which the independent activity of the individual no longer had room; which worked with the exactness of a machine and, throbbing with the dead rhythm of its own motion, unfeelingly obeyed the will of him who had set it in motion—this was Napoleon's political aim. And with iron persistency he pursued it and tried to give it life. Quite obsessed by this delusion, he strove to exclude every possibility which might lead to the formation of an independent opinion. Hence, his bitter fight against the press and all other means of expressing public thought. He said: "The printing press is an arsenal which must not be made available to the generality. Books must only be printed by persons who possess the confidence of the government."

In the brain of this terrible man everything was transformed into figures; only numbers decide; statistics become the foundation of the new statecraft. The emperor demanded of his counselors not only an exact statement and record of all material and technical resources of the whole country; he also demanded that "statistics of morals" should be kept, in order that he might at all times be informed of the most secret agitations among his subjects. And Fouché, that uncanny, specter-like snooper, who saw with a thousand eyes and heard with a thousand ears, whose soul was just as icy as that of his master, became the statistician of "public morals," which he registered by police methods, being quite well aware that his own movements also were watched by unknown spies and recorded in a separate register.

That Napoleon could never quite attain the last aim of his internal policy, that all his apparatus of government was wrecked again and again on men, was probably the bitterest pang of his power-loving soul, the great tragedy of his monstrous life, which even at St. Helena still burned within him. But the mad idea he pursued did not die with him. It is even today the basis of the will to power, which appears wherever the love of men has died and sacrifices pulsating life to the shadowy, pale, phantom forms of tyrannical lust. For all power is loveless, is inhuman in the nature of its being. It changes the hearts of the powerful into wolf-dens of hate and cold contempt for humanity, chokes all human emotion, and causes the despot to see his fellow man only as an abstract number to be used in calculating the execution of his plans.

Napoleon hated freedom on principle, as does every tyrant who has become clearly aware of the nature of power. But he also knew the price he had to pay for this, knew very well that to master mankind he must smother the man hidden in himself. It is significant that he says of himself: "I love power as an artist, as a violinist loves his violin. I love it in order to coax from it tones, melodies, harmonies." It is significant that this same man, who almost as a child was already evolving in his brain plans for power, uttered in early youth the ominous words: "I find that love is detrimental to society and to the personal happiness of man. If the gods were to free the world from love, it would be the greatest of blessings."

This feeling never left him, and when in later years he looked back on the separate phases of his life, there remained for him only this comfortless knowledge:

> There are only two levers which move men, fear and self-interest. Love is a stupid illusion, be assured of it. Friendship is an empty word. I love no one, not even my brothers—possibly Joseph a little, from habit and because he is older than I. And I love Duroc; but why? Because his character pleases me. He is earnest and resolute, and I believe the fellow has never shed a tear. I, for my part, know that I have no true friends.

How empty this heart must have been which through all the years pursued a phantom and was animated by only one desire—to rule. To this madness he sacrificed the bodies and souls of men after having first attempted to make their spirits fit into the dead mechanism of a political machine. But at last it was made clear to him that the age of the automatons had not yet arrived. Only a man whose soul was a desert could say: "A man like me cares nothing for the lives of millions of men."

Napoleon asserted that he despised men, and his uncritical admirers have rated this almost as a merit. He may in individual cases have found justification enough for it; for it is by no means the men of highest worth who crowd around the powerful. But if the matter is pursued more deeply one gets the impression that his demonstratively displayed contempt of men is to a large part pretense, intended to impress his contemporaries and posterity with the brilliance of his own achievements. For this apparent misanthrope was a first-class actor to whom the judgment of posterity was not a matter of indifference, who left no means untried to influence the opinion of future generations, who did not even shrink from the falsification of well-known facts in order to achieve this end.

It was not inner disgust which separated him from men, but his unfathomable egotism, which knew no scruples nor shrank from any lies, from any villainy, any dishonor—not from the meanest of crimes—in order to make himself dominant. Emerson rightly remarks: "Bonaparte was in a quite unusual degree devoid of every high-hearted emotion. . . . He did not even possess the merit of common truthfulness and honesty." And in another place in his essay on Napoleon he says: "His whole existence was an experiment under the best possible conditions to show of what intellect divorced from conscience is capable." Only as issuing from the disconsolate inner state of a man in whom his own greed for glory had utterly destroyed all social feeling are these words of Napoleon understandable: "The savage, like the civilized man, needs a lord and master, a sorcerer who keeps his fancy in check, subjects him to strict discipline, chains him, prevents his biting at the wrong time, clubs him, leads him to the chase. Obedience is his destiny; he deserves nothing better and has no rights."

But this heartless cynic, who in his youth had intoxicated himself with the *Contrat Social*, recognized to the uttermost the whole disastrous significance of this new religion on which in the last analysis his rule was founded. Thus, in one of those unguarded moments of complete truthfulness so rare with him, he allowed himself to be enticed into the statement: "Your Rousseau is a madman who has led us to this condition!" And on another occasion, somewhat pensively: "The future will show whether it had not been better for the world's peace if neither Rousseau nor I had ever lived."

Chapter 11

THE AUTHORITY PRINCIPLE IN GERMAN PHILOSOPHY. KANT AS THE ADVOCATE OF ABSOLUTE STATE POWER. KANT'S MORAL LAW. KANT'S CONCEPT OF SOCIETY. THE IDEA OF THE "ETERNAL PEACE" AND THE INTERNATIONAL LEAGUE OF STATES. KANT AND HERDER. FICHTE AND THE DOCTRINE OF THE INHERENT EVIL IN MAN. FICHTE AND MACHIA-VELLI. THE "SELF-CONTAINED COMMERCIAL STATE." FICHTE AND STATE SOCIALISM. FICHTE'S *ADDRESSES TO THE GERMAN NATION*. FICHTE AND NATIONAL EDUCATION. THE IDEA OF THE "HISTORIC MISSION OF THE GERMANS." HEGEL'S INFLUENCE ON HIS TIME. HEGEL'S DIALECTIC. THINKING IN CATEGORIES. HEGEL'S PHILOSOPHY OF HISTORY. HEGEL AND THE STATE. THE BELIEF IN FATE. HEGEL AND PROTESTANTISM. THE PRUSSIAN STATE PHILOSOPHER. HEGEL AND SOCIALISM.

IN sharp contrast with German literature and poetry stands German philosophy. Although it has not lacked occasional glimpses of light, German classical philosophy has never been a domain of freedom. Its best-known representatives have often flirted with freedom, but no real union ever resulted. One gains the impression that when life's brutal realities became too clearly felt, a few concessions, not too binding, were made to the awakened conscience in order to restore the disturbed equilibrium. In fact, the main trend of German philosophy was to organize bondage into a system and make of servitude a virtue which was consecrated by the famous "inner freedom."

What does Kant mean when he reduces his famous moral law to the formula: "Act so that the maxims of thy will could at all times serve as principles for general legislation"? Is not this to reduce man's ethical feeling to the pitiful concept of the law of a government? Coming from a man who was firmly convinced that man was inherently evil, this is not surprising. Only a man with this conviction could make the assertion:

> Man is an animal which, when living among others of its kind, needs a master. For he surely abuses his freedom in the presence of his equals, and although as a reasonable being he desires a law, his beastly selfish nature leads him to exempt himself whenever he can. Hence he needs a master who will break his individual will and compel him to obey a generally accepted rule whereby everyone can be free.

This is in fact but another form of the ancient and terrible dogma of original sin with its unavoidable conclusion. It is just this which prejudices all freer spirits against Kant. Thus Goethe wrote to Herder: "After using a full generation for the cleansing of his philosophic mantle of various foul prejudices, Kant has only defiled it again with the stain of innate evil, in order that Christians, too, may be persuaded to kiss its hem."

Even Schiller, who was strongly influenced by Kant, could not reconcile himself to the kernel of his ethics. To the poet and idealist who believed firmly in the good in man, the stern duty-concept of Kant, who had really no understanding of the significance of social instincts, must, indeed, have seemed repellent. It was with this in mind he wrote Goethe that with Kant there always remained something which, "as with Luther, reminds one of a monk, who although he has left his cloister still cannot quite rid himself of its traces."

Kant has often been called a republican and a democrat. These terms are very vague and prove nothing, for more than once in history they have been made to serve as a cloak for the most brutal forces. This curious republican was a stern advocate of unlimited state power, to rebel against which was in his eyes a capital crime—even when the executive instruments of the state acted contrary to the law and allowed themselves to be led into the most tyrannical acts. Thus Kant expressly declares in his *Theory of the Law:*

> The origin of the supreme power is for the people who are subject to it, in a practical sense, undiscoverable; that is, the subject, in view of the obedience he owes to it, should not speculate concerning its origin, as if of a doubtful law (*jus controversum*). For since the people, in order to judge concerning the supreme state power (*summum imperium*), must be regarded as already united under a general law-giving will, it cannot and dare not judge otherwise than as the existing head of the state (*summum imperians*) desires. Whether originally a real agreement among them (*pactum subjectionis civilis*) preceded it as fact, or whether the power came first and the law afterwards, are for the people who are now already under the law quite immaterial speculations. They would, however, prove dangerous to the state; for should the subject who now has discovered the final origin of the dominant authority rebel against it, he could quite legally be punished, exterminated, or declared outlaw and expelled from the state. A law which is so sacred, so inviolable, that merely to question it practically and thus to suspend its operation even for a moment, constitutes a crime, is represented as emanating, not from man, but from a supreme, blameless lawgiver. This is the meaning of the sentence, "All authority comes from God," which states, not the historical foundation of civil constitutions, but an idea, as a practical principle of reason: the existing power is to be obeyed, be its origin what it may.

When one compares thoroughly the reactionary concept of Kant with the ideas of the liberal school of thought in England which goes back to Locke, one realizes the shamefully reactionary aspect of this view, so daringly put forth at a time when beyond the German frontier the old régime was falling to ruins. Kant had already in his essay, *What is Enlightenment?* published in 1784, supported the despotism of Frederick II and praised the obedience of the subjects as the first maxim of political morality. His doctrine of the law, however, he develops in his later works —a proof that in this regard his ideas never changed. The "democrat" Kant was even ready to advocate slavery and to justify it as useful under certain conditions. He maintained that slavery was applicable to men who in consequence of their crimes had forfeited their civil rights. Such a man can, in the opinion of our philosopher, "be made simply a tool of another [of the state or of another citizen]."

The conservative point of view concerning the state and the respect of the subject for it, was virtually in Kant's blood. When in 1794 he received a reprimand from the royal government on account of an alleged disparagement of the Bible and Christian doctrine, he did not content himself with giving Frederick William II a written promise to refrain in the future from all oral and written expression concerning the Christian religion. Under the miserable conditions then existing in Prussia such an act was not only explicable, but also justifiable. But among the documents he left there were found these characteristic lines which had reference to the promise given to the king: "Recantation and denial of one's inmost convictions is contemptible, but silence in a case like the present one is the duty of a subject."

Kant, whose quiet Philistine existence never diverged from the prescribed paths of state guardianship, was not of a social nature, and could only with difficulty surmount his inborn aversion for any form of communion. But since he could not deny the necessity of associations, he accepted them as one accepts any necessary evil. Consequently, society appeared to him as a forced union held together solely by duty towards the state. Kant really hated every voluntary union, just as every good deed done for its own sake was repugnant to him. He knew nothing else but the stark, implacable "Thou shalt!"

One with such tendencies was hardly the proper man to formulate the fundamentals of a great social ethics, which is inherently the product of social communal life, finding its expression in every individual, and continually vitalized anew and confirmed by the community. Just as little was Kant capable of revealing to mankind great theoretical social insight. Everything which he produced in this field had been surpassed by the great enlightenment in France and England long before it saw the light of day in Germany.

That Kant, on account of his essay *On Eternal Peace,* and an earlier dissertation, *A View of General History in the Light of World-citizenship,* has lately been acclaimed as the intellectual father of the so-called "League of Nations," was to be expected in a generation which has long forgotten Lessing, Herder and Jean Paul; and only proves that the alleged "representatives of the German spirit" have also in this respect learned nothing. What Kant in reality strove for was no union of peoples, but a league of states, which for this very reason could never have accomplished the task he had planned for it. The experiences we have lately had with the international convention at Geneva have opened the eyes of all who are willing to see.

This was quite clearly perceived by Herder when, following in Lessing's footsteps, he declared himself against Kant's proposals and showed that an understanding among the nations can only be achieved by organic—meaning cultural—means, and never by mechanical means, that is, by the activity of "political machines." Herder explains that the forced organization which constitutes the state maintains itself primarily by continually creating external interests which run contrary to the interests of other states; and for this reason it is ill-suited to function as a mediator and adjuster. Therefore, he substituted for the idea of the international league of states advocated by Kant, his "association of all thinking men on all continents," proceeding from the correct view that mutual agreement between the human groups of the different countries is not achievable by dictation from above, but only from below upwards by the will of the people themselves. By this "all the prejudices of state interests, of native religion, and most foolish prejudice of all, of rank and class, are mitigated, confined, and made harmless." But, "such victories over prejudice are"—Herder maintains—"achieved from within outward, not from without inward."

Of quite another character was Fichte, who possessed a revolutionary vein that Kant lacked entirely. In fact, of all the representatives of German philosophy of that day, he was the only one who took an active part in the social and political life of his time. But a revolutionary temperament is, after all, no substitute for a libertarian viewpoint. Cromwell, too, and Robespierre, Mazzini, Lenin, Mussolini, and with them all other advocates of dictatorship, of the right or of the left, were revolutionaries. But the true revolutionary reveals himself in the ends that he seeks, not merely in the means that he uses, which are nearly always dependent on circumstances.

It is true that Fichte in his theory of law developed the view that "the final purpose of government is to make government superfluous." But he soon added cautiously that perhaps "myriads of years" would have to pass before man would be ready for such a condition. In the meantime

all his acts were in sharp contrast to this stated distant aim. For Fichte
was of a domineering, thoroughly authoritarian, nature; a man with freedom
always on his lips, but just the name of freedom, nothing more. Like
Kant, Fichte believed in the "innate evil" of man. He later modified his
teaching in many respects, but to this concept he always remained faithful.
It became even stronger in his mind as he came more and more under the
influence of the new romanticism in Berlin, headed at that time by Schleiermacher and the brothers Schlegel. Thus he could still write in 1812 in
the treatise on Machiavelli by which he sought—though vainly—to induce
the king of Prussia to take a decisive step: "The fundamental principle
of every theory of the state which is intelligent is contained in the following words of Machiavelli. 'Whosoever founds a republic (or any other
state) and gives it laws must recognize that all men are wicked, and that
all without exception will express their innate wickedness as soon as a
safe opportunity offers itself.' " One who believes this has no trace of
liberal spirit. It is this fatal belief in "innate evil" springing from the
theological concept of "original sin" which has served tyranny at all
times as a moral justification.

Fichte has given his conception concerning the relationship of men
to the state the best expression in his essay, *The Self-Contained Commercial State,* which he later declared to be his "most thoughtful work."
This essay, dedicated to the Prussian minister, von Struensee, contains the
plan of a so-called "reasonable" state, in which the life of the citizens
was regulated and prescribed to the last detail, so that they everywhere
and always felt the directing hand of a political Providence above them.
It is a police state in the worst sense, in which there is hardly room for
any kind of personal freedom. Fichte's ideal state is made up of various
classes strictly separated from one another, whose numerical strength
is determined by the government. His work is prescribed for every citizen
according to his class, and in such a manner that he cannot change his
occupation by his own choice. Following the principle that "the earth
is the Lord's, and man has only the duty to cultivate and use it profitably,"
all land is the property of the state, and the individual citizen is only
given a lease on it. The state has not only the task of guarding the citizen's
property, it must also see to it that every citizen receives the share which
has been appropriated to him by law. Since the citizen's property is under
the constant guardianship of the state, assurance is given that none shall
become too rich and likewise that none shall perish in poverty.

Instead of the current gold and silver coins (which the state is to call
in) paper or leather money is to be used to facilitate exchange within
the country. This is the more feasible as the frontier is closed, and
citizens are strictly prohibited from having any intercourse with the outer
world; so that he can maintain social relationships only with his fellow

citizens, of whose nature the state, of course, has sole direction. Only the state has the right to effect the necessary exchanges with other countries.

One can realize why so fanatical a worshiper of the state as Lassalle was so enthusiastic about Fichte. One can also realize that the very concept of such a monstrous state machine of officials and police as Fichte envisioned makes the mouths of the adherents of the Third Reich water, and that they, lacking ideas of their own, wish to attribute their intellectual output chiefly to Fichte. Fichte's theory of the state contains all the necessary assumptions for a state-capitalistic economic order under the political direction of the government after the pattern of the old Prussian class state, which today men often attempt falsely to call "socialism." While the citizen is to have his material existence secured, it is only at the cost of every personal freedom and of all cultural associations with other peoples. Of Fichte, too, we may reaffirm the old truth that no kind of social oppression would be anywhere near so intolerable for man as the realization of the philosophical plan of government of our sage.

Fichte is today regarded in Germany as the true prophet of the most genuine Germanism. He is lauded as the living embodiment of patriotic thought, and his *Addresses to the German Nation* are today again in everyone's home. In the interest of historical truth it must here be stated that Fichte's conversion into a German patriot and guardian of national interests occurred rather suddenly. He was in this regard as changeable as in his earlier atheism and republicanism, which in later years he completely dropped. Even in his *Fundamental Outlines of the Present Age* he was by no means enthusiastic over the national idea; and to the question, "Which is the fatherland of a truly developed Christian European?" he found the answer, "In general it is Europe; more especially, it is in every age that European state standing at the peak of culture."

Thus wrote Fichte still in 1805. In December, 1807, he began in the hall of the Berlin Academy the *Addresses to the German Nation*, which are remarkable not only as a powerful oral statement of his philosophical views, but also as the first revelation of the German patriot in him. His inner change was, therefore, effected somewhat hastily, proving that "the deep feeling of the holy cause of the nation" was not inborn.[1]

Fichte's speeches were a brave deed, for they were uttered, so to speak, in the shadow of French bayonets, and the speaker exposed himself to

[1] In his great work, *Der Atheismus und seine Geschichte im Abendlande* (IV: 73), Fritz Mauthner gives a very interesting description of Fichte, in which he remarks: "When he [Fichte] was accused of atheism in March, 1799, he sent to the Weimar government a threatening letter stating that in case of a public reprimand he would leave Jena and with several like-minded professors seek another sphere of activity already assured him. And he was not merely boasting. In Mainz, Forster, with the other clubmen, were enthusiastic for the French Revolution, and the French govern-

the danger of being seized by Napoleon's henchmen. That the latter was not to be trifled with, the execution of the book-dealer, Palm, proved quite sufficiently. But others have shown the same, and even greater, courage; and frequently for an incomparably more worthy cause. For what is the content of these speeches but a glorification of the power of the nationalist state? Their kernel is the national education of youth— according to Fichte the first and most important preliminary measure for the liberation of the country from the yoke of the foreign ruler, and the creation of a new generation familiar with the sacred mission of the nation. Hence the education of youth must not be intrusted to the church, for the church's realm is not of this world but is comparable to a foreign state, and its rulers are only interested in man's salvation after death.

Fichte's outlook was more earthly; his God was of this world. Hence, he would not give youth up to the priest, but rather to the state, although the latter only transferred the church's work into the political field with the same end in view: man's enslavement under the yoke of a higher power. It is futile to object that Fichte's theory of education opens many wide vistas, especially where he follows in the footsteps of Pestalozzi; all that is beside the point when we observe his objective. Education is character development, harmonious completion of human personality. But what the state accomplishes in this field is dull drill, extinction of natural feeling, narrowing of the spiritual field of vision, destruction of all the deeper elements of character in man. The state can train subjects, or as Fichte called them, citizens, but it can never develop free men who take their affairs into their own hands; for independent thought is the greatest danger that it has to fear.

Fichte raised national education to a systematic cult. He wished even to remove children from the home so that their national development would be exposed to no counter currents. Although convinced that such

ment was about to resuscitate the old university.· Fichte was to collaborate in a prominent position—perhaps the instigation came from General Bonaparte."

Of Fichte's attitude at the time his letter of May 22, 1799, to Professor Reinhold is also significant. One reads, "To sum up: Nothing is surer than that unless the French achieve an enormous supremacy, and effect in Germany, or at least in a large part of it, a change of conditions, in a few years, no man of whom it is known that ever in his life he entertained a liberal thought will find an abiding place there."

With what clear vision Fichte saw at the time events following the so-called "wars of liberation" showed clearly enough; the Holy Alliance, the Carlsbad Resolutions, the persecution of the demagogues—in short, the Metternich system—open reaction on the march, and along the whole line the brutal persecution of all who once had aroused the people in the fight against Napoleon. If a fatal disease had not removed Fichte in good time the powers that were would surely not have been satisfied to prohibit his *Addresses to the German Nation*, as was actually done. He would surely not have been treated more gently then were Arndt, Jahn, and so many others whose patriotic activity prepared and released the "wars of liberation."

a course would meet with great difficulties, he consoled himself with the thought that when once statesmen were found who were "themselves deeply convinced of the infallibility and the absolute truth of the propositions," then, "of such it was also to be expected that they would realize the state as the highest administrator of all human affairs, and, as the guardians of minors, responsible only to God and their conscience, they would have the full right to constrain their charges for their own good. For where does there now exist a state which doubts that it has the right to force its subjects into war service and to deprive parents of their children in order to make soldiers of them, whether one or the other or both of them desire it or not?"

This looks very like the man who in his theory of law developed the thought that "outside of the state there is no law," and coined these words: "Right is freedom according to a law." Of course, with Fichte, everything happens for the good of mankind. May Fate preserve us from such a good. Which involuntarily recalls to us the words of the Pestalozzi student, Hunziker, who speaks of "the state-instituted drill for the people's happiness."

The remaining ideas expressed by Fichte in his *Addresses to the German Nation* contain no trace of true liberal spirit, though much is said about freedom. Freedom, however, only according to Fichte's meaning, and that was of a most peculiar sort. But one thing those addresses have effected and effect still today: they have in a large measure contributed to the inculcation in Germany of that attitude of superiority which redounds so little to the credit of the German name. We are speaking here of the superstitious belief in "the historical mission of the Germans" which is again today flourishing like a weed in good soil. Since Luther, this curious illusion haunts all German history; but especially is it marked with Fichte and Hegel.[2] It even found its way into the literature of German socialism and was lovingly nursed by Lassalle. Houston Stewart Chamberlain and his countless successors, whose madness has defiled German spiritual life, before the World War were the heralds of "the German mission," determined to make the well-known words of Emmanuel Geibel come true:

[2] Herder refers to this craze, which has at length grown into a mental defect, when he makes the eccentric Realis of Vienna say:

"Germany's advantage consists of these four parts: that in the long night of deep ignorance she produced the first, the most, and the highest inventors, and in nine hundred years developed more thought than all the other four dominant peoples taken together, in four thousand. One can, therefore, say truthfully that God desired to make the world wise through two nations: before Christ through the Greeks, after Christ through the Germans. The Greek wisdom can be called the Old Testament of reason; the German, the New." (Herder, *Briefe zur Beförderung der Humanität* 4te Sammlung, 1794.)

By virtue of the German race
The world may yet attain to grace.

Fichte was, so to speak, the ancestor of the Chamberlains, Woltmanns, Hausers, Rosenbergs, Günthers, and countless others, who today construct the race theories and proclaim the "kismet of blood"! One cannot, however, put him into the same class with them; for he was, after all, a man of mental stature, which cannot be said of his dull successors.

Fichte in his *Addresses to the German Nation* supported the belief in "the world historical mission of the Germans" with particular passion, after the manner of an Old Testament prophet. It was especially the form and the linguistic rhythm of his speeches which had so great an influence on German youth. He has designated the German nation as destined by fate to be the "mother and reconstructor" of humanity. "Among all the newer nations it is you in whom the germ of human perfection is most definitely contained and to whom progress in the development thereof is intrusted." But this belief was not enough for him. He condemned and excommunicated everything which did not fit into his concept of what constitutes "Germanism"—which was only natural in such an obstinately authoritarian character. At the same time he did not fail to proclaim his own theory as the special, indeed, as *the* philosophy of the Germans and to reject the ideas of his great antagonists, Kant and Hegel, as "un-German"—a method which has always proved effective in Germany as its recent history has again clearly shown. . . . It is always the same story: man creates his god after his own image. Fichte was not mistaken when he said, "What kind of philosophy one chooses depends upon what kind of man one is." But when he made the attempt to impose his purely personal evaluations upon the whole nation, he arrived at the monstrous sophism whose tragic effect has not even today been overcome.

Among the representatives of classical philosophy in Germany, Hegel has affected his contemporaries most deeply. During his last years he was enthroned like an absolute monarch in the realm of the mind; hardly anyone dared to oppose him. Men who had already achieved a name in the most varied fields and those for whom a leading role was reserved in the future, sat at his feet and harkened to his words as if they came from an oracle. His thought influenced not only the best minds in Germany; it also found a decided echo in Russia, France, Belgium, Denmark and Italy. It is not easy today rightly to understand that mighty diffusion of ideas. Still stranger does it seem that Hegel's influence could extend to men of all political and social tendencies. Bred-in-the-bone reactionaries, and revolutionists heavy with the unborn future, conservatives and liberals, absolutists and democrats, monarchists and republicans, opponents and defenders of property—they all hung as if enchanted on the breasts of his wisdom.

For the most part this astonishing influence is not traceable to the content of the Hegelian doctrine; it was the peculiar dialectic form of his thought that captivated them. Hegel opposed the static concepts of his predecessors with the idea of an eternal becoming; so that he was less concerned to comprehend things in themselves than to trace their relationship to other phenomena. He interpreted in his own manner the Heraclitan thesis of the eternal flux of things, assuming an inner connection of phenomena such that each carries within itself its own opposite, which must of inner necessity operate to make room for a new phenomenon in its kind more perfect than the two forms of the becoming. Hegel called these thesis, antithesis and synthesis. But since, with him, each synthesis becomes at once the thesis of a new series, there is created an unbroken chain of which the individual links are firmly interlocked after an eternal divine plan.

Because of this concept, Hegel has been praised as the great herald of the evolutionary theory, but without justification; for his purely speculative concept has little in common with real evolutionary thought. The great founders of the evolution theory combined with these views the idea that organic forms exist not as separate units each for itself, but have rather descended one from another in such manner that the higher forms have developed from the lower. This process constitutes, so to speak, the whole content of the history of the organic world and leads to the appearance and development of the various species on earth, whose slow or rapid alteration is caused by changes in the environment and the external conditions of life. But to no serious researcher has it ever occurred to represent the process according to Hegel's view as an eternal repetition of the same tripartite scheme with the first form always by implacable necessity changing into its opposite in order that the general process of becoming may take its natural course. This speculative thought which knew how to work only with thesis and antithesis not only has no connection whatsoever with the actual phenomena of life; it stands in most violent contradiction to the real evolutionary idea based on the concept of organic becoming, which necessarily excludes any possibility that any species may change into its opposite. It must be rejected as the idle speculation of an errant imagination.

It was Hegel, too, who introduced that thinking in categories which has caused and is still causing such enormous confusion in men's minds. By endowing whole peoples with definite qualities and traits of character, a thing which at best can be affirmed only of the individual, and which, generalized, leads only to the most nonsensical conclusions, he conjured up an evil spirit which cripples thought and diverts it from its natural course, smoothing the way for our modern race theoreticians and the collective evaluations of an arrogant "national psychology." Whatever else Hegel wrote is now long forgotten, but his method of collective concept formation still haunts the minds of men and leads them only too frequently into the most daring assertions and the most monstrous conclusions, whose scope most of them hardly suspect.[3]

Hegel endowed every people which has played a historical part in the course of events with a special spirit whose task it was to execute God's plan. But every folk spirit is itself only "an individual in the course of world history," whose higher purpose it has to fulfill. For man, however, there remains little room in the spiritual world. He exists only in so far as he serves as a means of expression for some collective spirit. His role is therefore clearly prescribed for him: "The relation of the individual to it [the national spirit] is that he shall appropriate this substantial being, that it shall become his mind and art, in order that he may become something worth while. For he finds in the nation's existence a world already finished and firm into which he has to incorporate himself. In this, its work, the spirit of the people finds its world and is content."[4]

Since Hegel was of the opinion that in every nation which the "world spirit" has created as a tool for the execution of his mysterious plans there dwells a separate spirit which merely prepares it for its intended task, it follows that every nation is intrusted with a special "historic mission" whereby every form of its historic activity is determined in advance. This mission is its fate, its destiny, reserved for it alone and for no other people, and it cannot change its mission by its own powers.

Fichte tried to explain the "historic mission of the Germans" which he preached by their special type of history. In doing so he ventured the most extreme assertions, which time has long discredited. But at least he tried to justify this alleged mission on reasonable grounds. According to Hegel, however, the mission of a people is not a result of its history;

[3] In his excellent little work, *Rasse und Politik*, Julius Goldstein cleverly remarks: "The empty scheme of his [Hegel's] thought continues among the men, strange to say mostly foreigners, who think to have found in race the key to the understanding of the historical world. Gobineau, Lapouge, Chamberlain, Woltmann, stand under the dominance of a Hegelianism with naturalistic features. It is Hegelianism when, instead of the individualist spirit, the race spirit is called upon for an explanation of spiritual creation. It is Hegelianism when all contingency is banished from history and the destiny of nations is constructed from preconceived ideas as to what a race may or may not accomplish. It is Hegelianism when Germanism and Semitism are opposed to each other with logical exclusiveness and all profounder relationships of life between them are denied by a hard rationalistic formula. It is, finally, Hegelianism when the past and present course of history is explained from the one exclusive deciding factor of race without regard to the great variety of the forces operative in the various epochs."

[4] Hegel, *Lectures on the Philosophy of History*.

the mission which is intrusted to it by the world spirit constitutes, rather, the content of its history; and all this happens that the spirit may at last attain "to the consciousness of itself."

So Hegel became the modern creator of that blind theory of destiny whose supporters see in every historic event a "historical necessity," see in every end men have conceived a historical mission." Hegel is still alive in the sense that even today we speak quite seriously of the historic mission of a race, of a nation, of a class. Most of us do not even suspect that this fatalistic concept so crippling to man's activity had its root in Hegel's method of thought.

And yet there is expressed here only a blind belief which has no relationship whatsoever to the realities of life and whose implications are quite without proof. All this talk about the "compulsory course of historical events" and "the historically conditioned necessities" of social life—empty formulas repeated *ad nauseam* by the advocates of Marxism —what is it but a new belief in Fate sprung from Hegel's spectral world, except that in this case "conditions of production" has assumed the role of the "absolute spirit"? And yet every hour of life proves that these "historical necessities" have persistence only as long as men are willing to accept them without opposition. In fact there are in history no compulsory causes, but only conditions which men endure and which disappear as soon as men learn to perceive their causes and rebel against them.

Hegel's famous dictum, "What is reasonable is real, and what is real is reasonable"—words which no dialectic cleverness can rob of their real meaning—have become the *leitmotif* of all reaction, just because they raise acceptance of given conditions to a principle and try to justify every villainy, every inhuman condition, by the unalterability of the "historically necessary." The leaders of German socialism are merely imitating the sophistry of Hegel where they undertake, as they have thus far done, to discover in every social evil a consequence of the capitalistic economic order which, willy-nilly, one must endure until the time is ripe for its change or—according to Hegel—until thesis changes to antithesis. On what else does this notion rest but Hegelian fatalism translated into economic terms? We accept conditions and do not know that we are killing the spirit that resists existing wrongs.

Kant had set up unqualified submission of the subject to the power of the state as a principle of social morality. Fichte derived all right from the state and wanted to inculcate the view in all youth so that the Germans might at last become "Germans in the true sense of the word, namely, citizens of the state." But Hegel worshiped the state as an end in itself, as "the reality of the moral idea," as "God on earth." No one made such a cult out of the state, no one planted the idea of voluntary servitude so deeply in the minds of men, as he. He raised the state idea to a religious principle and put on a par with the revelations of the New Testament those ideas of right formulated by the state. "For it is now known that what is declared moral and right by the state is also divine and commanded by God, and that judged by its content there is nothing higher or holier."

Hegel more than once insisted that he owed his conception of the state to the ancients, more especially to Plato. What he really looked back to was the old Prussian state, that mis-birth which sought to compensate for lack of intelligence by barrack drill and bureaucratic stupidity. Rudolf Haym was quite right when he remarked with biting sarcasm that from Hegel "the lovely image of the ancient state received a coat of black and white paint." In fact, Hegel was merely the state philosopher of the Prussian government and never failed to justify its worst misdeeds. The introduction to his *Philosophy of Law* is a grim defense of the miserable Prussian conditions, an excommunicating curse against all who dared to shake the traditional. With a severity that amounted to a public denunciation he turned against Professor J. F. Fries (very popular among youth on account of his liberal ideas), because in his essay, *The German League and the German State Constitution,* he had dared to maintain that in a good community "life comes from below"—as Hegel scornfully put it, from the "so-called 'people.'" Such a concept was, of course, high treason in his eye, high treason against the "idea of the State," which alone endows people with life and for that reason is above all criticism. Since the state embodies in itself the "ethical whole" it is the "ethical itself." When Haym called this invective of Hegel "a scientific justification of the Carlsbad police system and the persecution of the demagogues" he said not a word too much.[5]

The Prussian state had an especial attraction for Hegel because he believed that he found exemplified in it all the necessary assumptions for the character of the state in general. Like de Maistre and Bonald, the great prophets of reaction in France, Hegel could recognize that all authority has its roots in religion. Hence, it was the great aim of his life to merge the state with religion most intimately into a great unit whose separate parts were organically intergrown with one another. Catholicism seemed to him little suited for this purpose—significantly, for the reason that it left too much scope for man's conscience.

In his *Philosophy of History* he says: "In the Catholic Church, however, the conscience can very well be opposed to the laws of the state. The murder of kings, conspiracies against the state, and the like have often been instigated and executed by the priests."

This is the Simon-pure Hegel, and one can understand why his

[5] Rudolf Haym, *Hegel und seine Zeit.* Berlin, 1857.

biographer, Rosenkranz, insists that it was his ambition to become the Machiavelli of Germany. It is certainly dangerous for a state when its citizens have a conscience; what it needs is men without conscience, or, better still, men whose conscience is quite in conformity with reasons of state, men in whom the feeling of personal responsibility has been replaced by the automatic impulse to act in the interest of the state.

According to Hegel, only Protestantism was fitted to this task, because the Protestant church has "accomplished the reconciliation of religion with law. There is no sacred, no religious conscience separate from secular law—or even antagonistic to it." Upon this road the goal was clear: from the reconciliation of religion with secular law to the deification of the state. And Hegel took this step with full consciousness of its logical correctness: "It is the way of God with the world that the state shall exist. Its foundation is the power of reason manifesting itself as will. In the idea of the state one must not have special states in mind, not special institutions, but rather the Idea, this actual God, considered in itself."

For all that, this high priest of authority at any price was able in the last section of his *Philosophy of History* to write these words: "For history is nothing but the evolution of the concept of freedom." It was, however, only the Hegelian freedom of which he spoke, and it looked exactly like the famous reconciliation of religion with law. For the peace of weak souls he soon after added these words. "Objective freedom, however, that is, the laws of real freedom, demand the subjugation of the casual will, for this is in general formal. In any event, if the objective is reasonable in itself, then the perception of this reason must correspond, and then the essential element of subjective freedom is also present."

The meaning of this passage is sufficiently obscure, as is everything that Hegel wrote, but it describes in reality nothing but the abrogation of the individual will in the name of freedom. The freedom that Hegel meant was, anyhow, only a police concept. One is involuntarily reminded of the words of Robespierre: "A revolutionary government is a despotism of freedom over tyranny." The lawyer of Arras, who went to bed with "Reason" and got up with "Virtue," would have made an excellent disciple for Hegel.

One is frequently reminded of the social-critical character of the neo-Hegelians ("Young Hegelians") in order to prove that such a trend of thought could only proceed from a revolutionary source. But with much more reason one could point to the fact that a whole legion of the most hard-boiled, bred-in-the-bone reactionaries have emanated from Hegel's school. Nor must we forget that it was just this neo-Hegelianism that carried a whole body of reactionary notions over into the opposite camp, where in part even today they still flourish.

Hegel's play with empty words, whose lack of content he knew how to hide by a symbology as pretentious as it was incomprehensible, has for decades artificially inhibited in Germany the inner urge for real knowledge. It has seduced many an able mind into pursuing the shadow forms of idle speculation instead of approaching life's realities and devoting heart and mind to a new organization of the conditions of social life.

> A man who speculates, I say to thee,
> Quite like a beast on barren heaths appears to me
> By wicked sprite in circles led around
> While all about is beautiful rich ground.

Goethe might well have been thinking of the Prussian state philosopher when he wrote these sprightly lines, for as a matter of fact Hegel was all his life led in circles by the spirits he had himself conjured up. Thousands followed him as the bearer of the torch of truth, never suspecting that it was but a will-o'-the-wisp that flickered over swamps and lured them ever deeper into the misty realm of a barren metaphysic.

Hegelianism in the form of Marxism acted on the great movement of socialism like mildew on a germinating seed. It scorned the hot, living words of Saint-Simon, "Remember, my son, one must be enthusiastic in order to accomplish great things"; and taught men to curb their longings and to listen to the regulated ticking of the clock which expresses that silent reign of unchangeable law, according to which all coming and going in history proceeds. Fatalism is the grave-digger of every burning desire, of every ideal yearning, of all overflowing power seeking expression and striving to transmute itself into creative activity. For it kills that inner faith and confidence in the justice of a cause which is at the same time faith in one's own power. Friedrich Engels boasts: "We German socialists are proud that we descend not only from Saint-Simon, Fourier, and Owen, but also from Kant, Fichte, and Hegel." It was largely this descent which gave socialism in Germany such a hopelessly authoritarian character. It surely would have profited German socialism more if it had taken its inspiration from Lessing, Herder and Jean Paul, instead of going to school to Kant, Fichte and Hegel.

To be a revolutionary means to compel social changes by the assertion of one's own power. It is fatalism to accept conditions because one believes one cannot change them. Only a fatalist in the worst sense could have said: "What is reasonable, that is real; and what is real, that is reasonable." Acceptance of the world as it is, is the intellectual preliminary to all reaction. *For reaction is nothing else but standing still on principle.* Hegel was a reactionary from head to heels. All libertarian feeling was foreign to him; it did not fit into the narrow frame of his fatalistic concepts. He was the stern, implacable advocate of a spiritless authoritarian principle, worse even than Bonald and de Maistre; for these only saw in the person of the monarch the living incarnation of all power, while Hegel made of a political machine, that crushes man with its merciless levers and gears and nourishes itself on his sweat and blood, a vessel of all morality, a "God on earth." This is his work in the light of history.

Chapter 12

THE RELATION BETWEEN SOCIETY AND STATE. FOLK AND STATE. THE STATE AS A POLITICAL CHURCH ORGANIZATION. NATIONAL CITIZEN-SHIP A POLITICAL CONFESSION OF FAITH. DEMOCRACY AS PIONEER OF MODERN NATIONAL CONSCIOUSNESS. LASSALLE ON DEMOCRACY AND THE NATION. NATION AND NATIONALISM. ECHOES OF THE FRENCH REVOLUTION IN GERMANY. SOCIAL CONDITIONS. FOREIGN RULE. PRUSSIA'S COLLAPSE. THE RISE OF THE NATIONALIST MOVEMENT. ARNDT AND FICHTE. SCHARNHORST AND GNEISENAU. THE ENDEAVORS OF THE BARON VON STEIN. CABALS OF PRUSSIAN JUNKERDOM. PRINCELY PROM-ISES. THE GERMAN DREAM OF FREEDOM AND THE GERMAN PRINCES. BETRAYED AND SOLD. GOETHE'S JUDGMENT CONCERNING THE SO-CALLED "WARS OF LIBERATION."

WE have seen under what circumstances the national state put in its appearance and gradually took on the democratic aspect which gave birth to the modern concept of the nation. Only when we view with open eyes the manifold ramifications of this most important social change in Europe will we get a clear idea concerning the real character of the nation. The old opinion which ascribes the creation of the nationalist state to the awakened national consciousness of the people is but a fairy tale, very serviceable to the supporters of the idea of the national state, but false, none the less. *The nation is not the cause, but the result, of the state. It is the state which creates the nation, not the nation the state.* Indeed, from this point of view there exists between people and nation the same distinction as between society and the state.

Every social unit is a natural formation which, on the basis of common needs and mutual agreement, is built organically from below upwards to guarantee and protect the general interest. Even when social institutions gradually ossify or become rudimentary the purpose of their origin can in most instances be clearly recognized. Every state organization, however, is an artificial mechanism imposed on men from above by some ruler, and it never pursues any other ends but to defend and make secure the interests of privileged minorities in society.

A people is the natural result of social union, a mutual association of men brought about by a certain similarity of external conditions of living, a common language, and special characteristics due to climate and geographic environment. In this manner arise certain common traits, alive in every member of the union, and forming a most important part of its social existence. This inner relationship can as little be artificially bred as artificially destroyed. The nation, on the other hand, is the artificial result of the struggle for political power, just as nationalism has never been anything but the political religion of the modern state. Belonging to a nation is never determined, as is belonging to a people, by profound natural causes; it is always subject to political considerations and based on those reasons of state behind which the interests of privileged minorities always hide. A small group of diplomats who are simply the business representatives of privileged caste and class decide quite arbitrarily the national membership of certain groups of men, who are not even asked for their consent, but must submit to this exercise of power because they cannot help themselves.

Peoples and groups of peoples existed long before the state put in its appearance. Today, also, they exist and develop without the assistance of the state. They are only hindered in their natural development when some external power interferes by violence with their life and forces it into patterns which it has not known before. The nation is, then, unthinkable without the state. It is welded to that for weal or woe and owes its being solely to its presence. Consequently, the essential nature of the nation will always escape us if we attempt to separate it from the state and endow it with a life of its own which it has never possessed.

A people is always a community with rather narrow boundaries. But a nation, as a rule, encompasses a whole array of different peoples and groups of peoples who have by more or less violent means been pressed into the frame of a common state. In fact, in all of Europe there is no state which does not consist of a group of different peoples who were originally of different descent and speech and were forged together into one nation solely by dynastic, economic and political interests.

Even where, influenced by the growth of democratic ideas, the effort toward national unity took the form of a great popular movement, as happened in Italy and Germany, the effort really started from a reactionary germ which could lead to no good outcome. The revolutionary efforts of Mazzini and his adherents for the establishment of a unified nationalistic state could but serve as hindrance to the social liberation of the people, whose real goal was hidden by the national ideology. Between the man Mazzini and the present dictator of Italy yawns a mighty abyss; but the development of the nationalistic system of thought from Mazzini's political theology to the fascist totalitarian state of Mussolini proceeds in a straight line.

A glance at the fresh-baked national states which appeared as a result of the World War gives us a factual picture which cannot be easily misunderstood. The same nationalities which before the War never ceased to revolt against the foreign oppressor reveal themselves today, when they have reached their goal, as the worst oppressors of national minorities, and inflict upon them the same brutal moral and legal oppressions which they themselves, and with full right, fought most bitterly when they were the subjected peoples. This ought to make plain to even the blindest that a harmonious living together of peoples within the framework of the national state is definitely impossible. But those peoples who in the name of liberation have shaken off the yoke of a hated foreign rule have gained nothing thereby. In most cases they have taken on a new yoke, which is frequently more oppressive than the old. Poland, Hungary, Jugoslavia, and the border states between Germany and Russia are the classic examples of this.

The change of human groups into nations, that is, into state peoples, has opened no new outlook for Europe; it has rather thrown up a strong bulwark of international reaction and is today one of the most dangerous hindrances to social liberation. European society was divided by this process into antagonistic groups which confront one another always with suspicion, and often with hate; and nationalism in every country watches with argus eyes to keep this morbid condition permanent. Wherever a mutual approach of peoples begins, there the adherents of nationalism always add new fuel to the flames of national antagonism. For the nationalist state lives by these antagonisms and would have to disappear the moment it was no longer able to maintain this artificial separation.

The concept of the national state rests, therefore, on a purely negative principle, behind which, however, very positive aims are hidden. For behind everything "national" stands the will to power of small minorities and the special interest of caste and class in the state. It is *they* who in reality direct the "will of the nation," for, as Menger rightly remarks, "The states as such have no purpose; only the rulers have." But that the will of the *few* may become the will of *all*—for only thus can it develop its full effectiveness—every form of intellectual and moral drill must be employed to anchor it in the religious consciousness of the masses and make it a matter of faith. Now, the true strength of a faith lies, in the fact that its priests draw sharply the lines which separate the orthodox from the adherents of any other religious communion. Without Satan's wickedness, it would go ill with God's greatness. *National states are political church organizations; the so-called national consciousness is not born in man, but trained into him. It is a religious concept; one is a German, a Frenchman, an Italian, just as one is a Catholic, a Protestant, or a Jew.*

With the spread of democratic ideas in Europe begins the rise of nationalism in the various countries. Only with the creation of the new state, which, at least in theory, secures for every citizen the constitutional right to participate in the political life of his country and to have a part in the choice of its government, could the national consciousness take root in the masses, and the conviction be bred in the individual that he was a member of the great political union of the nation, with which he was inseparably intergrown and which gave to his separate existence its content and purpose. In the pre-democratic period such a belief could take root only in the narrow circle of the privileged classes, remaining entirely alien to the great mass of the population. Quite rightly Lassalle remarks:

> The principle of free independent nationalities is the basis, the source, the mother and the root of the concept of democracy in general. Democracy cannot tread the principle of nationalities under foot without raising a suicidal hand against its own existence, without depriving itself of the support of every theoretical justification, without basically and on principle betraying itself. We repeat, the principle of democracy has its foundation and life source in the principle of free nationalities. Without this it stands on air.[1]

In this respect, too, democracy differs essentially from liberalism, whose field of view embraces mankind as a whole, or at least that part of mankind belonging to the European-American circle of culture or to one which has developed under similar social conditions. Since the point of view of liberalism starts with the individual and judges the social environment according as its institutions are useful or harmful to men, national limitations play but an unimportant part for its adherents, and they can exclaim with Thomas Paine: "The world is my country, all men are my brothers!" Democracy, however, being founded on the collective concept of the common will was more closely related to the concept of the state and made it the representative of the common will.

Democracy not only endowed the "national spirit" with new life; it also defined the concept of the national state more sharply than would ever have been possible under the reign of absolutism. Although the apostles of the latter, as French history clearly shows, constantly strove to unite the national forces ever more strongly and to put the whole administration of the country under a centralized direction, in doing this they always had the interest of the dynasty in view, even where they found it more advisable to veil their true intentions.

With the beginning of the democratic period all dynastic assumptions disappear, and the nation as such becomes the focal point of political events. Thus the state itself achieves a new expression. It now becomes

---

[1] Ferdinand Lassalle, *Der Italienische Krieg und die Aufgabe Preussens.*

in reality the national state by including all its inhabitants as equally privileged members of a whole and welding them together.

Filled with the principles of an abstract political equality, the representatives of democratic nationalism made a distinction between the nation and nationality. The nation they considered to be a political group which, united by community of language and culture, had collected itself into an independent state entity. As *nationalities*, on the other hand, they counted such groups of people as were subject to a foreign state and were trying to achieve their political and national independence. Democratic nationalism saw in the struggles of the suppressed nationalities which were trying to form themselves into nations the assertion of an inviolable right; and it acted in this spirit. If the individual citizen of a nation wished to enjoy in his own country all rights and liberties without hindrance, as guaranteed to him by the constitution, even so the nation as a whole should in its individual life be subject to no foreign power and be equal to all other nations in its political independence.

There is no doubt that these efforts were based on a sound principle, the theoretical equal right of every nation and nationality without regard to its political or social importance. But right here it was soon apparent that from the very beginning such equal rights could not be harmonized with the efforts of the state for political power. The more the rulers of the individual European states came to realize that their countries could not be closed against the entrance of democratic ideas, the more clearly they saw that the principle of nationality would serve most excellently as a cover under which to advance their own interests. Napoleon I, who because of his ancestry was less plagued by false prejudices than many representatives of legitimate royalty, understood quite thoroughly how to further his own secret plans with the aid of nationalist principles. Thus, in May, 1809, he sent from Schönbrunn his well-known message to the Hungarians in which he appealed to them to throw off the yoke of the Austrians. "I ask nothing of you," says the imperial message. "I only wish to see you a free and independent nation."

We know what this unselfish expression meant. Napoleon was just as indifferent to the independence of the Hungarians as, in his heart of hearts, he was to that of the French who in spite of his foreign descent had made him their national hero. What he really had at heart was his plans for political power. To realize these he played with Italians, Illyrians, Poles and Hungarians the same comedy he had played for fourteen years with the *grande nation*. How clearly Napoleon recognized the importance of the principle of nationality for his own political purposes is shown by a remark recorded by one of his companions on St. Helena: He could not marvel enough why, among the German princes, not a single one had been found with courage enough to use the idea of the national unity of

Germany, widely spread among the people, as a pretext for uniting the Germans under a definite dynasty.

Since then, the principle of nationality has assumed an important place in European politics. Thus, after the Napoleonic wars, England on principle supported the rights of the oppressed peoples on the continent only for the reason that she thereby created difficulties for continental diplomacy —which could but react to England's political and economic advancement. But of course the English diplomatists never for a moment thought of giving the Irish the same rights. Lord Palmerston directed his whole foreign policy by this method, but it never entered the mind of the cunning English statesman to help the suppressed nationalities when they most needed his assistance. On the contrary, he looked on with a most peaceful soul while their attempts at liberation perished under the claws of the Holy Alliance.

Napoleon III pursued the same cunning policy, pretending to be the defender of suppressed nationalities while having in view only the interests of his own dynasty. His part in the movement for Italian liberation, which resulted in the inclusion of Nice and Savoy in France, is convincing proof of this.

King Carl Albert of Sardinia likewise supported the movement for national liberation in Italy with all means in his power, as with clever prevision he had recognized what advantages would accrue to his dynasty. Mazzini and Garibaldi, the most radical supporters of revolutionary nationalism, had later to stand by and observe how the successor of the Sardinian garnered the fruits of their lifelong activities for himself as king of united Italy—which they had envisioned as a democratic republic.

That the national feeling took root so rapidly in France during the revolution and achieved such a mighty growth is principally traceable to the fact that the revolution had opened an enormous chasm between the French and old Europe, which the continued wars widened still more. For all that, the best and most valuable minds in all countries greeted the "declaration of human rights" with unmixed enthusiasm, firmly believing that now the era of liberty and equality had begun in Europe. Even many men who later risked everything to enflame in Germany the revolt against the foreign rule of Napoleon, greeted the revolution with inner joy. Fichte, Görres, Hardenberg, Schleiermacher, Benzenberg, and many others stood at first wholly under the spell of the revolutionary ideas emanating from France. It was the bitter disappointment of this craving for liberty which moved men like Jean Paul, Beethoven, and many others who formerly had been among the most glowing admirers of General Bonaparte—seeing in him the instrument of a coming social reconstruction in Europe—to turn from him after he had made himself emperor and began to show more and more clearly the intentions of the conqueror.

One can readily understand the unlimited enthusiasm of many of the best minds in Germany for the French when one views the hopeless political conditions which were a tragic reality in Germany on the eve of the revolution. The German empire was now only a group of countries rotting in their own filth, their ruling caste no longer capable of an inner creative impulse, and for that reason clinging the more closely to the old institutions. The frightful misfortune of the Thirty Years' War, whose hardly-healed wounds had been freshly opened by Frederick II's conquests, had marked the people of the unfortunate countries with its unmistakable stamp. "A generation filled with nameless woes," says Treitschke in his *German History*, "had broken the courage of the citizens and had habituated the little man to crawl before the mighty. Our free-spirited language learned the trick of abject submission, and came to contain that over-rich treasury of distorted, slavish forms of speech which even today it has not completely shaken off."

Two-thirds of the population at the beginning of the revolution was in a state of serfdom under unspeakably miserable conditions. The country groaned under the hard yoke of countless little despots whose heartless egoism did not shrink from peddling their own subjects as cannon fodder to foreign powers in order to fill their ever empty coffers with the blood money paid them for the lives of these miserable beings. All thoughtful historians are agreed that no liberation could come to this unhappy country from within. Even so grim a hater of the French as Ernst Morris Arndt could not dispute this conclusion.

So the French invasion had at first the effect of a cleansing thunder storm. The French armies brought the revolutionary spirit into the land and aroused in the hearts of its inhabitants a feeling of human dignity they had not known before. The spreading of revolutionary ideas beyond their frontiers was one of the most dreaded weapons of the French republic in its successful struggle against European absolutism; for it was most of all intent on separating the cause of the people from that of the princes. Napoleon never for a moment thought of giving up this invaluable weapon. So wherever his victorious flag floated over a nation he introduced far-reaching reforms in order to attach the inhabitants of the occupied territory to himself.

The peace of Lunéville in 1801 had forced the German emperor to recognize the Rhine as the frontier between France and Germany. According to the treaties the temporal rulers of the left shore of the Rhine were to be compensated by territories in the interior of the empire. So now began the shameful barter of the German princes with the "hereditary enemy" for every scrap of land which the one hoped to grab at the expense of the others, and all of them together at the expense of the people. The "noblest of the nation" fawned like whipped curs before Napoleon and his ministers for favorable consideration in the proposed partition. A comparable example of degradation of character, history has hardly shown. Quite rightly Freiherr von Stein told the Russian empress before the assembled court that Germany's ruin had been caused by the baseness of its princes. Stein surely was no revolutionary. He was an upright man who had the courage to proclaim a truth that was known to all. The German patriot, Ernst Morris Arndt, moreover, wrote with bitter contempt:

> Those who could help returned; the others were crushed. Thus stood the union of the mighty with the enemies, and no open shame marked the dishonored ones; they even dared to proclaim themselves as liberators; even those who carried on dishonorable trade in their own and others' honor. They bargained about the peace; there was much said about the German princes, never anything about the German people. Never had the princes stood so far from the nation as a separate party—indeed even opposed to it— and they did not blush before the gaze of a strong, virtuous, great people whom they treated as vanquished in order to participate in the loot. . . . Injustice is born from injustice, force from force, shame from shame, and, like the Mongolian empire, Europe will sink into ruins. . . . Thus you stood, and thus you stand, like traders, not like princes; like Jews with the money-bags, not like judges with the scales nor like marshals with the sword.[2]

After the battle of Austerlitz (1805) and the foundation of the Rhenish League there was nothing left to the Emperor Francis but to proclaim the dissolution of the German Empire: as a matter of fact it had not existed for a long time. Sixteen German princes had put themselves under Napoleon's protectorate and had reaped a rich harvest for this master example of patriotic attitude. But when patriotic historians make it appear as if, after this open treason to the nation, the Prussian monarchy was now the last bulwark of the German people against the foreign rule of the French, it is a deliberate falsification of historic facts. Prussia was internally just as diseased and morally rotten as the other parts of the empire. The debacle of 1806, the frightful defeat of the Prussian armies at Jena and Auerstädt, the shameful surrender of the fortresses to the French without even an attempt at any real resistance by the noble defenders, the flight of the king to the Russian frontier, the wretched machinations of the Prussian junkers (who in the midst of this gruesome catastrophe thought of nothing but to preserve their miserable prerogatives)—sufficiently characterize the then prevailing conditions in Prussia.

[2] E. M. Arndt, Geist der Zeit: Erster Teil, Kapitel VII.

The whole woeful history of the relations between the "exalted allies,"
Russia, Austria and Prussia, of whom each in turn, behind the others'
backs, worked for or against Napoleon, is a very witches' sabbath of
cowardly baseness and contemptible treason, of which the like in scope can
hardly be found in history.

Only a small minority of upright men whose patriotism was more than
lip-service dared resistance in the land by secret societies and open propaganda; which became constantly easier as Napoleon's military rule rested
more heavily on the population of the exploited countries, whose sons
were now being forced to fill the gaps the war had made in the French
armies. Neither the Prussian monarchy nor the Prussian kraut-junkerdom
was equal to such a task. On the contrary, they opposed all attempts which
threatened to endanger their privileges and treated men like Stein, Gneisenau, Scharnhorst, Fichte, Arndt, Jahn, and even Blücher, with undisguised
suspicion. Only when compelled did they yield to their urgency—and
betrayed them at the first opportunity. The characterless attitude of Friedrich Wilhelm III toward Stein and the cowardly cabals by which Prussian
officialdom sought to thwart the efforts of the German patriots, tell a very
eloquent tale. The Prussian monarchy, therefore, forms no exception in
this sad saga of the German princes, and Seume was quite right when he
wrote:

> Whatever might be hoped of the nation and for the nation the princes
> and the nobles are sure to destroy in order to preserve their senseless priv-
> ileges. Napoleon's best satraps are the German princes and nobles. . . . We
> have now actually reached the point when we, like Cicero, do not know
> whether we are to wish for victory for our friends or our enemies. Here are
> whips; yonder are scorpions.

And yet the men who worked for the national awakening of Germany
and took such an important part in the so-called "wars of liberation" were
by no means revolutionaries, although they were often enough denounced
as Jacobins by the Prussian junkers. Almost every one of them was king-
loyal to the bone and entirely untouched by a real libertarian thought.
But they had clearly recognized one thing: If a nation is to be formed
from serfs and hereditary subjects without any rights, and the great masses
of the people are to be aroused to fight against foreign rule, one must first
of all begin by abolishing the outrageous privileges of the nobles and must
secure for the man of the people the civil rights which have hitherto been
denied to him. Scharnhorst says:

> One must infuse in the nation a feeling of self-reliance. One must give
> it a chance to become acquainted with itself so that it may be interested in
> itself; for only thus will it learn to respect itself and compel respect from

others. To work toward this is all that we can do. To break the bonds of prejudice, to guide and nurse the rebirth and never to oppose free growth— beyond this our utmost effectiveness does not reach.

Also in the same way, Gneisenau, who in his memorial of July 1807 states that a European adjustment can be thought of only if one is resolved to emulate the French and by a constitution and the equalization of all classes to liberate the nation's natural forces:

> If the other states want to reëstablish this balance they must themselves reopen the sources of supply and use them. They must appropriate the results of the revolution and thus gain the double advantage of being able to oppose their own national power to a foreign one and also to escape the dangers of a revolution—which are not past for them for the simple reason that they have been unwilling to avoid a violent change by a voluntary one.

Hardenberg, who at the time of the peace of Tilsit was at Napoleon's behest dismissed by Friedrich Wilhelm, put it even more clearly. In his *Memorial for the Reorganization of the Prussian State,* September 12, 1807, he declares:

> The illusion that the revolution can best be opposed by clinging to old institutions and by harsh persecution of the principles it announces has contributed greatly to aiding the revolution and giving it a steadily growing extension. The force of these principles is so great, they are so generally accepted and so widespread, that the state which does not adopt them goes either to its own destruction or to an enforced acceptance of these principles. . . . Democratic principles within a monarchic government, this seems to be the most suitable form for the present spirit of the age.

These were the ideas then current among the German patriots. Even Arndt, who surely cannot be accused of French sympathies, had to recognize that the great revolution was an event of European importance, and he reached the conclusion: "All states, even those which are not yet democracies, will from century to century become more democratic."

And Baron von Stein, a thoroughly conservative spirit and an outspoken opponent of all revolutionary movements, could not escape the conclusion that a rebirth of the state and liberation from the foreign yoke were possible only if one should decide to abolish serfdom and to institute a national assembly. Nevertheless Stein was careful to add in the essay entitled his "Political Testament" prepared for him by Schön: "The right and the power of the king were always sacred to me, and must remain so to us. But that this right and this unlimited power shall express the good inherent in it, it seems to me necessary to give to the highest power the means whereby it can learn the wishes of the people and give life to their intentions."

These were surely no revolutionary ideas; and yet Stein encountered the greatest difficulty in instituting even the most modest reforms. It is well known that it was just the "noblest of the nation" who continually assailed him from behind and did not even shrink from treason to their country in order to thwart his patriotic plans. The facts are that while the famous *Edict of Liberation* of October 1807 abolished serfdom in name, its authors did not dare to touch the junker landowners in the least. Thus the former serfs became wage slaves and could at any time be driven from the land by their masters if they did not submit unconditionally to their will.

Likewise the *Edict of Regulation* of 1811, evolved under Hardenberg, was principally designed to incite the rural population to resistance against the French. The prospect held out to the former serfs of a change in the law of ownership which would enable them to become owners of land, was an attempt to make them the more inclined to fight against the foreign rule. But after the French armies had evacuated the country, the government shamelessly broke all its promises and left the population of the rural districts to the misery and poverty imposed on them by the junkers.

It was the force of circumstances which had induced the German princes to make their subjects all kinds of fair promises, to let them expect a constitution, from which the awakened citizenry promised themselves wonderful things. They had come to realize that only a "people's war" could free Germany from the French domination, no matter how much Austria was opposed to this idea. The events in Spain had spoken too clearly. So the noble lords suddenly discovered how dearly they loved the people and recognized—following their need, not their inclination—that an uprising of the masses was the last desperate resort to support their shaking thrones.

In the appeal of Kalisch the Russian czar appeared as a sworn guarantor for the coming free and united Germany, and the king of Prussia promised his faithful subjects a constitution. On the great masses who merely vegetated in mental stupidity even these promises would not have made a special impress; but the bourgeoisie, and especially the youth, were seized with patriotic enthusiasm and dreamed of Barbarossa's resurrection and the reconstruction of the ancient empire in all its power and glory.

For all that, Friedrich Wilhelm still hesitated and sought to protect himself against both sides. Even when the Russian victory and the burning of Moscow had destroyed Napoleon's giant army and driven it in desperate flight to France, the king could still not reach a resolution; for the interests of the Prussian dynasty were nearer to his heart than a nebulous Germany for which neither he nor his East-Elbian junkers had understanding. Only under the steadily growing pressure of patriotic passion did he finally decide on the war—because, in fact, no other course was open to him.

What was the opinion of the patriots at this time is clearly apparent from a curious letter of Blücher to Scharnhorst, dated January 5, 1813, where among other things he says (as nearly as its illiteracy can be imitated in English):

"Now is agen the time for what I advized allready in the yeer 9 (1809); naimly to call the hole nation to arms and, iff the princes are not willing, to chais them out of the country allong with Buonaparte: For not only Prussia allone but the hole German fatherland must be resurected and the nation reastablished." [3]

But it came out quite otherwise than the patriotic advocates of German unity had imagined. All the promises of the great ones vanished in smoke as soon as Napoleon was defeated and the danger of a new invasion was removed. Instead of a constitution came the Holy Alliance, instead of the hoped-for civil liberty came the Carlsbad Resolutions and the persecution of the demagogues. That misshapen child, the *Deutsche Bund* ("German League")—Jahn called it *Deutscher Bunt* [4]—had to serve as a substitute for the desired unity of the realm. The idea of unification was outlawed by the government. Metternich even expressed the opinion that there was "no more damnable idea than to desire to unite the German people into a German empire," and the investigating officials in Mainz were especially severe against Jahn because he had first advocated the "most dangerous doctrine of German unification"; which, by the way, was not at all correct.

Fichte's *Addresses to the German Nation* were prohibited, and the great patriots delivered over to the henchmen of reaction. Arndt was disciplined and indicted; Schleiermacher could only preach under police supervision; Jahn was put in chains and sent to prison—even after his acquittal he was for years restricted in his freedom. Görres, who in his *Rhenish Mercury*, called by Napoleon "the fifth great power," had contributed so greatly to the national revolt against the French, had to flee and seek protection in the land of the "hereditary enemy" from the police of the Prussian reaction. Gneisenau resigned. Boyen, Humboldt and others did the same. The *Burschenschaften* ("Students' Leagues") were dissolved and the universities put under the moral guardianship of the police.

Never has a people been so shamelessly and so thoroughly cheated of the fruits of its victory. It must, however, not be forgotten that it was only a small minority who had placed great hopes on the consequences of the overthrow of French dominion and really believed that the time had now arrived for German unification under the sign of civil liberty. The great masses were, as always, forced into the so-called "wars of liberation" and

[3] There were other field marshals who spelled as badly as Blücher.—*Translator*
[4] Jahn's misspelling "*Deutscher Bunt*," would mean something like "German patchwork," if anything—*Translator*.

simply followed their hereditary princes with dutiful obedience. Only thus can the unopposed subjugation of the population under the terrorism of the rising reaction be explained. Heine was quite right when in his articles about the "Romantic School" he wrote:

> When God, snow, and the Cossacks destroyed Napoleon's best forces we Germans received the All-Highest's command to shake off the foreign yoke, and we blazed up in manly wrath over the all-too-long-endured servitude, and we enthused ourselves with the good melodies and the bad verses of Körner, and we fought and achieved freedom; for we do everything that is commanded us by our princes.

Likewise Goethe, who had witnessed the wars of liberation and who went more deeply into things than did the mocker, Heine, held in this matter the same opinion. He said in a discussion with Luden soon after the bloody battle of the nations at Leipzig:

> You speak of the awakening and arising of the German people and are of the opinion that this people will not again allow itself to be deprived of what it has achieved and so dearly paid for with its blood and treasure, namely, freedom. But is the people really awake? Does it know what it wants and what it can achieve? And is every movement an uprising? Does he arise who is forcibly stirred up? We are not speaking here of the thousands of educated youth and men; we are speaking here of the mass, of the millions. And what is it that has been achieved or won? You say freedom. Perhaps it would be better if you were to call it liberation—liberation, that is, not from the yoke of the stranger, but from a strange yoke. It is true that I now see no Frenchmen, no Italians; but instead I see Cossacks, Bashkirs, Croats, Magyars, Cassubes, Samlanders, brown and other colored hussars. We have been accustomed for a long time to turn our glance westward and to expect all danger from there, but the earth extends also far to the east.

Goethe was right. While from the east there came no revolution there came the Holy Alliance, which for decades rested like an incubus on the people of Europe and threatened to stifle all spiritual life. Never had Germany suffered anywhere near as much under the French foreign rule as it did later under the shameful tyranny of its princely "liberators."

Chapter 13

CULTURE AND NATIONALISM. GERMAN ROMANTICISM. THE *"VERLORENE HEIMAT."* THE REDEMPTION IDEA. THE DOCTRINE OF THE *"URVOLK."* THE SHADES OF THE PAST. ARNDT'S HATRED OF THE FRENCH. KLEIST'S GERMAN "CATECHISM." LUDWIG JAHN, A PIONEER OF HITLERISM. ARROGANT GERMANISM. GERMAN JUNGLE SPIRIT. THE BURSCHENSCHAFT. ROME'S INFLUENCE ON ROMANTICISM. AFTER DAMASCUS. FREDERICK OF GENTZ. ADAM MÜLLER AND THE ROMANTIC IDEA OF THE STATE. LUDWIG VON HALLER AND NEO-ABSOLUTISM. FRANZ VON BAADER; AN EXCURSION INTO GERMAN MYSTICISM. GERMAN UNITY AS DREAM AND REALITY.

ALL nationalism is reactionary in its nature, for it strives to enforce on the separate parts of the great human family a definite character according to a preconceived idea. In this respect, too, it shows the interrelationship of nationalistic ideology with the creed of every revealed religion. Nationalism creates artificial separations and partitions within that organic unity which finds its expression in the genus Man, while at the same time it strives for a fictitious unity sprung only from a wish-concept; and its advocates would like to tune all members of a definite human group to one note in order to distinguish it from other groups still more obviously. In this respect, so-called "cultural nationalism" does not differ at all from political nationalism, for whose political purposes as a rule it serves as a fig-leaf. The two cannot be spiritually separated; they merely represent two different aspects of the same endeavor.

Cultural nationalism appears in its purest form when people are subjected to a foreign rule, and for this reason cannot pursue their own plans for political power. In this event, "national thought" prefers to busy itself with the culture-building activities of the people and tries to keep the national consciousness alive by recollections of vanished glory and past greatness. Such comparisons between a past which has already become legend and a slavish present make the people doubly sensitive to the injustice suffered; for nothing affects the spirit of man more powerfully than tradition. But if such groups of people succeed sooner or later in shaking off the foreign yoke and themselves appear as a national power, then the cultural phase of their effort steps only too definitely into the background, giving place to the sober reality of their political objectives. In the recent history of the various national organisms in Europe created after the war are found telling witnesses for this.

In Germany, also, the national strivings both before and after the "wars of liberation" were strongly influenced by romanticism, whose advocates tried to make the traditions of a vanished age live again among the people and to make the past appear to them in a glorified light. When, later, the last hopes which the German patriots had rested on liberation from the foreign yoke had burst like over-blown bubbles, their spirits sought refuge in the moonlit magic night and the fairy world of dreamy longing conjured up for them by romanticism, in order to forget the gray reality of life and its shameful disappointments.

In culture-nationalism, as a rule, two distinct sentiments merge, which really have nothing in common: for home sentiment is not patriotism, is not love of the state, not love which has its roots in the abstract idea of the nation. It needs no labored explanation to prove that the spot of land on which a man has spent the years of his youth is deeply intergrown with his profoundest feeling. The impressions of childhood and early youth which are the most permanent and have the most lasting effect upon his soul. Home is, so to speak, man's outer garment; he is most intimately acquainted with its every fold and seam. This home sentiment brings in later years some yearning after a past long buried under ruins; and it is this which enables the romantic to look so deeply within.

With so-called "national consciousness" this home sentiment has no relationship; although both are often thrown into the same pot and, after the manner of counterfeiters, given out as of the same value. In fact, true home sentiment is destroyed at its birth by "national consciousness," which always strives to regulate and force into a prescribed form every impression man receives from the inexhaustible variety of the homeland. This is the unavoidable result of those mechanical efforts at unification which are in reality only the aspirations of the nationalistic states.

The attempt to replace man's natural attachment to the home by a dutiful love of the state—a structure which owes its creation to all sorts of accidents and in which, with brutal force, elements have been welded together that have no necessary connection—is one of the most grotesque phenomena of our time. The so-called "national consciousness" is nothing but a belief propagated by considerations of political power which have replaced the religious fanaticism of past centuries and have today come to be the greatest obstacle to cultural development. The love of home has nothing in common with the veneration of an abstract patriotic concept. Love of home knows no "will to power"; it is free from that hollow and dangerous attitude of superiority to the neighbor which is one of the strongest characteristics of every kind of nationalism. Love of home does not engage in practical politics nor does it seek in any way to support the state. It is purely an inner feeling as freely manifested as man's enjoyment of nature, of which home is a part. When thus viewed, the home feeling compares with the governmentally ordered love of the nation as does a natural growth with an artificial substitute.

The impulse of German romanticism came from France. Rousseau's slogan, "back to nature," his conscious revolt against the spirit of enlightenment, his strong emphasis on the purely sentimental as against the clever systematic thought of rationalism, found beyond the Rhine also a notable response—especially in Herder to whom the romantics, nearly all of whom had been formerly in the camp of the enlightenment, were strongly obligated. Herder himself was no romantic. His view was too clear, his spirit too unroiled for him to enthuse over the romantic concept of the "purposelessness of all events." But his disinclination to everything systematic, his joy in the primordialness of things, his conception of the inner relationship of the human soul with all Mother Nature and, most of all, his deep sympathy and feeling of understanding for the spiritual culture of foreign people and past ages, brought him very close to the representatives of romanticism. In fact, the great service rendered by the romantics through their introduction of foreign literatures, their rediscovery of the German legends and folklore, can largely be traced to the inspiration of Herder, who showed them the way.

But Herder in all his thinking viewed mankind as a whole. He saw, as Heine so beautifully said, "all mankind as a great harp in the hands of a great master." Every people was for him a string, and from the harmonious union of the sounds of all the strings arose for him life's eternal melodies. Swept along by this thought he enjoyed the endless variety of the life of the people and followed with loving interest every manifestation of their cultural activity. He knew of no chosen people and had for the Negro and the Mongolian the same understanding as for the members of the white race. When one reads what he had to say concerning a plan for a "Natural History of Mankind in a purely Human Sense" one gets the impression that he had foreseen the absurdities of our modern race theoreticians and nationalistic fetish worshipers.

> Most of all, one must be impartial as the genius of mankind itself, have no preferred tribes, no favored folk on earth. One is easily misled by such a preference to ascribe to the favored nation too much good, to the others too much evil. And when the favored people prove only a collective name (Celts, Semites, Chuschites, etc.), which perhaps never existed and whose origin and continuity cannot be proved, then one has indeed written in sand.

The adherents of the Romantic School at first followed these trails and developed a number of fruitful ideas which had a stimulating influence on the most divergent schools of thought. But we are here interested solely in the influence they had on the development of the national idea in Germany. The romantics discovered for the Germans the German past and brought to light many of its features which had hardly been noticed before. They thoroughly reveled in this past, and their attempts to make it live again revealed many a hidden treasure and made many a silent string vibrate once more. And since most of their intellectual leaders were also inclined to philosophical reflections, they dreamed of a higher unity of life in which all phases of human activity—religion, state, church, science, art, philosophy, ethics and everyday affairs—are focussed like a bundle of sun-rays by the lens.

The Romantic School believed in a *"verlorene Heimat,"* a lost home, a past condition of spiritual perfection in which the oneness of life they were striving for was once existent. Since then there had occurred a sort of fall into sin. Mankind had gotten into a chaos of hostile segregation, so that the inner communion of the individual members was destroyed and each one was set up as a distinct part and lost his deeper relation to the whole. The attempts again to unite men into a whole have so far led to merely mechanical union, lacking the inner impulse of individual growth and purity. Hence, they have only increased the evil and destroyed the gaily colored variety of internal and external vital relations. In this respect France was for the romantics a repellent example, because there for centuries men had striven to embed every manifestation of life in a spiritless political centralism which falsified the primordial meaning of social relations and intentionally deprived them of their true character.

According to the romantic conception, the lost unity could not be restored by external means; it had rather to grow out of man's inner spiritual urge and then gradually to ripen. The romantics were firmly convinced that in the soul of the people the memory of that state of former perfection still slumbered. But that inner source had been choked and had first to be freed again before the silent intuition could once more become alive in the minds of men. So they searched for the hidden sources and lost themselves ever deeper in the mystic dusk of a past age whose strange magic had intoxicated their minds. The German medieval age with its colorful variety and its inexhaustible power of creation was for them a new revelation. They believed themselves to have found there that unity of life which humanity had lost. Now the old cities and the Gothic cathedrals spoke a special language and testified to that *"verlorene Heimat"* on which the longing of romanticism spent itself. The Rhine with its legend-rich castles, its cloisters and mountains, became Germany's sacred stream; all the past took on a new character, a glorified meaning.

Thus there gradually developed a sort of cultural nationalism whose inner import culminated in the thought that the Germans, because of their splendid past, which was now to be reborn among the people, were destined to bring to sick humanity the longed-for healing. Thus the Germans became in the eyes of the romantics the chosen people of the present age, selected by Providence itself to fulfill a divine mission. This thought occurs again and again in Fichte, whose philosophical idealism, together with the nature philosophy of Schelling, had the strongest influence on the romantics. Fichte had called the Germans an *"Urvolk,"* a primary people, for whom alone man's final redemption was reserved. What originally had sprung from the pious enthusiasm of an overintense poetic mood, and as such was rather harmless, assumed with Fichte the character of that construed antagonism which is at the base of all nationalism and already carries within itself the dragon's teeth of national hatred. From assumed national superiority to vilification and disparagement of everything foreign, it is as a rule but a step, which, especially in times of agitation, is very easily taken.

If the Germans were indeed an *"Urvolk"* as Fichte maintained and as others have repeated after him, a people which had more of the *"verlorene Heimat"* feeling than all other people, then no other nation could rival them or could even endure comparison with them. To maintain this contention to give the real or imaginary distinctions between them the meaning one desires, one is forced to conceive peoples as categories, not to take them as individuals. Thus began the work of idle speculation and construction, in which Fichte especially has achieved the extraordinary. For him the Germans were the only people who had character: "To have character and to be German are indubitably synonymous." From this it naturally follows that other peoples, and especially the French, have no character. It was discovered that there is no French equivalent for the word *"Gemüt."* Whereby it was proved that God had endowed only the Germans with so noble a gift.

From this and similar premises, Fichte gradually reaches the extremest conclusions: since the Frenchman has no *Gemüt* his mind is set solely on the sensual and the material, things naturally antagonistic to the inner chastity of the German so richly endowed with *Gemüt*. To *Gemüt* is due the "uniform honesty and loyalty" of the Germans. Only where *Gemüt* is lacking are cunning and guile at the bottom of the soul, qualities which the Germans freely leave to other people. True religion has its roots in the depths of the *Gemüt*. This explains why among the French that "spirit of enlightenment" had to develop which finally culminated in the crassest free thought and infidelity. The German, however, grasped the spirit of Christianity in its whole profundity, giving it a special meaning appropriate to its innermost essence.

Fichte also spoke of the *"Ursprache,"* the primitive speech of the Germans, meaning by this "a language which from the first sound uttered by this people has without a break developed from the actual common life of the people." Thus he reached the conclusion that only among an "*Urvolk*" possessing an "*Ursprache*" does intellectual growth penetrate life. Among other people, who have forgotten their *Ursprache* and have adopted a foreign language (to these of course belonged first of all the French), mental development and life each go their separate ways. From this assumption Fichte deduced certain political and social consequences in the life of a people; as when in his fourth *Address to the German Nation* he says: "In a nation of the first category the whole people are educable. The educators of such test their discoveries on the people and try to influence them. Whereas in a nation of the second category the educated classes separate themselves from the people and use the latter only as blind tools for the accomplishment of their plans."

This arbitrary assertion, whose nonsense is disputed every hour by life itself, is today the subject of most curious commentaries and is proclaimed to the German youth as the profoundest wisdom of the fathers. The higher one elevates one's own nation, the poorer and the more meaningless must everything else appear compared with it. All creative gift even is denied to others. Thus, Fichte maintains of the French "that they cannot raise themselves to the idea of freedom and of the legal state because by their system of thought they have missed the concept of personal values and cannot understand at all how other men or people can will or even think such a thing." [1] Of course only Germans were chosen for freedom because they had *Gemüt* and were an "*Urvolk*." Unfortunately, we hear today so often and so obtrusively of "German freedom" and "German loyalty" that we have become somewhat suspicious—for the Third Reich gives us none too clear a picture of what this alleged freedom and loyalty really consist of.

Most of the men who played leading parts in the nationalist movement in Germany before and after 1813 were rooted deeply in the spirit of romanticism; and from its descriptions of The Holy Roman Empire of the German Nation of medieval times, of the legendary world of ancient Germany, and of the magic of the native soil their patriotism drew rich nourishment. Arndt, Jahn, Görres, Schenkendorf, Schleiermacher, Kleist, Eichendorff, Gentz, Körner, were deeply imbued with romantic ideas; even Stein as he became older came ever more deeply under their influence. They dreamed of the return of the old realm of Austria's imperial banner. Only a few of them, with Fichte, saw in the king of Prussia the "*Zwingherr zur Deutschheit*," the compeller towards Germanism, and believed that Prussia was destined to establish the unity of the realm.

With most of these men the nationalistic idea reached its logical con-

[1] Fichte, *Über den Begriff des wahrhaften Krieges in Bezug auf den Krieg 1813.* Dritte Vorlesung.

clusion. It had begun as an enticing nostalgia for the *"verlorene Heimat"* and a poetic glorifying of the German past. Later, they got the idea of the great historical mission of the Germans; they made comparisons between the various peoples and their own and used for the embellishment of their own so much paint that there was hardly anything left for the others. The end was a fierce hatred of the French and an idiotic exaltation of Germanism which frequently bordered on mental aberration.

The same development can, however, be observed in every kind of nationalism, whether it be German, Polish or Italian; the only difference being that the "hereditary enemy" has for each nation a different name. Let no one say that it was the harsh experience of foreign rule and war, releasing all the worst passions in man, that led the German patriots to such one-sided and hatefilled modes of thought. What then, and also after the "wars of liberation," proclaimed itself as German patriotism, was more than a justified uprising against the foreign yoke; it was an open declaration of war against the character, the language and the spiritual culture of a neighboring people who—as Goethe said—belonged to "the most cultivated on earth," and to whom he himself "owed a great part of his education."

Arndt, who was one of the most influential men in the patriotic revolt against Napoleon's rule in Germany, knew actually no limits in his morbid hatred of the French:

> Hatred of the foreigner, hatred of the French, of their trifling, their vanity, their folly, their language, their customs; yes, burning hatred of all that comes from them, that must unite everything German firmly and fraternally; and German valor, German freedom, German culture, German honor and justice must again soar high and be raised to the old honor and glory whereby our fathers shone before most of the peoples of the earth. . . . What has brought you to shame must bring you to honor again. Only bloody hatred of the French can unite German power, raise again the German glory, bring out the noblest traits of the people and submerge all the lowest. This hatred must be imparted to your children and your children's children as the palladium of German freedom, and must in future be the surest guardian of Germany's frontiers from the Scheldt to the Vosges and the Ardennes.[2]

With Kleist the hatred of everything French rose to blind rage. He derided Fichte's *Addresses to the German Nation,* and saw in him nothing but a weak-willed school-master with whom impotent words had to do duty for courage, for action. What he demanded was a people's war such as the Spanish under the leadership of fanatical priests and monks were waging against the French. In such a war all means seemed to him per-

[2] E. M. Arndt, *An die Preussen.* January, 18I3.

220 NATIONALISM AND CULTURE

missible; poison and the dagger, breach of faith and treason. His *Catechism for the Germans, Modeled After the Spanish, for Old and Young,* which, significantly, is written in the form of a dialogue between a father and his child, displays the wildest manifestation of unrestrained national fanaticism, and in its frightful intolerance treads every human feeling under foot. Perhaps this gruesome fanaticism can be partly traced to the sick mentality of the unfortunate poet; on the other hand, the present time gives us the best possible understanding how such a mental attitude can be artificially trained and can spread with uncanny power if favored by particular social conditions.

Ludwig Jahn, who after Fichte's death became the spiritual leader of German youth and was regarded by it with almost divine veneration, carried Francophobia and nationalistic craze so far that he got on the nerves even of his patriotic fellow fighters. Stein called him a "grimacing, conceited fool" and Arndt a "purified Eulenspiegel." Jahn suspected everything and smelled everywhere foreign customs and French folly. Reading the biography of this peculiar saint one gets the impression of seeing in the "bearded ancient" an earlier pioneer of modern Hitlerism. His rude, presumptuous speech, his incredible arrogance, his hollow boasting, his delight in tying ideas into knots, his violent temper, his bold obtrusiveness, and most of all his boundless intolerance, which respected no other opinion and reviled every thought not in agreement with his own as un-German—all this makes him the ancestor of the present National Socialism.

Jahn really had no political ideas of his own. What mostly appealed to him was not medieval Germany, but primitive Germany; there he was at home, fairly wallowing in German primordialness. He proposed to create between Germany and France, a *Hamme,* a barrier, a sort of primitive forest filled with bisons and other wild beasts. A special frontier guard was to see to it that no intercourse whatever should take place between the two countries, so that German youth might not be contaminated by French rottenness. In his crazy hatred of France Jahn went so far as to preach publicly: "It comes to the same thing if one teaches his daughters French or trains them for whores." In the brain of this strange prophet everything became perverted and distorted; most of all, the German language, which he frightfully mistreated with his wild, fanatical "purification."

For all that, Jahn enjoyed not only the boundless admiration of German youth, but Jena University gave him an honorary doctor's degree and compared his tiresome boasting with Luther's eloquence. A distinguished philologist like Thiersch dedicated his German translation of Pindar to him, and Franz Passow, professor of Greek Literature at Weimar, declared that since Luther nothing so excellent had been written as

Jahn's *Teutsche Turnkunst* ("German gymnastics"). If the present Germany were not such a repellent example of how, under the pressure of special circumstances, a brainless phraseology supported by complicated illogic can impress wide sections of the nation and force them in a special direction, the influence of a confused mind like Jahn's would be difficult to understand. That this man could be accepted by German youth as Fichte's successor can only be explained by the low mental level of the younger generation itself. Even such a thoroughly nationalistic historian as Treitschke remarks in his *German History:* "It amounted to a social disease that the sons of an enlightened people could venerate a noisy barbarian as their teacher."

But this came about simply because the narrow-minded Germanism which became the fashion in Germany after the wars of liberation *had* to lead to mental barbarism. The morbid mania of *Auserwähltheit*, of "electness," necessarily led to intellectual estrangement from all general culture of the time and to a total misconception of all human relations. It was a time when the spirit of Lessing and Herder could no longer inspire the young generation; when Goethe lived beside, but not in, the nation. What resulted from it was the specific German patriotism which, according to Heine, consists in this, that in its supporters "the heart becomes narrower and shrinks like leather in cold weather; that they hate everything foreign; that they no longer wish to be citizens of the world, no longer Europeans, but only narrow Germans."

It is absurd to see in the men of 1813 the guardians of freedom; not one of them was moved by real libertarian ideas. Almost every one of them had his roots in a long-past age which could no longer open new outlooks for the present. This applies also to the Burschenschaft, the Students' League, whose shameful suppression by the victorious reaction is probably the main reason why even today it is praised for its libertarian activities. No one will deny that the Burschenschaft had idealistic features; but this is no proof that it had a libertarian mind. Its Christian-German mysticism, its grotesque rejection of all that is called "foreign custom" and "foreign spirit," its anti-Semitic tendencies which had been from of old in Germany the heritage of all reactionary movements, and the general confusion of its views—all these fitted it to be the champion of a mystical faith in which elements of the most diverse conceptions mingled in motley patchwork; not to be the banner-bearer of a new future. When after Kotzebue's murder by the student, Karl Sand, reaction dealt a destructive blow, and the infamous Carlsbad Resolutions suppressed all leagues of youth, the Burschenschaft could confront Metternich's creatures with nothing but those helpless and submissive verses of Binzer which end with the words:

The tie has been cut; it was black, red, and gold;
And God has endured it. His wish—who's been told?
The house it may fall; as fall it needs must;
The spirit lives in us, and God is our trust.

Real revolutionaries would have hurled different words against this brutal violation of deepest human dignity. When one compares the bold beginnings of German enlightenment and its great, all-dominating ideas of love and freedom of thought, with the sad results of an unfettered rampant "national consciousness," one realizes the enormous spiritual throw back which Germany has suffered and can appraise the whole grim meaning of Heine's words:

> There we now see the idealistic brutality that Jahn reduced to a system. It began as a shabby, loutish, unwashed opposition to a mental attitude which is the noblest, the holiest, that Germany has created; that is, against that humanity, against that general human fraternization, against that cosmopolitanism which our great spirits, Lessing, Herder, Schiller, Goethe, Jean Paul, and all Germans of culture have always venerated.

It is a curious phenomenon that the best-known representatives of the romantic school, who had contributed so much to the shaping of mystic nationalism in Germany, almost without exception landed in the camp of open political or clerical reaction. This was all the more remarkable since most of them had begun their literary careers as heralds of enlightenment and freedom of thought and had greeted the great revolution in the neighboring land with enthusiasm. If it was strange that a former Jacobin like Görres, who hailed the dismemberment of the German empire with wild joy, changed with such surprising rapidity into a fierce opponent of France, it was still more incomprehensible that the same Görres, who in his essay, *Germany and the Revolution* (1820), with manly resolution showed his teeth to the raging reactionaries, soon after threw himself into the arms of papism and in his clerical fanaticism went so far as to earn the endorsement of Joseph de Maistre.

Wilhelm and Friedrich Schlegel, Steffens, Tieck, Adam Müller, Brentano, Fouqué, Zacharias Werner, and many others, were swept away by the reactionary flood. Hundreds of young artists made pilgrimages to Rome and returned to the bosom of the Catholic Church, which was then reaping a good harvest. It was a very witches' sabbath of mad fanaticism and ardent rage for conversion which, however, lacked the inner vigor of conviction of medieval man. This was the end of that cultural nationalism which had commenced as a burning longing for the "*verlorene Heimat*" and ended in the slough of the deepest reaction. Georg Brandes did not exaggerate when he said:

As regards their religious attitude all the romantics, who were so revolutionary in poetry, submissively bent the neck as soon as they saw the yoke. And in politics it was they who guided the Vienna congress and drew up the manifesto for the abrogation of liberty of thought among the people—between a solemnity in St. Peter's Cathedral and an oyster dinner at Fanny Elssler's.[3]

But one must not compare most of these men with Gentz, to whom Brandes referred in these words; they were not in his class. Gentz, next to Metternich in whose pay he was, was chiefly responsible for the infamous Carlsbad Resolutions; he was a "rotten character," as Stein called him, a brilliant, venal scribbler who sold his pen to anyone who paid for it. He revealed to the English socialist, Robert Owen, in a moment of cynic frankness, the whole leitmotif of his miserable life in a few words when Owen—who did not know his real character—sought to win Gentz for his special plans of reform: "We do not wish to make the great mass wealthy and independent; how could we then rule them?" With Gentz one could perhaps compare only Friedrich Schlegel, who also degraded himself to become a purchased scribbler for Metternich. The rest of the heads of the Romantic School went the way of reaction quite independently, because all their ideas had a reactionary core. The fact that nearly all of them went the same road can very well serve as proof that there was something unhealthy about the whole movement which they never could overcome and which determined the course of their development.

The reactionary core of German romanticism is at once apparent from its view concerning the state, which traced directly back to theoretical absolutism. Novalis had begun by endowing the state with a special individual life of its own, treating it as a "mystic individual" and concluding that "the perfected citizen lives wholly in the state." But only that kind of man can live wholly in the state who is wholly filled by the state. Such a concept is naturally not in harmony with the liberal ideas of the period of enlightenment; it is their self-evident antithesis.

Adam Müller, the real state-theoretician of romanticism, most decidedly opposed the "Chimaera of natural rights" upon which most of the ideas of liberalism are based. In his *Elements of Statecraft* he most emphatically opposes the liberal concept, of which the most prominent representative in Germany had been Wilhelm von Humboldt, maintaining that "the state is not only a manufacturing, farming, and insurance institution or mercantile society," but "the most intimate union of the collective physical and spiritual wealth, the whole inner and outer life of a nation in one great energetic, infinitely active and living whole." Consequently, the state could never be the means for any special or definite end, as

[3] Georg Brandes, *Die romantische Schule in Deutschland*. Berlin, 1900, p. 6.

liberalism conceived it to be; it was rather, in its highest form, an end in itself, an end sufficient for itself, having its roots in the union of law, nationality and religion. If it often appeared as if the state was serving some special task, this, according to Müller's concept, was only an optical illusion of the theoreticians; in reality the state serves only itself and is not a means for anyone.

Karl Ludwig von Haller's shallow and shameless patchwork with the long-winded title *Restoration of Statecraft, or the Theory of the Natural Social State as Opposed to the Chimaera of the Artificial Bourgeois State*, was only a crude and lifeless repetition of the same ideas. But with Haller the reactionary trend is much more openly and demonstrably apparent. Haller on principle rejected the thought that civil society could have arisen from a written or unwritten contractual relation between the citizen and the state. The natural condition out of which all institutions of political society had gradually arisen is synonymous with the divine order, the origin of all things. The first outcome of this primal condition was, how-ever, that the strong ruled over all others, from which it is apparent that all power springs from a natural law founded in divine order. The mighty one rules, founds the state, declares the law—and all on the basis of his strength and superiority. The power he possesses is a gift from God and, coming from God, it is for that reason inviolable. From this it follows that the king is not the servant of the state, but must be its master. State and people are his property, a legitimate legacy received from God where-with to do as he pleases. If the king is unjust and harsh, this is certainly unfortunate for the subjects, but it does not justify their effecting a change by themselves. All that remains for them to do in such a case is to call on God to enlighten the ruler and guide him on the right way.

One can understand how thoroughly such a doctrine must have satisfied the crowned heads. Haller more especially pleased the Prussian crown prince, later Friedrich Wilhelm IV, who has been called "the romantic on the king's throne." Hegel's deification of the state was but a further step in the same direction and found such ready acceptance in Germany for the reason that the state concept of the romantics had smoothed the way for his ideas.

The one superior mind among the romantics, who even here went his own way, was the Catholic philosopher, Franz von Baader, whose diary contains a mass of profound reflections concerning state and society. Baader, who based his doctrine on man's original purity, most strenuously opposed Kant's concept of "innate evil" and especially fought the mania of govern-ment which smothers man's noblest talents and makes him incapable of any independent action. For this reason he praised anarchy as a healing force of nature against despotism because it compels men to stand on their own feet. Baader compared man infantilized by government to the fool who thought he could not walk until a conflagration taught him the use of his legs.

> Error and vice receive their great strength through materialization, authorization by institutions; for example, as law. And the latter is the great evil, the great bar to our capacity for perfection, which only government can cause. It is therefore incapable of achieving anything good, but very capable of achieving evil; for it, so to speak, makes folly and vice immortal, giving them a permanence they could not have of themselves.

Baader's state-critical concept does not hark back to liberalism, but to German mysticism. He had gone to school to Master Eckhart and Jacob Böhme and had reached a kind of theosophy which looked very sceptically at all temporal means of compulsion. What most attracted him to Catholicism was the universality of the church and the idea of Christendom as a world-embracing community held together only by the inner tie of religion and hence not in need of any external protection. Baader was a solitary, a deeply probing spirit, who inspired many but had no influence on the general course of German development.

Hence, neither romanticism nor its immediate practical result, the newly created national movement leading to the wars of liberation, could give Germany new spiritual outlooks for the free development of her tribes and peoples. On the contrary, the state-philosophical concepts of the romantic school only served reaction as a moral justification, while the absurd super-Germanism of German youth estranged all other peoples. And the strange thing happened that many of the advocates of the German national idea never realized that they owed their apparent liberation not to their German exclusiveness, but to those very "foreign influences" against which their "Germanism" fought with such Berserker rage. Neither Jahn's "acorn-eating Germanism" with its enthusiasm for the primitive forest nor Arndt's romantic dreams of a new German order of knighthood on the western front, nor the nostalgic call of the imperial herald, Schenkendorf, for a glorious return of the old empire, could have brought about Napoleon's downfall. It was the effect of foreign ideas and institutions taken over from abroad which accomplished this miracle. To shake off the foreign rule Germany had to accept at least a part of the ideas which the French revolution had called into life. The very fact that it was a "people's war" before which Napoleon's power bled to death proves how deeply democratic ideas had already penetrated into Germany; for at the root of all national exaltation lies consciously or unconsciously a democratic thought. It was this form of warfare which had enabled France to maintain itself against the whole of Europe. Hence the German princes, and more especially Austria, were almost to the last the bitterest opponents of a national uprising, behind which they saw the hydra of revolution lurking. They even feared with Gentz "that the national war of liberation might easily change into a liberating war." The establishment of the militia, indeed the whole army organization instituted by Scharnhorst in Prussia, was after the French pattern. But for this the French would still have been equal to their opponents even after the frightful catastrophe in Russia.

The idea of national education which had been brought so prominently into the foreground by Fichte, the universal military service, the legal compulsion which obligated the citizen to accept a definite office or perform definite duties as demanded by the state, and much else, were likewise taken over from the democratic teachings of the great revolution. German patriotism accepted this foreign intellectual property believing it to be of original German manufacture. This happened to Jahn, who wished to cleanse the German language with an iron broom of all foreign elements and never noticed that in the formation of the "original German" word *"turnen"* a Latin root is used.

The German unification movements of 1813 and 1848-49 were wrecked in both instances because of the treason of the German princes; but when the unification of the empire was brought about in 1871 by a Prussian junker the sober reality looked quite different from the brilliant dream that had once been dreamed. This was not the "return of the old empire" which had so stirred the yearnings of the romantics. Compared to that empire Bismarck's creation was but "as a Berlin barracks is to a Gothic cathedral"—as the South German federalist, Frantz, dramatically declared. Just as little was it like the liberal conceptions of a free Germany which was to lead the European family of nations in spiritual culture—as Hoffmann von Fallersleben and the pioneer fighters for German unity of 1848 had once prophesied. No, this misshapen political brat, got by a Prussian junker, was nothing more than a greater Prussia come to power, which had changed Germany into a gigantic barracks and with its insane militarism and its definite aims of world political power now assumed the same fateful role which Bonaparte had up to that time played in Europe. The very fact that it was just Prussia, the most reactionary and in its cultural history the most backward country, which assumed the leadership of all German peoples, left no doubt as to what would result from such a "creation." This was felt keenly by Bismarck's most important opponent, Constantin Frantz (whose weighty writings are as little known to the Germans as the Chinese language) when he expressed the opinion:

It must be generally admitted that it is an unnatural situation when the ancient Western Germany, which for centuries before Prussia was thought of had a history in comparison with which the history of Prussia looks very small indeed, and when speaking of the Mark Brandenburg was only dealing with the half-waste land of the Wends—that this old Germany with its primeval tribes of the Bavarians, Saxons, Franks and Swabians, Thuringians and Hessians, is now ruled by the Mark.[4]

The majority of the German patriots of 1813 refused to hear of a unified Germany under Prussian leadership, and Görres wrote in his *Rhenish Mercury* at the time of the Vienna congress that the Saxons and the Rhinelanders could not believe that four-fifths of the Germans should call themselves after the most distant one-fifth, which beside was half Slavic. In fact, the Slavic portion of the Prussian population was greatly increased by the conquest of Silesia and the partition of Poland under Frederick II and now amounted to two-fifths of the total population of the country. It is most comical that it should be just Prussia which later on so noisily announced itself as the chosen guardian of genuine German interests.

William Pierson, who was himself convinced of Prussia's historic mission for the accomplishment of German unity, described in his *Preussische Geschichte* very clearly the desire of the Prussian royalty for the creation of "the Prussian nationality" and proved against his will the old truth that it is the state which makes the nation, and not the nation the state:

The state achieved a definite nationality. The separate tribes belonging to it were more easily and quickly blended into a unified body since as Prussians all had the same name, all had the same colors, the black-and-white flag. *However, Prussiandom now developed itself as distinct from the rest of Germany, as all the more definitely a unique entity: the Prussian state stepped forth as something unique, something separate.*

That under these circumstances the national unity of the Germans created by Bismarck could never lead to a "Germanizing of Prussia" but inevitably to a "Prussianizing of Germany" was to be anticipated, and has been proved in every way by the course of German history since 1871.

[4] Constantin Frantz, *Der Föderalismus als das leitende Prinzip für die soziale, staatliche und internationale Organisation, unter besonderer Bezugnahme auf Deutschland.* Mainz, 1879. Page 253.

Chapter 14

SOCIALISM AND ITS VARIOUS TENDENCIES. INFLUENCE OF DEMOCRATIC AND LIBERAL IDEAS ON THE SOCIALIST MOVEMENT. BABOUVISM AND JACOBINISM. CAESARISTIC AND THEOCRATIC IDEAS IN SOCIALISM. PROUDHON AND FEDERALISM. THE INTERNATIONAL WORKINGMEN'S ASSOCIATION. BAKUNIN OPPOSED TO THE CENTRAL STATE POWER. THE PARIS COMMUNE AND ITS INFLUENCE ON THE SOCIALIST MOVEMENT. PARIAMENTARY ACTIVITY AND THE INTERNATIONAL. THE FRANCO-PRUSSIAN WAR AND THE POLITICAL CHANGE IN EUROPE. THE MODERN LABOR PARTIES AND THE STRUGGLE FOR POWER. SOCIALISM AND NATIONAL POLITICS. AUTHORITARIAN AND LIBERTARIAN SOCIALISM. GOVERNMENT OR ADMINISTRATION.

WITH the development of socialism and the modern labor movement in Europe, there became noticeable among the people a new intellectual trend which has not yet terminated. Its fate will be determined according as libertarian or authoritarian ideas win and hold the upper hand among its leaders. Socialists of all schools share the common conclusion that the present state of social organization is a continuous cause of most dangerous social evils and cannot permanently endure. Common also to all socialist schools is the conviction that a better order of things cannot be brought about by changes of a purely political nature but can be achieved only by a fundamental reform of existing economic conditions; that the earth and all other means of social production can no longer remain the private property of privileged minorities in society but must be transferred to the ownership and administration of the generality. Only thus will it be possible to make the end and aim of all productive activity, not the prospect of personal gain, but the satisfaction of the needs of all members of society.

But as to the special form of the socialist society, and the ways and means of achieving it, the views of the various socialistic factions differ widely. This is not strange, for, like every other idea, socialism came to men not as a revelation from Heaven; it developed, rather, within the existing social structures and directly dependent upon them. So it was inevitable that its advocates should be more or less influenced by the political and social movements of the time which had taken definite root in various countries. The influence which the ideas of Hegel had on the structure of socialism in Germany is well known. Most of its pioneers— Grün, Hess, Lassalle, Marx, Engels—came from the intellectual circle of German philosophy; only Weitling received his stimulus from another source. In England, the permeation of the socialist movements by liberal ideas was unmistakable. In France, it is the intellectual trends of the great revolution; in Spain, the influence of political federalism, which are most noticeable in their respective socialistic theories. Something similar can be said of the socialistic movement of every country.

But since in a common cultural circle like Europe ideas and social movements do not remain confined within any one country but naturally spread to others, it follows that movements not only retain their purely local color but receive also varied stimuli from without, which become imbedded, almost unnoticeably, in the indigenous intellectual product and enrich it in their own peculiar way. How strongly these foreign influences assert themselves depends largely on the general social situation. We need but remember the mighty influence of the French revolution and its intellectual repercussions in most of the countries of Europe. It is therefore self-evident that a movement like socialism gathers in every country the most varied assortment of ideas and is nowhere limited to one definite and special form of expression.

Babeuf, and the communist school which has appropriated his ideas, derive from the Jacobin world of ideas, the political viewpoint of which wholly dominated them. They were convinced that society could be given any desired form, provided that the political power of the state could be controlled. As with the spread of modern democracy in Rousseau's sense the superstitious belief in the omnipotence of the laws has deeply penetrated into men's consciousness, so the conquest of political power has, with this section of the socialists, developed into a dogma resting on the principles of Babeuf and the doctrine of the so-called "equals." The whole contest among these factions turned principally on the question how best and most securely to gain possession of the powers of the state. Babeuf's direct successors held fast to the old tradition, being convinced that their secret societies would one day achieve public power by a single revolutionary stroke and with the aid of a proletarian dictatorship make socialism a living fact. But men like Louis Blanc, Pecqueur, Vidal and others, maintained the view that a violent overthrow was to be avoided if possible, provided that the state comprehended the spirit of the times and of its own initiative worked towards a complete reorganization of social economy. Both factions, however, were united in the belief that socialism could only be achieved with the aid of the state and of appropriate legislation. Pecqueur had already prepared a whole book of laws for this purpose, a sort of socialistic *code Napoleon*, which was to serve as a guide for a far-seeing government.

Nearly all the great pioneers of socialism in the first half of the last century were more or less strongly influenced by authoritarian concepts. The brilliant Saint-Simon recognized, with great keenness of insight, that mankind was moving toward the time when "the art of governing men would be replaced by the art of administering things"; but his disciples displayed ever fiercer authoritarian temper and finally settled on the idea of a socialistic theocracy; then they completely vanished from the picture.

Fourier developed, in his *Social System*, liberal ideas of marvelous depth and imperishable significance. His theory of "attractive work" affects us especially today, at a time of capitalistic "rationalization of economy," like an inner revelation of true humanity. But even he was a child of his age and, like Robert Owen, he turned to all the spiritual and temporal powers of Europe in the hope that they would help him realize his plan. Of the real nature of social liberation he hardly had an idea, and most of his numerous disciples knew even less. Cabet's *Icarian communism* was infiltrated with Caesarian and autocratic ideas. Blanqui and Barbés were communistic Jacobins.

In England, where Godwin's profound work, *Political Justice*, had appeared in 1793, the socialism of the first period had a much more libertarian character than in France; for there liberalism and not democracy had prepared the way for it. But the writings of William Thompson, John Gray and others remained almost totally unknown on the continent. Robert Owen's communism was a strange mixture of libertarian ideas and traditional authoritarian beliefs. His influence on the trade union and coöperative movements in England was for a time very great; but gradually, and especially after his death, it died out to make room for practical considerations which little by little lost sight of the great aims of the movement.

Among the few social thinkers of that period who tried to base their socialistic efforts on a truly libertarian foundation, Proudhon was undoubtedly the most important. His analytic criticism of Jacobin tradition, of governmental systems, of the nature of government and blind belief in the magic power of laws and decrees, affects one like a liberating stroke whose true greatness has even today not been fully recognized. Proudhon perceived clearly that socialism must be libertarian if it is to be the creator of a new social culture. In him there burned the lambent flame of a new age, which he anticipated, clearly foreseeing in his mind its social structure. He was one of the first who confronted the political metaphysics of parties with the concrete facts of science. Economics was for him the real basis of all social life; and since with deep insight he recognized the sensitivity of economics to every external compulsion, he logically associated the abolition of economic monopolies with the banishment of all that is governmental from the life of society. For him the worship of the law to which all parties of that period were fanatically devoted had not the slightest creative significance; he knew that in a community of free and equal men only free agreement could be the moral tie of social relations.

"So you want to abolish government?" someone asked him. "You want no constitution? Who will maintain order in society? What will you put in place of the state? In place of the police? In place of the great political powers?"

"Nothing," he answered. "Society is eternal motion; it does not have to be wound up; and it is not necessary to beat time for it. It carries its own pendulum and its ever wound-up spring within it. An organized society needs laws as little as legislators. Laws are to society what cobwebs are to a beehive; they only serve to catch the bees."

Proudhon had recognized the evils of political centralism in all their detail and had proclaimed decentralization and the autonomy of the communes as the need of the hour. He was the most eminent of all the moderns who have inscribed the principles of federalism on their banners. To his fine mind it was quite clear that men of today could not leap at one bound into the realm of anarchy, that the mental attitude of his contemporaries, formed slowly during the course of long periods, would not vanish in the turn of a hand. Hence, political decentralization which would withdraw the state gradually from its functions seemed to him the most appropriate means for beginning and giving direction to the abolition of all government of men by men. He believed that a political and social reconstruction of European society in the shape of independent communes federally associated on the basis of free agreement would counteract the fatal development of the modern great state. Guided by this thought, he opposed the efforts at national unification of Mazzini and Garibaldi with political decentralization and the federalization of the communes, being firmly convinced that only by these means could the higher social culture of European peoples be achieved.

It is significant that it is just the Marxist opponents of the great French thinker who see in these endeavors of Proudhon a proof of his "utopianism," pointing to the fact that social development has actually taken the road of political centralization. As if this were evidence against Proudhon! Have the evils of centralism, which Proudhon clearly foresaw and whose dangers he described so strikingly, been overcome by this development? Or has it overcome them itself? No! And a thousand times no! These evils have since increased to a monstrous degree; they were one of the main causes of the fearful catastrophe of the World War; they are now one of the greatest obstacles to the solution of the international economic crisis. Europe writhes in a thousand spasms under the iron yoke of a senseless bureaucracy which abhors all independent action and would prefer to put all people under the guardianship of the nursery. Such are the fruits of political centralization. If Proudhon had been a fatalist he would have regarded this development of affairs as a "historic necessity" and advised his contemporaries to make terms with it until the famous "change of affirmation into negation" should occur. But being a real fighter he advanced against the evil and tried to persuade his contemporaries to fight it.

Proudhon foresaw all the consequences of the great development of the state and called men's attention to the threatening danger, at the same time showing them a way to halt the evils. That his word was regarded by but few and finally faded out like a voice in the wilderness was not *his* fault. To call him from this "utopian" is a cheap and senseless trick. If so, the physician is also a utopian who from a given diagnosis of disease makes a prognosis and shows the patient a way to halt the evil. Is it the physician's fault if the patient throws his advice to the winds and makes no attempt to avoid the danger?

Proudhon's formulation of the principles of federalism was an attempt to oppose by freedom the arising reaction, and his historic significance consists in his having left his imprint on the labor movement of France and other Latin countries and having tried to steer their socialism into the course of freedom and federalism. Only when the idea of state capitalism in all its various forms and derivatives has been finally overcome will the true significance of Proudhon's intellectual labors be rightly understood. When, later, the International Workingmen's Association came to life, it was the federalistic spirit of the socialists in the Latin countries which gave the great union its real significance and made it the cradle of the modern socialist labor movements in Europe. The International itself was a league of militant labor organizations and groups with socialistic ideas which had founded itself on a federalistic basis. Out of its ranks came the great creative thought of a social renaissance on the basis of a socialism whose libertarian purpose became more marked in each of its conventions and was of the greatest significance for the spiritual development of the great labor movement. But it was almost exclusively the socialists from the Latin countries who inspired these ideas and gave them life. While the social democrats of that period saw in the so-called "folk-state" the future political ideal and so propagated the bourgeois tradition of Jacobinism, the revolutionary socialists of the Latin countries clearly recognized that a new economic order in the socialistic sense demands also a new form of political organization for its unobstructed development. They also recognized that this form of social organization would have nothing in common with the present state system, but called, rather, for its historic dissolution. Thus there developed in the womb of the International the idea of a common administration of social production and general consumption by the workers themselves in the form of free economic groups associated on the basis of federalism, which at the same time were to be entrusted with the political administration of the commune. In this manner it intended to replace the caste of the present party and professional politicians by experts without privileges and supplant the power politics of the state by a peaceful economic order having its basis in the equality of interests and the mutual solidarity of men united in freedom.

About the same time Michael Bakunin had clearly defined the principle of political federalism in his well-known speech at the congress of the Peace and Liberty League (1867) and emphasized especially the significance of the peaceful relationship of the peoples to one another.

> Every centralized state, however liberal it may pretend to be, whatever republican form it may have, is nevertheless an oppressor, an exploiter of the working masses for the benefit of the privileged classes. It needs an army to keep these masses in check, and the existence of this armed force drives it into war. Hence I come to the conclusion that international peace is impossible until the following principle is adopted with all its logical consequences: Every people, whether weak or strong, little or great, every province, every community, must be free and autonomous; free to live and to administer itself according to its interests and special needs. In this right all people and communities are so united that the principle cannot be violated with respect to a single community without endangering all the rest at the same time.

The uprising of the Paris Commune gave the ideas of local autonomy and federalism a mighty impulse in the ranks of the International. When Paris voluntarily gave up its central prerogative over all other communities in France, the commune became for the socialists of the Latin countries the starting point of a new movement which opposed the central unification principle of the state with the federation of the communes. The commune became for them the political unit of the future, the basis of a new social order organically developed from below upwards, and not imposed on men automatically by a central power from above. Thus arose as a social pattern for the future a new concept of social organization, giving the widest scope for the individual initiative of persons and groups, in which, at the same time, the spirit of communion and of general interest for the welfare of all, lives and works in every member of the social union. It is clearly recognizable that the advocates of this idea had in mind these words of Proudhon: "The personality is for me the criterion of the social order. The freer, the more independent, the more enterprising the personality is in society, the better for society."

While the authoritarian wing of the International continued to advocate the necessity of the state and pleaded for centralism, the libertarian section within its body saw in federalism not only a political ideal for the future, but also a basis for their own organization and endeavors; for according to their conception the International was to provide the world a model of a free community, as far as this was at all possible under existing conditions. It was this concept which led to the internal strife between the centralists and federalists which was finally to wreck the International.

The attempt of the London General Council, which was under the immediate intellectual influence of Marx and Engels, to increase its sphere of power and to make the international league of awakened labor subservient to the parliamentary policies of definite parties, naturally led to the sharpest resistance on the part of the liberal-minded federations and sections which adhered to the old principles of the International. Thus happened the great schism of the socialistic labor movement which has not been bridged to this day; for this is a quarrel over inner antagonisms of fundamental significance, and its outcome must have decisive results not only for the labor movement but for the idea of socialism itself. The disastrous war of 1870-71 and the rising reaction in Latin countries after the fall of the Paris Commune, with the revolutionary events in Spain and Italy, where by oppressive laws and brutal persecutions every public activity was inhibited and the International forced into the hiding places of secret societies, have greatly favored the latest developments of the European labor movement.

On July 20, 1870, Karl Marx wrote to Friedrich Engels these words, very characteristic of his personality and his mental attitude:

> The French need a thrashing. If the Prussians are victorious the centralization of state power will be helpful for the centralization of the German working class; furthermore, German predominance will shift the center of gravity of West European labor movements from France to Germany. And one has but to compare the movement from 1866 till today to see that the German working class is in theory and organization superior to the French. Its dominance over the French on the world stage would mean likewise the dominance of our theory over that of Proudhon, etc.[1]

Marx was right. The victory of Germany did in fact mark the turning point in history of the European labor movement. The libertarian socialism of the International was forced into the background by the new state of things and had to abandon the field to the anti-libertarian views of Marxism. Living, creative, unlimited capacity for development of the socialist movement was replaced by a one-sided dogmatism which pretentiously announced itself as science but which in reality was based on

[1] *Der Briefwechsel zwischen Marx und Engels.* Stuttgart, 1913. Volume IV.

a mere historic fatalism leading to the worst fallacies, which slowly stifled every real socialistic idea. Although Marx had in youth exclaimed: "The philosophers have variously interpreted the world, but it is necessary to change it," he himself did nothing during his whole life except to interpret the world and history. He analyzed capitalistic society in his way, and showed a great deal of intellect and enormous learning in doing so, but Proudhon's creative power was denied him. He was, and remained, the analyst—a brilliant and learned analyst, but nothing else. This is the reason why he did not enrich socialism with a single creative thought, but enmeshed the minds of his followers in the fine network of a cunning dialectic which sees in history hardly anything but economics and obstructs every deeper insight into the world of social events. He even rejected and condemned as utopianism every attempt to attain clarity regarding the probable formation of socialistic society. As if it were possible to create anything new without being clear about the direction in which one is going! The belief in the compulsive course of all social phenomena led him to reject every thought about the appropriateness of social events—and yet it is this very thought that is the basis of all cultural activity.

With a change of ideas came also a change in the method of the labor movement. In place of those groups imbued with socialistic ideas and economic fighting organizations in the old sense, in which the men of the International had seen the germs of the coming society and the natural instrument for the reorganization and administration of production, came the present-day labor parties and the parliamentary activity of the working masses. The old socialist doctrine which taught the conquest of industry and of the land was forced gradually more and more into the background, and from now on one spoke only of the conquest of political power and so got completely into the current of capitalistic society.

In Germany, where no other form of the movement had ever been known, this development happened with remarkable quickness, and by its electoral successes had repercussions on the socialist movements of most other countries. Lassalle's powerful activity in Germany had smoothed the way for this new phase of the movement. Lassalle was all his life a passionate worshiper of the idea of the state in the sense of Fichte and Hegel, and had, moreover, appropriated the views of the French state-socialist, Louis Blanc, concerning the social functions of government. In his *Labor Program* he announced to the working class of Germany that the history of humanity had been a constant struggle against nature and against the limitations it had imposed on man. "In this struggle we would never have taken a step forward, nor would ever take one in the future, if we had made it, or wished to make it, alone, as individuals, everyone for himself. It is the state which has the function of bringing about this development of freedom, this evolution of the human race toward freedom."

His adherents were so firmly convinced of this mission of the state, and their faith in the state frequently assumed such fantastic forms, that the liberal press of that time often accused the Lassalle movement of being in Bismarck's pay. Proof of this accusation could never be found, but the curious flirtation of Lassalle with the "social kingdom," which became especially marked in his essay, *The Italian War and the Task of Prussia,* could very easily be ground for such a suspicion.[2]

As the newly created labor parties gradually concentrated all their activities on parliamentary action and maintained that the conquest of political power was the obvious preliminary to the realization of socialism, they created in the course of time an entirely new ideology, which differed essentially from the ideas of the First International. Parliamentarianism, which quickly came to play an important part in the new movement, enticed a number of bourgeois elements and career-seeking intellectuals into the camp of the socialist party, by whom the change of attitude was still further advanced. Thus there developed, in place of the socialism of the old International, a sort of substitute having nothing in common with it but the name. In this manner socialism gradually lost more and more the character of a new cultural ideal for which the artificial frontiers of the state had no meaning. In the minds of the leaders of this new trend, the interests of the national state became blended with the interest and spirit of their party until, gradually, they were no longer able to distinguish between them and became used to viewing the world and things through the glasses of the nationalist state. Thus it was inevitable that the modern labor parties gradually came to fit into the national state machine as a necessary part and greatly contributed to restore to the state the balance of power it had lost.

It would be wrong to regard these peculiar ideas simply as conscious treason on the part of the leaders, as has often been done. The truth is that we are here confronted with a slow assimilation of socialist theory into the thought-world of the bourgeois state, induced by the practical activity of present-day labor parties which necessarily affected the mental attitude of their leaders. The same parties which sallied forth under the flag of socialism to conquer political power saw themselves gradually forced by the iron logic of circumstances into the position where bit by bit they had to abandon their former socialism for bourgeois politics. The more thoughtful of their adherents recognized the danger, and sometimes exhausted themselves in fruitless opposition against the tactics of the

[2] The recently discovered letters between Bismarck and Lassalle published by Gustav Mayer in his valuable essay, *Bismarck and Lassalle,* throw a curious light on Lassalle's personality and are also psychologically of great interest.

party. This was necessarily without result, since it was directed solely against the excrescences of the party system and not against the system itself. Thus the socialist labor parties became, without the great majority of their members being conscious of it, buffers in the fight between capital and labor, political lightning-rods for the security of the capitalist social order.

The attitude of most of these parties during the World War, and especially after the War, proves that our view is not exaggerated, but fully in accord with the facts. In Germany, this development has taken an actually tragic form, with consequences which even today cannot be estimated. The socialist movement of that country had been completely emasculated by long years of parliamentary routine and was no longer capable of a creative act. This especially is the reason why the German revolution was so shockingly poor in real ideas. The old proverb, "Who eats of the pope dies of him," was proved by the socialist movement; it had so long eaten of the state that its inner life force was exhausted and it could no longer accomplish anything of significance.

Socialism could maintain its role as a cultural ideal for the future only by concentrating its whole activity on abolishing monopoly of property together with every form of government of men by men. Not the conquest of power, but its elimination from the life of society, had to remain the great goal for which it strove—which it could never abandon without abandoning itself. Whoever believes that freedom of the personality can find a substitute in equality of possessions has not even grasped the essence of socialism. For freedom there is no substitute; there can be no substitute. Equality of economic conditions for each and all is always a necessary precondition for the freedom of man, but never a substitute for it. Whoever transgresses against freedom transgresses against the spirit of socialism. Socialism means the mutual activity of men toward a common goal with equal rights for all. But solidarity rests on free resolve and can never be compelled without changing into tyranny.

Every true socialistic activity, the smallest as well as the greatest, must therefore be imbued with the thought of opposing monopoly in all its fields—especially in that of economics—and of guarding and enlarging by all possible means the sum of personal freedom within the frame of the social union. Every practical activity tending towards other results is misdirected and useless for real socialists. So must also be rated the idle talk about the "dictatorship of the proletariat" as a transitional condition between capitalism and socialism. History knows no such "transitions." There exist solely more primitive and more complicated forms in the various evolutionary phases of social progress. Every social order is in its original form of expression naturally imperfect; nevertheless, all further possibilities of development towards a future structure must be contained in each of its newly created institutions, just as already in the embryo the whole creature is foreshadowed. Every attempt to incorporate into a new order of things the essential parts of an old one which has outlived itself has up to now led always to the same negative result. Either such attempts were at the very beginning thwarted by the youthful vigor of social reconstruction or the tender sprouts and hopeful beginnings of the new forms were so confined and hindered in their natural growth by the old that they gradually declined and their inner life-force slowly died out.

When Lenin—much in the style of Mussolini—dared to say that "freedom is a bourgeois prejudice," he only proved that his spirit was quite incapable of rising to socialism, but had remained stuck in the old ideas of Jacobinism. Anyway, it is nonsense to speak of libertarian and authoritarian socialism. Socialism will either be free or it will not be at all.

The two great political trends of thought of liberalism and democracy had a strong influence on the development of the socialist movement. Democracy with its state-affirming principles and its effort to subject the individual to the demands of an imaginary "common will" needs must affect such a movement as socialism most disastrously by endowing it with the idea of adding to the realms the state already ruled the enormous realm of economics, endowing it with a power it never possessed before. Today it appears ever more clearly—and the experiences in Russia have proved it—that such endeavors can never lead to socialism, but must inevitably result in the grotesque malformation of state capitalism.

On the other hand, socialism vitalized by liberalism logically leads to the ideas of Godwin, Proudhon, Bakunin and their successors. The idea of reducing the state's sphere of activity to a minimum, itself contains the germ of a much more far-reaching thought, namely, to overthrow the state entirely and to eliminate the will to power from human society. Democratic socialism has contributed enormously to confirm again the vain belief in the state, and in its further development must logically lead to state capitalism. Socialism inspired by liberal ideas, however, leads in a straight line to anarchism, meaning by that, a social condition where man is no longer subject to the guardianship of a higher power and where all relations between him and his kind are self-regulated by mutual agreement.

Liberalism alone could not attain this highest phase of definite intellectual development for the reason that it had too little regard for the economic side of the question, as has already been explained in another place. Only on the basis of fellowship in labor and the community of all social interests is freedom possible; there can be no freedom for the individual without justice for all. For personal freedom also has its roots in man's social consciousness and receives real meaning only from it. The idea of anarchism is the synthesis of liberalism and socialism, liberation of economics from the fetters of politics, liberation of culture from all political power, liberation of man by solidaric union with his kind. For, as Proudhon says: "Seen from the social viewpoint freedom and solidarity are but different expressions of the same concept. By the freedom of each finding in the freedom of others no longer a limit, as the declaration of rights of 1793 says, but a support. The freest man is the one who has the most relations with his fellow men."

Chapter 15

FASCISM AS THE LAST RESULT OF NATIONALISTIC IDEOLOGY. ITS FIGHT
AGAINST THE WORLD OF LIBERAL IDEAS. MUSSOLINI AS OPPONENT OF
THE STATE. HIS POLITICAL CHANGE. GIOVANNI GENTILE, THE PHILOS-
OPHER OF FASCISM. NATIONALISM AS WILL FOR THE STATE. THE FASCIST
STATE IDEA AND MODERN MONOPOLY CAPITALISM. CONTEMPORARY
ECONOMIC BARBARISM. THE STATE AS DESTROYER OF THE COM-
MUNITY. FREEDOM AS SOCIAL CEMENT. THE EDUCATION OF MODERN
MASS-MAN IN LEADING STRINGS. THE FIGHT AGAINST PERSONALITY.
THE TOTALITARIAN STATE. NATIONALISM AS A POLITICAL REVEALED
RELIGION. SUBMERSION OF CULTURE. DECLINE OR RISE?

MODERN nationalism, which has found its fullest expression in Italian
fascism and German National Socialism, is the mortal enemy of every
liberal thought. The complete elimination of all libertarian thought is for
its advocates the first preliminary to the "awakening of the nation,"
whereby in Germany, most strangely, liberalism and Marxism are thrown
into one pot—a fact which, however, need no longer surprise us when we
know how violently the heralds of the Third Reich deal with facts, ideas
and persons. That Marxism, like democracy and nationalism, proceeds in
its fundamental ideas from a collective concept, namely from the class,
and for this very reason can have no relationship with liberalism, does not
trouble its pious Hitlerite opponents of today in the least.

That modern nationalism in its extreme fanaticism for the state has
no use for liberal ideas is readily understandable. Less clear is the assertion of its leaders that the modern state is thoroughly infected with liberal
ideas and has for this reason lost its former political significance. The fact
is that the political development of the last hundred and fifty years was
not along the lines that liberalism had hoped for. The idea of reducing the
functions of the state as much as possible and of limiting its sphere to a
minimum has not been realized. The state's field of activity was not laid
fallow; on the contrary, it was mightily extended and multiplied, and the
so-called "liberal parties," which gradually got deeper and deeper into
the current of democracy, have contributed abundantly to this end. In
reality the state has not become liberalized but only democratized. Its

influence on the personal life of man has not been reduced; on the contrary, it has steadily grown.

There was a time when one could hold the opinion that the "sovereignty of the nation" was quite different from the sovereignty of the hereditary monarch and that, therefore, the power of the state would be weakened. While democracy was still fighting for recognition, such an opinion might have had a certain justification. But that time is long past; nothing has so confirmed the internal and external security of the state as the religious belief in the sovereignty of the nation, confirmed and sanctioned by the universal franchise. That this is also a religious concept of political nature is undeniable. Even Clémenceau when, innerly lonely and embittered, he reached the end of his career, expressed himself in this wise: "The popular vote is a toy of which one soon tires; but one must not say this aloud, for the people must have a religion. Sad it is. . . . Sad but true." [1]

Liberalism was the outcry of the human personality against the all-leveling endeavors of absolute rule, and later against the extreme centralism and blind belief in the state of Jacobinism and its various democratic offshoots. In this sense it was still conceived by Mill, Buckle and Spencer. Even Mussolini, now the bitterest enemy of liberalism, was not so long ago one of the most passionate advocates of liberal ideas; he wrote:

> The state, with its monstrous terrific machine, gives us a feeling of suffocation. The state was endurable for the individual as long as it was content to be soldier and policeman; today the state is everything, banker, usurer, gambling den proprietor, shipowner, procurer, insurance agent, postman, railroader, entrepreneur, teacher, professor, tobacco merchant, and countless other things in addition to its former functions of policeman, judge, jailer, and tax collector. The state, this Moloch of frightful countenance, receives everything, does everything, knows everything, and ruins everything. Every state function is a misfortune. State art is a misfortune, state ownership of shipping, state victualizing—the litany could be extended indefinitely. . . . If men had but a faint idea of the abyss toward which they are moving the number of suicides would increase, for we are approaching a complete destruction of human personality. The state is that frightful machine which swallows living men and spews them out again as dead ciphers. Human life has now no secrets, no intimacy, neither in material affairs nor in spiritual; all corners are smelled into, all movements measured; everyone is locked into his cell and numbered, just as in a prison. [2]

This was written a few years before the "March on Rome"; the new revelation, therefore, came quite quickly to Mussolini, as so many

---

[1] Jean Martet, *Clémenceau Speaks.* Berlin, 1930, p. 151.
[2] *Popolo d'Italia,* April 6, 1920.

others; in fact the so-called "state concept of fascism" put in an appearance only after Il Duce had attained power. Until then the fascist movement glittered in all the colors of the rainbow as, not so long ago, did National Socialism in Germany. It really had no definite character. Its ideology was a motley mixture of intellectual elements from all sorts of sources. What gave it power was the brutality of its methods. Its reckless violence could have no regard for the opinions of others just because it had none of its own. What the state still lacked of being a perfect prison the fascist dictatorship has given it in abundance. Mussolini's liberal clamor stopped immediately as soon as the dictator had the state power in Italy firmly in his hands. Viewing Mussolini's rapid change of opinion about the meaning of the state one involuntarily remembers the expression of the youthful Marx: "No man fights against freedom; at the most he fights against the freedom of others. Every kind of freedom has, therefore, always existed; sometimes as special privilege, at other times as general right."

Mussolini has in fact made of freedom a privilege for himself, and to do this has brought about the most brutal suppression of all others; for freedom which tries to replace man's responsibility towards his fellow men by the senseless dictum of authority is sheer willfulness and a denial of all justice and all humanity. But even despotism needs to justify itself to the people whom it violates. To meet this necessity the state concept of fascism was born.

At the meeting in Berlin of the International Hegel Congress in 1931, Giovanni Gentile, the state-philosopher of fascist Italy, developed his conception of the nature of the state, culminating in the idea of the so-called "totalitarian state." Gentile hailed Hegel as the first and real founder of the state concept, and compared his state theory with the concept of the state as based on natural right and mutual agreement. The state, he maintained, is in the light of the latter concept merely the limit with which the natural and immediate freedom of the individual must be content if anything like a communal life is to be made possible. According to this doctrine the state is only a means for the improvement of man's condition, which in its natural origin is not maintainable—is, therefore, something negative, a virtue born of necessity. Hegel overthrew this centuries-old doctrine. He was the first to regard the state as the highest form of the objective intellect. He was the first to understand that only in the state can truly ethical self-consciousness be realized. But Gentile was not content with this endorsement of Hegel's state concept; he tried even to excel it. He criticized Hegel because, while he regarded the state as the highest form of the objective intellect, he still placed over the objective intellect the sphere of the absolute intellect; so that art, religion, philosophy, which according to Hegel belong to the latter intellectual realm, were in a certain conflict with the state. The modern state theory,

Gentile held, should so work out these conflicts that the values of art, religion and philosophy would also be the property of the state. Only then could the state be regarded as the highest form of the human intellect, being founded not on separateness, but on the common, the eternal, will and the highest form of generality.[3]

The purpose of the fascist state-philosopher is quite clear. If for Hegel the state was "God on earth," then Gentile would like to raise it to the position of the eternal and *only* God, who will endure no other gods above him, or even beside him, and absolutely dominates every field of human thought and human activity. This is the last word of a trend of political thought which in its abstract extreme loses sight of everything human and has concern for the individual only in so far as he serves as a sacrifice to be thrown into the glowing arms of the insatiable Moloch. Modern nationalism is only will-toward-the-state-at-any-price and complete absorption of man in the higher ends of power. It is of the utmost significance that modern nationalism does not spring from love towards one's own country or one's own people. On the contrary, it has its roots in the ambitious plans of a minority lusting for dictatorship and determined to impose upon the people a certain form of the state, even though this be entirely contrary to the will of the majority. Blind belief in the magic power of a national dictatorship is to replace for man the love of home and the feeling of the spiritual culture of his time; love of fellow man is to be crushed by "the greatness of the state," for which individuals are to serve as fodder.

Here is the distinction between the nationalism of a past age, which found its representatives in men like Mazzini and Garibaldi, and the definitely counter-revolutionary tendencies of modern fascism which today raises its head ever more threateningly. In his famous manifesto of June 6, 1862, Mazzini opposed the government of Victor Emmanuel, accusing it of treason and counter-revolutionary efforts against the unity of Italy, thus clearly making a distinction between the nation and Italian unity. His slogan, "God and the People!"—whatever one may think of it—was meant to inform the world that the ideas he followed emanated from the people and were endorsed by them. Undoubtedly Mazzini's doctrine contained the germ of a new form of human slavery, but he acted in good faith and could not foresee the historic development of his work for national democracy. How honestly he was devoted to this is most clearly shown by the difference between him and Cavour, who fully realized the significance of the national unification movement and therefore on principle opposed the "political romanticism" of Mazzini. Mazzini, Cavour said, forgot the state in his constant affirmation of freedom.

[3] We are here following the reports of the Congress in the *Deutsche Allgemeine Zeitung*, evening edition of October 21, 1931.

It is certain that the patriots of that time regarded the state and the nationalistic aims of the people as quite different things. This attitude doubtless sprang from an erroneous interpretation of historical facts, but it is just this erroneous conclusion which brings these men of "Young Europe" humanly closer to us, for no one will doubt their sincere love of the people. Modern nationalism is wholly lacking in such love, and though its representatives utter the word ever so frequently one always perceives its false ring and realizes that there is no genuine feeling in it. The nationalism of today swears only by the state and brands its own fellow-folk as traitors to their country if they resist the political aims of the national dictatorship or even merely refuse to endorse its plans.

The influence of the liberal ideas of the last century had at least brought it about that even the conservative elements in society were convinced that the state existed for the citizens. Fascism, however, announces with brutal frankness that the purpose of the individual consists in being useful to the state. "Everything for the state, nothing outside of the state, nothing against the state!" as Mussolini has expressed it. This is the last word of a nationalist metaphysics which in the fascist movements of the present has assumed a frightfully concrete form. While this has always been the hidden meaning of all nationalist theories, it has now become their clearly expressed aim. That they have so definitely outlined this aim is the only merit of its present representatives, who in Italy, and even more in Germany, are so dearly loved and so freely supported by the owners of the capitalistic economic system—because they have been so subservient to the new monopoly capitalism and have with all their power furthered its plans for the erection of a system of industrial serfdom.

For along with the principles of political liberalism the ideas of economic liberalism are also to be abrogated. Just as the political fascism of today tries to preach to man the new gospel that he can claim a right to live only in so far as he serves as raw material for the state, so also the modern industrial fascism tries to demonstrate to the world that industry does not exist for man, but man for industry, and that he exists merely to be useful to it. If fascism has assumed in Germany its most frightful and inhuman forms, this is largely the result of the barbaric ideas of German economic theoreticians and leading industrialists who have, so to speak, shown that fascism is the road. German captains of industry of world-wide fame, like Hugo Stinnes, Fritz Thyssen, Ernst von Borsig and many others, have by the brutal frankness of their opinions again furnished a proof into what abysses of cold contempt of humanity the human spirit can sink itself when it has abandoned all social feeling and deals with living men as if they were dead ciphers. In German scholarship there were always to be found "unprejudiced minds" who were ready to give the most monstrous and inhuman theories a "scientific basis."

Thus Professor Karl Schreber of the Institute of Technology at Aachen said that *for the modern worker the standard of living of the prehistoric Neanderthal man is quite appropriate and that for him the possibility of development cannot be considered at all.*

Similar ideas were advanced by Professor Ernst Horneffer of the University of Giessen, who in conventions of the German industrialists frequently plays star parts. At one of these meetings he declared: "The danger of the social movement can only be obviated by a division among the masses. Life's table is occupied to the very last place, and consequently industry can never guarantee to its employees anything more than bare existence. This is an unbreakable natural law. Hence all social politics is unspeakable stupidity."

Herr Horneffer has since made these humanitarian doctrines unmistakably clear in a special essay, *Socialism and the Death Struggle of German Industry,* in which he reaches the following conclusions:

> I maintain that the economic condition of the worker, basically and essentially, by and large, can in reality not be changed. The workers will once and for all have to be content with their economic condition, that is, with a wage only sufficient for the most necessary, the most urgent, the most indispensable requirements of life, in fact barely sufficient to sustain life. A fundamental change in the workers' economic status, their rise to an essentially different state of economic welfare, can never happen; this is a desire impossible of fulfillment for all time.

To the objection that under these circumstances it might easily happen that the wage would not suffice even for the most necessary demands of life the learned professor replies, with enviable peace of soul, that in such a case public charity would have to help, and if this did not suffice then the state as representative of the moral spirit of the people must step into the breach. Dr. F. Giese of the Technical High School of Stuttgart, who is an especially urgent advocate of the rationalization of industry according to "scientific methods," dealt with the early elimination of the modern laborer from every calling with these dry words:

> The directors of industry can view it as a simple biological law that today everywhere man's capacity for production in the competitive struggle must soon reach its end. The dyeing of the hair is customary in America, but we do not mistake this for a natural evolution toward which pity and patience would in practice perhaps be the worst sort of procedure for a technical treatment of men.[4]

The phrase, "technical treatment of men," is especially significant; it shows with frightful clearness into what byways capitalistic industrialism

[4] The meaning of the last sentence is far from clear in the German original.— *Translator*

has already led. Reading a heart effusion like the above, one comes to realize the deep significance of what Bakunin said regarding the prospects of government by pure scientists. The consequences of such an experiment would indeed be unthinkable.

That a system of mental gymnastics as senseless as it is brutal can today proudly proclaim itself as scientific knowledge is a proof of the asocial spirit of the time, which by the extremity of its system of mass exploitation and by its blind belief in the state has suppressed all of man's natural relations with his fellow men and forcibly torn the individual from the environment in which he had his deepest roots. For the assertion of fascism that liberalism, and man's need of freedom incorporated in it, atomized society and resolved it into its elements, while the state, so to speak, surrounded human groupings with a protective frame and thereby prevented the community from falling apart, is a specious fraud based at best on a gross self-deception.

Not the desire for freedom has atomized society and awakened asocial instincts in man, but the shocking inequality of economic conditions and, above all, the state, which bred the monopoly whose festering, cancerous growth has destroyed the fine cellular tissue of social relationships. If the social urge were not a natural need of man which he received at the very threshold of humanity as a legacy from hoary ancestors and which he has since uninterruptedly developed and extended, then not even the state would have been able to draw men into a closer union. For one can create no community by forcibly chaining elements which are basically antagonistic. It is true that one can compel men to fulfill certain duties if one has the necessary power, but one will never be able to induce them to perform the compulsory task with love and from inner desire. These are things no state can compel, be its power ever so great—for these there is necessary above all *the feeling of social union and of the innate relationship of man to man.*

Compulsion does not unite, compulsion only separates men; for it lacks the inner drive of all social unions—the understanding which recognizes the facts and the sympathy which comprehends the feeling of the fellow man because it feels itself related to him. By subjecting men to a common compulsion one does not bring them closer to one another, rather one creates estrangements between them and breeds impulses of selfishness and separation. Social ties have permanence and completely fulfill their purpose only when they are based on good will and spring from the needs of men. Only under such conditions is a relationship possible where social union and the freedom of the individual are so closely intergrown that they can no longer be recognized as separate entities.

Just as in every revealed religion the individual has to win the promised heavenly kingdom for himself and does not concern himself too greatly about the salvation of others, being sufficiently occupied with achieving his own, so also within the state man tries to find ways and means of adjusting himself without cudgeling his brain too much about whether others succeed in doing so or not. It is the state which on principle undermines man's social feeling by assuming the part of adjuster in all affairs and trying to reduce them to the same formula, which is for its supporters the measure of all things. The more easily the state disposes of the personal needs of the citizens, the deeper and more ruthlessly it dips into their individual lives and disregards their private rights, the more successfully it stifles in them the feeling of social union, the easier it is for it to dissolve society into its separate parts and incorporate them as lifeless accessories into the gears of the political machine.

Modern technology is about to construct the "mechanical man" and has already achieved some very pretty results in this field. We already have automatons in human form which move to and fro with their iron limbs and perform certain services—give correct change, and other things of that sort. There is something uncanny about this invention which gives the illusion of calculated human action; yet it is only a concealed clockwork that without opposition obeys its master's will. But it would seem that the mechanical man is something more than a bizarre notion of modern technology. If the people of the European-American cultural realm do not within reasonable time revert to their best traditions there is real danger that we shall rush on to the era of the mechanical man with giant strides.

The modern "mass man," this uprooted fellow traveler of modern technology in the age of capitalism, who is almost completely controlled by external influences and whirled up and down by every mood of the moment—because his soul is atrophied and he has lost that inner balance which can maintain itself only in a true communion—already comes dangerously close to the mechanical man. Capitalistic giant industry, division of labor, now achieving its greatest triumph in the Taylor system and the so-called rationalization of industry, a dreary barracks system drilled into the drafted citizens, the connected modern educational drill and all that is related to it—these are phenomena whose importance must not be underestimated while we are inquiring about the inner connections among existing conditions. But modern nationalism with its outspoken antagonism to freedom and its senseless, utterly extreme militaristic attitude, is only the bridge to a great and soulless automatism which would really lead to the already announced "Decline of the West" if not halted in time. For the present, however, we do not believe in such a gloomy future; rather, we are firmly convinced that even today mankind carries within it a multitude of hidden forces and creative impulses which will enable it victoriously to surmount the calamitous crisis now threatening all human culture.

What today surrounds us on all sides is comparable to a dreary chaos in which all the germs of social decay have fully ripened. And yet there are within the mad whirl of events also numerous beginnings of a new order developing apart from the ways of parties and of political life, hopefully and joyfully pointing toward the future. To further these new beginnings, to nurse and strengthen them so that they may not untimely perish, is today the noblest task of every fighting man, of every man who, though convinced of the instability of present conditions, refuses in tame submission to let fate take its course, but is ever on the lookout for something that promises a new upsurge of spiritual and social culture. But such an upsurge can occur only under the sign of freedom and social union, for only out of these can grow that deepest and purest yearning for social justice which finds expression in the social collaboration of men and smoothes the way for a new community. The leaders of the fascist and nationalist reactions know this very well; hence, they hate freedom as a sin against the holy spirit of the nation, which is in fact but their own evil spirit. So, Mussolini declares:

> Men are tired of freedom. They have celebrated an orgy with it. Freedom is today no longer the chaste and severe virgin for which the generations of the first half of the last century fought and died. For the enterprising, restless, rough youth now appearing in the dawn of modern history there are other values which have a much greater magic: *Order, Hierarchy, Discipline.* One must recognize once and for all that fascism knows no idols, worships no fetishes. Over the more or less decayed corpse of the goddess of freedom it has already marched, and it will if necessary return and march over it again. . . . Facts speak louder than the book; experience means more than a doctrine. The great experience of the after effects of the war now appearing before our eyes shows the decline of liberalism. In Russia and Italy it has been shown that one can rule without, over, and against the whole liberal ideology. Communism and fascism stand apart from liberalism.[5]

This is quite clear, even though the conclusions which Mussolini draws from this, his latest understanding, are open to refutation. That "one can rule against the whole liberal ideology" was known long before him; every rulership based on force had adopted this principle. The Holy Alliance was founded only for the purpose of eliminating from Europe the liberal ideas of 1789, in which year the first "declaration of human and civil rights" had been announced, and Metternich left no means untried to transform this tacit wish of the despots into reality. But in the long run his anti-humanitarian attempts had as little success as those of Napoleon before him, who had expressed opinions about freedom quite similar

[5] "Compulsion and Consent," in the fascist periodical, *Gerarchia*, April, 1922.

to those of Mussolini, and who had worked like one possessed towards the end of making every human emotion, every pulse-beat of social life, conform to the rhythm of his gigantic state machine.

But even the proud boast of fascism that it "knows no idols, worships no fetishes," loses all significance; for fascism has only thrown the idols from their pedestals, tumbled the pedestals into the dust, and put in their place a gigantic Moloch which seizes on the soul of man and bends his spirit beneath a Caudine yoke: The state everything; man nothing! The citizen's life aim is to find fulfillment in being employed by the state—"swallowed by the machine and spewed out again as dead ciphers." This constitutes the whole task of the so-called "totalitarian state" which has been set up in Italy and Germany. To achieve this end the spirit has been violated, all human feeling enchained, and the young seed from which the future was to grow crushed with shameless brutality. Not alone labor movements of whatever tendency became victims of the fascist dictatorship; everyone who dared to kick against the pricks or even to assume a neutral attitude towards the new rulers had to learn in his own person how fascism "marches over the body of freedom."

Art, the theater, science, literature and philosophy came under the shameful guardianship of a régime whose ignorant leaders hesitated at no crime to achieve power and confirm themselves in their new positions. The number of victims who in those bloody days when fascism seized power in Italy (and later on in both Italy and Germany) were murdered by inhuman wretches, runs into the thousands. Many thousands of innocent men were expelled from their homes and chased into exile, among them a long line of prominent scholars and artists of world-wide reputation, who in any other nation would have been regarded as honors to the land. Barbaric hordes forced themselves into the homes of peaceful citizens, plundered their libraries, and publicly burned hundreds of thousands of the best books. Other thousands were torn from the bosoms of their families, dragged into concentration camps where their human dignity was daily trodden under foot, and many were slowly tortured to death by cowardly hangmen or driven to suicide.

In Germany this madness assumed especially vicious forms because of the artificially trained racial fanaticism, directed mainly against the Jewish people. The barbarism of past centuries awoke suddenly to new life. A regular flood of vulgar incendiary pamphlets appealing to men's lowest instincts descended on Germany and muddied all the channels of public opinion.[6]

[6] Here is one little specimen from among thousands:
"There are two sorts of anti-Semitism, the higher and the lower. The first is intellectual, human, is a palliative, and consists in making laws which limit the Jewish sphere of influence. These laws make it possible for Jews and Gentiles to live

Realms which the wildest despotism had up to now left untouched, as, for example, the relations between the sexes, are now in Germany subject to the supervision of the state. Special "race officials" are appointed to guard the people from "racial shame," and to brand marriages between Jews or colored people and so-called "Aryans" as crimes, and to punish them. So that sexual ethics have at last happily arrived at the level of cattle-breeding. Such are the blessings of Hitler's totalitarian state.

Fascism has been hailed as the beginning of an anti-liberal epoch in European history springing from the masses themselves, and hence a proof that the "time of the individual" is past. But in reality there stands also behind this movement only the striving for political power of a small minority which has been clever enough to seize upon an exceptional situation for its special purposes. In this instance also the words of the youthful General Bonaparte prove themselves true: "Give the people a toy; they will pass the time with it and allow themselves to be led, provided that the final goal is cleverly hidden from them." And cleverly to hide this final goal there is no better means than to approach the mass from the religious side and imbue it with the belief that it is a specially selected tool of a higher power and serves a holy purpose which really gives its life content and color. This interweaving of the fascist movement with the religious feeling of the masses constitutes its real strength. For fascism also is only a religious mass movement in political guise, and its leaders neglect no means to preserve this character for it also in the future.

The French Professor Verne of the medical faculty of the Sorbonne, who was a delegate to the International Congress for the Advancement of Science meeting in Bologna in 1927, described in a French paper, *Le Quotidien*, the strange impression he received in Italy:

> In Bologna we had the impression of being in a city of ecstasy. The city's walls were completely covered with posters, which give it a mystical character: *Dio ce l'ha dato; quai a chi lo tocca!* ("God has sent him to us; woe to him who attacks him!") The picture of Il Duce was to be seen in all shop windows. The symbol of fascism, a shining emblem, was erected on all monuments, even on the celebrated tower of Bologna.

In these words of the French scholar is mirrored the spirit of a movement which finds its strongest support in the primitive devotional

together. Such measures are comparable to a board which is tied to the horns of cattle so that they may not hurt the others.—There is another sort of anti-Semitism which consists in the Gentiles who have reached the limit of pain, poverty, and patience simply killing the Jews. This anti-Semitism may be terrible, but its consequences are blessed. It simply cuts the knot of the Jewish question by destroying everything Jewish. It always arises from below, from the mass of the people, but is given from above, from God himself, and its effects have the enormous power of a natural force whose secret we have not yet fathomed." Marianne Obuchow, *Die Internationale Pest*, Berlin, p. 22.

needs of the masses and can only affect large sections of the population so powerfully because it most nearly satisfies their belief in miracles after they had felt themselves disillusioned of all the others.

We now observe the same phenomenon in Germany, where nationalism in an astonishingly short time developed into a gigantic movement and imbued millions of men with a blind ecstasy, wherein with faithful ardor they hoped for the coming of the Third Reich, expecting from a man who was totally unknown a few years ago, and had up to then given not the slightest proof of any creative capacity, that he would end all their distress. This movement also is in the last analysis but an instrument for the acquisition of political power by a small caste. For retrieving the position they had lost after the war every means was proper to them by which they might hope "cleverly to hide the final goal," as the cunning Bonaparte had liked to put it.

But the movement itself has all the marks of a religious mass delusion consciously fostered by its instigators to frighten their opponents and to drive them from the field. Even a conservative paper like the *Tägliche Rundschau*, some time before Hitler reached power, characterized the religious obsession of the National Socialist movement thus:

> But as to degree of veneration, Hitler leaves the Pope far behind. Just read his national organ, the *Völkische Beobachter*. Day after day tens of thousands worship him. Childish innocence heaps flowers on him. Heaven sends him "Hitler weather." His airplane defies the threatening elements. Every number of his paper shows the *Führer* in new attitudes under the spotlight. Happy he who has looked into his eyes! In his name we today in Germany wish one another and Germany "Good Luck!" "*Heil Hitler!*" Babies are given his auspicious name. Before his image fond souls seek exaltation at their domestic altars. In his paper we read about "Our Most Exalted Leader," with careful capitalization of these words designating Hitler. All this would be impossible if Hitler did not encourage this apotheosis. . . . With what religious fervor his masses believe in his mission to his coming Reich is shown by this version of the Lord's Prayer circulated among groups of Hitlerite girls:
>
> "Adolf Hitler, thou art our Great Leader. Thy name makes thy foes tremble. Thy Third Reich come. Thy will alone be law on earth. Let us daily hear thy voice, and command us through thy leaders, whom we promise to obey at the forfeit of our lives. This we vow thee! Heil Hitler!"

One might calmly overlook this blind religious fervor, which in its childish helplessness seems almost harmless; but this apparent harmlessness disappears immediately when the fanaticism of the enthusiasts serves the mighty and the power-seeking as a tool for their secret plans. For this deluded faith of the immature, fed from the hidden sources of religious feeling, is urged into wild frenzy and forged into a weapon of irresistible power, clearing the way for every evil. Do not tell us that it is the frightful material need of our day which is alone responsible for this mass delusion, robbing men weakened by long years of misery of their reasoning power and making them trust anyone who feeds their hungry longing with alluring promises. The war frenzy of 1914, which set the whole world into a crazy whirl and made men inaccessible to all appeals of reason, was released at a time when the people were materially much better off and the spectre of economic insecurity was not haunting them all the time. This proves that these phenomena cannot be explained solely on economic grounds, and that in the subconsciousness of men there are hidden forces which cannot be grasped logically. It is the religious urge which still lives in men today, although the forms of faith have changed. The Crusaders' cry, "God wills it!" would hardly raise an echo in Europe today, but there are still millions of men who are ready for anything *if the nation wills it!* Religious feeling has assumed political forms, and the political man today confronts the natural man just as antagonistically as did the man of past centuries who was held in the grip of the church's dogmatism.

By itself the mass delusion of the faithful would be rather unimportant; it always delves among the springs of the miraculous and is little inclined toward practical considerations. But the purposes of those to whom this delusion serves as means to an end are more important, even though in the whirl of mass events their secret motives are not generally recognized. And here lies the danger. The absolute despot of past times might claim to have his power by the grace of God, but the consequences of his acts always reacted on his own person; for before the world his name had to cover everything, both right and wrong, since his will was the highest law. But under cover of the nation everything can be hid. The national flag covers every injustice, every inhumanity, every lie, every outrage, every crime. The collective responsibility of the nation kills the sense of justice of the individual and brings man to the point where he overlooks injustice done; where, indeed, it may appear to him a meritorious act if committed in the interest of the nation.

"And the idea of the nation," says the Indian poet-philosopher, Tagore, "is one of the most powerful anaesthetics that man has ever invented. Under the influence of its fumes the whole people can carry out its systematic program of the most virulent self-seeking without being in the least aware of its moral perversion—in fact, feeling dangerously resentful when it is pointed out." [7]

Tagore called the nation "organized selfishness." The term is well chosen, but we must not forget that we are always dealing with the organized selfishness of privileged minorities which hide behind the skirts of

[7] Rabindranath Tagore, *Nationalism*. New York, 1917, p. 57.

the nation, hide behind the credulity of the masses. We speak of national interests, national capital, national spheres of interest, national honor, and national spirit; but we forget that behind all this there are hidden merely the selfish interests of power-loving politicians and money loving business men for whom the nation is a convenient cover to hide their personal greed and their schemes for political power from the eyes of the world.

The unexpected development of capitalist industrialism has furthered the possibility of national mass suggestion in a measure undreamed of before. In the modern great cities and centers of industrial activity live, closely crowded, millions of men who by the pressure of the radio, cinema, education, party, and a hundred other means are constantly drilled spiritually and mentally into a definite, prescribed attitude and robbed of their personal, independent lives. In the processes of capitalistic giant industry labor has become soulless and has lost for the individual the quality of creative joy. By becoming a dreary end-in-itself it has degraded man into an eternal galley slave and robbed him of that which is most precious, the inner joy of accomplished work, the creative urge of the personality. The individual feels himself to be only an insignificant element of a gigantic mechanism in whose dull monotone every personal note dies out.

While man was subduing the forces of nature, he forgot to give to his actions an ethical content and to make his mental acquisitions serviceable to the community. He himself became the slave of the tool he had created. It is this steady, enormous burden of the machine which weighs us down and makes our life a hell. We have ceased to be *men* and have become instead professional men, business men, party men. To preserve our "national individuality," we have been forced into the strait-jacket of the nation; our humanity has gone to the dogs; our relation to other nations has been changed into suspicion and hate. To protect the nation we sacrifice year by year enormous sums of our income, while the people sink into deeper and deeper misery. Every country resembles an armed camp and watches with inner fear and deadly suspicion every movement of its neighbor, but is always ready to participate in a conspiracy against him or to enrich itself at his expense. Hence, it must always be careful to entrust its affairs to men of elastic conscience, for only those have a fair prospect of maintaining themselves in the eternal cabals of internal and external politics. Saint-Simon recognized this clearly when he said: "Every people which embarks on conquest is compelled to let loose its most evil passions, is compelled to give its highest positions to men of violent character, to those who display the most cunning."

And added to all this is the constant dread of war, whose horrible consequences become every day more unimaginable and dreadful. Even our reciprocity treaties and agreements with other nations bring us no relief, for they are as a rule made with definite ulterior motives. Our national politics are supported by the most dangerous selfishness and can, therefore, never lead to effective weakening of national antagonisms, let alone to their long-desired total elimination.

On the other hand, we have increased and developed our technical ability to a degree which appears almost fantastic, and yet man has not become richer thereby; on the contrary he has become poorer. Our whole industry is in a state of constant insecurity. And while billions of wealth are criminally destroyed in order to maintain prices, in every country millions of men live in the most frightful poverty or perish miserably in a world of abundance and so-called "over-production." The machine, which was to have made work easier for men, has made it harder and has gradually changed its inventor himself into a machine who must adjust himself to every motion of the steel gears and levers. And just as they calculate the capacity of the marvelous mechanism to the tiniest fraction, they also calculate the muscle and nerve force of the living producers by definite scientific methods and will not realize that thereby they rob him of his soul and most deeply defile his humanity. We have come more and more under the dominance of mechanics and sacrificed living humanity to the dead rhythm of the machine without most of us even being conscious of the monstrosity of the procedure. Hence we frequently deal with such matters with indifference and in cold blood as if we handled dead things and not the destinies of men.

To maintain this state of things we make all our achievements in science and technology serve organized mass murder; we educate our youth into uniformed killers, deliver the people to the soulless tyranny of a bureaucracy, put men from the cradle to the grave under police supervision, erect everywhere jails and penitentiaries, and fill every land with whole armies of informers and spies. Should not such "order," from whose infected womb are born eternally brutal power, injustice, lies, crime and moral rottenness—like poisonous germs of destructive plagues—gradually convince even conservative minds that it is order too dearly bought?

The growth of technology at the expense of human personality, and especially the fatalistic submission with which the great majority surrender to this condition, is the reason why the desire for freedom is less alive among men today and has with many of them given place completely to a desire for economic security. This phenomenon need not appear so strange, for our whole evolution has reached a stage where nearly every man is either ruler or ruled; sometimes he is both. By this the attitude of dependence has been greatly strengthened, for a truly free man does not like to play the part of either the ruler or the ruled. He is, above all, concerned with making his inner values and personal powers effective in such a way as to permit him to use his own judgment in all affairs and to be independent in action. Constant tutelage of our acting and thinking has made us weak and irresponsible; hence, the continued cry for the strong man who is to put an end to our distress. This call for a dictator is not a sign of strength, but a proof of inner lack of assurance and of weakness, even though those who utter it earnestly try to give themselves the appearance of resolution. What man most lacks he most desires. When one feels himself weak he seeks salvation from another's strength; when one is cowardly or too timid to move one's own hands for the forging of one's fate, one entrusts it to another. How right was Seume when he said: "The nation which can only be saved by one man and wants to be saved that way deserves a whipping!"

No, the way to health can only lie in the direction of freedom, for every dictatorship is based on an extreme attitude of dependence which can never further the cause of liberation. Even when dictatorship is regarded as only a transitional state necessary to reach a desired goal, the practical activity of its leaders, even if they really have the honest intention to serve the cause of the people, forces them always farther from their original aim; not only because every provisional government, as Proudhon says, always strives to make itself permanent, but most of all because all power is inherently uncreative and therefore incites to misuse. One may think of using power as a means to an end, but the means itself soon grows into a selfish end before which all others vanish. It is just *because* power is unfruitful and cannot give birth to anything creative itself that it is compelled to draft the creative forces of society into its service. It is compelled to put on a false garment to hide its own weakness, and this circumstance seduces its leaders into false promises and conscious deception. By striving to make the creative force of the community subservient to its special ends it kills the deepest roots of this force and chokes the sources of all creative activity, which, while it welcomes stimulation, will not endure compulsion.

A people cannot be liberated by subjecting it to a new and greater power and thus starting again around the vicious circle of stupidity. Every form of dependency leads inevitably to a new system of slavery—dictatorship more than any other form of government, because it forcibly suppresses every adverse judgment upon the activity of its leaders and so inhibits in advance any better understanding. Every condition of dependence, however, has its roots in man's religious consciousness and cripples his creative powers, which can only develop properly in freedom. The whole of human history has up to now been a constant struggle between the cultural, creative forces of society and the power aims of particular castes, whose leaders put definite bounds to cultural efforts, or at least tried to do so. Culture gives man consciousness of his humanity and creative strength; but power deepens in him the sense of dependence and of slavish bondage.

It is necessary to free man from the curse of power, from the cannibalism of exploitation, in order to release in him those creative forces which can continually give his life new meaning. Power degrades man into a dead part of a machine set in motion by a superior will. Culture makes him the master and builder of his own destiny and deepens in him that feeling of communion from which everything great is born. Man's liberation from the organized force of the state and the narrow bondage of the nation is the beginning of a new humanity, which feels its wings grow in freedom and finds its strength in the community. Lao Tse's gentle wisdom holds good also for the future:

> To rule according to the Way is to rule without force:
> Just and equal give-and-take rules in the community.
> Where there is war, there grow thorns,
>   and the year is without harvest.
> The good man Is, and does not need force,
>   Is and does not rely on splendor,
>   Is and does not boast or glory,
>   Is and does not support himself on his deed,
>   Is and does not found himself on severity,
>   Is and does not strive after power.
>   Zenith means decline.
> All outside of the way is apart from the way.

BOOK II

Chapter 1

THE NATIONAL CONCEPT IN THE PROCESS OF TIME. THE NATION AS COMMUNITY OF DESCENT. THE NATION AS COMMUNITY OF INTEREST. DIVISION OF THE NATION INTO CASTES, RANKS AND CLASSES. NATIONAL INTEREST AND CLASS INTEREST. THE CONFLICT IN THE RUHR. POINCARÉ'S "NATIONAL POLICY." THE DEALINGS OF GERMAN HEAVY INDUSTRY WITH THE "HEREDITARY ENEMY" AGAINST GERMAN LABOR. THE "FOLK COMMUNITY" AT WORK. THE PENSIONERS OF THE GERMAN REPUBLIC. THE NATION AS COMMUNITY OF SPIRITUAL INTEREST. RELIGIOUS AND PARTY CONFLICTS. WORLD-PHILOSOPHICAL ANTAGONISMS. THE NATION AS COMMUNITY OF MORALS AND CUSTOMS. CITY AND COUNTRY. RICH AND POOR. THE NATIONAL TRADITION. MEMBERSHIP IN THE NATION AS THE RESULT OF POLITICAL EFFORTS. NORTH AND SOUTH AMERICA. THE NATION AND SOCIETY.

THE concepts of the nation and nationality have in the course of time undergone many changes, and have even today the same double meaning as the concept of race. During the Middle Ages the unions of fellow countrymen who were students in the universities were called nations. The famous University of Prague was divided into "four nations": Bavarians, Bohemians, Poles and Saxons. One also spoke frequently of a nation of physicians, of smiths, of lawyers, and so on. Even Luther makes a decided distinction between folk and nation in his pamphlet, *To the Christian Nobility of the German Nation,* designating as the nation the possessors of political power exclusively, that is, princes, knights and bishops, in contradistinction to the common people. This distinction prevailed for a considerable time, until gradually the demarcation between nation and people began to disappear in language. Frequently an unpleasant flavor was attached to the concept of the nation. Ludwig Jahn argues, thus, in his *German Folkways:*

> That which really is the highest, and was so regarded in Greece and Rome, is with us still a term of revilement: Folk and Nation! "He has gone among the folk," was said of the miserable deserters who for the sake of the money they got from the recruiting officer ran away, and will serve seven

259

potentates in one pair of shoes. "That's the regular nation," was colloquially said of Gypsies, thievish vagabonds, tramps, and Jewish peddlers.

There was a time when one was content to use the term "nation" of a human community whose members were born in the same place and were consequently held together by fundamental social relations. This concept corresponds best to the meaning of the Latin word *natio*, from which the term "nation" is derived. This is the more understandable since it is based on the more limited idea of home. But this concept does not correspond to the modern idea of the nation, nor is it in harmony with the national endeavors of the time, which seek to give the nations the widest possible boundaries. Were the nation in fact to comprise only the neighborhood where a man first saw the light, and were national consciousness to be defined only as the natural feeling of attachment between men who have been welded into a community by being born in the one place, then we could not speak of Germans, Frenchmen, Turks and Japanese, but at the most of Hamburgers, Parisians, Amsterdammers, or Venetians—a situation which actually existed in the city republics of ancient Greece and the federated communities of the Middle Ages.

Later, the concept of the nation became much broader, comprising a human grouping which had developed through a community of material and spiritual interests, and of morals, customs and traditions; hence, it represents a sort of "community of destiny," which holds within itself the laws of its particular life. This concept is not nearly as clear as the first; and is, moreover, in conflict with the daily experiences of life. Every nation includes today the most various castes, conditions, classes and parties. These not only pursue their separate interests, but frequently face one another with definite antagonism. The results are countless, never-ending conflicts and inner antagonisms which are infinitely more difficult to overcome than the temporary wars between the various states and nations.

The same nations which only yesterday faced each other on the "field of honor," armed to the teeth, to settle their real or imaginary difficulties by bloody wars, tomorrow or the day after make alliances of defense and offense with their former enemies against other nations with whom they had been previously allied by trade agreements or treaties of a political or military nature. But the fight between the various classes within the same nation can never be eliminated so long as these classes themselves exist and cleave the nation with eternal economic and political antagonisms. Even when by extraordinary circumstances or catastrophic events the class antagonisms are apparently overcome or temporarily allayed, as by the proclamation of the so-called "citizens' peace" during the World War, it is only a passing phenomenon arising from the pressure of circumstances, the real meaning of which is never clear to the great masses of the people. Such alliances have no permanency and they break apart at the first occasion for the lack of a real inner tie of community interests. A tyrannical system of government may under certain circumstances be able to prevent an open outbreak of inner conflicts, as has been done currently in Italy and Germany; but one does not abolish internal conflicts by preventing the people from speaking about them.

The love of his own nation has never yet prevented the entrepreneur from using foreign labor if it was cheaper and made more profit for him. Whether his own people are thereby injured does not concern him in the least; the personal profit is the deciding factor in such a case, and so-called national interests are only considered when they are not in conflict with personal ones. When there is such conflict all patriotic enthusiasm vanishes. Concerning the nature of the so-called "national interests" Germany got a lesson during the frightful years after the war which is not easily misunderstood.

After losing the war Germany found itself in a desperate situation. It had to give up economic spheres of great importance, and its export trade had been almost totally lost. Added to this were the extreme economic mandates of the victors and the breakdown of the old system. If the slogan about national unity had any meaning at all it had to be proved at this stage that the nation was indeed minded to face the newly created conditions unitedly and equitably to spread the load of misfortune over all sections of the population. But this never entered the minds of the owning classes. On the contrary, they tried to make profits from the situation. These patriots were bent solely upon gain, even though wide sections of their own people would be thereby impoverished.

It was the representatives of Prussian junkerdom and German heavy industry who during the frightful years of the war had secretly advocated the most ruthless annexation policy and by their insatiable greed brought on the great catastrophe of the debacle. Not content with the fabulous profits they had made during those years, they pursued the same ends when the war was over, and never for a moment considered sacrificing to the nation even a penny of their gains. The owners of German heavy industry got themselves relieved from the taxes which were deducted from the wages of even the poorest laborer. They raised the price of coal to unheard-of levels while the nation froze in front of cold stoves. They knew how to make enormous profits from the paper credits of the Reichsbank. (It was just this speculation with the monetary distress which it had itself caused that gave heavy industry the power to confirm its rule over the hungry nation.) Its representatives, under the leadership of Hugo Stinnes, really brought about the occupation of the Ruhr, causing the

German nation to lose fifteen billion gold marks—to which these industrialists contributed not a single penny.

The Ruhr conflict in its various phases of development is a splendid illustration of the capitalistic "interest" policy as a background for the national ideology. The occupation of the Ruhr was but a continuation of the same criminal power policy which led to the World War and for four years dragged people to the shambles. This conflict concerned exclusively the antagonistic interest of German and French heavy industry. Just as the great German industrialists were during the war the most pronounced advocates of the annexation idea and made the incorporation of Briey-Longuy one of the chief objects of German propaganda, so, later on, Poincaré's national policy followed the same line and represented the undisguised desire for annexation of French heavy industry and its powerful organization, the Comité des Forges. The same aims formerly pursued by the great German industrialists were now taken over by the representatives of French heavy industry, namely, the creation of certain monopolies on the continent under the direction of special capitalistic groups for whom the so-called "national interests" have always served as stalking horse for their own ruthless business interests. It was the union of the Lorraine iron mines with the coal fields of the Ruhr basin, in the form of a powerful amalgamation planned by French heavy industry, which was to secure for it an unlimited monopoly on the continent. And since the interests of the great industrialists harmonized with the interests of the gainers by the reparations and were favored by the military caste, so they worked from that side by every means for the occupation of the Ruhr.

But before it went so far there were negotiations between the German and French heavy industries for a peaceful, purely business-like solution of the question whereby both parties were to profit in proportion to their forces. Such an understanding would indeed have been achieved, for the great German industrialists did not give a hang for the national interest of the Reich, so long as their profits were secure. But as the owners of the British coal mines, to whom an amalgamation on the continent would have been a severe blow, doubtless held out to them the prospect of greater advantages, they suddenly rediscovered their patriotic hearts and let the occupation proceed. Together with the laborers and office employees who, ignorant of the inner connections, again allowed themselves to be used in the interest of their masters, they organized a passive resistance, and the press owned by Stinnes blew mightily into the national trumpet in order to rouse the country's hatred against the hereditary enemy. When the resistance collapsed, Stinnes and the other owners of German industry did not wait on the Stresemann government, but dealt directly with the French. On October 5, 1923, Stinnes, Klöckner, Velsen, and Vögler met the French general, Degoutte, and tried to persuade him to enforce the ten-hour day on the German workers who only the day before had been their allies in the passive resistance against the French cabinet. Could there be a better illustration of the nation as community of interest? [1]

Poincaré seized on Germany's alleged failure in the coal deliveries as a pretext for letting the French troops march into the Ruhr. This was of course only an excuse to give plain robber raids an appearance of legality, as is plainly proved by the fact that France was at the time richer in coal than any land in Europe with the sole exception of England. The French government even saw itself compelled to impose an extra duty of 10 percent on coal from the Saar in order to protect French coal in the home market. The fact is that 20 percent of this coal was being sent back into Germany and that only 35 percent of it was used in French industry.

On the other hand, the great German industrialists and their allies had by the ruthless defense of their special interests done everything to make the game easier for the French government. It was they who most bitterly opposed all attempts at the stabilization of the mark, since by inflation they could most conveniently sabotage the taxation of their industries and of the great landed estates and shift the load to the shoulders of the workers of their own country. As a result of these dark machinations not only did there arise a whole army of currency speculators and other profiteers who made enormous gains from the monstrous misery of the masses, but France was given the opportunity to gain extra advantage from Germany's monetary distress. Thus, according to the testimony of the former French Minister of Finance, Lasteyrie, Germany had by the end of September, 1921, delivered to France fuel to the value of 2,571 million francs for which, owing to the devaluation of the mark, it was credited with only 980 million francs. The business agencies of the good German patriots thus procured for the "hereditary enemy" a special source of income at the expense of the enormous exploitation of German workers and the declining middle class.

But when the Ruhr conflict was over and the industrialists of the occupied territory came to conclude the so-called Micum agreements, not one of them thought for a moment of the millions of profit they had made during the inflation period. On the contrary, they demanded of the Reich appropriate compensation for their loss, and the Luther-Strese-

[1] When the news of this conference sifted through to the public and it became known that General Degoutte had made it clear to the gentlemen that he was not minded to interfere in matters of internal German politics, the German workers' press accused Stinnes and company of treason to the country. Driven into a corner, the promoters at first flatly denied everything. But at the sitting of the Reichstag on November 20, 1923, the Socialist member, Wels, read the protocol of the conference prepared by the industrialists themselves, and any doubt concerning the occurrence of the meeting was finally removed.

mann government, without considering the state's right of eminent domain, made haste to hand them the trifle of 706,400,000 gold marks for the "Micum damages," for which the Reich was credited with only 446,-400,000 gold marks in the reparation accounts—a transaction such as has probably not often taken place in a state with a parliamentary government.

In short, the representatives of heavy industry, of the great estate owners and the stock exchange had never bothered their brains concerning the alleged community of national interests. It never occurred to them that in order to rescue the rest of the nation from helpless despair and misery after the war they might be content with smaller profits. They stole what they could lay their hands on, while the nation fed on dry bread and potatoes and thousands of German children died of undernourishment. None of these parasites ever heeded that their uncontrolled greed delivered the whole nation to destruction. While the workers and the middle class of the great cities perished in misery, Stinnes became the owner of fabulous riches. Thyssen, who before the war had approximately two hundred million gold marks, is today the owner of a fortune of a billion gold marks, and the other representatives of German heavy industry enriched themselves in the same proportion.

And how about the so-called "noblest of the nation"? The German people, who for years languished in hopeless misery, pay their former princes fabulous sums for "compensation," and servile law courts see to it that they do not lose a penny thereof. And we are dealing here not only with compensation paid to the "fathers of the country" overthrown by the revolution of November, 1918, but also to those who for years had been reckoned as descendants of little potentates whose lands had actually disappeared from the map for a hundred and thirty years. To the descendants of these former petty despots the Reich paid yearly the trifle of 1,834,139 marks. Among the princes who reigned until the outbreak of the revolution the Hohenzollerns alone collected compensation to the amount of 200,000,000 gold marks. The amounts paid to all the ex-princes exceeded the Dawes loan by fourfold. While the pittances for the poorest of the poor were continually shortened and did not even suffice for the most indispensable needs, it never occurred to any of these "nobles" to contribute a penny towards the lessening of this misery. Like Shylock they demanded their pound of flesh and gave the world a classic example of the nature of the "community of interest of the nation."

This does not hold for Germany alone. The alleged community of national interests does not exist in any country; it is nothing more than a representation of false facts in the interest of small minorities. Thus, during the Ruhr conflict the French press never tired of assuring the people that Germany must be forced to pay if France was not to be ruined and, just as everywhere else, this assertion was accepted as truth. But this does not alter the fact that of the immense sums which Germany was forced to pay to France after the war only a minimal portion ever profited the French nation as a whole or was used for the restoration of the destroyed territory. Here as everywhere else, the lion's share flowed into the bottomless pockets of privileged minorities. Of the 11.4 billion marks which Germany had paid as reparation to France up to December 31, 1921, only 2.8 billion were used for restoration; 4.3 billion were used for the payment of the occupation troops and the inter-allied commissions in Germany.

In France, just as in Germany, it is the suffering part of the working population from whose hides the owning classes cut their belts. While the representatives of giant capitalism made enormous profits in the countries participating in the war and almost smothered in their own fat, millions of luckless humans had to dung the battlefields of the world with their dead bodies. And still today, when only the forms of the war have changed, the working classes of society are the real sufferers, while landowners, industrialists and gentlemen of the stock exchange grind money from their misery.

When one takes a look at the modern arms industries of the various countries, employing millions of men and enormous capital, one gets a curious view of the "community of national interests." In these industries patriotism and the "protection of national interests" are quite openly a part of business. The sums spent by these industries for the stimulation of national enthusiasm are booked in the accounts like all other expenses for the guarding of business interests. But the national idea has up to now prevented no member of the arms industry from selling its instruments of murder and destruction to any state which has paid them the demanded price when it does not happen that important business interests are at stake. Just as little is the high finance of any country dissuaded by patriotic motives from loaning foreign states the necessary moneys for armament, even though the safety of their own country is endangered thereby. Business is business.[2]

[2] Deals of this sort are often used by these men to persuade their own states to give them new orders. Thus, Walton Newbold reports in his valuable book upon concrete cases from the business practices of the well-known arms firm, Mitchel and Company in England, which are very significant for the methods of the armament giants.

"Armstrong was a genius. His firm built for Chile the powerful cruiser, 'Esmeralda.' When the ship was completed he addressed himself to the British public and declared with every appearance of moral indignation that our [that is, the English] navy possessed no ship which could catch the 'Esmeralda,' escape it, or fight it successfully. He pointed out the danger such a ship might be to our commerce. The admiralty took this gentle hint and bought from Sir William Armstrong's firm most of the guns and armament for a new and improved 'Esmeralda.' Later on the

It is a quite normal phenomenon that the great enterprises of the international arms industry should unite in business to eliminate competition and increase profits. Of the numerous corporations of this kind we will here mention only the "Nobel Dynamite Trust," founded in 1886, which has English, French and Italian branches; and—especially—the "Harvey Continental Steel Company," which came into being in 1894 after the Harvey steel works in New Jersey had invented a new process of manufacturing thinner and stronger armor-plates which were immediately adopted by the various governments for their navies. The first directors of this international armor trust were Charles Campbell, Charles E. Ellis (of the firm of John Brown and Company, England), Edward M. Fox (Harvey Steel Company, New Jersey), Maurice Gény (Schneider and Company, France), Joseph de Montgolfier (Shipping and Railroad Company, France), Léon Lévy (president of Chatillon-Commentry Company, France), Josef Ott (Dillinger Iron Works, Germany),

same firm built for Italy a still better cruiser, the 'Piemonte,' and again Armstrong was able to enlist the world for his firm, and the South American states competed with one another and with Japan to obtain the first improved 'Piemonte' from the Elswick works. England likewise constructed a few Piemontes, which, while they were built in other places, were equipped with Armstrong cannons of the newest pattern!"

In another place Newbold reports:

"For nearly thirty years the firms of Sir William Armstrong and Sir Joseph Whitworth, who both manufactured guns, fought like cats and dogs to depreciate each other's products. Only on one point were they unanimous; both emphasized the opinion that all expenditure for the manufacture of armor-plate was to be regarded as uselessly wasted money, which had better be spent for guns. For both firms made only guns, no armor-plate. Ten years after this valiant fight against armor-plate, when the two firms had united, the first step of their successors was the erection of a marvelous plant for the manufacture of armor-plate."—(J. T. Walton Newbold, *How Europe Armed for the War*. London, 1916.)

These cases are by no means the worst and occur not only in "perfidious Albion." Every armament firm, without distinction of nation, pursues the same dirty methods and is very able to "correct" all given possibilities for good business so as to promote its profits. Here is only one example:

"On April 19, 1913, the delegate, Karl Liebknecht, supported by the Centrum's delegate, Pfeifer, made a statement in the Reichstag that stirred all Germany. Backed by indisputable documents he proved that Krupp, using a certain Brandt as intermediary, had bribed a number of subordinate officials of the general staff and the war office to obtain possession of important documents concerning pending arms orders. Furthermore, Krupp had officers of all ranks up to general and admiral in his service at the highest salaries, whose duty it was to procure arms orders for him. When this did not suffice, then, in company with other armament manufacturers like Mauser, Thyssen, Düren, Löwe, he bought a part of the press to whip up jingo patriotism and war sentiment. By an official search a part of these secret documents was found in the home of Herr von Dewitz, the assistant superintendent of the Krupp works. By this press propaganda a feeling of continuous danger from other nations was to be aroused and the German people made favorable to further expen-

Ludwig Klüpfel (A. G. Friedrich Krupp Company, Germany), Albert Vickers.

These men, whose paid press year after year was required to carry on the most shameful propaganda against other countries and nations in order to keep the "national spirit" alive among the people, had not the slightest compunction about allying themselves with the armament industries of other countries, if only for the purpose of more successfully exploiting their own. The notorious Putiloff case of January, 1914, clearly proves that not only did French and German capital work together in charming unity at the Putiloff works in St. Petersburg, but also that first-class experts of the armament industry of both countries assisted the Russians in the manufacture of heavy artillery. With grim irony the well-informed author of a book in which the monstrous venality of the national press was ruthlessly exposed wrote the following concerning these events:

The Putiloff works, incapable of filling the orders of the Russian government, had since 1910 had a community of interest with the Banque de l'Union Parisienne, which lent them 24 millions, likewise with Schneider ditures for war purposes. According to seasonal necessity the names of the threatening enemies were changed: When Krupp or Thyssen needed orders for machine guns, then it was the French or the Russians; if the dock yards of Stettin needed orders for battleships, then Germany was threatened by the English. Liebknecht had among his proofs a letter from the director of the Löwe arms factory to his Paris agent in the Rue de Chateaudun:

" 'If possible procure the publication in one of the French papers having the largest circulation, preferably *Figaro*, an article running something like this: "The French war ministry has resolved to speed up the manufacture of machine guns for the army and to increase the original orders by 100 percent. Please do your utmost to procure the spread of similar news.   (Signed)   von Gontard, Director."

"However, the report was not accepted in this form. The lie was too obvious, and the war ministry would at once have denied it. But a few days later there appeared, of course quite accidentally, in *Figaro*, *Matin*, and *Echo de Paris* a number of articles concerning the advantages of the new French machine guns and the predominance they gave to French armament.

"With these newspapers in his hand the Prussian delegate, Schmidt, an ally of German heavy industry, questioned the Reich's chancellor as to what the government intended to do to meet these French threats and restore the balance of armament. Bluffed and frightened, the Reichstag then by a great majority and without discussion voted the sums for the increase of the stock of machine guns. France quite naturally answered with a further strengthening of this type of arm. So, while *Figaro* and *Echo de Paris* kept the French people agitated by excerpts from the German papers, especially the *Post*, which Gontard owned, German public opinion was by similar means prepared for still further armament. The dividends of the Creusots, the Mausers, and the Krupps rose, the directors got larger salaries, and *Figaro* and *Echo de Paris* cashed a number of checks—and, as usual, the people paid." (*Hinter den Kulissen des Französischen Journalismus von einem Pariser Chefredacteur.* Berlin, 1925, p. 129.)

NATIONALISM AND CULTURE

of the Creusot works, who furnished them the plans for the 75 millimeter guns and the necessary engineers and technicians, and also with Krupp in Essen, who put the experience of the German heavy artillery manufacture and its experts and foremen at their disposal. Here we see how French and German engineers and artisans, united under the direction of officials and financiers of whom some belonged to a group from the Union Parisienne and others were related with the Deutsche Bank, were working on guns with which later on they were to shoot each other dead. It is a most marvelous thing, this rule of international capitalism.[3]

In 1906 a company was formed in England with the object of acquiring the Fiume branch of the firm of Whitehead and Company and taking over its management. Other English armament firms participated in the enterprise, whose board of directors in Hungary in 1914 consisted of the following persons: Count Edgar Hoyos (general director), Albert Edward Jones, Henry Whitehead (firm of Armstrong-Whitworth), Saxton William Armstrong Noble (manager for Europe of the Vickers firm), Arthur Trevors Dawson (managing Director of Vickers), and Professor Sigmund Dankl; as we see, nearly all English names, and representatives of the best-known and most powerful firms in the English armament industry.

Under the board of directors of this company the German U-boat, "Number 5," was built, which in the year 1914 sank the French armored cruiser, "Leon Gambetta," in the strait of Otranto with six hundred Frenchmen on board. One could cite a number of similar examples, but this would only mean a constant repetition of the same bloody tale. That in this respect there was no change even after the World War, the widely known Lord Robert Cecil proved emphatically at the gigantic demonstration of the Women's Peace Crusaders in London, in June, 1932, where Cecil launched a very sharp attack against the international armament industry and especially emphasized the sinister influence of the Parisian press. According to his statement, some of the greatest French newspapers had been bought by the interests of the steel and iron industry and were working day and night against the international disarmament conference. That the contemptible attitude of the so-called "League of Nations" in the Japanese-Chinese question can for the largest part be traced to the wretched machinations of the international armament industry is an open secret that sparrows now chirp from the housetops. Naturally international high finance pursued the same course.[4]

[3] *Hinter den Kulissen des Französischen Journalismus, etc.,* p. 252.
[4] There exists today a whole literature concerning this darkest chapter of the capitalistic social order. Besides the writings already referred to we may mention the following: *Generäle, Händler, und Soldaten,* by Maxim Ziese and Hermann Ziese-Beringer; *The Devil's Business,* by A. Fenner Brockway; *Dollar Diplomacy*

It is, therefore, quite meaningless to speak of a community of national interests; for that which the ruling class of every country has up to now defended as national interest has never been anything but the special interest of privileged minorities in society secured by the exploitation and political suppression of the great masses. Likewise, the soil of the so-called "fatherland" and its natural riches have always been in the possession of these classes, so that one can with full right speak of a "fatherland of the rich." If the nation were in fact the community of interests which it has been called, then there would not be in modern history revolutions and civil wars, because the people do not resort to the arms of revolt purely from pleasure—just as little do the endless wage fights occur because the working sections of the population are too well off!

But if we cannot speak of a community of purely economic and material interests within the nation, even less can we do so when so-called spiritual interests are in question. Not seldom have religious and philosophical problems profoundly stirred the nations and split them into hostile camps. It must be understood, however, that in such conflicts economic and political motives were also active, and frequently played important parts. We need but think of the bloody struggle in France, England, Germany and other countries between the adherents of the old church and the various factions of Protestantism which shook profoundly the inner balance of the nations, or of the sharp and frequently violent conflicts between democratic citizenry and representatives of absolute monarchy; we need but remember the murderous war between the Northern and Southern states of America for the maintenance or abolition of negro slavery—and thousands of other events in history—and we shall easily be able to estimate the worth of the assertion that the nation is the guardian of spiritual interests.

Every nation is today split by varying trends of thought into dozens of parties whose activity destroys the feeling of national unity and brands as a lie the fable of the community of intellectual interests of the nation. Each of these parties has its own party program, in pursuit of which it attacks everything which threatens it and uncritically adores whatever

by Scott Nearing and J. Freeman; *Oil and the Germs of War*, by Scott Nearing; and above all, the excellent essay by Otto Lehmann-Russbüldt, *Die blutige Internationale der Rüstungsindustrie*. It is significant that although up to now no attempt even has been made to question the frightful facts given by Lehmann-Russbüldt, the former German government denied this upright man a passport to prevent him from traveling abroad—because thereby the interests of the Reich would allegedly be endangered.

One finds it quite in order that civilized cannibals should make a business of organized mass murder and invest their capital in enterprises which have as a presupposition the wholesale killing of men while at the same time a man is socially ostracized who has the courage to brand publicly the shameless and criminal machinations of the dishonorable rascals who coin money from the blood and misery of the masses.

furthers its special purpose. And as any movement can only represent the views of a certain part of the nation, never the nation in its entirety, it follows that the so-called "intellectual interest of the nation" or the alleged "national thought" displays as many shades and colors as there are parties and movements in the country. Hence, every party asserts that in it the intellectual interests of the nation are best guarded, and in critical times each vilifies all other concepts and tendencies as antagonistic and even traitorous to the fatherland—a method which surely does not take very much intellect, but it has never failed so far. Germany and Italy are the classic witnesses to this.

Moreover, one finds this conflict of ideas and tendencies not only between parties which oppose one another as exponents of definite economic principles and political aims; one finds it also between movements which philosophically stand on the same ground and oppose one another solely for reasons of a subordinate nature. It is just in such cases that the battle between the various factions becomes ever more irreconcilable till it reaches a degree of fanaticism quite incomprehensible to the impartial spectator. A glance at the present party fights in the camp of socialism is proof of this. The further one pursues the matter the more clearly it appears that the unity of intellectual interests of the nation is in a very bad way. In reality, the belief in this unity is a delusion which will have permanence as long as the ruling classes of the national states succeed by external glamour in fooling the great masses of the population as to the real causes of social disintegration.

Moreover, the differences of economic interest and intellectual effort within the nation have naturally developed special habits and modes of living among the members of the various social classes. It is, therefore, very venturesome to speak of a community of national customs and morals. But the concept has only a very qualified value. Indeed, what community can there be in this respect between one of the members of the Berlin "millionaire quarter" and a Ruhr miner? Between a Bavarian lumber-jack and an East Elbian junker? Between a modern industrial magnate and a common laborer? Between a Prussian general and a Holstein fisherman? Between a society lady surrounded by every luxury and a cottage housewife in the Silesian mountains? Every larger country contains many distinctions of a climatic, cultural, economic and general social nature. It has its great cities, its highly developed industrial regions, its out-of-the-world villages and mountain valleys to which hardly a glimmer of modern life has penetrated. This endless variety of intellectual and material conditions of life precludes beforehand any close community of morals and customs.

Every rank, every class, every stratum of society develops its special habits of life into which a stranger penetrates with difficulty. It is by no means an exaggeration to maintain that between the working populations of different nations there is a greater community of general habits and customs than between the possessing and the non-possessing sections of the same nation. A worker who finds himself in a foreign country will soon find his sphere among the members of his trade or class, while the doors of another social class are hermetically closed against him in his own country. This applies, of course, to all other classes and sections of the population.

The sharp antagonism between town and country observable today in almost every land forms one of the greatest social problems of our time. To what degree these antagonisms can develop Germany learned during the hard times of the inflation, and the lesson will not quickly be forgotten. It was during the planned and organized starvation of the cities that the trenchant phrase was coined, "a people starving amid full granaries." Every appeal to the national spirit and alleged community of interest of the nation died out at that time like a cry in the wilderness, showing full clearly that the fairy tale of community of national interest bursts like a soap-bubble as soon as the special interests of a definite group make their appearance. But between town and country there exist not only antagonisms of a purely economic nature; there exists also between them a strong emotional aversion which has gradually arisen from differences in the conditions of social life and which today is very deep seated. There are very few townsmen who can completely penetrate into the mental processes and views of life of the peasant. It is probably still more difficult for the peasant to penetrate into the intellectual and moral life of the townsman, against whom he has for centuries nursed a mute hatred to be explained by the social relations which have up to now existed between town and country.

The same chasm exists between the intellectual leaders of the nation and the great masses of the working people. Even among those intellectuals who have for years been active in the socialist labor movement there are very few who are really able to understand the sentiments and thoughts of the workers. Some intellectuals even find the effort very painful, a situation which often gives occasion to tragic inner conflicts. Obviously we are dealing, in such a case, not with inborn differences of thinking and feeling, but with the result of a special mode of life arising from a different kind of education within a different social environment. The older a man grows, the harder he finds it to withdraw from those influences whose results have become second nature to him. This invisible wall which today exists between the intellectuals and the working masses of every nation is one of the main reasons for the secret mistrust with which wide sections of the laboring population quite unconsciously confront the intellectual and which has gradually condensed into the well-known theory of "the calloused fist."

It is vastly more difficult to provide a point of intellectual contact between representatives of capitalism and of the working population of a nation. For millions of workers the capitalist is only a sort of octopus who feeds on their flesh and blood. Many of them cannot understand that behind the capitalist's purely economic actions there may exist a purely human quality. The capitalist, on the other hand, usually observes the endeavors of the laborer as a total stranger; yes, often with openly displayed contempt, often felt by the workers as more oppressive and more humiliating than even their economic exploitation. While towards the workers of his own country the capitalist is always filled with a certain mistrust, often mixed with open antagonism, he shows to the possessing classes of other nations a continued attachment, even where he is not dealing with purely economic or political questions. This relationship may be impaired temporarily when the opposing interests are too strong; but the inner conflict between the possessing and the propertyless classes in the same nation never vanishes.

"Community of national tradition," likewise, amounts to little. Historical tradition is, after all, something quite different from that which is presented to us in the educational institutions of the state. In any event, the tradition is not the essential; far more important is the way in which the tradition is received, explained and felt by the various social castes within the nation. The concept of the nation as a "community of destiny," therefore, is as misleading as it is ambiguous. There are events in every nation's history which are felt by all its members as fateful, but the nature of the feeling is very different among different groups, and is often determined by the part which one or the other of the parties or classes has played in those events. When at the time of the Paris Commune thirty-five thousand men, women and children of the working class were put to death, the gruesome slaughter was doubtless felt by both parties as fateful; but while one class with pierced breasts and torn limbs covered the streets of the capital, their death gave the others the possibility of reëstablishing their rule, which had been very badly shaken by the lost war. In this sense the Paris Commune lives in the traditions of the nation. For the propertied class the revolt of March 18, 1871, is an "outrageous rebellion of the canaille against law and order"; for the working class it is "a glorious episode in the proletarian fight for freedom."

Volumes might be filled with similar examples from the history of all nations. Furthermore, the recent historical events in Hungary, Italy, Germany, Austria, and so on, give the best of instruction concerning the character of the "community of destiny of the nations." Brutal force can impose a common fate on a nation, just as it can arbitrarily create or destroy a nation; for the nation is not an organically evolved entity, but something artificially created by the state, with which it is most intimately intergrown, as every page of history shows. The state itself, however, is not an organic structure, and sociological research has demonstrated that everywhere and at all times it has appeared as a result of forceful intervention of warlike elements in the life of peaceful human groups. The nation is, therefore, a purely political concept arising solely from the adherence of men to a definite state. Also, in the so-called "law of nations," the word has exclusively this meaning, as is apparent from the fact that any man can become a member of any nation by naturalization.

How arbitrarily the adherence of whole groups of people to a nation is determined by the brutal compulsion of the stronger, the history of every country shows by numerous examples. Thus, the inhabitants of the present French Riviera went to sleep one evening as Italians and awoke next morning as Frenchmen because a handful of diplomats had so decided. The Heligolander was a member of the British nation and a faithful subject of the British government until Britain got the idea of selling the island to Germany; then the national membership of the inhabitants underwent a fundamental change. If on the day before this decision it was their greatest merit to be good English patriots, then after the transfer of the island to Germany this highest virtue became the greatest sin against the "spirit of the nation." There are many such examples, and they are characteristic of the whole formative history of the modern state. One need but glance at the stupid and stumbling provisions of the Versailles treaty to get a classic example of how nations are artificially manufactured.

And just as the stronger can today and at all times decide upon the national membership of the weaker according to his pleasure, so it was and is also empowered to end the nation's existence arbitrarily if for reasons of state this appears to him desirable. Read the reasons on which Prussia, Austria and Russia based their intervention in Poland and prepared the partition of that land. They are stated in the famous pact of August 5, 1772, and are truly a shining example of conscious mendacity, nauseating hypocrisy, and brute force. It is merely because these phenomena have heretofore been given so little consideration that we have such curious illusions concerning the real nature of the nation. It is not "national differences" which lead to the formation of the various states; it is the states which artificially create national differences and further them on principle, for these have to serve the states as moral justification for their own existence. Tagore has stated this inherent antagonism between the nation and society in these splendid words:

A nation, in the sense of the political and economic union of a people, is that aspect which a whole population assumes when organized for a mechanical purpose. Society as such has no ulterior purpose. It is an end in itself. It is a spontaneous self-expression of man as a social being. It is a natural regulation of human relationships so that men can develop ideals of life in cooperation with one another.[5]

The contrast between the political organization of North and South America serves as an excellent example of the fact that a nation does not organically evolve itself, create itself, as is often asserted, but is rather the artificial creation of the state mechanically imposed on various human groups. In North America the Union succeeded in combining all the land between the Canadian and Mexican borders, between the Atlantic and Pacific oceans, into a powerful federated state, a process greatly furthered by favorable circumstances of various kinds. And this happened in spite of the fact that the United States contained the most motley mixture of people assembled from all the nations and races of Europe and of other continents; so that it has been rightly called the melting-pot of the nations.

South and Central America, however, are separated into sixteen different states with sixteen different nations, although the racial relation between these peoples is incomparably closer than it is in North America, and the same language—with the exception of Portuguese in Brazil and various Indian tongues—prevails in all. But the political evolution of Latin America was of a different order. Although Simon Bolivar, the "liberator" of South America from the Spanish yoke, sought to create a federated state for all South American countries, his plan did not succeed; for ambitious dictators and generals, like Prieto in Chile, Gamarra in Peru, Flores in Ecuador, Rosas in Argentina, opposed this project by all possible means. Bolivar was so disappointed by the machinations of his rivals that shortly before his death he wrote: "In South America there is neither trust nor faith; neither among men nor among the various states. Every treaty is here but a scrap of paper and what are here called constitutions are but a collection of such scraps."

The result of the power lust of small minorities and dictatorially inclined individuals was the creation of quite a number of national states, which in the name of national interest and national honor waged war against one another quite as we do. If political events in North America had developed as they did in the lands of the southern continent, then there would be today Californians, Michiganders, Kentuckians and Pennsylvanians, just as in South America there are Argentinians, Chileans,

[5] Rabindranath Tagore, *Nationalism*, New York, 1917, p. 19.

Peruvians and Brazilians. Here is the best proof that the nation's existence is founded purely on political endeavor.

Whoever yields to the illusion that community of material and intellectual interest and identity of morals, customs and traditions constitutes the real nature of the nation, and from this arbitrary assumption tries to deduce the necessity of national endeavors, deceives himself and others. Of this kind of unity nothing is discernible in any of the existing nations. The force of social circumstances is always stronger than the abstract assumptions of all nationalistic ideology.

Chapter 2

THE NATION AS COMMUNITY OF LANGUAGE. LANGUAGE AND CULTURE. FOREIGN CONSTITUENTS IN LANGUAGE. PURISM AND THE DEVELOPMENT OF LANGUAGE. LITERARY LANGUAGE AND POPULAR SPEECH. RELIGION, SCIENCE, ART, PROFESSION, ETC., AS MEDIATORS OF NEW LANGUAGE VALUES. LANGUAGE AND IMAGERY. THE SIGNIFICANCE OF LOANWORDS IN LANGUAGE DEVELOPMENT. ORIENTAL SYMBOLISM IN LANGUAGE. FOREIGN MATERIAL IN NATIVE GUISE. SPEECH AND THOUGHT. NATURE AND LANGUAGE. WORK AND LANGUAGE. THE SYMBOLISM OF LANGUAGE. LINGUISTIC ATAVISMS. THE ILLOGICAL IN LANGUAGE FORMATION. CONSTANT CHANGE IN LINGUISTIC EXPRESSION. THE INADEQUACY OF PSYCHOLOGICAL LANGUAGE THEORIES. THE INFLUENCE OF THE CULTURAL CIRCLE VERSUS THE TIE OF COMMUNAL SPEECH. THE DEVELOPMENT OF THE ENGLISH LANGUAGE. IDIOM AND LANGUAGE. THE BELIEF IN THE *URSPRACHE*. CONCERNING THE COMMON GENEALOGY OF THE ARYAN LANGUAGES. PEOPLES THAT CHANGE THEIR LANGUAGE. NATIONS WITH DIFFERENT LANGUAGE DISTRICTS.

OF all the evidences which have been cited for the existence of a national ideology, community of language is by far the most important. Many see in community of language the essential characteristic of the nation. A common language is, in fact, a strong tie for any human grouping; and Wilhelm von Humboldt says with some reason: "The true homeland is really the language." Karl Julius Weber saw in language the real characteristic of nationality: "In nothing does the national character, the imprint of the mental and spiritual power of a people, express itself so clearly as in its language."

Likewise, the best known representatives of nationalistic ideas in the last century, like Schleiermacher, Fichte, Jahn and the men of the German League of Virtue; Mazzini, Pisacane, Niemojowsky, Lelewel, the "Young Europe," and the German democrats of 1848, confined their concept of the nation to the realm of a common language. Arndt's song, "What is the German's Fatherland?" shows this. It is significant that Arndt as well as Mazzini based their efforts at national unification not on popular speech, but on the written language, so as to include the largest possible fatherland.

A common language naturally appears highly important to the advocates of the national idea because it is a people's highest means of expression and must, in a certain sense, be regarded as a sample of its intellectual life. Language is not the invention of individual men. In its creation and development the community has worked and continues to work as long as the language has life in it. Hence, language appeared to the advocates of the national idea as the purest product of national creativeness and became for them the clearest symbol of national unity. Yet this concept, no matter how fascinating and irrefutable it may appear to most, rests on a totally arbitrary assumption. Among the present existing languages there is not one which has developed from a definite people. It is very probable that there were once homogeneous languages, but that time is long past, lost in the grayest antiquity of history. The individuality of language disappears the moment reciprocal relations arise between different hordes, tribes and peoples. The more numerous and various these relations become in the course of the millenniums, the larger borrowings does every language make from other languages, every culture from other cultures.

Consequently, no language is the purely national product of a particular people, nor even of a particular nation. Towards the development of every one of our cultural languages peoples of the most various origins have contributed. This was inevitable, because a language as long as it is spoken at all continually absorbs foreign elements in spite of all the noise of the purification fanatics. For every language is an organism in constant flux; it obeys no fixed rules, and flies in the face of all the dicta of logic. Not only does it make the most diversified borrowings from other languages, a phenomenon due to the countless influences and points of contact in cultural life, but it also possesses a stock of words that is continually changing. Quite gradually and unnoticeably the shadings and gradations of the concepts which find their expression in words alter, so that it often happens that a word means today exactly the opposite of what men originally expressed by it.

In reality, there exists no cultural language which does not contain a great mass of foreign material, and the attempt to free it from these foreign intruders would lead to a complete dissolution of the language— that is, if such a purification could be achieved at all. Every European language contains a mass of foreign elements with which, often, whole dictionaries could be filled. How, for instance, would the German or the Dutch language look if all the words borrowed from French or Latin were removed from it, not to speak of words of other origin? How, the Spanish language, without its countless elements borrowed from the Germans and the Arabs? And what a mass of German, English, and even Turkish words has penetrated into the Russian and Polish tongues! Similarly, the Hungarian language contains a great number of words of Italian and Turkish origin. Rumanian consists only one-half of words of Latin descent; three-eighths of its stock of words are from the Slavic, one-eighth from the Turkish, Magyar and Greek. In the Albanian, until now, only five or six hundred original words have been distinguished; all the rest is a mixture of the most varied elements. Fritz Mauthner remarks very correctly in his great work, *Contributions to a Critique of Language*, that it is owing simply to "the accident of point of view that, for example, we speak of the French language as Romance and of the English as Germanic." And it is well known that the Latin language itself, from which all the Romance languages trace their descent, contained a body of words of Greek origin, to the number of several thousand.

For the development of every language the acceptance of foreign elements is essential. No people lives for itself. Every enduring intercourse with other peoples results in the borrowing of words from their language; this is quite indispensable to reciprocal cultural fecundation. The countless points of contact which culture daily creates between people leave their traces in language. New objects, ideas, concepts—religious, political, and generally social—lead to new expressions and word formations. In this, the older and more highly developed cultures naturally have a strong influence on less developed folk-groups and furnish these with new ideas which find their expression in language.

Many of the newly acquired elements of speech gradually adapt themselves so completely to the phonetic laws of the adopting language that eventually their origin can no longer be recognized. We quite involuntarily feel that words like *Existenz, Idee, Melodie, Musik, Muse, Natur, Religion,* and a hundred others are foreign words in the German language. And the speech of political life is completely permeated with foreign words. That *Bourgeoisie, Proletariat, Sozialismus, Bolschevismus, Anarchismus, Kommunismus, Liberalismus, Konservatismus, Fascismus, Terrorismus, Diktatur, Revolution, Reaktion, Partei, Parliament, Demokratie, Monarchie, Republik,* and so on, are not German speech elements, we recognize at the first glance.

But there is also a great mass of words of foreign descent in the German language which have in the course of time become so colloquial that their foreign origin has been completely forgotten. Who would, for example, regard as strangers such words as *Abenteuer, Anker, Artzt, Bezirk, Bluse, Bresche, Brief, Essig, Fenster, Frack, Gruppe, Kaiser, Kantor, Kasse, Keller, Kelter, Kerker, Kette, Kirsche, Koch, Koffer, Kohl, Kreuz, Küche, Lampe, Laune, Markt, Mauer, Meile, Meister, Mühle,*

Müller, Münze, Oel, Orgel, Park, Pfahl, Pfau, Pfeffer, Pfeiler, Pfirsich, Pflanze, Pforte, Pfosten, Pfühl, Pfütze, Pfund, Pöbel, Prinz, Pulver, Radieschen, Rest, Schüssel, Schule, Schwindler, Schreiber, Siegel, Speicher, Speise, Strasse, Teller, Tisch, Trichter, Vogt, Ziegel, Zirkel, Zoll, Zwiebel, and countless others? [1]

Very frequently the foreign word changes in the course of time so completely that its mutilated form sounds like other words and we involuntarily give it a quite different meaning. Thus *Armbrust* (crossbow) has nothing in common with either *Arm* (arm) nor *Brust* (breast), but instead goes back to the Latin word *arcubalista,* meaning arc-thrower, or catapult. Likewise *Ebenholz* (ebony) has no relation to *eben* (smooth), but again goes back to the Hebrew word, *hobnin,* from *obni,* meaning stony. The German *Vielfrass* (wolverine), which, construed as a Germanic word, equals "much-eater," "glutton"—originates from the Norwegian *fjeldfross* (mountain-cat). *Murmeltier* (marmot) does not come from *murmeln* (to murmur), but was formed during the Middle Ages from the Latin *murem,* accusative of *mus* (mouse), and *montis* or *montanum*—that is, "mountain mouse." The word *Tolpatsch* first appeared in the seventeenth century in southern Germany. It was a popular designation for Hungarian soldiers. The word owes its origin to the Hungarian *talpas,* meaning flat-foot. (In modern German, *Tolpatsch* means blockhead, booby—also the dodo.) *Ohrfeige* (box on the ear) comes from the Dutch word *veeg* (blow). *Trampeltier* goes back to the Latin *dromedarius.* *Hängematte* (as if from German roots meaning hanging mat) comes from the South American word *hamaca.* From the thieves' jargon comes *Kümmelblättchen* (three-card monte), which has nothing in common with *Kümmel* (caraway seed), but with the Hebrew word *gimel* (three). Likewise, the word *Pleite,* so much used today, is of Hebrew origin and comes from *pletah* (flight). French has left many traces in our language. Thus the quite senselessly conjoined *mutterseelenallein,* about which there plays for us today all the sickly sentimentality of *deutsches Gemüt,* comes from *moi tout seul* (I, quite alone). *Fisimatenten* comes from *fils de ma tante* (son of my aunt). The German words *forsch* and *Forsche* have the French base, *force.* When we say that we throw our lives into the *Schanze* (*in die Schanze schlagen*) this has nothing to do with *Schanze* (bulwark); the expression comes instead from the French *chance*—equaling the Eng-

[1] A similar list of usually unsuspected foreign words in English follows: alms, bond, bomb, boom, boon, brief, calm, camp, cane, cape, card, case, cash, catch, cave, cell, cellar, cent, center, chafe, chain, chair, chalk, chance, change, chant, charge, chart, chase, chief, church, circle, city, claim, clerk, cloak, clock, cook, cross, dean, doll, dour, doubt, due, duke, dupe, duty, ease, fail, farm, fate, feast, fig, grand, habit, haste, ink, just, lamp, luck, male, master, mile, oil, park, pest, place, plain, plant, part, port, post, pound, prince, school, seal, street, toll—and so on indefinitely.
—*Translator*

lish chance. Hence also, the expression *"zuschanzen"* (*Jemanden etwas zuschanzen*—give someone an opportunity). The formerly much used word, *Schwager*, for coachman, we doubtless owe to the French *chevalier*.

Such examples can be given for every language by the thousands. They are characteristic of the spirit of language and of the development of human thought in general. It would be quite erroneous to credit this intrusion of foreign speech elements simply to the written language. Because through this the ideas of the educated classes find expression it is often quite unreasonably assumed that the popular speech is better guarded against the intrusion of foreign elements and that it quite instinctively repels them. It is admitted that in the language of the educated, and especially in that of scholars, we have gone too far in the use of quite arbitrarily selected foreign words; so that we can with reason speak of a "caste language." When we consider that in the well-known Heyse *Dictionary of Foreign Words* there are no less than a hundred thousand expressions derived from a dozen different languages which are all supposed to be used in German, we may indeed regard this abundance with a secret dread. Nevertheless, it is quite mistaken to assume that popular speech offers any great resistance to the intrusion of foreign words. The fact is that also in those dialects of all European cultural languages in which the speech of the people finds purest expression we find a body of foreign words. There are quite a number of South German dialects in which, without much difficulty, plenty of Slavic, Romance, and even Hebrew, elements can be observed. Likewise, the Berliners regularly use such Hebrew words as *Ganef, Rebach, Gallach, Mischpoche, Tinef, meschugge,* and so on. We also remember the well-known words of William II, *"Ich dulde keine* MIES*macher!"* The word *Kaffer*, which is used everywhere in Germany to describe a foolish or stupid man, has no relation to the South African tribe of Kafirs, but has its root in the Hebrew *kafar*, meaning village.

It frequently happens that the original meaning of borrowed words is completely lost and is replaced by other ideas which have hardly any resemblance to the fundamental meaning of the word. One can make very interesting discoveries in this field, open surprising vistas into the inner connections of things. Thus, in my Rhenish-Hessian home, a cross-eyed man is in the popular tongue called a *Masik*. The word comes from the Hebrew and means demon or goblin. In this case the word's original meaning was changed considerably, but we recognize quite clearly the associations involved; for a cross-eyed person was formerly regarded as being "possessed by demons" or as having an "evil eye."

In southwestern Germany one hails a drunken man with a friendly, *"Schesswui,"* from the French *je suis*, I am. One discharged from employment explains that he has been *"geschasst"* from the French *chasser*, to

chase. *Mumm* comes from the Latin *animus* (*animum* in the accusative);
Kujohn, from the French *coion* (rogue); *Schmanfut* is from *je m'en fus*
(I don't give a damn!). Quite a number of blunt foreign expressions
found in the writings of that talented maker of language, Johann Fischart,
who borrowed from Rabelais, survive even today in popular speech.
Furthermore, there are quite a number of foreign words out of that
region which have penetrated into the written language and have common currency in southern and southwestern Germany. We need but think
of *schikanieren, malträtieren, alterieren, kujonieren, genieren, pussieren,*
and a hundred other expressions. The man of the people uses these words
freely and their German rendering would sound strange to him. It is,
therefore, completely wrong to prate about the natural purity of the
popular tongue, which nowhere exists.

In expressing our thoughts we ought, of course, to use German terms
so far as these are at our disposal. The very feeling of language demands
this. But we also know that in our best speech there is today a mass of
foreign elements of whose origin we are no longer conscious. We know,
furthermore, that in spite of all endeavors of so-called "speech purifiers"
it is unavoidable that these should continually find admittance into the
various languages. Every new intellectual development, every social movement which transcends the narrow frontiers of a country, every new device
borrowed from other people, every advance in science with its immediate
effects in the field of technology, every change in the general means of
intercourse, every change in world economics with its political consequences, every development in art, causes the intrusion of newly borrowed
words into the language.

Christianity and the church caused a regular invasion of Greek and
Latin word-structures which were unknown before. Many of these expressions have so thoroughly changed in the course of time that the stranger
is no longer recognized. We need but think of such words as *Abt, Altar,
Bibel, Bischof, Dom* (cathedral), *Kantor, Kaplan, Kapelle, Kreuz, Messe,
Mönch, Münster, Nonne, Papst, Priester, Probst* (provost), *Teufel,* and
a long list of others used by the Catholic church. The same phenomenon
was repeated with the spread of Roman law in German lands. The change
of legal systems to conform to the Roman pattern brought us a whole
body of new ideas which necessarily found admission into the language.
In general, by contact with the Roman world, the language of the German people became permeated with new expressions and word-forms,
which the Germans, in their turn, conveyed to their Slavic and Finnish
neighbors.

The development of militarism and army organization brought a
whole flood of new words from France, which the French in their turn
had borrowed from the Italians. Most of these words have retained their

foreign imprint completely. Think of *Armee, Marine, Artillerie, Infanterie, Kavallerie, Regiment, Kompanie, Schwadron, Bataillon, Major, General, Leutnant, Sergeant, Munition, Patrone, Bajonett, Bombe, Granate, Schrapnell, Kaserne, Baracke, equipieren, exerzieren, füsilieren, chargieren, rekrutieren, kommandieren,* and countless other words from military life.

The introduction of new foods and drinks has enriched our language with a long line of totally foreign expressions. There are *Kaffee* and *Zucker* from the Arabic, *Tee* from the Chinese, *Tabak* from the Indian, *Sago* from the Malayan, *Reis* from the Latin-Greek, *Kakao* from the Mexican. We will not speak of the new words with which science daily endows the language, nor of the countless coined words which the language of art contains. Their number is quite beyond reckoning. Today sport, which is spreading in Germany quite uncannily, has adorned the language with many English and American technical expressions that hardly enhance its beauty. Even when one tries hard to eliminate these foreign words and replace them by German expressions quite monstrous results sometimes follow.

But we are dealing not alone with so-called loan-words taken from a foreign language and in some form transferred to our own. There is another phenomenon in the development of every language for which the term loan-translation has been coined. When a hitherto unknown idea from another cultural circle penetrates into our mental or social life it does not always happen that, together with the new idea, we accept a foreign expression into our language. It frequently occurs that we translate the newly acquired concept into our own language by creating from the material at hand a word structure not previously used. Here the stranger confronts us, so to speak, in the mask of our own language. In this manner came words like *Halbwelt,* from demi-monde; *Aussperrung,* from lock-out; *Halbinsel,* from peninsula; *Zwieback,* from biscuit; *Wolkenkratzer,* from skyscraper, and a hundred similar creations. In his *Critique of Language,* Mauthner mentions a number of these "bastard translations," as he calls them; words like *Ausdruck* (expression), *Bischen* (particle), *Rücksicht* (regard), and *Wohltat* (beneficence). Of such loan translations there are a great number in every language. These have an actually revolutionary effect on the course of development of the language, and show us most of all the unreality of the view which maintains that in every language the spirit of a particular people lives and works. In reality every loan-translation is but a proof of the continuous penetration of foreign cultural elements within our own cultural circle—in so far as a people can speak of "its own culture."

Let us take into account how strongly the oriental imagery of the Old and New Testament has affected the heritage of all European languages. We are thinking not only of short phrases like "mark of Cain," "judgment of Solomon," "Job's comforter," "to bear one's cross," and so on, which are quite colloquial; more involved figures from the Bible have penetrated into all languages so deeply that they have become fully naturalized in everyday speech. Here are some examples which could easily be multiplied many times: to sell one's birthright for a mess of pottage; for a camel to pass through the eye of a needle; to gird up one's loins; a wolf in sheep's clothing; heaping coals of fire on one's head; to drive out the Devil with Beelzebub; to put new wine into old bottles; to hide one's light under a bushel; not worthy to tie the shoe-laces of another; being wise as a serpent and harmless as a dove; straining at a gnat and swallowing a camel; a voice crying in the wilderness; poor as Job; a light dawning on us; to speak with fiery tongues; to be like unto whited sepulchers; to wash one's hands of guilt; and a whole line of others of the kind.

In fact, loan-translation is one of the most curious things in language. Who thinks deeper here will reach conclusions which completely dispel the fairy tale of the immaculate conception of national speech. Loan-translations testify eloquently how strongly culture unites mankind. This bond is so enduring because it has, so to speak, tied itself and has not been imposed on man by external pressure. Compared with culture, so-called "national consciousness" is but an artificial creation serving to justify the political ambitions of small minorities in society.

Culture knows no such subterfuge, if only for the reason that it was not mechanically made, but has grown organically. It is the sum total of all human activity and motivates our lives unconditionally and without pretense. Loan-translations are nothing but intellectual borrowings by various groups of people within a certain cultural circle—and even beyond it. This influence, the so-called "national consciousness" opposes vainly, and Fritz Mauthner remarks with good reason:

> Before the intrusion of national consciousness, before the beginning of purist movements, the mass of the people borrowed from the treasury of foreign speech. Afterwards, such loans were avoided, but all the more numerously foreign concepts were brought into the language by translation. There are modern people of such touchy national feeling that they have driven purism to the utmost extreme (Neo-Greeks and Czechs). But they can isolate only their language, not their world concepts, their whole intellectual situation.[2]

For speech is not a special organism obeying its own laws, as was formerly believed; it is the form of expression of human individuals socially united. It changes with the spiritual and social conditions of life

[2] Fritz Mauthner, *Die Sprache*, Frankfurt a/M 1906, p. 55.

and is in the highest degree dependent on them. In speech, human thought expresses itself, but this is no purely personal affair, as is often assumed, but an inner process continually animated and influenced by the social environment. In man's thoughts are mirrored not only his natural environment, but all relations which he has with his fellows. The closer the union to which we belong, the richer and more varied the cultural relations we maintain with our fellow men, the stronger are the reciprocal effects which unite us with our social environment and continually influence our thought.

Thinking is, therefore, by no means a process which finds its explanation solely in the mental life of the individual; it is likewise a reflection of the natural and social environment which crystallizes in man's brain into definite concepts. From this point of view the social character of human thought is undeniable; and as speech is but the living expression of our thought, its existence is rooted in the life of society and conditioned by it.

This is, indeed, apparent from the fact that human speech is not inborn, but only acquired by man through his social relations. It is not maintained that by this concept all the riddles of thought and speech have been solved. In this field there is very much for which we have no sufficient explanation; and the well-known opinion of Goethe, that really "no one understands another, and no one on hearing the same words thinks what another thinks," has certainly profound meaning. There are still many unknown and mysterious things in us and around us concerning which the last word has not yet been spoken. However, we are not dealing here with such problems, but solely with the social character of thought and speech, which in our opinion is undeniable.

Concerning the origin of language, likewise, we have until now only been able to surmise, but Haeckel's assumption that man commenced his evolutionary course as a mute being appears to us to have little probability. It is reasonable to assume that man, who had inherited the social instincts of his predecessors in the animal kingdom, was already, upon his appearance on the human plane of life, endowed with certain expressions of speech—however crude and undeveloped these might have been. For language in its widest sense is not the exclusive property of man, but can be clearly recognized in all social species. That within these species a certain mutual understanding takes place is undeniable according to all observations. It is not language as such, but the special forms of human speech, the articulate language which permits of concepts and so enables man's thoughts to achieve higher results, which distinguish man in this respect from other species.

It is probable that human speech was at its beginning limited to certain sounds derived from nature, to which were probably added expressions denoting pain, pleasure or surprise. These sounds became habitual within the horde for the designation of certain things and were inherited by the progeny. With these first paltry beginnings the necessary preconditions for the further development of speech were given. But speech itself became for man a valuable instrument in the struggle for existence and has doubtless contributed most to his fabulous rise.

By communal work, obligatory for the whole horde, there gradually arose also a series of special designations for the tools and objects of daily use. Every new invention, every discovery, contributed to the enrichment of the previously acquired store of language, and this evolution in time led to the formation of definite word pictures or symbols from which a new mode of thinking had to result. Although language was primarily only an expression of thought, it now reacted on thought and influenced its course. The image import of words, which originally sprang from purely sensual impressions, gradually progressed to the mental and created thereby the first precondition for abstract thinking. From this arose that curious reciprocal action between speech and human thought, which during cultural development has become ever more varied and complicated, so that we can with some reason maintain that "language thinks for us."

But it is these very image-expressions, the so-called "word symbols," that have most influenced the course of events and changed their original meanings so thoroughly that they frequently turn into their opposites. This happens, as a rule, against all logic; but then language is not amenable to logic, a fact which seldom occurs to most of the language purifiers. Many words gradually disappear from a language without any clear reason—a process which we can very well observe at the present time. Thus, the old *Gasse* had to yield precedence to *Strasse*; *Stube* is being crowded out by *Zimmer*; *Knabe* had to yield to *Junge*; *Haupt*, to *Kopf*; *Antlitz*, to *Gesicht*. On the other hand, some words whose original meaning has been lost nevertheless maintain themselves in the language. Thus we still speak of a *Flinte*, a *Feder*, a *Silbergulden*, although the flintlock long ago passed into history, and we have almost forgotten that our fathers and grandfathers made their writing implements from the plumage of a goose, and although *gulden* really means golden and can consequently have nothing in common with silver. We enjoy a man's "dry humor," and never suspect that the latter word, derived from the Latin, originally meant wetness, juice or moisture. But language accomplishes still stranger things. Thus, a knight returning to his castle from a fight was *entrüstet*, meaning that he took off his armor, but we now put on our armor when we become *entrüstet* (indignant). Every language contains a number of such contradictions, the only explanation being that men gradually give to certain things and events new meanings without being conscious of it.

The German philologist, Ernst Wasserzieher, in some excellent studies from which the above examples were taken, has described impressively the symbolism of language and has shown that we speak almost exclusively in images without noticing it.[3] When peasant women *lesen* (glean) ears of grain in a field, when we *übertreten* (overstep) a puddle, when our image mirrors in a brook, these are real processes which need no further explanation. But when we *lesen* from a newspaper, *übertreten* the law, or a man's soul is mirrored in his eyes, then the symbolism of language is at work, visualizing for us certain processes for which sensual perception can only serve as godfather.

These conceptual images are not only subject to constant change, but every new phenomenon of social life creates new word-forms which were quite incomprehensible to former generations because they lacked the social and mental bases for these new structures in language. The World War, with its immediate accompanying effects in all fields of economic, political and social life, gives an excellent example of this. During it a number of new words were introduced into the language which no one would have understood before the War, for example: drumfire, gas attack, flamethrower, fieldwalker, shock troop, smoke screen, barrage fire, camouflage. Such new formations appear in the course of time in all fields of human activity, and owe their creation to the constant change in the conditions of life. In this manner language changes within certain periods so completely that later generations, looking backward and viewing its creation, find it stranger and stranger, until finally a point is reached where it is no longer understood and has meaning only for the scholar engaged in research.

Already the language of Schiller and Goethe has disappeared. The speech of Fischart, Hans Sachs and Luther presents many problems to us, and frequently requires an explanation to bring the men of that time and their concept of life within our comprehension. The further we hark back—say to the time of Walter von der Vogelweide and Gottfried von Strassburg—the darker and less understandable becomes the meaning of the language, until we finally reach a point where "our own language" appears to us like a foreign tongue whose puzzles we can only solve by the aid of translations. Let one read a few stanzas from the famous *Heilandhandschrift*, allegedly composed by an unknown Saxon poet at the instigation of Louis the Pious not long after the conversion of the Saxons to Christianity. This German from the first half of the ninth century sounds to us today like a foreign language; and just as strange to us are the men who spoke it.

The language of Rabelais was hardly understood in France a hundred years after his death. The modern Frenchman can understand the original text of the great Humanist only with the aid of a special dictionary.

[3] *Bilderbuch der deutschen Sprache; Leben und Weben der Sprache.*

By the establishment of the French Academy in 1629 the French language was given a strict guardian that endeavored with all its power to eliminate from it popular expressions and figures of speech. This was called "refining the language." In reality it deprived it of originality and bent it under the yoke of an unnatural despotism from which it was later obliged forcibly to free itself. Fénélon, and also Racine, gave this sentiment various expression; Diderot wrote quite plainly.

> We have impoverished our language by all too much refinement. Frequently we have only a particular word at our disposal for the expression of a thought, so we prefer to let the thought's force fade because we are afraid to use a new and allegedly ungenteel expression. In this way a number of words have been lost to us which we gladly admire in Amyot and Montaigne. The so-called "good style" has banished them from the language only for the reason that they were used by the people. The people, however, who always strive to imitate the great, after a while refused also to use these words, so that in the course of time they were forgotten.

The language of Shakespeare presents many puzzles even to the educated Englishman, not only because much ancient speech-stuff survives in it which is no longer used in modern English, but principally because the poet uses many words in a sense which does not correspond to their modern meaning. Back to the *Canterbury Tales* of Geoffrey Chaucer is a very difficult journey, while the original text of the songs of Beowulf is unknown territory to the modern Englishman.

To the Spaniard of today the original of *Don Quixote* presents many difficulties; and these become increasingly insurmountable as he approaches the old text of *El Cid*. The deeper we penetrate into the past of a language, the stranger it appears to us; to attempt to discover its beginning would be a vain undertaking. Who could, for example, definitely state when in Italy and France men quit speaking Latin and began to speak Italian and French? Who could say when the corrupted *lingua Romana rustica* changed into Spanish, or better still, Catalonian? Language alters so gradually that succeeding generations are hardly conscious of the change. With this we reach a point of great significance for our investigation.

The defenders of national ideology maintain that nationality represents a natural inner unity and is in its deepest being something permanent, something unchangeable. Although they cannot deny that the conditions of mental and social life of every nationality are subject to change, they try to save themselves with the assertion that these changes affect only the outer conditions and not the real nature of the nationality. Now if language were in fact the special token of the national spirit, then it would have to represent a special unity which is defined by the nature of a nation and reveals the special character of every people. In fact, such assertions have not been wanting.

Fichte, even, attempted to derive a nation's character from its language. With the full arrogance of his extreme patriotic enthusiasm he asserts of the German language that it reveals the vigor of a natural force which gives it life, power, and expressiveness, while the people of the Latin tongues, more especially the French, have at their disposal only an artificial, purely conventional language which does violence to their nature (and in which the real character of those people is revealed). Later, Wilhelm von Humboldt also developed a complete theory which was to prove that in the structure and expressiveness of a language the special nature of a people reveals itself. "Language is, so to speak, the external expression of the spirit of a people. Their speech is their spirit, and their spirit is their speech. One cannot express too strongly the identity of the two." [4]

Since then, similar theories have appeared frequently The attempts of Vierkandt, Hüsing, Finck and others illustrate this. In all these attempts, some of them presented very brilliantly, the wish was father to the thought. They all bear on their face the mark of the manufactured. One feels that they are artificially wound up. Real and indisputable proofs for the correctness of these theories have nowhere been given. Hence, the well-known philologist, Sandfeld-Jensen, is quite right when he disputes Finck's statement that "the structure of the German language should be regarded as the expression of the German world concept," and declares that Finck never gave proof for his assertion and that other researchers could with just as good grounds have reached quite a different conclusion. Says Sandfeld-Jensen, "In this difficult field, usually called folk-psychology, one constantly runs danger of being pushed off the firm ground and losing oneself in empty philosophizing." [5]

No, language is not the result of a special folk-unity. It is a structure in constant change in which the intellectual and social culture of the various phases of our evolution is reflected. It is always in flux, protean in its inexhaustible power to assume new forms. This eternal change in language accounts for the existence of old and new, living and dead, languages.

But if language constantly changes, if it readily yields to foreign influences and always has an open door for the progeny of another species, then it is a faithful reflection of culture in general. This fact also gives proof that by the aid of language we can never penetrate into the mysterious "nature of the nation" which allegedly is always the same at bottom.

[4] *Einleitung über die Verschiedenheit des menschlichen Sprachbaues und ihren Einfluss auf die geistige Entwicklung der Menschheit.*
[5] *Die Sprachwissenschaft.* Leipzig-Berlin, 1923.

As we conscientiously pursue the origins of a language, we find that it has fewer and fewer relations with the cultural circle to which we belong, the chasm which separates us from the men of past ages becomes ever wider, until at last all is lost in an impenetrable mist. When a Frenchman or an Englishman, be he thinker, statesman or artist, today presents certain thoughts to us, we readily understand him, although we do not belong to the same nation; we do belong to the same cultural circle and are united by invisible ties, the spiritual currents of our time. But the feeling and thinking of men of past centuries remains for us largely strange or impenetrable even when they belong to the same nation; for they were subject to other cultural influences. To bring those ages closer to us we need a substitute which replaces reality—tradition. But where tradition sets in, there begins the realm of fiction. Just as the first history of every people is lost in mythology, so also in tradition the mythical plays the most important part.

It is not alone the so-called "historical conception" which makes events of past ages appear to us in a "special light"; allegedly "objective" history, too, is never free from mythological haziness and historical mistakes. Usually these occur quite unconsciously; everything depends on how strongly the personal attitude of the historian has influenced his interpretation of the received tradition and, consequently, the picture he has made. In this personal attitude of the historian, the social environment in which he lives, the class he belongs to, the political or religious opinions he holds, all play an important part. The so-called "national history" of every country is a great fable having hardly any relationship to actual events. Of the "history" taught in the school books of the various nations we will not even speak. There, history is perverted on principle. Human predisposition, inherited prejudices and traditional concepts, to touch which we are either too cowardly or too lazy, very frequently influence the judgment of even earnest researchers and tempt them to arbitrary judgments having little in common with historical reality. No one is more subject to such influences than the protagonists of nationalistic ideas; for them all too frequently a wish-concept must serve as a substitute for sober facts.

That the origin and evolution of a language does not proceed according to national principles nor spring from the special conception of a particular people is clear for everyone who is willing to see it. Let us glance at the evolution of English, today the most widely spread of all European tongues. Of the speech of the Celtic tribes who inhabited the British Isles before the Roman invasion certain dialects have to this day survived in Wales, the Isle of Man, Ireland, the Scottish Highlands and French Brittany. But "British" in this sense has no relation whatsoever with modern English either in sentence structure or vocabulary. When during the first century the Romans subjected the land to their rule, they naturally tried to introduce their language among the people. Presumably the spread of the Latin tongue was confined primarily to the towns and the larger settlements in the southern part of the country where Roman rule had taken strongest root. At any rate, it was inevitable that during almost four centuries of Roman occupation many words were adopted from that language. It is even very probable that in this manner, in the course of time, a special local Latin would have evolved, from which, just as in Italy, France and Spain, a language would have developed.

This development was completely destroyed when in the sixth century the Low German tribes, the Angles, Saxons and Jutes, invaded Britain and conquered the land after protracted struggles with warlike tribes of the north. Then the speech of the conquerors gradually became the language of the land, although many words from the local dialects were adopted. With the Danish invasions of the eighth and tenth centuries new Germanic idioms entered the language of the country—an influence which even today can be clearly recognized. Finally, after the invasion of the Normans under William the Conqueror, the language was thoroughly permeated with Norman French, so that there occurred not only a decided increase of the old speech heritage by so-called loan-words, but also a profound change in the spirit and structure of the language. From these manifold transitions and mixtures of tongues there evolved gradually the modern English speech.

Every language has had a similar evolution, even though the separate phases of the process cannot always be so clearly followed. Not only has every language in the course of its development received many foreign language elements into its stock of words, but very frequently even the grammatical structure of the language has been profoundly changed by close touch with other people. A classic example is the modern speech of the various Balkan states. The various languages can be traced to quite different language roots; nevertheless, these languages have, according to the enlightened testimony of eminent philologists, a remarkably unified imprint, not only in respect to their phraseology, but also in the evolution of their syntax. Thus, for example, in all of them, the infinitive has been more or less lost. One of the most curious phenomena in the evolution of languages is the Bulgarian. According to the united opinion of well-known philologists like Schleicher, Leskien, Brugman, Kopitar and others, the Bulgarian is much closer to the old Slavic church language than any other modern Slavic tongue; yet, besides two thousand Turkish and about one thousand Greek words, it has absorbed numerous expressions from the Persian, Arabic, Albanian and Rumanian. The grammar of the Bulgarian language has assumed quite new forms. Thus the definite article is attached to the noun, as in Albanian and Rumanian. Furthermore, Bulgarian is the only one among the Slavic tongues which has completely lost its seven cases and has replaced them by prepositions, as in Italian and French.

Of such examples comparative philology knows a great number. This is one reason why modern philology comes more and more clearly to recognize that all former classifications of languages according to various original groups can at best be regarded only as a technical device corresponding but little to reality. We know today that even the Tibetan-Chinese and the Ural-Altai and Semitic languages are interspersed with a mass of Indo-Germanic speech elements, as was also the Old Egyptian. Of the Hebrew language it is maintained that while it is Semitic in its structure, in its vocabulary it is Indo-Germanic. G. Meinhof, one of the best experts on African languages, even maintains that Semitic, Hamitic, and Indo-Germanic languages belong to the same speech circle.

But it is not alone foreign influences which affect the evolution of a language. Every great event in the life of a people or a nation which steers its history into new courses leaves deep marks on its language. Thus, the great French Revolution resulted not only in profound changes in the economic, political and social life of France; it also caused a complete about-face in language and burst the fetters which the vanity of the aristocracy and the literary men under aristocratic influence had imposed on it. Especially in France the language of the court and of the salon and of literature had been so immensely "refined" that it seemed to have lost all vigor of expression and spent itself only in sophistications. Between the language of the educated and of the great masses of the people there yawned an abyss just as unbridgeable as the chasm between the privileged classes and the proletariat. Only the revolution stayed the decline of the language. It endowed the newly awakened political and social life with a great number of forceful and popular expressions, most of which maintained themselves, although during the years of the reaction every effort was made to eliminate from the language all expressions reminiscent of the revolution. In his "Neology," published in 1801, Mercier mentions over two thousand words unknown in the age of Louis XIV; yet the number of new creations emanating from the revolution was by no means exhausted. Paul Lafargue says, in a very remarkable essay: "New words and expressions assailed the language in such number that newspapers and periodicals of that time could have been understood by the courtiers of Louis XIV only by means of a translation." [6]

Popular speech is, in fact, a chapter in itself. If we choose to regard language as the essential characteristic of a nation we are likely to over-

---

[6] This essay, from which we have borrowed some passages concerning the development of the French language, first appeared in a Parisian periodical, *Era Nouvelle*. A German translation appeared in a supplementary number of *Die Neue Zeit*, No. 15, under the title, "*Die französische Sprache vor und nach der Revolution.*"

look the fact that mutual understanding between the various members of the same nation is often possible only by the common written language. This language, however, which every nation only gradually evolves, is, compared, with popular speech, an artificial creation. Hence, written language and popular speech are always antagonistic, the latter only unwillingly submitting to external compulsion. It is certain that all written language developed first from a particular dialect. Usually this dialect belongs to a region more advanced economically and culturally, whose inhabitants on account of their higher mental development have also a larger vocabulary which gradually gives them a certain predominance over the dialects of others. This development is clearly observable in every country. Gradually the written language absorbs words of other dialects, and so the possibility of linguistic understanding within a larger territory is furthered. Thus we find in Luther's translation of the Bible, which is based on the High Saxon dialect, quite a number of expressions borrowed from other German dialects. Many words which Luther uses in his translation were totally unknown in Southern Germany, so that they could not be understood without a special explanation: for instance, *fühlen*, *gehorchen*, *täuschen*, *Lippe*, *Träne*, *Kahn*, *Ufer*, *Hügel*, and so on. Taken from High German dialects are *staunen*, *entsprechen*, *tagen*, *Unbill*, *Ahne*, *dumpf*; while *Damm*, *Beute*, *beschwichtigen*, *flott*, *düster*, *sacht*, are of Low German origin.[7]

It is, therefore, the written language, not the popular speech, that serves as a means of understanding in a wider circle. The man from Ditmar or East Prussia is practically in a foreign country when he comes to Bavaria or Swabia. To the Frieslander the so-called *"Schwitzerdütsch"* sounds as foreign as French, although he has the same written language. That a South German is quite helpless among the various dialects of the Low Germans everyone knows who has had even the least experience. We meet the same phenomenon in the speech of every nation. The Londoner can hardly understand the Scotch dialect; the Parisian is entirely a stranger to the French of the Gascon or the Walloon; while to the Provençal the secrets of the Parisian argot are forever closed, without a special study. The Italian of the Neapolitan is less difficult to the Spaniard than to the Venetian or the Genoese. The speech of the Andalusians is very distinct from that of the Castilians—not to speak of the Catalonians, who have their own language.

The philologist who could draw a definite line between dialect and language is yet to be born. In most cases it is quite impossible to determine where a dialect ceases and a separate language begins. Hence the uncertainty about the number of the languages on earth, put by some philolo-

[7] See W. Fischer, *Die deutsche Sprache von heute*. Berlin-Leipzig, 1918.

gists at about eight hundred and by others at fifteen hundred to two thousand.

The speech free from dialects, however, which is created from the written language, is never able to convey to us properly the spirit and the special character of the idiom. Every translation from a foreign language has its deficiencies which can never be quite surmounted. Yet it is easier to translate from one language into another than to translate a dialect of one's own language into the common written language. The bare occurrence of things can be conveyed, but never the living spirit, which stands and falls with the idiom. All attempts to translate Fritz Reuter into High German have so far failed and must always fail, just as it would be love's labor lost to try to translate into the written German the *Alemannische Gedichte* of Hebel, or the dialect poets like Friedrich Stoltze, Franz von Kobell, or Daniel Hirtz.

Frequently, the question whether a speech is to be regarded as a dialect or as a distinct language is purely a political affair. Thus, Dutch is today a separate language because the Hollanders have their own state organization. If this were not so, Dutch would probably be regarded as a Low German dialect. The same relationship exists between Danish and Swedish. In Germany as well as in Sweden there seem to exist greater differences between various dialects of the country than between German and Dutch or between Swedish and Danish. On the other hand, we see how under the influence of an especially intense nationalism a dead language can be awakened to new life, as the Celtic in Ireland, and Hebrew in the Jewish colonies in Palestine.

But speech everywhere takes quite curious courses and constantly presents new puzzles which no philologist has up to now been able to solve. It is not so very long since we believed that all existing and all vanished languages could be traced to a common original language. Doubtless the myth of the lost paradise played a part in this. The belief in a first pair of mankind logically leads to the concept of a common original language (Hebrew was naturally accepted)—the "sacred language." Advancing knowledge concerning man's origin put an end to this belief also. This definite break with the old conception first cleared the way for an evolutionary-historical examination of language. The consequence was that the whole mass of arbitrary preconceptions had to be abandoned as being in hopeless disagreement with the results of modern philological research. Thus, among others, fell the hypothesis of a regular evolution of language according to definite phonetic laws, which had been maintained by Schleicher and his successors. Gradually the conclusion was reached that the slow formation of a language is no law-determined process at all, but happens quite without rule or order. When later the theory of the legendary "Aryan race" also gently dissolved, together with the

fanciful speculations which had attached themselves to the alleged existence of such a race, the hypothesis of a common origin for the so-called
Indo-Germanic languages, frequently called "Aryan," was badly shaken
and can hardly be maintained today.

> The fable of a common genealogical tree of the so-called Aryan lan-
> guages can, after the skeptical labors of Johannes Schmidt, be no longer main-
> tained, and is carefully avoided by leading philologists. I see the time as not
> far distant when the concept of language kinships will no longer be used
> at all, when the similarity of speech elements can for the larger part be
> traced to adoptions and the lesser part left unexplained, when we finally
> quit trying to apply the methods of history when dealing with prehistoric
> times and the science of tradition to the time without traditions. The genea-
> logical tree-building of comparative philology achieved its triumphs for a
> time out of which literary sources may have come down to us, but not his-
> torical connections. When we recognize these connections in the light of
> historical time there exist no longer any daughter languages, there are only
> adoptions by the weaker culture from the stronger (wherein often enough
> fashion, religion, or war-glory decided what is weaker and what is stronger).
> There are individual adoptions and mass adoptions, adoptions from a special
> culture branch and adoptions from a whole culture.[8]

The origin and formation of the different languages is wrapped in such
impenetrable darkness that we can only feel our way forward with the
help of uncertain hypotheses. All the more is caution commanded in a field
where we can so easily go hopelessly astray. But one thing is sure; the
idea that every language is the original creation of a particular people
or a particular nation and has consequently a purely national character
lacks any foundation and is only one of those countless illusions which in
the age of race theories and nationalism have become so unpleasantly
conspicuous.

If one maintains, however, that speech is the characteristic expression
of nationality, then one must naturally prove therefrom that a people
or a nation ceases to exist when, for one reason or another, it has abandoned its speech, a phenomenon by no means rare in history. Or do we
believe that with a change in speech there also occurs a change in the
"national spirit" or the "soul of the nation"? If this were true, it would
prove that nationality is a very uncertain concept, lacking any substantial
basis.

Peoples have in the course of history frequently changed their language, and it is for the most part only a question of accident what language
a people uses today. The people of Germany present no exception in this
respect; they have with relative ease accepted not only the morals and

[8] Fritz Mauthner, *Die Sprache*, p. 49.

customs of foreign peoples, but also their languages, and have forgotten their own. When the Normans in the ninth and tenth centuries settled in Northern France it was hardly a hundred years before they had completely forgotten their own language and spoke only French. At the conquest of England and Sicily in the eleventh century the same phenomenon was repeated. The Norman conquerors in England forgot their acquired French and took over the language of the acquired land, whose development, however, they strongly influenced. In Sicily and Southern Italy, however, the Norman influence vanished entirely or left scarcely a trace. The conquerors were lost entirely in the native population, whose language (and, frequently, oriental customs) they had accepted. And not the Normans alone. A whole line of Germanic peoples have in their wanderings and conquests surrendered their own language and accepted another. We may mention the Lombards in Italy, the Franks in Gaul, the Goths in Spain, not to mention the Vandals, Suevians, Alani, and many others. Peoples and tribes of the most varied stems have had to accept the same fate.

When Ludwig Jahn, the great German patriot, who on principle could not endure a Frenchman, uttered the words: "In its mother tongue every people honors itself, in the treasury of its speech is contained the charter of its cultural history. A people which forgets its own language abandons its franchise in humanity and is only playing a super's part on the world stage," he unfortunately forgot that the people to which he belonged, the Prussians, were also one of the peoples who had forgotten their language and had abandoned their franchise in humanity. The Old Prussians were a mixed people in which the Slavic element was by far predominant, and they spoke a language related to the Lettish and Lithuanian, which maintained itself until the sixteenth century. The philologist, Dürr, therefore, rightly maintains: "There are few, perhaps no, peoples who in the course of history have not changed their language; some of them several times."

In this respect the Jews are remarkable. Their original history, like that of most peoples, is totally unknown; but we may assume that they entered history as a mixed people. During the Jewish rule in Palestine two languages were in use there, Hebrew and Aramaic, and in religious services both languages were used. A considerable time before the destruction of Jerusalem there was in Rome a large Jewish congregation with considerable influence which had adopted the Latin language. In Alexandria also there lived numerous Jews, whose number was increased by countless fugitives after the failure of the rebellion of the Maccabees. In Egypt, Jews adopted the Greek language and translated their sacred writings into Greek, and at the last the text was studied only in these translations. Their best minds participated in the rich intellectual life of the Greeks and wrote almost entirely in their language.

When at the beginning of the eighth century the Arabs invaded Spain, many Jews streamed into the land, where, just as in the north of Africa, a considerable number of Jewish settlements already existed. Under the Moorish rule the Jews enjoyed very great liberties, which permitted them to take prominent part in the cultural upbuilding of the land—at that time an oasis in the midst of the spiritual darkness wherein Europe was sunk. And Arabic became the speech of the Jewish people. Even religio-philosophical works like the *Moreh Nebuchim* ("Guide of the Erring") by Moses ben Maimon (Maimonides) and the *Cosari* of the celebrated poet, Jehuda Helevi, were written in Arabic and only later translated into Hebrew. After the expulsion of the Jews from Spain many families went to France, Germany, Holland and England, where already existed Jewish communities which had adopted the speech of their hosts. Later, when cruel persecution of the Jews occurred in France and Germany, streams of Jewish refugees went to Poland and Russia. They took their old Ghetto German, largely interpenetrated with Hebrew expressions, into the new home, where in the course of time many Slavic words drifted into their speech. Thus developed the so-called Yiddish, the present speech of the Eastern Jews, which during the last forty years has created a fairly voluminous literature that can very well endure comparison with the literature of the other small peoples of Europe. We are here dealing with a people which in the course of a long and painful history has frequently changed its language without thereby losing its inner unity.

On the other hand, there are a number of instances where community of language does not coincide with the frontiers of the nation at all, and again others where in the same state various languages are used. Thus, by language, the native of Rousillon is much more closely related to the Catalonians, the Corsican to the Italians, the Alsatian to the Germans, although for all that they all belong to the French nation. The Brazilian speaks the same language as the Portuguese; in the other South American states Spanish is the language. The Negroes of Haiti speak French, a very corrupt French, which is, nevertheless, their mother tongue—for they have no other. The United States has the same speech as England. In the lands of North Africa and Asia Minor, Arabic is the common language. Of similar examples there are a great number.

On the other hand, in even so small a country as Switzerland, four different languages are used: German, French, Italian and Romansh. Belgium has two languages, Flemish and French. In Spain, besides the official Castilian, there are Basque, Catalonian and Portuguese. There is scarcely a state in Europe that does not harbor foreign language groups to a greater or less extent.

Language is, therefore, no characteristic of a nation; it is even not always decisive of membership in a particular nation. Every language is permeated with a mass of foreign speech elements in which the mode of thought and the intellectual culture of other peoples lives. For this reason, all attempts to trace the so-called "essence of the nation" to its language fail utterly to carry conviction.

Chapter 3

RACE RESEARCH AND RACE THEORY. CONCERNING THE UNITY OF THE GENUS MAN. THE ALLEGED ORIGINAL RACES OF EUROPE. CONCERNING THE CONCEPT "RACE." THE DISCOVERY OF THE BLOOD-GROUPS AND THE RACE. PHYSICAL CHARACTERS AND MENTAL QUALITIES. GOBINEAU'S THEORY OF THE INEQUALITY OF THE RACES OF MEN. THE ARYANS. HISTORY AS RACE CONFLICT. RACE THEORY AND SEIGNORIAL RIGHT. CHAMBERLAIN'S RACE THEORIES. CHAMBERLAIN AND GOBINEAU. THE GERMAN AS THE CREATOR OF ALL CULTURES. CHRIST AS A GERMAN. PROTESTANTISM AS A RACE RELIGION. "GERMANDOM" AND "JEWDOM" AS OPPOSITE POLES. THE POLITICAL ENDEAVORS OF CHAMBERLAIN. LUDWIG WOLTMANN'S THEORY. RACE THEORY AND HEREDITY. THE INFLUENCE OF THE NATURAL ENVIRONMENT. MODERN RACE THEORIES. THE "RACE SOUL." RACE CHARACTERISTICS OF THE GERMAN BEARERS OF CULTURE. THE POWER OF ACQUIRED CHARACTERS. HUNGER AND LOVE. RACE IN THE WORLD WAR. THE NORDIC THEORY. DENUNCIATION OF OTHER RACES. THE CONSEQUENCES OF A DELUSIVE CONCEPTION. CONTRADICTIONS IN MODERN RACE LITERATURE. MEN AND IDEAS IN THE LIGHT OF RACE THEORY. RACE AND POWER.

BESIDES the concepts already discussed concerning the character of the nation there is another which today is very clamorous and has gained many adherents, especially in Germany. We are here speaking of "community of blood" and of the alleged influence of race on the structure of the nation and on its spiritual and cultural creative endowment. From the very beginning we must make here a clear distinction between purely scientific investigations concerning the origin of races and their special characteristics, and the so-called "race theories" whose advocates have ventured to judge the mental, moral and cultural qualities of particular human groups from the real or imaginary physical characteristics of a race. The latter undertaking is extremely risky, inasmuch as we are quite uncertain not only of the origin of races, but of the origin of men in general, and have to rely solely upon hypotheses, not knowing how far they correspond to reality, or fail to do so.

Scientific authorities are not agreed in their opinions as to the age of the human race. It was some time before they were willing to place the first appearance of man on earth as far back as the Glacial Epoch. However, the opinion is lately gaining ground that man's past can be traced back to the Tertiary Period. We are also completely in the dark concerning man's original home. Decided differences of opinion among the most noted representatives of biological science have again been brought sharply to the front during recent years by the results of the Cameron-Cable expeditions in South Africa and the Roy Chapman Andrews American expedition in Outer Mongolia. The question also remains unanswered whether the appearance of mankind was confined to a definite region or occurred in various parts of the earth approximately at the same time. In other words, whether the genus Man sprang from a single stem and the differences of race were subsequently caused by migrations or changes in the external conditions of life, or whether difference of race was due to descent from different stems from the very beginning. Most researchers today still maintain the standpoint of monogenesis and are of the opinion that mankind goes back to a single original source and that race distinctions appeared only later through change of environment. Darwin maintained this point of view when he said: "All human races are so immensely closer to one another than to any ape that I am inclined to view them as descending from a single form." What has caused prominent men of science to adhere to the unity of the human species is principally the structure of the human skeleton, which determines the whole bodily formation, and which among all races shows an astonishing similarity of structure.

To all these difficulties must be added the fact that we are not at all clear about the concept of "race," as is seen from the arbitrary way men have played about with the classification of existing races. For a long time we were content with the four races of Linnaeus; then Blumenbach produced a fifth and Buffon a sixth; Peschel followed at once with a seventh and Agassiz with an eighth. Till at length Haeckel was talking of twelve, Morton of twenty-two, and Crawford of sixty races—a number which was to be doubled a little later. So that as respectable a researcher as Luschan could with justice assert that it is just as impossible to determine the number of the existing races of men as of the existing languages, since one can no more easily distinguish between a race and a variety than between a language and a so-called dialect. If a white North European is set beside a Negro and a typical Mongolian the difference is clear to any layman. But if one examines thoroughly the countless gradations of these three races one reaches a point at last where one cannot say with certainty where one race leaves off and the other begins.

The Gothic word, *reizza*, really had only the meaning of rift or line.[1] In this sense it found admission into most European languages where it gradually was called upon for the designation of other things and still is. Thus in English we understand by "race" not only a specific animal or human group with definite hereditary physical characteristics, but the word is also used for contests in speed, as for instance, horse-race. Also we speak of the race of life, and a mill-race. In France, the word acquired, among other meanings, also a political meaning, as applied to the succession of the various dynasties. Thus the Merovingians, the Carolingians and the Capets were spoken of as the first, the second and the third race. In Spanish and Italian also, the word has a similar variety of meanings. Later, it was used mainly by breeders of animals—until gradually it became the fashionable slogan for particular political parties. Thus we have become used to connect the word race with a concept which is itself unclear. As eminent an anthropologist as F. von Luschan dared to say: ". . . yes, the word race itself has more and more lost its meaning and had best be abandoned if it could be replaced by a less ambiguous word."

Since the discovery of the famous human skeletal remains in Neanderthal (1856) scientific research has made about a hundred similar discoveries in various parts of the earth, all of which are traceable to the Glacial Age. We must, however, not overestimate the knowledge gained from them, for nearly all are single specimens with which no certain comparisons can be made. Besides, bone remnants alone give us no idea whatsoever concerning the skin color, hair and superficial facial structure of these prehistoric men. From the skull structure of these human specimens only one thing can be stated with a certain degree of definiteness, namely, that in these discoveries we are dealing with at least three different varieties, which have been named after the places where they were discovered. So we now speak of a Neanderthal race, an Aurignac race and a Cro-Magnon race. Of these, the Neanderthal man seems to have been the most primitive, whereas the Cro-Magnon man, both from his skull structure and the tools discovered, seems to have been the most developed scion of the European population at that time.

In what relationship these three races—assuming that we are really dealing with races—stood to each other and where they came from, no one knows. Whether the Neanderthalers really originated in Africa and emigrated to Europe, or whether they had inhabited great sections of our continent for thousands of years until about 40,000 years ago they were driven out by the immigrating Aurignac race, as Klaatsch and Heilborn assumed, is of course only hypothesis. It is equally questionable whether the Cro-Magnon man is in fact the result of a mixture of the Neanderthal

[1] Some English philologists trace the verb "to write" to *reizza*, as it originally meant to mark something.

and the Aurignac man, as some investigators have assumed. Entirely mistaken is the attempt to derive the present European races from these three "original" races, since we cannot know whether in these varieties we are really dealing with original racial types or not. Most probably not.

Not only in Europe are pure races wanting; we also fail to find them among the so-called savage peoples, even when these have made their homes in the most distant parts of the earth, as, for example, the Eskimos or the inhabitants of Tierra del Fuego. Whether there were once "original races" can hardly be affirmed today; at least our present state of knowledge does not justify us in making definite assertions which lack all convincing proof. From this it appears that the concept of race does not describe something fixed and unchangeable, but something in a perpetual state of flux, something continually being made over. Most of all we must beware of confusing race with species or genus, as is unfortunately so often done by modern race theorists. Race is only an artificial classification concept of biological science used as a technical device for keeping track of particular observations. Only mankind as a whole constitutes a biological unit, a species. This is proved primarily by the unlimited capacity for cross-breeding within the genus man. Every sexual union between offspring of the most widely different races is fruitful; also unions of its progeny. This phenomenon is one of the strongest arguments for the common origin of human kind.

With the discovery of the so-called blood groups it was at first believed that the problem of race had been solved; but here, too, the disillusionment followed swiftly. When Karl Landsteiner had succeeded in proving that men can be distinguished according to three different blood groups, to which Jansky and Moss added a fourth, it was believed that this difference in the blood, a fact of great importance especially for medical science, would establish the existence of four primary races. But it was soon discovered that these four blood groups can be found among all races, though blood group three is rare among American Indians and Eskimos. Above all, it was shown that a long-skulled blond with all the marks of the Nordic race may belong to the same blood group as a dark-skinned Negro or an almond-eyed Chinese. Doubtless a very sad fact for those race theorists who have so much to say about the "voice of the blood."

The majority of race theoreticians maintain that so-called "race characteristics" are a heritage created by nature itself unaffected by external life conditions and are transferred unchanged to the progeny, providing that the parents are racially related. Hence, the race destiny is a blood-fate which none can escape. By race characteristics we mean primarily the shape of the skull, the color of the skin, the special kind and color of the hair and eyes, the shape of the nose, and the size of the body. Whether these characteristics are indeed so "inalienable" as race theorists maintain, whether they can really be changed only by crossing of races, or whether natural or social environment cannot also effect a change of purely physiological race characteristics, is for science a chapter far from closed.

How the special characteristics of the various races originally appeared we can today only guess, but in all probability they were in one way or another acquired by a change in the natural environment—a view held today by the most prominent anthropologists. There exist already quite a number of established facts from which it appears that physical race characteristics may be changed by external life conditions and the change inherited by the descendants. In his excellent work, *Race and Culture*, Friedrich Hertz records the experiments with mollusks and insects by the two researchers, Schröder and Pictet, who by changes in environment succeeded in altering the nutritional instincts, mode of ovulation and of pupation, and the procreative instinct so thoroughly that the changes were transmitted by inheritance, even though the modified conditions were later removed. The experiments which the American scholar, Tower, made with the Colorado beetle are well known. Tower exposed the insects to colder temperatures and by these and other influences succeeded in effecting a change in certain characteristics which also were inherited by the progeny.

E. Vatter records the experiences of the Russian anthropologist Ivanowsky during the three-year famine period in Russia after the war. Ivanowsky had made measurements of 2,114 men and women from the most varied parts of the country at half-yearly intervals, so that every individual was examined six times. Thereby it was discovered that the cross-section of the body was reduced an average of four to five centimeters, and the circumference of the head as well as its length and breadth was reduced and the cephalic index changed. This was true among the Great Russians, as also among the White and Little Russians, Syrians, Bashkirs, Kalmucks, and Kirgizes. (Among the Armenians, Grusians, and Crim-Tartars it was raised.) Likewise, the percentage of shortheads had increased, and the nasal index had become smaller. According to Ivanowsky, "The unchangeableness of anthropological types is a fable." [2]

Change of food, of climate, influence of higher temperatures, greater humidity, and so on, unquestionably result in alterations of certain body characteristics. Thus the well-known American anthropologist, F. Boas, was able to prove that the skull formation of the descendants of immigrants showed a marked change in America, so that, for instance, the descendants of short-headed Oriental Jews became longer-headed, and the long-headed Sicilians became shorter-headed; the skull, that is, tends to assume a certain form of cross-section. [3] These results are the more

[2] Ernst Vatter, *Die Rassen und Völker der Erde*. Leipzig, 1927, p. 37.
[3] F. Boas in *Die Zeitschrift für Ethnologie*, 1913; Band 45. Compare also the same author's *Kultur und Rasse*. Zweite Auflage, Berlin, 1922.

remarkable because they deal with a change in bodily characteristics which can only be explained by the action of external influences on the so-called "hereditary purity of the race." Of quite especial, and in its results as yet quite incalculable, significance are the results achieved in late years by the action of Roentgen and cathode rays. Experiments made at the University of Texas by Professor J. H. Miller yielded results which lead us to anticipate a complete revolution in theories of heredity. They not only prove that artificial interference with the life of the germ-mass leading to a controlled change in the race characteristics is possible, but also that by such experiments the creation of new races can be effected.

From all this it appears that bodily characteristics are by no means unchangeable and that a change can be effected even without racial cross-breeding. It is even more monstrous to infer mental and spiritual characteristics solely on the basis of bodily ones and deduce from them a judgment about moral worth. It is true that Linnaeus, in his attempts at a racial classification of humanity, took moral factors into consideration when he said:

The American is reddish, choleric, erect; the European, white, sanguine, fleshy; the Asiatic, yellow, melancholy, tough; the African, black, phlegmatic, slack. The American is obstinate, contented, free; the European, mobile, keen, inventive; the Asiatic cruel, splendor-loving, miserly; the African, sly, lazy, indifferent. The American is covered with tattooing, and rules by habit; the European is covered with close-fitting garments and rules by law; the Asiatic is enclosed in flowing garments and rules by opinion; the African is anointed with grease and rules by whim.

But Linnaeus was not in his scheme conforming to any political theories. The very naïveté of mentioning tattooing, clothing and greasing of the body along with forms of government proves the innocence of his effort. But, however odd the notions of the Swedish naturalist may seem to us today, we still have no right to laugh at them in view of the shameful flood of so-called race literature that has rolled over us during the last two decades, with nothing better to offer than Linnaeus could say two hundred years ago. For when the Swedish scholar brought tattooing, clothes and greasy black bodies into combination with forms of government, he did far less harm than when today men try to deduce the capacity for culture, the character and the moral and spiritual disposition of the separate races from the color of their skins, the curve of their noses or the shape of their skulls.

The first attempt to explain the rise and fall of peoples in history as a play of race antagonisms was made by the Frenchman, Count Arthur Gobineau, who during his diplomatic career had seen many distant lands. He was a fairly prolific writer, but we are interested here only in his *magnum opus, Essai sur l'inégalité des races humaines* ("Treatise on the Inequality of the Races of Men"), which first appeared in 1855. According to his own statement, the Parisian Revolution of February, 1848, gave Gobineau the first impulse toward the formulation of his ideas. He saw in the revolutionary occurrences of that time only the inevitable consequences of the great upheaval of 1789-94, amid whose violent convulsions the feudal world fell in ruins. Concerning the causes of this collapse he had formed his own judgment. For him the French Revolution was nothing else than the revolt of the Celto-Romanic race mixture that for years and years had lived in intellectual and economic dependence on the Franco-Norman master caste. This caste was made up, according to Gobineau, of the descendants of those Nordic conquerors who had at one time invaded the country and subjected the Celto-Romanic population to their rule. It was this race with its blue eyes, its blond hair and its tall figure that held for Gobineau the sum-total of all mental and physical perfection, whose superior intelligence and strength of will in themselves guaranteed to it the role which it was, in his opinion, destined to play in history.

This idea was by no means entirely new. Long before the time of the French Revolution it had bobbed up in the minds of the aristocracy. Henri de Boulainvilliers (1658-1722), author of an historical work which was not published until after his death, maintained that the French nobles of the ruling caste were descended from the Germanic conquerors, while the great mass of the bourgeoisie and the peasantry was to be regarded as the progeny of the conquered Celts and Romans. Boulainvilliers tried on the basis of this thesis to justify all the privileges of the nobles, in opposition to both the people and the king, and demanded for his class the right to keep the government of the country always in their hands. Gobineau adopted this theory, extending it considerably to apply to the whole of human history. But since he—as he himself once said—"believed only that which seemed to him worth believing," it happened inevitably that he pushed on to the most daring conclusions.

Just as Joseph de Maistre once declared that he had never met a human being, but only Frenchmen, Germans, Italians, and so on, so also Gobineau maintained that the abstract human being existed only in the minds of philosophers. In reality the human being is only the expression of the race to which he belongs; the Voice of Blood is the Voice of Fate, from which no people can escape. Neither the climatic environment nor the social conditions of life have any influence worth mentioning on the constructive power of peoples. The driving force in all culture is race, above all the Aryan race, which even under the most unfavorable conditions is capable of the greatest achievements so long as it avoids mixture with less worthy racial elements. Following the classification of the French naturalist, Cuvier, Gobineau distinguished three great racial groups, the white, the yellow and the black. Each, according to Gobineau, represented a separate experiment of God in the creation of man; God had begun with the Negro, coming round at last to the creation of the White Man in His own image. Among these three great racial groups there existed no inner relationship, since they were descended from different stems. Everything outside of these three basic races was racial mixture—for Gobineau, mongreldom—which had come into being by interbreeding of white, yellow and black.

It is clear that in Gobineau's opinion the white race is far superior to the other two. It is in the best sense a "noble race," for besides its physical beauty it possesses also the most distinguished mental and spiritual qualities—above all, mental breadth of view, superior capacity for organization, and in particular that inner urge of the conqueror which is entirely lacking in the yellow and black races and which gives to the Aryans alone in history the power to found great states and civilizations.

Gobineau distinguishes ten great culture periods in history, which include all the significant epochs in human civilization, and attributes them exclusively to the activity of the Aryan race. The origin, development and decay of these great epochs constitute, according to his understanding, the entire content of human history; for civilization and degeneration are the two poles about which all events turn. Gobineau, to whom the idea of organic evolution was entirely unknown, tried to explain the rise and decay of the great civilizations by the degeneration of races, or rather, of the ruling race, since for him the mass of less important beings which constitutes the great majority in every state exists only for the purpose of being governed by the racially pure conquerors. Changes in social relationships and institutions are to be attributed solely to changes of race. The decay of a dominion and its culture occurs when a great deal of other blood is mixed with that of the conquerors' caste. From this ensues not only an alteration in external race characteristics, but also a change in the spiritual and mental impulses of the master race which leads to gradual or rapid decay. In this inner decay of the noble race is found the final and authentic explanation of the decline of all great cultures.

The stronger the component from the white race in the blood of a people, the more prominent will be its cultural activity, the greater its power of building a state; while too strong an infusion of Negro or Mongolian blood undermines the creative cultural characteristics of the old race and gradually brings about its inner dissolution. In contrast with Chamberlain and most of the exponents of modern race theories, Gobineau was thoroughly pessimistic about the future. He could not escape the conclusion that the Germanic race, this "last bud upon the Aryan stem," as he called it, was doomed to inevitable destruction. The wide dissemination of republican and democratic ideas seemed to him an unfailing sign of inner decay; they foretold the victory of "mongreldom" over the Aryan Noble Race. According to Gobineau only a monarchy can accomplish anything lasting, since it contains in itself the basic law of its being, while a democracy is always dependent on external powers and so can do nothing important. Only the degenerate blood of the mixed race demands democracy and revolution. On this point Gobineau is close to the views of Joseph de Maistre, the standard-bearer of reaction, with whom he has much else in common, including actually hair-raising distortion of historical facts and almost inconceivable naïveté of ideal interpretations. Although de Maistre found the root of all evil in Protestantism, it came to the same thing in the end, for democracy was for de Maistre a political variety of Protestantism.

On one point Gobineau is sharply at issue with all later advocates of the race theory: he has no sympathy with nationalistic ambitions and regards the notion of the "fatherland" with outspoken antagonism. Because of his aversion to everything that savored of democracy no other position was possible. Then, too, it was from the French Revolution that the idea of the fatherland and the nation received the special imprint they bear today. This was enough to make Gobineau despise it as a "Canaanitish abomination" which the Aryan race had, against its will, taken over from the Semitic. As long as Hellenism had remained Aryan, the idea of the fatherland had been entirely alien to the Greeks. But as the intermixture with the Semites progressed farther and farther, monarchy had to give place to the republic. The Semitic element impelled toward absolutism, as Gobineau put it; still the Aryan blood which was still active in the mixed race of the later Greeks was opposed to personal despotism such as was common in Asia and arrived logically at the despotism of an idea—the idea of the fatherland.

On this point Gobineau is thoroughly consistent: his hostility to the idea of the fatherland is the immediate and deliberately derived product of his race theory. If the nation were in fact a community of descent, a race-unity, then the race instinct must be its strongest cementing material. If, however, it is made up of the most varied race constituents—a fact which no race theorist dares to dispute—then the notion of race must act on the concept of the nation like dynamite and blow to bits its very foundation. More talented and imaginative than any of his successors, Gobineau recognized clearly the opposition between race and nation; and between the pure-race ruling stratum of the nation and the "mongreldom" of the great masses he had drawn a sharp line which our nationalistically inclined race theorists have tried in vain to bridge over. The notion that the great masses of the nation are merely Helots who must without choice submit to the rule of a privileged caste determined by blood is in fact the greatest danger to national cohesion.

The admirers of Gobineau have tried to account for the master's attitude on this point by explaining that he cherished in his mind an ideal fatherland corresponding to his innermost feeling and that he did not fail to take into account that patriotic need which is said to dwell in every man. But such an explanation is without value. If man can arbitrarily set up for himself the fiction of an ideal fatherland, that merely proves that the notions of the fatherland and the nation are fictitious concepts which can be drilled into the individual and can at any time be driven out by other fictions. Gobineau was a fanatical opponent of the equality of human rights; therefore the Revolution appeared to him as a desecration of divinely established order. His whole race ideology was merely the product of a profound wish: to implant in men a belief in the unalterability of social inequality. As Malthus had explained to the "superfluous" that life's table did not have places for all, so Gobineau wished to prove to the world that the enslavement of the masses is ordained by fate and is a law of nature. Only when the instincts of the inferior mixed race begin to work in the blood of the master caste does the belief in the equality of everything in human form arise. For Gobineau this belief was an illusion which must lead irrevocably to the destruction of all social order.

Although little recognition was accorded Gobineau in his native France, even his purely literary work receiving less appreciation than it deserved, he exercised upon the development of race opinions elsewhere, especially in Germany, an influence that is not to be underestimated. Through his acquaintance with Richard Wagner, in whose home he first made the acquaintance of Schemann, the German biographer and translator of Gobineau, there was later formed the so-called "Gobineau Society" which looked after the dissemination of his work on race and further advanced the notions of the imaginative Frenchman to whom, in spite of all his scientific shortcomings, there cannot be denied a certain greatness which is entirely lacking in his later followers.

A much stronger influence on the development of the race doctrine in Germany, and also outside it, was exercised by the Englishman, Houston Stewart Chamberlain, whose work, *Die Grundlagen des 19. Jahrhunderts* ("Foundations of the Nineteenth Century") (1899), was rather widely circulated. Chamberlain enjoyed the special favor of William II, whom he knew how to approach from his most vulnerable side. He compared William's reign to a "rising morning" and testified that he was "really the first emperor." For such bald flattery the present Lord of the Castle of Doorn had a very receptive ear, so it could not fail that Chamberlain by high command advanced into the ranks of the great contemporary minds. The *Grundlagen* found a rapid sale among the members of the ruling caste in Germany. In order to assure for his work the widest possible circulation, a special fund was established; the Kaiser endorsed the work in person and so became benefactor to many a German private or state library and to all the schools of the Reich. According to von Bülow's malicious statement, William used to read whole sections of the book to the ladies of his court, until they fell asleep.

As a rule Chamberlain is regarded merely as the perfecter of Gobineau's race theory; emphasis, however, is always laid on his mental superiority. It is impossible to oppose such a view too strongly. Chamberlain was merely the beneficiary of Gobineau, without whom his *Grundlagen* would be unthinkable. No one who has carefully compared the two works can avoid this conclusion. Chamberlain first became acquainted with Gobineau's racial philosophy of history in the home of his father-in-law, Richard Wagner, and appropriated its essential features for his own work.

From Chamberlain, no more than from Gobineau, do we discover what, exactly, "race" is. He is the finished mystic of the race idea, which in him condenses into a devoutly believed race mythology. External characteristics, like the shape of the skull, texture and color of the hair, the skin, the eyes, have for him only a qualified meaning; even language is not determinative. Only the instinctive feeling of cohesiveness which reveals itself through the "voice of the blood" is determinative. This "feeling of race in one's own bosom," which is subject to no control and cannot be scientifically apprehended, is all that Chamberlain has to tell us about race.

Like Gobineau, Chamberlain sees in every great culture period the undeniable product of the German intellect and with cool assurance appropriates for his Noble Race the cultural wealth of all peoples and of all the great minds that mankind has ever produced. The Germans are the salt of the earth; they have been endowed by Nature herself with all the mental and spiritual qualities which fit them to be "masters of the world." This alleged historical destiny of the Germans follows so clearly for the author of the *Grundlagen* from all previous history that any doubt about it is stricken dumb. It is Germans who as leading caste have played an important role even among non-Germanic folk-groups, such as the French, the Italians, the Spaniards, the Russians; it is due only to their influence that a culture was able to develop in these lands at all. Even the great cultures of the Orient arose in this way. Under the influence of German blood they rose to undreamed-of greatness, and then went down as mental elasticity relaxed and the will to power was quenched in the deteriorating master caste by blood mixture with inferior races. Even Chamberlain did not deny that race-crossing can be advantageous to cultural development so long as it involves only the mixture of related races; for a noble race builds itself up only gradually by intermixture with other races of more or less the same worth. It is at this point that Chamberlain's concept parts company with Gobineau's. For Gobineau race stands at the beginning of all human history. It has its definite physical and mental characteristics which are transmitted by heredity and can be changed only by crossing with other races. And since he was convinced that in the course of thousands of years the blood of the noble race had been constantly debased and its precious qualities lost by mixture with yellow and black races, he looked toward the future with gloomy eyes. Chamberlain, on whom Darwin's theory had not been quite without effect, saw in race not a starting point, but a product of evolution. According to his view the race arises through natural selection in the struggle for existence, which eliminates the incapable and preserves only the able individual for the propagation of the species. Consequently, the race is the end-product of a continuous process of splitting-off from a related genus.

But if the race is a product of evolution and not its starting-point, then the production of noble races for the future also is guaranteed, provided that the ruling upper stratum of a nation takes to heart the teaching of history and wards off the threatening "race chaos" by a suitable race hygiene. For the strengthening of his position Chamberlain appeals to the experience of breeders and shows us how a noble race of horses, dogs or swine comes into being. It is true, he forgets the essential point, namely, that the crossings of the human races in the course of millennia have been carried on under very different circumstances from those followed in the so-called "ennobling experiments" in the stables of breeders. For Gobineau we should rightly read: In the beginning was the Race. Therefore the nation meant nothing to him, and the idea of the fatherland was just a cunning invention of the Semitic mind. Chamberlain, however, who believed in the breeding of a noble race, wished to train the nation to racial purity. And since the German nation seemed to him best fitted for this purpose, because in its veins, according to his opinion, Germanic blood flowed purest, he saw the Teuton as the Bearer of the Future.

After Chamberlain had fitted out the noble Germans with every conceivable mental and spiritual trait in a really big way, there remained nothing for the peoples of any other descent except to surrender unconditionally to the proud master race and in the shadow of its overtowering greatness to drag out a humble existence. Since these others are merely the culture-dungers of history, it is so much the worse for them if they cannot see it.

According to Chamberlain the opposition between Romanic peoples and Germans constitutes the whole content of modern history. And since the Romanic world, which had risen out of the great "chaos of peoples," had bound itself for good or ill to the "materialistic aims" of the Catholic church; had of necessity so to bind itself, since the voice of the blood left it no other choice, therefore Protestantism became for him the great achievement of Germanic culture. The German is the specially chosen minister of the Protestant mission, through which Christendom is first made aware of its true content. That the Christian had thoughtlessly chosen the Jew, Jesus, for his savior was surely a bitter pill; it was too late to undo that. But was it not written in the Gospel that Christ first saw the light in Galilee? And immediately the "instinct of the race" came to Chamberlain's aid and informed him that in just this part of Palestine extensive crossing of races had occurred and, above all, that in Galilee Germanic stocks had settled. Must one not, then, admit that Christ had been a German? It was, in fact, unthinkable that out of "materialism-drunken Jewry" a doctrine could come to whose spiritual content the Jewish mind is completely opposed.

Chamberlain revealed an utterly morbid hatred of everything Jewish. He even ventured to assure his credulous readers that a Germanic child, the keenness of whose senses had not yet been ruined or blunted by the prejudices of adults, could tell instinctively when a Jew was near him. Yet he found it possible to speak highly of the Spanish Jews, the so-called "Sephardim," while he could never severely enough disparage the "Ashkenazim," the Jews of the northern countries. To be sure, he based his preference for the Sephardim on the assumption that they were in reality Goths who had been converted to Judaism in large numbers—a recognition which came to the great master of unproved assertion rather tardily, as it first appears in the third edition of his book. How the Goths, those genuine branches of the noble tree of Germandom, in spite of their "mystic inclination" and their inborn sense of "religious profundity," which according to Chamberlain are the heritage of their race, could throw themselves into the arms of "materialistic Judaism" with its "dead ritualism," its "slavish obedience," and its "despotic God" remains an unsolved mystery. In this case the "race in their own bosoms" must have failed outright; otherwise the wonder is not to be explained. Chamberlain's work on race swarms with similar assertions. There is hardly another work which reveals such unexampled unreliability in the material used and such reckless juggling with bare assumptions of the most daring type. As to this, not only the opponents, but also many outspoken believers in the race theory, like Albrecht Wirth, Eugen Kretzer and others, are fully agreed. Even so self-satisfied an advocate of the race theory as Otto Hauser speaks of Chamberlain's work as "the *Foundations of the Nineteenth Century* which so frequently lacks factual basis." [4]

Like Gobineau, Chamberlain is a fanatical opponent of all liberal and democratic ideas and sees in them a danger to Germanism. For him, freedom and equality are antagonistic concepts; who desires equality must sacrifice to it his personality, which alone can be the basis of freedom. But

[4] *Die Germanen in Europa*. Dresden, 1916, p. 5.

the freedom of Chamberlain is of a quite peculiar kind. It is the "freedom which the state is able to protect only on the condition that it shall limit it." "Man does not become free by being granted political rights; rather, the state can grant him political rights only when he has attained inner freedom; otherwise these alleged rights are always misused by others." [5]

This utterance proves that Chamberlain had never understood the nature of either freedom or the state. But how could he? Fatalism is the exact opposite of the concept of freedom, and no fatalism bears so plainly the Cain's brand of hostility to freedom as the Kismet of race. Chamberlain's concept of freedom is that of the well fed and satisfied, to whom order is the first duty of the citizen, and who accepts such rights as the state hands out to him. Before such freedom no despot has ever trembled; but any trivial right that man wins by struggle against the tyranny of tradition brings the sweat of anxiety to the despot's brow. Chamberlain's "inner freedom" is just an empty word; only where the inner sentiment of freedom is transformed into liberating deed has the spirit of freedom a genuine homestead. "He who is occupied with nature and with 'force and matter' must, if he is honest, let freedom go," opines Chamberlain. We think, however, that he who does not constantly strive to convert freedom into "force and matter" must always remain a slave. An abstract conception of freedom that cannot inspire its possessor to strive to the limit for the attaining of his rights is like a woman to whom nature has denied the gift of fertility. Chamberlain's concept of freedom is the illusion of impotence, a cunning inversion of the inner feeling of serfdom which is incapable of any action. Ibsen had a very different view of freedom when he wrote:

> You can never get me to regard freedom as synonymous with political liberty. What you call freedom, I call freedoms; and what I call the struggle for freedom is nothing but the constant, livihg assimilation of the idea of freedom. Who possesses freedom otherwise than as something to be striven for possesses it only as a thing without life or spirit, for the idea of freedom has always this quality, that it constantly expands as one assimilates it, so that if during the struggle one pauses to say: Now I have it! he merely shows that he has lost it. But to have just this dead kind—a certain static view of freedom—is characteristic of state organizations; and it is just this that I have called worthless. [6]

Chamberlain never stood still on the road to freedom, because he never found himself on that road. His criticism of democracy has its basis in the past; he is the man who looks backward, the man to whom every product

---

[5] *Demokratie und Freiheit.* Munich, 1917.

[6] Letter to George Brandes of February, 1871, in *Henrik Ibsens samtliche Werke in deutscher Sprache.* Zehnter Band, Berlin, 1905.

of revolution was hateful because it carried on its face the mark of its revolutionary origin. That which is today called democracy can be overcome only by forces which look not to the past, but to the future. The remedy lies not in what has been, but in the continual enlargement of the concept of freedom and its social applications. Even democracy did not overcome the will to power, because it was shackled to the state and dared not shake the privileges of the possessing classes. But Chamberlain did not find his base in the future; his gaze was fixed unchangingly on the past. Therefore he condemned even the constitutional monarchy as essentially alien to the Germanic spirit and advanced the idea of an absolute monarchy over a "free people"—whatever he meant by that. He was one of those unswerving ones who opposed to the very last every limitation of the royal power in Prussia and, like all his predecessors and successors in the race theory, stood squarely in the camp of undisguised political and social reaction.

One would think that a work like the *Grundlagen,* which offers no opening for earnest understanding, which has regard neither for social relationships nor for the slow process of spiritual endeavor, and in which actually only the violent whim of the author is revealed, would be wrecked on its own mad contradictions. But it worked quite otherwise. It became for the ruling castes in Germany a destiny. So profound was the infatuation which this work induced that the former Kaiser could write in his memoirs: "Germanism in all its glory was first revealed and preached to the astounded German people by Chamberlain in his *Grundlagen des 19. Jahrhunderts.* But, as the collapse of the German people showed, without effect."

That the dethroned champion of divine right even today holds the German people responsible for the collapse is quite as delightful a revelation of the "lordly German spirit" as is the sorry role of those who with slavish exaltation revered the hopeless fool as "German Emperor" only to turn upon him after his downfall and kick him like maddened asses— even to brand him as an "offspring of the Jews."

What Chamberlain had begun so gloriously was continued in the same spirit by men like Woltmann, Hauser, Günther, Clauss, Madison Grant, Rosenberg, and many others. Woltmann, the former Marxist and Social Democrat, who one fine day threw over the class struggle and took up the race struggle instead, tried to supply historical proof for what Gobineau and Chamberlain had asserted about the origin and character of foreign cultures. He assembled an enormous mass of material which supposedly went to prove that all distinguished persons in the cultural history of France and Italy had been of German descent. To reach this conclusion he had examined the portraits of several hundred prominent personalities of the Renaissance period and was in a position to announce to an astonished world that most of them had blond hair and blue eyes. Woltmann was completely obsessed by his blue-eyed-blond theory and went into raptures every time he thought he had discovered a new blondling.[7]

One utterly fails to see what such assertions are meant to prove. That there are Germanic elements in the population of France and Italy, no one has ever questioned. Both peoples are racially just as mixed as are the Germans, as are all the peoples of Europe. France and Italy were repeatedly overrun by Germanic tribes, just as the numerous human floods of Slavic, Celtic and Mongolian tribes poured over Germany. But to what extent the culture of a people is determined by race is a question to which science has as yet found no answer, nor is likely to find one. We are here depending merely on conjectures which can never serve as substitutes for actual facts. We do not yet know one thing definitely about the causes behind even purely external characteristics like color of hair and eyes.

And so the whole portrait-diagnosis of Woltmann and his successor, Otto Hauser, is utterly worthless. It is the most utterly unreliable means that could be produced for the establishment of definite characters. In the picture books of our race astrologers such "documents" look very fine and serve there their full purpose, but for the earnest student they offer hardly even a point of attack. The work of painters is not photography, which incorruptibly gives back what is before it. It must from the first be valued as the reproduction of what the inner eye of the artist perceives; and this inner picture which hovers before the artist, and without which no work of art can be produced, not seldom misrepresents the original from a factual standpoint. Also, the personal style of the artist and the school to which he belongs play an important part in the work. To what genuine investigator, for example, would it occur to try to establish the characteristics of a race from portraits by our present-day cubists or futurists? Besides which, the very same portraits which serve Woltmann as proofs of the Germanic origin of the French and Italian cultures supply to other advocates of the race theory a basis for quite different views. For example, Albrecht Wirth, who also thinks that he recognizes in race the determinative factor in historical development, explains in his *Rasse und Volk:* "In this view is involved a strange error; that Woltmann and his adherents discovered in so many geniuses and men of talent in France and Italy Germanic features. To unprejudiced eyes the very pictures which Woltmann gives as illustrations show just the opposite: Bashkir, Mediterranean, and Negro types."

In fact, in the whole long portrait gallery which Woltmann displays

[7] Ludwig Woltmann, *Die Germanen und die Renaissance in Italien;* 1905. *Die Germanen in Frankreich;* 1907.

to the world in support of his thesis, there is hardly a type that could stand as genuinely representative of the Germanic race. In every one of them unmistakable characteristics of the hybrid are more or less clearly shown. If the researches of Woltmann and Hauser were to lead us to any "law of history" at all, it could be only to this: that racial inbreeding gradually undermines spiritual vigor and has as its consequence a slow decline, while racial interbreeding imparts to the capacity for culture ever new vigor and favors the production of personalities of genius. The same holds good also for the German bearers of culture, and Max von Gruber is not wrong when he says:

> And when we apply racial standards to the bodily characteristics of our greatest men we find, indeed, in many of them Nordic characters, but in none of them only Nordic characters. The first glance reveals to the expert that neither Frederick the Great, nor Baron von Stein, nor Bismarck was pure Nordic; the same is true of Luther, Melanchthon, Leibnitz, Kant, and Schopenhauer, as also of Liebig and Julius Robert Mayer and Helmholtz, of Goethe, Schiller, and Grillparzer, of Dürer, Menzel, and Feuerbach, and even of the greatest geniuses of that most German of all the arts, music, from Bach and Gluck and Haydn to Bruckner. They were all hybrids; the same is true of the great Italians. Michelangelo and Galileo were, if Nordic at all, still not pure Nordic. To the characteristics from the North apparently ingredients from other races must be added in order to produce the happiest combination of characters.[8]

However much Woltmann may insist that "Dante, Raphael, Luther, and so on, were geniuses not because they were hybrids, but in spite of it," and that "the foundation of their genius is their heritage from the Germanic race," it remains but empty preaching so long as we are not in a position to establish indisputably and to confirm scientifically the influence of race on the intellectual characteristics of mankind. By just the same logic could we affirm that the spark of genius in Luther, Goethe, Kant or Beethoven was to be attributed to the presence of "Alpine" or "Oriental" blood in them. Nothing would be proved by this; the world would merely be richer by one more assertion. In fact, during the War there were found on the other side of the Vosges men like Paul Souday and others who explained that all the great personalities that Germany had produced were of Celtic, and not German, descent. Why not?

The latest advocates of the so-called race doctrine take great pains to give a scientific appearance to their views and appeal especially to the laws of heredity, which play such an important part in modern natural science, and are still the subject of so much controversy. By heredity, biology means chiefly the fact, firmly established by common observation,

[8] "*Volk und Rasse*" in *Süddeutsche Monatshefte*, 1927.

that plants and animals resemble their parents and that this resemblance is apparently traceable to the fact that the descendants arise from bits of the same protoplasm and so develop from the same or similar hereditary primordia. From this it follows that in protoplasm there reside peculiar forces which by the separation of the tiniest portions can transmit the whole to the descendants. Thus men came to recognize that the real cause of inheritance must be sought in a particular condition of the living cell-stuff which we call protoplasm.

However valuable this recognition may be, it has hardly brought us nearer to the real solution of the problem. Instead it has proposed for science a whole set of new problems, whose solution is no less difficult. In the first place, it is necessary to establish the processes in protoplasm which control the development of particular characters, a task attended by almost insurmountable difficulties. And we are just as much in the dark as to the inner processes which precede inheritance. Science has, it is true, succeeded in establishing the existence of so-called chemical molecules and even the existence of certain fairly well-developed organs within the cell-structure, but the specific arrangement of the molecules and the inner causes of the differences between the protein groups in dead and in living substance are still unknown to us today. One can safely say that in this perplexing realm we rely almost entirely on assumptions, since none of the numerous theories of heredity has been able to lift the veil of the Magi that still hides the actual processes of inheritance. We have profited much by the observations on hybridization and their interpretation; but of course these deal less with the explanation of causes than with the establishment of facts.

Seventy years ago the Augustinian monk, Gregor Mendel, busied himself in his quiet cloister garden at Brünn with twenty-two varieties of pea-plants and achieved the following results: when he crossed a yellow with a green variety, the descendants bore all yellow seeds and the green appeared to be completely eliminated. But when he dusted the yellow hybrids with their own pollen, the vanished green appeared again in their descendants, and in a definite ratio. Of every four seeds in plants of the second generation, three were yellow and one was green. The characteristics of the green variety had, therefore, not disappeared; they were merely hidden by the characteristics of the yellow. Mendel speaks, therefore, of recessive or concealed, and dominant or concealing, characters. The recessive character—in this case green-seededness—in renewed fertilizations showed itself constant in heredity so long as self-fertilization was strictly controlled and no new crossing occurred. The dominants, however, segregated regularly in each new generation. A third of their progeny were pure dominants, which bred true in later generations; the other two-thirds "mendeled," that is, they segregated in reproduction again in the same proportion of 3:1. In the same ratio the process continued indefinitely.

Countless experiments by well-known botanists and zoologists have since then confirmed Mendel's rules in the large. They also agree very well with the results of modern cytology, or cell-theory, as far as the growth and division of the cell can be observed. One can, therefore, agree that these rules have validity for all organic beings up to man and that in nature as a whole a unified plan of control of the processes of heredity obtains; but this recognition does not dispose of the countless difficulties which have thus far prevented our deeper insight into this mysterious occurrence. It is clear from the Mendelian laws of heredity that the characters of the parents are transmitted to the offspring in a definite ratio. On the other hand, cytological research has shown that the hereditary primordia of a living being are to be sought in those carefully separated nuclear parts in the germ cell which we call chromosomes. And all that science has more or less certainly established seems deducible from this: that the hereditary primordia enter into the germ cell in pairs, and that in each pair one element comes from the sperm cell of the father, the other from the egg cell of the mother.

But since one cannot believe that all the hereditary primordia of both parents are transmitted to each of their offspring, because in that case their number would become greater with each succeeding generation, one comes to the conclusion that only in the nucleus of the soma- or body-cells of a living being are all the hereditary primordia present; the germ cell always suppresses finally a part of the nuclear factors so that it receives only one-half of all the primordia, that is, only one member of each character-pair. One learns that in the general body cell of man there are 48 chromosomes, but the germ cell when ready for fertilization contains only 24. But this is not to say that man possesses only 24 character-pairs that function as bearers of heredity. In every chromosome several members of different character-pairs may be present, so that in the offspring the most varied combinations may appear. Since, however, every fertilization is really a crossing, even when it occurs between beings of the same race, because in nature no two individuals are exactly alike, it follows that from every instance of fertilization the most manifold results may ensue. From only two different hereditary factors there would arise in two generations four varieties; from three pairs, eight varieties; from four, 16; from ten, 1,024; and so on. From these clearly obvious possibilities of combination any comprehensive view of the results of the processes of heredity becomes not merely increasingly difficult, but actually impossible.

And we were still speaking only of purely physical characteristics. When we turn to mental or moral characters the processes become much more involved, because here no segregation or fixation of separate qualities is possible. We are, then, not in a position to separate mental characteristics into their components and to differentiate one part from another. Intellectual and moral characters are given us as wholes; even if we agree that the Mendelian laws of heredity apply in this field, we still have no means of subjecting their operation to scientific observation.

And when it becomes clear that pure races are nowhere to be found, in fact, have in all probability never existed; that all European peoples are merely mixtures and present every possible racial make-up, which both without and within each nation are only to be distinguished by the proportion of the separate constituents; then only does one get an idea of the difficulties which beset the earnest student at every step. If, further, one keeps in mind how uncertain the results of anthropologic research in regard to the different races still are today, how defective still is our knowledge of the inner processes of heredity, then one cannot avoid the conclusion that every attempt to erect on such uncertain premises a theory which allegedly reveals to us the deeper meaning of all historical events and enables its exponents infallibly to judge the worth of the moral, mental and cultural qualities of the different human groups must become either senseless play-acting or clownish mischief. That such theories could find such wide circulation, especially in Germany, is a serious sign of the mental degradation of a society that has lost all inner moral strength and is therefore concerned to replace outworn ethical values with ethnological concepts.

Of the present-day advocates of the race theory, Dr. Hans Günther is the best known and the most disputed over. His numerous writings and especially his *Rassenkunde des deutschen Volkes* have had an extraordinary circulation in Germany, and in wide circles have achieved an influence that one dares not underestimate. What distinguishes Günther from his predecessors is not the content of his doctrine, but the pains he takes to surround it with a scientific mantle, in order to endow it with an outer dignity which does not belong to it. As a basis for his views Günther has collected a great mass of material, but that is all. When it becomes necessary to establish scientifically conclusions of decisive significance, he fails completely and reverts to the methods of Gobineau and Chamberlain, who relied entirely on a wish-concept. For him the Aryan moves clear into the background; the Germanic man has also played out his part; Günther's ideal is the "Nordic race," which he endows with precious native qualities as generously as Gobineau does the Aryans and Chamberlain the Germans. In addition he has enriched the classification of European races by one new component, and has equipped the already existing divisions with new names without, by this, adding anything to our knowledge.

The American scholar, Ripley, who first attempted to write an anthropological history of European peoples, contented himself with three principal types, which he designated as the Teutonic, the Celtic-Alpine and the Mediterranean races. Later there was added to these three a fourth, the Dinaric race, and it was thought that in these four fundamental types the chief components of Europe's racial make-up had been recognized. Besides these four principal races there are also in Europe Levantine, Semitic, Mongolian and Negro strains. Of course, one cannot represent these four types as pure races; we are merely concerned here with a working hypothesis for science, to enable it to undertake a classification of European peoples on more or less correct lines. The mass of European peoples is the result of crossings among these "races." These themselves, however, are merely the product of certain mixtures which in the course of time have taken on particular forms, as is the case in every instance of race formation. Günther added, superfluously, a fifth to these four principal races, the so-called "East-Baltic race." Along with this new discovery he effected a rebaptism of the Alpine race which he called the "Eastern" (ostisch). There was no reason at all for this change, and his bitterest opponent in the racial camp, Dr. Merkenschlager, may have been right when he assumed that Günther, in this renaming of the Alpine race, had the purpose merely of "representing it to the sentiment of his readers as 'contaminated' and to enable the unthinking masses to interpret it as Oriental-Jewish."

Like nearly all of the present-day race theorists Günther in his discussions starts from the modern theories of heredity. He uses as his foundation especially the hypothetical assumptions of neo-Mendelism. According to these conceptions the hereditary primordia are not subject to any external influence, so that a change in the hereditary factors can occur only through crossing. From this it follows that man and all other living beings are to be regarded merely as the products of particular hereditary primordia which they received before their birth and which can be turned from their predestined course neither by the influence of the natural or social environment, nor by any other forces.

Here lies the essential error of every race theory, the reason for their inevitably false conclusions. Günther, and with him all the other advocates of race theories, proceed from assumptions which can in no way be proved and whose untenability can always be shown by examples from daily life and from history. One could take these assertions seriously only if their proponents were in a position to adduce conclusive proofs of these three points: first, that hereditary primordia are in fact unchangeable and are not affected by the influences of the environment; second, that physical characters must be taken as unmistakable signs of particular intellectual and moral qualities; third, that the life of man is determined entirely by congenital factors and that acquired or imparted characters have no essential influence on his destiny.

As to the first question, we have already shown that science knows a whole series of firmly established facts which prove irrefutably that action of the environment on the hereditary factors does occur and produce changes in them. The fact that numerous investigators have succeeded in effecting a modification of hereditary factors by radiation, changes of temperature, and so on, testifies to this. Besides, we have the effects of domestication, the importance of which has been brought out with special strength by Eduard Hahn and Eugen Fischer. Indeed, Fischer was led to declare: "Man is a product of domestication, and it is domestication that has caused his great variability, or contributed to it."

Concerning the second point, no sophistry will help. Not a shadow of proof can be adduced to show that external racial characters like the shape of the skull, the color of the hair, slimmer or sturdier build, have any relation to mental, spiritual or moral factors in mankind; so that, for example, a tall, blond, blue-eyed Nordic because of his external physical characters should possess moral and mental qualities which one would not find in descendants of some other race. Our race ideologists claim this, it is true, but their doctrine is completely untenable, and based on assertions for the correctness of which they have not the slightest proof.

We have already emphasized that in the long line of persons of genius who deserve credit for the intellectual culture of Germany there is hardly one whose appearance corresponds even halfway to the ideal concept of the "Nordic man." And it is precisely the greatest of them who are physically farthest from the fanciful picture of the Günthers, Hausers and Clausses. We need but think of Luther, Goethe, Beethoven, who lacked almost completely the external marks of the "Nordic race," and whom even the most outstanding exponents of the race theory characterize as hybrids with Oriental, Levantine and Negro-Malayan strains in them. It would look even worse if one should go so far as to apply the blood-test to the champions in the arena of the race struggle like Hitler, Alfred Rosenberg, Goebbels, Streicher, for example, and give these worthy representatives of the Nordic race and the national interest the opportunity to confirm their rulership of the Third Reich by virtue of their blood.[9]

[9] The well-known race hygienist of Munich, Max von Gruber, President of the Bavarian Academy of Science and a leading mind in the race movement in Germany, certainly an unprejudiced witness, has drawn the following picture of Hitler: "Today I saw Hitler close-up for the first time. Face and head of a bad race, a mixture. Low, retreating forehead, ugly nose, wide cheek-bones, little eyes, dark hair. A tiny tooth-brush mustache, only as wide as his nose, gives his face a defiant aspect. His expression is not that of a self-controlled commander, but of a crazy emotionalist. Repeated twitchings of the facial muscles. Final expression that of happy self-satisfaction." (*Essener Volkswacht* of November 9, 1929.)

If it is indisputable that men like Socrates, Horace, Michelangelo, Dante, Luther, Galileo, Rembrandt, Goya, Rousseau, Pestalozzi, Herder, Goethe, Beethoven, Byron, Pushkin, Dostoievsky, Tolstoi, Balzac, Dumas, Poe, Strindberg, Ibsen, Zola, and hundreds of others were of mixed race, this is surely a proof that external race-marks have nothing to do with the intellectual and moral qualities in man. It is really amusing to observe with what excuses our modern race fetishists try to overcome these difficulties. Thus, Dr. Clauss accounted for Beethoven's inconvenient race affinities quite simply by declaring: "Beethoven was, so far as his musical ability is concerned, a Nordic man. The style of his work proves this clearly enough; and this is not altered at all by the fact that his body—anthropologically considered, that is, just the mass and weight of his body —perhaps was fairly pure Oriental." [10]

As we see, the purest metempsychosis. What mysterious forces were at work when the "Nordic race-soul" of Beethoven was stuck into a vile Oriental body? Or did, perhaps, the Jews or the Freemasons have a hand in it!

There remains the last question, whether the qualities which man acquires during the course of his life or which are imparted to him by the culture in which he lives have actually no influence on his inherited factors. If this could be proved, then indeed should we be compelled to speak of a "Kismet of the blood" which no one could withstand. But how does the matter stand in reality? The power of the acquired characters reveals itself every day in our lives and constantly conceals the inherited factors with which we began our life journey. As examples we may take the two strongest impulses—which in all living beings and in men of every race and clime reveal themselves as equally powerful—hunger and love. Man has surrounded these two instincts in which the whole vital energy of the individual and the race exhausts itself, with such a network of age-old customs and usages, which in the course of time have been erected into definite ethical principles, that the inborn urge in most cases no longer asserts itself against this web of imparted and acquired concepts. Do we not see every day how in our great cities thousands of miserable, starving human beings silently sneak past the rich display in the show-windows of our food stores? They devour these splendors with greedy eyes, but very seldom does one of them dare to yield to the inborn impulse and take what would serve for the satisfaction of his most urgent needs. Fear of the law, dread of public opinion, inculcated respect for the rights of property of others prove stronger than the drive of the inborn impulse. And yet we are dealing here with acquired characters which are no more transmissible by heredity than are the calloused hands of the blacksmith.

[10] *Rasse und Seele.* Munich, 1925, p. 60.

The child confronts these things quite without comprehension until it gradually learns to adjust itself to them.

And love? With how many prohibitions, duties and grotesque customs has man hedged in this most elemental of his impulses. Even among primitive peoples there exist a great mass of morals and customs which are sanctified by usage and respected by public opinion. Human imagination invented the cult of Astarte in Babylon and that of Mylitta in Assyria, the sexual religions of India and the asceticism of the Christian saints. It created all the institutions of sexual behavior: polygamy, polyandry, monogamy, and all of the forms of promiscuity from the "sacred prostitution" of the Semitic peoples to the sequestration by the state of the women of the street. It brought the whole gamut of sexual passion under strict rule and developed definite views which today are deeply rooted in the minds of men. And yet here are at work also merely acquired concepts, customs, institutions, which have found emotional expression in definite trained-in characteristics. And it is just these characteristics which direct the love-life of man into definite courses and constantly impel the individual to quite distressing suppression of his inborn impulses. Even the most cunning sophistry cannot avoid these facts.

Every phase of human history shows us the powerful influence of religious, political and moral ideas on the social development of men, the strong influence of the social conditions under which they live and which in their turn react on the form of their ideas and opinions. This eternal reciprocal influence constitutes the whole content of history. Hundreds of thousands of men have gone to their death for particular ideas, very often with the most frightful accompaniments, and have by their conduct defied the strongest inborn impulse that exists in every living being. And this has happened under the overpowering influence of acquired ideas. Religions like Islam and Christianity have drawn peoples of all races into their bonds. The same may be said of all the great popular movements of history. We need but think of the Christian movement in the decaying Roman Empire, of the great movements of the time of the Reformation, of international floods of ideas like liberalism, democracy or socialism, which have been able to exert their proselyting power upon men and women of every social class and enlist them under their banners. The peoples of the "Nordic race" have been no exception to this rule.

Our race alchemists have tried to save their faces by maintaining that the peoples of the Nordic race have all too often been misled by ideas that are racially alien to them and for which they had no real inner inclination. They call this incomprehensible invasion by "foreign custom" and "foreign spirit" one of the most lamentable aspects of Germanism and of the Nordic race in general. Such outbursts, which are quite common with Günther, Hauser, Neuner, and others, seem rather odd. What sort of remarkable race is this which allegedly feels itself drawn toward foreign ideas and foreign customs as iron is drawn to the magnet? This unnatural phenomenon might easily make us think that we have here a morbid degenerate form of the "Nordic race-soul"—which otherwise is shown clearly enough by the whole "race" rubbish of our time. It is still more remarkable that the enraptured worshipers of the Nordic wonder-race constantly strive to eliminate these moral blemishes of their idol and in the same breath announce that race is destiny. If this is true, what is the use of all the indoctrination? Of what use that Günther and his "Nordic Ring"—a sort of Blue-Blond International—try by all means to prevent a war between the Nordic peoples in the future; or that Otto Hauser proclaims to an astonished world that the principal strategists of the World War on both sides were blond Nordics and honors the French General Joffre as a "blond Goth"? All the worse if this is so. It then merely proves that blond Nordics on opposite sides have killed one another for a cause which according to their blood was alien to them; above all it proves that the inborn "voice of the blood" could not prevail against the economic and political interests about which the war was fought.

The French race ideologist, Vacher de Lapouge, once announced that in the twentieth century "we shall kill one another by the millions because of one or two degrees more or less in the cephalic index," and that "by this sign, which will replace the biblical shibboleth and kinship of language, related races will recognize one another, and the last sentimentalist will live to see a mighty extermination of peoples." Even the bald and terrible reality of the war was less fantastic than the bloodthirsty imagination of this race fetishist. In the World War we did not smash skulls because they were a little longer or shorter, but because the opposing interests within the capitalistic world had grown to such a degree that the war seemed to the ruling classes the only available way by which they could hope to escape from the blind alley into which they had gotten themselves. In the late World War the most various races fought shoulder to shoulder on both sides. We even drew black men and yellow into the catastrophe with us, without any hindrance from the "voice of the blood," to let themselves be slaughtered for interests which were certainly not their own.

Peoples have not infrequently undergone a fundamental change in their morals and customs which could in no way be traced to racial crossing. According to the unanimous testimony of all recognized race theorists, men of the Nordic race are today most numerous in the Scandinavian countries, especially in Sweden. But these very Swedes, Norwegians and Danes have in the course of their history experienced a profound change in their ancient ways of living. Those very countries which were once hated and feared as the home of the most warlike tribes in Europe now harbor the most peaceful population on the continent. The famous "spirit of the Vikings" which is supposed to have been the outstanding characteristic of Nordic race is, in these same Scandinavian lands, as good as extinguished. The phrase "born pacifists," which was invented by Günther and his satellites especially to bring the so-called "Oriental man" into moral disrepute, fits no one better than the present-day Scandinavians. They merely show that the latest destiny-faith of race is the shallowest fatalism that has ever been devised; it is the most pitiful and degrading surrender of the spirit to the cannibalistic delusion of the "voice of the blood."

In order to prevent the submersion of the "Noble Race" they have hit, in Germany, on the grand idea of "nordification," which has led cunning minds to the most daring proposals. The nordification theory has during the past ten years called forth a whole flood of literary productions than which anything more grotesque would be hard to find. No other country can approach Germany in this. Most of those strange saints who obtrude themselves in Germany today as reformers of sexual relations wish to put procreation under the controlling hand of the state. Others stand openly for the legal introduction of polygamy in order to put the Nordic race the quicker on its somewhat weakened legs. And, so that the lord of the family may come into his rights "in the midst of this effeminate old world"—as Alfred Rosenberg, Hitler's spiritual adviser, so picturesquely expresses it—Herr Richard Rudolf in his essay, *Geschlechtsmoral*, defends polygamy, not only because it provides a means for raising the fecundity of the Nordic race to its highest capacity, but also because this institution better corresponds to the polygamous instincts of the male.

Inspired adherents of nordification a few years ago called to life a special movement for the advocacy of the so-called "Midgard marriage" whose sponsors proposed the founding and financing of special settlements where Nordic men and women selected for this purpose should, in loving collaboration, devote themselves to the exalted task of preventing the decline of the noble race. There were to be ten women for every man. The marriage was to be regarded as a sort of bond of pregnancy which was to last only till the birth of the child, unless both the mates expressed a wish to prolong the union. In his book, *Weltanschauung und Menschenzüchtung*, Health Commissioner F. Dupré advocated a so-called "temporary marriage" which was to serve merely for breeding purposes. A state-appointed "Council of Elders" was to supervise these matters. "The couple must be brought together purely for the purpose of propagation," declares this curious elaboration. "When this has been accomplished they are to separate. . . . The expenses of this breeding are to be borne by the state." Very much like Hentschel, the inventor of the "Midgard marriage," Herr Walther Darré, later Germany's National Socialistic Minister of Nutrition, sets to work, in his book, *Neu-Adel aus Blut und*

Boden ("A New Nobility from the Blood and the Soil"), for the breeding of a new nobility on special *Hegehöfen* ("breeding farms"). Herr Darré wishes to bring the propagation of the nation under constant supervision by establishing "breed-wardens." For this purpose special "herdbooks" and "family records" are to be prepared for all women. All virgins are to be divided into four classes to whom on the basis of special "breeding laws" marriage is to be permitted or denied according to their racial characteristics and fitness for childbearing. On March 12, 1930, the National Socialists introduced in the Reichstag the following addition to Article 218 of the Criminal Code:

> Whoever undertakes artificially to restrict the natural fertility of the German people to the injury of the nation, or by word, writing, print, picture, or in any other way to assist such attempts, or whoever by mating with members of the Jewish blood-community or of the colored races contributes or threatens to contribute to the corruption and disintegration of the German people shall be punished by imprisonment for racial treason.

On December 31, 1931, the national administration of Hitler's Storm Troopers issued a decree that after January 1, 1932, a marriage license should be issued to every Storm Trooper by a so-called "Race-office." This curious document, which pleads for the "preservation by hygienic heredity of a distinct German-Nordic species," and makes reference to a "book of kinship of the S. S.," gave us the first foretaste of the glories of the Third Reich. It is characteristic that the same crowd which peddles its "German idealism" so insistently and with such profound moral enthusiasm combats the "materialistic debasement" of Germany, values sexual relations purely from the viewpoint of the breeder and would reduce the love-life of men to the level of the breeding stall and the stud-farm. After the "rationalization of industry," the rationalization of sexual intercourse—what a future!

But all the talk about nordification is entirely worthless because all the conditions for such a process are lacking. Even if the race were not a mere idea, but an actual living unity whose characteristics were transmitted to their progeny in their entirety, still such a project could not be undertaken. A farmer may be in a position to breed his oxen, cows or swine for the production of meat, milk or fat, but to breed human beings for definite moral and intellectual characteristics is quite another matter. All experiments which have so far been made on plants and animals have shown that a race never enters a mixture as a whole. So long as human beings with like or with very similar racial characteristics keep to themselves and propagate only within their own circle their peculiar characters reappear more or less conjoined and in like relations. When, however, mixture with other racial elements occur, then race is not inherited as a compact unity, but each separate character by itself or in separate con-stellations. Therefore, not only may both pure and mixed characters occur in the offspring; there exists for each of them the possibility of every conceivable combination of the parental hereditary primordia.

There are no longer any pure races, least of all in Europe. The so-called "fundamental races" of Europe are today so thoroughly jumbled together that racially pure peoples are simply not to be found. This holds true especially for Germany, which because of its geographical situation in the heart of the continent seems to have been made for a highway for tribes and peoples. At the time of the migration of peoples Nordic tribes left the old homeland in troops and moved towards the south, where the Nordic blood gradually fused with that of the indigenous "race-alien." Slavic tribes, which invaded the land from the east, took possession of the half-emptied territories and spread in the north as far as the Elbe and in the south as far as the Regnitz. Up to the middle of the eleventh century the Thuringian Forest was called the Slavenwald, and one can recognize in the appearance of the population there the strong influence of Slavic blood even today. The ancient population of Germany was com-pletely recast by these continued intermixtures of blood. The Germans have long ceased to correspond to the description that Tacitus once wrote of the Germanic people. Not only have the physical characteristics altered, the mental and spiritual characters, too, have undergone a profound change. Among the sixty millions which today inhabit Germany there is probably hardly one person whom one could describe as a pure Nordic. It is, therefore, one of the strangest delusions that men have ever harbored that out of this variegated mixture there can be redistilled one of the old "basic races." One must, in fact, be a race-theoretician to be able to think such things. The whole nordification Utopia is as Brunhold Springer cleverly remarks—"not an undertaking, but an Old-German community play." [11]

It is the extremes which mutually attract one another, especially in the love of the sexes. The blond will always be more drawn to the brunette than to one of his own type. It is the strange that charms and allures and sets the blood astir. The very fact that there are no pure races and that all peoples are mixtures proves that the voice of nature is stronger than that of race or of blood. Even the strictest castes of India were not able to preserve their racial purity. The "Nordic man" of Günther and his followers is a purely imaginary picture. The belief in a race which unites in itself every feature of physical beauty along with the most exalted qualities of mind and spirit is a wonder-faith, a dream notion, which cor-responds to nothing in the past or the future.

If the Nordic race were in fact the miraculous entity from which every

[11] Brunhold Springer, *Die Blutmischung als Grundgesetz des Lebens*. Berlin.

human culture has proceeded, how came it that in its Nordic homeland it was unable to bring forth any culture worth mentioning? Why did its "inborn culture-making capacity" unfold only in distant zones and far from its native soil? Why must we go to Greece and Rome to find a Sophocles, a Praxiteles, a Pericles, a Demosthenes, an Alexander, an Augustus, a hundred others, who are honored by the Günthers, Woltmanns and Hausers as representatives of the Nordic race? The fact is, alas, that the Nordic man revealed his celebrated culture-building powers only in another environment and in association with foreign peoples. For the "proud Viking voyages" with which the books on race are all ablaze could hardly be described as cultural activities. On the contrary, they all too frequently threatened culture and laid waste valuable elements of it, as the robber-raids of Goths, Vandals, Normans and other Germanic tribes show clearly enough.

All modern race theorists are, however, agreed that the capacity for state-making was the most important characteristic of Nordic man, which destined him alone to be the leader and guide of peoples and nations. If this is true, how is it that Nordic man in those very Nordic lands never set up a great kingdom, like, for example, that of Alexander, the Roman Caesars, or Genghis Khan, but always stayed shut up in little communities? It really seems rather odd that this crowd which has so much to say about the state-building genius of the blond Nordic, in the same breath bewails the eternal disunion of the Germanic tribes as one of the most lamentable manifestations of their character and warns the present-day Germans of the fatal consequences of this bad habit of their forebears. Such a state of affairs is surely hard to reconcile with the capacity to weld together great kingdoms and nations; a fact—we may remark in passing—that is no great misfortune. The impulse of the Germanic tribes to split up, which is quite proverbial, goes very poorly, in fact, with their alleged capacity for state-building. The blond Nordic acquired this only in foreign parts when the power-concepts of the Roman Empire came to him as a new revelation—and a catastrophe.

We do not mean to deny to "Nordic man" cultural capacity or other valuable characters. Nothing is farther from our intent than to fall into the opposite error from that of the race ideologists. But we guard ourselves with all modesty against the immeasurable arrogance of those persons who dare to deny to other races not only all deep feeling for culture but every idea of honor and fidelity. In the end, all the talk about the "race soul" is nothing but an idle playing with imaginary ideas. The method which brings all human groups mentally and spiritually under a single norm is a monstrosity which can but lead to the most perniciously erroneous conclusions. It is not to be disputed that men who have reproduced for centuries in the same territory and under the influence of the same natural and social environment have certain outer and inner characters in common. These resemblances are more manifest between members of the same family than in a tribe or a people; and yet what immeasurable contrasts of character one finds when one goes deeper into the mental and spiritual make-up of the individual members of a family. In general the so-called "collective character" of a people, a nation or a race expresses merely the personal views of individuals which are taken up by others and thoughtlessly repeated.

What, for instance, are we to think when Günther in his *Rassenkunde des jüdischen Volkes* has this to say about the so-called "Oriental race"? "This race came out of the desert and their mental attitude inclines them to allow formerly cultivated lands to become desert again." This is empty prattle based on nothing at all. In the first place, we lack any historical evidence that this race in fact came out of the desert; and in the next place, who is to produce proof that in the members of this race there really resides the instinct to "let cultivated lands become desert again"? But Günther needed this construction of history to convince his readers of the utter worthlessness of the Jews. Yet, in Palestine, the Jews were an agricultural people; their whole legislation was built around this fact. The Arabs changed Spain into a garden of which great portions became desert again after the expulsion of the Moors.

Fear of the Jews has developed among the advocates of the race theory into a genuine race panic. It is admitted, of course, even in those circles, that actually no such thing as a Jewish race exists, and that the Jews, like all other peoples, are a mixture of every possible racial element. Modern race theoreticians go so far as to assert that along with Levantine, Oriental, Hamitic and Mongolian blood, even a drop or two of Nordic blood flows in the veins of Jews! Nevertheless, it seems that of all races the Jewish has the worst inheritance. There is hardly any evil quality that hostile imagination has not attributed to the Jew. He was the real inventor of socialism, and at the same time he let capitalism loose in the world. He has infected all countries with his liberal ideas and loosened all bonds of authority; still, his religion is a creed of strictest authority, a cult of the utmost despotism. He caused the War and invoked the revolution. He seems to have just the one secret purpose of hatching out subtle conspiracies against the noble Nordic man. We are assured that mixture of blood destroys the original characteristics of a race and diverts the course of its mental and spiritual tendencies. How comes it, then, that so highly mixed a race as the Jews have for two thousand years been able to preserve their religious system in spite of the horrible persecutions they have endured because of it? Must one not infer from this that there are in history other factors than hereditary racial characteristics? And how comes it that the Jews could poison the whole world with their "modernistic spirit" if the ideas of man are only the outcome of hereditary factors inherent in his blood? Must we not conclude from this either that the Jew is much more closely akin to us by blood than our race ideologists are willing to admit or that the blood-determined hereditary characteristics are too weak to withstand foreign ideas?

But the attacks of modern race doctrine are not directed solely against the Jews; in even greater force they are massed against a section of their own people, against the offspring of the so-called "Alpine race" which Günther rebaptized "Eastern." When Günther, Hauser, Clauss and their associates speak of the Eastern peoples they become downright malicious. That the Eastern race settled in the very heart of Europe is, according to Günther, a great misfortune, for with its "impure blood" it constantly threatens the exalted Nordic, whose mixture with this "talentless," "uncreative" race leads only to ruin. The Eastern is the exact opposite of the Nordic man. If in the latter the "spirit of the commander" finds its most distinguished expression, in the former lives only the "sullen soul" of the pikeman capable of no great campaign. The Eastern is the "born pacifist," the "mass man"; hence his preference for democracy, which grows out of his need to pull down everything superior to himself. He has no heroic traits and no feeling at all for the greatness of the fatherland and the nation. The Easterns are the "men of Jean Paul, already plentiful enough, in fact, far too plentiful, in Germany." They make good subjects, but they can never be leaders; only the Nordic man is a predestined leader (see Hitler and Goebbels). But that is not all.

"Sexual intercourse among near relatives, also between brothers and sisters and parents and children, is, I am assured by country doctors, said not to be unusual in those districts settled by Easterns. The Eastern mind, perhaps because of its origin, is not acquainted with the idea of incest." [12]

Otto Hauser has the worst things to say about Eastern man, of whom he presents the following charming picture:

> He will do anything for money. He would unhesitatingly sell his honor if he had any. He is the born democrat and capitalist. . . . The Eastern man is more lascivious than the pure races or than the other mixed races. He makes men and women dance naked on the stage or wrestle with one another. He loves to read about perversions and practices them when he can afford it. He enslaves woman and is enslaved by her. He advocates individualism in the sense that everyone is to do what he pleases, violate girls and young boys, employ any means in social, mental, or political contests. And though it is contrary to all rules of sportsmanship to grasp an opponent by the genitals, he, who advocates in general the freeing of all desire, likes to make use of the practice when he wants to drag down to his own level

---

[12] L. F. Clauss, *Rasse und Seele*, p. 118.

those inconvenient geniuses whom he, the devoid of genius, cannot beat in fair fight.[13]

In another place in his works Hauser tells his readers:

The Eastern is vulgar in his sexuality. One cannot be with him half an hour before he begins telling not merely indecent stories, but his own sex experiences and possibly even those of his wife; and the women entertain the listeners with accounts of their menstrual difficulties. His brats bedaub the walls with vulvas and phalluses and make dates for sexual intercourse at public comfort-stations.

One can hardly trust one's eyes when one reads such stuff. The first impression is that one is dealing with a diseased mind, for this joyous wallowing in the imagined sexuality of another surely springs from a perverted disposition and a morbid imagination incapable of healthy perceptions. Let us be clear about the monstrousness of these accusations which are published thus to the whole world. They throw this filth at a whole body of human beings, numbering millions in their own countries, and ascribe to them alleged "character traits" which really spring only from their own diseased and unclean imagination. This sort of "demonstration" is characteristic of the methods of the present-day race ideologists; it also is typical of the mental degradation of the men who do not hesitate even to draw on the secrets of the comfort-station in order to hang something on the "racial enemy" and so to satisfy their own dirty instincts. And this poison has been poured into the country for years by countless books, pamphlets and newspaper articles. Let no one be surprised if this sowing of dragon's teeth shall some day germinate. For the absurdity of the present-day nationalistic movement in Germany is just this: that it rests on the race theory and that its advocates in their blindness fail to see that they are destroying with their own hands the strongest bulwark of the nation, the inbred feeling of national cohesion.

If one is not sufficiently deluded to be able thus to insult the members of his own nation, he can easily see how this race fatalism must operate against other peoples. Out of the short-sighted belief in the divinely ordained superiority of the noble race follows logically the belief in its "historical mission." Race becomes a question of destiny, a dream of the renewal of the world by the conscious will of Germankind. And since one cannot admit that all peoples will view the approaching destiny from just the same angle of vision, war becomes the only solution. Experience has shown us where that leads. The belief that "In Germankind the world once more its weal will find" (*Am deutschen Wesen einmal noch die Welt genesen*) rouses in just those classes which had the greatest influence on

---

[13] *Rasse und Kultur.* Braunschweig, p. 69.

the fate of Germany the conviction of the inevitability of the "German war," of which they talked so much in Chamberlain's circle. In a widely circulated work in which war is hailed as "midwife of all culture" Othmar Spann declares: "We must desire this war just to prove that all its burden will rest on us, that we alone must fight it out with all the power that the lordly Germanic race has manifested throughout the millennia." [14] ·

This spirit was cherished through the decades and gradually reared to that fatalistic delusion which views all history under the aspect of race. Spann was not the only one who played with the race war of the future. At the conference of the *All-deutscher Verband* ("All-German Union") of November 30, 1912, the question of the coming war held the most prominent place. There was talk of the "decisive struggle between the collective Slavic peoples and Germankind" by Baron von Stössel and others; and Dr. Reuter-Hamburg declared that it "is our chief task to inform the people about the real grounds of the war which is probably coming," which is to be regarded only as a "battle of united Slavism against Germanism." When the German administration brought in its new safety proposals in April, 1913, Bethmann-Holweg based the new provisions on the necessity of preparing for the threatened clash between Slavs and Germans. Although the groupings of the powers at the beginning of war must prove to every person of insight that there could be no talk here of a "war of the races," there were still not lacking those who saw in the frightful catastrophe only the inevitable impact of races. Even so widely known a historiographer as Karl Lamprecht published in the *Berliner Tageblatt* of August 23, 1914, an essay in which he spoke of a "war of Germandom and Latin [Catholic] Slavdom against the invading Oriental barbarism."

> Lamprecht discovered then that Scandinavia, Holland, Switzerland, and America had been led by racial feeling to favor the German cause, and he announced jubilantly "Blood will tell!" The illusion of having America as an ally even led him to proclaim the living future of a "Teutonic-Germanic race!" And since very finally England did not fit into this scheme, the great historian emphasizes: "Just observe that the central land of the British world-empire is no longer dominated by a pure Germanic spirit, but rather by the Celtic." [15]

If the race theory can produce such incurable delusion in the brain of a scholar of worldwide renown, need we wonder at the crazy presumption of an economist like Sombart, who at that day of the world could announce: "Just as the German bird, the Eagle, soars high above all other animals on earth, just so shall the German feel himself exalted above all that

[14] *Zur Soziologie und Philosophie des Krieges*, 1913.
[15] F. Hertz: *Rasse und Kultur.*

mankind which surrounds him and which he sees at an infinite distance beneath him." [16]

We do not maintain that only the German is capable of such deluded notions. Every belief in a chosen religion, nation or race leads to similar monstrosities. But we must recognize that among no other people has the race theory found such wide acceptance or inspired a literature of such general circulation as among the Germans. It seems almost as if the Germany of 1871 had wished to make up for what its greatest spirits before the foundation of the empire, because of their broadly humanistic attitude, had fortunately omitted.

The exponents of race doctrine find themselves in the enviable position that they can venture the most extravagant assertions with no need to trouble themselves about intelligible proofs. Since they themselves know that most of these assertions cannot be maintained on the basis of their scientific value, they appeal to the infallibility of the race instinct, which allegedly gives clearer insight than is vouchsafed to the painstaking experience of scientific research. If this famous instinct of race were real and demonstrable to everybody it would get along very nicely with science, since the "inner voice" or "race in one's own bosom" would bring certainty to men on every difficult question, even when science failed. But in that event we should expect at least the most distinguished advocates of the race theory to be in complete agreement and to voice a certain unanimity in their conclusions. But here is just the trouble. There is hardly a single question of fundamental importance about which those in the camp of the race ideologists are even halfway agreed. Often their views are so far apart that no bridging of the difference is conceivable. Just a few instances of this from the thousands:

In his work, *Rasse und Kultur*, Otto Hauser informs us that the Greeks "were a strictly blond people who, quite of themselves, attained to a height of culture that will always arouse admiration, will always serve as a model as long as the related Nordic blood flows in any people, in any human being." Woltmann, Günther, and others have said the same thing in other words—basing their opinion, doubtless, on the same "Nordic instinct" which permeates the related blood through the millennia. But Gobineau, the real founder of the race theory, found nothing good to say of the Greeks; rather he constantly disparaged them in every way, because of his ingrained hatred of democracy. In his 1,200-page *Histoire des Perses* he praises the culture of the Persians in exaggerated terms and pictures Greece as a half-barbaric country with no culture of its own worth mentioning. Gobineau even denies to the Hellenes every moral quality

[16] Werner Sombart, Händler und Helden, *Patriotische Besinnungen*. Munich, 1915, p. 143.

and declares that they had no understanding of the sentiment of honor—as we see, the purest "Oriental."

For Chamberlain, Christianity is the highest expression of the Aryan spirit; in the Christian faith the Germanic soul reveals itself in its true profundity and divorces itself most definitely from every Semitic religious concept. For Judaism is the complete antithesis of the Christian religion; any philosophic synthesis of the Jewish and the Germanic mind, even in religion, is quite unthinkable. On the other hand, Albrecht Wirth sees in Christianity a product of the Jewish-Hellenic mind, which undertook, as the "despised Jew fled from the misery of the outer world, to erect about it a higher inner world." [17] While Eugen Dühring condemns Christianity utterly because by its influence the Judaizing of the Aryan mind was accomplished.[18] Ludwig Neuner accuses the Frankish kings of having stolen from our ancestors and utterly destroyed "the ancient, indigenous faith that sprang from a childlike view of nature" and forcing on them instead "a harsh system of religion of outspokenly international character." [19] Then Erich Mahlmeister assures us, in his essay, *Für deutsche Geistesfreiheit:* "Christianity is of an unmanly, slavish nature, directly opposed to the German nature." On the person of Christ he passes judgment thus: "The outcast traitor to his country of a hatred race is the God before whom the German is expected to bend his knee."

Günther, Hauser, Clauss, see in Protestantism a spiritual movement of the Nordic race, and Lapouge, as well, sees in it "the attempt to adapt Christianity to the specific type of the Aryan race." Chamberlain, too, is a decided opponent of the Catholic church and refers in his *Grundlagen* to the Semitic origin of the Papacy. He sees in the latter the exact antithesis of the Germanic spirit, which recognizes no priestly caste and is emotionally opposed to a world hierarchy. For him, therefore, the Reformation is the revolt of Nordic man against the Semitic Caesarism of Rome and one of the greatest deeds of Germanism in general. Against this, Woltmann exalts the Papacy as the glorification of Germanism and takes great pains to demonstrate the Germanic descent of most of the popes. He was especially impressed by that "child of the Goths," Hildebrandt, who sat on the papal throne as Gregory VII and was the real founder of the temporal power of the Papacy. Otto Hauser, however, explains this patent confusion of the Germanic spirit as follows: "It is characteristic of the power hunger of Nordic man that he is able to employ all his force in every undertaking and unhesitatingly makes use of every means to an end. We know how extremely frivolous was the attitude of many of the

[17] *Das Auf und Ab der Völker.* Leipzig, 1920, p. 84.
[18] *Die Judenfrage als Frage der Rassenschädlichkeit für Existenz, Sitte und Kultur der Völker.* See also, *Sache, Leben und Feinde.*
[19] *Deutsche Gott-Natur-Kunde.*

popes toward the Papacy and Christianity. So, while the Papacy was represented for a while by an almost uninterrupted line of Germans, it was nevertheless an un-German, un-Nordic idea." [20]

How are we to find our way in all this? What sort of strange thing is this "Nordic racial soul"? It glimmers with all the colors of a chameleon. It is popish and antipopish, Catholic and Protestant. The Voice of the Blood in it is opposed to the rulership of a privileged priestly caste and rejects the thought of a world hierarchy, but at the same time its representatives exert every effort to bring the world under the yoke of the Papacy, whose forms are derived from "the Oriental despotism of the Semites"; and the matter becomes still more interesting when we learn that Ignatius Loyola, the founder of the Jesuit Order, was a blond-haired descendant of Germans—as Woltmann and Hauser assert. Here, as in the case of Beethoven, it seems that a dirty trick was played on nature. Think of it: Loyola, a blond-haired, blue-eyed German, the warlike herald and acknowledged preacher of the counter-Reformation; and Martin Luther, the "soul of the German Reformation," a dark-haired man, of stocky figure, with brown eyes, who exhibits so plainly the outward characteristics of the "Eastern" that even Günther, Hauser and Woltmann cannot deny this! That Gobineau in his work on race and elsewhere makes laudatory mention of the controlling hand of the Catholic church, and in his *Ottar Jarl* damns heartily every heresy against Holy Mother Church, does not tend to simplify the matter. And, as if all this were not enough, Hauser assures us that the Reformation was a "movement of the blood" and indicates the "displacing of the mixed-race spirit by the Nordic." [21] And he says this just after he has, a few pages farther back, drawn for us this picture of the men of the Reformation: "What was left of Germany had reached the lowest point of its cultural and racial ebb about 1500. The Germans were at that time usually so ugly that Dürer and his forerunners and contemporaries in their realistic paintings are almost never able to present a beautiful, clear-cut, noble countenance, only features of a quite beastly repulsiveness; and even in their representations of the divine personages and saints from sacred history they were very seldom able to depict a halfway beautiful being because they had not even models to follow." But these men of the "racial ebb," after all, made the Reformation. How explain that this "movement of the blood" which displaced the "mixed-race spirit" occurred just at the time when, according to Hauser's own statement, Germany had reached the "lowest point of its cultural and racial ebb"?

Let one take any period whatever of human history and one stumbles always on these same contradictions. There is, for example, the great

[20] *Die Germanen in Europa*, p. 112.
[21] *Rasse und Kultur*, p. 331.

French Revolution. It is mere matter of course that one finds among the exponents of the race theory no trace of understanding of the economic, political and social causes of that great European upheaval. Just as gypsies read the fate of a man in the lines in his hand, so the soothsayers of the race theory read from the portraits of the leading spirits of that storm-lashed time the whole story of the Revolution and its "blood-determined" causes. "We know that a man must of necessity behave as his appearance indicates, and that this law can manifest itself as well in the most primitive as well as in the most complicated and confused fullness of expression, that it must remain always and everywhere the timeless and unchanging law of the inheritance of life." [22]

This masterly exposition, which disposes of the most difficult question with which science has dealt for many decades as if it were the most matter of course affair in the world, is quite astounding. "We know!" Who knows? How do we know? Who established this "law" of which our author speaks? No one! No science! We are dealing here merely with an empty assertion that is not worth a bad penny. In fact, the author tried from the portraits of Louis XVI, Mirabeau, Madame Roland, Robespierre, Danton, Marat, to establish the inner law of their behavior and to infer it from the degree of their racial mixture. Unfortunately this deduction rests on no law but merely on imagination, which is neither "timeless" nor "unchanging." There may be men whose character is written on their forehead, but there are not many of them; for types like Karl and Franz Moor live only in works of fiction; in actual life one seldom meets them. No one is able to recognize the mental and moral characters of a man from his external features; the most expert physiognomists could hardly read the importance of any of the great personages of history from their faces. This ability is usually revealed only when one knows with whom he is dealing; and it would not have been so easy for the author of our selected work to pass judgment on persons like Mirabeau, Robespierre, Marat or Danton if these men had their historic roles still to play.

Gobineau saw in the great revolution only the revolt of "Celto-Romanic mongreldom" against the Germanic ruling class of the French nobility and damned the whole tremendous movement with the virulent hatred of the royalist, who on principle condemned every attempt to destroy the divinely ordained order. The revolution was for him the slave-revolt of men of baser race, whom he already despised because they were the exponents of those modern revolutionary and democratic ideas in Europe which had struck a death-blow at the ancient master caste. Chamberlain judged the revolution from a like point of view, since he, like Gobineau, saw in democracy and liberalism the deadly foe of the Germanic spirit. In contrast, Woltmann saw in the revolution a demonstration of that

[22] A. Harrar, *Rasse Menschen von Gestern und Morgen.* Leipzig, p. 86.

same Germanic spirit and in support of this view tried to prove that most of the leading minds of the revolution were of German origin. While for Gobineau the slogan of the revolution, "Liberty, Equality, Fraternity," was merely the utterance of a completely unleashed racial mixture, Hauser tells us: "The demand for liberty, equality and fraternity is genuinely Protestant, but it holds good only for the selection which Protestantism makes, only for groups like that." In another place in the same work he says: "The revolution begins as the work of Germans and Germanoids and on the basis of a Germanic idea; it finds an echo in all those of higher race; but it ends in the witches' sabbath of the unshackled impulse of the baseborn mass, which has made use of the Germanic 'heavenly light' only 'to be beastlier than any beast.' " [23] Now does this mean that the Germanic descent of the French nobility of which Gobineau tells us was just an idle boast, or are we here dealing with an annihilating war of Germans against Germans, a sort of race-suicide?

That Marx and Lassalle were Jews by descent is, for men of the stamp of Philipp Stauff and Theodor Fritsch and their kind, the best proof that the socialist doctrine is based on the Jewish mentality and is alien to the racial feeling of Nordic man. That the enormous majority of the founders of socialism were non-Jews and that the socialist movement found quite as easy entrance into Germanic countries as into Romanic and Slavic has for these gentlemen just as little significance as the fact that Marx and Lassalle were influenced most deeply and permanently in their mental development, not by the ideology of Judaism, but by the philosophy of Hegel. As for the idea of socialism itself, Woltmann explains, that it has its most convinced adherents in the German sections of the proletarian population on account of their blood, because in the Germanic elements the urge to freedom finds strongest expression. Gobineau, on the contrary, recognizes in socialism a typical sign of Mongolism and the covetousness of the born slave, hence his outspoken contempt for the workers, to whom he denies any sustained cultural ambition. Driesmans designates the socialists as "Celto-Mongolians." Chamberlain scents in the socialistic movement everywhere the influence of Jewish ideology, which in this movement pursues its aim of utterly destroying the Germanic spirit in Germans. Dühring, however, declared categorically: "The Jewish social democracy is a reactionary gang whose state-enforced activities tend, not toward freedom and good husbandry, but toward the universality of bondage and exploitation through enforced service to the state in the interest of leading Jews and associations of Jews." [24] And so that nothing might be lacking to this crazy pot-pourri, the "rough riders" of the race theory in Germany declared a holy war against Judaized Marxism and proclaimed a so-called

[23] *Die Germanen in Europa*, pp. 149-150.
[24] *Sache, Leben, und Feinde*, p. 207.

"national socialism" that probably presents the most gruesome enlivening of capitalistic platitudes with worn-out socialistic slogans that was ever thought of. Under this banner, and with the lovely motto, "Germany, awake! Judah, perish!" they made their way into the Dritte Reich.

But crazier still was the picture when the advocates of the race theory set themselves to subject to the Nordic blood-test the great personalities of history. What they got out of it could be written on no single parchment, though it were made from the skin of the famous Cloud-cow Audumla of the Norse saga. First, there is Goethe, whose character portrait in the race-books is suspiciously shaky. The appearance of this "most German of all Germans" is certainly very little like the representation of a Germanic man. To begin with, he lacked the "sparkling sky-blue eye," the blond hair and several other features which alone make the 100 percent Nordic. Regardless of this, Chamberlain rates him as the most perfect genius of the Germanic race and recognizes in *Faust* the ripest product of the German mind. Albrecht Wirth is of the opinion, in which anthropologists seem to be fairly well agreed, that Goethe was a non-Nordic; and most anthropologists see in him a product of the Alpine race. Lenz recognizes in Goethe a Levantine-Germanic hybrid. Dühring questions the Aryan descent of Goethe and believes that he recognizes in him Semitic traits. Hans Hermann goes farthest of all. In his *Sanatorium of Free Love* he presents this picture of the greatest of German poets: "One looks now at Goethe; these protruding brown eyes, this nose slightly hooked at the tip, this long body with its short legs, with even a slightly 'melancholy' expression; and we have before us the very prototype of a descendant of Abraham."

Lessing, whose creative work was of such decisive and profound significance for the intellectual development of Germany, is honored by Driesmans as the living embodiment of the German spirit. Dühring, on the contrary, sought to adduce proofs that the author of *Nathan* had Jewish blood in his veins. Even the noses of Schiller and Richard Wagner aroused the scorn of the race snifflers, and Schiller was as good as done for when Adolf Bartels, the literary pope in the present Hitlerite state, traced the "un-Germanic" in Schiller's works to Celtic admixtures in his blood.

For Chamberlain Napoleon I was the living embodiment of all Non-Germandom. But Woltmann discovered in him a blond-haired German, and Hauser opines: "If one sees in him a 'Corsican' one assigns him to a group in which he is an exception; in the North Italian nobility, however, to which he belongs, one finds all the splendid condottieri of the Renaissance and perceives at once that he is to be counted with these." [25] As to this, we may note that the notion that Napoleon sprang from a line of

[25] *Rasse und Kultur*, p. 14.

condottieri is merely the thoughtless adoption of an assertion of Taine's. The fact is that in the whole tribe of the Bonapartes there was not a single condottiere—neither in the line from Treviso nor in that from Florence—though probably there is Saint Bonaventura. Wherefore Mereshkowski quite properly inquires: "Why should the blood of these supposititious robbers (condottieri) have run stronger in the veins of Napoleon than that of the actually provable saint?"

But enough of this unpleasant game, which one could keep up indefinitely without becoming any the wiser. It is neither the conclusions of science nor the voice of the blood which is responsible for the ideas of the founders of the race theory, but their strongly asocial sentiment, which makes them walk rough-shod over every feeling of human dignity. To no one so well as to them does the old saying of Goethe apply: "We are able to understand correctly how anyone will think about any particular matter only when we know what is his sentiment toward it." It was not their doctrine that shaped their sentiment; it was the sentiment that gave form and content to the doctrine. But this sentiment is rooted in the very foundations of all spiritual, political and social reaction: in the attitude of masters towards their slaves. Every class that has thus far attained to power has felt the need of stamping their rulership with the mark of the unalterable and predestined, till at last this becomes an inner certainty for the ruling castes themselves. They regard themselves as the chosen ones and think that they recognize in themselves externally the marks of men of privilege. Thus arose in Spain the belief in the *sangre azul*, the "blue blood" of the nobility, which is first mentioned in the medieval chronicles of Castile. Today they appeal to the blood of the "noble race" which allegedly has been called to rule over all the peoples of the world. It is the old idea of power, this time disguised as race. Thus one of the best known defenders of the modern race idea declares with noble self-assurance: "All Nordic culture is power culture; all Nordic talent is talent for matters of power, for matters of enterprise and world-making, whether in the material or in the spiritual realm, in the state, in art, in research." [26]

All advocates of the race doctrine have been and are the associates and defenders of every political and social reaction, advocates of the power principle in its most brutal form. Gobineau stood squarely in the camp of the counter-revolution and made no bones about his purpose of attacking by his teaching "democracy and its weapon, the revolution." The slave-owners of Brazil and of the southern states of North America appealed also to his work to justify Negro slavery. Chamberlain's *Grundlagen* was an open declaration of war against all the achievements of the last hundred years in the direction of personal freedom and the social equalization of men. He hated everything which had sprung from the

[26] L. F. Clauss, *Rasse und Seele*, p. 81.

revolution with grim bitterness and remained to the last the bellwether of political and social reaction in Germany. In this respect the representatives of the modern race theory differ in not the slightest degree from their predecessors except that they are more soulless, outspoken and brutal, and therefore more dangerous at a time when the spiritual in people is crippled and their emotions have grown callous and dull because of the war and its horrible after-effects. People of the brand of Ammon, Günther, Hauser and Rosenberg, are in all their undertakings ruthless and hidebound reactionaries. What that leads to, the Third Reich of Hitler, Goering and Goebbels shows us realistically. When Günther, in his *Rassenkunde des deutschen Volkes* speaks of a "gradation in rank of the Germans according to their blood" his concept is thoroughly that of a slave-people who are arranged in a definite order of ranks that reminds us of the castes of the Indians and the Egyptians. One comprehends how this doctrine found such ready acceptance in the ranks of the great industrialists. The *Deutsche Arbeitgeberzeitung* wrote thus about Günther's book: "What becomes of the dream of human equality after one takes even a single glance at this work? Not only do we regard the study of such a work as this as a source of the highest interest and instruction; we believe, too, that no politician can form a correct judgment without investigation of the problems here dealt with."

Of course! No better moral justification could be produced for the industrial bondage which our holders of industrial power keep before them as a picture of the future.

The race theory first appeared as an interpretation of history. But with time it has acquired a political significance, and it has crystallized today in Germany into a new ideology of reaction in which lurk future dangers that cannot be overlooked. He who thinks that he sees in all political and social antagonisms merely blood-determined manifestations of race, denies all conciliatory influence of ideas, all community of ethical feeling, and must at every crisis take refuge in brute force. In fact, the race theory is only the cult of power. Race becomes destiny, against which it is useless to struggle; therefore any appeal to the basic principles of humanity is just idle talk which cannot restrain the operation of the laws of nature. This delusion is not only a permanent danger to the peaceful relations of peoples with one another, it kills all sympathy within a people and flows logically into a state of the most brutal barbarism. Whither this leads is shown in Ernst Mann's *Moral der Kraft*, where we read: "Who because of his bravery in battle for the general welfare has acquired a serious wound or disease, even he has no right to become a burden to his fellow men as cripple or invalid. If he was brave enough to risk his life in battle, he should possess also the final courage to end his life himself. Suicide is the one heroic deed available to invalids and weaklings."

Thus we should happily attain the cultural level of the Papuans. Such lines of thought lead to total depravity and inflict on all human feeling deeper wounds than one suspects. The race theory is the leitmotif of a new barbarism which endangers all the intellectual and spiritual values in culture, threatening to smother the voice of the spirit with its "voice of the blood." And so belief in race becomes the most brutal violence to the personality of man, a base denial of all social justice. Like every other fatalism, so also race-fatalism is a rejection of the spirit, a degrading of man to a mere blood-vessel for the race. The doctrine of race when applied to the concept of the nation proves that this is not a community of descent, as has been so often asserted; and as it dissects the nation into its separate components it destroys the foundations of its existence. When in spite of this its adherents today so noisily proclaim themselves the representatives of the national interests, one can but recall the saying of Grillparzer: "The course of the new education runs from humanity through nationality to bestiality."

Chapter 4

CONCERNING THE CONCEPT OF CULTURE. CULTURE AS ETHICAL STAND-
ARD OF VALUE WITH KANT, HERDER AND OTHERS. CULTURE AND CIVILI-
ZATION. CULTURE AS CONSCIOUS RESISTANCE TO THE NATURAL COURSE
OF EVENTS. NATURE PEOPLES AND CULTURE PEOPLES. CULTURE IN THE
STRUGGLE AGAINST TYRANNY AND LUST FOR POWER. SOLIDARITY AS
THE MOST EFFECTIVE PROMOTER OF CULTURE. RELATION OF SEPARATE
HUMAN GROUPS TO THE GENERAL COURSE OF CULTURE. CULTURAL
VITALIZATION BY FOREIGN INFLUENCES. VICTORY OF THE HIGHER CUL-
TURE OVER POLITICAL SUPPRESSION. CULTURAL FITNESS AND ASSIMI-
LATION BY THE STATE.

BEFORE we go further into the relation of the national state to the
general course of culture it is necessary to define as sharply as possible
the concept of culture, so as to avoid confusion. The word "culture,"
the general use of which is a rather recent matter, embodies no very
clearly defined idea—as one would infer from the multiplicity of its
applications. Thus one speaks of culture of the soil, of physical, spiritual
and mental culture, of the culture of a race or a nation, of a man of
culture, and other like matters, and in each instance the word means something different. It is not very long since we gave to the concept of culture
an almost purely ethical meaning. One spoke of the morality of peoples as
we today speak of their cultures. In fact, up to the end of the eighteenth
century and later men employed the concept "humanity," which is a
purely moral concept, in the same sense in which we today use the word
culture, and one cannot say that such application was less appropriate or
less clear.

Montesquieu, Voltaire, Lessing, Herder and many others thought of
culture only as a moral concept. Herder, in his *Ideas for a Philosophy of
the History of Mankind*, had laid down the principle that the culture of
a people is higher in proportion as it expresses the spirit of humanity.
Besides, even today, ethical feeling is for many the essential content of
all culture. Thus, Vera Strasser declares, in a much-noticed work, that
"the progress of culture consists in this: that every individual shall suppress the bestial and develop the spiritual," which by the contrast selected

reveals clearly that the spiritual is thought of as primarily a moral concept.[1]

Kant, also, saw in morality the essential characteristic of culture. Proceeding from the standpoint that man is a being in whom the inclination toward seclusion is matched with the impulse toward sociability, he thought he saw in the conflict of these two attitudes the "great instrument of culture" and the real source of ethical feeling in man. By it man was first enabled to overcome his natural crudity and to ascend the steps of culture, which, according to Kant's own utterance, "comprises the social worth of man." Culture seemed to him the final purpose of nature, which in man attained to consciousness of itself. According to Kant's view, culture carries in itself many obstacles which seem to hinder the free growth of humanity, but which really serve this final purpose. Holding this opinion he thought he saw in every form of expression of culture a fingerpost that pointed to the great goal toward which humanity strives.

Later, attempts were made to differentiate culture and civilization. Civilization was to mean merely the subjugation of external nature by man, while culture was to be valued as intellectualizing and spiritual refinement of physical existence. Based on this definite divisions were made of the phenomena of social life and conceived art, literature, music, religion, philosophy and science as separate spheres of culture; while technical skill, industrial life and political organization were gathered under the heading of civilization. Others wanted to recognize in science, too, only a manifestation of civilization, since its practical application constantly influenced and transformed the material life of man. Each of these attempts has its peculiar advantages, each also its inadequacies; for it is not a simple matter to draw lines of division here, even when we recognize that this is only an attempt to set up a classification that shall make the study of actual occurrences easier.

The Latin word *cultura*, which had been almost forgotten, was originally applied almost exclusively to agriculture, animal-breeding and similar matters which represent a conscious attack by man upon the course of natural events; it had very nearly the meaning of rearing or cultivating. Such an approach involves no contradiction; it can also be conceived as a particular shaping of events which attaches itself to the long course of natural occurrences. It is very probable that only the Christian theologic way of thinking was the cause of this setting up of an artificial opposition between nature and culture by its placing of man *above* nature and its belief that nature was created entirely for man's sake.

When we take culture to mean simply man's conscious attack on the blind operation of natural forces, with the possibility of distinguishing between lower and higher forms of cultural process, there is no longer

[1] *Psychologie der Zusammenhänge und Begebenheiten.* Berlin, 1921.

any possibility of misinterpretation. Thus understood, culture is the conscious resistance of man against the course of nature, to which resistance alone he owes the preservation of his species. Countless genera which once inhabited the earth perished in the early glacial period because nature had deprived them of food and of their old conditions of life. But man struggled against the altered conditions and found ways and means to escape from their destructive influence. In this sense the whole course of his development and dispersal over the earth has been a constant struggle against the natural conditions of his environment, which, in his way, he has tried to change to his advantage. He made for himself artificial utensils, weapons and tools, learned to use fire, and adapted himself by appropriate clothing and shelter to the circumstances under which he was compelled to live. Thus he made, so to speak, his own climate and was enabled to change his residence and to defy the natural conditions of his life. Thus understood, the appearance of man is the beginning of culture, and human life is merely its content. Ludwig Stein made an illuminating presentation of the contrasting concepts, nature and culture:

> The unbroken regularity in the succession of events which goes on without definite purpose and independent of human activity, we call *nature*. What human beings have elaborated, planned, striven for, achieved, shaped purposively and deliberately, we call *culture*. What grows freely from the soil without any demands upon human labor is a natural product; but what takes shape only by the intervention of human labor is an artifact or culture-product. By pursuing conscious purposes and by a developed system of adapting these purposes to available means human effort controls the unconsciously adaptive creative activity of nature. By means of tools, which men as an imitative being makes in the approximate likeness of his own members, and with the help of institutions and labor-saving devices which he has invented, man speeds up the monotonous, tedious course of natural processes, and makes them serve his own ends. The type of the natural status is, therefore: *mastery of man by his environment;* the essence of the cultural status, on the other hand, is: *mastery of his environment by man.*[2]

This definition of the concept is simple and clear; it has the further advantage that it simply presents the relation between nature and culture without setting up an express opposition between them. This is important; for if one holds the view that man also is only a part of nature, one of its creatures who stands neither above it nor outside it, then neither does his work fall outside the general frame of nature, whether we call it culture, civilization, or something else. Viewed thus, culture is only a special manifestation of nature, and its beginning is linked with the appearance of man upon earth. *His* history is the history of culture in its manifold gradations; and yet he belongs, like every other being, to the same totality

---

[2] *Die Anfänge der menschlichen Kultur*, Leipzig, p. 2.

of things that we call nature. It is culture that assures him of his place in the great realm of Nature, who is *his* mother also. Of course, one can speak only of a relative mastery of nature by man, for even the most advanced culture is not yet in a position completely to control nature. A tidal wave suffices to destroy his carefully built dams, to drown his planted fields, and to send his well-built ships to the bottom of the sea. An earthquake annihilates in a few minutes painful products of a century of creative activity. The progress of culture is therefore only a gradual mastery of nature by man, which with his advancing development becomes ever better planned and surer of its goal without ever becoming absolute.

With this view the artificial distinction that has been set up between "nature peoples" and "culture peoples" disappears. Such a distinction corresponds in no way to actual facts, since there are no tribes or peoples anywhere entirely without a culture. Indeed, Friedrich Ratzel, the actual founder of the anthropo-geographical theory of history, stated, in his *Völkerkunde*, that there is to be found no essential difference between nature peoples and culture peoples, but merely differences in the degree of their culture, so that one can in reality speak only of culturally poorer and culturally richer peoples.

The different forms of the cultural life have of themselves given rise to certain distinctions, and even though it is hardly possible to draw sharp lines between the separate fields of activity of human culture, still we cannot get along without them, for our brains are so constructed that we can proceed only with the help of the crutches of concepts. So it was the presentation of the purely political history of separate states, whose content was limited almost exclusively to the enumeration of dynasties, the description of wars and conquests and the explanation of the different systems of government, which undoubtedly gave the first impulse to profounder cultural interpretations of history. We came to see that these one-sided presentations by no means exhaust the unlimited abundance of cultural events but rather make indecent display of their most unfruitful aspect. For, just as the forces of nature are not all of service for human purposes, so also, not all the occurrences in the social environment man has built up further his higher development. Some of them, in fact, operate as dangerous obstacles to this development.

Even slavery and despotism are manifestations of the general cultural movement; for they, too, represent a conscious attack on the natural course of things. But these are in the last analysis only defects of social culture, and their disastrous effects are brought more and more clearly to the consciousness of man in the course of his history. The long list of social upheavals and the uncounted uprisings against old and new systems of rulership bear witness to this. As man continually strives to impart to his natural environment more and more of his own character, his own development impels him in ever increasing measure to eliminate the evils of his social environment, to advance the intellectual development of his species and to lead it toward ever higher perfection. It is the essential core of all culture that man does not submit blindly to the rough caprice of natural processes, but struggles against them in order to shape his fate by his own standards; so he will some day break those chains which he forged for himself while ignorance and superstition still interfered with his freer insight. The farther his mind forces its way along the winding road of his social evolution, the broader become the purposes he holds before him, the more consciously and insistently will he try to influence the course of this evolution and to make all social occurrences serve the higher ends of culture.

Thus we advance, urged by an inner longing and spurred on by the influence of the social institutions under which we live, toward a social culture which will no longer know any form of exploitation or slavery. And this coming culture will work the more beneficently the more clearly its representatives recognize in the personal freedom of the individual and the union of all in the solidaric bonds of a sense of social justice the mainspring of their social activity. Freedom, not in the abstract sense of Hegel, but conceived as a practical possibility which guarantees to every member of society that he may develop to the fullest all those powers, talents and capacities with which nature has, endowed him, without hindrance by authoritative compulsion and the inevitable effects of an ideology of brute force! Freedom of the person on the basis of economic and social justice! Only by this is man offered the possibility of bringing to full flower that consciousness of his personal responsibility which is the firm foundation of each and every freedom, and of developing the vital sense of his unity with his own kind to a stage where the wishes and desires of the individual spring from the depths of his social feeling.

Just as in nature the brutal struggle for existence that is fought out with tooth and claw is not the only mode of maintaining life; just as along with this crude manifestation another and much more involved form of the struggle for existence is in operation which finds expression in the social banding together of the weaker genera and in their practical rendering of mutual aid; so also in culture are manifested different forms of human activities which employ the more primitive or the finer traits of man. And just as in nature that second type of struggle for existence is far more effective in preserving the individual and the race than the brutal war of the so-called "strong" against the "weak"—a fact which is shown satisfactorily by the astounding retrogression of those species which have no social life and in their struggle with the environment have to rely merely on physical superiority [3]—so also in the social life of mankind

---

[8] Peter Kropotkin, *Mutual Aid, a Factor of Evolution.*

the higher forms of moral and intellectual development slowly achieve victory over the brute forces of political forms of rulership, which have thus far only served to cripple every higher cultural development.

We are led to conclude, then, that if culture is simply a constant subduing by man of the primitive processes of nature, and the political endeavors within the social structure which throughout his life circumscribe man and subject his creative activities to the external compulsion of rigid forms, then it is in its essence everywhere the same despite the ever increasing number and the endless diversity of its special forms of expression. Then the notion of the alleged existence of purely national cultures, each of which constitutes by itself a closed whole and carries within itself the laws of its origin, is no more than a wish-concept which has nothing in common with life's realities. The universal which lies at the foundation of all cultures is infinitely more important than the difference in their outer forms, which are for the most part determined by the environment. For every culture springs from the same urge and strives consistently toward the same goal. Everywhere it begins at first as a civilizing force that sets up artificial limits to the rough, unbridled rule of nature and enables man to satisfy his essential needs more easily and with less interference. Later there grows out of it quite spontaneously the aspiration for worthier organization and loftier spirit in social and individual life that is deeply rooted in the social sentiment of man and must be regarded as the driving force in every higher culture. If one wishes to get a clear picture of the relations and closer connections of the various groups of human beings with this thing we call culture he might make use of this comparison:

Over the broad surface of the ocean the sun unceasingly draws up watery vapors to the skies. Clouds form, and float, wind-driven, to the land where they discharge their garnered fullness and fall to earth as fruitful rain. By millions the raindrops hide themselves within the bosom of the earth, and then from countless springs gush, laughing, out again upon its surface. Rivulets are formed, cut through the land in every direction, swell to a brook, a river. The river rolls its floods down again to that same sea in which it had its beginning. Through endless time the circuit has gone on with irresistible certainty, unchanging; and it will continue in unbroken sequence as long as the cosmic conditions of our solar system themselves endure unchanged.

It is not different with the cultural work of peoples, with every creative activity of the individual. What we in general designate as culture is at bottom only a great all-embracing unity of the "Occurring," which is gripped by a restless, uninterrupted transforming and makes itself apparent in countless forms and structures. Always and everywhere the same creative urge is hungry for action; only the mode of expression differs and is adapted to the environment. Just as every spring, every brook, every river is in its depths allied to the sea, into whose tides it ever pours itself anew, so also is every separate culture cycle only part of the same all-embracing unity, from which it draws its deepest and most original forces and into whose lap its own creative work always falls again at last. Like the brooks and rivers are all the culture forms that through the millennia have followed one another or have existed side by side. They are all rooted in the same primitive soil, to which they are in their depth allied as are the waters to the sea.

Cultural reconstructions and social stimulation always occur when different peoples and races come into closer union. Every new culture is begun by such a fusion of different folk elements and takes its special shape from this. This is quite natural, for only through outside influences do those new needs, those new understandings arise which constantly struggle for expression in every field of cultural activity. The desire to preserve the "purity of the culture" of a people by the deliberate elimination of foreign influences—a notion which is today advocated with great zeal by extreme nationalists and adherents of the race doctrine—is just as unnatural as it is futile, and merely shows that these peculiar fanatics for cultural autonomy have not understood at all the profound significance of the cultural process. Such distorted ideas have about the same meaning as saying to a man that he can attain to the highest state of manhood only if he eliminates woman from his life. The result would be the same in both cases.

New life arises only from the union of man with woman. Just so a culture is born or fertilized only by the circulation of fresh blood in the veins of its representatives. Just as the child results from the mating so new culture forms arise from the mutual fertilization of different peoples and their spiritual sympathy with foreign achievements and capacities. One needs a strong dose of mental short-sightedness to dream of withdrawing an entire country from the spiritual influences of the wider cultural circle to which it belongs, especially today when peoples are more than ever bent on the mutual enlargement of their cultural aspirations.

But even if the possibility existed, such a people would not experience an uplift in their cultural life, as the exponents of cultural autonomy so strangely insist. All experience indicates rather that such inbreeding would lead inevitably to a general stunting, to a slow extinction of culture. In this respect it is with peoples as it is with persons. How poorly that man would fare who in his cultural development had to rely entirely on the creations of his own people! This quite apart from the fact that it is utterly useless to talk of such a possibility, since even the wisest is in no position to say which among the cultural possessions of a people they actually worked out for themselves and which they took over in one form or another from others. The inner culture of a man grows just in the measure that he develops an ability to appropriate the achievements of other peoples and enrich his mind with them. The more easily he is able to do this the better it is for his mental culture, the greater right he has to the title, man of culture. He immerses himself in the gentle wisdom of Lao-tse and rejoices in the beauty of the Vedic poems. Before his mind unfold the wonder-tales of the *Thousand and One Nights,* and with inner rapture he drinks in the sayings of the wine-loving Omar Khayyam or the majestic strophes of Firdusi. His soul absorbs the profundities of the Book of Job and swings in rhythm with the *Iliad.* He laughs with Aristophanes, weeps with Sophocles, reads with enjoyment the humorous incidents of the *Golden Ass* of Apuleius, and hears with interest Petronius' portrayal of conditions in declining Rome. With Maistre Rabelais he treads the tastefully decorated halls of the happy Abbey of Thélème and with François Villon he wanders past the Ravenstone. He tries to fathom the soul of Hamlet and rejoices in Don Quixote's lust for deeds. He presses through the terrors of Dante's Hell and grieves with Milton for the lost Paradise. In one word, he is everywhere at home, and therefore knows better how to value the charm of his own homeland. With unprejudiced eye he searches the cultural possessions of all peoples and so perceives more clearly the strong unity of all mental processes. And of these possessions no one can rob him; they are outside the jurisdiction of the government and are not subject to the will of the mighty ones of the earth. The legislator may be in a position to close the gates of his country to the stranger, but he cannot keep him from making his demands upon the treasure of the people, its mental culture, with the same assurance as any native.

Here is the point at which the preponderant importance of culture over any political-national frontier-fixing reveals itself most clearly. Culture unlooses the shackles that the theological spirit of politics has fastened on the peoples. In this sense it is in its deepest essence revolutionary. We indulge in profound reflections about the evanescence of all existence and demonstrate that all the great kingdoms which have played a world-commanding role in history were irrevocably doomed to downfall as soon as they had attained the highest peak of their culture. A number of well-known historians have even maintained that we have to do here with the inevitable operation of a definite law, to which all historic process is subject. But really the fact that the decline or downfall of a kingdom is not in any way equivalent to the decline of a culture should indicate to us where the actual causes of the downfall are to be sought. A political rulership can go down without leaving behind it a trace of its former existence; with a culture it is quite otherwise. It can, as it were, wither in a country where it has been disturbed in its natural growth. In this event it looks for new possibilities of development outside its old circle of operation, gradually enters upon new fields and fertilizes there germs that were in a sense waiting for fertilization. Thus there arise new forms of the cultural process, which doubtless differ from the old, but nevertheless carry in them its creative forces. Macedonian and Roman conquerors could put an end to the political independence of the tiny Greek city-republics; they could not prevent the transplanting of Greek culture deep in Inner Asia, its growth to new bloom in Egypt, nor its intellectual vitalizing of Rome herself.

This is the reason why peoples of less developed culture could never actually bring under subjection peoples of higher cultural status even when they far excelled them in military strength. It is possible to completely subjugate only very small populations which because of their numerical weakness could be easily ground down; so to subdue any larger people which has been welded together in the course of many centuries by a common culture is unthinkable. The Mongols could easily deal with the Chinese militarily; they were even in a position to set up a man of their tribe as despot of the Celestial Kingdom; but they had not the slightest influence on the inner structure of the social and cultural life of the Chinese peoples, whose distinctive customs were hardly disturbed by the invasion. On the other hand, the primitive culture of the Mongols could not hold out against the much older and immeasurably finer culture of the Chinese, and was, in fact, so completely absorbed by it that it left not a trace behind. Two hundred years sufficed to transform the Mongolian invaders into Chinese. The higher culture of the "conquered" proved itself stronger and more effective than the brutal military power of the "conquerors."

And how often was the Apennine Peninsula, the present Italy, overrun or quite inundated by foreign tribes. From the times of the migrations of peoples to the invasion by the French under Charles VIII and Francis I, Italy was the constant object of attack by countless tribes and populations whom ancient yearning and, above all, the prospect of rich booty, drew southward. Cimbri and Teutons, Lombards and Goths, Huns and Vandals, and dozens of other tribes rolled their rude troops through the fertile vales of the peninsula, whose inhabitants suffered severely from the continuous invasions. But even the most powerful and the cruelest of the conquerors succumbed to the higher culture of the country, even though they opposed it at first with outspoken hostility or contemptuous disdain.[4] They were all gradually drawn into it and compelled to new ways of living. Their native strength has merely served to bring to that

[4] Thus Procopius tells us in his story of the wars of the Goths and Vandals of a significant utterance of Luitprand: "When we wish to insult an enemy in public and hold him up to scorn, we call him a Roman." The Germanic tribes were espe-

ancient culture new vitalizing factors and to fill its veins with their fresh blood.

History knows many similar instances. They serve repeatedly to demonstrate the infinite superiority of cultural processes over the pitiful stupidity of political endeavors. All efforts of conquering states to assimilate the population of new-won territories by the brutal exercise of power —suppression of the native language, forcible interference with traditional institutions, and so on—have been vain; more than that, in most instances, their effect has been just the opposite of what the conqueror sought to accomplish. England has never been able to win the loyalty of the Irish; her violent treatment has only deepened and widened the abyss that separates the two peoples and increased Irish hatred of the English. The "Germanizing efforts" of the Prussian government in Poland made the lives of the Poles more difficult and bitter, but they were not able to change their temper or make them friendlier to the Germans. Today we behold the fruits of this senseless policy. The Russifying policy of the tsarist government in the Baltic provinces led to shameful outrages against human dignity, but it brought the people no closer to Russia and was of profit chiefly to the resident German barons whose brutal exploitation of the masses it greatly furthered. The supporters of imperial policy in Germany might persuade themselves that they could win the affection of the Alsatians for Germanism by their "dictatorial decrees," but, although the people were German both in language and customs, Germany failed to achieve that end. Just as little will the present efforts of the French at assimilation in Alsace be able to instill into the inhabitants a love for France. Almost every great state has within its borders national minorities which it treats in this manner; the result is everywhere the same. Love and loyalty cannot be compelled; they have to be earned; and force and suppression are the least fitting means to this end. The national-suppression policy of the great states before the War developed in the suppressed nationalities an extreme nationalism which finds expression today in the according by the new-made states of the same treatment to their national minorities which, as national minorities, they themselves once received —a phenomenon showing all too clearly that little states follow in the footsteps of great ones and imitate their practices.

We can just as little convert a people by force to alien morals, customs and modes of thought as we can force a man into the frame of an alien individuality. A fusion of different tribes and racial elements is possible only in the realm of culture, because here no external compulsion arises, only an inner need, to meet which every member makes its special contribution. Culture rests neither on brute force nor on blind faith in authority;

cially hostile to all instruction and educative influence because, in the opinion of Procopius, they saw in these the enervation of their warlike activities.

its effectiveness is based on the free acceptance of all that has resulted from collaborative efforts for spiritual and material welfare. The decisive matter here is the natural need, not the blind edict from above. For this reason, in all the great epochs, culture has marched hand in hand with the voluntary union and fusion of different human groups; in fact, these two factors are mutually necessary. Only voluntary determination which in most cases arises quite unconsciously is able to unite men of different descent in their cultural efforts and in this way to produce new forms of culture.

Here the situation is the same as it is with the individual. When I take up the work of a strange author who reveals new things to me and arouses my mind no one compels me to read the book or to appropriate its ideas. It is merely the mental influence that affects me and that will perhaps later be erased by influences of another kind. Nothing compels me to make a decision that is repugnant to my inmost nature and does violence to my mind. I appropriate the alien matter because it brings me pleasure and becomes a part of my spiritual being; I assimilate myself to it until at last there is no boundary between myself and the alien matter. It is in this way that all cultural and mental occurrences are brought about.

And this natural, unforced assimilation goes on without any oversight, without any evident analysis, because it grows out of the personal requirements of the individual and corresponds to his mental and spiritual experiences. Any cultural process goes on the more peacefully and with the less friction, the less political motives are in evidence; for politics and culture are opposites which can never be fundamentally reconciled. They are striving in different directions, always widely divergent; their allegiance is to different worlds.

Chapter 5

NATIONAL-POLITICAL UNITY AS HINDRANCE TO CULTURAL DEVELOP-
MENT. THE REDISCOVERY OF GREECE. POSITION OF RELIGION IN GREECE.
CONCERNING THE DESCENT OF THE HELLENES. GREEK THOUGHT. IDEAS
ABOUT MAN AND THE UNIVERSE. SCIENCE AND PHILOSOPHY. MANY-
SIDEDNESS OF HELLENIC CULTURE. POETRY. DRAMA. COMEDY. THE THE-
ATER AS BAROMETER OF PERSONAL FREEDOM. PHYSICAL CULTURE.
ARCHITECTURE. GREEK STYLE. SCULPTURE. PAINTING. ART AS A PRIN-
CIPLE OF LIFE. THE NATIONAL-POLITICAL DISUNION OF GREECE. IN-
FLUENCE OF THE NATURAL ENVIRONMENT ON THE MANIFOLDNESS OF
HELLENIC CULTURE. CHARACTER OF THE GREEK *POLIS*. PECULIARITY
OF GREEK COLONIZATION. PARTICIPATION OF THE INDIVIDUAL IN PUB-
LIC AFFAIRS. OLYMPUS AS A SYMBOL OF THE POLITICAL CONDITIONS.
THE PERSIAN WARS. REASONS FOR THE VICTORY OF THE HELLENES.
CULTURAL UNITY AND POLITICAL UNITY. THE PELOPONNESIAN WAR
AND THE QUESTION OF NATIONAL UNITY. SIGNS OF COLLAPSE. ALEX-
ANDER BRINGS ABOUT THE POLITICAL UNITY OF GREECE AND DESTROYS
THE SOURCES OF HELLENIC CULTURE.

WE referred in the first part of this work to the irreconcilable opposition between the political endeavors of small minorities in history and
the culturally creative activity of socially allied human groups, and tried
to make the results of this inner antagonism as clear as possible to the
reader. Everything else follows from this. Before all, it follows that in
periods when political thought and action prevail in society, cultural creation, and especially its higher forms, fall into decay and collapse. If it
were otherwise, then culture would have been in fullest bloom in times
of highest perfection of national political power and would have withered
in times of national dissolution. But history everywhere shows us the
opposite. Greece and Rome are the classical witnesses of this, but not the
only ones; the history of all times and all peoples bears eloquent testimony
to it. Nietzsche had recognized this very clearly when, in his well-known
utterance on the resurrection of the spirit, he said: "On the political sick-
bed a people usually renews its youth and finds again the soul it lost in

seeking and maintaining power. Culture is most deeply indebted to times of political weakness."

About the outstanding importance of the ancient Grecian culture, peoples are fairly well agreed. Even if one is of the opinion that this culture has been too highly idealized by the enthusiastic partisans of classical antiquity, one still cannot deny its monumental importance. The immoderate over-estimation which was at one time accorded to classical antiquity is easily explained. One must not forget that with the development of the Christian church Europe for centuries almost entirely lost its connection with Greek intellectual life which, of course, seemed to Christian thought essentially alien and revolting. By the rediscovery of the Greek language and the universal awakening of minds toward the close of the Middle Ages, man became again spiritually united with ancient Hellas. On the Humanists of the sixteenth century this ancient world, which so suddenly emerged from oblivion, and which, seen from a distance, glittered with a thousand hues, must have made an actually bewitching impression; especially since it suggested immediate comparison with the present when the church was more and more vigorously combating the new conceptions of the universe with torture and the stake. Without doubt, Greek culture had, along with its illuminating and alluring features, also profound social defects, which one must not overlook if one wishes to form a clear picture of its total character. Thus, one must not forget that in Greece, as in every other state of antiquity, slavery existed, even though—except in Sparta—the treatment of slaves was much more humane than, for example, in Rome. In many Greek communities it was even customary to set free those slaves who acquired a Greek education. It also happened sometimes, under unusual circumstances, that part of the slaves were adopted into the master-class. This happened in Sparta at the time of the Archidamian war when the privileged caste had been greatly weakened by its losses and had to deal with an uprising of the helots. The same thing occurred repeatedly in Athens.

Also, the history of Greece is by no means entirely free from persecutions of ideas. Socrates had to drink the hemlock. Protagoras had to flee, and his book, *About the Gods*, was publicly burned. Diogenes of Appolonia and Theodorus "the Atheist" were subjected to persecutions. Even poets, like Diagoras of Melos and Aeschylus, were sometimes in peril of their lives, and Euripides was threatened with a public indictment because of his "godless ideas." Of course, these occasional persecutions cannot be compared even remotely with the persecutions of heretics during the Middle Ages. The basic assumptions for the latter were entirely lacking in Greece. There was neither an organized priestly caste nor a church. The country lacked also any start toward political unity, the supporters of which are always inclined to suppress free thought and to raise persecution of certain ideas to a system. However, there existed, of course, among the people themselves all sorts of superstitions; and in many places, especially in Delphi, this had developed under the influence of the priests into a fanatical orthodoxy; but this had only local importance, since all organized connection with other parts of the country was lacking.

Despite such defects, the intellectual greatness of Grecian culture is undisputed. A culture which could influence the totality of European peoples for so long and in such diverse fields, with an irresistible power which has not yet exhausted itself today though its creators vanished from history two thousand years ago, may easily be overvalued; it can hardly be overlooked.

No man of profound insight will try to maintain that the Greeks originated among themselves all the contributions they have made in the various fields of cultural life. The greatness and significance of every culture lies just here: its intellectual and social effectiveness cannot be confined within political or national boundaries. Perhaps a state can be created with the sword, but not a culture; for this stands above all state organizations or lordly institutions, and is in its innermost essence anarchistic; even if one could overlook the fact that thus far political bondage has been the greatest hindrance to any higher cultural development. That Greece was influenced in its development by other cultures is perfectly obvious, and one would have to be a race-theorist to deny it. Besides, the Greek mythology itself bears witness to these foreign influences—as in the legends of Cadmus, Cecrops, Danaos, and others. In recent times there has been hardly a year in which scientific research has not brought to light new material that reveals more clearly the Oriental and Egyptian influence upon the shaping of Greek culture. Thus, the Semitic elements in the poetry of Homer have been repeatedly brought out. Of quite especial importance were the excavations of Heinrich Schliemann in Asia Minor which laid bare the remains of an ancient culture now called the Mycenian. Then, in 1900, came the excavations of the English scholar, Evans, on the island of Crete, bringing to light the vestiges of a very much older culture, which can be assigned to a time at least two thousand years before our chronological era.

These splendid results of archeological research have, of course, opened up to historiography new and hitherto quite unknown fields, but they have also produced a whole series of new problems, at the solution of which science has thus far worked in vain. Thus, it is today undecided whether there were intimate connections between the Cretan and the Mycenian cultures, or whether we are here dealing with two distinct developments. The question whether the creators of these two cultures should or should not be regarded as Greeks remains quite unsolved. There have been discovered in Crete, it is true, thousands of clay tablets bearing strange inscriptions; but science has not succeeded in deciphering them, and we wait still the many facts they might tell us. It was proved long ago that other languages were once spoken in Greece. A whole series of place-names, like Athens, Thebes, Corinth, Olympus and Parnassus, are still veiled in darkness; they have no sort of relation to the Greek language—belong, indeed, to no Indo-Germanic speech. Besides, Herodotus tells us that in his travels he visited various cities in which the Pelasgians spoke a peculiar language, which he designated as "barbaric." According to the sagacious inferences of Moritz Hoernes the Cretan-Mycenian culture is, so to speak, the connecting link between the ancient cultures of Egypt and the Orient and that of Greece [1]—a view that is constantly winning wider acceptance. The fact is that the active intellectual life of Greece first developed in the East, where intercourse with Egyptians, Phoenicians and Persians was most active.

But we are not here dealing with the question of how far Grecian culture was influenced by other cultures, but merely with the fact that it is one of the most splendid and all-embracing cultures that humanity has ever produced. It affected the whole subsequent development of the peoples of Europe more deeply and more permanently than did any other culture, and its remote effects are still becoming clearer and clearer. Before all, there is the kind of thought process which the Greeks brought closer to us than any other people of antiquity. Their peculiar gift for scientific observation and deductive reasoning, often enabling them to recognize facts which were not scientifically established until many centuries later, had much more kinship to our present ways of thinking than had the mysteries of the Egyptians or the Babylonians. Though it is today beyond question that the Greeks got their first knowledge of astronomy and other matters from the Oriental peoples, still they organized this knowledge with a luminous clarity and developed it to a height which no other people in ancient history was able to attain. Their highly developed mathematics is glorious evidence of this. The very fact that among the Egyptians, the Chaldeans, the Persians, all knowledge about nature was kept in the possession of the priests and Magi, while in Greece science and factual-theoretical thinking were carried on by men who had no connection of any kind with a priestly caste, is characteristic of the general status of intellectual life.

Although only fragments of the ideas of the Grecian thinkers have come down to us, and much of this only at second hand—principally from Aristotle and Cicero—and the transmission was not without some distortion of the original text, still the little that we now possess gives a clear enough understanding of their intellectual productiveness. Even in the old Ionic nature philosophies one encounters that luminous keenness of observation

[1] *Kultur der Urzeit.* Band II, 1912.

combined with clarity of expression which is so characteristic of the think-ing of the Greeks. Thales, Anaximander, Pherecydes, Anaximenes, and others based everything on the study of nature, which gave to their teach-ings from the very beginning a distinctive stamp. On the basis of the statements of Anaximenes, who was already acquainted with the move-ments of the constellations and of the polestar, and the ideas of the Pytha-goreans, Aristarchus of Samos arrived at last at the conclusion that the earth turns on its axis once every twenty-four hours and that the earth and all the planets revolve about the sun once every year, while the sun and the fixed stars remain motionless in space. Of course the Greeks lacked any scientific hypotheses such as we have command of today, as a basis for their teachings. But the way in which they constructed for themselves a picture of the universe which quite overshadows everything that for fifteen hundred years the men of a later period believed in as unassailable truth, is very significant.

The ancient sages brought the same interest to the consideration of the changes in matter. The well-known division of matter into four basic elements—earth, water, air and fire—which is ascribed to Empedocles, controlled the ideas of men for many centuries and was at last only over-thrown by the results of modern chemistry. The "atomists" took a decisive step toward the construction of a picture of the universe on natural founda-tions when they tried to establish the nature of matter. Of course, one cannot put the theories of a Democritus or a Leucippus without change on a level with the modern atomic theory of a Dalton or an Avogadro; the ancient lacked almost all the preparatory ideas for such. The thing about their theories, however, that arouses our astonishment even today is the magnitude of the undertaking, the all-embracing character of the concept, at a time when the most basic preliminaries of our present-day attainments in physics and chemistry were completely unknown. Since the atomists attributed every phenomenon to natural causes, they banished from their conception of the universe accident and whim, and, consequently, that manner of thought which tries to find a special purpose in all things. One can, therefore, understand why Bacon so greatly admired Democritus and preferred his doctrines to those of Aristotle and his blind Christian fol-lowers.

There have come down to us scarcely four hundred lines in all of Empedocles' great didactic poem about nature. He has been called the earliest forerunner of the Lamarckian-Darwinian theorists and, with the necessary limitations, the characterization may be allowed to stand. Empedocles recognized in love and aversion the two primitive forces which manifest themselves as attraction and repulsion and to whose opera-tion the origin and dissolution of all things may be traced. Men, animals and plants are composed of the same materials, but the mixture is different for each species. In the course of incalculable ages, by numberless combinations and separations, plants gradually came into existence, then animals. At first nature produced all organs separately: arms without shoulders, heads without necks, and so on; and finally only those forms persisted which were capable of existing independently.

It is even asserted of Xenophanes, the alleged founder of the Eleatic school of philosophy, that he tried to explain the fossil imprints of plants and animals in stone as relics of once-living species that had become extinct. Xenophanes recognized also the anthropomorphism that underlies every belief in divinities, and asserted, many centuries before Feuerbach, that in God man reveres his own nature.

But not only the conception of things and the universe, the ways of thinking also early attracted the attention of the ancient thinkers and led them to the conviction that only through observation and experience could they arrive at definite laws and generalizations. This method seemed to them the first requisite for any knowledge whatever; by such a way of thinking the practical sciences, too, would necessarily be brought to fullest fruition. In fact, the geometry of Euclid reached a perfection such that it could survive for over two thousand years without revision of its content or change in its form. Not until the most recent time have new paths been opened up in this field. The same is true of the scientific experiments of Archimedes, who, with his theory of the lever, and so on, first laid the foundation for a science of mechanics.

The same freedom of thought is noticeable in all other fields as well. We encounter it in the philosophic schools of the Sophists, the Cynics, the Megarics and, later, the Stoics, who concerned themselves chiefly with the relations of men to society and its various institutions. From the rapid development of intellectual and social life in the Greek cities there gradually arose entirely new ideas about the causes of ethical feeling and the relations of men to one another. The ancient belief in the gods, which finds in the Homeric poems an expression as childlike as it is natural, was dwindling away. Philosophy had opened new perspectives to the thoughts of men and had shown them how to become the masters of their own destinies. Thus arose a transvaluation of all traditional moral concepts, which was carried, especially by the Cynics and the Sophists, to the utmost limit, till Socrates demonstrated the true basis of all ethical feeling in social communal life. "Virtue," said he, "is not a gift from the gods, but the proved knowledge of what is really good and enables men to live without constraining others, to act justly and to serve, not merely themselves, but the community. Without this a society is unthinkable." Later the Epicureans and the Stoics built further on this basis and developed their theories concerning the ethical consciousness of man.

Besides, a large number of the Greek thinkers busied themselves with the question of public economy and of the political structure of social life, and individuals among them arrived at most far-reaching conclusions. In this the ancient traditions of a Golden Age, which poetry had kept alive among the people, played a not inconsiderable part and gradually shaped themselves into the doctrine of "natural right" which was so zealously advocated, especially by the Cynics. As a result of these ideas there developed gradually a totally new attitude toward social institutions and toward foreign peoples, which found its ripest expression in the teachings of Zeno, the pupil of the Cynic, Crates, and the Megarian, Stilpos, and culminated in the complete rejection of any exercise of force in society.

There is hardly any other period in history which displayed such a lofty and many-sided intellectual life. But our admiration becomes still greater when we contemplate the array of Hellenic letters. The very oldest of the poetic works of the Greeks that have come down to us, the *Iliad* and the *Odyssey,* exhibit a poetic perfection of such strength and beauty that they are properly regarded as the very epitome of epic poesy. Close interweaving of a naïvely sensuous conception of the universe with the deepest impulses of the human heart, overpoweringly colorful splendor of landscape, intimate intergrowth of the human soul with external nature and, above all, joyous spontaneity in depiction, reach here a height of perfection such as was seldom attained in later times, and only by the very great. The epic was succeeded by the didactic poem, as the inventor of which old Hesiod of Askra was honored. In the place of the wonderful and the adventurous of the ancient epic poetry, there appeared dependence on the native soil, feeling for the useful business of everyday life, deliberate contemplation of things.

The deeply implanted feeling of the Greeks for that most romantic of all arts, music, which finds such charming expression in the ancient myths of Amphion and Orpheus, led to the early development of lyric poetry to an unexampled height. If epic composition limited itself to the graphic depiction of the past, lyric poetry created its matter out of the inner experiences of the poet and wedded the rhythm of the verse to the notes of the lyre and the flute, and so gave utterance to every stirring of the soul. Thus, the poet became an indispensable guest at every public celebration, and cities competed with one another in devices to attract him within their walls. A long line of the most celebrated exponents of lyric poetic art came from the island of Lesbos, which came to be known as the native land of the lyric, in the narrower sense. There wrote Terpondros, the actual creator of Melian poesy, who fused together music and verse with such consummate art that the legend ran that he had found again the lost lyre of Orpheus. The lyric reached its zenith on Lesbos in that noble pair of poets, Alcaeus, the violent hater of tyrants, and the great poetess, Sappho, whose intoxicating love poems are among the

loveliest that were ever written. Arion, too, the singer of the Dionysian
festivals and inventor of the dithyramb, hailed from Lesbos. In Anacreon
of Taos, the enthusiastic singer of love and wine, the lyric of the ancients
found its most graceful and joyous representative. With him wrote Ibycus
of Rhegium, Simonides of Ceos and, above all, Pindar of Thebes, whom
Quintilian honored as the "prince of lyricists." Pindar was also famous
throughout Greece as a writer of scholia. These scholia, or table songs,
intended to lend added zest to the pleasures of the table, spread throughout all Hellas.[2] And we should here think, too, of the former slave, Aesop,
the waggish composer of animal fables, whose humorous tales went from
mouth to mouth. Every city had its singers and poets, and there is scarcely
another period in history in which, in so small a country and in such a
comparatively short time, such an astonishing number of poets and thinkers
made their appearance as in the little communities of Greece.

The Hellenes reached the summit of their poetic art in the drama,
which developed from the ancient festival plays in honor of Dionysus, or
Bacchus. Dramatic poetry had a long line of more or less notable forerunners, of whom Epigenes of Sicyon, Thespis of Icaryon and, especially,
Phrynichus, author of the tragedy, *The Capture of Miletus,* are oftenest
mentioned. But the drama reached its highest perfection after the Persian
wars, in the time of Athenian bloom, when Aeschylus, Sophocles and
Euripides, a constellation of three, illumined all Hellas with their glory,
surrounded by poets like Philocles, Euphorion, Xenocles, Nichomachus
and many others. Of the two hundred pieces by Aeschylus only seven have
come down to us, among them his great tragedy *Prometheus Bound,* in
which the daring temper, the gigantic power and the magnificence of his
ideas are revealed at their strongest. It is said of Sophocles that he wrote
far more than a hundred dramas, of which, however, only seven have been
preserved. From these we get an idea of the greatness of his genius, which
finds its most perfect expression in his *Antigone.* Of the work of Euripides,
the "poet of enlightenment," as he has been called, more has been saved.
Of the two hundred dramas that have been ascribed to him nineteen have
been preserved to posterity. His art was soberer than that of Aeschylus

[2] In the scholia political motives often found expression, such as hatred of tyranny,
and so on. Here is a strophe from the paean to the tyrannicides, Harmodius and
Aristogeiton, that is ascribed to Kallicrates:

"Myrtle I'll weave round my murderous blade
Like Harmodius and Aristogeiton
When at the thrice-holy feast unto Pallas
They struck down the tyrant, Hipparchus.
Always your fame will endure on the earth,
Dear Harmodius and Aristogeiton,
Because when you struck down the tyrant
You set Athens upright and free again."

and Sophocles and it was said, even in his lifetime, that while Sophocles represented men as they should be, Euripides showed them as they are. That he had the power to move men mightily by his representation is shown by his demonic depiction of passion, in which he was excelled by none.

Greek comedy developed from beginnings similar to those of tragedy; it, too, grew out of the ancient festival plays, and was especially associated with the phallic choruses. But it was in Athens that comedy first reached its highest development. There Cratinus wrote, of whom it is told that even Pericles, the greatest statesman of Greece, did not escape his biting satire; and with him were Crates, Eupolis, Pherecrates and others, who were, however, completely overshadowed by Aristophanes, that "spoiled darling of the graces." Of the fifty-four comedies of Aristophanes only eleven have been preserved, but these suffice to give us a picture of the renowned poet who knew how to combine the most withering scorn with the most gracious suavity. His biting wit knew no bounds; he lashed men and institutions with the boldest unrestraint and without a trace of prudery. Although he was very conservative in his opinions his devastating mockeries halted neither before gods nor official persons, and he lustily shook his cap and bells at the most sacred things.

It was no accident that comedy and the drama reached their highest perfection just when the Athenian democracy was in fullest bloom. The utterly unrestricted presentation of comedy at that time shows a much better understanding of personal freedom than do the most beautiful descriptions in republican constitutions. For the spirit of a time is not defined by the dead letter of its laws, but by the living actions of its men, which first give it its imprint.

If, finally, we cast a brief glance at what the Greeks brought forth in architecture, sculpture and painting, we shall be able to estimate the whole greatness and depth of their culture. History knows many peoples which have done very great things in special fields of cultural creation; but the Greeks are perhaps the only people who were able to achieve the highest in *every* field of culture. It was this which gave to their creation that inner balance which for the last two thousand years has constantly aroused the astounded admiration of the greatest minds. One understands what Goethe meant when he said of Greek art: "For all other cultures one must make allowances; to the Greek alone one is always a debtor."

For the Greeks, art was not a private interest of individuals, which they pursued as if it were some sort of sport, but a creative activity that was intimately intergrown with their whole social life, and without which they could not conceive existence. The Hellenes were perhaps the only people that ever understood how to make an art of living itself; at least no other people is known to us among whom the intimate connection of art with every phase of personal and social life is so clearly and impressively apparent. A community like Athens, which spent more for the support of its theater and its dramatic art than it did on the wars with the Persians, which threatened the entire political existence of ancient Hellas, is hardly conceivable to us today, in this time of state barbarity when bureaucracy and militarism absorb enormously the greatest part of the national incomes of all so-called "civilized" peoples. But it was only in such a community that art could develop to such a height.

This is especially true of architecture, the most social of all arts, development of which is completely dependent on the understanding that men bring to it socially. Only in a country where the individual constantly took the liveliest kind of part in public affairs, and could easily keep track of those affairs, could architectonic skill reach such perfection. Among the Babylonians, the Egyptians, the Persians and other peoples of antiquity, architecture as an art was limited to the palaces and tombs of the kings and the temples of the gods. Among the Greeks we first find it applied to all the purposes of public life and to personal use.

Besides, the Grecian temple breathed a very different spirit from the sacred buildings of Oriental peoples, whose shapeless massiveness express the whole oppressive and crushing weight of gloomy religious systems and rigid priestly dogmas. There hovers over the religious ideas of the Greeks the poetic glamour of a cheerful view of life, which regarded the gods as also human and was burdened with no life-hating dogmas. A healthy sensuality governed the life of the Greeks and set its mark even on their conceptions of divinity. The Hellene prostrated himself in the dust before no god. The idea of sin was utterly foreign to him; he never blasphemed against his humanity. Thus culture became for him a worldly celebration of the joy of life. Songs, dances, farces, tragedies, athletic contests, associated with joyous feasts where wine and love played no small part, followed one another in colorful sequence and gave to the religious festivals their characteristic note. And this did not occur behind thick temple walls, but under the blue sky, in the midst of lovely natural settings which supplied a fitting frame for these joyous exercises. This sense of the joy of life inevitably revealed itself in the works of man. Taine has sketched the peculiarity of architectonic achievement in Hellas in these words:

> There is nothing ceremonial, peculiar, torturedly artistic, about this building; it is a rectangle surrounded by a row of pillars; three or four geometrical forms at the foundation support the whole, and the symmetry of the plan becomes apparent through the repetition of these and the opposition of them one to another. The crowning of the gable, the deck-plate of the capital, all accessories and all detail equally make clear the peculiar

character of every member, and the diversity of the coloring completes the emphasis and the elucidation of these values.[3]

This special type of architectonic artistry, this graceful, flexible beauty, in which every line blends into a brilliant, harmonious whole, is found everywhere in Hellas: in the temple of Zeus at Olympia, in Apollo's temple in Phigalia, in the Theseum, in the Parthenon; from the propylea of the Acropolis to the splendid works of Ictinus, Kallicrates and so many other masters.

No art was so widespread among the Hellenes as sculpture. It surpasses, in fact, everything that peoples have ever done in this field and constantly astounds us by the fabulous abundance of its creations. In the time of the Roman invasion Roman generals plundered the art treasures of Greece to an extent unheard of. The reports even state that in Rome and its immediate vicinity over sixty thousand Greek statues were set up. Yet, in spite of this, Pausanias, who lived in the second century after Christ, in the time of the Roman emperors, Hadrian, Antoninus Pius and Marcus Aurelius, could say after his great journey through Hellas that the whole country, from coast to coast, was like a great museum of art. According to Winckelmann, Pausanias tells of twenty thousand statues which he had seen himself.[4] From these figures one can form an approximate estimate of the lavish abundance of Greek sculpture and of its wide distribution. The care of the naked body became for the Greeks a regular cult. Public games and athletic contests were a part of every festival, and offered to the eye of the artist the human body in every conceivable posture, giving ever new inspiration for the exercise of his creative power.

Along with the individual masters there developed in such centers as Athens, Corinth, Argos and Sicyon, whole schools of sculpture. And what a horde of great artists do we find here. Agelades, who worked in Argos, was celebrated as the teacher of the three great masters, Phidias, Myron and Polycletus. Phidias is known as the creator of the forty-foot-high statue of Zeus in his temple in Olympia. Also the colossal bronze statue of Athena Promachos on the Acropolis in Athens, which could be seen from afar by mariners at sea, was his work. We can form only an imperfect idea of Phidias' gigantic statue of the Athena of the Parthenon, for, like so many others of that period, it has completely disappeared. Later there developed the new Attic school, which attained the height of its power in the works of Scopas of Paros and, above all, of Praxiteles of Athens. The rediscovered statue of Hermes to the north of the Olympian temple gives us an idea of the perfected art of Praxiteles. And the great sculptors, Euphranor of Corinth and Lysippos of Sicyon, must not be left unmen-

[3] Hippolyte Taine, *Philosophy of Art*.
[4] J. J. Winckelmann, *Geschichte der Kunst des Altertums*, 1764.

tioned. Of the hundreds on hundreds of less well-known masters we know usually not even the names.

Of course, fewer by far of the works of Greek painters have been preserved. From the accounts of the ancients we gather that a great number of famous schools existed in every part of the country, like the Ionic school of painters in Asia Minor, especially in Ephesus—where Zeuxis and Parrhasius worked—the schools of Sicyon, Paestum, and so on. Polygnotus from the island of Thasos is usually spoken of as the first painter of outstanding importance; but Apelles seems to have produced the greatest works in the field of painting; the ancients are filled with his praise.

The art of the Greeks found expression in every object of daily use; it swept like a transfiguring inspiration over every phenomenon of public and private life, as we can see from the numberless vases with their charming paintings and from the unearthed gems, cameos and engraved precious stones of the most varied kinds that so arouse our admiration. One can hardly overestimate the outstanding greatness and the infinite many-sidedness of this people, even though one does not lose sight of their darker side and counts it in for its full worth. No other people in ancient history has been able to exert such power of attraction on the greatest minds of all later times. Countless books have been written in every language about every branch of their rich creative activity, and even now hardly a year passes which does not bring to light new and important material concerning the culture of ancient Hellas.

If one turns to observe what was the status among the Greeks of that national and political unity which is asserted to be the indispensable preliminary to the development of any kind of culture among a people, one comes to conclusions that are utterly destructive of this view. Ancient Hellas never knew what national unity meant, and when towards the end of its history national-political unity was forcibly imposed on it from without, it was the end of Grecian culture, which then had to find another home for its creative activities. The Greek spirit simply could not endure the national-political experiment, and was gradually extinguished in the countries in which its force had poured forth most strongly for centuries.

What united the Grecian tribes and peoples was their common culture, which revealed itself everywhere in thousands upon thousands of different forms—not the artificially woven bond of national-political community, in which no one in Greece felt any interest and the essence of which was always alien to the Hellenes. Greece was politically the most dismembered country on earth. Every city took zealous care lest its political independence be assailed; for this the inhabitants of even the smallest of them were in no mind to surrender. Each of these little city-republics had its own constitution, its own social life with its own cultural peculiarities; and this it was that gave to Hellenic life as a whole its variegated wealth of genuine cultural values. Albrecht Wirth has rightly said: "The achievements of the Greeks were the more astounding the more they were, as a people, torn and divided. No one ever succeeded in uniting their infinity of different tribes for any collective deed, in any single opinion. . . . They all always valued highly their membership in their own folk-group, but they did not possess enough power of sacrifice, enough political feeling to weld them into one great whole; to subordinate to it their separate ambitions." [5]

But it was just this lack of political feeling which quickened the cultural activity of the Greeks, yes, which first made them spiritually susceptible to it. When Aristotle was collecting the material for his work on the constitutions of the Hellenes he found himself under the necessity of extending his undertaking over a hundred and fifty-eight municipalities, each of which presented a political entity in itself and, because of its autonomy, had its own peculiar social characteristics. Even the topography of the whole peninsula was highly favorable to such a development of social life. The land is mountainous in parts and enjoys a mild and delightful climate, which without doubt exerted a strong influence on the minds and souls of the inhabitants. Lovely and fruitful valleys cut across the landscape in every direction; the sea penetrates deep into the land in countless bays, and provides on three sides the most wonderful coastline one could conceive of. Added to this, a multitude of larger and smaller islands connect the peninsula with Asia Minor almost like a bridge. This entire rich natural setting was unusually variable and could but inspire in men reflections that would have been denied them anywhere else. Every part of the country had its peculiar character, which helped to give a definite stamp to the activities of the inhabitants. Thus was awakened and furthered that rich diversity of intellectual and social life which is so characteristic of ancient Hellas.

As to the Greeks themselves, it is today becoming constantly clearer to us that they were neither a homogeneous people nor a pure race. Everything indicates, rather, that we have to do here with an exceptionally happy intermixture of different folk and race elements fused into spiritual unity by a common culture. The assertion that the Hellenes were a people of the Germanic race which invaded the peninsula and gradually subdued the resident population, is, in that sweeping form, confirmed by no intelligible proof. The harder scientific research tries to penetrate the veil that still covers the primitive history of Greece, the more does it bring to light facts which indicate exactly the opposite. That the peninsula suffered from frequent invasions of foreign tribes that pressed in from the north is unquestioned. But we are still far from a clear understanding of the racial affiliation of those tribes, whose origin is completely lost in the mists of

[5] *Volkstum und Weltmacht in der Geschichte.* Leipzig, p. 18.

unrecorded time. Most of these invasions occurred in a prehistoric epoch and kept large sections of the country in constant ferment, as we learn from the traditions of the Greeks themselves. By these migrations and continual conflicts whole populations were driven out of their homeland and fled to the islands in the Aegaean or to the coast of Asia Minor. The greatest of these migrations was that of the Dorians, which is believed to have occurred about eleven hundred years before our era, and which gave rise to great changes in the social life of the country.

But these migrations from the north were certainly not the only ones; and there is much ground for believing that long before these invasions Asiatic tribes had already forced their way into the future home of the Hellenes. Numerous traces of Asiatic influence in the mythology of the Greeks and, very emphatically, the names of many cities and localities, bear witness to this. How far the influence of the Semitic Phoenicians extended on the Grecian mainland has not yet been incontestably established; that this influence could have been no small one is shown by the fact that a great number of the islands that were later Grecian, such as the Cyclades, the Sporades, Rhodes, Cyprus and Crete, were colonized by the Phoenicians long before the existence of Greek society. The Carian people of Asia Minor also left distinct traces in Greece. Only from them can we derive the names of the citadel of Karia in Megara and of the legendary King Kar.

Of the Dorians, Aeolians and Ionians, which are usually regarded as the three principal lines of the Greeks, the Ionians, the most highly endowed and culturally most advanced of them all, seem to have the smallest infusion of Hellenic blood. A large number of famous historians have made mention of the extensive intermixture of the Ionians with Semitic and other Oriental peoples. Ernst Curtius—and others with him—have even placed the original home of the Ionians in Asia Minor. In support of this view Curtius urges, chiefly, that only in Asia Minor can the existence of an Ionian country be historically established. Of course, this does not prove that the Ionians really stem from there. They might merely have migrated into Asia Minor and established a settlement there.[6] Herodotus, too, referred in different places to the non-Hellenic origin of the Ionians, especially of the Athenians, and designated them as descendants of the Pelasgians, who only later adopted the Greek language.

From all this one fact emerges clearly, that the Greeks present no particular national-political unity, nor one of race and descent, and that all assertions to the contrary rest merely on vague surmises and indefinite wish-concepts. Quite in accord with our earlier conclusions, unity was found only in the Greek culture, which spread from the west coast of Asia

[6] Ernst Curtius, *Geschichte Griechenlands* and *Die Jonier vor der jonischen Wanderung.*

Minor and the islands of the Aegean to Sicily and southern Italy. To this must be added separate settlements in the Crimea, on the eastern shores of the Black Sea, and at the mouth of the Rhone.

It must, therefore, have been other causes which furthered the growth of such an outstandingly rich and splendid culture as the Hellenic; and we do not feel that we go astray when we see by far the most important and decisive of these causes in the political separateness and national diversity of the country. It was this healthy decentralization, this internal separation of Greece into hundreds of little communities, tolerating no uniformity, which constantly roused the mind to consideration of new matters. Every larger political structure leads inevitably to a certain rigidity of the cultural life and destroys that fruitful rivalry between separate communities which is so characteristic of the whole life of the Grecian cities. Taine depicts very clearly this political status in ancient Hellas:

> To modern eyes the Greek state seems like a miniature painting. Argolis had a length of forty to fifty and a breadth of twenty to twenty-five miles; Laconia was of about the same size; Achaia is a narrow strip of land on the flank of a mountain range that slopes down to the sea. All Attica does not equal the half of one of our smallest [French] departments; the territory of Corinth, Sicyon and Megara extends for only an hour's journey; in general, and above all in the islands and the settlements, a state was merely a city on the coast with a circle of farms about it. From one acropolis one looked across to the acropolis or the mountains of a neighbor city. In such a narrow enclosure everything is clear and easily understood; the intellectual fatherland has about it nothing of the gigantic, the abstract and the indefinite, as with us; the mind can embrace it, it is identified with the physical fatherland; both are outlined in the mind of the citizen by distinct boundaries. To conceive of Athens, Corinth, Argos or Sparta, he thinks of the recesses of its valley or of the outline of its city. He is acquainted with all of its citizens, just as he can picture all its boundaries, and the narrowness of his political enclosure, like the form of his corporeal enclosure, supplies him in advance with that middling, limited type in which all his intellectual conceptions will be shaped.[7]

These words reveal to us the whole nature of the Grecian city. In such a miniature state man's love of the homeland identifies itself completely with his love of the community. Homeland and fatherland are still one and the same and have nothing in common with the abstract modern idea of the fatherland. Therefore, the so-called "national idea" was always entirely alien to the Greeks, and even in times of most pressing danger could not strike root among them. In Homer one finds not the slightest trace of national fellowship, and there is nothing to show that the national idea was any more appealing to the Greeks in the bloom of their culture.

[7] *Philosophy of Art*, p. 319.

It was merely the consciousness of belonging to a common culture that held the Greek cities together. That is the reason why the colonizings of the Greeks had quite another character than those of all the other peoples of antiquity. The Phoenicians thought of their colonies primarily as associates in trade. For the Romans they played the part of subject territories, which were economically drained by the mother country and were entirely dependent on the Roman state. Not so with the Greeks. They founded their colonies with the same notion as their cities in the closer homeland —as independent organizations, which were, indeed, linked to the mother country by the same culture, but which otherwise felt in themselves the pulse beat of their own separate lives. A colony had, moreover, its own constitution, was a *polis* in itself, and competed with the cities of the homeland in the independent development of its own cultural life.

Since the area of the Greek municipality extended to only a few square miles every citizen was easily able to keep track of the entire public life and to form his own judgment about everything—a circumstance of great importance, which is utterly inconceivable in our modern state organization with the wide ramifications of its governmental machinery and the complicated gearing of its bureaucratic institutions. Hence the perplexed helplessness of the citizen of the modern state, his exaggerated overvaluation of governmental proclamations and of political leadership, which deprive him of all personal initiative. Since he is, of course, not in a position to keep track of all the fields of activity of the modern state and its internal and external policy, and is, on the other hand, so firmly convinced of the unalterable fixedness of all these functions that he believes he would sink into a bottomless quicksand if the political equilibrium were at all disturbed, his feeling of his own personal unimportance and dependence upon the state becomes strengthened, and his belief in the absolute necessity of political authority—which today is deper seated in man than his belief in the authority of God—becomes deeper still. So, at best, he dreams only of a change of the persons at the head of the state and does not comprehend that all the inadequacies and evils of the political machine which constantly oppress him depend on the very existence of the state itself and hence always recur in any of the various forms it may assume.

Not so with the Greek. Since he could more easily get a view of the inner workings of the *polis* he was in a better position to pass judgment on the conduct of his leading men. He had their earthbound humanity always before his eyes and was the more interested in his own affairs because his intellectual agility was not crippled by blind faith in authority. In no country were the great men so exposed to the judgment of public opinion as in Greece at the time of its highest cultural development. Even the greatest and most undeniable merit afforded no protection in this regard. Men of the stature of a Miltiades, a Themistocles, had to experience this in their own persons. In this way public life in Greece was kept always in flux, and no one fixed ordering of affairs could persist for long. Thus were the personal freedom and possibilities of development of the individual best safeguarded; his initiative did not exhaust itself on the dead forms of a central state authority. In this condition of intellectual freedom lay the sources of that magnificent culture the powerful development of which cannot otherwise be explained. Sir Francis Galton mentions, correctly, that Athens alone, most important of the Greek city-republics, and the one where spiritual freedom was most at home, in the course of a single century, from 530 to 430 B.C., produced not fewer than ten of the most outstanding men of Grecian history, namely, Miltiades, Themistocles, Aristides, Cimon, Pericles, Thucydides, Socrates, Xenophon, Plato, Aeschylus, Sophocles, Euripides, Aristophanes and Phidias. The English scholar adds that only Florence, where under similar conditions a culture as rich, even if of altogether different type, developed, can be compared with Athens in this respect.[8]

This spirit of creative activity reached its high state of perfection in every city of Greece with the exception of Sparta, which never freed itself from the domination of the aristocracy, while all the other cities were finding the way to democracy. In Sparta, therefore, the idea of political sovereignty played the decisive role, to which everything else was subordinated. True, it is undeniable that in Athens, Thebes and Corinth forces were always present that worked for a political sovereignty in the country; but that merely proves that every form of the state stands as a hindrance in the way of culture, even when its power is ever so limited. But the complete political and national separateness of Greece took the strength out of these efforts toward an extension of power; even where they had a passing success it was only momentary, and never attained the status of an established political order such as is proper to all great states. Nietzsche, years ago, recognized the internal opposition between *polis* and culture and characterized the allegedly necessary connection between them as a delusion.[9]

Not only did Greece know no unified national state; it had never learned to recognize a priestly hierarchy like that of the Babylonians, the Egyptians or the Persians, after which as prototype the Papacy was later formed. And since there was no church, there was also no theology and no catechism. The religion of the Hellenes was an airy structure, in the development of which the poets had a much greater share than the priests. The religious concepts did not support the dogmatism of a theological caste and were scarcely any hindrance to freedom of thought. The Greek thought of his gods differently from most other Oriental peoples.

[8] *Hereditary Genius, Its Laws and Consequences*, 1869.
[9] *Menschliches Allzumenschliches*, Chap. 8.

He clothed them with all the qualities of human greatness and human weakness, and faced them, therefore, with that rare simplicity which gives to his religious concepts a peculiar tone to be found among no other people of antiquity. This is also the reason why the idea of hereditary sin remained always alien to the Hellenes. Schiller was quite right when he said that while in Greece the gods were regarded as human, man had to feel himself divine. All Olympus was, so to speak, a faithful copy of the rich Hellenic cultural life with its internal political separateness, its colorful manifoldness and constructive power, its constant rivalry and its utter humanness and all-too-humanness. In Hellas, too, man mirrored himself in his gods. Only when one sees clearly what a crippling influence the Christian church exerted for centuries on the intellectual life of Europe, how it has supported every despotism and remains today the unconquered stronghold of every intellectual and social reaction, does one comprehend what a chasm yawns between the religious experiences of the Greek and the dead, soul-shackling dogmas of the Christian church.

There are few periods in history when the necessary conditions for the unfolding of a great culture were so prodigally provided as in ancient Hellas. What might seem to the modern statesman the great defect in the Hellenic world, the extreme political dividedness of the country, was the greatest blessing for the rich and unrestricted development of its cultural strength. How little of the feeling for national unity there was among the Greeks was shown most conspicuously at the time of the Persian wars. If there ever was a time calculated to awaken a national consciousness among the Greek tribes, this was the time, when Persian despotism had set itself to put an end to the freedom and independence of the Greek cities. The danger which threatened the Hellenes then was equally great for all. No one could have had the faintest illusion about this; everyone knew what a Persian victory meant for the Greek community. But it was just at that time of greatest danger that the political disunion of the Hellenes became most noticeable.

Already at the time of the victorious expedition of Harpagon who, under orders from the Persian King Cyrus, brought most of the Greek cities in Asia Minor under Persian domination (546-545 B.C.), and later at the time of the Ionic revolt (499-494 B.C.), there were two occurrences of far-reaching importance, which might be regarded as a foretaste of the later Persian wars, and which showed so unmistakably the complete lack of any unified national effort among the Greeks that a unified resistance against the Persians never came to pass. Miletus, which was so cruelly punished at the suppression of the Ionic revolt, on the occasion of the military expedition of Harpagon, left the other cities altogether in the lurch in order to negotiate a favorable peace with the Persians. Only a few cities carried on the war to the bitter end. Most of them when they saw that any resistance to the Persians was vain, preferred to abandon the old soil and to found for themselves a new home at a distance. The Spartans refused any help whatever to the revolting Greek cities in Asia Minor—which simply cannot be reconciled with a strongly developed national feeling. The Athenians supported the Ionic revolt, chiefly because the tyrant Hippias, whom they had exiled, had found asylum at the Persian court and from there had instigated continuous cabals against his native city. These petty potentates, who before the introduction of the republican form of the state had established themselves in almost every Grecian city, allowed themselves to be controlled by no national considerations and were always ready to perform the most menial services for the Persian despots in exchange for assistance in suppressing the struggles for freedom put up by their own people. The machinations of men like Pisistratus in Athens, Aleutos in Thessaly and the Spartan king, Demaratus, prove this.

When at last the Persian king, Darius, got his hands free he sent a great army against Eretria and Athens, which cities he especially hated because of their support of the Ionic revolt; still it was clear that his attack was directed at all Greece, for Persian power was not safe in Asia Minor until the Hellenes there were deprived of the possibility of receiving aid from the cities of the mother country. The danger was great, the more so because the tyrant, Hippias, was with the Persian army and, as a Greek, could render them many a useful service. Despite this there is no trace of a kindling of national consciousness among the Hellenes. Sparta's attitude was ambiguous, as always—this, despite the fact that the Persian emissaries who were sent to demand earth and water as tokens of sub-mission were thrown into a well with the suggestion that they would there be able to collect for themselves what they wanted. Many cities on the islands and also on the mainland had submitted almost without resist-ance, among them the greater part of the Boeotians. Even the closest neighbors of the Athenians, the inhabitants of the island of Aegina, would risk no resistance to the Persian army and preferred surrender to probable capture.

When at last at Marathon it came to a decisive combat between the land forces of the Persians and the Greeks, in which the latter faced an overwhelmingly superior force, the Athenians took the field almost alone, for, except for a thousand hoplites whom the Plataeans had sent, no other aid was at hand. Even the Spartans, who had entered the war against the Persians, appeared on the field only after the battle and contributed noth-ing to the tremendous victory of Miltiades and his troops. By the victory at Marathon the danger which had threatened Hellas was for the time being averted and the Persian generals were compelled to lead their troops back to Asia. Nevertheless, it must certainly have been clear to everyone that, though the danger was certainly postponed for a while, it was by no means ended. There was no vestige of a doubt that the Persian despotism would set all its forces at work to get even for the defeat it had suffered. The whole situation was so unequivocal that no one in Hellas could have misunderstood it. One might, therefore, have expected that the Greeks would have availed themselves of the short breathing spell to prepare better to face the approaching danger. If there had existed in Greece the slightest trace of that "national spirit" of which uncritical historians have so much to say, it would by all means surely have revealed itself in such a perilous situation. But there occurred nothing which one could point to as revealing a strengthening of the national consciousness. Internal conditions in Greece remained the same. Sparta, whose military and political prestige had been greatly impaired by the Athenian victory at Marathon, from then on directed its whole political activity to obstructing in every way the rapid development of Athens. This presented to the Spartan aristocracy a much more important problem than the Persian danger.

When, then, in 480 B.C., ten years after the battle of Marathon, the Persian king, Xerxes, threatened Greece with an enormous army on land and a mighty fleet along its coast, the general situation of the Greeks was not better by a single hair than on the occasion of the first Persian attack. Even then there appeared no trace of national unanimity in the face of the frightful danger which threatened all alike. At first there was universal panic. Still no one thought of a common defense of "national interests." Thebes, within whose walls the so-called "Median party" had achieved a strong influence (fostered, beyond a doubt, by the Persian despot) submitted to the enemy without resistance; several tribes in the more central parts of the country followed suit. Boeotians, Thessalians and Achaeans tried by submission to escape the danger which threatened them.

But even the famous assembly on the Isthmus, to which the few cities that had resolved on resistance sent representatives, presented anything but a picture of national resolution. First of all, the Spartans could not be induced to throw their entire military power into the northern part of the country to confront the advancing hostile army. They were clearly quite willing to allow Central Greece to be laid waste, and there is hardly a doubt that the ruling caste in Sparta would gladly have seen Athens destroyed by the Persians and themselves thus freed from an embarrassing rival. The whole role of the Spartans at this time was just as ambiguous as it had been ten years before in the war against Darius. When at last, in order to avoid making their secret purposes all too manifest, they were compelled to consent to putting up a resistance to the Persians at Thermopylae, they sent Leonidas with only three hundred Spartan citizens and about a thousand Perioecae, with whom a few other tribes joined.

Altogether, the number of heavy-armed soldiers was less than four thousand, a ridiculously small number compared to the gigantic horde of the Persians. When Grote and other celebrated narrators of Grecian history express doubts of the sincerity of the Spartans, their reason is only too evident in the light of the historical facts.

Even later when, after the disastrous defeat of his fleet at Salamis, Xerxes was compelled to retreat across the Hellespont with the greater part of his army, Sparta continued to pursue the same equivocal tactics. Xerxes, it was true, had withdrawn into Asia, but he had left behind in Thessaly a strong army under his general, Mardonius, who was to winter there in order to renew the war in the spring. But just at this final decisive battle, the Spartan king, Pausanias, who had the supreme command of the fighting forces of the Hellenes, displayed such an appalling lack of decision that it seemed to hint at treachery. The end of Pausanias, who on a later occasion was led into open betrayal of the interests of the Greeks, justifies the suspicion that even at that time he had struck a secret bargain with Mardonius. This supposition gains probability if we take into consideration that before the opening of hostilities Mardonius had made a secret proposal to the Athenians that they should enter into an alliance with him, promising that their independence should be in no way impaired. The Athenians proudly rejected the proposal, and it is easy to conjecture that Mardonius at once tried it on Pausanias and from him met with a better response. At any rate, the whole behavior of Pausanias before the battle of Plataea lends itself to such an interpretation.

If in spite of their superiority and in spite of their secret machinations the Persians were still decisively defeated, it was because the troops of the Hellenes, who fought for their independence and their freedom, and who had to lose nothing less than their all, were animated by a very different spirit than the gigantic army of the Persians, welded together by the will of a despot, and in large part merely impressed for the war from foreign populations. For this reason the Greeks won despite their national divisions and their political disunion, without their having been aware of these as weaknesses.

The attempt of many historians to interpret the later Peloponnesian war as a struggle over the national unity of Greece is without any secure foundation. Mauthner has strikingly commented on the unreasonableness of this assertion:

Let one only think, for example. that during the nearly thirty-years-long Peloponnesian war the idea of a Hellenic nationality practically did not make its appearance; of course, a man like Alcibiades, who under the stress of wrath and need put his inventive talent at the disposal, now of his fellow Athenians, now of the hostile Spartans, now of the hereditary enemy in Persia, was even at that time an exception; but even among the simple

Greeks those were rare who had formed any conception of their nationality, who as conscious Pan-Hellenes or All-Grecians desired the end of the war. The idea of nationality was not yet effective, despite their love for their homeland, for their city.[10]

In that long and bloody conflict in which Greece slashed at its own flesh and gnawed at its own vitals, the struggle was not over the national-political unity of the Grecian tribes, but over the question: autonomy or hegemony? What was to be decided was which of the larger cities should hold the leadership: Athens, Sparta, Thebes or Corinth. After the Persian wars culture, especially in Athens, had expanded into fullest bloom; but the victory over the Persians had contributed strongly to the extension of the consciousness of political power. The Athenians, who, with their allies, continued the war against the Persians and wished to secure for the Grecian cities in Asia Minor liberation from the Persian yoke, was not actuated by purely economic motives. The principal ground of their behavior was undoubtedly the conviction that an alliance of free cities in Asia Minor would constitute a strong bulwark against further attacks by the Persian despotism. While the Spartans and the other Peloponnesian cities had withdrawn from the war, Athens, and the cities which had identified themselves with her undertakings, founded the Delian-Attic League, which was at first a free federation of independent communities; within its framework every city enjoyed the same rights. But this was ended with the development of the hegemony, which gradually conceded to Athens greater and greater privileges which she could hold only at the expense of her allies. This brought the political motive ever more sharply into the foreground of social life.

This is precisely the curse of every power of whatever sort: that its holders misuse it. Against this manifestation no reform helps, no safety valve in the constitution, however farsightedly devised; for it springs from the innermost nature of power itself and is therefore inevitable. It is not the external form, but power *as such,* that leads to misuse; the striving after power opens gate and door to all the foul and fateful passions of man. When Goethe once spoke of the ruin that politics works on character, he may well have been thinking of that obsession with power which lies at the foundation of all politics. Everything which seems to us base and contemptible in private life becomes—when statesmen use it—patriotic virtue, provided that success treads on its heels. And since with the extension of power more and more economic wealth falls into the laps of its possessors, there develops a system of venality and corruption that gradually undermines all social morale, without which no community can long endure. So power becomes a terrible scourge to social life and its

---

[10] Fritz Mauthner, *Der Atheismus.* Band I, p. 102.

creative cultural forces. Even the Grecian *polis* proved no exception to this rule, and fell into inner dissolution just in the proportion that political ambition got the upper hand in it.

Moreover, it was shown then, and has ever since been constantly confirmed, that war, which hopeless fools celebrate as the rejuvenation of social life, usually affects the victor more injuriously than the vanquished. Because as one of its consequences it enriches immoderately certain sections in the community, displaces the earlier limits of well-being and thus disturbs the social equilibrium to such a degree that it becomes constantly more difficult to speak of a community of social interests; and the class contrasts in society manifest themselves more strongly and more undisguisedly. It happened thus in Athens also. Hand in hand with the luxuriant growth of a money oligarchy went the impoverishment of the lower sections of the people; the destruction of the ancient foundations of their society. On this and on her slave economy Greece was at last to wreck herself.

The struggle for the hegemony, which found such overpowering expression in the Peloponnesian war, at the same time initiated the decline of Greek culture and prepared the way for the subjugation of Greece by the Macedonian monarchy, for it led everywhere—in Athens, in Sparta, in Thebes—to the same inevitable results. The one pleasing phenomenon in the struggle for leadership is the fact that none of the larger cities was able to maintain its predominance for any length of time, because the sense of freedom of the Hellenes always impelled the individual cities to revolt and to shake off the yoke that had been imposed on them. But the war lasted too long and undermined completely the foundations of social life. After the termination of hostilities all the cities were so exhausted that they were no match for the approaching Macedonian peril. The less so because, owing to the upsetting of customs and the decay of all moral principles which resulted from the war and the struggle for power, the Macedonian king was able to keep agents in almost every city who worked actively in furtherance of his plans. In fact, the moral depravity was most complete exactly at the time when Demosthenes was vainly striving to arouse Hellas to a united defense against the Macedonian peril.

Alexander of Macedon at last established the national political unity of Greece with the sword, by bringing the whole country under his own overlordship. He was the real founder of that so-called "Hellenism" which servile historians have acclaimed as the zenith of Greek culture. In reality, it was an intellectual decline, incapable of any renewal of its life. Alexander laid the foundation for a unified Grecian kingdom, and in doing this he destroyed the inexhaustible diversity of that rich cultural life which was so characteristic of the Greek communities at the time of their bloom. The former citizens of free cities became subjects of the unified national state, which directed all its forces to reducing every manifestation of social life to the dead level of its political purposes. "Hellenism" was merely a substitute for a culture which could flourish only in freedom; it was the triumph of the uncreative exploiter over the creative spirit of the Greek city.

Most historiographers honor Alexander as the great disseminator of Hellenic culture over the enormous territories of his kingdom. But they overlook the fact that he, unmindful of his own victory over the Persian military power, fell, in thought and action, ever more under the spell of Persian notions of dominion and set himself to the task of transplanting these to Europe. Grote is entirely right when in his *History of Greece* he maintains that Alexander did not make Persia Grecian, but Greece Persian, thus strangling forever the further development of its culture; yes, that his actual purpose was to convert Hellas into a satrapy, as the Romans later made it into a province of their world realm. Under his rule and that of his successors the springs of the ancient Grecian culture dried up. For a long time men fed on its abundance, but it developed no new products. National-political unity sounded the death-knell of Hellenic culture.

—just as among the Greeks—along with the new political forms,
remnants of the old gentile system survived for a long time. In
the transformation from purely social union to political organiza-
accomplished only very gradually; in fact, about in the measure
natural union of the old gentile system was loosened by the
ion of private property, and the family achieved an influence which
all power into the hands of the head of the family. Thus the
customary law was more and more displaced by the enactments
state, which gradually grew into the Roman law.
ese inner transformations of course affected also the relations with
oring communities. It is easily seen that with the rapid growth of
its lands would soon become inadequate for the production of
uffs to meet the needs of the inhabitants; thus the first hostilities
e neighbors may have arisen. So we have the first battles growing
the desire to conquer the land of the neighboring communities and
e these subject to Rome. But the conquered territories must be held
ist be safeguarded against uprisings of the old population, and this
be accomplished only by a strong military organization, in the de-
ent of which the Roman state little by little completely sunk itself.
was built up a new system of outspokenly militaristic character.
rly, responsibility for public affairs had rested on the popular
ly, the *comitia curiata* which was still made up after the pattern
ancient gentile system, but already under Numa, the successor of
lus, influences were at work which led to decisive alterations in the
and tended strongly to give it a purely political character. The
ditions for this transformation are to be looked for in those internal
ns of Roman society into classes which were already plainly notice-
nder the earliest kings. It is sheer nonsense to try to see in patricians
lebeians members of two different races which held toward one
r in some measure the relation of conquerors and conquered. The
fact that some of the descendants of the same family might belong
patricians and others to the plebeians disposes of this view. In
we are here dealing with two different social statuses which grew
the system of private property and of the inequality of economic
ions. In this view the patricians are to be regarded as the represen-
of the big farmers while the plebeians were gathered from the ranks
small farmers, who in consequence of the increasing inequality of
sions came ever more and more under the yoke of their rich fellow
ns.
ne society of earliest Rome was divided into family-clans, each
d by a chieftain or king clothed with the powers at once of high
and general. Beside the king there stood the council of the leading
f the clans, on whom rested the actual guidance of the affairs of the

Chapter 6

THE PREHISTORY OF ROME. THE ETRUSCANS. THE FOUNDING OF THE
CITY OF ROME. PATRICIANS AND PLEBEIANS. ROME AS MILITARY AND
POLITICAL CENTER. CONQUEST AS A PRINCIPLE OF STATE. THE NATURE
OF THE ROMAN STATE. DICTATORSHIP AND CAESARISM. FROM NA-
TIONAL-POLITICAL UNITY TO WORLD DOMINION. RELIGION IN THE
SERVICE OF THE STATE. ROME AND CULTURE. THE STRUGGLE OF "GENU-
INE ROMANISM" AGAINST THE HELLENIC SPIRIT. CATO AND SOCRATES.
INVASION BY GRECIAN CULTURE. A PEOPLE OF IMITATORS. ART IN ROME.
CONTEMPT FOR LABOR. LITERATURE AS STATE-PURPOSE. THE THEATER
IN ROME AND IN ATHENS. THE "GOLDEN AGE." THE *AENEID* OF VIRGIL.
THE COMPLAINT OF HORACE. PHILOSOPHY AND SCIENCE IN ROME. CON-
QUEST AS A MONETARY TRANSACTION. ROME AS WORLD VAMPIRE. CON-
CERNING THE DECLINE OF ROME. INCREASING INFLUENCE OF MILITARY
LEADERS. SOLDIERY AND PEASANTRY. ROMAN LAW. THE PROLETARIAT.
SLAVE UPRISINGS. CHARACTERLESSNESS AND SLAVERY ON PRINCIPLE.
CAESARISM AND PRETORIANISM. DEGENERATION AND CHRISTIANITY.
THE END OF THE EMPIRE.

WHENEVER we speak of Greece we also think of Rome, an association
of ideas that is established in our school days. Our concept of "classic
antiquity" embraces Greeks and Romans as peoples of the same cultural
circle; we speak of a "Graeco-Roman culture period" and associate with
this the idea of profound inner connections which never existed, never
could have existed. It is true that we were told of certain characters
distinguishing the Greeks from the Romans. Against the cheerful independence of the Greeks we were shown the stern sense of duty of the
Romans; "Roman virtue" wrapped in its coarse toga served us in some
measure as antithesis to the frank joy of living of Hellas. Above all,
however, the schools praised the highly developed political sense of the
Romans, which enabled them to forge the whole Italian peninsula into
a firm political unity, a thing the Greeks could never accomplish in their
own country. And all this was so presented to us as to convey with certainty the impression that Romanism was merely a necessary extension
of the Grecian conception of life which, in a sense, it merely carried to its

conclusion. Without doubt there were connections between the Hellenic and the Roman culture, but these were of a purely superficial nature and had not the slightest relation to the peculiar modes of thought or the intellectual and cultural aspirations of the two peoples. Even if there were available proofs of the view that the Greeks and the Romans are to be regarded as descendants of the same people (one which in prehistoric times had its dwelling in the Middle Danube Basin and of whom they say one part wandered into the Balkans while the other forced its way into the Apennine peninsula), this still would be no proof of the interdependence of the Greek and the Roman cultures. The very wide difference in the social development of the two peoples would in that event merely show that different environments had influenced decisively the hereditary characteristics of the Greeks and the Romans and forced the course of their social life into different paths.

Concerning the primitive history of the Romans we know no more than about the early home of the Grecian tribes. With them, too, everything fades into the thick haze of mythological tradition. Famous authorities on Roman history (like, for example, Theodor Mommsen), even maintain that many of these legends, especially the myth of the founding of the city of Rome by the brothers Romulus and Remus, were invented much later with the conscious political purpose of giving a national Roman stamp to institutions taken over from the Etruscans and to delude the people into a belief in their community of descent. That the peninsula had already in prehistoric times been inundated repeatedly by Germanic and Celtic tribes cannot today be doubted; but in all probability immigrations from Africa and the Levant by the sea-route had also taken place, and this long before the colonization of Sicily and South Italy by the Phoenicians—and a few centuries later by the Greeks.

It is certain that the so-called Italic peoples did not belong to the original inhabitants of the peninsula, as was once widely accepted. The Italics were rather a people of Indo-Germanic origin which had crossed the Alps in prehistoric times and settled on the plains of the Po Valley. Later, driven out by the Etruscans, they withdrew to the middle and southern parts of the country, where they probably mixed with the Japygo-Messapians. The time of their entrance is veiled in utter darkness. On their arrival they encountered the Ligurians, who probably came from Asia Minor. Later the Ligurians completely vanished from the canvas; but their territories once extended over all the northern part of the peninsula, the Alps, Southern France, and as far as Northern Spain, where they mixed with the Iberians.

Among all the peoples, however, who played a part before the foundation of Rome and exerted very strong influence on the development of Roman civilization the Etruscans take first place. We are still altogether

uncertain about the origin of this remarkable [...] search has not yet succeeded in deciphering thei[...] realm extended in early times from the extrem[...] of the Tiber, which was called by the ancients [...] control, undisturbed for centuries, was first bro[...] of the Romans. But even at the founding of [...] important part. Among the Roman kings Ta[...] pressly designated as Etruscan, while Numa Po[...] were called Sabines by the Roman historiograph[...]

Beyond doubt the great structures of ancient [...] the Capitoline temple, and so on, were erected [...] none of the Latin tribes were highly enough de[...] accomplished such works. It is now generally [...] Rome is of Etruscan origin and probably goes [...] Ruma. In the semi-historical traditions of the [...] Etruscans are mentioned as one of the three ab[...] they ascribed the founding of the city. From a [...] Romans proper enter history as an already mix[...] circulated the blood of several races.

The immediate occurrences which led to th[...] Rome lie wholly in the dark. Many historians a[...] founding of the city can be traced back to the [...] springtime," a widespread custom among the La[...] which the young men of twenty years of age left [...] tion to establish elsewhere a home of their own. [...] this custom, and it is not impossible that Rome [...] It is also clear from the traditions that the Pa[...] settled, while the other six hills were added to t[...] and were, in fact, held by different tribes. The [...] ments into the city of Rome followed much lat[...] position to establish historically its immediate caus[...] a considerable part in it, a view that gains cr[...] tradition that the tribal fathers of the city of Ro[...] all sorts of fugitives, to whom the young settle[...] The legend of the rape of the Sabine women al[...] colonists were no very pleasant neighbors.

Very little of the primitive history of the I[...] but that little shows clearly that they were a peop[...] breeders. Their social life was based on the so-ca[...] separate family-clans gradually united with oth[...] tions, from which in time there proceeded a fe[...] had bound themselves together into a union for c[...] community out of which Rome later arose exhib[...]

which—
strong [...]
genera[...]
tion wa[...]
that th[...]
institut[...]
deliver[...]
ancient[...]
of the [...]

Th[...]
neighb[...]
the citi[...]
food s[...]
with th[...]
out of [...]
to mak[...]
and m[...]
could [...]
velopm[...]
There [...]
Forme[...]
assemb[...]
of the [...]
Romu[...]
system[...]
precon[...]
divisio[...]
able u[...]
and p[...]
anothe[...]
simple[...]
to the [...]
reality[...]
out of [...]
condit[...]
tative [...]
of the [...]
posses[...]
citizer[...]

T[...]
heade[...]
priest[...]
men [...]

community. Because of the close relation between the king and the leading men it was altogether natural that he should select his officials from their ranks. Because of the economic preponderance of the big farmers it resulted that they came gradually to hold all the important offices and used them to foster and build up their own interests and privileges, so that the poorer part of the population was brought more and more under their mastery. Out of this situation developed the first beginnings of a caste of nobility, which worked for the abolishment of the old gentile system so that the conquest of foreign territories might proceed more systematically. These undertakings were definitely begun under Numa; but it was not until the time of Servius Tullius that there occurred the great about-face by which Roman society acquired that unique political stamp. The city of Rome became the focus of all the surrounding and the conquered territories. In the place of the ancient institutions there arose a political-military structure based on five classes with unequally apportioned rights. The council of leading men was replaced by the Senate, in which only patricians had seat and voice, being thus raised to the status of a hereditary aristocracy. The different classes were divided into military centuries, kept always ready for service in war. In place of the old *comitia curiata* came the *comitia centuriata* corresponding to this new division. Each class had its separate centuries; their relative electoral weight was determined by their possessions.

There is no doubt that by this new division the people were shamefully cheated; still, because remnants of the old order were cunningly mixed with the new, most of them were unaware of it. Thus came into being that aristocratic-democratic state system, the internal organization of which was based on conquest and spoliation. The whole people was welded into an army and the government pursued with relentless persistence its aim of bringing the whole peninsula under Roman rule and forging it into a vast political unity. Only from this point of view can the relation between patricians and plebeians be rightly judged. It would be quite the reverse of the truth to try to see in the plebeians merely an oppressed class whose efforts were directed at the abolition of privilege and the establishment of a new economic order. They were not thinking of anything of the sort. Rather, their sole concern was to become participants in the privileges of the patricians and obtain an equal share of the spoils of war. There was no fundamental difference between the two ranks; they were equally obsessed by the "Roman spirit"; both were ready to make slaves and to oppress other peoples; both strove for the same opportunities for exploitation.

But the military character of the Roman state, ever bent on conquest, actually brought it about that the patricians had to yield to the demands of the plebs. They did not do this willingly; they defended their privileges

with obstinate determination, even forbidding marriage between patricians
and plebeians. In consequence of the state's cold-blooded policy of conquest, especially in the era of the republic, ever heavier demands were laid
upon the poorer population, and the gulf between the two classes was
constantly widened. However, the Roman policy demanded soldiers; it
was this necessity which had gradually compelled the patricians to share
their privileges with the plebs. Along with these concessions there was set
up a new nobility to support that imperial world-policy which was to bring
all important countries of the then known world under the power of Rome
and build up the Roman state into that frightful plunder-machine which
in all the history of the peoples of the earth has no parallel.

Some historians assert that it was during the reign of the emperors
that Rome first became the robbers' cave of the world, into the insatiable
mouth of which the freedom and the wealth of peoples disappeared. Without doubt what they called the "Roman spirit" was most effective under
the empire; but one must be blind not to recognize that the poisonous
bloom of Caesarism was sown in the time of the republic. In it were prepared the indispensable preliminaries for every possible further development of unlimited power. Under the republic arose the fateful institution
of the dictatorship, which justified on principle every abuse of power and
smothered at its birth every liberty of man. The constitution of the
republic placed two consuls at the head of the state, who were armed
with all the powers of the former kings. In emergencies the consuls with
the consent of the Senate could appoint a dictator who was clothed with
unlimited authority. The dictator had the right to suspend all existing
laws and to demand from all officials of the state unconditional obedience;
he could suspend all those rights of freedom and security guaranteed to
citizens by the constitution. Only a state which was based entirely on war
and the subjugation of other peoples could have called into being such a
terrible institution.

From dictatorship to Caesarism is only a step. The empire was merely
the ripened fruit of a system which had established power as the basic
principle of life. Hegel was entirely right when he said that "Rome was
from the very beginning an artificial, forced, not-primeval thing," and
that "the Roman state, geographically and historically, rested on the
impetus of violence." The will to power, in which the "spirit of Rome"
is so perfectly embodied, created that gruesome ideology which debases
the individual into the spiritless tool of the state, the insensate automaton
of a higher power; which justifies every means for the realization of its
aims. The much praised "Roman virtue" was never anything else than
state-slavery raised to a principle and stupid selfishness unmitigated by a
trace of sympathy. Both flourished in republican Rome quite as luxuriantly
as in Rome of the Caesars. Even Niebuhr, who was in general an unre-

strained admirer of the Roman state-policy, states in his *Roman History* that "from the earliest times down the most frightful vices prevailed, insatiable lust of power, conscienceless contempt for the rights of foreigners, unfeeling indifference to the sufferings of strangers, avarice, robbery, and a settled exclusiveness from which arose a quite inhuman hard-heartedness not only towards slaves but even towards fellow citizens." The pillars of the Roman state were calculating and methodical in their policy; they shrunk from no baseness, no infamy, no treachery, no breach of faith which promised advantage to their plans. *They* were the real inventors of the "reason of state" which in the course of time has grown into a frightful curse to every principle of humanity and justice. Not for nothing was a she-wolf the symbol of Rome; the Roman state in truth had wolf-blood in its veins.

Though at first the subjugation of the Italian peninsula was the aim of Roman policy, there appeared quite logically after its attainment, that ambition for world dominion which has such unmistakable attraction for every state with pretensions to power. The Italian peninsula, with its long coast-line, was too freely exposed to the attacks of hostile powers to permit the inauguration of any larger plans until the country was politically united and well fortified. The entire mainland is by nature a great geographic unit, and the principal aim of the crafty Roman policy was directed towards converting this geographical unity into a political unity. By a series of internal wars one people after another was made subject to the Roman state. In general the treatment accorded these Italian tribes by the conquerors was milder than that which they later practiced towards other subjugated peoples. This was clearly owing to well-considered political reasons, for the Roman statesmen dared not imperil their rulership over the Italian mainland by continual uprisings of the conquered populations if they were to pursue further their high-flown plans; hence their tenderness. The irruptions of the Gauls favored this cunning policy, since it made the indigenous populations so much the more dependent on the protection of Rome. Thus there developed in the course of time a feeling of closer cohesiveness that gradually solidified into the "national idea": not only in Rome, but over the whole peninsula, men felt themselves to be Romans.

Only after the political unification of the mainland had been accomplished could Roman policy set itself larger undertakings, which its leaders then pursued with unscrupulous greed and stern persistence, never allowing themselves to be frightened off by temporary setbacks. With these wider aims before their eyes there grew in the Romans an inner assurance of their strength and that peculiar arrogance towards other peoples which is characteristic of world-conquerors. Rome, once she became the focus of the world, believed herself rightfully called upon to subject all other peoples to her rulership. Her successes won for her a "historic mission" long before Hegel set this notion at the foundation of his theory of history. In the *Aeneid*, the national epic of the Romans, Virgil gave this fixed idea a poetic expression:

> Others will polish more charmingly bronzes that stand as if breathing,
> Carve, I am certain, as easily, faces in marble as lifelike,
> Plead in the courts with an eloquence finer, and measure with gnomon
> Courses of stars in the heavens and tell us the hours of their rising.
> Be thou, O Roman, concerned about wielding world-mastering power!
> Thine be such arts, then; and after, thine be it to scorn and to strike down
> Proudly the man who would set up a world where the people are peaceful!

After the fall of Carthage and Corinth these ideas grew with the Romans to an inner conviction, a sort of political religion; so arose gradually that monstrous mechanism of the Roman state, supported by force and plunder, which Kropotkin described in striking words:

> The Roman dominion was a state in the true sense of the word. To our own day it remains the ideal of the legislator and the legal expert. Its institutions covered a mighty realm as with a fine-meshed net. Everything converged on Rome; economic life, military life, legal relations, property, education, even religion. From Rome came the laws, the judges, the legions to protect the country, the office-holders, the gods. The collective life of the realm culminated in the Senate, later in the Caesar, the all-powerful and all-knowing, the God of the realm. Every province, every district had its tiny capitol, its fragment of the Roman sovereign, which guided its collective life. A single law imposed from Rome ruled throughout the realm. This realm was in no sense a union of citizens; it was a herd of subjects.[1]

In fact, Rome was the state *par excellence*, the state which was completely bent upon a gigantic centralization of all social forces. No other state has been able to maintain so long its worldwide dominion; no state has exerted such a commanding influence on the later political development of Europe and upon the form of its legal institutions. And that influence has even today not completely vanished; in the years since the World War it has even increased. The "idea of Rome," as Schlegel called it, is still the basis of the policy of all modern Big States, even when the forms of this policy have taken on a different appearance.

If everywhere in the history of Greece we meet with the spirit of autonomy and complete national dismemberment, in Rome we find, from the very outset, the idea of an all-embracing political unity, which found its most perfect expression in the Roman state. No other empire developed the idea of political unity to such a degree and planted it so deeply in actual life. It runs through all of Roman history and forms, so to speak, the leitmotif of its collective content.

[1] *The State: Its Role in History.*

Chapter 6

THE PREHISTORY OF ROME. THE ETRUSCANS. THE FOUNDING OF THE CITY OF ROME. PATRICIANS AND PLEBEIANS. ROME AS MILITARY AND POLITICAL CENTER. CONQUEST AS A PRINCIPLE OF STATE. THE NATURE OF THE ROMAN STATE. DICTATORSHIP AND CAESARISM. FROM NATIONAL-POLITICAL UNITY TO WORLD DOMINION. RELIGION IN THE SERVICE OF THE STATE. ROME AND CULTURE. THE STRUGGLE OF "GENUINE ROMANISM" AGAINST THE HELLENIC SPIRIT. CATO AND SOCRATES. INVASION BY GRECIAN CULTURE. A PEOPLE OF IMITATORS. ART IN ROME. CONTEMPT FOR LABOR. LITERATURE AS STATE-PURPOSE. THE THEATER IN ROME AND IN ATHENS. THE "GOLDEN AGE." THE *AENEID* OF VIRGIL. THE COMPLAINT OF HORACE. PHILOSOPHY AND SCIENCE IN ROME. CONQUEST AS A MONETARY TRANSACTION. ROME AS WORLD VAMPIRE. CONCERNING THE DECLINE OF ROME. INCREASING INFLUENCE OF MILITARY LEADERS. SOLDIERY AND PEASANTRY. ROMAN LAW. THE PROLETARIAT. SLAVE UPRISINGS. CHARACTERLESSNESS AND SLAVERY ON PRINCIPLE. CAESARISM AND PRETORIANISM. DEGENERATION AND CHRISTIANITY. THE END OF THE EMPIRE.

WHENEVER we speak of Greece we also think of Rome, an association of ideas that is established in our school days. Our concept of "classic antiquity" embraces Greeks and Romans as peoples of the same cultural circle; we speak of a "Graeco-Roman culture period" and associate with this the idea of profound inner connections which never existed, never could have existed. It is true that we were told of certain characters distinguishing the Greeks from the Romans. Against the cheerful independence of the Greeks we were shown the stern sense of duty of the Romans; "Roman virtue" wrapped in its coarse toga served us in some measure as antithesis to the frank joy of living of Hellas. Above all, however, the schools praised the highly developed political sense of the Romans, which enabled them to forge the whole Italian peninsula into a firm political unity, a thing the Greeks could never accomplish in their own country. And all this was so presented to us as to convey with certainty the impression that Romanism was merely a necessary extension of the Grecian conception of life which, in a sense, it merely carried to its conclusion. Without doubt there were connections between the Hellenic and the Roman culture, but these were of a purely superficial nature and had not the slightest relation to the peculiar modes of thought or the intellectual and cultural aspirations of the two peoples. Even if there were available proofs of the view that the Greeks and the Romans are to be regarded as descendants of the same people (one which in prehistoric times had its dwelling in the Middle Danube Basin and of whom they say one part wandered into the Balkans while the other forced its way into the Apennine peninsula), this still would be no proof of the interdependence of the Greek and the Roman cultures. The very wide difference in the social development of the two peoples would in that event merely show that different environments had influenced decisively the hereditary characteristics of the Greeks and the Romans and forced the course of their social life into different paths.

Concerning the primitive history of the Romans we know no more than about the early home of the Grecian tribes. With them, too, everything fades into the thick haze of mythological tradition. Famous authorities on Roman history (like, for example, Theodor Mommsen), even maintain that many of these legends, especially the myth of the founding of the city of Rome by the brothers Romulus and Remus, were invented much later with the conscious political purpose of giving a national Roman stamp to institutions taken over from the Etruscans and to delude the people into a belief in their community of descent. That the peninsula had already in prehistoric times been inundated repeatedly by Germanic and Celtic tribes cannot today be doubted; but in all probability immigrations from Africa and the Levant by the sea-route had also taken place, and this long before the colonization of Sicily and South Italy by the Phoenicians—and a few centuries later by the Greeks.

It is certain that the so-called Italic peoples did not belong to the original inhabitants of the peninsula, as was once widely accepted. The Italics were rather a people of Indo-Germanic origin which had crossed the Alps in prehistoric times and settled on the plains of the Po Valley. Later, driven out by the Etruscans, they withdrew to the middle and southern parts of the country, where they probably mixed with the Japygo-Messapians. The time of their entrance is veiled in utter darkness. On their arrival they encountered the Ligurians, who probably came from Asia Minor. Later the Ligurians completely vanished from the canvas; but their territories once extended over all the northern part of the peninsula, the Alps, Southern France, and as far as Northern Spain, where they mixed with the Iberians.

Among all the peoples, however, who played a part before the foundation of Rome and exerted very strong influence on the development of Roman civilization the Etruscans take first place. We are still altogether uncertain about the origin of this remarkable people, since scientific research has not yet succeeded in deciphering their inscriptions. The Etruscan realm extended in early times from the extreme north clear to the banks of the Tiber, which was called by the ancients an Etruscan stream. Their control, undisturbed for centuries, was first broken by the growing power of the Romans. But even at the founding of Rome they still played an important part. Among the Roman kings Tarquinius Superbus was expressly designated as Etruscan, while Numa Pompilius and Ancus Marcius were called Sabines by the Roman historiographers.

Beyond doubt the great structures of ancient Rome, the *cloaca maxima*, the Capitoline temple, and so on, were erected by Etruscan engineers, for none of the Latin tribes were highly enough developed culturally to have accomplished such works. It is now generally accepted that the name Rome is of Etruscan origin and probably goes back to the tribe of the Ruma. In the semi-historical traditions of the Romans, moreover, the Etruscans are mentioned as one of the three aboriginal peoples to whom they ascribed the founding of the city. From all this it follows that the Romans proper enter history as an already mixed people, in whose veins circulated the blood of several races.

The immediate occurrences which led to the founding of the city of Rome lie wholly in the dark. Many historians are of the opinion that the founding of the city can be traced back to the *ver sacrum*, the "sacred springtime," a widespread custom among the Latin tribes, in obedience to which the young men of twenty years of age left their old place of habitation to establish elsewhere a home of their own. Many cities arose through this custom, and it is not impossible that Rome owes its existence to it. It is also clear from the traditions that the Palatine Hill was the first settled, while the other six hills were added to the city only subsequently and were, in fact, held by different tribes. The merging of these settlements into the city of Rome followed much later, and we are not in a position to establish historically its immediate causes. Probably force played a considerable part in it, a view that gains credence from the ancient tradition that the tribal fathers of the city of Rome gathered about them all sorts of fugitives, to whom the young settlement offered an asylum. The legend of the rape of the Sabine women also indicates that the first colonists were no very pleasant neighbors.

Very little of the primitive history of the Romans is known to us, but that little shows clearly that they were a people of farmers and cattle-breeders. Their social life was based on the so-called gentile system. The separate family-clans gradually united with others into tribal organizations, from which in time there proceeded a federation of tribes which had bound themselves together into a union for defense and offense. The community out of which Rome later arose exhibited a political unity in which—just as among the Greeks—along with the new political forms, strong remnants of the old gentile system survived for a long time. In general, the transformation from purely social union to political organization was accomplished only very gradually; in fact, about in the measure that the natural union of the old gentile system was loosened by the institution of private property, and the family achieved an influence which delivered all power into the hands of the head of the family. Thus the ancient customary law was more and more displaced by the enactments of the state, which gradually grew into the Roman law.

These inner transformations of course affected also the relations with neighboring communities. It is easily seen that with the rapid growth of the city its lands would soon become inadequate for the production of food stuffs to meet the needs of the inhabitants; thus the first hostilities with the neighbors may have arisen. So we have the first battles growing out of the desire to conquer the land of the neighboring communities and to make these subject to Rome. But the conquered territories must be held and must be safeguarded against uprisings of the old population, and this could be accomplished only by a strong military organization, in the development of which the Roman state little by little completely sunk itself. There was built up a new system of outspokenly militaristic character. Formerly, responsibility for public affairs had rested on the popular assembly, the *comitia curiata* which was still made up after the pattern of the ancient gentile system, but already under Numa, the successor of Romulus, influences were at work which led to decisive alterations in the system and tended strongly to give it a purely political character. The preconditions for this transformation are to be looked for in those internal divisions of Roman society into classes which were already plainly noticeable under the earliest kings. It is sheer nonsense to try to see in patricians and plebeians members of two different races which held toward one another in some measure the relation of conquerors and conquered. The simple fact that some of the descendants of the same family might belong to the patricians and others to the plebeians disposes of this view. In reality we are here dealing with two different social statuses which grew out of the system of private property and of the inequality of economic conditions. In this view the patricians are to be regarded as the representatives of the big farmers while the plebeians were gathered from the ranks of the small farmers, who in consequence of the increasing inequality of possessions came ever more and more under the yoke of their rich fellow citizens.

The society of earliest Rome was divided into family-clans, each headed by a chieftain or king clothed with the powers at once of high priest and general. Beside the king there stood the council of the leading men of the clans, on whom rested the actual guidance of the affairs of the community. Because of the close relation between the king and the leading men it was altogether natural that he should select his officials from their ranks. Because of the economic preponderance of the big farmers it resulted that they came gradually to hold all the important offices and used them to foster and build up their own interests and privileges, so that the poorer part of the population was brought more and more under their mastery. Out of this situation developed the first beginnings of a caste of nobility, which worked for the abolishment of the old gentile system so that the conquest of foreign territories might proceed more systematically. These undertakings were definitely begun under Numa; but it was not until the time of Servius Tullius that there occurred the great about-face by which Roman society acquired that unique political stamp. The city of Rome became the focus of all the surrounding and the conquered territories. In the place of the ancient institutions there arose a political-military structure based on five classes with unequally apportioned rights. The council of leading men was replaced by the Senate, in which only patricians had seat and voice, being thus raised to the status of a hereditary aristocracy. The different classes were divided into military centuries, kept always ready for service in war. In place of the old *comitia curiata* came the *comitia centuriata* corresponding to this new division. Each class had its separate centuries; their relative electoral weight was determined by their possessions.

There is no doubt that by this new division the people were shamefully cheated; still, because remnants of the old order were cunningly mixed with the new, most of them were unaware of it. Thus came into being that aristocratic-democratic state system, the internal organization of which was based on conquest and spoliation. The whole people was welded into an army and the government pursued with relentless persistence its aim of bringing the whole peninsula under Roman rule and forging it into a vast political unity. Only from this point of view can the relation between patricians and plebeians be rightly judged. It would be quite the reverse of the truth to try to see in the plebeians merely an oppressed class whose efforts were directed at the abolition of privilege and the establishment of a new economic order. They were not thinking of anything of the sort. Rather, their sole concern was to become participants in the privileges of the patricians and obtain an equal share of the spoils of war. There was no fundamental difference between the two ranks; they were equally obsessed by the "Roman spirit"; both were ready to make slaves and to oppress other peoples; both strove for the same opportunities for exploitation.

But the military character of the Roman state, ever bent on conquest, actually brought it about that the patricians had to yield to the demands of the plebs. They did not do this willingly; they defended their privileges with obstinate determination, even forbidding marriage between patricians and plebeians. In consequence of the state's cold-blooded policy of conquest, especially in the era of the republic, ever heavier demands were laid upon the poorer population, and the gulf between the two classes was constantly widened. However, the Roman policy demanded soldiers; it was this necessity which had gradually compelled the patricians to share their privileges with the plebs. Along with these concessions there was set up a new nobility to support that imperial world-policy which was to bring all important countries of the then known world under the power of Rome and build up the Roman state into that frightful plunder-machine which in all the history of the peoples of the earth has no parallel.

Some historians assert that it was during the reign of the emperors that Rome first became the robbers' cave of the world, into the insatiable mouth of which the freedom and the wealth of peoples disappeared. Without doubt what they called the "Roman spirit" was most effective under the empire; but one must be blind not to recognize that the poisonous bloom of Caesarism was sown in the time of the republic. In it were prepared the indispensable preliminaries for every possible further development of unlimited power. Under the republic arose the fateful institution of the dictatorship, which justified on principle every abuse of power and smothered at its birth every liberty of man. The constitution of the republic placed two consuls at the head of the state, who were armed with all the powers of the former kings. In emergencies the consuls with the consent of the Senate could appoint a dictator who was clothed with unlimited authority. The dictator had the right to suspend all existing laws and to demand from all officials of the state unconditional obedience; he could suspend all those rights of freedom and security guaranteed to citizens by the constitution. Only a state which was based entirely on war and the subjugation of other peoples could have called into being such a terrible institution.

From dictatorship to Caesarism is only a step. The empire was merely the ripened fruit of a system which had established power as the basic principle of life. Hegel was entirely right when he said that "Rome was from the very beginning an artificial, forced, not-primeval thing," and that "the Roman state, geographically and historically, rested on the impetus of violence." The will to power, in which the "spirit of Rome" is so perfectly embodied, created that gruesome ideology which debases the individual into the spiritless tool of the state, the insensate automaton of a higher power; which justifies every means for the realization of its aims. The much praised "Roman virtue" was never anything else than state-slavery raised to a principle and stupid selfishness unmitigated by a trace of sympathy. Both flourished in republican Rome quite as luxuriantly as in Rome of the Caesars. Even Niebuhr, who was in general an unrestrained admirer of the Roman state-policy, states in his *Roman History* that "from the earliest times down the most frightful vices prevailed, insatiable lust of power, conscienceless contempt for the rights of foreigners, unfeeling indifference to the sufferings of strangers, avarice, robbery, and a settled exclusiveness from which arose a quite inhuman hard-heartedness not only towards slaves but even towards fellow citizens." The pillars of the Roman state were calculating and methodical in their policy; they shrunk from no baseness, no infamy, no treachery, no breach of faith which promised advantage to their plans. *They* were the real inventors of the "reason of state" which in the course of time has grown into a frightful curse to every principle of humanity and justice. Not for nothing was a she-wolf the symbol of Rome; the Roman state in truth had wolf-blood in its veins.

Though at first the subjugation of the Italian peninsula was the aim of Roman policy, there appeared quite logically after its attainment, that ambition for world dominion which has such unmistakable attraction for every state with pretensions to power. The Italian peninsula, with its long coast-line, was too freely exposed to the attacks of hostile powers to permit the inauguration of any larger plans until the country was politically united and well fortified. The entire mainland is by nature a great geographic unit, and the principal aim of the crafty Roman policy was directed towards converting this geographical unity into a political unity. By a series of internal wars one people after another was made subject to the Roman state. In general the treatment accorded these Italian tribes by the conquerors was milder than that which they later practiced towards other subjugated peoples. This was clearly owing to well-considered political reasons, for the Roman statesmen dared not imperil their rulership over the Italian mainland by continual uprisings of the conquered populations if they were to pursue further their high-flown plans; hence their tenderness. The irruptions of the Gauls favored this cunning policy, since it made the indigenous populations so much the more dependent on the protection of Rome. Thus there developed in the course of time a feeling of closer cohesiveness that gradually solidified into the "national idea": not only in Rome, but over the whole peninsula, men felt themselves to be Romans.

Only after the political unification of the mainland had been accomplished could Roman policy set itself larger undertakings, which its leaders then pursued with unscrupulous greed and stern persistence, never allowing themselves to be frightened off by temporary setbacks. With these wider aims before their eyes there grew in the Romans an inner assurance of their strength and that peculiar arrogance towards other peoples which is characteristic of world-conquerors. Rome, once she became the focus of the world, believed herself rightfully called upon to subject all other peoples to her rulership. Her successes won for her a "historic mission" long before Hegel set this notion at the foundation of his theory of history. In the *Aeneid*, the national epic of the Romans, Virgil gave this fixed idea a poetic expression:

> Others will polish more charmingly bronzes that stand as if breathing,
> Carve, I am certain, as easily, faces in marble as lifelike,
> Plead in the courts with an eloquence finer, and measure with gnomon
> Courses of stars in the heavens and tell us the hours of their rising.
> Be thou, O Roman, concerned about wielding world-mastering power!
> Thine be such arts, then; and after, thine be it to scorn and to strike down
> Proudly the man who would set up a world where the people are peaceful!

After the fall of Carthage and Corinth these ideas grew with the Romans to an inner conviction, a sort of political religion; so arose gradually that monstrous mechanism of the Roman state, supported by force and plunder, which Kropotkin described in striking words:

> The Roman dominion was a state in the true sense of the word. To our own day it remains the ideal of the legislator and the legal expert. Its institutions covered a mighty realm as with a fine-meshed net. Everything converged on Rome; economic life, military life, legal relations, property, education, even religion. From Rome came the laws, the judges, the legions to protect the country, the office-holders, the gods. The collective life of the realm culminated in the Senate, later in the Caesar, the all-powerful and all-knowing, the God of the realm. Every province, every district had its tiny capitol, its fragment of the Roman sovereign, which guided its collective life. A single law imposed from Rome ruled throughout the realm. This realm was in no sense a union of citizens; it was a herd of subjects.[1]

In fact, Rome was the state *par excellence,* the state which was completely bent upon a gigantic centralization of all social forces. No other state has been able to maintain so long its worldwide dominion; no state has exerted such a commanding influence on the later political development of Europe and upon the form of its legal institutions. And that influence has even today not completely vanished; in the years since the World War it has even increased. The "idea of Rome," as Schlegel called it, is still the basis of the policy of all modern Big States, even when the forms of this policy have taken on a different appearance.

If everywhere in the history of Greece we meet with the spirit of autonomy and complete national dismemberment, in Rome we find, from the very outset, the idea of an all-embracing political unity, which found its most perfect expression in the Roman state. No other empire developed the idea of political unity to such a degree and planted it so deeply in actual life. It runs through all of Roman history and forms, so to speak, the leitmotif of its collective content.

[1] *The State: Its Role in History.*

Of course, Rome never thought of granting to the conquered lands outside of the Italian peninsula which were incorporated into the realm as provinces, political or national rights of any kind. The foreigner—even when his country had been conquered by the Romans—was utterly without rights in Rome. It is characteristic of the mode of thought of the Romans that their language had for the ideas "foreigner" and "enemy" only the one word, *hostis*. It is, moreover, an entirely erroneous notion that the Roman state concerned itself only with the economic exploitation of the subject peoples and in other respects was guided in its treatment of the conquered by cosmopolitan ideas. Hand in hand with military and political subjugation, went the Romanizing of the conquered territories; and this was carried out with implacable consistency. Only towards religions did the Romans display a certain broadmindedness—so long as these were in no way dangerous to their supremacy. And in this connection we must not forget that in Rome even religion was completely subordinated to the purposes of the state. There was, therefore, no church which could stand out as a rival to the state. Every cult was under the supervision of the state. The Senate regulated all religious affairs, as is clear from innumerable decrees. The priests were subordinate officers of the state; and, besides, the highest priestly positions were all in the hands of the leading statesmen or of the Senate.

To a world-dominion like Rome every cult is equally acceptable so long as it subordinates itself to the state. Alexander of Macedon had already given an instructive example in this respect by making toleration of foreign religious systems an instrument of political power. He rendered to Apis of the Egyptians or to the God of the Jews the same honors as to Zeus of the Greeks. "Such a toleration," remarks Mauthner, "which was really indifference, became first with the Romans a genuine instrument of their permanent imperialism, their policy of world conquest." If, however, a religion became bothersome or actually dangerous to the state, tolerance quickly ended and persecution set in. This was the basis of the attacks on the early Christians, whose doctrine struck at the very foundations of the empire, and who refused to render divine honors to the person of the emperor. Religious persecutions in Rome always sprang from political motives.

The religion of the Romans displayed little that was primitive. They borrowed elements of religious faith from every possible people and incorporated them in their own body of ideas. It is today the fairly unanimous opinion that they derived a large part of their ancient cult from the Etruscans. This is especially true of their belief in demons and of the meticulously regulated ceremonial of their worship, which played a part in every phase of their daily life. Elisée Reclus remarks pointedly:

The ceremonials of the tribunals, the governmental palaces, the temples, the private dwellings, which the Romans followed almost without change for centuries, were likewise adopted from the Etruscans. From whatever point of view one regards it one cannot avoid the conclusion that the Roman people was nourished on the substance of the Etruscans, much like those insects which find their food all ready in the brood-cells that have been prepared for them.[2]

In no case can one identify the religion of the Romans with that of the Hellenes, as is so often done. It is true there are found in their cult many borrowings from the Greeks; the same is true for a number of their gods. But one cannot infer from this an essential relation between the two religions. A sober, unpoetic people like the Romans had no understanding at all of the cheerful activity of the Greek Olympus. The free, spontaneous behavior of the Hellenic gods was hard to harmonize with the Roman sense of order. Religion meant to the Romans spiritual bondage, as is revealed in the very derivation of the word. Bondage, however, simply did not go down with the Hellenes; in this sense they were not religious. Zeus was to them simply the father of the gods, otherwise endowed with exactly the same excellences and the same weaknesses as all the other gods. The dignified Jupiter of the Romans, however, was quite especially the guardian god of the capitol and of the Roman state.

The polytheism of the Greeks was the product of a poetically illumined mysticism, in which the various natural forces were embodied in the individual divinities. Among the Romans, the divinity often embodied nothing more than an abstract principle with a practical application. Thus they had gods of the frontier, of concord, of welfare, of theft, of pestilence, of fevers, of contentment, of worry, to whom the faithful could resort in special cases. The residences of the gods were arranged just like the Roman state: each god had his particular post, where nobody else had any business. For the Roman religion, like everything else, was designed to be practical and purposive; their whole cult exhausted itself in a ritual as rigid as it was spiritless. Even the cults of the Egyptians, the Syrians, the Persians and others, which later found a home among the Romans, had to adapt themselves to the peculiar character of the Roman state. The idea of political unity stood among the Romans ahead of every other consideration, a firm article of faith which must not be distorted and need not be explained.

If the assertion were true that national or political unity is the indispensable condition for the unhampered cultural development of a people, then the Romans should have overshadowed completely all other peoples in history as to both creative power and cultural activity, for among no

[2] *L'Homme et la Terre*, Volume II.

other people were these concepts so firmly and so universally held as among them. Furthermore, the dominance of Rome extended through a period of twelve hundred years; no other world power has lasted so long. Therefore no one can assert that the Romans did not have sufficient time to bring their cultural capabilities to full development. In spite of this, not even the most fanatical admirer of the Roman state and the "political genius" of the Romans would venture to assert that they were a culturally creative people or that they could be compared, even in a dream, with the nationally and politically completely disunited Hellenes. The mere thought of such a comparison would be treason to all culture. All distinguished minds whose mental vision has not been dimmed by the will to power are agreed that the Romans were, by and large, an unimaginative people with purely political interests, and that because of this purely political obsession they had no comprehension of the deeper significance of culture. Their actual cultural achievements were of trifling significance; in no field of culture did they make a single outstanding contribution; they remained always a race of imitators. Of course, they knew how to appropriate the creative products of others and to exploit them for their own special ends. At the same time, they always infected them with death-germs, for one cannot with impunity constrain cultural effort in political forms.

Every people possesses certain creative endowments and capabilities, and it would be ungracious to deny all such to the Romans. But these natural abilities were limited by the external conditions of the social environment and constrained into definite directions. Or, to speak with Nietzsche, every people—just as every man—has control over only a certain total of powers and capacities, and so much of this total as is expended for world-dominion or in political effort is necessarily withheld from cultural activity. This is the same thought which Hegel clothed in the words: "The Roman principle was fixed entirely on dominion and military power. It had no intellectual focal point as an aim to occupy and to satisfy the mind." The strained unity of the state structure was not of a type to give free range to the cultural capacities of the Romans. On the contrary, its entire twelve-hundred-year-long history gave conclusive proof that political unity is one thing and creative cultural activity is another thing.

The Romans tortured their natural talents to death on the Procrustean bed of political unity. Every creative idea was crippled by the rigid framework of their military and bureaucratic machine. They had made of the state an earthly Providence which guides everything, determines everything, decides everything; and in doing this they smothered at its birth every impulse toward spontaneous, independent activity. They sacrificed the whole world—and themselves—to this Moloch. The more extended and powerful the Roman state made itself in the course of the centuries, just so much more man shrank in spiritual worth and social importance; just so much more completely his sense of personality shriveled and with it his urge to cultural creation, which can endure no political coercion.

The Romans reveal this especially in their art, which among every people represents the high point of cultural creativeness. Until after the complete subjugation of all the countries bordering on the Mediterranean one cannot speak of a Roman art at all. Everything in Rome which could be assigned to the field of representative art up to that time was of either Etruscan or Grecian origin. The influence of the Etruscans is already easily recognizable in the earliest days of Rome. Later, out of the Grecian settlements at the south of the peninsula, there issued this other influx, which for the first time brought the Italic people into close contact with the art of the Hellenes. From the conquest of Greece after the second Punic war and the forcible incorporation of the country in the Roman realm, came that immediate union which was to be for the Hellenes of a later time a fatality, but which brought into Rome the first forms of a higher culture. The Roman commanders robbed the Greek cities of their most splendid treasures and dragged off to Rome everything transportable. Of the fabulous wealth of stolen art treasures we can hardly form a just estimate. Taine informs us in his *Philosophy of Art:* "When Rome had completely plundered the Grecian world she possessed a population of statues almost equal to her people. They estimate today the number of the statues which, after all the centuries and all the destructions, have been found in Rome and its environs at more than sixty thousand."

But the Romans had no sort of inner understanding of this art. They decorated their homes and their cities with Greek pictures, somewhat as today rich American upstarts buy Rembrandts and Van Dycks, because they thought they owed it to their station. Whence could they have gotten such an understanding?

The glad enjoyment of life of the Oriental Aryans, the joy of the Hellenes in nakedness, in the beauty of human nature, is in its every detail completely alien to the Roman. He has no splendid holiday plays, he honors no poets and writers, and he carries prudery so far that a son-in-law is not allowed to bathe with his father-in-law. What distinguishes the Roman is his intensity, his method. He must know that his house and his state is in order. His family life is strictly regulated and therefore extremely dull; he names his daughters "Fifth" and "Sixth," and he puts his son to death if he is disobedient. Unlike most Aryans he sets a high value on externals, on keeping up appearances. Gravity, dignity, decorum—these are his favorite expressions, words which on the lips of the facetious and undignified Cicero become doubly impressive.[3]

[3] Albrecht Wirth, *Volkstum und Weltmacht*, p. 40.

Holding such a concept of life it is surely no wonder that the so-called "genuine Romans" met the intrusion of Greek modes of life always with a certain shyness or even a definite hostility. With many this aversion took quite peculiar forms. Thus Cato the Elder warned his son against Greek physicians, asserting that the Greeks had entered into a conspiracy against the Romans in which the physicians were assigned the duty of poisoning all Roman citizens with their medicines.[4] The same Cato pronounced Socrates a loud-mouthed, turbulent agitator who well deserved his fate. He also prophesied that when Rome had become saturated with the teachings of Greek philosophy it would lose its dominion over the world. This hard-boiled slave-driver and heartless usurer divined instinctively that culture and world dominion were irreconcilable opposites, either of which could assert itself only at the expense of the other.

How completely and stupidly insensitive the Romans were to every higher cultural experience up to the end of the second Punic war is shown by the cruel and utterly inhuman destruction by the Roman commander, Lucius Mummius, of Corinth, the loveliest city in Greece. Not content with slaughtering all of the population capable of bearing arms, selling the women and children into slavery, and giving the city over to plunder by a rough soldiery, he set fire to it and finally left not one stone upon another. Shortly before the same fate had been dealt out to Carthage where flames raged for seven days, laying waste the land. Over it a plow was driven as symbol of Roman pitilessness.

But despite all this, Rome could not escape the influence of Hellenic culture, and all the warnings of Cato and his adherents were but wasted on the winds. Roman armies could strike down Greece by force of arms, could make Hellas into a Roman province, but they could build no dam against the flood of Hellenic culture. The Roman poet, Horace, has put his recognition of this into words:

Hellas, o'erpowered, o'erpowered her unlettered masters,
Carrying art into Latium gently to conquer it.
Crude Saturnine verse disappeared. Finer taste then expelled
The harsh and repellant, though long did the traces still show there
Of earlier rudeness, and have not yet utterly vanished;
For the Roman's mind tardily turned toward Grecian letters.
After the Punic wars, languidly resting, he thought to inquire
What he could use out of Sophocles, Thespis, and Aeschylus.
Soon he was trying to clothe them worthily in Latium's speech.

[4] There is nothing new under the sun. Today we have Julius Streicher, the bosom friend of Hitler, with whom anti-Semitism has taken an actually pathological form, asserting that the Jewish physicians have entered into a conspiracy to poison the German people.

No, Rome could not escape this peaceful invasion of a higher culture, more perilous to the Roman spirit than Hannibal or the incursions of the barbarians. The developing pan-Hellenism caused a profound change in the rubbishy beginnings of primitive Roman poetry. Whole troops of Greek architects, painters, sculptors, goldsmiths, bronze-founders, ivory-carvers, worked in the palaces of the Roman aristocracy—among them many slaves who had been forcibly dragged to Rome. And among these slaves were a large number equipped with all the riches of Hellenic education, who seemed called to bring to their masters a higher intellectual and spiritual culture. For all this, the Romans never progressed in their practice of the arts beyond a slavish imitation of foreign originals; and it is characteristic that in the whole history of Rome, a history of more than twelve hundred years, we find not more than half a dozen really great artists, that is, artists inspired with ideas of their own, while almost every Grecian city—Sparta alone excepted—can marshal a whole troop of them.

Even the so-called "Golden Age" has little to offer that can be designated as truly Roman art. Joseph Strzygowski has shown conclusively that Roman art in the time of the empire was merely the last phase of declining Hellenism, whose centers were to be found in Asia Minor, Syria and Egypt. At that time there were manifest in Hellenism strong Oriental influences gradually leading to the creation of the so-called Byzantine art, which in its essence was not Roman.[5] Only in architecture did the Romans actually produce a new style; but even here we must not forget that most of the show buildings of the time of the empire were constructed under the direction of foreign architects. At first the Romans borrowed their building art from the Etruscans, as is shown clearly by the characteristic form of their earlier temples. Later, when the influence of late Hellenic culture was growing constantly stronger in Rome, the Grecian spirit became more plainly operative in architecture, although the Etruscan type long remained unmistakably present. From the Etruscans the Romans learned the art of building arches and vaults, which the former had brought with them from the East. It was by the practical application and further development of this art that they were later able to carry through those mighty public works which even today strike us with astonishment. The art of vaulting led, then, in its further development to the construction of the cupola, which presented a new principle in architecture. The magnificent effect of this style reached its highest expression in the Roman Pantheon, the erection of which is attributed to Apollo of Damascus.

That in painting the Romans never got beyond mediocrity is known to everybody. They never had any profound feeling for music. As late as 115 B.C. the old-Roman patriots in the Senate forbade the use of musical

[5] Joseph Strzygowski, *Orient oder Rom?* 1901.

instruments—only the primitive Italian flute found grace in their eyes. Of course this measure was not permanently enforced, it disappeared before the advance of Hellenism, but even much later music was still consigned entirely to the hands of Grecian slaves. It was quite characteristic that in the field of plastic art the Romans failed almost completely. Although they adorned their cities with the stolen glories of Greece, they left sculpture entirely in the hands of Hellenic artists whom they had brought to Rome as slaves. So there developed in Rome the neo-Attic school which produced quite outstanding works. All the world-renowned works of that period, the caryatides of the Pantheon, the Borghese gladiator, the Venus de Medici, the Farnese Hercules, were made by Greeks. It is true we do not know the creator of the Apollo Belvedere, but there is no doubt that he was a Greek; the bungling efforts of the Romans in plastic art permit no other conclusion.

No people is entirely original in its artistic creation. Even the Greeks were intellectually stimulated and fertilized by other cultures; but they used the foreign matter in their own way, so that it became a part of their own thought and feeling. This is the reason why when we look at a Greek work of art which we know to have been produced under foreign influence we do not feel the foreign element, or at most perceive only a slight disturbance of the intrinsically Hellenic determination of the work. With the Hellenes one never feels that they are imitating foreign stuff; everything is experienced, sympathetically felt, inside them. With the Romans one can generally lay his hand on the imitation at once. This is not a matter of the lack of technical knowledge; it is evidence, rather, of the utter lack of sympathetic understanding with which the Roman artist really viewed the foreign original. Even during the blossoming period of Roman culture the educated Roman got no closer to the essence of Greek art. Friedlander, in his *Sittengeschichte Roms*, remarks with full justice:

> As a matter of fact, in spite of all the old and new artistic pomp of Rome and the Roman dominion, representative art never acquired an influence on the Roman population as a whole; Roman literature when viewed in its entirety gives convincing and unanswerable proof of this. Out of so large a number of poets and writers of various periods, most of whom stand at the peak of the education of their period and serve us as fully accredited representatives of it, hardly one betrays either interest or understanding for formative art. In this so highly varied literature, covering a period of centuries and touching all important tendencies and interests, which during the first centuries after Christ (that is, in the period of the empire before the dominance of Christianity) directed its attention especially upon the present, and even searched into its intellectual status with manifold praisings and blamings, there is found scarcely a trace of understanding of the true essence

of art and no expression of a comprehension of the splendor of its achievements. Wherever it is mentioned it is either with outright misunderstanding
or at least without warmth or sympathy. However many individual Romans
may have succeeded in penetrating into the essence of Greek art, for Roman
culture at large it remained always remote and strange.

This misjudgment of art, which with Cato and the Old-Roman party
passed over into openly avowed contempt, is found everywhere. The
writings of Cicero are strewn with contemptuous remarks about art and
artists. The gigantic development of slavery in Rome led naturally to a
profound contempt for labor, in which the prosaic Romans also included
art. A well-known saying of Plutarch is in this connection extraordinarily
significant. (By the way, this alleged teacher of the Emperor Hadrian
was a born Greek, in whose work, however, the Roman way of thinking
often achieves surprisingly clear expression.)

"No respectable young person," says Plutarch, "who sees the Zeus
in Pisa or the Hera in Argos will on that account wish to be a Phidias
or an Apelles; for though a work may be acceptable and pleasing to us
it by no means follows that its creator deserves our envy."

The same phenomena manifest themselves in the literature of the
Romans. Despite its many-sidedness it remains on the whole a literature
of imitations. One looks in vain for a Sophocles, an Aeschylus, an Aristophanes; with a few exceptions it all breathes the spirit of dullest mediocrity.
On the whole, literature was in Rome always one of the luxuries of a
privileged minority and was never able to strike root in the people itself.
The Golden Age (from 80 B.C. to 20 B.C.) offers no exception to this.
In Athens the production of a play by Sophocles or Aristophanes was an
event that stirred the whole population. In Rome there was hardly any
feeling for such matters, and Horace complains bitterly that the people
would rather be entertained by the performance of a rope-dancer or a
street clown than be instructed by the production of a drama. Like everything in Rome, so also literature served, above all, the purposes of the
state. Cato the Elder declared this openly and devoted a whole work
to it. In the time of the republic literature amounted to little; under
Caesarism it was in the service of the court. No other literature, therefore,
is so filled with the most disgusting flattery of the great ones of the earth
as is the Roman. In no other does the spirit of servility and boot-licking
display itself so openly and shamelessly. There never was a time in which
poet and artist rolled so deep in the dust as in that Golden Age.

A genuine literature was first produced in Rome through Greek influence, on which account the Roman literature has with justice been called
a dim reflection of dying Hellenism. What had previously appeared in
Rome as literature hardly deserves the name. This holds good especially
for the Saturnine verses, inartistic holiday songs with meager content and

of a wooden lifelessness. An epic such as most peoples possess was altogether lacking to the Romans. There exists no connection between the mythical history of Rome and Roman literature. (The attempt to create an epic was first undertaken in the time of the empire to flatter the vanity of the Caesars.) Then came the Fescennines, burlesque wedding songs, usually recited extemporaneously, and later the Atellanes, named for the Oscan city of Atella, in which already Greek influences made themselves felt. But these early starts toward a primitive literature vanished entirely from the canvas when Hellenism made its way into Rome and Greek education became the shibboleth of the privileged castes.

The first poets, who are usually regarded as the founders of Roman literature, were Livius Andronicus, Gnaeus Naevius and Quintus Ennius, three Greeks, the first of them a manumitted slave who translated Homer into Latin. It is a unique phenomenon that a people that played in history such a long and world-dominating part should owe the beginnings of its literature to foreigners. Plautus and Terence, the immediate successors of these three, were completely permeated by the Hellenic spirit and presented in their work chiefly paraphrases of Greek originals. Moreover, Terence came from Carthage and was brought to Rome as a slave, where he was later freed by his master in recognition of his merit.

But the opportunities for the development of dramatic art were not the same in Rome as in Greece, and especially in Athens. In Hellas the drama was able to attain great heights only because its natural development was subjected to no external restraints. Every art requires the utmost conceivable freedom in order to maintain its life at its full greatness—dramatic art more than any other. Such freedom never existed in Rome. In Athens there was a most intimate connection between the theater and the public life of the community, and even a Pericles, like any other man, had to endure complacently the attacks from the stage. In Rome such audacity would have been regarded as assault upon the sanctity of the state. When one of the first dramatists in Roman literature, the Greek Naevius, dared, in one of his comedies, to ridicule a distinguished patrician, he was forced to make public apology and sent into exile, where he died. For this reason the drama could never strike root among the people. What interest could the average Roman find in it? The stuff that was presented to him on the stage was borrowed from the life of a foreign people in whose mental and spiritual experience he was not able to participate. Material which would have been able to seize and hold his attention, the representation of the actual occurrences of public life in which he himself was involved, was banned from the stage.

The poets of the time of the republic were completely under the domination of the Hellenic literature, and by far the greater part of their work is confined to the more or less free translation of original Greek texts. The single literary type which then and later showed a degree of independence was the satire, especially after Lucillius had given it the form of the satiric poem, in which, of course, he also took his hint from Greek prototypes. Under the empire literature fell completely under the patronage of the court. Even its most important representatives, Virgil, Horace, Ovid, Tibullus, Propertius, could not free themselves from these unworthy fetters, and despite their ability were compelled to burn incense before the emperor and his favorites and to celebrate their godlike virtues. Thus the famous and greatly over-praised *Aeneid* of Virgil, in which he tried—in imitation of Homer—to create for the Romans a national epic, would probably never have been written if it had not occurred to the poet to elevate the Trojan Aeneas to the position of progenitor of the Julian family from which the Emperor Augustus was descended. From the circumstance that Virgil, in his will, directed that his still unpublished heroic poem should be burned, one could almost conclude that the poet had in an outburst of self-respect felt ashamed of his debasement. The poets of the Golden Age were separately and collectively dependent on the rich and the powerful in the state, whose favor could be purchased only by self-abasement and contemptible flattery. After Messala, Maecenas, Augustus had gathered about them whole courts of poets who basked in the gracious effulgence of their patrons, it became in time the fashion for every rich upstart to keep his own poets, for whose success he provided and who in turn attended to his deification. Horace, who always tried to resist the enticements of Augustus (whom, nevertheless, he deified most unworthily), has confided to us in his *Epistles* how the prosaic need of bread spurred him to poetic creation. Having told us how fate drove him from his "good Athens" back to Rome, the poet comes to his confession:

> When from my service there Philippi summoned me homeward,
> Dispirited, wings clipped, robbed of the herds in my pastures,
> Yes, of the pastures themselves, then grim-poverty, shameless,
> Drove me to verse-making. Now that I have means to live by
> Where is there hemlock enough to cleanse me completely,
> If it should seem to me better to sleep than to make verses?

This peculiar confession of one of the greatest Roman poets, which is not wanting in inner tragedy, is characteristic of the conditions of the time. To worm into a poet's post was the dearest wish of a horde of hunger-driven beings who had acquired a more or less thorough education in Greek and now tried to find a market for it by reciting rhymed flatteries to the great for wages. In the Golden Age it was practically the profession of the poet to renounce his manhood and become a salaried flatterer of the rich and powerful. One need but peruse the repulsive adulation of their patrons by Martial and Statius to realize to what a state literature had come in that age, when everything was for sale. It is significant that it was just the most horrible and cruel despots who were most glorified by their poets. Caesarism rested like a mountainous weight on the whole of public life; it transformed the nation into a horde of lackeys among whose leaders the poets took first place. The situation became ever more pitiful and revolting as the inner disruption under the shameless dominion of the Caesars progressed. Persius, Petronius, and especially Juvenal, have pictured for us the general moral foulness of their time. Juvenal in particular was a first-rate depicter of customs, and his satires, especially the sixth, display an actually uncanny power of description.

If one takes the literature of Rome as a whole, one comes to the conviction that it is poorer in independent productions than any other and cannot endure the slightest comparison with the rich and creative literature of the Hellenes. It is entirely dependent on the latter, and its representatives, with a very few exceptions, set themselves with a truly slavish diligence at the imitation of the Greeks. Even so splendid a work as the *Golden Ass* of Apuleius, which without doubt ranks among the proudest contributions of Roman authorship, would never have come into being without the intellectual stimulation and constructive power of the Greeks. The loveliest part of that work, the charming episode of Cupid and Psyche, shows this with the utmost clarity. Only in the writing of history, which appealed more to the practical Roman than did the flowery pomp of poetry, was a certain originality of presentation noticeable, especially when the writer was dealing with events within his own experience. But even here one must not overlook the fact that the "Roman idea" lay at the foundation of almost all of the writings.

In philosophy the Romans were even more dependent on the Greeks than in anything else. They enriched the world by not a single idea, but were content to pursue old lines of thought and to reproduce them in weakened form. And one must not think of the schools of the philosophers in Athens and other Grecian cities. Such phenomena were altogether unknown in Rome. Here no Socrates spoke publicly to all the citizens; philosophy was at home only in the palaces of the rich, for whom it was the fashion of the moment, as were art and literature. The patriots of the Old Roman party fought philosophy with the same virulence they had displayed toward Hellenic art. In 173 B.C. the adherents of the doctrines of Epicurus were expelled from Rome; twelve years later all philosophers and rhetoricians were banished from the capital, because there was recognized in their teachings a danger to the state. The penetration of Hellenism into Rome gave wider scope to philosophy, but its teachers were always regarded with a certain distrust, and persecutions of philosophers, especially of the Stoics, were carried on under almost all of the Roman emperors.

394 NATIONALISM AND CULTURE

Of the philosophic systems of the Greeks only Epicurianism, Stoicism, and Skepticism found wide acceptance among the educated Romans. But the adherents of these doctrines did not enrich the concepts of the Greeks with any ideas of their own. When they attempted originality they lost themselves in a shallow eclecticism which entirely lacked inner force of conviction. There was a time when Cicero was honored as a profound thinker; today, it has long been recognized that he never produced a single original idea but confined himself to preparing the most superficial compilations conceivable from the works of Greek thinkers—many of whom were first thus made known to us, even if in greatly weakened form. Mauthner has rightly said: "Cicero would have no place in a history of philosophy, at the most only in a history of the history of philosophy or a history of philosophical terminology; he whose vanity was almost greater than his later fame had definitely committed himself to dependence on the Greeks—himself poor in thoughts, rich only in unminted words." [6]

The illuminating didactic poem of Lucretius, *De rerum natura* ("Concerning the Nature of Things"), is without doubt a splendid presentation of the doctrines of Epicurus, but it is nothing more. This holds also for the line of thought of Pliny, Lucian and the other Roman Epicureans. Much the same may be said of the Roman Stoics; they likewise contributed to their doctrine no ideas of their own, and by far their greatest importance lay in the field of political life. Most of the satirists were found among the Stoics, and in Rome satire offered the only opportunity of hurling stones from concealment at the windows of the high-placed. The Stoics strove for a reform in social conditions; for this reason they sometimes drew upon themselves the wrath of the despots, which often expressed itself in rigorous persecutions. Many of them went pretty far in their ideas; for example, Seneca opposed slavery, and in many of his letters, especially in the nineteenth, reached genuinely socialistic conclusions. Of course we must not neglect to mention that one cannot very well harmonize Seneca's life with his teachings; he had to face in the Senate the accusation that he had accumulated his wealth (he left behind 300,000,000 sesterces, say about 15 million dollars) by wangling legacies and practicing the vilest usury.

There is no field of intellectual life in which the Romans distinguished themselves by originality and independence of thought. We must, therefore, count it as a special merit that they had such capacity for appropriating the discoveries and inventions of others and exploiting them for their own purposes. Their intellectual dependence on the Greeks appears clearly in every field of their scientific activity. At no point did they progress beyond the elementary foundations of Greek science; in many respects they fell far short even of this. This held good especially for their

[6] *Der Atheismus usw.* Band I, p. 161.

astronomy and their conception of the structure of the universe. From the Alexandrians they took over the Ptolemaic system, by which the inspired conception of Aristarchus of Samos was pushed into the background for a whole thousand years until Copernicus led the human intellect back into the right path. Of course, in Rome, science, too, merely served the interests of the state. And in accord with this all education was also debased, reaching under the empire that state of insipid, outworn windiness that Schlosser has so strikingly depicted:

> The universal regimentation of the intellect had expelled all vigor and naturalness from life; science was just the handmaid of vain and vulgar ends; the numerous schools, teachers and students were victims in equal degree of empty imagination, overbearing pride, false taste and lack of conviction. Behind the lauded elegance of conversation and the intellectual playing with concepts, ideas and information, lurked hardness of heart, emptiness of soul, selfishness of sentiment and extremely superficial understanding.

A people among whom political effort was rated much higher than any contribution of intellect, could achieve nothing different. Just as religion was to the Romans nothing but the epitome of spiritual bondage, so also in the state they revered the principle of political and social bondage which culminated in the complete subjection of man to the political machine. That the state idea, which with them rested from the very beginning on a military basis, gradually developed into Caesarism and reached its highest point in the elevation of the emperor to the station of an actual God, was the natural consequence of that strict authority principle which will submit to no examination and is inaccessible to every human approach. Rudolf von Jehering, the well-known law scholar, passed his judgment on the Romans in these words:

> The Roman character with its virtues and its faults may be designated as a system of disciplined egoism. The chief principle underlying this system is that the subordinate must be sacrificed to the higher, the individual to the state, the particular instance to the abstract rule, the moment to the permanent condition. A people among whom in the presence of the highest love of freedom the virtue of self-subjection has still become second nature, is called to mastery over others. But the price of Roman greatness was surely a dear one. The insatiable demon of Roman selfishness sacrificed everything for its ends: the blood and happiness of its own citizens as readily as the nationality of foreign peoples. The world which belongs to it is a soulless world, robbed of its loveliest possessions, a world ruled not by human beings, but by abstract maxims and rules—a huge mechanism admirable for the firmness, the regularity and the certainty with which it operates, for the power which it develops, crushing to bits everything which opposes it, but just a machine, whose master was at the same time its slave.[7]

[7] *Geist des Römischen Rechts.* Leipzig, 1852. Vol. I, p. 298.

A state whose whole history was founded on the principle of conquest and which through all phases of its long historical development adhered to this principle with undeviating consistency came of necessity to a complete surrender of every human consideration. War was its proper element, brutal robbery its life purpose, to which every other was subordinated. Thus came into being that shameful bondage which was in fact the essence of "true Romanism." A state in which, from the first, every citizen had to be a soldier and in which no citizen could be clothed with public office who had not taken part in at least ten battles, could but brutalize its population. In fact the Romans were a people of savage disposition. Even the invasion of Hellenism was able to change this but little, since its influence reached effectively only a small privileged minority and hardly touched the great masses.[8]

In two fields, however, the Romans revealed an originality of thought and its practical application which no one can justly refuse to recognize—though it is true that these were concerned with social institutions which can hardly be said to have advanced culture. The Romans were the real creators of militarism and the inventors of that brutal and soulless system which we call "Roman law" and which is still today the theoretical basis of the legal constitutions of all so-called "civilized states." Roman law, based only on cold-blooded calculation of the most purely material interests, admitting into its theory no ethical considerations whatever, was the natural result of the Roman state concept. The Roman state was a military state, a power-state in the strictest sense; it knew only one right, the right of the stronger. Therefore Roman law could be nothing else than the most brutal violation of every idea of natural right. It laid the foundation for the dreary formalism of our modern lawbooks, in which vital being is smothered under abstract maxims. And this was not changed at all by the so-called "equality before the law," which was always a lie practically, and theoretically had in view only the equality of slaves who

[8] Richard Wagner, who in his revolutionary days recognized very clearly the significance of freedom for culture in general and for art in particular, in his work, *Kunst und Revolution* ("Art and Revolution"), broke out thus about the inner savagery of Romanism: "The Romans, whose national art early gave way before the developed art of the Greeks, employed the services of Grecian architects, sculptors and painters; their wits took up Greek rhetoric and versification; great public amphitheaters were opened, but not to the gods and the mythical heroes, not to the free dancers and singers of the sacred choruses; rather, wild beasts, lions, panthers and elephants, had to tear each other to tatters to delight Roman eyes; gladiators—slaves who had been trained to strength and skill—had to ravish the Roman ear with their death-rattle. These brutal world-conquerors took delight only in positive reality; their imagination could deal only with the materially actual. They permitted the philosopher who timidly fled from public life to devote himself to abstract thought; as for themselves, they loved to give themselves over in public to displays of concrete murder, to see before them examples of actual, physical human suffering."

found themselves at the same level of degradation. Heinrich Heine, who from the bottom of his soul hated the brutal inhumanity of the concepts of Roman law, poured out his heart in these words:

> What a frightful book is the *Corpus Juris*, the Bible of egoism! I have always hated their legal code as I have hated the Romans themselves. These robbers wished to safeguard their booty, and what they won by the sword they tried to protect by the law; therefore the Roman was at the same time soldier and lawyer, presenting a blend of the most revolting type. Actually we have to thank those Roman thieves for the theory of property—which had previously been just a fact—and the development of that doctrine in all its despicable consistency is that lauded Roman law which lies at the base of all our modern state institutions, although it stands in glaring contradiction to religion, morals, human feeling and reason.[9]

Never before had any legislation given to the concept of property a form so inhuman, cruel and egoistic. "Property is the right to use and to misuse one's possessions," declares the Roman law. This view, which is still today the legal basis of every exploitation and every economic monopoly, was subject to no limitations except those based on reasons of state. All attempts of later experts in law to cloak or to mitigate the cynical brutality of this declaration have been but futile raising of dust-clouds. Proudhon gave this striking expression:

> They have tried to justify the word "misuse" by explaining that it must not be taken to mean an arbitrary misuse in defiance of morals, but merely as indicating the unlimited control of the owner over his possessions. That is an empty, meaningless distinction, which merely serves to accentuate the sacredness of property, and by which the pleasure of possession is neither destroyed nor disturbingly affected. The owner may let his fruit rot on the trees, he can sow his fields with salt, he can pour the milk of his cows on the sand, he can convert a vineyard into a desert, turn a park into a vege-table garden, quite at his own pleasure. Is this all misuse, or is it not? In every consideration of property use and misuse are hidden together.[10]

Who accords to property such power must necessarily rate the worth of a man very low. This is shown especially in the Roman law of debt and in the position given to the head of a family. According to the law of the twelve tables a creditor had the right to hail a debtor before the court and, if no one would go security for him or assume his debt, to sell him into slavery. If several creditors had claims to present against the same debtor, then the law gave them the right to kill him and cut him in pieces. The simple objective fact of the debt was decisive, and no con-

[9] *Memoiren*, 1854.
[10] P. J. Proudhon, *Qu'est-ce que la propriété ou recherches sur le principe du droit du gouvernement.* Paris, 1840.

siderations of humanity could be urged against it. The right of possession
of an owner stood above the life and freedom of a man.

One finds the same pitiless feature also in Roman family law. The
head of the house held power of life and death over the members of his
family. He could expose a child at its birth or sell it into slavery; he could
also pass judgment of death on any of his dependents. On the other hand,
a son could make no complaint against his father, since he was regarded
merely as the father's bondsman. This dependence he could end only by
founding a household of his own, which he could do only by his father's
permission. Hegel, himself an unreserved advocate of the authority
principle, remarks strikingly: "For the harshness which the Roman
suffered from the state he was compensated by the harshness which he
exercised in his family—serf on the one hand, despot on the other. This
constituted the greatness of Rome; its peculiarity was harsh insistence on
the unity of the individual with the state, with the law of the state, with
the mandate of the state." [11]

The whole criminal law of the Romans was one of deliberate brutality
and barbarous cruelty. One could object that cruelty in the imposition of
punishment was at that time the general custom; but what gives its
peculiar tone to the Roman law of punishment is the circumstance that
here, too, every detail was patterned on reasons of state, and every human
consideration regarded with cold indifference. Thus in a long series of
cases children could be punished for the faults of their parents; about
which the wise Cicero placidly remarks: "The harshness that punishes
children for the misdeeds of their parents grieves me, but still it is a wise
provision of our laws, for by it the father is by means of the strongest of
all bonds, by means of the love that he feels for his children, bound to
the interest of the state."

These provisions and some others were in later times made milder,
but the inner core of their nature was not changed. What was the lot of a
slave under such a system of laws is easily guessed. The slave was completely without rights and was, indeed, hardly regarded as human; at
best he was thought of as one who had been human. The slightest disobedience, the slightest insubordination, or even things for which he was
not responsible at all, were requited with bestial vengeance. Such an unfortunate might have his tongue torn out, both hands chopped off, his eyes
put out, boiling lead poured down his throat; after such unspeakable
tortures he might be nailed to the cross or thrown to wild beasts to be
devoured—all this by the unquestioned right of the master.

The admirers of the Roman state idea make every effort to overbalance
the lack of any deep feeling for culture among the Romans, which even
they are compelled to recognize, by unstinted praise of the "spirit of

[11] *Philosophie der Geschichte.*

Roman legislation" which, regarded as a work of art, they find actually astounding. But against this, even, there is much to be said. No less a man than Theodor Mommsen in his *Römische Geschichte* passes the following judgment on Roman law:

> Men are accustomed to praise the Romans as the people especially endowed for jurisprudence and to regard with astonished admiration their excellent systems of laws as if it were a mystic gift from heaven, perhaps chiefly to spare themselves some of their shame at the contemptible status of their own laws. A glance at the incomparably shaky and undeveloped Roman criminal law should reveal the untenability of these muddy notions even to those to whom it seems too simple to say that a healthy people will have healthy laws; a diseased people, diseased ones.

Only such a state could arrive at so completely developed a system of militarism. Militarism and a military establishment are not the same thing, although the existence of a standing army is to be regarded as the first prerequisite of militarism. Militarism is to be appraised first of all as a psychic condition. It is the renunciation of one's own thought and will, the transformation of man into a dead automaton guided and set in motion from without, carrying out blindly every command without being conscious of his own personal responsibility. In one word, militarism is the meanest and most degraded form of that slave-spirit raised to the status of a national virtue which despises all the rules of reason and is devoid of all human dignity. Only a state like the Roman, where man was valued merely as a mechanical part of an all-assimilating machine, and brutal force was esteemed the highest principle of policy, could bring about such a cruel distortion of the human mind and so lay the foundations of the shameful system that still lies like a mountain weight on the peoples and is even today the deadly foe of all higher cultural development. Militarism and Roman law are the inevitable results of the "Roman idea," that conception which is today confusing minds more than ever. No revolution has thus far been able either to chain the "Roman idea" or to cut the cord that binds us to a long-vanished past. For the Greeks, the institutions of their communal life were a means to an end. In Rome, the state was an end in itself; man existed for the sake of his institutions, whose slave and vassal he was.

Much has been written about the downfall of the Roman empire, and every conceivable explanation of that gigantic collapse has been brought forward. Some see the cause in the "over-refined culture," others in the utter neglect of morals. Nowadays one school has much to say about a "subversion of the soul of the race"—whatever this empty phrase may mean—and tries hard to represent the decline of Rome as a "race catastrophe"—though in this, the fact that Rome itself issued from a so-called "racial chaos," which this did not prevent the Romans from playing their historic part in world history to the end, is deliberately overlooked. Yet the actual causes of the downfall of the Roman empire are much more clearly apparent than are those of most other historical events. If one examines all the details of this gigantic collapse without allowing oneself to be misled by artificially constructed preconceptions, one must reach the same conclusion as the English historian, Gibbon: "The wonder is, not that Rome fell, but that the downfall was so long delayed." But even for this delay there is an explanation: the Roman state machine was so strongly constructed and men were so universally convinced of its unshakable stability that it, so to speak, ran itself and overcame all obstacles for a long time after its foundation had quite rotted away. Rome was the victim of its own blind power mania and its inevitable accompaniments. Ceaselessly, in deluded blindness the leaders of the Roman state strove to extend the boundaries of their dominions, and no means was for them too brutal or too revolting. They themselves released the catastrophe that was one day to overwhelm them.

The fabulous prodigality of the privileged classes at the time of the downfall, the unscrupulous exploitation of every people, the complete demoralization of public and private life, were not the results of a physical racial degeneration, but the inevitable consequences of that cruel insatiability which had thrown an entire world into chains. The end of such a policy was necessarily complete disruption of all social life.

The *might* of Rome ground to powder everything that came in contact with it, without distinction of people or race. Even the Nordic peoples showed themselves in this matter incapable of resistance, and their "Germanic blood" afforded them no protection against the universal corruption of a system of oppression carried to the bitter end. At best they could only get the cruel machine temporarily into their own hands, and, doing this, they became at the same time its unconditional slaves and were ground up in its pitiless cog-wheels just as all before them had been.

The signs of the downfall were clearly recognizable in the time of the republic. The empire was only the heir of the republican war policy and brought it to its full expansion. So long as it was concerned with the subjugation of the small populations on the Italian peninsula there was little profit in it for the conquerors, for Italy was a relatively poor country. But the old conditions were fundamentally changed after the Second Punic War. The enormous riches which flowed into Rome led to the development of a gigantic capitalistic robber-economy which completely destroyed all the foundations of the old social structure. Salvioli, who followed every ramification of this system to its last details, convincingly describes its consequences:

After the splendid victories which opened Africa and Asia to the Romans the realm attained its widest expansion. Especially out of Asia, that fairy-land of art and industry, that high school of luxury and taste, that unquench-able source of advancement for farmers-of-state and proconsuls, the most pitiless and brutal force squeezed a stream of gold and silver. This did not cease to drench Italy till the source itself was exhausted. The treasures which had been accumulated in the Orient, in Gaul, in the whole world, and those which the miner's craft still produces today, all were poured together into Rome as spoils of war, as tribute, as the fruit of plundering, and as taxes; all the other parts of Italy received their share, even if a modest one, of the general prosperity. Rome became and remained for some centuries the great market for metallic wealth. A raging transport of power-lust and ava-rice had seized upon this simple warrior-peasant people, so that it measured the fame of its commanders by the quantity of gold and silver which they brought to their triumphal processions. And these made it their practice to bleed conquered peoples white and to sell to allies the favor of Rome at the highest price they could get. To this avarice nothing was any longer sacred; right and reason were shamelessly trodden into the mud. King Ptolemy of Cyprus was known to be the possessor of a well-filled state treasury and of royal ceremonial vessels; so a law was promptly passed which gave the Roman Senate the right to inherit from a wealthy "ally" during his lifetime. The Senate regarded the treasures of all the world merely as Roman private property, the conquered could not call a penny their own. . . . This colossal stream was not allowed to flow in quite without interruption; victorious commanders, proconsuls and tax-farmers, who were all hungry for the riches of conquered kings and peoples, saw to this. Thousands of traders and ad-venturers followed the legions, paying cash for the booty which had been divided among the soldiers and taking from the conquered countries anything the commanders might have left.[12]

Thus arose that disastrous regime of speculators and chiselers whose sole purpose in life was gain, and who strove to extract a profit from every-thing without caring in the least what the consequences were. The most shameful usury developed into a murderous system which, slowly perhaps, but surely, must at last undermine the very foundations of the collective economic life. There arose great capitalists and capitalistic stock companies which farmed from the state the collection of taxes from entire countries and provinces. This saved the state much labor and vexation, but the last drop of blood was pumped out of the veins of the countries that fell into the claws of these vampires, for they spared nothing that aroused their avarice. In the same way they farmed the departments of the state and the mining enterprises from the government; they supplied the legions with the necessary equipment, and constantly amassed greater capital; they organized the slave trade on mercantile principles and supplied the

[12] J. Salvioli, *Der Kapitalismus im Altertum*. Stuttgart, 1922, p. 26.

great works with their human material; in a word, they were always there, if there was profit to win.

The virtuous men of the republic participated in these robberies with the utmost complacency and amassed great fortunes as usurers, slave-dealers or real estate speculators. Cato, who in our schools is still honored as the personified virtue of ancient Romanism, was in reality a shameless hypocrite and cold-blooded usurer, to whom no means was too reprehensible for furthering his selfish ends. He sounded, one might say, the correct note for his time when he coined the saying: "It is the first and most sacred duty of man to make money"! Plutarch puts into his mouth as his very last utterance the characteristic words: "The business of the conquerors pleased the gods, but the business of the conquered pleased Cato." Still, Cato constituted no exception among the "virtuous Romans" of his day. Even the famous tyrannicide, Brutus, whom tradition clothes with all the trimmings of strictest uprightness, was quite as heartless a usurer as Cato and thousands of others, and his business practices were often of so questionable a character that even Cicero, that undefeated attorney of usurers and speculators, avoided looking after his affairs in court.

By far the most important cause, however, that helped to seal the doom of Rome was the ruin of the small landholders, who had been the strongest bulwark of Roman superiority. The constant and successful wars forced the small peasantry, hungry for foreign riches, ever farther along that dangerous road which has thus far always been the fatal road of the conqueror. The crushing of the Etruscan cities in the north and the conquest of the Grecian colonies in the south of the peninsula had already powerfully stirred the avarice of the Romans. Then, when they first successfully waged war in the out-land and began to pursue a world policy, everything else followed of itself. A world policy and a prosperous peasantry are things which in the long run cannot be reconciled. The peasant who husbands his farm is grown into the soil that he tills. Continuous war, with the uninterrupted withdrawal of thousands of men from husbandry, must in the course of time work ever more disastrously. A system under which twenty-five out of every hundred men were from the seventeenth to the forty-fifth year of their age always under arms must inevitably lead to the downfall of the ancient peasant husbandry. Moreover, the state had openly raised the trade of robbery to a policy, and this accumulation of wealth by force seemed to the peasants more profitable than the tiresome tilling of the soil. So the peasant gradually became estranged from the land. During the long wars the Roman peasantry slowly bled to death. Contemporary writers even assert that by the end of the Second Punic War Rome had lost half of its earlier population. Along with this, small landholding moved more and more swiftly toward

its end, and there developed in its stead the *latifundia,* of which Pliny
says quite truthfully that they were the downfall of Italy and the
provinces.

In the earliest days of Rome the land question already played a significant role, a fact which found clear enough expression in the long
struggles between patricians and plebeians. In this stern conflict the
plebeians at last won equal rights with their former opponents, and
the famous Licinian-Sextine laws, whose wording has come down to us
only in mutilated form, provided that thereafter the two classes should
share alike in the division of public lands. The law also provided that the
larger landholders must employ a prescribed number of free laborers
proportionate to the number of the serfs each employed. After the end of
the Second Punic War, however, these provisions were, in general, not
enforced. Hundreds of small farms lay quite untilled because their owners
had fallen in battle. The state had, moreover, come into the possession of
vast tracts of land by the confiscation of the property of all of the partisans
of Hannibal in Italy. The greater part of these fell into the hands of
speculators, and land speculation assumed horrible forms. Contemporary
writers are unanimous in their description of the base devices by which
the small owners were robbed of their holdings.

> Unsated avarice
> Moves back the boundary-stones of neighboring fields.
> Thou over-ridest everywhere
> The peasants' hedges. Outcast wander forth,
> Husband and wife, upon their backs
> Their goods; in their arms, miserable children.[13]

Even though in some parts of the realm the small holdings were not
completely abolished, nevertheless many thousands of small landowners
were ruined by the plan for managing the latifundia. The latifundia,
when they were not allowed to lie fallow or converted into pasture land,
were tilled by so-called "serfs," whose lot was the hardest of all of the
slaves. By this sort of husbandry the productivity of agriculture was
constantly diminished, as always happens with slave labor. Great masses
of free laborers, because of this slave-labor, were deprived of their means
of subsistence; while the importation of grain from Sicily and Africa completely wiped out innumerable small peasants.

In the cities a similar picture presents itself. There slave industry in
the homes of the rich cut off the means of living for small artisans and
plunged them into the abyss with the small peasants and agricultural
laborers. These latter wandered by thousands into the cities and swelled
the ranks of the ruined beggar proletariat that had completely lost the

---

[13] Horace, *Odes.* Book II.

habit of productive occupation and served the state only as bearers of babes. This homeless, idle, purposeless mass, which had become used to living on the refuse of the rich, offered to political adventurers and up-starts of every sort a claque whose paid support was useful to their avaricious plans. Already under the republic the sale of their votes had become for the proletariat a comfortable source of income. The rich bought the votes of the poorer citizens and so were enabled to hold the most important positions and to bequeath them to their children, so that certain state offices remained almost constantly in the possession of the same families. A candidacy for a public post was quite hopeless unless the candidate was in a position to bribe the electors by the distribution of gifts or the exhibition of public games—usually gladiatorial combats.

Under such conditions it was inevitable that the influence of victorious commanders upon the course of political affairs should become constantly greater, thus first smoothing the road to Caesarism. In fact the change from republic to monarchy was accomplished in Rome without any difficulty worth mentioning. Men like Caesar, Crassus, Pompey, expended enormous sums in molding public opinion. The later Caesars made use of these same methods, making of the proverbial *panem et circenses* a buttress of inside politics. Cruel gladiatorial combats had to be used to keep in good humor the depraved proletarian masses of the cities. Thousands upon thousands of the strongest slaves were carefully trained in special schools to slaughter one another in the arena before the eyes of brutalized crowds, or to measure their strength in combat with that of starving wild beasts. "Every sort of monstrous horror," says Friedländer, "took place in the arena; for there was hardly a form of torture or fright-ful death known to history or literature that was not offered to the people in the amphitheater for their entertainment." The murderous games often lasted for weeks; thus it is said that Trajan once had 10,000 slave com-batants driven into the arena, where the gruesome exhibition continued for a hundred and twenty-three days. What a devastating effect the constant viewing of such revolting cruelty had on the character of the people needs no description.

It was a necessary consequence of the continuous wars that Rome became in time unable to enlist from the ranks of her free population enough men fit to bear arms. Julius Caesar had, in fact, begun to incor-porate in his armies hired foreign soldiers. Later commanders developed the employment of mercenaries into a complete system and created by its use that military monarchy, the seeds of which the republic had planted. But the foreign mercenaries, who later were made up chiefly of Celts, Germans and Syrians, lacked those ideological assumptions in which the ancient Romans were reared and trained. To them the thievery of the soldier was merely a profitable trade; the "Roman idea" troubled them very little, since its essence was quite alien to them. Therefore the Caesars had always to take care to keep their pretorian hordes contented, if they did not wish to imperil their rulership. The last words of the Emperor Severus to his two sons, "Keep your soldiers loyal and care for no one else in the world!" were the watchword of Caesarism.

But since none of the Caesars was quite sure of his rulership and had always to protect himself against rivals from the ranks of his generals and his favorites, the army became a constantly more expensive instrument, and its maintenance a constantly greater burden. And so the pretorians gradually became the controlling element in the state, and the Caesars were often no better than their prisoners. They supported some rulers and hurled others from the throne according as they saw greater profit from the one side or the other. Every election of an emperor was accompanied by a thorough plundering of the state treasury, which must then be refilled by the employment of every forcible means. Thus the provinces were constantly, and at ever shorter intervals, squeezed dry like a sponge; and this gradually led to a complete exhaustion of all economic forces. To this must be added that Roman capitalism developed no sort of productive activity, but lived only by plunder, which necessarily hastened the catastrophe.

The farther Caesarism proceeded along its perilous course, the larger became the number of parasites who fastened themselves on the mass of the people. It went so far that emperors had to pledge their "personal property" to the exchequer or to pawnbrokers to raise money for their soldiers. Marcus Aurelius was once compelled, when he needed money, to sell at public auction all his portable possessions including the art treasures of his palaces and the costly wardrobe of the empress. Others found it more profitable to make away with wealthy contemporaries in order to confiscate their possessions. Nero, for instance, when he learned that one-half of the soil of Africa was in the hands of only six persons, had all six of them murdered so that he might inherit from them.

All the earlier attempts to put an end to the evil were without result and were suppressed by the owning class with bloody cruelty. Thus, the two Gracchi had to pay for their daring with their lives; and it went no better with Cataline and his fellow conspirators, whose real objective has never been made entirely clear. And the numerous slave revolts which periodically convulsed the realm, and of which the uprising under Spartacus seriously endangered Rome itself, were all without lasting result. This could have been because the majority of the slaves were filled with the same spirit as were their masters. Here can be applied also the saying of Emerson, that the curse of slavery is that one end of the chain is forged round the ankle of the slave, the other round that of his owner. The slave revolts in Rome were uprisings of mistreated and desperate men who lacked any lofty purpose. So if a brief success was achieved by the revolting slaves they knew no better course than to imitate the role of their former masters. So utterly had the spirit that breathed out of Rome corrupted men and weakened in them all impulse toward freedom. There could be no talk of a mutual alliance of the oppressed, because even the beggar-proletariat of Rome regarded the slaves as inferiors. And so it came about that slaves had to help the possessing class to suppress the Gracchi, and proletarians helped them to put down the revolt of Spartacus.

What could be the end of a status where all intellectual power was crippled and every ethical principle trodden into the mud? As a matter of fact the whole history of Roman Caesarism was a long chain of frightful horrors. Treason, assassination, beastly cruelty, crazy confusion of ideas and morbid greed prevailed in tottering Rome. The rich gave themselves over to the most excessive indulgence and the poor knew no other desire than to be able to participate, ever so modestly, in that indulgence. A little gang of monopolists ruled the realm and organized the exploitation of the world according to well-established principles. At the court of the Caesars one palace revolution followed another, one bloody outrage wiped out its forerunner. And everywhere peeped the eye of the snooper; no one was secure in his most private affairs. An army of spies infested the land and sowed distrust and secret suspicion in every heart.

Never before had the spirit of authority celebrated such triumphs. Rome first provided the conditions for that contemptible status which we might call slavery on principle. And while the spirit of basest slavery was completely unmanning the masses of the people, the delusion of grandeur of the rulers was growing in inverse proportion, because no one dared to oppose their cruel whims. The most honored members of the Roman Senate, overcome with awe, threw themselves in the dust before the God-emperors and paid them divine honors. A Caligula could cause his horse to be chosen a member of the sacerdotal college; a Heliogabalus could have his made a Roman consul. Human cowardice swallowed even this.

Upon this road there could be no longer any halt. In insane blindness Rome had wasted the wealth of the world; and when this was quite exhausted its power collapsed like a decayed building in whose timbers the worms have long been at work. For such a people liberation by its own effort was no longer possible, because every earnest resolution, every independent impulse had been crushed out of it. Under the long-continued domination of a power system developed to the point of madness, serfdom had become for it a habit, degradation had become a principle. The revolt against the "Roman idea" came in the form of Christianity. But dying Rome revenged herself even in her hour of dissolution by infecting with her poisonous breath the very movement in which it seemed that new hope for an enslaved world might be looked for, and transforming it into a church. So out of the world dominion of the Roman state there developed the world dominion of the Roman church; in Papism Caesarism celebrates its resurrection.

Chapter 7

ROME AND GREECE AS SYMBOLS. VISIGOTHIC FEUDALISM IN SPAIN. THE
ARABIAN CULTURE. THE PRIME OF THE SPANISH CITIES AND THE AU-
TONOMY OF THE TOWNS. POLITICAL DECAY AND ZENITH OF MOORISH
CULTURE. THE WAR BETWEEN CROSS AND CRESCENT. THE SPANISH
FUEROS AND CITY CONSTITUTIONS. THE CORTES. FEDERALISTIC SPIRIT
OF SPAIN. THE VICTORY OF THE UNIFIED NATIONAL STATE. THE IN-
QUISITION AS INSTRUMENT OF POLITICAL POWER. CONQUEST OF THE
COMUÑEROS AND GERMANIAS. THE DETERIORATION OF CULTURE UNDER
DESPOTISM. THE PERIOD OF FREE CITIES IN ITALY. UPSURGE OF THE
INTELLECTUAL LIFE. EXPANSION OF THE ARTS AND CRAFTS. THE GUILDS
AND THE TIME OF FEDERALISM. THE ADVOCATES OF NATIONAL UNITY
AS DEADLY FOES OF FEDERATION. MAZZINI'S DREAM AND PROUDHON'S
SENSE OF REALITY. ABSOLUTISM AS DESTROYER OF FRENCH FOLK CUL-
TURE. LITERATURE AND LANGUAGE IN THE STRAIT-JACKET OF DES-
POTISM. THE REGIMENTATION OF INDUSTRY. NATIONAL UNITY AND
THE END OF INTELLECTUAL CULTURE IN GERMANY. BISMARCKISM.
GLANCES INTO THE FUTURE.

GREECE and Rome are merely symbols. Their whole history is just a
single instance of the great truth that the less the political sense is developed in a people, the richer are the forms of its cultural life; and the
more political endeavors get the upper hand, the deeper sinks the general
level of spiritual and social culture, the more completely natural creative
impulse, all deep spiritual feeling—in a word, everything human—dies
out. The spiritual is supplanted by a dead technique in affairs which takes
account only of calculations and neglects all ethical principles. Cold
mechanization of forces takes the place of vital influx in all social activities.
Organization of social forces is no longer a means to the higher ends of
the community, something that has become organic and is always in flux;
it becomes a dreary end-in-itself and leads gradually to a retardation of
all higher creative activity. And the more man becomes aware of the
inner incapacity, which is only the result of this mechanization, the more
desperately he clings to the dead form, and for any remedy looks to that
technique which is devouring his soul and laying waste his mind. Rabin-

dranath Tagore, who as an Asiatic surveys western civilization with something of detachment, has set forth the deeper meaning of these events
in pithy words:

> When the organization-machine begins to embrace wide territory and
> machine workers become parts of the machine, then the human person dis-
> solves into a phantom, everything that was human becomes machine and
> turns the great wheel of politics without the slightest feeling of sympathy
> and moral responsibility. It may well happen that even in this soulless per-
> formance the moral nature of man still tries to assert itself, but the ropes
> and pulleys creak and groan, the threads of the human heart become en-
> tangled in the gears of the human machine, and only with difficulty can the
> moral will call up a pale, mute image of what it was striving for.[1]

Therefore, national-political unity, which always means technique at
the expense of culture, is no nutrient medium for the creative formative
force of a people. It is rather the greatest hindrance to any higher intellectual culture, because it pushes all important social undertakings into
the political field and subjects every social enterprise to the oversight of
the national machine, which stifles in men any urge toward higher ends
and forces all the impulses of social life into definite forms adapted to
the purposes of the national state. The "art of ruling men" has never
been the art of educating men, since it has at its disposal nothing but that
type of intellectual drill which is set upon bringing all life in the state
under a single specific norm. Education means the release of the natural
dispositions and capacities in men for independent development. The
educational drill of the national state strangles this natural expansion of
the inner man by forcing upon him from without matters which, though
originally alien to him, still must be made the leitmotif of his life. The
"national will," which is only a cautious paraphrase of the will to power,
operates always as a crippling force upon every cultural process; where it
overbalances, culture suffers, the sources of creative urge are quenched,
because nourishment has been withdrawn from them to feed the all-
devouring machine of the national state.

Greece brought forth a great culture and enriched mankind for thousands of years, not *in spite of*, but *because of* its political and national
disunion. Because it never knew political unity each separate member
could develop in freedom and could give expression to its own peculiar
character. Greek culture grew great upon the minute division and complete
separation of the efforts at political power. Because the cultural creative
urge which throve so mightily in the Hellenic community, for a long time
greatly outweighted the power-urge of small minorities and so afforded
a much wider scope for personal freedom and independent thought—

[1] *Nationalism*, p. 17.

because of this, and only because of this, the rich diversity of the cultural impulses found an unlimited field of activity and were not crippled against the rigid bars of a unified national state.

Rome knew nothing of this inner cleavage; the notion of political autonomy was entirely foreign to her leading men, and the idea of political unity runs through all the epochs of her long history. In the field of political centralization Rome achieved the highest that a state can achieve; but for just this reason the Romans produced nothing that was culturally important and remained a highly uncreative people to whom it was denied even to penetrate deeply into the meaning of foreign cultural creations. They completely exhausted all the social forces at their disposal in struggles for political power, which became more violent with each success and at last loosed a genuine power-madness; they had respect for no humanity and could find neither time nor understanding for any other endeavors. The natural cultural endowments of the Romans were shipwrecked on the Roman state and its struggle to obtain and hold world dominion. Political technique swallowed all original cultural enterprise and sacrificed all social forces to a ravenous machine, until at last there was nothing left to sacrifice and the soulless mechanism could but collapse of its own weight. This is the inevitable end of every policy of conquest, which Jean Paul so strikingly pictured: "The conqueror: O, how often art thou like thy Rome! Filled with the conquered treasures of the world, filled with statues of the gods and the great, thou art surrounded by deserts and death. About Rome there is nought green but poisonous swamps, everything lies empty and waste and no hamlet looks toward Saint Peter's. Thou alone swellest up with thy sins mid the tumult, as corpses swell up in a storm."

But these phenomena are not confined to Greece and Rome; they recur in every epoch of human history and thus far have led everywhere to the same results. This is a sign that we contemplate here a certain necessity in the course of events which arises of itself from the valuation that a people sets on cultural activity or the pursuit of political enterprises.

Let us cast a glance at the history of Spain. When the Arabs invaded the Iberian peninsula from Africa the kingdom of the Visigoths was already in a condition of internal decay. After their subjugation of the country the Goths had taken away from the conquered inhabitants three-fourths of the land and converted it into endowments for the dead hands of the church and the nobility. From this there developed, especially in the southern part of the country, an overlordship of the great landowners, and with it a crude feudal system under which the productivity of the soil constantly diminished. The country which had once been the granary of Rome became less and less fertile and in a few centuries was transformed into a desert. By the cruel persecutions of the Jews, especially under

Sisebut, who was completely under the influence of the church, economic life was dealt a severe blow, for business and industry lay in great part in the hands of Jewish groups. After Sisebut had caused a law to be proclaimed under which the Jews had only the choice of turning Christian or of being scalped and sold as slaves, one hundred thousand Jews migrated into Gaul and another hundred thousand into Africa, while ninety thousand were baptized. Besides this, there were the endless struggles for the throne in which poison and the dagger, treachery and assassination played no small part. Only so can we explain how the Arabs were able to conquer the country in so short a time and with no resistance worth mentioning.

After the last Gothic king had been decisively defeated by the Arabian general, Tarik, the Arabs and their allies streamed into the country in great hordes, and there developed the first beginnings of that glorious culture-epoch, which made Spain for centuries culturally the foremost land in Europe. This is usually called the period of Arabic culture in Spain, but the designation is perhaps not quite correct, for the Arabs proper constituted only a tiny fraction of the invading Moslems. The Berbers and Syrians were much more numerous, and besides these there came also great numbers of Jews, who took a prominent part in the upbuilding of that great culture. It was chiefly the Arabic language which united these different race and folk elements.

The country which under the Gothic feudalism had been laid completely waste was in a short time transformed into a flourishing garden. By the construction of numerous canals and a system of artificial irrigation the cultivation of the soil was developed to a degree never before seen in Spain and never since reached. In the fruitful fields flourished date-palms, sugarcane, indigo, rice and many other useful plants which the Arabs had introduced. Countless cities and villages covered the glorious country. According to the descriptions of the Arabian chroniclers Spain was in cities the richest country in Europe, the only one in which the traveler, besides numerous villages, could find two or three cities in a single day's journey. On the banks of the Guadalquivir there were in the period of bloom of Moorish culture six great cities, three hundred towns and twelve hundred villages.

In the ore-filled mountain ranges mining reached a pitch which even today it has not regained. In the numerous cities, moreover, handicrafts and industry flourished luxuriantly and spread welfare and the necessities of a higher culture over the whole country. Weaving and spinning alone employed more than two million people. In Cordova alone a hundred and thirty thousand people were supported by the silk industry; the same was true in Seville. The finest fabrics—arras, damask and costly carpets— were produced in countless workshops and, especially in foreign lands, were highly prized. Arabic filigree and inlaid work were world-famous. Spain at that time produced the most precious steel weapons, the most gorgeous leatherware, the most beautiful pottery, with a golden glaze which cannot be produced today. Paper was introduced into Europe by the Arabs, by whom it was manufactured in Spain, replacing the very expensive parchment. In short, there was hardly any branch of industry which was not developed to the most perfect state of craftsmanship.

Hand in hand with this splendid development of handicrafts and industry, art and science developed to a degree which still calls out our unqualified admiration. While in the tenth and eleventh centuries all Europe could show scarcely a single public library and could boast of only two universities that were worthy of the name, there were in Spain at that same time more than seventy public libraries of which the one in Cordova alone contained six hundred thousand manuscripts. In addition, the country possessed seventeen famous universities, among which those at Cordova, Seville, Granada, Malaga, Jaen, Valencia, Almeria and Toledo were especially outstanding. Many students came from distant countries to study in the Arabian high schools, and carried back to their homelands the knowledge they had acquired there—which contributed not a little to the later growth of science in Europe. Astronomy, physics, chemistry, mathematics, geometry, philology, geography, reached in Spain the highest stage at that time known anywhere. Medicine in particular made an advance which had not been possible for it in Christian countries because the church threatened with death the dissectors of cadavers. Artists and scholars united in special associations for the pursuit of their studies. There were regular congresses of all branches of science where the latest achievements of research were announced and discussed, which naturally contributed greatly to the spread of scientific thought.

The Arabs made great contributions in the fields of music and poetry, and their graceful forms had a strong influence on the poesy of Christian Spain. What the Arabs accomplished in architecture borders often on the miraculous. Unfortunately, most of their best works fell as sacrifices to the barbarity of the Christians. Even where the savage fanaticism of the bearers of the cross did not level everything to the earth, they did sufficient damage to splendid works of art by crude mutilation. Nevertheless, structures like the Alcazar of Seville, the great Mosque of Cordova, and above all the Alhambra, in which the Moorish style attained its highest perfection, give us, even today, an idea of that wonderful period. In the Mosque at Cordova, which after the expulsion of the Moors was converted into a Christian church, the powerful impression of the interior with its nineteen bronze portals and forty-seven hundred lamps was in great part destroyed by a barbaric reconstruction, so that Charles V could with justice hurl at the church administration of the time the accusation: "You have built here what could just as well have been built elsewhere; and have destroyed that which existed nowhere else in the world."

What gave the Moorish style its distinctive character was the abundance of that unusual ornamentation of the walls and interiors known as arabesque. Since the Koran forbids to the followers of Islam the representation of mén and animals in picture or image, the fancy of the Moors hit upon that mysterious play with lines which in its delicate and inexhaustible richness of forms so deeply stirs the spirit—so that one may with justice speak of a "fairy tale in lines." Wide scope was afforded to the art of the architect because the cities at that time were very populous and extended in area. Thus at the height of Moorish culture Toledo counted two hundred thousand inhabitants, Seville and Granada four hundred thousand each. Of Cordova the Arabian chroniclers tell us that it embraced more than two hundred thousand houses, among them six hundred mosques, nine hundred public baths, a university and numerous public libraries.

Moreover, this highly developed culture unfolded in a time of political decentralization which was uninfluenced by the monarchic form of the state. Even when Abder Rachman III raised himself to the Caliphate he was compelled to make the most far-reaching concessions to the feeling for personality and the sense of independence of the population; he knew only too well that a sharp centralization of the powers of the state would immediately stir up a conflict with the ancient tribal notions of the Arabs and the Berbers which might shake his entire realm. The country was divided into six provinces, which were administered by viceroys. The great cities had their city governors, the smaller towns their cadis, the villages their directors or *hakims*.

These officials were, however, in a measure only intermediaries between the government of the realm and the municipalities. The administration of the latter was entirely independent; especially where whole tribes of family-groups dwelt together unlimited autonomy prevailed. Arabs, like Berbers, lived according to their ancient laws and constitutions and permitted no interference by the authorities in their community affairs. The Christians enjoyed equal freedom and chose their chiefs from among themselves. These latter, with the bishops, directed the administration of the congregations and were responsible to the government for the fulfillment by their fellows in the faith of their obligations as citizens and for the just collection of the taxes. The bishops were selected freely by the congregations, but had to be confirmed by the caliphs, who had succeeded to the customary rights of sovereignty of the Gothic kings. The civil affairs of the Jews as citizens were ordered in a similar fashion, their head rabbi functioning chiefly as head of the congregation.[2]

[2] Gustav Diercks, *Geschichte Spaniens von den frühsten Zeiten bis auf die Gegenwart.* Berlin, 1895. Band II, S. 128.

In fact the rulers of the Ommayad dynasty never succeeded during the three hundred years of their dominion in drawing the reins tighter and instituting a more unified government in the country. Every attempt in this direction led to endless uprisings, refusals to pay taxes, occasional secessions of single provinces, and even to forcible deposition of the caliph. Thus the realm was a rather loose structure, which immediately dissolved into its separate constituents when, in 1031, Hischam III abdicated as caliph and abandoned his former activity with the resigned words: "This race was made neither to rule nor to obey." Cordova then became a republic, and the former kingdom split into a few dozen taifas, tiny states, which no longer obeyed a central governing power. At just that time Moorish culture attained its highest bloom. The little communities strove to excel one another in the development of the intellectual life and the arts and sciences, and the collapse of state authority did not the slightest harm to this cultural development. On the contrary, it rather furthered it by guaranteeing to it freedom from injurious political restrictions.

In Christian Spain, too, one can see clearly how the tide of cultural development rises and falls according as the power of the state confines its activities within definite limits or assumes a scope which frees it from all internal restrictions and delivers to it all fields of social life. When the Visigoths were defeated by the Arabs a part of their scattered army fled into the mountains of Asturia. There they established a miserable little state from which they kept up constant attacks on the territory occupied by the Arabs. Thus developed that endless war between cross and crescent which lasted over seven hundred years. Out of it arose that cooperation of the church with the nationalistic endeavors of the Spaniards which gave to the later unified Spanish state its characteristic stamp, and to Spanish Catholicism that peculiar structure which it had assumed in no other country.

When, then, in the course of these bloody and bitter struggles the Arabs lost more and more territory, there arose, at the beginning of the twelfth century, in the north and west of the peninsula, a host of other Christian states, like Aragon, Castile, Navarre and Portugal, which, because of unceasing struggles for the throne, were constantly in one another's hair and did not emerge from this internal confusion until, at the end of the fifteenth century, Ferdinand the Catholic, of Aragon, and Isabella of Castile came to reign over the various states. In the smaller states there existed at first the elective monarchy, from which only later evolved hereditary succession to the throne. But even when, by the capture of Granada, the last bulwark of Islam in Spain had fallen and the first foundation for a unified national state had been laid by the marriage of Ferdinand and Isabella, there still elapsed a considerable time before the monarchy could bring all the social institutions of the country under its control. "In economics, in methods of administration, and from the political point of view it was still no nation," as Garrido remarked. "Its unity was embodied only in the person of the king, who ruled over several kingdoms, of which each had its own legislature, constitution, money, even its own system of weights and measures. . . ." Before the unified national state could develop its full power it had to get rid of the ancient rights of the towns and provinces, whose liberties were anchored in the *Fueros* or city constitutions; this was no small job.

When the Arabs had come into the country only a small part of the population, principally the noblemen, had fled into the rough mountainous land to the north. The great majority of the Iberian and Romanic inhabitants, as well as a much greater part of the poorer Gothic population, remained quietly on their ancient homesteads, especially when they saw that the conquerors were treating them with mercy and consideration. Many were even converted to Islam. But all, Moslem and Christian, enjoyed the advantages of the free local administration of the Arabs, Berbers and Syrians; and this assured them of a wide scope for their love of independence. When, now, the Spaniards in the course of this endless struggle with the Arabs had gained possession of one or another city or a new district, they were compelled to respect the old rights of the community and to leave them undisturbed. In those places where the conquest had been preceded by long battles with the population and had been achieved either by a massacre of the inhabitants or by driving them into flight, the conquerors found it necessary to grant to the new settlers a *Fuero* which guaranteed to them far-reaching local rights and liberties. This was the only way to get an effective hold on the recaptured territories and attach them to the victors. Spanish literature contains a large number of important works upon the history of these city and country communities and their *Fueros*, from which we gather that the city administration rested with the popular assembly, to which the inhabitants were called every Sunday by the ringing of the bells in order to discuss all the public affairs and interests and to adopt resolutions.[3]

The spirit which prevailed in these communities was thoroughly democratic and looked zealously after the local rights of the municipality, prepared at any time to defend them by all means at their command and to protect them against the attacks of the nobility and the crown. In these struggles the corporations of the manual laborers of the city played an important part; these constituted everywhere a very useful factor in the rich and changing history of the Spanish municipalities, in which the affairs of the people were incorporated. Thus Zancada remarks:

[3] Eduardo Hinojosa, *El origen del régimen municipal en Castilla y León*.

Among the various causes of the communal uprising there is one common factor which greatly favored that popular organization. This factor, which commanded great power, was the craft unions of the working population, which had arisen as reaction against the tyranny of the feudal barons, and under whose protection the manual laborer was able to secure respect for his rights; these unions were, in general, an outstanding means for the betterment of the social and economic status of the craftsmen.[4]

As in other countries at that time, so also in Spain, the municipalities united into larger and smaller federations in order more effectively to protect their ancient rights. Out of these alliances and the city *Fueros* there developed in the separate Christian states the *Cortes*, the first attempts at popular representation, which took form in Spain a whole hundred years earlier than in England. In fact, the memory of the free municipalities, the *Municipios Libres*, was never completely lost in Spain and stepped into the foreground in almost all the uprisings which periodically disturbed the country for centuries. Even the Cantonalist Revolution of 1873 was undertaken in this spirit. Today there is in all Europe no other country in which the spirit of federalism is so deeply alive in the people as it is in Spain. This is also the reason why the social movements in that land even today are characterized by a libertarian spirit which we no longer find in the same measure in any other country.

It was some time before any definite culture could be noticed at all in the Christian states in the northern part of the Iberian peninsula. Among the remnants of the Visigothic population social life retained for four hundred years very primitive forms, so that one could not speak at all of any higher independent culture among them. Diercks remarks in his *Geschichte Spaniens:*

> The culture of northern Spain was, then, entirely different from that of the southern part of the peninsula. Here we see all branches of material and spiritual culture come to flower; the state organization, on the other hand, remained at a relatively very low level and was little changed; thus the institutions which were formed in the north carried along with them the development of the state and the exacting control of legal institutions.

This is a fact of the greatest importance. Of its significance, however, Diercks is apparently not at all aware. Exactly *because* in Arabian Spain the power of the state could never really be centralized, culture was able to develop there undisturbed, while it was for a long time unable to make itself felt in the north where the struggles for political power pushed all other interests into the background. Only after the capture of Zaragossa and Toledo did any great change appear there, and in this the Moorish influence was of decisive importance.

[4] Praxiteles Zancada, *El Obrero en España.* Barcelona, 1902, p. 44.

Only Catalonia, and above all, Barcelona, constitute an exception, for they, long before any other Christian state in Spain, reached a high degree of social and intellectual culture. This was owing to their intimate relations with Southern France, which before the crusade against the heretical Albigenses was one of the countries most highly developed, intellectually and culturally, in all Europe. Besides, the Catalonians did not feel themselves bound by the pope's prohibition and they carried on a flourishing trade with the Arabian states of the south, which, of course, brought them into closer contact with Moorish culture. Thus there developed in Catalonia a freer spirit and a higher standard of cultural life than in any of the other Christian states of the peninsula. This difference, of which royal despotism made the Catalonians still more vividly aware by its forcible suppression of their ancient rights and liberties, changed them into sworn enemies of Castile, and created that sharp antagonism between Catalonia and the rest of Spain which has not even yet been completely overcome.

So long as the royal power—which grew constantly firmer after the marriage of Ferdinand of Aragon with Isabella of Castile—was still compelled to respect the ancient rights of the municipalities and the provinces, there flourished in the cities the rich culture which had been transmitted to them by the Arabs and which gradually stimulated them to independent creation. At the beginning of the sixteenth century all the industries were still in full bloom. As Fernando Garrido tells us, the Spaniards had learned wool-combing and dyeing from the Arabs; and the weaves of Leon, Segovia, Burgos, and Estramadura were the best in the world. In the provinces of Cordova, Granada, Murcia, Seville, Toledo, and Valencia the silk industry flourished and supported the greatest part of the local population. Life in the cities resembled the industry of a beehive. And along with the handicrafts the arts, especially architecture, reached a glorious expansion; the cathedrals of Burgos, Leon, Toledo and Barcelona bear notable testimony to this.

Of course the internal antagonisms of the several states, especially those of Castile, with the other parts of the country were not at once overcome. Therefore the royal power could not at once launch its attack on the municipalities and was often obliged to submit to the control of the Cortes, which alone could supply it with the money that it needed for its undertakings. But the powerful Cardinal Ximenes de Cisneros, Confessor to Queen Isabella, had already planned the campaign against the "special rights" of the municipalities. One of the most effective weapons in the struggle for the triumph of kingly absolutism was the Inquisition, which is often regarded merely as the creature and tool of the church—incorrectly; for the Inquisition was only a special department of the administrative apparatus of the kingdom which helped to strengthen the power of absolutism and bring it to full expansion. Since in Spain the efforts for the erection of the unified national state were most intimately intergrown with the unity of religious belief, the church and the monarchy worked together. Still, the church was in great measure just a tool in the hands of royal despotism, whose plans it helped to carry out and to which, by its savage fanaticism, it gave that peculiar tone which is lacking to the absolutism of all other countries. In fact, it was by the Spanish kingdom that the Inquisition was first raised to that frightful importance that has loaded it with the curses of all later generations. In his book about modern Spain, Garrido gives us some statistics of the Abbé Montgaillard according to which, from 1481 to 1781, 31,920 persons were burned alive and 16,759 were burned in effigy. The total number of persons who were sacrificed—and whose property was confiscated by the state—reached 341,029. This estimate, Garrido adds, is very moderate.

Ferdinand the Catholic had already tried to impose limitations on the ancient municipal rights in various parts of the country and had been successful in many instances, but he had to proceed cautiously and to conceal his real purposes under all sorts of subterfuges. Under Charles I (the German Emperor, Charles V) the crown continued its efforts in this direction with redoubled zeal, and so brought about the great uprising of the Castilian cities in 1521. At first the rebellion achieved a few small successes, but a little later the army of the *Comuñeros* was disastrously defeated at Villalar; and Juan de Padilla, commander-in-chief of the revolt, was executed. Almost at the same time the revolt of the *Germanias,* the brotherhoods and craft guilds, in the province of Valencia was put down after a terrific battle. As a result of these victories the crown was in a position to put a bloody end to the ancient municipal constitutions which had been in force in the Christian states of Spain since the beginning of the eleventh century. When, therefore, under Philip II the revolt of the Aragonese was drowned in the blood of the rebels of Saragossa and Chief Justice Lanuza was beheaded at the command of the constitution-smashing despot, absolutism was firmly in the saddle and was never seriously shaken by the later uprisings in other parts of the country.

So the unified national state was established under the dominion of an absolute monarchy. Spain became the first of the great powers of the world, and its political exertions strongly influenced European policy. But with the triumph of the unified Spanish state and the brutal suppression of all local rights and liberties there dried up the sources of all material and intellectual culture, and the country sank into a condition of hopeless barbarism. Even the inexhaustible streams of gold and silver that flowed in from the young Spanish colonies in America could not check the cultural decline; they only hastened it.

By the cruel expulsion of the Moors and the Jews Spain had lost its best craftsmen and farmers; the ingenious irrigation works fell into ruin, and the most fertile regions were transformed into deserts. Spain, which as late as the first half of the sixteenth century was still exporting grain to other countries, was already in 1610 compelled to import it, despite the fact that the population was steadily diminishing. After the capture of Granada there were dwelling in the country almost twelve million persons. Under Philip II the number of inhabitants had fallen to about eight million. A census which was taken in the second half of the seventeenth century gave 6,843,672 inhabitants. Although formerly Spain could not only supply her own colonies with all the manufactured products they needed but could also export considerable quantities of silks, cloth and other manufactures to foreign countries, at the end of the seventeenth century three-fourths of her people were clothed in foreign fabrics. Industry had fallen into utter ruin, and in Castile and other regions the government was compelled to lease land to foreigners. Above all, under the unceasing oppression men had lost all joy in work. Whoever could in any way manage it became a monk or a soldier, and the intellectual darkness was impenetrable. Labor was so despised that the Academy of Madrid in 1781 offered a prize for an essay which should show that a useful handicraft in no way degraded a man nor derogated from his personal dignity. According to Garrido:

> Misery had lowered pride and slain freedom. Superstition brought about the most frightful of all scourges, that wealth fell, for the greater part, into the "dead hand." The mania for establishing primogenitures and endowing the church with property was carried so far that at the beginning of the revolution of this century [the nineteenth] more than three-fourths of all the land in the country was subject to servitudes.

One might here mention that it was just at the time of absolutism that Spanish literature and painting reached its highest point. But let us not deceive ourselves. What was here produced was merely the intellectual precipitate of a past time; it inspired only a few of the foremost minds, whose works were appreciated by a small and dwindling minority and awakened no response among the people themselves. Therefore Diercks remarks very justly:

> If along with the governmental ruin came distinguished achievements in several fields of culture, if poetry and painting flourished vigorously, the fact must not deceive us as to the real causes of the general ruin, and it could not check it. Similar contradictions are offered as well by the cultural life of other countries. The surviving vital force of the people made itself effective in the only fields where, under the weight of spiritual and temporal despotism, it could be active.[5]

[5] *Geschichte Spaniens.* Band II, p. 394.

The high development of Russian literature under tsarism is an excellent illustration of the correctness of this view. Anyway, this glorious upsurge of Spanish literature did not last long, and its sudden collapse served to make it all the more noticeable later.

Italian culture never stood at a higher level than during the time, from the twelfth to the fifteenth century, when the whole peninsula was split into hundreds of tiny communities and there could be no talk at all of political unity. During that period the free cities were veritable oases of a higher intellectual and social culture of an astounding diversity and a creative vigor never since reached. If we leave out of consideration the city-republics of ancient Hellas there never was another period in the history of European peoples which produced in so short a time so great a wealth of works of culture. The English scholar, Francis Galton, stated in his works that Florence alone produced in that strange epoch more minds of distinction in every field of culture than all the monarchic states of contemporary Europe together.

In fact the Italian cities at that time were like fruitful seed-beds of intellectual and cultural activity, and they revealed to European humanity wholly new perspectives of a social development which later, by the appearance of the national state, the influence of business capital and the growth of political ambitions, was diverted into quite other lines. In the Italian cities was born that spirit which revolted against the enslaving influence of the church. Here, too, the two philosophical currents of nominalism and realism reached their highest pitch, after having been vitalized by Arabian intellect, and because of the stimulus they had received, even before the appearance of Humanism, were looking for new roads to knowledge. For the real meaning of these two movements—particularly of nominalism in the later phases of its development—consists in this, that they were trying to set philosophic thought, which for a thousand years had been under the intellectual guardianship of ecclesiastical theology, once more on its own feet. Only when one becomes clearly conscious of the distorted thought processes of Christian scholasticism can one correctly value this unmistakable change in the ways of judging spiritual matters. For four hundred years the thought of the scholastic was occupied with the most trivial questions and lost itself in the rubbish of a dead formalism which could open no new outlooks to the human mind. For several decades Christian theologians quarreled over how many spirits could stand on the point of a needle; what sort of excrement the angels emitted; whether, and how, Christ had completed his task of salvation; whether he came to earth as a pumpkin, a beast or a woman; whether a mouse which nibbled at the Host devoured the body of Christ; and what the consequences would be if he did. These and similar questions engaged the minds of the literate for centuries, and their hair-splitting explanations passed as signs of profoundest learning.

In the cities developed the first preliminaries of the rebirth of science, which with the ascendancy of the ecclesiastical mind had fallen into utter decay. In 1209 a church council at Paris forbade to ecclesiastics the study of those writings about natural history which the Christian world had received from the ancients. As far back as the tenth century there existed in Salerno a high school of the sciences, especially of medicine, where mostly Arabian and Jewish physicians served as teachers. These schools contributed greatly to the spread of Arabic learning and Arabic education in Italy, and so throughout the rest of Europe, by which the first stimulus to the reawakening of science was given. A long line of distinguished discoveries fall in that glorious epoch, many of which supplied the indispensable preliminaries for the great outburst of discovery at the end of the sixteenth century. The magical personality of Leonardo da Vinci, who was not only one of the greatest masters of all time in the most diverse fields of art, but also proved himself a thinker of the first rank in every branch of scientific research, and achieved, especially in mechanics, quite outstanding results, is in its astounding many-sidedness and the greatness of its genius justly the symbol of that wonderful time in which the creative urge of man achieved such powerful expression.

In the cities the handicrafts rose to a greatness never known before. Human labor came again to be honored and was no longer counted a disgrace. In the city municipalities of Northern Italy there were produced the finest embroideries, the most splendid silken stuffs. Every city competed in the production of inlaid steelware, splendid goldsmith's work, and objects of everyday use. Blacksmith's work, metal-casting, mechanical devices, and all the other branches of handicraft, reached a perfection which by its inexhaustible diversity and its fineness and sincerity of execution even today calls forth our admiration.

What was produced in every field of art during that blossom-time of culture excels everything that had made its appearance since the downfall of the Hellenic world. Countless monumental buildings in every city of the peninsula still reveal to us the spirit of that mighty epoch, in which the pulse beat of the community was so strong, and artists, craftsmen and scholars worked together to bring forth the best of which they were capable. In the cathedrals and council houses of the cities, their bell-towers and city gates, in the erection of which the entire population collaborated, is revealed the "creative genius of the masses," as Kropotkin called it, in its full greatness and endless diversity. It filled every undertaking with its spirit, breathed life into dead stones, embodied all the passionate longing that slumbers in men and yearns for fulfillment, and knit the tie that bound them into a community. What then brought men together for a common effort was the vivid consciousness of an inner unity, which had its roots in the community—that invisible unity which is not imposed on the individual from without, but is the natural result of his social experience. Because man at that time felt always the living tie that bound him to all others there was no need to impose social connections upon him forcibly from without. Only out of this spirit could a free production arise which released all the creative forces in man and so brought the social life of the community to full expansion. In this way were the social prerequisites for the mighty architectural achievements of that great epoch first brought into being.

Like architecture, sculpture and painting ripened to a greatness whose like is to be found only in the Hellenic communities. From the creation of the South-Italian school of sculpture in the first half of the thirteenth century, and the work of Niccola Pisano in Tuscany, to the masterpieces of Donatello, Verrocchio, Sansovino and Michelangelo, almost every city brought forth its own line of distinguished sculptors, to whose abilities the spirit of the community gave wings. Never in so short a time were so large a number of important painters produced, such a wealth of great and greatest works brought to life. From Cimabue to Giotto, from the fresco painters of the later thirteenth century to Fra Angelico, Masaccio, and Masolino, from Pisanello and Castagno to Filippo Lippi, from Piero della Francesca and his circle to Mantegna and his numerous imitators, from Lorenzo di Credi to Verrocchio, Ghirlandajo and Botticelli, from Perugino to Bellini and Leonardo da Vinci, from Correggio, Giorgione, del Sarto, to Titian, Michelangelo and Raffaello, distinguished masters arose in almost every city and gave to painting an exalted status it had never known before. Many of the great masters displayed an astounding versatility and worked at the same time as painters, sculptors, bronze-founders, architects and craftsmen. Thus Pindemonte called Michelangelo the "man with four souls," because he painted the Last Judgment, carved the statue of Moses, vaulted the cupola of Saint Peter's, and wrote sonnets of terrific expressive power. In this way there was shaped in the Italian cities a culture which in a few centuries completely changed the aspect of the country and gave to its social life a trend which it had never possessed before.

At the same time the Italian language also was developing, and with it the literature of the country. At first the style of the Sicilian troubadours was dominant, but the Tuscan dialect came more and more into the foreground and, because of the rich culture of the Tuscan cities, steadily gained in influence. Poets like Guinicelli, Cavalcanti and Davanzati wrote in it; but the powerful poetry of Dante first gave to the language the irresistible vigor of expression, the plastic form and delicate coloring, which enabled the poet to depict everything that stirs the soul of man. Along with Dante worked Petrarch and Boccaccio to shape that instrument of the soul—a language.

That splendid culture which spread from Italy over most of the cities of Europe and in them also gave the impulse to a reshaping of social life unfolded at a time when the country was completely split up politically and the idea of national unity had as yet no power over the minds of men. The whole country was covered with a network of self-contained communities which defended their local independence with the same zeal as did the city-republics of ancient Hellas. In the municipality artists and craftsmen in their brotherhoods and guilds cooperated in a common task. The guilds were not merely the directors and administrators of economic life, they constituted also the sole basis for the political structure of the community. There were no political parties nor professional politicians in the modern sense. Each guild elected its representatives to the municipal council, where they carried out the instructions of their organizations and tried by conference with the delegates from other organizations to reach a settlement of all important questions on the basis of free agreement. And since every guild felt itself closely identified with the general interests of the city, things were decided by the vote of the corporations represented. The same procedure held in the federations of cities, the tiniest market town had the same rights as the richest municipality, since it had joined the alliance of its own free choice and had the same interest in its efficiency as all the other communities. At the same time every guild within the city and every city within the federation remained an independent organism which had control of its own finances, its own courts, its own administration, and could make and dissolve treaties with other associations on its own motion. Only the common requirements of the same tasks and the same interests brought the several guilds and municipalities together into corporate bodies of similar type so that they might carry out plans of wider scope.

The great advantage of this system lay in the fact that each member of a guild as well as the representatives of the guild in the corporation could easily keep track of all its functioning. Everyone was dealing with matters which he understood exactly and making decisions about them—matters about which he could speak as expert and connoisseur. If one compares this institution with the legislative and administrative bodies of the modern state, its moral superiority becomes instantly apparent. Neither the voter, today, nor the man who is said to represent him, is in a position that enables him to supervise in any degree (not to say completely) the monstrous mechanism of the central political apparatus. Every delegate is compelled almost every day to decide upon questions of which he has no personal knowledge and about which he must rely on the judgment of others. That such a system must inevitably lead to the worst sort of maladjustment and injustice is indisputable. And since the individual voter is, for the same reason, in no better position to keep track of and to control the acts of his so-called "representatives," the caste of professional politicians, many of whom have in view only their own advantage, is able more easily to profit by the confusion and the gate is opened wide for every kind of moral corruption.

Next to these notorious evils which are today so unambiguously and so glaringly evident in every parliamentary state, the so-called "centralized representation" is the greatest hindrance to any social progress, standing in direct contradiction to all principles of natural development. Experience teaches us that every social innovation first permeates one little circle and only gradually achieves general recognition. For just this reason federalism offers the best security for unrestricted development, since it leaves to every community the possibility of trying out within its own circle any measures which it may think fitted to advance the welfare of its citizens. The community is, therefore, in a position to apply practical tests and so to subject immediately to the proof of positive experience any proposed innovations. It thus exerts an enlivening and stimulating influence upon neighboring communities, which are thus themselves put in a position to judge of the fitness or unfitness of the innovations. With the central representative bodies of our time such an education in social views is completely excluded. In such a structure, in the very nature of things, the most backward sections of the country have the strongest representation. Instead of the most advanced and intellectually active communities leading the others by their example, we have just the opposite; the most downright mediocrity is always in the saddle and every impulse toward innovation is nipped in the bud; the most backward and intellectually sluggish sections of the country put fetters on the culturally most developed groups and cripple their initiative by their opposition. The best electoral system cannot alter this fact; it often serves only to make the situation harsher and more hopeless; for the reactionary germ lies in the system of central representation and is not at all affected by the varying forms of the suffrage.

If one compares the superlative culture of the great federalistic epoch in Italy with the rubbishy culture of the unified national state which had hovered so long before the eyes of the Italian patriots as the highest goal of their ambition, one comprehends at once the enormous difference between the two organizations. Their cultural outcomes were quite as different as the intellectual assumptions underlying their whole social structure. The adherents of national unity, and especially Mazzini, who had staked his very life on this idea, were firmly convinced that a united Italy was destined to march at the van of all the peoples of Europe to initiate a new period in human history. With all the visionary exaltation of his political mysticism Mazzini declared:

> In me survives the faith in Rome. Within the walls of Rome life has twice unfolded as unity of the world. While other peoples vanished forever after the completion of a fleeting destiny, and none came twice to the front, life there went on eternal and death was never known. . . . Why should there not arise out of a third Rome an Italian people, whose emblem floats before me; why not arise a third and greater unity, which shall set in harmony earth and heaven, right and duty, which, not to the individual but to the peoples, to the free and equal, shall speak a luminous, unifying word about their mission in this earthly vale?

Mazzini believed in the divine destiny of Italy in the coming history of Europe with the mystic rapture of one divinely possessed; for him it was the intellectual concept of the *Unita Italiana* through which alone could the "historic mission" of Italy be set to work. For him national unity was first of all a question of power; for, though the people was always on his lips, still this people remained for him always an abstract concept which he constantly strove to adapt to the requirements of his national state. Only out of political unity could Italy acquire the strength which would fit it for the fulfillment of its alleged mission. Hence Mazzini's outcry against federalism:

> This young Italy is unitary; for without unity there is no real nation, because without unity there is no power, and Italy, surrounded by unitary nations, which are strong and jealous, must, above all, be powerful. Federalism would reduce it to the powerless condition of Switzerland, and under stress of necessity it would fall under the influence of one or another of the neighboring nations. Federalism would give new life to the rivalries of different localities, which today are quenched, and so lead Italy back to the Middle Ages. . . . Seeking the destruction of the unity of the great Italian family, federalism would render utterly vain the mission that Italy is called to fulfill for humanity.[6]

Mazzini and his adherents hoped from the erection of the unified national state a mighty upsurge of Italian culture, which, once it was freed from the fetters of foreign domination, would unfold to an undreamed-of greatness. Before everything, however, Italian unity was to establish the freedom of the people and put an end to every type of slavery. How often had the Italian patriots celebrated in extravagant words the natural urge toward freedom of the Italians and with a quite especial pride boasted of it to the French. Carlo Pisacane, the fiery socialist patriot (who was, it is true, no adherent of Mazzini's political metaphysics

---

[6] *Allgemeine Unterweisung für die Verbrüderung des Jungen Italien,* 1831. (*Aus Mazzinis "Politischen Schriften."* Leipzig, 1911.) Band I, p. 105.

though he esteemed him highly as a man, and who gave his life for the liberation of his country in 1851), in his great work, *Saggi storico-politici-militari sull' Italia,* passes a very unfavorable judgment on the French. He called them a people without a sense of freedom who, indeed, always had freedom on their lips, but were inwardly completely enslaved and, moved by their thirst for glory, cast themselves on the neck of any despot who came along. With this he contrasted the instinctive love of freedom of the Italians, who could never be induced in sheepish surrender to assign their destiny to a dynasty; and he kept repeating that a united Italy could never be built by the power of a privileged minority, but must arise from the freedom of the people. Mazzini and his followers had no better opinion of France and made no secret of their sentiments.

These men had no slightest intimation that their efforts must lead immediately to just that condition which they urged against the French as a reproach. No unified state has thus far opened new outlooks to cultural aspirations, but has always led to the degradation of all higher cultural forms. Every national-political unity results in an extension of the struggle of small minorities for political power, which always has to be purchased by a lowering of intellectual culture. Above all, however, national unity has never yet established the freedom of a people, but has always merely reduced its implicit slavery to a definite norm, which is then proclaimed as freedom. Though Pisacane might cherish the illusion that a genuine nation could harbor in its bosom no privileged classes, orders or castes, experience has thus far always shown us that the national state is constantly busied in setting up new privileges and in dividing the people into castes and orders, because its very existence is based on this division. How clearly and forcibly had Proudhon told Mazzini and his adherents what Italian unity would bring to the people:

> Every original characteristic in the various districts of a country is lost by the centralization of its public life—for that is the proper name for this so-called "unity." A centralized state of twenty-six million souls, such as Italy would become, suppresses all liberties of the provinces and municipalities in favor of a higher power—the government. What is this unity of the nation in reality? It is the merging of the separate folk-groups in which men live, and which differ from one another, into the abstract idea of a nation, in which no one breathes, and no one is acquainted with another. . . . To govern twenty-six million people who have been robbed of all dominion over themselves calls for a gigantic machine; then to set this machine in motion, a monstrous bureaucracy, a legion of officials. To protect it from within and without, there is required a standing army, officers, soldiers, mercenaries; these will from now on represent the nation. Fifteen years ago the number of officials in France was estimated at six hundred thousand. The number has not diminished since the *coup d'état.* The strength of the army and the navy

is proportionate to this number. All this is indispensable to unity. This is the usual cost of a state, a cost which, because of centralization, is constantly increasing, while the freedom of the provinces is constantly diminishing. This grandiose unity calls for fame, glitter, luxury, an imposing civil list—embassies, pensions, benefices, and so on. In such a unified state everyone has his hand out, and who can count the chiselers? The people! Who says unified nation means a nation that is sold to its government. . . . And the profits of such a unified regimen? They are not for the people but for the ruling classes and castes in the state.[7]

The brilliant Frenchman had recognized clearly the moving principle of efforts at unity. Everything which he prophesied for the Italians has been made good to the very last letter. If Pisacane and his friends believed that only in France could it happen that an entire nation would put itself in the hands of any adventurer who made great promises, and especially who gratified their thirst for glory, the example of Mussolini has since shown us that national-political unity prepared Italy for exactly the same sort of thing. For this also is a result of governmental centralization. The more completely personal initiative and the impulse to self-reliance is smothered in man, the stronger in him becomes the belief in the "strong man," who is to end all his troubles. Moreover, this belief is just a bit of political religion which is deeply implanted in the nature of man by the feeling of dependence on a higher power.

What Proudhon so clearly foresaw because his mental perspective was not clouded by blind faith in the state, our modern socialists—from social democracy to the various factions of Russian Bolshevism—cannot see even today, because the egg shells of their Jacobin ancestors still stick to them. National unity brought to Italy only the bureaucratizing of public affairs and the debasement of higher cultural activity for the advantage of the political plans of its statesmen and their mistress, the bourgeoisie. The delight of the modern bourgeoisie in the unified state is so great merely because it opens an outlook for their policy of exploitation such as a federation of small communities could never afford. For the material interests of small minorities in a country the unified national state has always been a blessing. For the freedom of the people and the shaping of higher forms of culture it has always been a misfortune.

How the efforts at centralization of the unified national state worked out in France has been shown in the first part of this work. Here, too, the accumulation of all political authority in the hands of the king went on at the expense of all the local rights and liberties of the municipalities and the provinces till it reached the dimensions of that unbounded policy of world power typified by Louis XIV and plunged France and the con-

---

[7] *La Fédération et l'Unité en Italie*, Paris, 1862, p. 25.

tinent of Europe into an abyss of misery and intellectual barbarism. One must not allow himself to be blinded by the pompous splendor of the French court, which brought in poets and artists from all over the world to strengthen its prestige and to deify the person of the ruler. For the French autocracy, art served the same ends as formerly for the Roman Caesars.

The monarchistic state in no way advanced the development of a popular literature and art, as is so often thoughtlessly asserted. On the contrary, it first created the wide gulf between the people and literature, which in no other country was so sharply apparent as in France of the *ancien régime*. This came about because French despotism pursued its aims with a rare consistency and was always intent on subjecting to its will every sphere of social life in order to implant the spirit of authority in every stratum of the people. Before the effective establishment of the monarchy a rich culture flourished in the cities of France, especially in the southern part of the country, where intellectual life was freer and more active than in the north, the most important stronghold of royal power and ecclesiastic scholasticism. The lyric poetry of medieval France, extraordinarily rich in content, owes much to the graceful flexibility of the Provençal language. Even more important, it drew upon popular sources and found its surest basis in life itself. The poetic spirit of the South hovered about the Provençal minnesingers and troubadours and gave to their art its form and its implicit moving force. But the troubadours were not merely singers of ballads, they were also the heralds of popular opinion, and their *sirventes* or "battle-hymns" influenced social events to a high degree. In these songs there stands out strongly a burning hatred for Rome and the domination of the church. Not for nothing was the South the land of heretics and dissenting sects, feared in equal measure by pope and king.

The *fabliaux*, strange mixture of epic and didactic poesy, which were sung or recited by wandering minstrels (*conteurs*) and which concerned themselves with everything which gave purpose or content to the life of man, had an even deeper hold on the people. In these songs satire played an important part and not rarely served to set public opinion in motion. The Christian mystery plays, which often had a genuinely insidious and blasphemous content, attained also in medieval France their first regularly artistic form, out of which the drama was later developed. At that time there still existed an intrinsic alliance between the people and literature. And with Francois Villon, who has been called the actual creator of French poetic art, this alliance is evident in every strophe; his *Great Testament* provides glorious evidence of this. Likewise Rabelais, the brilliant satirist and opponent of romanticism, who understood his time better than any other man, stood with both feet in the life of the people; so that his two immortal works, *Gargantua* and *Pantagruel*, remain today genuine folk-books.

With the victory of absolutism and the unified national state this relation was changed fundamentally. This became quickly apparent after Louis XI (that sinister being who has been called "the spider of Europe" and who carried out his plans with a mad obsession that shrank from no means that promised success) had broken the resistance of his great vassals and so laid the actual foundation for the absolutist unified state. Francis I, who is generally acclaimed as having made available to Frenchmen the higher intellectual culture of the Italian Renaissance, selected Machiavelli's Prince as his model and in his patronage of classic studies pursued a quite definite political purpose. In the old *fabliaux*, mystery plays, and folk songs there still lived the memory of a past which had tried to free itself from royal despotism. Francis determined that from that time on, poetry was to avail itself of classical material and turn its mind toward Rome, instead of attaching itself to the customs and institutions of an epoch which might awaken in the people a yearning for the things they had lost.

What Francis I had begun his successors and their priestly satellites carried on with stubborn zeal. So literature became court literature—and entirely estranged from the people. Poets no longer drew upon the rich popular sources which, under despotic domination, withered more and more. As once in Rome, so now at Versailles and in Paris, all art revolved about the person of the king and the sanctified institution of the monarchy. Men took every conceivable pains to bind poetic creation by fixed rules and sacrificed the living spirit to a dead erudition which had lost all relation to real life. Everything was regimented and bureaucratically ordained, even the language. All the instruments of power had been earlier employed to eradicate along with the heretics of the South also their language, the Provençal. In 1635 Richelieu established the French Academy in order to subordinate language and poetry to the authoritarian ambitions of absolutism. Only what from above was found correct in style and unobjectionable was to be allowed to achieve immortality; nothing else had a right to exist. Boileau in his *Art Poétique* gave to poetry in general a definite plumb-line which was followed with slavish assiduity not only in France but in other countries, and so for a long time closed every new outlook for the development of literary art. All the French classics suffer from this restriction of the spirit and seem to us unrelated to the world and lacking in inner warmth. When Corneille was so daring as to disregard the prescribed rules in his *Cid*, the Cardinal quickly made him see reason by setting the Academy in action against him. Thus it had happily come to pass that language, literature and art were bureaucratized. Can one wonder that even Voltaire, who in his dramatic works went the academic way, found Shakespeare a "savage"?

Only a few poets of that enslaved period constitute a glorious exception. First of all comes Molière, the unique, in whom the spirit of Rabelais still lived and gave to his genius the power to overstep the narrow bounds and to tear the solemn mask of vain pretence from the hypocritical countenance of his time. No wonder that the French Academy failed to add his name to the troop of the "immortals" or that the Archbishop of Paris threatened readers of *Tartufe* with excommunication. Perhaps it was fortunate for the poet that he died young; such a rebellious head as his was exposed to dangers of many kinds in that time of rigid forms and majestic mendacity. La Fontaine, too, and Lesage, must be named here. The exquisite fables of the former have kept their freshness of coloring because he discarded rigid rules and turned back to the inexhaustible wealth of ideas of the old *fabliaux*. Lesage, who with such masterly skill had told those wholesome truths to his contemporaries in *The Devil on Two Sticks* and his delightful *Gil Blas*, was the actual creator of the modern novel.

It was at that time, too, when every expression of life was adjusted to the spirit of authority and absolutism, that Bossuet wrote his *Discours sur l'histoire universelle*, thus becoming the founder of the theological concept of history purposing to proclaim the system of royal despotism as a divinely ordained reality over which man had no power, since its foundations lay in the plan of Providence itself. Every revolt against the system or the sacred person of the monarch became a revolt against God and a capital crime against church and state. The unintelligent theology which was then taught in the Sorbonne permitted no scientific explanations. Thus, the church rendered invaluable service to the temporal despotism, for it left no means untried to plant the principle of authority deep in the consciousness of every subject.

And it was not only language, art, and literature that were placed under the control of a special authority. Crafts and industry, also, were brought under regimentation by the state and could no longer make independent decisions. Definite methods were prescribed by the state for all the industries in the country, and an army of officials took care that no one of them deviated by a hair's breadth from the established norm. In his great work, *De l'industrie française*, Jean de Chaptal has pictured the whole monstrosity of this crazy system in its every detail and has shown how every creative instinct was deliberately smothered and every new idea condemned to suppression. Thus, the tailor was told how many stitches to use in sewing a sleeve into a coat; the cooper, how many hoops he must put on a barrel. The state bureaucracy not only determined the length, width and color of the fabrics that were woven; even the exact number of threads in each weave was prescribed, and a widespread police system saw to it that every prescription was meticulously observed. Violations were strictly dealt with, being punished by confiscation or destruction of the goods. In serious cases destruction of tools and workshops, mutilation of offenders, even the death penalty, were employed. That under such circumstances the entire industrial system of the country must have been crippled is clear. Just as under serfdom agricultural production constantly diminished, so the royal ordinances destroyed industry and drove the country toward the abyss. Only the revolution put an end to this insane condition.

But one chain not even the revolution could break: the chain of authoritarian tradition, the basic principle of absolutism. It changed the old forms, it is true, but the deeper purport was not touched, and it merely continued what the monarchy had begun long before. Just as today in Russia Bolshevism carries to the extreme the authoritarian state-concept of tsarism by suppressing indiscriminately all free exchange of ideas and therefore all creative impulse in the people, so, then, the Jacobins carried the political centralization of society to its ultimate conclusion and so became, like their later imitators in Russia, the real leaders of the counter-revolution. The revolution gave France the republic, but this could have meaning only if it represented the opposite of autocracy and safeguarded right with the same determination with which the monarchy had hitherto safeguarded power. The republic must become the symbol of the true community of the people, in which every movement really comes from the people and rests on the freedom of man. To the royal dictum: "I am the state!" the republican enfranchisement must reply: "We are the community!" Man must come to feel that he is no longer bound by the decisions of a higher power, that his fate from now on rests in his own hands and in his cooperation with his fellows. The republic could bring to the people something genuinely new only by replacing the ancient principle of guardianship with the creative activity of freedom, intellectual coercion by education for intellectual independence, the mechanical operation of a directing power by organic evolution.

The revolution did, indeed, free the people from the yoke of royal power, but in doing so it merely plunged them into deeper bondage to the national state. And this chain proved more effective than the strait-jacket of the absolute monarchy because it was anchored, not to the person of the ruler, but to the abstract idea of the "common will," which sought to fit all efforts of the people to a definite norm. Thus, they landed happily back in the old absolutism that they thought they had overthrown. As the galley-slave dragged the ball at his leg, so the new citizen dragged through life the abstract idea of the nation, which had been set up as the reservoir of the "common will" and, doing this, forgot the art of standing on his own feet, which the revolution had scarcely restored to him. The "republicans" gave to the republic as content absolutism dressed up as the nation, and so destroyed the genuine community of the people of the *res publica*. What the men of the Convention had begun, their imitators in all subsequent popular uprisings followed undeviatingly: they retained absolutism under the name of freedom and followed slavishly the tradition of the Great Revolution, whose counterfeit glory still today outshines all the signs and symbols of genuine liberation.

Proudhon had understood this truth in its full profundity; to him, therefore, all the efforts of political parties to get power into their hands were simply different demonstrations of absolutism under false colors. He had come to see that anyone who undertakes a social revolution by the conquest of political power comes inevitably to deceive himself and others. For power is, in its very essence, counter-revolutionary, an outgrowth of the concepts of absolutism, in which every system of exploitation has its roots. Absolutism is the principle of authority which is most logically represented in the state and the church. Until this principle is overthrown the so-called "culture nations" will continue to sink deeper and deeper into the bog of power-politics and a dead industrial technique; this, too, at the cost of that freedom and manhood out of which alone there can grow for us a higher social culture. Ibsen felt this when he said:

> The state must go! Nor will I have anything to do with revolution! Undermine the state concept; establish free choice and its intellectual implications as the sole determinant for a union—that is the beginning of a freedom that is worth something! A change in the form of government is nothing but a fussing about degrees—a little more or a little less—all of it's just nonsense. Yes, my dear friend, all that counts is not to let yourself be frightened by the venerableness of ownership. The state had its roots in time; it will reach its growth in time. Greater things than it will fall; all religion will fall.[8]

The same experiences run through the history of all peoples; they lead everywhere to the same results. National-political unity has never and nowhere vitalized the development of the intellectual culture of a people; on the contrary, it has always set limits to it, because it always sacrifices the best forces in the people as a whole to the unlimited ambition for power of the national state and so dries up the deeper sources of intellectual progress. As we have seen, the periods of so-called "national disunion" have always been up to now the great culture periods of history, while the epochs of "national unity" have always brought degradation and ruin to all the higher culture forms.

In ancient Germany culture reached its zenith in the free cities of the Middle Ages in the midst of a world of cultureless barbarism. They were the only places where art and handicraft could expand, where free thought

[8] Letter to Georg Brandes, February 17, 1873. *Briefe von Henrik Ibsen.* Berlin, 1905, p. 159.

still had a place and a social spirit kept men united. The mighty monuments of medieval architecture and art are still great witnesses to a cultural development which belonged among the most glorious that German history can display. But the history of the more recent intellectual culture in Germany is also only a confirmation of that old truth, which so few, alas, have thus far understood. All great intellectual achievements in this country hark back to the time of its "national disunion." Its classic literature from Klopstock to Schiller and Goethe, the art of its Romantic School, its classic philosophy from Kant to Feuerbach and Nietzsche, its music from Beethoven to Richard Wagner—all of it falls in the time before the founding of the Reich. With the victory of the German national state begins also the decline of German culture, the drying up of its creative forces, and along with this collapse the triumph of Bismarckism, as Bakunin has styled the senseless combination of militarism and bureaucracy. Nietzsche was quite right when he said: "When the Germans began to interest the other peoples of Europe it was because of a culture which they now no longer possess, yes, which they have, with blind zeal, shaken off as if it were a disease; and yet they knew of nothing better to put in its place than the political and national delusion." [9]

And Constantin Frantz, the South German Federalist and opponent of Bismarck, opines: "One needs but contemplate the situation existing today in every field of art, which the proclamation of the new empire at Versailles represents, and the nature of this new creation stands out with all desired clarity: a company in glittering uniforms before which a few gentlemen in black coats play an utterly humble part, the whole as prosaic as it is unfolklike—the inauguration of militarism could not reveal itself more drastically." [10]

In fact, national unity turned Germany into an enlarged Prussia, which felt itself called to pursue world politics. The barracks became the high school of the new German mentality. Germany became great in the fields of technique and applied sciences, but narrow-minded and poor of soul. Worst of all, she lost that great universal attitude of Lessing, Herder, Goethe, Schiller, Jean Paul and Heine, which once had been the pride of the Germans. This is not a plea either for particularism or for the small state. What we urge is the complete elimination of the power principle from the life of society and, consequently, the supplanting of the state in every form by a higher social culture founded on the freedom of man and his free union with his fellow men. This does not, however, alter the fact that the larger a state is, the stronger the instruments of power which it commands, the more dangerous it is to human freedom and the demands for higher forms of intellectual and cultural

[9] *Werke*, V: 179.
[10] *Die preussische Intelligenz und ihre Grenzen*. Munich, 1874, p. 53.

life. These are most imperiled in a central, unified state. Carlo Pisacane
had recognized this clearly when he wrote in his *Saggio sulla Rivoluzione:*

> Every government, even a despotism, is once in a while in a position to
> advance science and to attract to it brilliant men and great minds; be it thus
> to make some concessions to the spirit of the time, be it because this accords
> with the personal ambitions of the head of the state. From this one can
> deduce the fact that the more governments there are in a country the greater
> is the probability that the general darkness will be illuminated by at least a
> few sparks of intelligence.

One could perhaps cite England as counter-evidence and show that
here culture took a great upsurge in spite of the national state, especially
in the age of Queen Elizabeth. But one must not forget that only under
the Stuarts was genuine absolutism able to claim an overwhelming success
there, and that the English state never succeeded in centralizing public
life to the degree which was reached in France, for example. The English government had always a strongly developed liberal opposition against
it, which was deeply rooted in the people and which gave to the whole
of English history its peculiar character. The fact is that in no other
country did so much of the ancient municipal constitutions persist as in
England, and that the English city government is today, so far as local
independence is concerned, the freest in Europe. But that in England
also the central powers of the state were always trying to shackle the
economic and cultural life of the country, and that the shackles were only
broken by the revolution, has already been more fully developed in the
first part of this work.

In his political masterpiece, *Du Principe Fédératif*, Proudhon gave
expression to the thought: "Either the twentieth century will introduce
the era of federation or mankind will be plunged for another thousand
years into purgatory. The true problem which delays the redemption is
in reality no longer the political, but the economic problem."

Now the twentieth century has thus far brought us, not federalism, but
an unlimited strengthening of centralization. Whither this development
of matters has led us the World War showed; it is shown also by the
frightful chaos of our political and economic conditions, by the startling
unspirituality of the time and by the complete lack of any higher cultural
feeling. We find ourselves actually in purgatory, and no one can predict
when the hour of our redemption will sound. But that the solution of the
problem of which Proudhon spoke is possible only within the framework
of a federation of free communes on the basis of social community interests
is becoming today more and more an inner certainty for everyone who
has recognized the dangers of the immediate future and does not wish
to throttle man slowly with state capitalism.

Chapter 8

THE ESSENTIAL IDENTITY OF ALL CULTURE. THE DANGER OF THE COL-
LECTIVE CONCEPT. COMPARATIVE PSYCHOLOGY OF PEOPLES. INFLUENCE
OF THE SOCIAL IMPULSE. INDIVIDUAL AND MASS PSYCHOLOGY. JUDG-
MENT ABOUT FOREIGN PEOPLES. THE PICTURE OF ONE'S OWN NATION
AS A WISH-CONCEPT. THE SYMBOL OF THE NATION. THE ILLUSION OF
A NATIONAL CULTURE. CULTURE'S FREEDOM FROM FRONTIERS. CAPI-
TALISM AS TEMPORARY RESULT OF SOCIAL EVOLUTION. THE RA-
TIONALIZING OF CAPITALISTIC ECONOMY. THE "AMERICANIZING" OF
EUROPE. THE INFLUENCE OF CAPITALISTIC ECONOMY ON MODERN
STATE POLICY. THE FORM OF THE STATE NO EXPRESSION OF PECULIAR
NATIONAL ENDOWMENTS. THE MODERN CONSTITUTIONAL STATE. THE
NATURE OF PARTIES. THE PARLIAMENTARY MACHINE. ECONOMIC IN-
DIVIDUALISM AND THE CAPITALISTIC STATE. ECONOMIC NATIONALISM.
POLITICAL RECONSTRUCTIONS OF THE PRESENT TIME.

THERE is no culture of any sort of which it could be asserted that it arose altogether independently and without outside influences. It is true that we have long been accustomed to "organize" the so-called history of culture according to definite points of view, somewhat as a druggist puts up his stuff in little boxes, vials and cartons, but one cannot maintain that we have gained much by this. While we were busy working out very thoroughly the "inner contrasts" between different culture patterns, we lost the ability rightly to value the common features which lie at the foundation of every culture; we can no longer see the forest for the trees. Spengler's *Decline of the West* is only a belated, though completely logical, result of this obsession. The surprising achievements of modern ethnology and sociology gave renewed keenness to our understanding of the striking similarity of the social and cultural development in different human groups and led to a revision of the traditional views. Wherever scientific research has undertaken the investigation of a past culture epoch, it has come upon the remains of still older cultures or of blendings and transfers which plainly reveal the invigorating influence of earlier social patterns.

"We can't fall out of this world," as Grabbe says. This utterance constantly reminds us of the Essential and Universal which unite all human beings with one another and which, in spite of all the peculiarities arising from differences in climate and in external conditions of life, quite harmonize the inner equilibrium between the different human groups. We are all children of this earth and subject to the same laws of life, which find their most elementary expression in hunger and love. And because we are, by and large, of the same physiological species, because the natural environment in which we live acts on us to the same degree, even if the external conditions are not everywhere the same, therefore the intellectual and spiritual precipitates which the external surroundings produce in us are much more similar than most people suspect. Everywhere man struggles for the preservation of his species and, within the species, for his personal existence; everywhere the bases of his behavior are the same. The natural environment and the inborn impulses which have been transmitted to him by the unbroken chain of his ancestors and which operate in the unconscious of our minds give rise everywhere to the same primal forms of religious experience. The struggle for existence leads in all regions to definite forms of economic and political life, which frequently display an astonishing similarity even when we are dealing with peoples of different race who are widely separated from one another by continents and oceans. All this shows that our thinking and doing, because we all possess the same physiological properties and the same sensitivity to the influences of the environment, are subject to the same fundamental laws of life, in comparison with which all the differences of expression play a quite subordinate role. Usually, we are dealing only with difference in degree, which springs merely from more developed or more primitive cultural requirements.

Since Hegel and others taught us to think in abstract general concepts, that manner of thinking has become the fashion. We have grown used to working with psychological quantities and thus we arrive at the most far-reaching generalizations without most of us even suspecting that we have been made the victims of arbitrary assumptions from which must ensue the most misleading conclusions. After Lazarus and Steinthal, following in the footsteps of Herbart, had, with all conceivable ingenuity, constructed the so-called "comparative psychology of peoples," the drift in this direction went merrily onward and led us with compelling logic to the abstract idea of a mass-, class- and race-soul and similar ideas created by intellectual acrobatics, according to which one can think everything and nothing. Thus Dostoievsky became the type of the Slavic soul as Goethe became the revealer of the German soul. The Englishman appears to us as the living embodiment of sober understanding to whom any sentimental consideration of things is denied; the Frenchman as the representative of frivolous vainglory; and the Germans as a "people of poets and thinkers." We get drunk on this tumult of words and are happy as kings when the language is enriched with a new verbal fetish. We speak in all sobriety of an "individual people," yes, even of an "individual state." By which one is by no means to understand men who belong to a certain people or are citizens of a certain state; no, one is dealing in this case with an entire people or an entire state as if they were individuals with definite traits of character and peculiar psychic properties or intellectual qualities. Let us understand clearly what that means. An abstract structure, like *state* or *people*, that merely conveys to us a sociological concept, is endowed with definite properties which are perceptible only in the individual and which, applied to a generalization, must irrevocably lead to the most monstrously deceptive conclusions.

How such constructions come into being Lazarus has shown us with complete clarity in the argument of his *Psychology of Peoples*. After he had quite unthinkably transferred the properties of the individual to entire peoples and nations he explained profoundly that the separate man comes into the question at all merely as representative of the collective intellect and only as such can be a transmitter of ideas.[1] Following the thought processes of Wilhelm von Humboldt, Lazarus and Steinthal relied chiefly upon the difference of languages, the organic structure of which they tried to deduce from the special intellectual type of each people. To this peculiar intellectual and spiritual endowment they traced also the difference in the religious ideas of the peoples, their forms of government, their social institutions and their ethical concepts, and ascribed to every nation a particular type of feeling and thought which it could voluntarily neither accept nor reject.

Since then we have learned that language as expression of the special "intellectual and spiritual status" of a people does not enter into the question at all, since there is no longer any people which has retained its primitive language or has not changed its language in the course of its history, as has been already brought out. The same holds true for the different forms of government, social institutions, moral views and religious systems. Despite this, men continued along the lines that had been opened up by Lazarus and Steinthal. Gustav Le Bon became the founder of "mass psychology"; others discovered the psyche of the class; while the Gobineaus, Chamberlains, Woltmanns and Günthers luckily found the "race soul." They all pursued the same method: they transferred the peculiar properties of the individual to nations, classes and races, and thought that they had thus transformed an abstract construct into a living organism. This is the same method by which man made his gods: he transferred his own character to the pale creature of his imagination and then set it up as the master of his life. Who would doubt that the inventors

[1] Moritz Lazarus, *Das Leben der Seele*. Berlin, 1855-57.

of the various collective psychologies, who have constructed their schemes
in the same way, will of necessity reach the same results? Every collective
concept developed in this way becomes a Saturn, who in this case devours,
not his children, but his parents.

When men began to work with the concept of mass psychology they
meant by it at first merely that man, when he is together with many
others of his kind and because of some stimulus is seized with the same
excitement, is subject to a special emotion, which leads him under the
circumstances to acts which he would not perform if alone by himself.
So far, so good. Without doubt there are such moods; but here, too, we
are always dealing with a mood of the individual, not with a mood of
the mass as such. Emotions of this sort doubtless arise from the social
impulse of man and merely show that this is an essential feature of his
human existence. In this way arise moods of general sorrow and of general rejoicing and animation, just as, indeed, every profound psychic
experience of the individual arises from the immediate influence of his
social environment. A mass expression of human feeling such as we can
observe in demonstrations by rather large numbers of men is impressive
just because here the sum of the elementary force of all the individual
emotions makes itself felt and so affects extraordinarily the state of mind
of the individual.

Moreover, similarities of feelings among individuals shows itself not
only in association with great masses, but with other accompanying
phenomena, which is merely to say that, regardless of all the differences,
there are present in human beings certain common basic instincts. Thus,
enforced loneliness and enforced companionship induce in many individuals
altogether similar emotions, which often even lead to the same behavior.
The same thing is observed in many phenomena of sickness, in sexual
excitement, and on a hundred other occasions. One can therefore speak
only of an individual psychic or intellectual condition, for it is only in
the individual that the physiological prerequisites for emotions of any
sort or for mental impressions are present; they are not to be found in
abstract entities like the state, nation or mass. We can just as little conceive the occurrence of a thought without the functioning of the brain
or of sense impression without the mediation of the nerves as we can
of the digestive process without the appropriate organs. Just for this
reason every collective psychology lacks that firm basis on which alone
any useful comparison could rest. But the adherents of these theories are
undisturbed by such trifles and generalize merrily. What they bring forth
is sometimes very cleverly constructed, but that is all.

Membership in a particular class, nation or race has for a long time
not been decisive for the total thought and feeling of the individual;
just as little can the essential nature of a nation, race or class be distilled

from the manner of thought and fundamentals of character of individuals. Every larger or smaller social structure includes persons of every conceivable trait of character, intellectual endowment and effective behavior-instincts, in which every shade of human thought and feeling find expression. Among the people who belong to such a group there exists usually a vague feeling of relationship, which is not in any way inborn, but is acquired, and is of little significance in judging the group as a whole. The same is also true of physical and intellectual similarities that have their origin in the conditions of the environment. In every instance the special characteristics of the individual throughout his entire development stand out much more sharply than do certain common features which have arisen in particular human groups in the course of time. Indeed, Schopenhauer had already recognized this when he said:

> Besides, individuality greatly outweighs nationality and in any given human being deserves a thousand times more consideration. National character, since it has to do with the crowd, will never be anything fairly to boast about. It is rather that human limitation, perversity and baseness appear in every country in a different form, and we call this the national character. Disgusted by one of them, we praise another until this, too, has earned our disgust. Every nation speaks scornfully of every other—and they are all right.

What Schopenhauer says here about nationality and national character can be applied without change to every other collective concept. The properties which the "psychologists of the crowd" ascribe to or invent for their collective structures very seldom correspond to reality; they are always the result of personal wish-concepts, and are therefore to be valued only as fanciful structures. The race or nation whose qualities the race- or folk-psychologist tries to represent is always like the picture which he had made of it in advance. According to the affection or aversion which he feels for it at the given moment will this race or nation seem brilliant, chivalrous, faithful, idealistic, honorable, or intellectually inferior, calculating, faithless, materialistic and treacherous. Let one compare the different judgments which were passed during the World War by members of every nation upon other nations, and one will be unable to entertain any illusions about the true significance of such estimates. The impression would be still more devastating if one should bring into comparison also the estimates of earlier periods and contrast them with the later; say, the hymn of the French romantic, Victor Hugo, about the German peoples or the ode of the English poet, Thomas Campbell, "To the Germans"; and as contrasting pieces to these the effusions of respectable contemporaries in both countries concerning these same Germans. Though just here we are speaking of Englishmen and Frenchmen, the Germans would provide no better examples. Let one read the hot-headed judgments of German race-theoreticians about the alleged inferiority of the Britons and the degeneracy of the French, and one understands at once the maxim of Nietzsche, "to associate with no man who had a share in the deceitful race-fraud." How greatly opinion about foreign nations is affected by altered circumstances and momentary moods is shown by the productions of two French authors whom Karl Lahn has presented in his valuable and frank little book, *Frenchmen*. Thus, Frédéric-Constant de Rougemont was able to say this for the Germans:

> The German comes into the world to a spiritual life. He lacks the light, simple cheerfulness of the Frenchman. His soul is rich, his temperament sensitive and profound. He is tireless at work, persistent in undertaking. No people has a higher moral code, among none do men attain a greater age. . . . While the inhabitants of other countries make it their boast that they are Frenchmen, Englishmen or Spaniards, the German embraces all mankind in his unprejudiced love. Just because of its location in the center of Europe the German nation seems to be at once the heart and the dominating reason of mankind.

Let us compare these utterances with the estimate of these same Germans by the Dominican Father Didon in his book, *Les Allemands:*

> I have never encountered among present day Germans, not even at that age when men are most accessible to chivalrous ideas, any sublime emotion that reached beyond the horizon of the German fatherland. The frontier shuts the Germans in body and soul. Self-interest is their highest law. Their greatest statesmen are merely clever utilitarians. Their self-seeking policy, which is more avid of profit than of glory, has never felt the slightest misgivings about the country which unresistingly and blindly accepts its oracles. The Germans make allies for themselves but no friends. Those whom they bind to themselves are impelled either by interest or fear; they are thinking of the difficulties of the future. How can men be free from fear when they are at the mercy of a power that is not inspired by justice and when the dominance of self-interest is unlimited? . . . Germany's preponderance in Europe means universal militarism, a rule of terror, violence and selfishness. Times beyond number have I tried to discover among them any kind of sympathy for other nations; I have never been so fortunate as to find it.

The two judgments utterly destroy one another, but without doubt— each in its own way—they have influenced public opinion in France. There is, of course, a certain explanation for the sweeping contradiction which we find here. The two estimates come from two different men; one was uttered before, the other after, the Franco-German war of 1870-71. Then, in the "great period of shams," which hot-headed boobies called the "steel bath of the folk rejuvenation," people were quicker at the trigger in passing judgment and had learned besides to modify a judgment to fit the circumstances. Thus, the *Popolo d' Italia,* the organ of the later dictator Mussolini, laid down the following admirable estimate of the Rumanians before they had entered into the War and declared themselves upon the side of the allies:

> Let us finally quit calling the Rumanians our sister nation. They are no Romans even if they adorn themselves with that noble name. They are a mixture of those barbarian primitive peoples who were subjugated by the Romans, with Slavs, Pecheneges, Chazars, Avars, Tatars, Mongols, Huns, Turks and Greeks, and one can easily imagine what sort of ragbag that produced. The Rumanian is still today a barbarian and inferior individual, who, to the universal scornful amusement of Frenchmen, apes the Parisians and likes to fish in muddy waters when there is no danger that he will get himself into trouble. He showed this clearly in 1913.

Hardly, however, had the Rumanians entered the war on the side of the allies when this same journal of Mussolini's wrote of them:

> The Rumanians have now proved gloriously that they are worthy sons of the ancient Romans from whom, like ourselves, they are descended. They are, therefore, our next of kin, who now, with that courage and determination which distinguishes them, have joined in the struggle of the Latin and Slavic races against the German, in other words, the struggle for freedom, culture and right against Prussian tyranny, arbitrary rule, barbarism and selfishness. And just as the Rumanians showed in 1877 what they were capable of at the side of our brave Russian allies against Turkish barbarism, so will they now also throw their sharp sword into the scale against Austrian-Hungarian-German barbarism and unculture and bring these to their knees. Of course, nothing else was to be expected of a people which has the honor to belong to the Latin race, which once ruled the world.[2]

It would be a grateful task carefully to gather and contrast with one another similar estimates which were made of the various nations during the world war. Such a collection would furnish better evidence of the worldliness of our time than the finest commentaries of our historians.

If the judgment of the so-called race- or folk-psychologists about foreign nations is as a rule unjust, one-sided and artificially constructed, the continued glorification of a man's own nation to the derogation of all others affects one as utterly silly and childish, provided one still has any feeling for such things. Let us think of a man who misses no opportunity to parade himself as the very paragon of wisdom, talent and virtue, and while thus burning incense to himself disparages all others and treats them as inferiors. One would certainly take him for a vain booby or an imbecile and treat him accordingly. But when our own nation is concerned

[2] We take these two citations from the clever essay, *Rasse und Politik,* by Prof. Julius Goldstein, p. 152.

we take up with the wildest delusions and are not at all ashamed to deck ourselves in all the virtues and to regard the others as peoples of the second rank—as if it were by our own merit that we came into the world as Germans, Frenchmen or Chinese. Even discriminating minds are subject to this weakness, and the Scottish philosopher, Hume, knew what he was saying when he declared:

> When our nation gets into a war with another we abhor the hostile nation with all our heart and call it cruel, faithless, unjust and violent; we ourselves, however, and our allies we hold to be honorable, reasonable and gentle. We designate our treacheries as cleverness, our cruelties become for us necessities. In short, our faults seem to us small and insignificant, and not infrequently we call them by the name of that virtue which is most like them.

Every collective psychology suffers from these defects and is compelled by the logic of its own assumptions to proclaim empty wishes as concrete facts. By this it arrives automatically at conclusions of the sort for which self-deception smooths the way. It is especially unfortunate to speak of a "national culture" in which the special "mind" or the special "soul" of each people allegedly finds expression. The belief in the national culture-soul rests upon the same illusion as the "historical mission" of Bossuet, Fichte, Hegel and their numerous successors.

Culture as such is never national, because it always extends beyond the political frame of the state structure and is confined by no national frontier. A brief glance at the various fields of cultural life will easily confirm this. We will disregard any artificial distinction between civilization and culture for the reasons earlier advanced. Our survey will extend, rather, over all the fields in which man's conscious attack upon the crude natural course of events has found expression—from the material structure of economic life to the most highly developed forms of intellectual creativeness and artistic activity; for what Karol Câpek has so beautifully clothed in words holds good also for us:

> Every human activity which has as its purpose the perfecting, the enlightening and the ordering of our life is cultural. There is no yawning cleft between culture and everything else. I would not assert that the roar of the motors is the music of the present. But the roar of the motors is one of the voices in the polyphony of the cultural life, just as the heavenly notes of the violin, or the words of the orator, or the shouting on the field of sport are voices in this polyphony. Culture is not a section or a fragment of life, it is its sum and center.

It would be a vain undertaking to prove the national origin or content of the capitalistic economic system under which we live. Modern capitalism has carried the monopolizing of the means of production and of social wealth in the interest of small minorities to an unbelievable length and in doing so has delivered the great mass of the working population over to all the cruelties of wage slavery; but it is neither the result of any national undertakings, nor has it, ideologically, the slightest element in common with such undertakings. It is true that the supporters of capitalistic economy under certain circumstances are favorable to national undertakings, but their favor is always a matter of calculation, for the "national interests" to which they commit themselves are always really their own interests. No economic order of the past has so openly and ruthlessly sacrificed all so-called "national principles" to the rapacity of small minorities in society as the capitalistic order.

The shaping of capitalistic economic methods progressed in all countries with such astounding uniformity that one can understand why the economists and economic-politicians constantly harp upon the "determinism" of this development and see in every manifestation of the capitalistic system the inevitable result of iron economic laws, whose effects are stronger than the will of its human agents. In fact, capitalism has shown in every country which it has thus far captured, the same phenomena, the same effects upon the collective life of men without distinction of race or nation. If here and there, small differences are noticeable, this is not the result of peculiar national characteristics but of the various degrees of capitalistic economic development.

This shows itself today very clearly in the development of the great capitalistic industries in Europe, and especially in Germany. It is not long since everywhere strong opinions were based upon the fabulous development of American industry and its methods of work. Men sought to find in these methods the inevitable operation of a peculiar American mentality which could never be harmonized with the temperament of Europeans and especially of Germans. Who today would have the courage, in view of the latest results of our collective economic life, to defend this assertion —as untenable as it is arrogant? The famous, or much better, the notorious rationalizing of industry, with the help of the Taylor system and Ford's continuous operation, has within the last few years made greater advances in Germany than in any other country. We have long understood that Taylorism and Fordism are not at all specific products of the American mentality, but obvious phenomena of the capitalistic economic order as such, the sentimental German promoter is just as receptive to their advantages as the most hard-boiled Yankee, whose purely materialistic attitude we could formerly not sufficiently condemn.

The fact that these methods first arose in America is no proof that they are based on the American mentality and are to be esteemed as peculiar national characteristics. Their methods did not come even to

Ford and Taylor as a special gift from heaven; these men, too, had their predecessors and pacemakers who arose out of capitalistic industry and were certainly not destined for this role by peculiar national endowment. Continuous operation, stop-watch, and "scientific management," as they have christened the minute calculation of every muscular movement in work, have arisen gradually out of capitalistically controlled industry and have been fostered by it. It is of slight significance for the general character of mechanical production whether this or that machine finds its application first in Germany or in America. The same is true of the methods of work which grow out of the development of modern technique.

The endeavor to make production yield the greatest results with the smallest expenditure of power is closely bound up with modern machine production and with capitalistic economy in general. The constantly accelerated harnessing of natural forces and their technical employment, the constant refinement of mechanical apparatus, the industrializing of agriculture and the growing specialization of labor, bear witness to this. That the latest manifestations of industrial capitalism were noticeable in America earlier than elsewhere has not the slightest relation to national influences. In a country which has been so unusually favored by nature, and in which industrial development set out at such a gigantic pace, the extremes of capitalistic economic life necessarily mature earlier and stand out in sharper forms. Fred Taylor, who found his starting point in these fantastic industrial processes and whose mind was restrained by no ancient traditions, recognized with a sure instinct the utterly unlimited possibilities of this development. Constant increase of the productive capacity in industry was the slogan of the time and led to continuous further improvements of the mechanical apparatus. Under these circumstances was it such an unheard of phenomenon that a man hit upon the idea of adjusting the machine of flesh and bones to the rhythm of the machine of steel and iron? From the Taylor system to the traveling belt was only a step. Ford was the beneficiary of Taylor and his much praised genius consists only in his having developed Taylor's methods farther for his own purposes and having adapted them to the new conditions of mass production.

From America these methods gradually spread over all Europe. In Germany rationalization within a few years brought about a complete transformation of industry as a whole. Today, French industry bears its brand. The other countries follow at a little distance—must follow if their economy is not to fall to the rear. Even in Bolshevist Russia they follow in the same path and speak of a "socializing of the Taylor system" without considering that they thus seal the fate of socialism, which the Russian Revolution was to realize.

What is true of this latest phase of capitalistic development is true of the development of capitalism in general. It has begun everywhere with the same attendant phenomena. Neither the national boundaries of the various states nor national and religious traditions were able to check its advance. In India, China, Japan, we observe today the same phenomena which were presented to us by early capitalism in Europe, except that the progress of development is today everywhere much more rapid. In all modern industrial countries the struggle for raw materials and for markets, which is so indicative of the nature of capitalistic economy, leads to the same results and puts its stamp upon the foreign policy of the capitalistic states. These manifestations proceed everywhere with a strang uniformity, and in almost the same shapes. Nothing, however, nothing at all, in this indicates that forces are here in operation that are traceable to the peculiar national endowment of one or another people.

The transition from private to monopoly capitalism, which we can observe today in every industrial country, goes on everywhere. Everywhere it is shown that the capitalistic world has entered upon a new phase of its development which yet more openly expresses its true character. Capitalism today breaks through all frontiers of the so-called "national economic fields" and works ever more unequivocally for a condition of organized world economy. Capital, which formerly felt itself bound up with certain national interests, develops into world capital and is concerned with building up the exploitation of all mankind on uniform principles. We see today how in place of the earlier national economic groups there are crystallizing out ever more distinctly three great economic entities: America, Europe and Asia; and there is no reason why the development in this direction should not keep on, so long as the capitalistic system can hold out at all.

If formerly free contract was the great slogan of the political economists, who saw in the "free play of forces" the necessary operation of an iron economic law, today these already antiquated forms are more and more yielding the field to the strategy of collective capitalistic organizations which undertake to eliminate contract entirely by setting up national and international trusts in order to achieve uniform control of prices. If formerly the mutual competition of private owners in industry and trade took care that entrepreneurs and merchants should not be able to raise their prices to quite too high a level, today the promoters of the great economic cartels are in a position easily to suppress all private competition and in the thoroughness of their control to prescribe prices to consumers. Corporations like the Internationale Rohstahlgemeinschaft and a hundred others show clearly the course of this development. Together with the ancient private capitalism, vanishes also its catchword of laissez-faire, to make way for the economic dictatorship of modern collective capitalism. No, our present economic system has not a single national vein in its body; just as little as the economic systems of the past, as economics in general.

What is said here of modern industrial capitalism is true also of trade and bank capital. Its administrators and beneficiaries feel themselves everywhere safe in the saddle. They conspire to bring on wage wars and organize revolutions; they provide modern politics with the necessary slogans with which to conceal behind the veil of misleading ideas the cruel and insatiable greed of small minorities. By means of a venal and thoroughly mendacious press they modify and shape "public opinion," and with cold cynicism disregard every mandate of humanity and of social morality. In a word, they make personal profit the starting point of every discussion and are always ready to sacrifice to this Moloch the weal and woe of mankind.

> Whenever innocent souls catch the scent of deep political reasons or of national hatred there is open to them no recourse except to the conspiracies instigated by the pirates of finance. They exploit everything: political and economic rivalries, national hostilities, diplomatic traditions and religious antagonisms. In all the wars of the last quarter-century one finds the hand of high finance. The conquest of Egypt and the Transvaal, the annexation of Tripoli, the occupation of Morocco, the partition of Persia, the carnage in Manchuria, and the international blood-bath in China on the occasion of the Boxer uprising, the Japanese wars—everywhere one stumbles upon the big banks. . . . The hundreds of thousands of men that the war will cost—what does that matter to finance? The mind of the financier is concerned with columns of figures which balance. The rest is none of his affair; he does not even possess imagination enough to include human lives in his calculation.[3]

Capitalism is everywhere the same in its objectives; likewise, in the selection of its means. Its devastating effects on the intellectual and emotional life of men are also everywhere the same. Its practical operation in all parts of the earth leads to the same results and imprints on men a peculiar stamp which had not been known before. If one follows these phenomena with a watchful eye one cannot avoid the conclusion that our modern economic system is the symbol of a definite epoch and in no way the result of special national exertions. The forces of every nation have had a part in bringing about this condition. If one wishes really to grasp its inner nature, the one must dive into the intellectual and material assumptions of the capitalistic epoch; but it would be a vain task to try to judge the economic foundations of this and of all past social epochs from a so-called national point of view.

This is just the reason why the so-called "economic nationalism" of

[3] P. Kropotkin, *La science moderne, etc.* Paris, 1913, p. 294.

which there is so much talk today, and which has cast its spell over even outspoken socialists, is so hopelessly highflown. From the fact that the old national economic entities are today being more and more completely crushed by the world economy of the international trusts and cartels men have rather prematurely drawn the conclusion that all economy is to be transformed and reconstructed on the basis of the special endowments and capabilities resident in each people because of their national peculiarities. Thus, one regards operations in the coal industry and its different branches and the proceeding of fiber-stuffs as occupations which are best suited to the national industrial instincts of Englishmen, while one says of the Germans that they are best fitted for the potash industry, lithography, the chemical trade and optics. Thus, it is believed that to each people can be assigned a special industrial activity which best fits his national endowment, and that in this way a reorganization of the whole economic life can be arrived at.

In reality, these ideas are merely a new edition of similar lines of thought which once played an important role in the works of the old English economists. Then, too, it was thought necessary to establish that Nature herself had destined certain peoples for industry and others for agriculture. This illusion long ago went into the discard, and its latest ideological recoinage will be accorded no better end. Men as individuals can be subjected to industrial specialization; whole peoples and nations, never. This and similar lines of thought suffer from the same defect that is found in the foundation of every collective concept. A man may very well, because of certain inborn characteristics and capabilities, belong among the chemists, the farmers, the painters or the philosophers; but a people as a whole never permits itself to be subjected to an abstract assumption, because every one of its members exhibits peculiar inclinations and requirements, which become apparent in the rich manifoldness of their undertakings. This very many-sidedness, in which natural endowments, capacities and inclinations mutually supplement one another, constitutes the genuine essence of every community. Who overlooks this has no understanding whatever of the organic structure of the community.

What has been said here about the economic side of social culture applies also to the political forms of social life. These also can be judged and valued only as products of definite epochs, never as typical manifestations of any kind of national ideology whatever. It would be a futile undertaking to examine all past forms of the state in the light of their national character and content. In this field also, we have to do with a social development which gradually penetrated to every part of the European culture circle, and just for this reason was connected with no specific national norm. Even the most decided supporters of "national thought" cannot deny that the transition from the "state with subjects" to the "national constitutional state" occurred in all Europe under the same social assumptions and often in quite similar forms.

The absolute monarchy, which almost everywhere in Europe preceded the present constitutional state, was originally just as intimately interwoven with the ancient feudal economy as was, later, the parliamentary system with the economic order of private capital; and as the latter was confined by no national boundaries, so also the parliamentary form of government served not merely a particular nation, but all the so-called "culture nations" as the political frame for their social activities. Even the manifestations of decay of the parliamentary system, which one can observe everywhere today, reveal themselves in every country in similar forms. However much Mussolini might insist that modern fascism was a purely Italian product which could not be imitated by any other nation, the history of the last ten years has already shown how arrogant and baseless the claim was. Fascism also—regardless of its exaggerated nationalistic ideology—is merely a product of the spirit of our time, born of a definite situation and nourished by it. The general economic, political and social status which arose in consequence of the World War led in all countries to similar efforts; which is merely evidence that even the most extreme nationalism is, in the final view, to be regarded as a tendency of the time which develops under specific social conditions and which in no way embodies the special "national spirit" of a particular people.

The modern politician is, in every country with a parliamentary government, determined by the same norm and pursues everywhere the same aims. He is a type which is found in every modern state and is shaped by the peculiarities of his profession. Attached to his party, to whose "will" he gives expression, he is always striving to make its opinion the dominant one and to defend its special interests as general interests. If he rises slightly above the average intellectual level of the usual party leader he knows quite well that the alleged will of his party is merely the will of a small minority which gives direction to the party and determines its practical activity. Always to hold the party firmly in hand and so to guide its adherents that each believes he is guided by his own will is one of the characteristic manifestations of the modern party system.

The nature of political parties, upon which every parliamentary government rests, is in every country the same. Everywhere the party is distinguished from other human organizations by its endeavor to attain to power. It has the conquest of the state inscribed on its banner. Its whole organizational structure imitates that of the state; and just as the government is constantly guided by reasons of state, the party is guided always by considerations of its special reasons of party. An action, or an idea, is for its adherents good or bad, just or unjust, not because it agrees with the personal judgment and convictions of the individual, but because it is advantageous or disadvantageous to the undertakings of the party, furthers its ends or is a hindrance to them. And here the voluntary discipline which the party imposes upon its adherents proves itself, as a rule more effective than the menace of the law, because servitude on principle is always deeper rooted than that which is imposed on men by external force.

So long as a party has not attained the public influence for which it strives it stands in opposition to the existing government. But an opposition is such a necessary institution for the parliamentary system of government that if it did not exist one would have to invent it, as Napoleon III once cynically remarked. If the party becomes stronger, so that the heads of the state must reckon with its influence, they make to it all sorts of concessions and under some conditions invite its leaders into the government. But the very existence of political parties and their influence in public life contradicts most strikingly the illusion of an alleged "national consciousness"; for it shows only too clearly how hopelessly divided and shattered the artificial structure of the nation is.

Now, as regards parliamentary government as such, there are, indeed, in the individual countries certain differences, which, however, are to be regarded merely as formal deviations and not at all as essential differences. Everywhere the parliamentary machine operates by the same methods and with the same routine. The discussions in the legislative bodies serve, in a measure, merely as theatrical exhibitions for the public and have not at all the purpose of convincing opponents or weakening their convictions. The position of the so-called "representatives of the people" in the vote upon the various questions which come up for debate is determined in advance in the separate party caucuses, and not even the eloquence of a Demosthenes would be able to change it. If the parliament would merely confine itself to voting and abstain from all public discussion of the separate proposals, the results would not differ by a hair. The oratorical exhibitions are, by and large, merely a necessary adjunct to keep up appearances. This is the same in France as it is in England and America, and it would be a waste of time to try to discover special national features in the practical procedure of the separate parliaments.

The whole development in Europe up to the modern constitutional state has proceeded everywhere in more or less similar form for the same reasons, since conditions underlay it which were effective not merely for a particular nation but forced themselves with the same irresistible logic upon all the peoples of the continent, however much the supporters of the old regime might struggle against them. Perhaps temporary differences can be discovered, for the great transformation did not take place in all the countries at the same time, but its manifestations were everywhere alike and were fostered by the same causes. Furthermore, this is proved also by the rise and spread of the so-called mercantile theories which exerted such a decisive influence upon the internal and external policies of the absolutist states of the sixteenth, seventeenth and eighteenth centuries. These theories found famous advocates in every country in Europe: in France, Bodin, Montcrétien, de Watteville, Sully, Melon, Forbonnais and others; in England, Raleigh, Mun, Child, Temple, and so on; in Italy, Galiani, Genovesi and their successors; in Spain, Ustariz and Ulloa; in Holland, Hugo Grotius and Pieter de Groot; in Austria and Germany, Becker, Hrneck, Seckendorff, Justi, Süssmilch, Sonnenfels and many others. Here, too, we are dealing with a general intellectual drift which arose from the social status of Europe.

The more the absolutist state operated in the different countries as an unsurmountable obstacle to any further social development, the more clearly the destructiveness of its political-economic tendencies were revealed, the more unequivocally apparent became, in course of time, the striving for political reconstruction and new understandings of economic theory. The insane extravagance of the courts in the midst of starving peoples, the shameless prodigality of the favorites and mistresses, the collapse of agriculture because of the feudal privileges and a monstrous system of taxation, the threat of state bankruptcy, the unrest of the peasants who were hardly regarded as human by the privileged orders, the destruction of all moral ties, and the heartless indifference in those striking words of Pompadour which have achieved such pitiful fame, *"Après nous le déluge!"*—all this could but prepare the way for the overthrow of the old régime and lead to new views of life. Whether this occurred from within, as in Holland, England and France, or was effected from without, as in Germany, Austria and Poland, is of little importance.

So there arose critics of absolutism and social reformers like Montesquieu, Rousseau, Voltaire, Diderot and many others, who had been preceded in Holland and England by thinkers with similar ideas. The school of the physiocrats, also, which made war upon mercantilism, regarded agriculture as the real source of the wealth of the people and sought the liberation of economy in general from all state ordinances and regulations, was produced by the same causes. The famous saying of Gournay, *"Laissez faire, laissez aller!"* which was later to serve the Manchester school as a motto, had originally a quite different meaning. It was an outcry of the human spirit against the iron compulsion of state guardianship, which threatened to smother every demonstration of social life. It was becoming more and more impossible to breathe freely and men were beginning to yearn for sunlight and air. The ideas of Quesnay, Mirabeau, Beaudeau, de la Rivière, Turgot and others with surprising promptness, found militant supporters in Germany, Austria, Poland,

Sweden, Spain and America. Under their influence and that of David Hume, Adam Smith developed his new theory and became the founder of the classical national economics which soon spread through all countries, just as did the critique of socialism which followed close on its heels.

Here, too, we are dealing with phenomena of the time which were born of the general social conditions of a definite period and which gradually led to a reconstruction of the state and a renewal of economic life. But Saint-Simon already recognized that even this form of political life is not the last when he said: "The parliamentary and constitutional system, which seems to so many to be the last miracle of the human intellect, is merely a transitional dominion between feudalism, on whose ruins we are living, and whose fetters we have not yet completely shaken off, and a higher order of affairs." The more deeply we look into the current structure of political and economic life, the more clearly we recognize that its forms have arisen from the general course of social development, and therefore cannot be measured by national principles.

Chapter 9

GENIUS AND THE NATION. GOETHE ON THE ORIGINALITY OF OUR
THOUGHT. FORERUNNERS AND CO-WORKERS. THE COPERNICAN PICTURE
OF THE UNIVERSE AND THE EVOLUTION THEORY AS EXAMPLES. THE
HELIOCENTRIC SYSTEM OF THE UNIVERSE AMONG THE ANCIENTS. THE
PTOLEMAIC SYSTEM OF THE UNIVERSE. THE DOCTRINE OF COPERNICUS.
JOHANNES KEPLER AND GALILEO. NEWTON'S LAW OF GRAVITATION.
THE FORERUNNERS OF NEWTON. LAPLACE AND KANT. THE DEVELOP-
MENT OF ASTRO-PHYSICS. THE PRELIMINARIES FOR RELATIVITY. THE
THEORY OF EVOLUTION IN ANTIQUITY. THE SHAPING OF THE IDEA OF
EVOLUTION UP TO THE EVE OF THE FRENCH REVOLUTION. LAMARCK
AND GOETHE. THE FORERUNNERS OF DARWIN. THE DOCTRINE OF DAR-
WIN AND WALLACE. SOCIAL DARWINISM. KROPOTKIN'S THEORY OF
"MUTUAL AID." THE PRESENT STATUS OF THE THEORY OF EVOLUTION.
THE INFLUENCE OF THE IDEA OF EVOLUTION ON ALL BRANCHES OF
HUMAN THOUGHT.

JUST as the structure of economic and political social forms is not
bound up with particular peoples, races or nations, so also the thought
and feeling of the individual does not follow definite national lines, but
is always influenced by the ideas of the time and the cultural circle to
which he belongs. Great pioneer ideas in the fields of science and of philosophic thought, new forms of artistic expression, never arise from a whole
people or an entire nation, but always merely from the creative power
of enlightened minds, in whom genius is revealed. How a genius arises
no one has yet determined. A genius may come out of any people, but
what special merit the people or the nation has in this no one can say.
However, there is no people, no nation, no race of geniuses, there never
has been one; it is because of this that the endeavors of our modern race
fatalists are so hopelessly muddled and senseless. But even genius does
not owe everything to its own powers; even the greatest mind does not
stand outside of time and space; he is, like all others, bound to the past
and the present. This is what is significant in genius, that it lends voice
and form to what lies slumbering in many, and forms a unified concept
of the separate results of the intellectual development of a period. The

mind of the genius is a *universal mind*, which builds out of all that has gone before it a new world-picture and thus opens to mankind new outlooks on life. The deeper it is rooted in its social environment the more precious are the fruits which it brings to maturity. No one has felt this more deeply than did Goethe, who said:

At bottom, however, we are all collective beings, pose however we please. For how little we have, and how little we are that we can, in the strictest sense, call our own! We must all receive and learn as well from those who were before us as from those who are with us. Even the greatest genius would not get far if he wished to owe everything to what he had within him. But very many worthy men do not understand this and, with their dreams of originality, grope half their lives in the dark. I have known artists who boasted of having followed no master, rather of owing everything to their own genius. The fools! As if that happened anywhere! And as if the world were not pressing on them at every step and, in spite of their stupidity, making something out of them! . . . Perhaps I may speak of myself and tell modestly how I feel. It is true that during my long life I have undertaken and accomplished a great variety of things of which, perhaps, I might boast. But what did I have, if we want to be honest, that was really my own except the ability and the inclination, too, to see and to hear, to decide and to choose, and to animate what I had seen and heard with my own spirit and reproduce it with some skill. I owe my works in no way to my own wisdom alone, but thousands of things and persons outside me offered me the material for them. There came fools and wise men, clear heads and muddled ones, childhood and youth, as also ripe old age: all told me how they felt, what they thought, how they lived and worked, and what experiences they had gathered; and I had nothing more to do than to seize and reap what they had sown for me. At bottom it is just all nonsense, whether one gets something out of himself or whether he gets it from others; whether one works through himself or works through others: the chief thing is that one have a great will and possess skill and persistence to carry it out; all the rest does not matter.[1]

We are always dependent upon our predecessors, and for this reason the notion of a "national culture" is misleading and inconsistent. We are never in a position to draw a line between what we have acquired by our own powers and what we have received from others. Every idea, whether it be of a religious, an ethical, a philosophic, a scientific or an artistic nature, had its forerunners and pioneers, without which it would be inconceivable; and it is usually quite impossible to go back to its first beginnings. Almost invariably thinkers of all countries and peoples have contributed to its development.

Let us take as examples two theories that penetrate deeply and shake

[1] J. P. Eckermann, *Conversations With Goethe in the Last Years of His Life.* 1823-1832.

to their very foundations all previous conceptions, as do the Copernican system and the Darwinian theory of evolution. These two doctrines not only transformed fundamentally the views of men about the structure of the universe and the development of life upon earth; in doing this they worked with genuine revolutionary effect upon every other field of human thought and brought about a complete overturning of all previously known science. But here, too, the new knowledge broke its path only gradually—until in the course of time enough factual material was accumulated so that a brilliantly gifted mind could draw from it the necessary conclusion and give to the new views a clear foundation.

To what beginnings the idea that the earth turns on its own axis and, together with the other planets, moves around the sun, goes back historically, will perhaps never be ascertained. Albert Einstein, the honored founder of the theory of relativity, remarks with justice that, especially where the fundamental principles of physics are concerned, man is always stumbling on something earlier, so that it is almost impossible to follow any line of discoveries back to its first beginning. Even if we were unanimous in honoring Aristarchus of Samos as the first great forerunner of the Copernican system, we should still always entertain the suspicion that he may in turn have drawn upon Egyptian sources.[2] No objection can be urged against the concept on this account, because this is shown anew in the history of every new invention and discovery. Not even from the most brilliant brain does a new idea spring full-grown, like Minerva from the head of Jupiter. It is, therefore, indisputable that the idea of a heliocentric universe was grasped in a premonitory fashion by bold thinkers long before Copernicus and, by a few, was given a more or less convincing foundation. The Italian scholar, Schiaparelli, has set this forth clearly in a special monograph, *I Precursori del Copernico*.

That the Greeks were deeply indebted to the Babylonians and the Egyptians for their knowledge of astronomy and physics is today quite beyond question, so it does not matter whether or not the Ionian natural philosopher, Thales of Miletus, was in fact a pupil of the Babylonian thinker, Berossus. Certainly there existed between Greece and the countries of the Orient very close connections, which must have had their intellectual effects. Thus, it was said of Pythagoras that he traveled in Egypt and the East and acquired there a great part of his knowledge of astronomy and mathematics. In fact the school of the Pythagoreans was distinguished for its bold conception of the structure of the universe. Plutarch relates of the Pythagorean, Philaos, that according to his teaching the earth and the moon move in an oblique circle about the central fire.

It is known with certainty that Aristarchus of Samos developed the theory of a heliocentric universe. It is true that his essay on the subject

[2] A. Moszkowski, *Einstein, Einblick in seine Gedankenwelt.* Berlin, 1921.

has been lost, but we find in Plutarch and in the "calculation of the sands" of Archimedes short sketches of the theory of Aristarchus, from which we learn that he maintained that the earth turns on its own axis and also moves about the sun as center, while the stars and the sun remain motionless in space. We do not know how widespread such teachings were, but it is easily conceivable that the adherents of the geocentric system, which places the earth at the center of the universe, were in the majority, since direct observation seemed to speak for them. Even the famous system of the Alexandrian, Ptolemy, as he had developed it in his *Almagest*, which held captive the minds of men for a millennium and a half, had its forerunners and was merely the completion of the great work which Hipparchus of Nicaea had begun three hundred years before. Hipparchus, moreover, owed much of his doctrine to the Chaldean astrologers.

That the Ptolemaic system could endure so long without contradiction was owing chiefly to the influence of the Church. Religion had set up the earth as the center of creation, had elevated man to the position of crown of creation, the image of God himself. It, therefore, did not suit the church that the earth should lose its point of vantage as the center of all things, and circle about the sun like all the other planets. Such an idea was incomprehensible to the religious temperament and might give rise to serious consequences. This was the reason why the church fought the doctrine of Copernicus so long and so bitterly. In Rome, until the resolution of the Cardinals of the Inquisition which Pius VII sanctioned in September, 1823, no book could be printed or publicly circulated in which the theory of a heliocentric universe was advocated. How many secret opponents of the Ptolemaic system there were during the long period of its unlimited dominion can, of course, not be determined. Only under the influence of the rediscovered writings of the ancients, which were first transmitted to the European peoples in any large measure by the Arabs, did there develop, especially in the Italian cities, a new spirit which set itself against the authority of Aristotle and Ptolemy. Bold thinkers like Domencio Maria Novara (1454-1504) revealed to their pupils the "Pythagorean doctrines" and evolved the idea of a new picture of the universe. Copernicus, who in those years was pursuing his studies at Bologna and Padua, fell completely under the sway of this new intellectual movement, which doubtless gave him the first impulse toward the development of his theory. Actually he was in the years 1506-1512 laying the foundations of his theory, which he enlarged later in his principal work, *Concerning the Revolution of the Heavenly Bodies*, which appeared in 1543. This work had been preceded by an essay, long since lost, entitled *A Short Sketch of the Probable Movements of the Heavens*, which was rediscovered by the Copernican scholar, Curtze, and published in the seventies. Even if Copernicus did not hit upon the idea of the helio-centric system quite of himself, still his is the indisputable merit of having developed and established the new conception on scientific principles.

In his famous seven theses Copernicus defended the notion that there is only one center for the stars and their orbits; that the center of the earth is not the center of the universe, but merely the center of the moon's orbit and its own mass; that all the planets revolve about the sun, which stands at the center of their orbits; that the distance from earth to sun is, in relation to the width of the firmament, smaller than the semi-diameter of the earth in relation to the distance from earth to sun, and hence vanishes when compared with the size of the firmament; that what seems to us a movement of the heavens is not such, but is due to a motion of the earth, in which the earth and its immediate environment rotates daily, while its two poles retain constantly the same direction; that the heavens, on the other hand, remain immovable quite to their uttermost limit; that what seems to us a movement of the sun is not due to that star, but to the earth and its orbit, in which we move about the sun like all the other planets, the earth having, therefore, a twofold movement; that the advance and retrogression of the planets is not a consequence of *their* movement, but of that of the earth—that the multi-plicity of heavenly phenomena finds, therefore, its complete explanation in the movement of the earth.

To this new theory of Copernicus history offers few comparable intel-lectual achievements; yet with it the proud structure of the heliocentric system of the universe was not quite finished. From the beginning it found a flock of enthusiastic supporters, but still more opponents, so that it was able at first to make its way only gradually. At the outset the new theory met with the best reception in Germany, where the power of the church had been badly shaken by the Reformation. From this we must not con-clude that Protestantism was any more favorably inclined to it. That was not at all the case. Luther and Melanchthon were just as uncompre-mending and hostile toward the new doctrine as the pope; but the new church had not yet had time enough to cement its power, and for this reason could not be so dangerous to the daring novelty as the Catholic Church in the Latin countries. In Italy Giordano Bruno, to whom the Copernican system had rendered good service as the basis for his nature philosophy, had to atone for his boldness at the stake (1600); while Galileo, the most brilliant teacher of the new view of the universe, perhaps escaped the same fate only by letting himself be moved to renounce his alleged errors before the Tribunal of the Inquisition.

The theory of Copernicus received a powerful impulse from the German astronomer, Johannes Kepler, the most distinguished pupil of Tycho Brahe, to whom he doubtless owed very much. Kepler developed in his *New Astronomy* and in a later work his famous three laws, by which he brought out with astounding cleverness and after long and vain experiment, a mathematical proof of the correctness of the Copernican system. This brilliant thinker, whose intellectual greatness could not protect him from the bitterest misery, showed to his contemporaries that the paths of the planets are not actually circles, but ellipses, which, however, differ very little from true circles. Most important of all, he showed how the distances of the planets from the sun could be calculated from their periods of revolution, and what relation the velocity of their movement at different points in their orbits bears to their distance from the sun. Kepler had already grasped as a presumption that great unity of the cosmic laws which Newton later developed so brilliantly.

Almost at the same time, but independently of Kepler, Galileo Galilei of Pisa achieved a deeper insight into the operation of mechanical forces and established the laws of falling bodies, the motion of the pendulum, and projectiles, which put him in a position to answer all physical objections to the heliocentric system. But even in this field there had been a forerunner. Thus, the Genevan, Michel Varo, had already in 1585 clearly recognized the interrelation of the mechanical laws, and Simon Stevin of Brügge (1548-1620) had tried, independently of him, to establish practically the principle of those laws. Besides these two, there were still other isolated thinkers who were active with more or less success in the same field. After they began to puzzle out the diaries of Leonardo da Vinci it became clearer and clearer that this genuinely universal intellect had anticipated Galileo and many another in several respects, as, for example, the explanation of the law of falling bodies, the wave theory and a few more.

With the help of the telescope which he constructed Galileo succeeded in making a considerable number of important discoveries in celestial space. Thus, by the discovery of the moons of Jupiter he offered convincing proof that there actually were heavenly bodies which did not revolve about the earth. All in all, the invention of the telescope led to a whole series of similar discoveries, which were made in different countries and quite independently of one another. We need only recall here the observations of the Jesuit Father Christopher Scheiner in Ingolstadt, of Johannes Fabricius in Osteel, Friesland, and of Thomas Harriot in Isleworth, England.[3]

After Kepler had succeeded in establishing the movements in space mathematically by his three fundamental laws, and Galileo had formu-

---

[3] The development and perfection of the telescope was advanced by members of all nations. Galileo was by no means the inventor of the astronomical telescope, as has been often asserted; he himself told that he was guided in the setting up of his instrument by a discovery of some Belgian. It is certain that the telescope was invented in

lated the general principles of the force of gravity as these are revealed on the earth, the idea lay ready to hand that the same laws operate not only upon our planet but in the entire universe and that they determine the movements of the heavenly bodies. Francis Bacon (1561-1621), who has been called the father of the inductive method, already dreamed of a time when the human mind would succeed in tracing all events in space to the same uniform physical laws.

It was Isaac Newton (1642-1727), the brilliant English mathematician and natural philosopher, who helped the doctrines of Copernicus and Kepler to a final effective victory by his formulation of the so-called "law of gravitation." Newton established that the force which makes an apple that has been loosened fall to the ground is the same which holds the planets in their orbits in space. He recognized that the force of attraction which resides in every body increases with its mass at such a rate that a body twice as heavy attracts another twice as strongly. Along with this he discovered, too, that the attractive force of a body increases or diminishes with its smaller or greater distance from another body, and that it is inversely proportional to the square of the distance; that, therefore, a body of the size of the earth but twice as far away from the sun, is pulled by the sun only one fourth as forcibly.

Newton reduced this relation to a definite formula. With the aid of the infinitesimal calculus—a mathematical method which makes possible calculation with infinitely small magnitudes, and which the English thinker conceived almost simultaneously with the German philosopher, Leibnitz—he was able to prove the correctness of his discovery. This is set forth in his celebrated work *Principia Mathematica*. In this he also furnished the best confirmation of the heliocentric system of Copernicus and of the three laws of Kepler. Since then the law which bears Newton's name has been the basis of all astronomical calculations. But, just as Newton's brilliant discovery had its known anticipators, like Edmund Halley, Robert Hooke, Christopher Wren and others, who had all busied themselves with the problem of gravitation, so the theory was in no way a finality. In its turn, like every other great discovery, it gave the impulse to farther researches and observations. On the results of the Newtonian theory rested the splendid contributions of the famous mathematician, Leonhard Euler of Basel, and of the two Frenchmen, Alexis Clairvault and Jean le Rond d'Alembert. Here, too, we may mention the Danish astronomer, Olaf Römer, who as early as 1675—before the appearance

Holland during the first decade of the seventeenth century, and the two spectacle makers, Hans Lippershey and Zacharias Jansen, were actually named as the inventors. Individual instruments, however, had been constructed before this. The invention was, so to speak, in the air, and its further development was aided by minds of every nation.

of Newton's principal work—on the basis of the Copernican system, had undertaken a measurement of the velocity of light from the occurrence of eclipses of the moons of Jupiter.

Newton's intellectual achievement gave the impulse to numerous new discoveries which smoothed the way for that great theory which the French astronomer, Pierre Laplace (1749-1827), set forth in his two works, *Exposition du système du monde* and *Traité de la mécanique céleste*, in which he gave an explanation of the origin of our planetary system and traced all events in space to the operation of purely physical forces. But even his theory did not put the capstone on the structure of the new conception of the universe; it was essentially corrected, broadened and extended by men like Friedrich Gauss, J. L. Lagrange, P. A. Hansen, A. L. Cauchy, J. C. Adams, S. Newcomb, H. Dylden, F. Tisserant, and numerous thinkers of all peoples and nations.

Astrophysics, also, which acquired such a splendid impetus during the course of the last century, developed in the same manner. Before the genius of Gustav Kirchhoff had succeeded in establishing the chemical composition of the sun by his discovery of spectrum analysis, a whole troop of thinkers and investigators had preceded him in the various countries; men like W. H. Wollaston, Joseph Fraunhofer, W. A. Miller, L. Foucault, A. J. Angström, Balfour Stewart, G. Stokes and many others, on whose results Kirchhoff depended, while he brilliantly extended them and wrought them into a synthetic whole. On the other hand, the discovery of spectrum analysis opened the way for innumerable new inventions and discoveries which because of their abundance cannot even be mentioned here.

It is, therefore, indisputable that in the creation and development of our modern picture of the universe brilliant minds of all countries have contributed, of whom only a few of the best-known names could be mentioned briefly. Further, the relativity theory of Albert Einstein, with the help of which he has succeeded in solving the mystery of the orbit of Mercury in a manner as surprising as it is brilliant, would have been impossible without these countless predecessors. Let the incorrigible race fanatics enjoy themselves in proving from traditional portraits of Copernicus, Galileo or Laplace the membership of these men in the Nordic race; no one will envy them their childish sport. Wherever intellect speaks nationality and race vanish like mist before the wind, and it would be a senseless undertaking to try to judge a social idea, a religion or a scientific theory by its national content or according to the racial characteristics of its leaders.

We have seen how Poles, Germans, Italians, Frenchmen, Englishmen, Danes, Swedes, Dutchmen, Belgians, Swiss and others have worked for the victory of the heliocentric system. That intellectual structure was born of their united labor; to its development a whole world contributed; and its character cannot be determined by any political confession of faith nor by special national characteristics. When we are dealing with intellectual phenomena the universal in human thought becomes most clearly apparent and can be dammed in by no national limits; or, as Goethe so strikingly put it: "There is no patriotic art and no patriotic science. Both belong, like every exalted good, to the whole world, and can be fostered only by the general free cooperation of all who live at the same time, with constant regard for what remains known to us from the past."

What has been said here in a few words about the development of the Copernican theory holds good in still greater degree for the modern theory of evolution, which in such an astonishingly short time led to a complete reconstruction of all traditional concepts and hypotheses. Leaving out of consideration the heliocentric system, there is hardly any doctrine which has had such a deep and lasting effect upon the whole of human thought as the idea of a gradual development of all natural forms and manifestations of life under the influence of the environment and the external conditions of life. The new theory led not merely to a complete revolution in all fields of the natural science; it developed also quite new points of view in sociology, history and philosophy. Even the religious leaders, who at first fought the idea of evolution most bitterly, found themselves compelled to make far-reaching concessions to it and, after their fashion, to accommodate themselves to it. In a word, the idea of evolution has taken such complete possession of us and influences our whole thought to such a degree that we can today hardly conceive of any other view.

However, even this idea, which seems to us today so self-evident, did not burst suddenly upon the world, but like all great intellectual achievements only gradually matured and won general acceptance. How far back the first glimmerings of the theory of evolution extend historically will perhaps never be established. It is certain that the idea of a natural development of all things was already fairly widespread among the earliest of the Greek thinkers, and very probably would have guided the whole intellectual life of the European peoples into quite different channels if under the domination of the church the writings of the ancient sages had not remained so long unknown. As it was, they were transmitted only in fragments and in greatly diluted form to the men of a later epoch, who were controlled by quite different ideas.

Already among the Ionian philosophers, and especially in Anaximenes, we find the idea of a primal substance in which there resides a generative and transforming force revealing itself in production and alteration of living beings on the earth. Empedocles appears to have had a very profound grasp of this conception when he expressed the opinion that the different living forms owe their origin to special combinations of the primal substance. This bold and unique thinker was already explaining the evolution of organic beings through adaptation to their environment, since, according to his view, forms suitably equipped would be able to maintain themselves, while the others would disappear. In Heraclitus and the Greek atomists, as well as among the Epicureans and others, references are found to a gradual evolution and transformation of all manifestations of life. These Lucretius later assembled in his famous didactic poem and they have thus come down to us. Moreover, it is clear from the work of Lucretius that the ancient thinkers were by no means dealing with a vague notion to which later generations have attributed a meaning corresponding to their own way of thinking, but with a clear conception, and while this was very often based on insufficient grounds, its kernel is unmistakable.

It was only by the prevalence of Christian dogmatism, which had committed itself completely to the biblical legend of the creation and would permit no other view, that these brilliant beginnings of a theory of evolution were for fifteen centuries pushed into the background— though the idea itself never completely disappeared. It reappeared in the Middle Ages with the Arabian philosophers, Farabi and Avicenna, although in a very peculiar form strongly influenced by neo-Platonism. It likewise found expression in the noteworthy work, *Mekor Chaim*, of the Jewish Cabalist, Avicebro (also translated into Latin), reminiscent in some respects of the German mystic, Jacob Böhme, in which the Cabalist, recognizably came close to a premonition of the idea of an eternal development of all things.[4] The Scottish scholastic, Duns Scotus, also came very close to the idea of a development of the universe on the basis of definite physical laws.

Under the influence of the great discoveries of Copernicus, Kepler, Galileo and other enlightened minds of that period the idea of evolution made a new beginning. Bernardo Telesio, the great Italian scholar and philosopher, and one of the first to contradict the ideas of Aristotle which had dominated the Middle Ages, had undertaken in his work, *De Rerum Natura*, to trace all natural events to the operation of natural laws, seeking to explain every manifestation of the universe by the motion of its elements, thus coming at least close to the concept of universal evolution in nature. Before all, however, mention must be made here of Giordano Bruno, in whose pantheistic line of thought the idea of evolution is clearly reflected. Bruno, who in the shaping of his doctrine reached back to the ideas of Democritus and the ancient atomists, combined their views with

---

[4] Salomon Munk, in his book, *Mélanges de philosophie juive et arabe*, produced proof that Avicebro was none other than the great Jewish poet-philosopher, Ibn Gabirol.

the Copernican conception of the universe and—following in the footsteps of the Epicureans—arrived at the conviction that the universe is unlimited, an idea which was obviously unknown to Copernicus, since he represented the universe as bounded by the sphere of the fixed stars. The multiplicity of forms in which matter appears arises, according to the view of the great Italian nature philosopher, of itself, without any external impulse. "Matter," so Bruno argues, "is not formless; rather, it conceals within itself the germs of all forms, and since it unfolds what it carries hidden within it, it is, in truth, the mother of nature and of all living beings."

The French physicist and empiricist, Gassendi, also appropriating the doctrine of Epicurus, traced the origin of the world to the play of the atoms, which he thought of as endowed with the power of self-movement. He saw in the atoms the primal particles of all things out of which everything arises and moves toward completion. It is interesting to observe how strongly the ideas of the ancient Grecian nature philosophers, which had suddenly awakened to new life, influenced the thought of the best minds from a considerable time before the discovery of Copernicus up to the time of the French encyclopedists. Thus, the work of Lucretius was at the time of Voltaire in the hands of all educated people. Demonstrably it was chiefly the teaching of the ancient atomists which suggested to thinkers like Descartes, Gassendi and others the idea that a gradual development underlies all events in nature. Nor can we here pass over the brilliant Jewish thinker, Baruch Spinoza, who explained all phenomena of the process of the universe as owing to implicit necessity, and not only had a conception of the general idea of evolution, but anticipated some of its most fundamental hypotheses, such as, for example, the impulse of self-preservation.

On the eve of the great revolution France was the center of a new development in human thinking which has been rightly designated as the intellectual introduction to the later social upheaval. The ancient views of the universe and man, of state and society, of religion and morals, underwent a fundamental transformation. The publication of the famous *Encyclopedia* was a pretentious attempt to subject the whole body of human knowledge to a rigorous examination and to set it up again on new foundations. Such a time could but be extremely propitious for the advancement of the doctrine of evolution. In fact, we find among a whole line of the thinkers of that period of ferment more or less definite beginnings toward the theory of evolution, by which the later researches were inspired. Maupertuis attempted to account for the origin of organic life from atoms endowed with sensitivity. Diderot, the most universal intellect of this period, undertook to depict the origin and shaping of religions, moral concepts and social institutions as a graduated development, having as predecessors in this field thinkers like Bodin, Bacon, Pascal and Vico.

Condorcet, Lessing and Herder struck out along similar lines and saw in the whole of human history a constant process of transformation from lower to more complicated and higher forms of culture.

La Mettrie recognized that we know nothing essential about the nature of motion and matter, but that man is, nevertheless, in a position to establish by observations the sole difference between inorganic and organic matter; that is, that the latter is self-regulating, but for this very reason uses up its vital forces and dissolves after the death of the living being into its inorganic constituents. And, just as the organic develops out of the inorganic, so out of the organic develops the mental. According to La Mettrie's theory all higher forms of existence are subject to exactly the same laws as the whole of organic and inorganic nature. Therefore he set up no artificial boundary between man and beast and saw in both only different results of the same natural processes. Robinet came to similar conclusions and held to the standpoint that all functions of the mind were dependent upon those of the body. Holbach, in his *Système de la nature*, brought together these different views and, taking off from strictly materialistic lines of thought, developed the idea of a gradual genesis of the different living forms on the basis of the same uniform natural laws.

In Germany Leibnitz, who tried to counteract the materialism of the French thinkers, repeatedly exposed himself to the attacks of La Mettrie and his sympathizers. Yet his theory of monads, which has unmistakable points of contact with the views of modern biology, led him also to the idea of a gradual formation of the universe, as has been so often pointed out by modern exponents of the theory of evolution. Kant had an even clearer understanding of the idea of evolution than Leibnitz when, in his *Allgemeine Naturgeschichte und Theorie des Himmels*, he maintained that the whole system of the universe had evolved from revolving nebulae, the chaotic motions of primal matter gradually assuming fixed and permanent orbits. Kant saw in the universe the result of the operation of physical and mechanical forces and held the conviction that the cosmos had gradually shaped itself out of chaos and in the course of an enormous period of time would sink into it again and begin the process anew. He saw the world as a continuous play of becoming and dissolving. Hegel, too, saw in the course of nature an uninterrupted process of development and, in the metaphysical fashion that was peculiar to him, he transferred these ideas to human history; it was to this circumstance that he chiefly owed his great influence over his contemporaries. The theory of evolution was already unmistakably in the air. It would lead us too far to develop more fully here to what a degree thinkers like Malpighi, Malebranche, Bonnet and others, each in his own way, helped on the idea. The word "evolution" was already in frequent use among men of science in the first half of the eighteenth century, a proof that the idea of evolution dwelt more and more in men's thoughts.

Among the forerunners of the modern theory of evolution as it found expression with Darwin and his numerous successors, the French natural philosopher, Buffon, deserves especial regard, because his views are to be thought of less as the outcome of philosophical speculation than of practical experiments and earnest, laborious research. Buffon was one of the most intellectual men of his time, and the full significance of many of his inspirations was not properly recognized until long afterward. His *Natural History* was not merely a greatly conceived attempt at a rational explanation of the course of events in the universe; it developed in many other fields also a great many fruitful ideas. Thus he demonstrated from practical examples that alteration of plant and animal species can arise from many causes—his idea being quite the same as Darwin's was later. Buffon recognized also that the process of evolution can never reach a definite end, and deduced from this that science would be able by tests and observations to establish beyond question certain manifestations of it. It is, therefore, easy to understand how a man of such splendid gifts could have such a great influence on thinkers like Goethe, Lamarck and Saint-Hilaire.

At the beginning of the nineteenth century the idea of evolution had everywhere found its way into all unprejudiced minds. Its most distinguished advocate at that time was Goethe, in whose brilliant personality the prophetic vision of the poet was in the happiest way combined with the keen and sober gift of observation of the investigator. Goethe was powerfully stimulated by Buffon in his studies in natural history and developed as early as 1790, in his *Über die Metamorphose der Pflanzen*, ideas which lie wholly within the line of thought of the theory of descent; as when he traced the origin of all the organs of a plant to "metamorphosis," that is to the modifications of a single organ, the leaf—an idea which occurred later to Lamarck. Goethe applied the same ideas to the animal world also and gave us in his vertebrate theory a splendid example of penetrating keenness of observation. Moreover his concept of the geological changes in the earth's surface crust contains several ideas that were only later worked out and established more fundamentally by Lyell and Hoff.

A unique forerunner of the evolution theory was Erasmus Darwin, the grandfather of Charles Darwin, who (doubtless influenced by Lucretius) in his comprehensive didactic poem, *Zoonomia*, tried to account for the origin of the universe and of all life on the earth on an evolutionary-historical basis, and expressed many ideas that come surprisingly close to our modern view.

The German nature philosopher, Treviranus, in his work *Biologie:*

oder die Philosophie der lebenden Natur, which appeared in the years 1802-1805, advocated the idea that all higher living beings have developed from a small number of primitive original forms and that every form of life is the result of physical influences which differ only in the direction and the degree of effectiveness of their operation. Lorenz Oken, a contemporary of Goethe, quite independently of him developed the view that the cranium is made up of vertebrae and is only a continuation of the spinal column, and concluded that every living being is composed of cells and that all organic life on the earth had originated in a primal plasma. Oken also made an attempt to reclassify the whole plant and animal world according to descent.

This long line of bold thinkers of every nation, who, with justice, are called the pioneers of the modern theory of evolution, came to an end with the French zoologist, Lamarck, still a pioneer, but most effective. In his *Philosophie zoologique,* which appeared in 1809, he assembled the more or less developed ideas of his predecessors, together with his own theories, and gave them a definite scientific basis. He assailed the doctrine of the unalterability of species and concluded that these seem to us unalterable merely because the process of transformation is too gradual to be comprehended within the brief span of a human life. These transformations are, nevertheless, indisputable, and are conditioned by alterations in climate, means of subsistence and other phenomena of the environment. He concludes:

> It is not the organs, that is, the nature and structure of the body-parts of an animal which have produced its habits and special capabilities; but, on the contrary, its habits, its manner of life, and the conditions under which the individuals from which it descends were forced to live, have in time determined its bodily structure, the number and condition of its organs and capabilities.

The great reaction which was noticeable everywhere in Europe after the Napoleonic wars and which in the time of the Holy Alliance of unhappy memory not only exerted a crippling influence on the whole of political and social life, but also put bonds upon the thoughts of men and raised against the further expansion of the evolutionary doctrine a dam which had to be broken down before any further advances in this direction could be thought of. Art, science and philosophy fell under the dominion of the reactionary course of ideas, and a new spirit had to be born in Europe before a new impetus could be given to the theory of evolution. There were few glimpses of light in that long period of intellectual stagnation, and even they were scarcely noticed. Thus the English scholar, W. C. Wells, as early as 1813, developed with some clearness the idea of natural selection. He recognized that a dark skin made men more capable of withstanding the dangers of a tropical climate, from which he deduced that originally only those individuals were able to survive in tropical regions whom nature for some reason or other had blessed with a dark skin. Of course, Wells confined himself in his researches to definite types and made no attempt to test the general validity of the idea.

The most important thing appearing in that dark period was Charles Lyell's *Principles of Geology*, which came out in 1830. This work, in which the English geologist attacked Cuvier's theory of cataclysms, was to prove of fundamental significance for the further shaping of the theory of evolution. Cuvier's authority in the field of natural history had till then been undisputed. Now Lyell maintained that all the changes in the surface of the earth were brought about, not by sudden catastrophes, but by the unceasing operation of the same forces which are even today continuously at work. This theory, which Goethe had already postulated, was the necessary assumption for the whole evolutionary-historical line of thought; only by means of it was the idea of a gradual modification of species, adapting themselves to the gradual alterations of the earth's crust, made properly intelligible and scientifically thinkable.

In the same year in which Lyell's work was given publicity there took place in the Paris Academy that notable controversy between Cuvier and Saint-Hilaire which Goethe followed with such lively interest despite his extreme old age. Cuvier defended the doctrine of the permanency of species, while Saint-Hilaire undertook to prove their alterability through adaptation to the conditions of the environment. But the spirit of the time was against him, and Cuvier emerged victorious before the scientific world from a learned debate in which there was no lack of platitudes. All in that field of science were on his side and had only scorn and derision for his opponent. It looked as if the theory of evolution was done for once and for all, for Cuvier's doctrine was hardly attacked at all during the next three decades. (Even after the appearance of Darwin's epoch-making work the specialists in France, Germany and other countries hesitated to take under consideration the ideas developed there, and a considerable time passed before they were able to resolve upon an earnest examination of the new theory.) Neither did the idea of a natural selection among organic beings, to which the English investigator, Patrick Matthew, gave expression in the appendix to his book on ship-building and indigenous culture, meet with acceptance. The theory of evolution seemed, in fact, to be dead. Only with the decline of political and social reaction in Europe and the collapse of Hegel's doctrines did the demand for scientific thought in Europe come again into its own. Then the theory of evolution awoke to new life and even before the appearance of Darwin's work found courageous advocates in men like Spencer, Huxley, Vogt, Büchner and others.

The decisive victory of the doctrine of evolution was the appearance in 1859 of Darwin's great work, *The Origin of Species by Means of Natural Selection;* in which connection it is worth noting that Darwin was not a specialist in the usual sense but, one might say, devoted himself to natural science as a hobby. We are confronted here with the same phenomenon which we can observe so frequently in connection with great discoveries and revolutionary intellectual achievements, and which merely affords further proof that in every field authority leads to ossification and sterility, while the free unfolding of ideas is always creative.

Contemporaneously with Darwin the English zoölogist Alfred Russell Wallace, who was then pursuing his researches in Borneo, arrived at the same results, independently establishing the theory of natural selection in the same way as did Darwin. But the latter had in the course of his extended research gathered such a wealth of material and reviewed and elaborated it with such genius that Wallace modestly stepped back and conceded priority to his friend.

Darwin set to work very cautiously with the results of his rich experience, mostly achieved during that notable trip around the world on board the "Beagle" (1831-36), guarding himself against any generalizations that could not be established beyond cavil. So almost a quarter century went by before he laid his work before the public. Meanwhile he had spared no pains, but had conferred diligently with breeders and husbandmen to learn what experience had taught them. The experiments which had been carried out on domestic animals and cultivated plants in the course of artificial breeding served to confirm his conclusion that similar processes took place in nature and led to the origin of new species. So he was able with complete assurance to let the world know of the results of his prolonged studies and to support his conclusions with an inexhaustible array of facts.

Darwin came to the conclusion that alteration of species in nature is not the exception, but the rule. His observations had convinced him that related species were descended from a common ancestral form, and that the differences among them had been brought about in the course of time by changed conditions of life, migrations, changes in feeding habits and changes of climate. He supported this view chiefly by embryological researches by which he showed that the differences between embryos of the various genera of animals are much smaller than those between the developed individuals. So there was a quite special importance in the discovery that organs which serve the same purpose have in the embryo very similar forms even though they may have later, in the separate species, quite different appearances—a fact for which the only explanation can be that the different species have sprung from a common origin. The changes which appeared later were gradually transmitted to the descendants, and in such manner that the entire sequence of acquired characters is repeated in the embryo.

Darwin recognized that adaptation of the different living beings to their environment is the most important law of life, and that species and individuals maintain themselves in the so-called "struggle for existence" the more easily in proportion as they possess the ability of adapting themselves to environmental conditions. Thus, the theory of descent and the doctrine of natural selection were the cornerstones of the modern idea of evolution and opened to it the broadest outlook upon every field of human research. Without them the splendid results of modern anthropology, physiology, psychology, sociology, and so on, would have been quite impossible. The impression produced by Darwin's work was overpowering. The idea of evolution had become so utterly strange to men during the period of political and intellectual reaction that most scholars regarded it as little more than a fairy tale. One can understand the powerful influence of the Darwinian theory upon his times only if one looks at what famous investigators who were his contemporaries had to say about it. Thus, Weismann, in his *Vorträge über die Deszenztheorie* declares:

> One cannot understand the effect of Charles Darwin's book on the origin of species if one does not know how completely the biologists of that time had abandoned general problems. I can only tell you that we younger men of the period, who were studying in the fifties, had no suspicion that a theory of evolution had ever been set forth, for no one spoke about it, and it was not even mentioned in lectures. It was as if all the teachers in our universities had drunk of Lethe and had completely forgotten that any such thing had ever been discussed, or even as if they were ashamed of these philosophical excursions of natural science, and wanted to protect youth from that sort of thing.

In his first work Darwin had left the question of the descent of man untouched on purpose; still it lay in the nature of his theory that man could not occupy an exceptional place in nature. It was, therefore, only logical that well-known investigators like Thomas Huxley and Ernst Haeckel should draw from the newly acquired understanding the inevitable conclusion and set man in his place as a member of the long line of organic living beings. By this the opponents of Darwinism were, of course, still more aroused against the new doctrine, especially after Huxley had published his book, *Evidences of Man's Place in Nature;* but no obstacles could bar the way of the victoriously advancing ideas. Not until 1871 did Darwin, in his great work, *The Descent of Man and Natural*

Selection with Regard to Sex, take a stand upon this much disputed problem and answer it in accord with his first work.

But the theory of the great English thinker was by no means finished with this book; just as little as was the theory of Copernicus in his time. It rather gave the impulse to new investigations and reflections by which some of Darwin's ideas were corrected and others carried further. Darwin, indeed, understood clearly that his theory needed much more work, knew only too well that ideas also must go through a definite process of development. Thus, for example, the idea of natural selection as it had been developed by Darwin and Wallace in the course of time underwent much change to set its importance in correct relation to that of the other factors which cooperate with it in the modification of species. On the basis of the Darwinian theory of descent Spencer was able to prove that the countless genera of animals and plants on the earth had developed from a few simple organisms. Haeckel was able to go so far as to construct a family tree for the entire animal kingdom inclusive of man. In his *Natürliche Schöpfungsgeschichte* the German scholar attaches a special importance to the "biogenetic law" according to which the individual development of a living being is in high degree a brief and rapidly completed recapitulation of all the changes of form through which the entire ancestry of the genus has passed in the course of its natural evolution, and which are dependent on the physiological processes of inheritance (reproduction) and nutrition. This new insight into the processes of evolution led in turn to a whole series of new interpretations in the most widely separated fields of scientific investigation, by which the limits of our knowledge were very notably extended.

Darwin and Wallace believed that they had found an adequate explanation of the alterations in living forms in the mechanical selection of the best, and were convinced that this selection occurred as the result of a constant struggle between the different species—and also within the same species—in the course of which the weak species and individuals succumbed and only the strong were able to survive. We know that Darwin was strongly influenced in the development of this theory by the reading of Malthus' book on the population problem. He later greatly revised this opinion and, especially in his work on the origin of man, reached essentially different results. But the theory of the "struggle for existence" as it was first presented, in incomplete and one-sided form, exercised a powerful influence on a whole line of distinguished investigators, especially on the founders of the so-called "social Darwinism." Men came to regard nature as a monstrous battlefield on which the weak were pitilessly trodden down by the strong and, in fact, believed that within every genus there went on a sort of perpetual civil war arising from natural necessities. A large number of scholars, among them Huxley and Spencer, at first saw human society also in this light and were of the firm conviction that they were on the track of a natural law of universal validity. Thus Hobbes' "war of all against all" became once more the unalterable course of nature, which could be changed by no ethical considerations, and the advocates of "social Darwinism" never tired of mouthing the gloomy declaration of Malthus that the table of life is not spread for everyone. This notion no doubt arose from the bourgeois attitude of the scholars without their being themselves aware of it. Capitalistic society had made the principle of free competition the cardinal point of economics; what, therefore, was simpler than to see in this merely an extension of that same struggle which, according to the view of many distinguished Darwinians, was to be seen everywhere in nature, and which not even man could escape? In this way justification was found for every human exploitation and oppression, by tracing it to the operation of an inexorable natural law. Huxley, in his well-known work, *The Struggle for Existence and Its Bearing on Man,* had with the consistency that was characteristic of him unreservedly advocated this point of view, and thus, contrary to his intention, forged a weapon for social reaction which even today is occasionally made to serve it as a means of defense. The thinkers of the period took these things the more seriously because the most of them were so firmly convinced of the inexorable struggle in nature that they assumed it unconditionally without taking the trouble to examine the assumption carefully.

There were at that time only a few supporters of the Darwinian theory who questioned the correctness of this view. To this few belonged most notably the Russian zoologist Kessler, who as early as 1880 at a natural science congress in St. Petersburg announced his opinion that along with the brutal struggle with tooth and claw in nature there prevails still another law which finds expression in mutual assistance within the society of living species and contributes essentially to the maintainance of the race. This idea, which Kessler merely referred to hurriedly, was given a far-reaching application by Peter Kropotkin in his well-known work, *Mutual Aid—a Factor of Evolution.* Kropotkin showed, on the basis of a wealth of factual material, that the presentation of nature as an unlimited battlefield was only a caricature of life which does violence to the real facts.[5] Like Kessler, he also emphasized the importance for the preservation of the species of its members' living together in societies and the instincts of mutual aid and solidarity which grow out of it. This second form of the struggle for existence seemed to him of incomparably

[5] Kropotkin first published his work in separate installments in the English periodical *Nineteenth Century* (September, 1890, to June, 1896). His latest work, *Die Ethik* (Berlin, 1923), which unfortunately was not completed, constitutes a valuable supplement to the earlier publication.

greater importance, as well for the preservation of the individual as for the maintainance of the race, than the brutal warfare of the strong against the weak, a view which is confirmed by the noticeable degeneracy of those species which have no social life and try to maintain themselves by their mere physical superiority. While Kessler was of the opinion that the instinct of sympathy is a result of parental affection and the care of offspring, Kropotkin took the standpoint that we are dealing here simply with a result of social living together which man inherited from his animal ancestors, who, like him, lived in societies. Thus regarded, man was not the creator of society, but society the creator of man. This view, which has since been accepted by numerous investigators, is, especially for sociology, of wide applicability, for it throws a new light on the whole evolutionary history of man and stimulates most fruitful reflections.

It would lead us too far to enter in detail into all the numerous evolutionary factors of the Darwinian theory. The theory of selection and, more especially, the problem of heredity, have given rise to a whole series of scientific investigations which have advanced the evolutionary doctrine in general even if their outcome has not always been very successful. Many theories which were thus set up appear, perhaps, all too daring and too lacking in foundation; still one must not forget that it is not the positive results alone that serve to advance an idea. Hypotheses also can inspire to new considerations and greatly accelerate research. This is especially true of the Weismannian theory of inheritance and of all the attempts at explanation in this field that have been made by meritorious investigators like Mendel, Naegeli, de Vries, Roux and their numerous followers, as also by the advocates of neo-Lamarckianism, and by the defenders and opponents of the mutation theory. The most of these attempts at explanation have, beyond doubt, contributed to the further development of the theory of evolution, though they are in detail far too complicated for one to estimate with certainty their actual importance for the future. It would be labor lost, to attempt a survey of an intellectual phenomenon of such enormous range as the modern theory of evolution according to its national constituents. A whole army of thinkers and investigators of all peoples and nations, of whom only a few of the best-known names can here be mentioned, has contributed to the universal upbuilding of this theory and given it intellectual impetus. No nation could escape its influence. It has directed the entire thought of the men of our cultural circle into definite lines, revalued all previous assumptions concerning man and the universe and brought forth an entirely new conception of all the problems of life. What importance, after all, have all the trifling peculiarities distinguishing members of different human groups—which at the best are all that can be established and which are, in the end, only results of trained-in understandings, ideas and habits—in comparison with the overpowering effect of an idea or concept of the universe which applies to all men with equal force and strides on across all artificially constructed national boundaries. No, the human mind will not permit itself to be bound in the chains of artificially created prejudice and will not endure the restraint of national limitation. The individual man may be held temporarily or permanently under the spell of a national ideology, just as perhaps the man of science may be influenced by the inbred prejudices of his class or station; but no power is in a position to give a national stamp to science as such or to fix the thought of a people by the artificial norms of a so-called "national idea." Whither such attempts lead, the present conditions in Germany and Italy show us with complete clarity. The mere fact that the national-minded in every country persuade themselves that they must enforce their peculiar lines of ideas upon all others, if necessary even against their will, is the announcement of intellectual bankruptcy of nationalism of every sort. If national sentiment were in fact a clearly recognizable spiritual phenomenon which shaped itself in men into a kind of instinct, then this feeling would be alive in every one of us and would assert itself with compelling necessity, and there would be no need to cultivate it and force it upon the consciousness of men artificially.

We have purposely brought up for consideration the Copernican system of the universe and the theory of evolution, because in them the universal character of human thought shows most clearly. To achieve the same result it would suffice to have brought out any special branch of science, a philosophical theory, a social popular movement or a great discovery. Every bit of scientific knowledge, every philosophical consideration of man and the universe, every social movement which is born of the conditions of the time, every practical application of acquired knowledge in technique and industry, is fostered and built up by members of all nations. One can just as little speak of a national science as of a national system of the universe or a national theory of earthquakes. Science as such has nothing in common with national ambitions, it stands rather in unmistakable opposition to them, for while it is without doubt one of the most effective factors that unite men and bind them to one another, nationalism is an element that estranges them from one another and always tries to make their natural intercourse difficult and hostile. It is not the nation which shapes the thought of our species and inspires and equips it for new experiments; it is the culture circle to which we belong that brings to maturity everything intellectual in us and constantly stimulates it. No national isolation can withdraw us from this influence; it can only contribute to our cultural impoverishment and the curtailment of our intellectual endowments and capacities, as is shown today with terrifying consistency especially in Germany.

Chapter 10

ART AND NATIONALITY. ARTISTIC PRODUCTION AND WORLD PHILOSO-
PHY. THE PERSONALITY OF THE ARTIST. STYLES AND SOCIAL FORMS.
THE ARBITRARINESS OF DESIGNATIONS OF STYLE. ARCHITECTURE AND
COMMUNITY. NECESSITY AND ESTHETICS. INFLUENCE OF MATERIAL ON
STYLE. THE BRIDGE BETWEEN EGYPT AND BABYLON. FROM GRECIAN
TEMPLE TO HELLENISTIC STYLE OF ART. CONNECTION BETWEEN ETRUS-
CAN AND GRECIAN FORMS. ARCHED STRUCTURES. TRANSITION TO THE
CHRISTIAN CHURCH STYLE. THE CENTRAL TYPE AND CAESARISM. THE
BYZANTINE STYLE. THE MIGRATION OF PEOPLES AND THE ROMANESQUE
STYLE. THE TRANSITION TO GOTHIC. GOTHIC AS SOCIAL STRUCTURE.
THE RENAISSANCE. DEVELOPMENT OF TYPES OF SPACE TREATMENT.
MICHELANGELO AND THE TRANSITION TO THE BAROQUE. ABSOLUTISM
AND THE SHAPING OF THE BAROQUE. THE STYLE OF THE JESUITS.
DOWNFALL OF THE OLD REGIME AND THE ROCOCO IN ART. THE CAPI-
TALISTIC WORLD AND THE CHAOS OF STYLE. FACTORY. WAREHOUSE.

"BUT, art?" someone will say. Does not the peculiar soul of every
people speak in that? Are not the differences which reveal themselves in
the art of different peoples results of their national peculiarities and
determined by them? Does there not live in every work of art a certain
something that can only be felt nationally and which the offspring of
another people or a foreign race will never rightly understand because
he lacks the special organ needed for its emotional comprehension? Those
are questions which one often meets when the "essence of national art"
is under discussion.

First let us just picture to ourselves how a work of art comes into
being—everywhere, be it understood, without distinction of race or nation.
When, for instance, we look at a landscape, what we behold may produce
in us various effects. It may impel us to grasp in detail the things which
the eye perceives, to distinguish them from one another in order to
recognize their peculiar properties and to discover their relation to the
environment. Perhaps a naturalist would at first approach things with
this purely intellectual attitude and so arrive at purely scientific interpretations, which he keeps in mind and elaborates. But we may also make a

purely emotional appraisal of the same landscape; we may be affected merely by the splendor of its colors, its vibrations and tones, without concerning ourselves about the special type of its material structure. In this case our experience of what we see is purely esthetic, and if nature has endowed us with the needful ability to reproduce what we have seen, there results a work of art. Certainly our visual impressions cannot always be separated so neatly as we have suggested here, but the more profoundly the purely emotional, the so-called "mood," permeates a work of art, the better does it deserve the name. For this very reason art is never a mere imitation of nature. The artist does not simply give back what he sees, he animates it, breathes into it that mysterious life which alone has power to awaken the strange mood which is the peculiar property of artistic feeling; in a word, the artist *"wirkt Seele ins All"* ("puts a soul into everything"), as Dehmel has so strikingly phrased it.

That an artist can devote his art to the service of a particular world philosophy and work in its spirit is so clear a truth that it needs no proof. At the outset it matters little whether this philosophy be of a religious, an esthetic or a generally social character. Therefore, even the "national idea"—whatever that means—can animate the artist and influence his creations. But a work of art is never the result of an inborn national feeling that is of determinative importance for its esthetic qualities. Philosophies are acquired by man and come to him from without. How he reacts to them is a question of his personality, a result of his individual endowment, and in no way the effect of a peculiar national quality. The personal quality of the artist reveals itself in his style, the peculiar tone that is revealed in everything he produces.

Of course, the artist does not stand outside of space and time; he, too, is but a man, like the least of his contemporaries. His ego is no abstract image, but a living entity, in which every side of his social being is mirrored and action and reaction are at work. He, too, is bound to the men of his time by a thousand ties; in their sorrows and their joys he has his personal share; and in his heart their ambitions, hopes and wishes find an echo. As a social being he is endowed with the same social instinct; in his person is reflected the whole environment in which he lives and works and which, of necessity, finds expression in his productions. But how this expression will manifest itself, in what particular manner the soul of the artist will react to the impressions that he receives from his surroundings, is in the final outcome decided by his own temperament, his special endowment of character—in a word, his personality.

How utterly art is the highest manifestation of an existing community of culture, how little it can be regarded as the result of alleged racial peculiarities or national emotional complexes, is revealed especially by architecture. Its various styles are always bound up with a particular period of time, never with a definite nation or race. Whenever in the life of the European peoples there has occurred a rearrangement of social forms and their spiritual and material assumptions, new styles appeared in art in general and in architecture in particular, which gave expression to the new ambitions. These changes in the artistic formative impulse were confined to one country or one nation just as little as were the social changes from which they arose. Rather, they spread over the whole European culture circle to which we belong and out of whose womb it was born. Antique, Gothic, Renaissance—to mention only the best-known styles—do not simply embody special trends in art; they are also to be regarded as forms of expression of the social structure and the intellectual acquirements of definite epochs.

The more clearly the thinking man recognized the gap which opens between the antique, with its classical art forms and the later developed Christian world and the formative impulses peculiar to it, the more strongly was he impelled to search out the esthetic reasons for this contrast. This occurred first when men made comparisons between the art products of the two epochs; and the rediscovery of the antique was an immediate incitement to such comparisons. In this they scarcely took into account the deeper evolutionary processes which underlay the two social structures and their intellectual effects. Such comparisons always lead to definite judgments of value, which are made to serve abstract thought as concrete symbols. But a judgment of value is always preceded by a concept of purpose. When these comparisons were instituted between different styles, the judgment depended on the degree to which any particular style fitted in, or failed to fit in, with certain assumptions. In this manner Lessing, Goethe, Schiller, Winckelmann and their numerous successors arrived at the conclusions in their theories of art. They saw in art merely the purpose of representing the beautiful; and since the Greek ideal of beauty seemed to our classicists the most perfect, it acquired for them an absolute significance; it was for them, consequently, the beautiful, measured by which every other style must seem crude and imperfect. So, while following the trail of the antique, they arrived at many valuable discoveries, yet left the heart of the question untouched.

The beautiful is a much debated concept, which has a special meaning, not merely for peoples of different regions and different culture circles; the ideal of beauty of the same people or the same cultural community— if one may speak of such a thing—is constantly subject to great variations. What today seems to the individual an ugly fad, tomorrow achieves recognition as a new concept of beauty. We are therefore of the opinion that in art in general there is no definite goal, only a way in which the formative impulse of man finds expression. Following up the forms in which this impulse reveals itself is a very attractive undertaking, nothing more. It furnishes us no stopping point for the alleged purpose of art; for in this field, also, purpose has only a relative, never an absolute, meaning. Scheffler has beautifully clothed this idea in words: "Just as no single mortal possesses all of truth, just as truth is, rather, divided up among all, so also art as a whole is not in the possession of any one people or any one definite time. All styles together are just art." [1]

Just as in natural science, so also in the history of art, the theory of catastrophes has long since been abandoned. No style sprang suddenly into existence of itself without points of contact with earlier styles. Every historian of art is in a position to demonstrate how one style gradually developed from another, in just the same way, in fact, as did the different forms of social life. That, of course, does not prevent the conflict of opinions about the worth of the various types of style from becoming often very sharp. So it has recently become common to acclaim the Gothic as bearer of the "Germanic spirit" and to play up its peculiar beauty in opposition to that of antique and Renaissance art. In fact, if one compares a Grecian temple with a Gothic cathedral one finds a quite overpowering difference between them. But to conclude from this that the contrast in style is the outgrowth of race or nationality is a monstrous absurdity. If Gothic was in fact the result of definite racial endowment or of a special national formative urge, then it is hard to understand why men like Lessing, Goethe, Schiller, Winckelmann and others, honored as the most outstanding representatives of the German race, committed themselves to unconditional approval of the classical antique. Goethe, who was in his younger years strongly attracted by the Gothic—as is shown by his observations on the cathedral at Strassburg—later turned more and more decisively to the antique ideal of beauty and made no secret of his low estimate of everything Gothic. Ought not this to prove to us that all theories which seek to find in artistic feeling in general and in the creative activities of artists in particular merely a revelation of the genius of the race or the nation are based on vain imaginings which have nothing in common with the realities of life?

There is one peculiar thing to note in connection with theories of art and style. They have the advantage that they bring definite differences between artistic creations more clearly before our consciousness, but their weak side is that they all proceed from assumptions which accord with the arbitrary views of their founders. When one tries to uphold his preference for one particular style over the others there are frequently brought out contrasts of a purely abstract nature which may fulfill the purpose of exalting special details, but are of little value for the clarifying of the real problem. Even the designations which have been given to the different styles have usually been chosen very arbitrarily and seldom cor-

[1] Karl Scheffler, *Der Geist der Gotik*. Leipzig, 1921, p. 14.

respond to any clearly defined idea. Thus the word "Renaissance" in no way covers the concept which we associate with it today; for the culture of that period represents very much more than a rebirth of the antique. It was a complete overturning of all traditional notions and social concepts, which naturally made itself felt in art also. In place of the medieval society with its countless religious and social ties, its mysticism and its other-worldly urge, there appeared a new order of things to which the great discoveries of the time and the rapid transformation of all economic conditions were highly favorable. The Renaissance was, therefore, by no means a repetition of antique life forms, but a great unchaining of new impulses in every sphere of life. It could not be a rebirth of the antique, because it could not arbitrarily shake off the fifteen-hundred-years-old traditions of Christianity, but was bound up with these throughout its development.

Still more arbitrary is the designation "Gothic" for the art of the Christian Middle Ages; it recognizably has not the slightest relation with the people called Goths. Vasari, from whom we have taken over this designation, meant to express by it merely the contrast with the art of the Renaissance; and his violent attacks upon the principles of the Gothic show clearly that he wanted the term to be associated with the idea of the crude, coarse and barbaric. The case is no better with expressions like "baroque" and "rococo," concerning the original meaning of which we are today not at all clear. It was only later that these words took a more or less definite meaning, which nearly always differed essentially from their original significance. Hence, the great majority of the more recent style psychologists have long been convinced that a special style is not associated with a people or a nation. Thus, Scheffler, who took the standpoint that "the Gothic spirit brought forth at every stage the forms of unrest and suffering, the Grecian, on the other hand, the forms of peace and happiness," is of the opinion that both styles, the Grecian and the Gothic, have appeared among all peoples and at the most widely separated times. It was in this sense that he related to the concept of the Gothic, prehistoric and Egyptian, Indian and baroque, antique and modern, remote and near. We cannot commit ourselves to Scheffler's conclusions in general, because they suffer from the same defects as all other theories of style: from unproved and unprovable arbitrary assumptions. His assertion that the Grecian style is to be regarded as the feminine, and the Gothic as the masculine element in art is at the best an ingenious association of ideas. On one point, however, Scheffler was absolutely right: the idea which we usually associate with the Gothic was not confined to the Christian Middle Ages, although it found perhaps its most complete expression at that time. There was undoubtedly a great deal that was Gothic in the art of the ancient Egyptians and Assyrians. Many of the

Indian temples, too, convey to us the impression of demonic feeling, unlimited fertility of form and powerful upreach which are characteristic of Gothic. Just so one can recognize in many modern factory buildings and warehouses similar features, so that one is almost tempted to speak of a Gothic of industry.

Nietzsche developed a similar idea when he tried to establish in Grecian art itself two different tendencies which in some form or other recur in every period. One—Nietzsche calls it Apollinian—seems to him the expression of purely creative forces, which are surrounded by the "radiant glory of beauty" and which by their moderation and philosophic calm affect us like a dream. The other tendency—which he designates as Dionysian—is surrounded by a thousand mysteries and dark forebodings like a delirium with the upsurge of which "the subjective vanishes in utter self-forgetfulness." Nietzsche finds this feature not in Greek culture alone. "Even in the German Middle Ages impelled by the same Dionysian force ever growing bands rolled on, singing and dancing, from place to place. In these Saint John and Saint Vitus dances we recognize again the Bacchic choruses of the Greeks, with their earlier history in Asia Minor and on to Babylon and the orgiastic Sakaeae." Nietzsche put the contrast in these splendid words:

> We have thus far depicted the Apollinian and its opposite, the Dionysian, as artistic forces which burst forth from Nature itself *without the mediation of the human artist,* and in which their artistic impulses first find satisfaction directly: sometimes like the imaginary world of a dream whose completeness lacks any connection with the intellectual heights of the artistic imagination of the individual, and again like a delirious reality, which again takes no account of the individual, but even tries to destroy the individual and dissolve him in a mystic feeling of unity.[2]

Whether we wish to avail ourselves of the old concepts of the "classic" and "romantic," or whether instead of these we like to designate this polarity of styles, felt by everyone, as "realistic" and "idealistic" or as "impressionistic" and "expressionistic," or whether we give preference to the expressions of those logomachists who speak of the "art of abstraction" of the Nordics and its opposite, the "art of intuition" of the Greeks, or with Nietzsche like to speak of an Apollinian and a Dionysian expression of emotion in art, matters at bottom very little. What Nietzsche had recognized very clearly is the fact that the much-debated contrast which he tried to fix in the concepts of the Apollinian and Dionysian cannot be regarded as at all a problem of the North and the South or as a contrast between races and nations, but rather as an implicit dualism in human nature, which occurs among all peoples and human groups.

[2] *The Birth of Tragedy.*

Above everything we must avoid generalizing individual phenomena in the history of a people or a period in order to build up for it a collective character. The Greeks were certainly a people filled with the joy of life, but it would be senseless to suppose that the implicit tragedy of life was hidden from them and that the Greek never knew anguish of spirit or tormenting emotional disturbances. It is just as misleading when certain culture psychologists and style theorists represent the Middle Ages to us as a time of agony of soul and primal demonic impulses in which man was too much concerned over the terrors of death and the gloomy problem of the approaching day of retribution to appreciate the joyous and peaceful aspects of life. The Middle Ages, too, knew joy of life, had their festivals of cheer, their earthbound sensualities, which often enough are manifested in their art. One need but recall the ultra-realistic sculptures on countless ecclesiastical and secular buildings of that time to find eloquent testimony to this. Every period has its delusions, its spiritual epidemics, its Saint John's and Saint Vitus's dances. The Christian Middle Ages were no exception to this rule. We are, however, often so much concerned with the illusory ideas of others that we never become conscious of our own. And yet our own time offers us a lesson in this regard that it is not easy to misunderstand.

Pain and joy are the high points of human feeling, which recur in all times, under every sky; they are the two poles about which our spiritual life revolves, and alternately they set their stamp on our physical being. And as the individual man can never remain permanently in a state of deepest agony of soul or ecstatic happiness, still less can an entire people, a whole period. The greater part of a human life lies between suffering and joy. Pain and bliss are like Siamese twins; despite all antitheses, they are still linked together, so that we cannot imagine one without the other. That is also true for the creative expression of the two emotions in art. As every man is sensitive to the feelings of joy and pain, so we find in the art of every people evidence of both emotional complexes, which alternately fade out and wax strong. Only the two taken together, with their thousands on thousands of modulations, shadings and changes, convey to us an idea of art as a whole. Scheffler recognized this clearly when he concluded:

> The ideal thing for the understanding of art is to get close to that imaginary point outside the earth's orbit of which Archimedes dreamed. It must have no reservations, no limits; life, art, must for it become one enormous whole, and every bit of art history must be like an extract from a universal history of art. Even the patriotic point of view has no validity. The manner in which all races, peoples and individuals have had their share in the eternal life of artistic form is too great a miracle to be reducible to the nationalistic. But if the national point of view must thus be given up, that is, if the scien-

tific connoisseur may not even participate in the impelling will of his nation, how much less can he follow his little personal will, his own natural impulse, and coin from it apparently material arguments.

So long as our acquaintance was limited to the styles of the European peoples and their relatives it was comparatively easy to survey the fine arts, and especially architecture, as a whole and to make definite classifications. But with the extension of our knowledge much of this is changed. It is not yet possible to establish beyond dispute the basic relations between the different styles of architecture of ancient peoples, especially when they did not belong to the European culture circle, although some important results have already been achieved in this direction. Countless connecting links of the tectonic creations which certainly once existed have in the course of the millennia disappeared without leaving a trace, either because the material could not withstand the ravages of time or because influences of some other kind hastened the destructive processes. So it has gradually ceased to be customary in scientific circles to speak of an Egyptian, an Assyrian, or a Persian art simply, though this may still happen often enough in everyday life and in school instruction. With the deeper penetration into the history of Greece there dawns on us for the first time the knowledge that the antique itself had its antiquity, its Middle Ages, its later and its latest period, a matter which is made clear to us especially by the development of architecture from pre-Homeric times to the rise and decline of "Hellenism." It is in style that the culture content of a period best reveals itself, because it in a certain degree reflects an ensemble of all the social strivings of a period. But most important of all there is revealed here also the stimulating influence that comes from without and often gives rise to new forms of style. This mutual stimulation runs through the history of all peoples and constitutes one of the fundamental laws of cultural development in general.

This can be observed in architecture better than in any other field of art, for it is the most social of all arts and in it is always manifest the will of a community. In architecture the purposive is most intimately blended with the esthetic. It was not the whim of the artist that built a pyramid, a Grecian temple, a Gothic cathedral; it was a generally experienced faith, a common idea, that made those works arise under the hand of the artist. It was the Egyptian cult of the dead that impelled to the construction of the so-called "*mustabas*" and the pyramids. The pyramid is nothing more than a gigantic tomb which in its external form reflects the social character of a definite epoch. Just so, the airy temple of the Greeks could come into being only among a people that constantly played about under the open sky and would not allow themselves to be shut up in enclosed rooms. The Christian cathedral had to be able to take in an entire community; this purpose underlay its whole structural type, and in spite of all the alternations of external form remains always the same.

Architecture has been called an art of moods, and so it is, and in much higher degree than any of the other arts; but this is true only because architecture gives such overpowering expression to the spirit of the community as to summon a collective mood in which every personal emotion dissolves. Scheffler has depicted this effect of the architectonic work of art by showing how it is the weight of a universal idea that is here revealed to the beholder. The impression is so powerful because what is transmitted to man is not a mood pointing to some inner relation between the work and its creator, even when he is known. When looking at a picture there comes to the mind of the beholder quite of itself an implicit contact between the work of art and the master who brought it to life. From the picture he gets in some measure a feeling of the personality of the artist, feels the stirring of his soul. But with the architectonic work of art the creator remains for him just a name; here it is not an individual will that speaks to him; here towers the will of a community, which always seems like an anonymous primal force. Scheffler concludes from this that "the architect is only the pupil of the spirit of his time, only the intelligent instrument of fruitful technical concepts. He is rather the one led, than the leader." [3]

But the inner aspirations and the will of a community, as they are manifested in its religious ideas, its customs and general social philosophy, do not change suddenly, but only gradually, even when the changes are caused by catastrophic occurrences. Even revolutions can create nothing new of themselves; they merely release the hidden forces that have been slowly developing in the body of the old organism till the external pressure can no longer withstand them and they break their way out. The same phenomenon can be observed in the development of the various styles in art, and especially in architecture. True, we may observe revolutionary changes, and the apparently sudden appearance of new styles. But if we go into matters a little more deeply, we recognize clearly that a long development preceded the periods of revolution, and that without these nothing new could ever have been constructed. Every new form develops organically from those already existing and as a rule still carries on its back for a long time the shell of the egg it came from.

If one brings into immediate juxtaposition two utterly different styles, for example, the Grecian and the Gothic, there is, of course, a whole world between them and no point of contact can be recognized. But if one studies the slow growth of various styles, taking note of all connecting links and transitional types, then one recognizes a slow maturing of the

[3] *Der Architekt.* Frankfurt a/M, 1907, p. 10.

various forms and structures. Like all others, this development has its periods of stagnation and of vigorous forward drive, though nothing can long interrupt the steady progress of the whole movement. This is quite natural, for art itself is merely one of the many manifestations of cultural constructive progress, and in its way gives expression to this. So here, too, the several stages of the development of style are of longer or shorter duration according as the stream of social events glides slowly on or suddenly swells to a flood and overflows its banks. But the steps in the development can never be mistaken; out of every form there grows another; nothing arises just of itself; all is in flux; everything moves.

The question of style arises not merely from the conception of the artist; it is also in great measure dependent on the material which he has at his disposal. Every material, be it wood, clay or stone, demands its own peculiar treatment, has its own peculiar effects, which the artist recognizes fully and takes into consideration in his work. It is, therefore, not without reason that men have spoken of the spirit of the material. There are art historians to whom the commanding influence of the material seems all-important. Naumann, for example, could maintain that the Gothic style owed its origin immediately to the soft, workable sandstone of the Ile de France, where the Gothic first took on visible form. This assertion may be too sweeping, but we must recognize that there is a large measure of truth underlying it. Let one think of the builder's art in ancient Egypt, of the origin of the pyramids. Or let one take the structures of the Babylonians and Assyrians, who because of the lack of wood and stone were almost entirely dependent on the fabrication of dried or baked clay bricks. Brick construction led to quite peculiar types of style; only from it could the rounded arch and, gradually, the vaulted dome, have arisen.

Of course the mighty structures of the ancients did not arise all at once, but in the course of a long cultural development in which, in Egypt as well as in Babylonia, peoples of the most widely different descent took part. In a very stirring and scholarly work of the Egyptologist, Henry Schäfer, the gradual growth of the builder's art among the peoples of the Nile Valley is very convincingly presented: [4] how stone construction gradually developed from clay-, brick-, wood-, and reed-hut structure, and how its inventors tried at first to imitate in stone the ancient types. From the older sepulchres, which because of their casket-like shape the Arabs called *mustabas*, that is, "rest-banks," arose gradually the pyramids, by piling these stone caskets one upon another. The famous terraced pyramids of Sakkarah and the "flat" pyramids of Dashoor, still display for us the several transitions which led at last in the Fourth Dynasty to the marvelous structures at Gizeh.

[4] Heinrich Schäfer, *Die Leistung der ägyptischen Kunst*. Leipzig, 1929.

Schäfer shows us to what a degree the majestic buildings of the peoples of the Nile Valley stimulated all the neighboring peoples and transmitted to them the rectangular type of structure—indeed, of stone construction in general. That already in very early times there was cultural intercourse between the Egyptians and the prehistoric population of what was later Greece, is today no longer disputed by any prominent investigator; also, the results of the excavations of Evans and others in Crete reveal clearly connections with Asia and Egypt. It is becoming ever more probable that the peculiar Egyptian columnar type of the structures of Deir-el-Bahri and Beni Hassan was not without influence on the creations of the Greeks. Likewise, the intercourse between the Egyptians and the numerous peoples that occupied the Levant, especially that region of primeval culture through which flow the Euphrates and the Tigris, are being brought more clearly to light by the more recent investigations. It is true that we are not yet in a position to establish in detail the manifold actions and reactions of this intercourse, even in a preliminary way. Still, we shall probably not go astray if we accept the view that there occurred here a mutual stimulation which proceeded from peoples of various races and was not without influence on the development of the several styles. It would be quite inconceivable that two such mighty culture systems as Egypt and Babylon, which developed at the same time and in closest proximity to one another, should have had no relationship with one another. It is probable that these reciprocal influences already existed before the lordship of the Pharaohs on the Nile or the dominion of the Babylonian and Assyrian kings on the Tigris and the Euphrates had been thought of. One can even accept with tolerable certainty that the great intermixtures of races and peoples, which from earliest antiquity has played so large a part in those regions, was one of 'the most important causes of the development of the two cultures.

As in the Egyptian, so also in the Babylonian and the Assyrian art of building, there can be observed a gradual development of styles, which was perhaps caused and fostered by the intrusion of new peoples. When the peoples involved were simple nomadic tribes which possessed no culture worth mentioning they were quickly absorbed by the ancient culture. But it was quite otherwise when the realm was invaded by more highly developed peoples. In this event, after the termination of military conflict, new art-forms appeared, which gradually blended with those already in use and led to new types of style. Unfortunately, the building material which was available to the peoples along the Tigris and the Euphrates, unlike the stone structures of Egypt, was not of a sort to resist time. It is therefore not easy to reconstruct from the ruins of this long-past culture any complete picture of it. Still, the strong influence of the Persian invasions upon the ancient style of building can be clearly recognized. If the ruins of the ancient royal palaces of Chorsabad are compared with those of Persepolis the difference leaps to meet the eye. The Medes and Persians, who, as is well known, were not, like the Babylonians and the Assyrians, Semitic peoples, brought from their home-land a style of wooden construction which now sought for itself new means of expression under different conditions and under the influence of the Assyrian forms. The slender columns in Xerxes' palace at Persepolis with their fantastic capitals bear witness to this new development. These structures have not, of course, the mighty dimensions of the gigantic palaces of Chorsabad, but they are distinguished by a more graceful pattern and, especially, by a greater harmony of the external and internal elements of structure. In the ancient buildings at Susa, which are related to the palaces of Persepolis, Greek influence is already apparent.

If the inner connections in the building art of the Egyptian and Levantine peoples are, in their details, still largely unknown to us, we have a much better picture of the gradual development of the various styles of building in Europe. It is true that here, also, the beginnings are veiled in darkness, for the earliest Grecian temples that we know stand already at a very high stage of perfection. Still, the excavations at Tiryns and Mycenae in Asia Minor and those at Knossos and Phaestos in Crete have proved clearly that here, too, the stimulation of Egypt and the Levant had been felt. This is shown especially by numerous ornaments from Crete, like, for example, the symbols of fertility, which point to the tree of life of the Assyrians. In Mycenae, similar connections can be traced.

In the Greek temple we see for the first time a work of art that presents a close-knit unity. Interior and exterior form an undisturbed harmony. The whole structure follows a natural law by which every form arises of itself. Upon a three-stepped socle arise the columns and the walls of the cella, which encloses the sacred quadrangle. They carry the entablature that serves to support the saddle-shaped roof. The most important achievement of the Grecian art of building is the harmonious shaping of the cornice and its connection with the horizontal cover of the outer hall and with the gable. The external and internal ornamentation in a measure grew out of the whole structure. The works of sculpture and painting occupy just the place that seems destined for them by the whole and derive their correct values only from their relations in space. The whole structure seems like a happy combination of mathematical forms and musical feeling. As remarkably typical as the Grecian temple is, it lends itself to manifold variations, so that the creative genius of the artist is in no wise restricted and he never needs to repeat himself. The great variety in the forms of the columns, especially the rich choice among the capitals, as expressed in the Doric, Ionic and Corinthian styles, produced ever varying impressions. The intrinsic completeness of the Greek structure has, in fact, such an overpowering effect that one understands why the later defenders of classic art would admit the validity of no other ideal of beauty.

The last art form that Greece produced, the so-called "Hellenic" style, which developed chiefly in Asia Minor and Egypt, is the connecting link with the Roman style. The Roman temple is a blending of Grecian and Etruscan forms. Here the use of columns is combined with the arch and wall which the Etruscans brought with them out of Asia. This style led to a whole series of other creations, out of which there grew, in turn, a large number of later styles. Thus there was developed from the so-called barrel-vault, which resembled a cylinder split lengthwise, the later cross-vault, which consisted of two such half-cylinders intersecting at right angles and blending together. The form of room thus produced later played an important part in the development of Christian church architecture.

The practical Romans were not content to restrict the use of the forms received from the Etruscans and the Greeks merely to their temples, they applied them also in the construction of numerous buildings which served purely secular purposes. In this way they developed the most important type of enclosed room in architecture, the basilica. The basilica was at first a large, rectangular hall in the heart of the city which served the merchants and the city officers as a council hall, but which very early found use also as a place for the settlement of legal differences. The middle space was shut off lengthwise by two rows of columns, which separated from it at right and left two narrow lateral corridors, above which there was often a gallery. It is unmistakable that the later Christian master builders borrowed the most important forms of their arrangement of rooms from the ancient basilica.

The development of the barrel-vaulted room led logically from the cross-vault through various intermediate types to the creation of the cupola, which found such perfect expression in the Pantheon at Rome. The Pantheon is the most perfect central-domed building. Its designation as a monument to the Julian imperial family makes clear to us that the building was not regarded as the assembly hall of a community but merely as an enclosed space surrounding the statue of the Caesar. The effect of the interior is, in fact, fascinating. The cupola, which admits from above a uniform light, offers no point that arrests the eye and gives the beholder the feeling of gently soaring upward. The Oriental influence is more noticeable in the Pantheon than in any other example of the Roman vaulted structure.

It was formerly thought that the domed buildings of the Arsacides and the later Sassanides in Persia were to be traced to Roman influence;

today we are coming more and more clearly to recognize that the influence operated in the opposite direction. In his *Architektonische Raumlehre* Ebe takes the standpoint that this type of building is to be regarded as a continuation of Mesopotamian beginnings, which later also served the Christian-Byzantine as well as the Islamic architecture as a starting point. In general, we are fairly sure today that in the development of the Byzantine style, which made its appearance with the spread of Christianity, Persian, Syrian, and even Egyptian influences coöperated strongly. It is true that the beginnings of Byzantine architecture have not been preserved for us. Still, the Oriental influence is unmistakable in the structures of the later periods. A number of celebrated historians of style have expressed the opinion that the beginnings of Byzantine art occurred on the Ionian coast of Asia Minor, because there the influences of the various types of style focused like rays from a burning-glass, constantly offering new stimuli to the artist. In fact, that part of the Orient produced a whole line of distinguished masters of Byzantine architecture; among others, Anthemius of Tralles and Isidoros of Miletus, the two builders of the celebrated church of Saint Sophia at Constantinople, which is held to be the most perfect product of Byzantine architecture.

The Byzantine church-building presents essentially the fusion of two spacial types, which—considered purely esthetically—seem to avoid one another, yet gradually to grow together into a unity; the oblong of the Christian basilica, and the central-domed structure. Such a union gave wide scope to the architect's impulse to design, and led to manifold products in style. In fact, Byzantine art had a strong influence on all Europe and the countries of the Orient and for centuries dominated artistic production. The numerous buildings that date from the early Middle Ages in Constantinople, Italy, Greece, Palestine, Syria, Armenia, and so on, bear witness to this. From the tenth to the twelfth centuries there still persisted a revival of the Byzantine style which, in the Greek Catholic countries, persists even today. The building art of the Mohammedan peoples also harks back to the Byzantine style. Its first products, the mosques at Jerusalem and Damascus, are pure Byzantine and were erected by Byzantine masters. Whether the further development of Mohammedan architecture may properly be designated as "Islamic style," as is often done, is very questionable. Such uniformity as it possessed was owing merely to the fact that the Mohammedan religion had helped to determine the internal framing of the mosque, just as the Christian had determined the spacial arrangement of the church building. Quite outside of this, however, an enormous number of different forms are to be found in Islamic building. Islam, which in its victorious progress through the East swept every land, from the shores of the Ganges to the banks of the Ebro, learned in its course the styles of every possible people and race, and evaluated all of them after its fashion. Thus there are found in the Islamic builder's art Persian, Semitic, Egyptian, Indian, Byzantine and antique elements, which asserted themselves in manifold ways and later had their effect upon the building art of the Christian West.

Out of the oblong of the Christian basilica there developed gradually a new style which set its stamp upon European architecture from the tenth to the thirteenth century. We are speaking of the Romanesque type of building, which in its beginnings harks back to the late Roman style, but which attained its highest development in the northern countries. The word "Romanesque" as a designation for a definite manifestation of style is, if possible, even less appropriate than the term "Gothic" or "Renaissance." French archeologists gave the word currency at the beginning of the eighteenth century to indicate the unity of a style which up to that time had been called in different countries sometimes Lombard, sometimes Rhenish, Norman, or by yet some other name. Of course, the alleged uniformity left much to be desired, and the inventors of the new term had in mind at first only certain details from the Roman antique, such as the rounded arch in combination with columns, which were of little importance in the total picture. In this Romanesque style of building also there can be distinguished the influence of a whole series of different styles, which in many regions gave it a quite distinctive stamp. Let one think of the Romanesque structures erected in Sicily of the time of the Norman domination by Saracen master-builders and show unmistakable features of Islamic style. Just so the Byzantine influence on the Romanesque churches of Northern Italy is so manifest that one speaks with entire justice of a Byzantine-Romanesque style.

Among the peoples of the northern countries the Romanesque reached a special perfection. By the prolonged tempests of the migrations of peoples and by the Roman world these peoples had been aroused and stimulated to higher creativeness. For them Christianity, which among the Romans had already sunk into corruption, had a very special significance in that it enabled them to reëstablish their community of opinion, which had suffered many a shattering blow during the storm and stress of the great migrations and the endless wars. They developed in their own way the principles of a Christian art of building which they had received from the South, and although much of the crude and awkward still clung to their work at first, they betrayed a healthy originality which held within it much of greatness.

The essential feature of Romanesque architecture consists in the supplanting of the flat-roofed, column-supported basilica by the vaulted oblong, in which pillars more and more displaced columns, which at the last found application only as adornment. By the use of the cross-vaulted basilica there developed gradually a new type of room, which displays a definite tendency to movement upward. The further the development proceeded, the more strongly evident became this feature. The arches became constantly steeper, the framework became constantly more slender. The tower was an essential part of the structure, which more and more grew to be integral with it and, viewed from without, gives it a distinctive character. This development at last flowed into the Gothic and at the same time reached its end. Nothing more could be done in this direction. Gothic was, in fact, the final consequence, the finished product of that principle of vertical construction, which in this latest phase of its development fairly tore itself away from the earth and with impetuous impulse soared aloft. It is stone turned to ecstasy, which beholds the heavens and thinks to escape from every earthly bond.

And yet it would be a mistake to wish to see in the Gothic merely an expression of religious feeling; for it was at the same time the result of a definite form of social life, of which it was in large measure the symbol. Gothic is the artistic precipitate of a culture which in a certain measure presented a synthesis of personal initiative and mutual coöperation. In an appendix to Whewell's *History of the Inductive Sciences* the English scholar, Willis, remarks concerning this form of the Christian style of building:

A new decorative construction had arisen, which did not conflict with and disturb the mechanical construction, but aided it and made it harmonious. Every member, every buttress, became a supporter of the load; and by the number of the supports which assisted one another and the resulting sharing of the weight the eye was satisfied of the stability of the structure, despite the peculiarly meager look of the separate parts.

Gustav Landauer, who in his excellent essay *Die Revolution* took the above citation from Kropotkin's splendid book, *Mutual Aid,* attaches to it this fine comment:

The man of science intended here simply to depict the nature of the Christian style of building; but because he had hit upon the correct, the true content of this style, and because the building of this great period is an epitome and a symbol of its society, he had unintentionally put into words a picture of that society: freedom and union; abundance of supports, which lend assistance to one another.

That is unreservedly right; so right that one can get no clear picture of the building art of the Gothic at all without going deeply into the medieval social structure and apprehending that rich manifoldness which finds faithful expression in Gothic architecture. Like medieval society with its uncounted unions, sworn brotherhoods, guilds, municipalities, federalistic in character and unaware of the principle of centralism, the Gothic cathederal is not a centralized structure, but a structure of articulated members, in which every part breathes with its own proper life and is, despite this, organically connected with the whole. Thus, the Gothic building becomes a symbol in stone of an articulated, federated social structure, in which even the smallest part attains effectiveness and contributes to the maintenance of the whole. It could only arise out of a society so rich and of such varied structure, in which every part, consciously or unconsciously, strove toward a common goal. The cathedral was a collective creation in the production of which every section, every member of society, joyously took part. Only through the harmonious cooperation of all the forces in the community, supported by the spirit of solidarity, could the Gothic building arise and become the majestic embodiment of that community which lent it a soul. There was here revealed a spirit which built its own house from within outward, finding it easier to follow its own untamed creative impulse than the laws of esthetics, and which in time created a beauty of its own sort embodying that harmony of every part which best accorded with its innermost essence.

Gothic has often been acclaimed as the profoundest revelation of German mood and German nature; in truth it embodies only the mood and the nature of a particular culture period, with roots running back to the tenth century, which from the eleventh to the fifteenth centuries spread over all Europe. That epoch, of an inner compactness which still arouses the admiration of the investigator, arose not from the special endeavors of a particular people. It was rather the result of a collective creativeness, the living expression of all the intellectual and social tendencies which then inspired European humanity and stirred it to new creative activity. Unfortunately, this very period is most shamefully misjudged by the majority of those historians who are under the influence of the modern idea of the state. A few historians in every country constitute a glorious exception, and to these we owe it chiefly that an understanding of this much misinterpreted period has been revived, at least for a minority. Among them, Georg Dehio, in his splendidly conceived work on German art, has ably shown that Gothic was not the fruit of a particular people or a special race. He says:

> Quite certainly the French were the first to assemble the elements of Gothic construction into a logical system, the first, also, to recognize their value as expression of the Gothic mood, the Gothic world feeling, or whatever else you wish to call it. And by this they are assured of the honor of making a contribution of wide historical application.
>
> It is, however, incorrect to go still further and proclaim this mood, this world feeling, as, in any exclusive sense, a quality of the French mind traceable to hereditary peculiarities. In itself race is a very questionable principle of explanation for phenomena falling within the same time limits. How about

it, if one is dealing with a mixed people? Is it the Gallic or the Latin or the Germanic in the Frenchman that found its expression in Gothic? It is enough just to ask the question in order to realize that the question cannot be asked at all. Gothic is not to be explained by the tradition of blood; it is the artistic synthesis of the culture that was created and lived out in common by Nordic men in a temporary phase of its development. It was a time-product of world-citizenship at the height of the Middle Ages, which grew out of the idea of the Romanic-Germanic family of peoples—this was the true progenitor of Gothic style.[5]

It was among the Frankish tribes of the Ile de France and in Picardy that the Gothic style first found its fullest expression after it had successfully passed through all the transitional stages. From there, Gothic gradually spread over all Europe and assumed in each region a distinctive form. Often differences made themselves manifest even in the same country, and not seldom in the same town, revealing to us the manifold influences of the time. If the Gothic never attained in Italy to that extreme perfection it reached in many localities in Germany, this is in no way to be traced to the difference of race or nationality. Here the influences of the past played a decisive role, which of necessity operated in Italy quite otherwise than in Germany. In Italy the traditions of the antique had never been completely suppressed; then, too, the bitter opposition of the church to the "pagan tradition" could not be changed in this connection. Echoes of the antique were always noticeable there, and the development of the Gothic style of building could not escape these influences. The same phenomenon can also be observed in many parts of France, where the basic principle of the Romanesque type of building was never quite eliminated from the Gothic structures. In England, again, the principle of vertical construction was carried to the extreme of the perpendicular style which presents a special form of Gothic. Of similar phenomena, which we can perceive in the various phases of development of every great style period, there are a great many.

With the dissolution of medieval society and the ancient city culture Gothic art also sank slowly into its grave. The beginning Renaissance was the initial stroke of a new period in the history of European peoples and necessarily led also to a new style in art. It is a mistake, however, to regard the Renaissance as purely an affair of the arts. Every great transformation of style is the expression of social changes and can be correctly understood only through these. The Renaissance was a cultural event of European importance from the effects of which no people could escape. If one wishes to estimate correctly its influence on the cultural structure of Europe, one must contemplate it as a whole. For what is usually designated as French, Italian or German Renaissance, or appears in the

[5] *Geschichte der deutschen Kunst.* Band I, p. 215.

works of the historiographers as Humanism, Reformation or Rationalism, are parts of a single whole which is understandable by us in its entirety only in the light of the inner connections of all of its separate results. Thus regarded, the Renaissance was the beginning of a mighty overturning in all spheres of personal and social life, which led to a reshaping of all the forms of European culture. All earlier norms and concepts had lost their grip, the most firmly held theories and ideas had begun to totter, old and new tumbled together in a crazy chaos, until there were gradually shaped out of it completely new elements of social existence.

That such a far-reaching historic occurrence should produce even in the arts a fundamental overturning of all traditional styles, was inevitable and needs no further explanation. In fact, the Renaissance led to a renewal of the ancient concepts of style, a fact which was revealed with especial clarity in architecture. Yet even here one is unable to speak of a sharp break with the past. It is true that the Renaissance was the starting point for a new conception of life and of artistic structure, but its connections with what had been are, despite this, plainly discernible. Here, too, the separate forms penetrate one another, and the new is articulated with the old. Gustav Ebe remarks:

> The great epoch of Renaissance art which, arising in Italy, expanded at first over the Western European countries and at last took in the compass of the whole world, is generally conceived as a re-acceptance of the antique-Roman artistic traditions; and this view even goes so far as to assume that the Renaissance, at least in its purest Italian form, drew its whole stylistic apparatus from Roman sources. Meanwhile, independently of the formal stylistic treatment, which expressed itself in a sharp contrast with Gothic, steady advance in the development of spacial types was making itself felt, and it was growing up entirely on the soil of medieval achievements. And in this last mentioned field appears also no sharp break with the next preceding, but a logical further development of the old types, corresponding to the ideas and demands of the time, in a reconstruction which perhaps would not be conceivable without the aid of the antique-sounding terminology.[6]

The correctness of this observation is obvious. In the artistic treatment of space the architecture of the Renaissance, despite all the stylistic contrasts which separate it from the forms of the Middle Ages, signifies merely a new generation. The external forms change and adapt themselves to the new demands and intellectual currents. The man who turns his ardent gaze from heaven and once more beholds the earth about him clings fast to the earthly. Buildings lose the vertical character which had found its highest perfection in the Gothic and could not be surpassed. In place of the high-uplifted there appeared again the wide-spread on the

---

[6] *Architektonische Raumlehre.* Dresden, 1900. Band II, p. 1.

earth; the horizontal feature becomes the decisive character of the new building. It no longer grows from within up toward heaven; it is shaped plastically from without, according to definite principles and new artistic assumptions. Proportion becomes once more the measure of everything and assigns to every part its fixed, irrevocable place. The spacial arrangement is clearly thought out and is supported by definite leading principles of organization. The building often terminates in a heavy cornice crown; and the separate stories, too, are sharply marked off from one another by cornices, by which the horizontal character of the whole is still more strongly emphasized. This feature stands out with especial clarity in the palaces of the Italian Renaissance. The column, also, comes again into use, as is shown in an especially charming manner in the courts of the Renaissance buildings in Italy surrounded by loggias and porticos.

In the ecclesiastical buildings the central principle, which had been completely suppressed by the Gothic, became dominant again. For the most part the centralized structure was surmounted by a cupola, which brought out still more forcibly the enclosed character of the structure. Even if the connection with Byzantine and antique prototypes is unmistakable, nevertheless, masters like Brunelleschi, Bramante, and especially Michelangelo, were able to bring out entirely new effects of incomparable weight and concentrated strength. It is true that it was necessary to combine the centralized type of building with the oblong in various ways to adapt it to practical demands, but it was just these experiments which, especially in the late Renaissance, gave the impetus for a wealth of the most distinctive style-forms. Michelangelo's design for Saint Peter's in Rome is the most powerful expression of this new style, so to speak, its last word. Bramante, to whom the construction of the cathedral had been intrusted, in his design had surrounded the principal cupola with four small cupolas, each of which was, however, to have its own life and present in itself a finished whole. But Michelangelo, who carried on the work after the death of Bramante, took from the four small cupolas all individuality and subjected them almost violently to the domination of the principal dome. Thus every part was robbed of its independence and incorporated into a central unity which almost crushed the life out of its separate parts. Michelangelo developed this feature to the extreme; but he also opened entirely new outlooks to the art of building and spiritualized it to a degree that makes his creation imperishable.

The Renaissance, which had dissolved all traditional norms into nothing and which, especially in the last phase of its development, came close to a serious skepticism which operated to cripple its loftier efforts, would necessarily have foundered here if it had not been permeated by a certain deeper yearning which kept it looking for new shores. None felt this more deeply than the great Florentine, whose tormenting figures reflect the inner struggle of his own soul. A Faust nature like Michelangelo's could not be content with even the most ostentatious externalities. He strove always for a subjectivizing of art and knocked at many a gloomy portal which had thus far opened to no one. This feature is also revealed distinctively in his tectonic creations. His work becomes a living entity breathing forth every passion of the human soul, every secret quest, every rebellious defiance, and above all that Titanic urge for the superhuman which is so characteristic of the whole product of the master, enabling him even then to progress beyond the horizon of the Renaissance.

The social culture of the Renaissance issued, it is true, chiefly from Italy, but since it found everywhere in Europe the needed intellectual and social background, it wakened in every country a lively echo and developed into a world style in which was mirrored the social culture of a particular epoch. Its boundaries are far too wide to permit it to be restricted to the narrow frame of national ideas. Like the Gothic, it gave birth to various styles growing out of special environments. If the development which the Gothic had attained in Germany was never reached in Italy because the tradition of the antique hindered it there in a peculiar manner, just so the art of the Renaissance was never able completely to overcome the vital tradition of the Gothic in Germany. The same sort of thing can be shown of the Renaissance in England, France or Spain. Everywhere the special environment and the traditions of the past affected the development of style. But these peculiarities and deviations do no damage to the picture as a whole; on the contrary they merely set up a complete image and mark the kinship of the ambitions which everywhere were nourished from the same sources. It was neither the special character of the race nor the peculiarity of the national temperament that called the art of the Renaissance to life; it was the great social upheaval which convulsed all Europe, and which everywhere gave the stimulus for the development of new types of style and new conceptions of art in general.

From the art of the Renaissance there developed logically the baroque which was the characteristic artistic style of the seventeenth century and in many countries, especially in Germany, was dominant well into the eighteenth century. Here, again, we are confronted with no sharp break with the past, in whose stead had arisen with primal abruptness something new, but with a gradual development which slowly crystallized out of the Renaissance type of style, influenced, like every other style, by the social reconstructions in the life of the European peoples. Out of the bewildering chaos of the Renaissance period there was gradually shaping the great European state in the guise of the absolute monarchy. Powerful dynasties developed or confirmed their position in the most important countries after the resistance of the cities and the noble vassals had been overcome. A new power had arisen which brought even the church under its control and made it serve its ends. With the help of its huge armies and its bureaucratic administrative apparatus the monarchy succeeded in sweeping all hostile forces from the field and in suppressing by force the ancient rights and freedoms of the municipalities. The person of the king became the embodiment of absolutely complete power, the court became the center of all social life. The state took all the functions of society into its own hands or under its supervision and set its imprint on all social performance. Legislation, jurisprudence, the entire public administration, became the monopoly of royalty; society was almost completely merged in the state. This transformation in the whole social life forced the thought and feeling of the subjects into definite lines prescribed by the state. Everything seemed to exist merely to further the purposes of the dynasty. It was the time of the "Sun Kingdom," whose representative could utter the words: *"L'état c'est moi!"*

In a state of society in which every public activity had its special rule and everything was ruled and regulated from above to the smallest detail there was hardly offered to art the possibility of free creativeness. Its representatives were in the service of the autocrat and had hardly any other task than to proclaim the glory of His Divine Grace. As once the splendor of the cathedrals and of the religious festivals of the church had shone like a glowing aureole, so now the pomp of the palaces and the royal courts formed a halo for the monarchy and imparted to its power a mystic glory. In this wise arose the great buildings of the period of absolutism; the Louvre in Paris, the palace and the park at Versailles, the Escorial at Madrid, the Zwinger in Dresden, and so on; and since every petty despot must have his Versailles the new style spread over every country. Only in connection with this social reconstruction in Europe can the art of the baroque be rightly understood. The term itself, derived from the Portuguese word *baroque,* which means a very irregular pearl formed by the fusion of several close-packed units, is in itself utterly unimportant, and was at first used merely in derision.

In reality, baroque means a new style which arose from the Renaissance, but had its roots in a new conception of art. In sharp contrast with the Gothic, the Renaissance, following in the footprints of the antique, had proclaimed harmony as the most profound, indeed, as the only, expression of the beautiful. The baroque established a new esthetic criterion by putting *power* in the place of harmony. In this the influence of the social reconstruction in Europe was revealed plainly. The power concept of the absolute monarchy filled the mind of the time. Power became beauty, expression of a new artistic feeling, which was gradually impressed completely into the service of royalty. The majesty of the monarch radiated its splendor over everything and subjected to itself every emotion in social life. And this blazing glory of absolute, unlimited power, with which at the height of its development, royalty was able to surround itself, was revealed also in the architecture of that time, and proclaimed its omnipotence in thunderous accords. The overwhelming power of the absolutist state, which tolerated near the person of the ruler nothing claiming equality of birth and impressed the stamp of its purpose upon everything, gave to the art of the baroque that deeply imprinted courtly-representative character which is so characteristic of the whole seventeenth century. Just as Jesuitism had made it its task to subjectivize once more the power of the church, so the advocates of absolutism endeavored now to spiritualize the coercive character of the monarchy and to make men forget its true origin. Thus royalty took on that glamor of superhuman grace that finds expression even in its buildings. In fact, the baroque building often seizes on the beholder with the intrinsic power of a mystic revelation and fills the soul with awe.

The church buildings of the period pursue the same lines and bring to highest effectiveness the omnipotence of an absolute principle of power. Under the influence of Jesuitism, which embodied, historically, the organized counter-Reformation, there developed the so-called "Jesuit style." New problems of space force their way into the foreground and produce in the minds of the faithful an overpowering effect, forcing their emotions with irresistible power under the yoke of its universally dominating influence. The house of God is transformed into a show-place, which is adorned with gorgeous ornamentation and often arouses a feeling of passionate excitement such as flows only from ecstasy. Waves of mystic terror seem to surge through the holy place. The external structure as well as the inner furnishing are designed to whisper to men of the omnipotence of a Higher Will that strides triumphant over every earthbound thing.

The baroque style finally ended in rococo. The icy majesty and stiff solemnity of courtly ceremonial became tiresome at last and aroused the need for warmer and more intimate forms. The so-called "Regency style," which arose under the regency of Philip of Orleans, takes this need into account and is the beginning of a new style of expression that gradually grew into the rococo and reached its zenith under Louis XV. In place of the unapproachable and majestic, which with rigid dignity rejected every intimacy, there appeared the graceful and charming, pursuing airy fantasies and amorous intrigues seeking only to delight, and no longer weighed down with the burden of representing a social system. Thus, there arises a new style, which reveals itself chiefly in the decoration of interiors. The wall loses its massive character and becomes transformed into a plastic frame, its spaces covered with scrolled lines, flower-motifs and other elements of a cheerful ornamentation. The walls blend into the ceiling, which is adorned with delightful figures in stucco. The colors lose their harshness and dissolve into soft tones. The huge mirrors of the apartments help to push back the natural limits of the room and deceitfully conceal its material dimensions.

Especially charming is the delicate porcelain, the elegance of which was not without influence on the whole development of the rococo. Furniture, too, loses its heavy awkward forms and is adapted to the interior arrangement. A goading unrest, arising from a refined sensitivity, dominates men and things and operates like a mysterious drug on the overkeen nerves of the upper strata of society. The new style corresponds exactly to the mental status of the privileged castes. A profound alteration in the more intimate customs becomes evident in those circles, and in rococo we find its emotional precipitate.

The principle of power, to which the absolute monarchy had been able in the time of its ascending development to give a metaphysical significance, lost more and more of this character, and in the circle of favorites and parasites came to be valued merely for its practical results. People began to make fun of the strenuous glory-seeking and the stiff pomp of a time of alleged greatness which no longer impressed anyone. All that which earlier had produced the impression of the proudest and most majestic unapproachability affected people now like a silly parody and involuntarily gave the intellectuals an opportunity to exercise the satiric impulse and display the sharpness of their wits. Royalty was already an embalmed corpse merely awaiting burial. When Louis XIV identified the state with his person he was giving the proudest expression to the innermost essence of absolute monarchy: the king everything, the people nothing! But later, when Madame Du Barry with blunt familiarity called her royal gallant, *"La France,"* it was the grimmest mockery of all that royalty "by the grace of God" set itself up to be. The monarchy was ready for the downfall that waited not far in the future. In the tempests of the Revolution the fragile culture of the rococo fell in ruins, together with the old society which had produced it. Amid agonized convulsions and violent shocks a different world took shape, a new generation arose, that looked out toward new horizons.

What the generation hoped and longed for has never become a reality, and the words "Liberty, Equality, Fraternity" are still but the echo of a dream. The bourgeois society, which had entered into the inheritance of the old régime, was able, it is true, to charm into life the abstract image of the modern nation, but it was denied to it to form a genuine community having its roots in the needs of all and based on the principles of social justice. Its new economic order, which raised the "war of all against all" to a principle, necessarily begot that heartless egoism, so characteristic of the capitalistic world, that marches on over corpses. This society was not in a position to create social ties between men and peoples; it merely made the antagonisms wider and more unbridgeable and led logically to the World War and the gigantic chaos of our times.

It could, therefore, create no new intellectual outlooks for architecture. Here, too, it furthered only the play of antagonisms and led to that peculiar stylelessness that has been characteristically designated as "stylistic chaos." Let one think of the plan and the outlook of our modern industrial cities, of the comfortless ugliness of the barrack tenements, of the silly façade structures with their impudent swagger that convert the street into a dreary canyon, and one has the impression that all the aberrant tastes of the time have been invited to make themselves at home. Not without reason has our generation coined the term "junk." A society which has lost all natural feeling of the ties binding man to man, and allow the individual to drown in the chaos of the mass, could arrive at no other results. Wherever today there develops in public buildings or in modern settlements a really new style, it always springs from the inner yearning for a new community which shall free men from the slavery and emptiness of their present existence and give their lives purpose and content again.

In the end, this epoch, too, with its extremely developed industrialism, its factories, warehouses and barracks, with its incurable divisions in society and the chaos in the building arts that arises from these, is a proof of how little national consciousness means at bottom. It is the time—and the material, spiritual and intellectual conditions of the time—that everywhere attains expression and in the last issue determines also the utterances of art.

Chapter 11

THE PERSONAL IN PAINTING. LEONARDO AND MICHELANGELO. CONCEPTION OF LIFE AND CREATIVE URGE. THE COMMUNAL FEATURES OF AN EPOCH AND THEIR INFLUENCE ON ART. ALBRECHT DÜRER AND THE REFORMATION. THE GERMAN ELEMENT IN DÜRER'S ART. FOREIGN INFLUENCES. REMBRANDT AND NATIONAL CITIZENSHIP. THE ARTIST AS VICTIM OF THE NATIONAL FOLLY. GOYA AND THE SPIRIT OF THE REVOLUTION. THE ARTISTIC IDEAL OF THE PRIVILEGED. ROCOCO AND REVOLUTION. DAVID AND THE ROMAN GESTURE IN THE FRENCH REVOLUTION. THE RULE OF THE BOURGEOIS. DAUMIER AGAINST THE "RULE OF THE PAUNCHES." JUSTICE AND MILITARISM IN THE MIRROR OF DAUMIER'S ART. THE AWAKENING OF LABOR. THE PROBLEM OF LABOR IN MODERN ART. MILLET AND MEUNIER. THE ARTIST IN THE STRUGGLE AGAINST THE SOCIAL ORDER. ART TREND AND NATIONAL PECULIARITY. THE UNIVERSALLY HUMAN IN ART. POWER OF THE IMAGINATION.

WE HAVE treated the development of architecture at some length because here the transitions in style and the influence of the social environment upon artistic production are most clearly apparent. But it would be a mistake to assume that in the other arts the "national peculiarity" of the artist has any more decisive influence on the character of his work. The personal always takes first place in artistic work and gives it its special note. Two artists who are born in the same place, belong to the same time, and are related in the same way to the influences of their social environment, display fundamentally different reactions to the impressions which they receive and which more or less strongly influence their creations.

Michelangelo and Leonardo da Vinci were both Florentines, both lived in the same time, both were gripped by the spirit of their epoch; still they differ from one another as do day and night, and not merely in their purely human qualities. The works of these two men belong in quite different worlds, and even the boldest national fantasy cannot bridge the abyss that separates them.

There is in Leonardo's art something siren-like, softly calling from bottomless depths. The enigmatic smile of his female figures issues from an inner world withdrawn from everything temporal, in which the soul seems filled with an enticing yearning. It seems like a dreamy play of the senses that can never become truth. And like a dream, too, those strange landscapes that have nothing earthly in them. Misty distances enchant the eye, awakening melodies of dreamy depth and more than human loveliness. Let one think of the landscapes of the *Virgin of the Rocks,* the *St. John,* or the *Mona Lisa.* All the figures to which Leonardo imparted life are nymph-like, including his madonnas, which are touched by no breath of Christian tradition. Everything is surrounded with a veil of the most delicate sensuality, which stirs deep vibrations in the soul, and out of which one thinks he hears soft echoes of the harmony of the spheres. This same strange current runs through all the work of Leonardo, recurring again and again in inexhaustible diversity. It is this current which so allured his contemporaries and posterity, like the news of a remote fairyland, which no mortal being had ever entered: always and everywhere the half-veiled glance, that peeps out from darkly enigmatic depths and seem like a vision from another world.

Of what an utterly different sort was Michelangelo, the powerful creator of titanic figures, on which he imposed the curse of his own life. Himself a giant who wants to take every heaven by storm and always feels himself held back by the weight of his own spirit, one struck down by Fate, in whose gloomy soul rage superhuman forces, who can never find satisfaction in his work and still is driven by an inner compulsion to work restlessly on, because he can do nothing else. In his demonic figures lives the torment of loneliness and gloomy brooding about which hover all the terrors of eternity. Many of his figures impress us like an Alpine weight. Let one think of the Jeremiah of the Sistine Chapel, of the sybils and painted caryatids of the gigantic ceiling; or even of the mighty masonry of the Medicean chapel in Florence. This Day, this Night, this Morning, this Evening, on which rests the burden of all the thousands of years, and in which the sorrow-filled soul of the artist is mirrored. Even the Leda being mated with the swan shows the same expression of leaden weight and arouses no feeling of sensuous passion. In other figures rages the storm of passionate wrath, as in the colossal statue of Moses, in whose gigantic body every muscle is tensed, and on whose forehead shows the mood of the thunder-storm. Even the Christ of the *Last Judgment* and the troop of naked giants which fills the background breathe the same spirit.

It is a difference in world philosophy that here finds expression. In the art of Leonardo that Humanism survived which is not the spirit of a nation, but the spirit of an epoch, its culminating point, and at the same time its most comprehensive expression. In the works of Michelangelo, Humanism was utterly suppressed to make place for the striving after superhuman things, which dared to knock at the secret gates of all heavens and of every hell, driven by the heat of enthusiasm and the fanatical desire for a law that should not be human law. The man who withstood both emperor and pope, who in Gianotti's dialogues defended tyrannicide—"because the tyrant is not a human being, but a beast in human form"—lived also in his work.

That which is revealed at first glance in the work of a great artist who puts spiritual problems into visible shape is not the accident of his nationality but the deeply human in him which belongs to all times and teaches us to understand the speech of all peoples. Compared to this the assaults of the local environment—however important they may be as indexes for the technical and historical judgment of his work—play a very small part. But even the quite local touches in a work of art do not give it a national character; for within every nation, and especially every great nation, there are a multitude of local influences that peacefully work together in motley mixture but can never be assembled within the narrow frame of a fictitious concept of the nation.

What Leonardo, for example, wished to give expression to in his *Mona Lisa* was the manifold emotions of the human soul, the hidden ebb and flow of profound inner feeling. In it he followed the most delicate oscillations of mood, and the woman whom he had, so to speak, discovered for art, gave him a superlative starting point in this. The enigmatic countenance of Mona Lisa reflects all the extremes of human emotion; the adorably radiant and the abysmally demonic, cheerful innocence and cunning calculation, undesirous purity and ruinous sensuality. It is the artist's own soul that radiates from this picture; himself a Faust, who follows every obscure path, aching with the urge for knowledge, is yet unable to force his way to the Ultima Thule. It is just this profound experience of the innately tragic in the human soul that imparts to his work its peculiar greatness. With Michelangelo, also, every work is transformed into an expression of the experiences of his own soul: "And always it became an image of my own anguish, bore the gloomy lines of my own brow." In this profoundest emotion of the man and the artist there breathes no breath of national feeling. How little, how trifling, is all the bungling assertion of national influence in contrast with this struggling humanity that is always striving for the superhuman.

Just as in history the alleged national currents are forced quite into the background by the universal flood-stream of the time, so also in art. Thus we could hardly picture to ourselves the art of Albrecht Dürer without the Reformation and its countless undercurrents. Only if one keep clearly in mind the storm and stress of that time of ferment in which old and new were so completely churned together can one understand the strange combinations that are revealed in Dürer's work. We cite Dürer because he has been so often and so baselessly styled the "most German of all German painters." Such a designation really means nothing at all. If one wants to designate as German the master's deep feeling for the tender inspirations and spiritual radiations of his native soil, by all means let him do so, but this in no way expresses the distinctive essence of Dürer's art. Lafarge was quite right when he said: "But the German side of his work is its limitation. The national or race side of any work of art is its weakness. What is called German is probably nothing more than the form of a less lengthy civilization." [1]

In Dürer's art lives that strange dreamland which the surroundings of his homeland had called into being in his soul, people with the creatures of his fantasy which are born of the landscape, breathe its atmosphere and feel its sunrise sky above them. Works like *Jerome at Home*, the *Flight into Egypt*, the *Saint Anthony*, *The Knight*, *Death and the Devil* and many others, are illuminated by that strange gleam from his native soil that is so comforting to the eye. But in this same artist in whose soul is mirrored all the magic of his northern homeland lives also the alluring longing, the silent rhythm, of sunlit fields through which his feet have wandered. This influence, this voice from the distant South, is impressively revealed in the work of the master. When Scheffler declares that "in a painter like Dürer the Gothic has entered into a most noteworthy combination with the Grecian," he is merely giving expression to this feeling in other words. Dürer had absorbed into himself the whole creative urge of the Italian Renaissance and saturated every fiber of his being with it. The influence of Italian masters like Verrocchio, Leonardo, Mantegna, Bellini, Raffaello, Pollajuole and many others, find plain expression in many of his works. Verrocchio's equestrian statue of Colleoni stirred Dürer deeply, and one can definitely accept it that without this influence works like the *Saint George* and *Ritter, Tod und Teufel* would never have come into existence. The Renaissance landscape, also, and, above all, the love of the naked human body, which is one of the most typical characteristics of the Renaissance, had an unmistakable influence on Dürer's art.

Dürer absorbed everything foreign, sucked it in at every pore, till it became a part of himself. Thus there mingled in his work the confused and twilight wonderings of the Northland and the clear and cheerful impressions of the South, which brightened and clarified his brimming fancy and supplied the current of his art as a whole. Even the deeply human in his work, that is brought so close to us especially by his figure of Christ, is in no way a "revelation of his German soul," but a revelation of the spiritual aspirations of his time. Here speaks to us Dürer the Humanist, who follows every human emotion to its utmost depths. The deeply human feature of Dürer's art appeals to us, too, in the well-known

[1] John Lafarge, *Great Masters*. New York, 1906.

self-portrait of the master in the Munich Pinakothek—a silent brooder with searching eyes, whose gaze seems to be directed inward. One feels that behind that brow the great problems of the time are struggling to take shape, but the profound earnestness beaming from his countenance tells us also that this brain will not solve every riddle. We think involuntarily of the winged woman in the *Melancholy* of the master, who, sunk in gloomy brooding, gazes into an enigmatic distance, over which spreads mysteriously the glow of comet and of northern light.

If there were in reality such a thing as a national art, then such an artist as Rembrandt, and with him a legion of others, would be inconceivable. For the "national feeling" of his contemporaries had for the work of the greatest artist that little Holland ever produced nothing but scorn and derision. Its spokesmen had so little comprehension of Rembrandt's greatness that they calmly allowed him to perish in misery and took not the slightest notice even of his death. Only long after his demise did Rembrandt slowly find his way into the ranks of the immortals so that today he serves his country as the symbol of its "national spirit."

The citizenry of the Netherlands, which once carried on a desperate fight for the liberation of the country from the yoke of Spanish despotism, came out victorious in that struggle. A new spirit entered into every class of the population and brought the little country to an undreamed of height. In every city there was excitement and motion; everywhere, a surplus of vital energy. There still survives in the pictures of Franz Hals a last precipitate of the spirit of this time of impudent upstarts, intoxicated with its own vigor. But this unbridled spirit was rather quickly curbed; the desire for orderly conditions became more and more noticeable among the citizens, and with the rising development of business and of mercantile capital these assumed more and more stable form. Thus there developed gradually that comfortable Philistinism that lived only for its material interests and endeavored to regulate all life by fixed rules.

To Rembrandt this bourgeois-national orderliness became the curse of his life. So long as he tried, as he did at first, to satisfy the taste of his unimaginative public, he got along after a fashion. Until the artist in him was aroused! Then it was all over with the cheap popularity of the master, and the irreconcilable antagonism between him and the "nation" became increasingly evident. This antagonism finds in his works a completely conscious expression raised to a mordant sharpness. The artist became a rebel against his time and drew with keen clarity the boundary between his art and the national Philistinism of his land. Let one think of that Samson in the Kaiser Friedrich Museum in Berlin, who threatens his father-in-law with his clenched fist, or of that angry Moses in Dresden, who is dashing to pieces the tables of the law in grim rage, and one feels that it is Rembrandt himself who is smashing the bourgeois orderliness on which his life was to be wrecked.

Even in his later work, which reveals the quality of the artist in full maturity, when he had long ceased to vent his ire on complacent profiteers, he came no closer to the national feeling of his country. On the contrary, the chasm between his art and the national lack of taste became ever wider and deeper, until at last he established his residence in the middle of the Ghetto of Amsterdam where the exiled Jews from Spain and Portugal unveiled to his keen eyes a new world strangely unlike the gray uniformity of Dutch life of his day. There he gradually forgot the old environment and reveled in all the colorful dreams of the Orient. What he had earlier surmised and in various ways developed became for him the profoundest spiritual experience. So he became the mighty magician of the brush, who flooded with spirituality everything corporeal and laid bare the hidden landscape of the soul. And so doing he became the bearer of a new art which was trammeled by no national ties, and was therefore to become an inner revelation for men of a later time.

There runs also through Rembrandt's art a deep social current. Let one cast a glance at the Christ of the "Hundred Guilder Print," [2] that savior of the despised and the outcast, surrounded by ragged beggars, the sick and the lame, who in torment pant for salvation. For beggars, drunkards and tramps were the constant companions of the artist during his last years, when, in order to be able to endure existence at all, he sought forgetfulness in carousal. And let us not here forget those last self-portraits of the master, out of which there stares at us a drink-wasted countenance marked by anguish of soul—perhaps the most terrible indictment of the nation that any artist ever put on canvas.

Every great art is free from national limitations and affects us so overpoweringly just because it rouses in us the hidden stirrings of our humanity, reveals the mighty unity of mankind. Let one sink himself in the creations of Francisco Goya from which radiates all the warmth of southern plains. Still, behind the outer forms of southern surroundings dreams the soul of the artist, stand ideas and problems that were revolving in his brain, and which were not simply the problems of his country, but the problems of his time. For every art of vital strength brings out the value of the spiritual contribution of its epoch, which is struggling for emotional expression. And right here there enters that purely human quality that overcomes the foreign and sets us on our native soil.

One need not be a Spaniard to be able to appreciate the art of Goya in all its greatness. The onrush of a new time that strode steelshod over a perishing world rumbles from out his work and seems like the twilight

[2] Originally called *Christ Healing the Sick*, the etching came later to be named for a price once paid for it.—*Translator*

of the gods, the battle to the death of everything that is. His portraits of the Spanish royal family and the entire courtly setting are gruesome examples of an inexorable urge for the truth that made no concessions and stripped from divinely established royalty the last fragment of the tinsel of majesty. Only the human, the all too human, finds expression here. Nietzsche's saying, "Often corruption sits on the throne—and often the throne on corruption," becomes reality here in both its aspects.

And what holds good of Goya's paintings holds good in still higher degree of the etchings of the master. Here his rebellious temper takes on actually demonic forms. His *Desastres de la Guerra* are more horrible than anything ever said against war. In these frightful drawings there lies no slightest glimmer of heroic sentiment, no patriotic inspiration of any sort, no glory of the great leaders of battle; only the human beast is here depicted in every phase of his murderous activity. A revolutionary in the boldest sense of the word here speaks to us in a language understood by all peoples that strips the last rags from the rotten body of patriotic hypocrisy; a really great man here passes judgment on the organized murder of peoples. Goya's all-destroying spirit made pause before no sanctity. With grim scorn and angry contempt he broke through all the bounds of antiquated traditions and reverend notions. He writes his *Mene tekel* above the gates of the old society, and opposes the heads of state and church just as implacably as he does the whole chaotic mass of dead conventions and inherited prejudices of his contemporaries. When the signal fires of the French Revolution flamed up also in Spain, then the artist jubilated over the new time which was to come. But these unbounded hopes were quickly shattered; and with Ferdinand VII on the throne, blackest reaction boldly reared its head and scoffed at all the dreams of a coming freedom. The Inquisition was reëstablished in its old rights, all the young germs perished before the pest-laden breath of a bloody despotism, and dense darkness spread over all the land. Even Goya's dream had been dreamed out. In utter silence, filled with a grim contempt for mankind, he lived withdrawn from all the world in his country house near Madrid, alone with the offspring of his hellish fantasy which his hand conjured forth upon the walls—frightful figures of a silent world of specters, surrounded by the madness of every terror, compared to which Dante's Hell seems happy and peaceful—till the aged artist no longer felt safe even in this loneliness from the malice of the despot, whom people called the "Tiger," and dragged his withered body off to France, where death closed at last his tired eyes.

However strongly the advocates of "art for art's sake" may emphasize that art is timeless, still the art history of every epoch shows us by innumerable examples how irresistibly the intellectual and social currents of the time come to expression in its art. Let one compare the works of the rococo painters with the creations of Jacques-Louis David, and one recognizes at the first glance that in the short time that lies between the two a scene of mighty dimensions in world history has been enacted.

The trenchant phrase of Pompadour, "After us the deluge!" stood invisible above the gates of the old society, a world of hypocritic appearances, as fragile as its dainty porcelain and its slender, curved-legged furniture that seemed made rather to be looked at than to be used. Its speech is graceful and select, its social forms are of involved courtliness. It has no more feeling for the heroic gestures of Corneille or for the stiff dignity of Racine. Only the intimate, the dainty, still has attraction for its supporters. Their passion is the pastoral play, the gallant adventure, which make no further demands on one; and if the debilitated body is not in shape to follow up the tumult of the senses, then artificial means must be employed to reinforce the erotic impulse. Everything seems ornate, softened, over-refined in this theatrical world; everything coos, smiles, minces, dances, lures, sighs amorously, smells of musk and cosmetics and never for an instant thinks of the fact that outside a whole people is perishing in shocking misery. And when from time to time a dull growl of hatred disturbs the dainty joys of this eternal holiday, they seem for a while bewildered and anxious, then quickly turn with graceful wantonness to some new madness. To shut themselves away from all the realities of the world outside, not to see what is, was the motto of that society, to which Mozart has so delightfully given sound and rhythm in his *Figaro*.

Watteau's *Embarkation for the Island of Cytherea* could serve that time as a slogan. A company of enamored rococo people in the midst of a lovely landscape before a placid body of water, awaiting the vessel that is to transport them to the dream-fields of the blissful. Here the woe and suffering of the world is forgotten; no rough gale penetrates into this hidden paradise. All life seems wrapped in fragrance and delight—a faithful image of the gay society, which lived as if in a garden of love and walled up every entrance so that no uninvited guest could disturb their pleasures. What inspired Watteau was yet more delicately and perfectly depicted in the works of Lancret, Boucher, Fragonard and others. Everything great, solemn, stern, which might awaken in the beholder serious or tormenting reflections, is lacking here. Life is lived under the sign of Venus, the erotic is its only content. It is not the naïve, almost undesirous nakedness of a past time, which gives the artist the opportunity to trace all the motives for the activities of the human body—not even the blunt sensuality which stands out so crudely in the works of Rubens. Here something else appears. A gentle quiver goes through these female bodies, which often have not quite reached their bloom, as in Boucher's figures of girls. Something like a lascivious shudder runs through this naked flesh, pregnant with hidden pleasures and panting for the joys of secret love. It is a world of rapturous charm, the carefree world of Arcadia, where the tender sky seems never beclouded by a sorrow; almost too lovely to be true. One has the feeling of sitting out a cheerful play on which the curtain will shortly be rung down.

But the pastoral idyll was to have a sudden end. Too frightful was the price that must be paid for the pleasures of a tiny minority of privileged idlers, too horrible the suffering that ground to earth the millions born of the dust, whose death rattle died out unheard amid the carouse of the love-feast. The catastrophe did not come suddenly. Since the death of Louis XV revolts of the hungry peasantry had become a constantly recurring phenomenon. Because the unrest was confined to narrow limits, as a rule, the government was able to suppress it with comparative ease; but the disturbances occurred again and again, and they became constantly more bitter. The signs were there, but there were only a few who wanted to understand them; and still fewer who could summon up the courage to interpret them correctly. But at last the storm broke, and, wildly howling, tore through the rotten framework of the old society so that everything came crashing down together. A thunder storm had broken over Cytherea; fiery bolts set the old trees ablaze, and through the pleasant walks, where hitherto there had been heard only the billing and cooing of lovers, roared the thunder's mighty voice announcing the beginning of new time. The firm walls which had so safely shut off the fields of the blessed from the outer world, fell in ruins; and aroused masses rolled in compact troops through the quiet closes of a lost paradise—the miserable and enslaved of uncounted years. None had had pity on them; now they, in turn, knew no mercy, and with rough fists and clenched teeth they made their own law.

The lovely dream was dreamed out, the last illusion burst like a glittering bubble. The awful twilight of the gods had come and proclaimed the end of every rapturous feast and gallant shepherd play. The world no longer smelled of perfume and rouge, but of sweat and blood, of powder and lead. Out of a herd of ragged subjects there had come forth a nation which took the field against all the world. These are no longer rococo men—these soldiers who tread the world stage and plunge into battle to the strains of the Marsaillaise to safeguard the achievements of the revolution. A new idea had been born, the idea of the fatherland; the insurgent masses themselves had stood sponsor for it; it seemed to them the integrating bond that held all forces together in the service of the revolution against her enemies. For patriotism meant in those days fidelity to the revolution. Out of the former subject there had been made a citizen, who now felt that he, too, had a part in the common responsibility for the fate of his country. All unwordliness had vanished; there were no dreamers any more.

This new state of affairs forced art also into different roads and became the creator of another new style. This new art found its most important representative in Jacques-Louis David. Himself an enthusiastic, indeed, a fanatical advocate of democracy in Rousseau's sense, he belonged also among the men who had overthrown the monarchy and declared war to the knife against the old society. An outspoken Puritan in politics, he felt himself powerfully drawn to Robespierre and believed, like the latter, that virtue could be enforced by the terror. His very first works, the *Oath of the Horatii, Brutus,* the *Death of Socrates* reveal the harshness of his inexorable character. What a distance lies between these works and the productions of a Boucher or a Fragonard! Two worlds stand here ruggedly opposed, utterly without a point of contact. Muther depicts this contrast very effectively when he says of David:

> He showed us a new puritanical generation that could no longer make use of the trifling art of the rococo, the man, the hero who dies for an idea, for the fatherland. He gave to this man a powerful musculature, like a fighter plunging into the arena. And he also brought color and the language of line into harmony with the heroism of the day. What in the rococo period had been flattering and vague, in David is hard and metallic. What in line had been caressing and fawning, is with him rigid discipline. In the place of the irregularity, the spirals, and the curved trifles came the straight line, the bolt-upright posture of the training-field, the movement of the soldier on parade.[3]

There are few artists whose work so completely coincide with the man as does David's. His personality is of one piece with the events of his time—is fully rooted in them. Even his relations with Napoleon show this. How he regarded the latter is revealed by the pictures which represent General Bonaparte, especially the well-known portrait in which the field-marshal, with his clear-cut, narrow face and his calm self-conceit, gazes defiantly into the distance, confident that he will not miss the right road. To David, the Jacobin and Tribune of the People of 1793, who had expected from the dictatorship the setting up of the ideal society, the saber-dictatorship of the first consul and, later, emperor, must have seemed a necessity. He would never have allied himself with the Bourbons, whom he hated bitterly to the day of his death, for they were for him the visible supporters of the old régime. But he was allied to Napoleon by an inner kinship of nature which bridged the external antagonisms. David could not do otherwise. The historical man in him impressed its stamp on his individuality and showed his art its way.

We know the story of Mademoiselle de Noailles who had commissioned the artist to try his skill once upon a Christus. When the picture

[3] Richard Muther, *Geschichte der Malerei.* Leipzig, 1909. Band III, p. 128.

was finished the Savior of mankind had become an implacable Cato, always ready to hurl at the world his heartless *"Ceterum censeo."* When the lady expressed her astonishment at this conception of the Savior the artist answered brusquely, "I have long known that there is no more inspiration to be drawn from Christianity!" Certainly not for David, for forgiveness was not in his line. Leonidas, Cato, Brutus, Spartans and Romans—as he saw them—were his ideal figures. Romanism had become popular at that time. Men assumed Roman names, called themselves Romans, and the men of the Convention competed with one another in the effort to behave like members of the Roman Senate. Their speeches had the Roman cut, their carriage the rigid dignity that used to stalk about beneath the toga, inaccessible to any consideration of humanity. Many took their parts seriously: Saint-Just, Robespierre, Couthon are examples of this; the others followed them because it was the fashion.

It is of symbolic significance that the creators of the modern nation were at the hour of its birth already set upon dressing their idol in the garb of a foreign people and imparting to it the forms of expression of a time long past. The greatness of the nation, which hovered before the men of the great revolution, was in reality only the omnipotence of the new state, which now began to stretch its iron limbs preparatory to initiating a new epoch in the history of Europe. For the revolution was not just an occurrence in French history, but an event of European importance, which brought under its spell in equal measure all the members of the same cultural circle. David's art heralded this dawning time and embodied all its historical greatness without being able to overcome its defects and weaknesses. Thus seen, he was not merely the creator of a new style and of new esthetic concepts which gave full expression to the rigid forms of the revolutionary epoch; considered even from a purely sociologically standpoint, his work is of imperishable significance.

Much has changed since then. Periods of reaction and of revolution have followed one another in varied sequence and influenced the intellectual and social development of the European peoples. Many a vantage point that seemed to have been won for all time was lost again in the unending struggles of the times. What, however, no reaction could again turn back, was the fact that the revolution had for the first time set the masses permanently in motion and had brought them to believe that they would get their rights only by struggle. At first it was the ideals of political radicalism which set these masses astir; then came the great ideas of socialism, which powerfully affected the thought and feeling of men and gave a deeper and more comprehensive meaning to the revolution. A new stratum of society was aroused to a sense of its own life: the class of working people, which defiantly stretched its limbs and from then on took part in public affairs. And no one would ever again put them down after the recognition slowly dawned on them that their labor kept society alive. This movement of the masses, the most characteristic phenomenon of modern history, had also to find its expression in art and literature. The great reaction which spread over all Europe after the overthrow of Napoleon was able for a time to suppress this movement on the surface, but it was not in a position to destroy in the minds of the peoples the memory of the heroic time of the revolution. The revolutionary hurricane had shaken society too deeply. The French Revolution had thrown a new bond around the peoples of Europe that no government could destroy. All the revolutionary occurrences in Europe up to the middle of the second half of the last century had been inspired by its ideas and had set the masses in motion. In Delacroix's painting, *Freedom on the Barricades,* these ambitions are given powerful expression. Exultant passion roars out of it. The mass goes into action, fights, dies, falls into ecstasies, seized by the intoxication of the moment, which reflects the secret yearning of the centuries. And that current never disappears again from the art of our time.

Up to the year 1848 the "Fourth Estate" fought the battles of the bourgeoisie in the struggle against the last bulwarks of the old régime. But the bloody tragedy of June put an end to all the illusions about the harmony of the classes and revealed with dreadful clarity the yawning abyss that had opened between the new upstarts and the awakened working class. It must have been clear even to the blindest that the paths of the new holders of power could never be the paths of the working people. A new social type had gradually taken shape in the years since the great revolution: the "bourgeois," the repulsive misbirth of the citizenry that had once taken part in the storming of the Bastille and had let loose the revolution. But the sons and the grandsons had in them no more of that unrestful spirit; they hated nothing more than revolt and fermenting riot. The bourgeois loves order, which allows him to pursue his business with proper deliberation. His heart beats in his pocketbook, and to this he sacrifices ruthlessly all deeper social feeling. With the revolting greed of the upstart he tries to subject everything to himself and to oppress everyone as suits him. He is intellectually limited, plebeian and loutish in behavior, comfortable and self-satisfied, a born Philistine, but ready for any baseness when he thinks his property is threatened.

Louis-Philippe was the worthy representative of this class, whose type he even illustrated physically: a fat banker's face, with rolling double chin and crafty glance, in which lurked sly cunning and clever business sense. After those hot July days of 1830 two hundred nineteen Bourgeois deputies had palavered off this scion of the House of Orleans on the French as their king. They called him the "citizen king," and no crowned head ever wore his title with better right than did Louis-Philippe. The period of this man's government was one of the most shameful that France has ever had to endure. The infamous slogan of the Minister Guizot, "Get rich!" was written on the body of this miserable system, which during the eighteen years of its duration stirred up such frightful bitterness in the people.

In Honoré Daumier there arose a terrible and implacable opponent of the miserable régime. Daumier was a genuinely great man who was able to give to his drawings, although they were designed for the demands of the moment, an eternal worth. He was utterly inexhaustible in his attacks upon the ruling system and its chief representatives, spied out its every weakness and lashed them with burning scorn. He aimed the sharp darts of his diabolic wit at the king. He depicted him in every conceivable situation: as a harlequin, a ropedancer, a swindling stockbroker, even as a criminal. Louis-Philippe had nothing majestic about him, and no one could take from him what he had never possessed; but Daumier sketched him in his pitiful weak humanity as the typical symbol of bourgeois society, with his stove-pipe hat as "citizen's crown," his thick umbrella under his arm—the veritable "king of the paunches," to whom the mind is merely ballast, the prototype of the gluttonous Philistine always pregnant with petty commonplaces.

Not even prison made Daumier any more docile, and when the "government of the paunches" put into effect the infamous September law of 1835, by which all political caricatures were forbidden and the freedom of the press practically suspended, the artist turned upon the bourgeois himself and made him the target of his infernal mockery. He fairly stripped him naked to the gaze of all beholders and pointed out every hidden wrinkle in his dreary Philistine soul. We see him on the street, in the theater, on his promenades in the Bois, in the tavern, by the side of his loved spouse, in the bath, in his bedroom, and come to know thoroughly every aspect of his unintellectual existence. Daumier's uncompromising pencil preserved for us a whole gallery of types that belong among the most imperishable that art has ever produced. Unexcelled are his drawings of Robert Macaire, the type of the cunning sharper and cutpurse, who is always busy coining into money the intellectual limitations of his dear fellow men and, together with his friend, Bertram, attends to the plucking of those who are not quite all there. A well-known Parisian playwright had put this type on the stage in a melodrama, and Daumier availed himself of the clever idea, of which he made an unexampled success. Under his cunning hand the entire period became the era of Robert Macaire. The clever rascal, who is firmly convinced that the stupidity of his gallant contemporaries has no limit whatever, with calm arrogance engages in every field of human activity and plays his star role with the expert air of the connoisseur who knows just what men will swallow. The variations that Daumier was able to play with this type of charlatan were quite inexhaustible.

Never was an artist so intimately intergrown with his social environment as was Daumier. Even if he had not uttered for us his *"Je suis de mon temps,"* we should know it. A single glance at his work is enough to tell us that he was a "child of his time." Well said! Of his time. Not of his people or his nation, for his art reached far beyond the frontiers of France; his work is the cultural possession of the entire world. Daumier felt the pulse-beat of his age, recognized its slightest stirrings and saw, above all, its profound debasement. He saw with the keen eye of the artist, which nothing escapes; therefore he saw more deeply than most of his contemporaries who stood with him on the same side of the barricades. Thus, he already recognized the entire hollowness and triviality of the legislative assembly while parliamentarism was still in the flowering springtime of its sins. Let one contemplate the ideal figures that grin back at us from the drawing of the "legislative paunch." Never have the so-called "representatives of the people" and members of the government been so pitilessly unmasked as here. Here the very innermost things were brought to the surface. Those charming contemporaries were a company of intellectual zeros, who for narrow-mindedness, windiness, complacent self-satisfaction, petrifaction of brain, petty intrigue and brutal indifference represent about the worst that can be gathered under the heading, "popular representation." And then the delicious figures of his *"représentants réprésentés"* of the period of 1848-49, figures of irresistible drollery and gruesome realism, in which the unintelligence and impotence of the parliamentary system is more eloquently portrayed than the most skillful pen could do it.

Daumier was a fervent worshiper of freedom and remained one till death closed his eyes. He felt truly that freedom cannot be hemmed in by the narrow frame of a constitution, that it cannot breathe, must suffocate, as soon as it is delivered over to the hair-splitting of advocates and lawmakers. What an expressive language is spoken by the plate, "The constitution puts Liberty into a hypnotic sleep!" And that other drawing where the constitution is fitting a new dress on Liberty, who pleads anxiously, "Don't take off too much, please!" Ah, the time has not yet come, will never come, when—as Georg Büchner expects in *Dantons Tod* —the pattern of the state will be like a transparent garment that clings close to the body of the people so that every beat of a blood-vessel, every tensing of a muscle, every twitch of desire will show clearly through it. Even the best state constitution is inevitably a strait-jacket for freedom. Besides, the worthy tailors of the constitution have in every country cut away so much of the stuff of freedom that what is left makes hardly a decent nightshirt. And then that splendid picture: *The Constitution on the*

Operating Table. An unconscious woman lies stretched out on a table; about her stand the doctors in their operating gowns and listen to the explanations of the professor. Uncanny goblins, those political surgeons, repulsive and of revolting ugliness. One feels with horror what it means to intrust confidingly to these fellows the safety of hard-won freedoms. Is not even this operating room haunted by the ghost of Robert Macaire? How modern this plate seems. Just as if it were dedicated to Herr Brüning and the Weimar constitution. Yes, everything in Daumier is modern, for the bigoted faith in the miraculous power of the constitution has not yet become, by a long way, a dead dream. Daumier might very well have felt as did Bakunin, who said in this connection: "I do not believe in constitutions and laws; the best of constitutions could not satisfy me. We need something else: storm and life and a new, lawless, and therefore free, world." [4]

And as Daumier had chosen the men of the legislative bodies as the target of his bitter scorn, so also he hated their executive instruments with all the passion of his southern temperament. The whole of bourgeois justice was to him just the whore of that society of the paunches which he so profoundly despised. It is in this light that he portrays for us its administrators; living embodiments of sanctimonious pretense and infamous knavery, slayers of souls who think in formulas and whose feeling has grown dull in the routine of legal violence and intellectual rape. These plates, too, still have the same force, for in this respect nothing has changed, and justice is still today the organized revenge of privileged castes which press the law into their service.

Daumier's art depicted the spirit of things, and the individual supporters of existing institutions he used merely to give expression to this spirit. Thus he attacked war and its instigator, militarism, also. It is not the external that excites him, the immediate causes that lead to war. His gaze penetrates deeper and shows us that horrible bond which still chains the men of today to the past and in an evil hour awakens to new life the seemingly dead. Daumier knew, too, that militarism was not just the existence of standing armies. He had recognized clearly that here we have to deal with a special state of mind which, once it is artificially bred in him, transforms man into an unfeeling automaton that obeys every command blindly and takes no account of the consequences of his deed. This artificial crippling of the conscience and of individual reflection, which breaks down in man all moral control, all sense of personality, is the first presupposition of every militarism without distinction of flag or uniform. By expressing in his pictures just this Daumier went far beyond the narrow bounds of nationally conditioned situations and treated

---

[4] Marcel Herwegh, *Briefe von und zu Georg Herwegh: "Brief Bakunins an Herwegh aus dem Jahre 1848,"* München, 1898.

war and militarism as the unwholesome results of a system which in every land, through the same fundamental conditions of life produces the same effects. Here speaks to us an artist in whom the man has conquered the citizen of the state! to whom humanity as a whole is more precious than that artificial creation, the nation, and that so variable concept, the fatherland, despite which he was devoted with all his heart to his native country. It is this all-embracing character of his view that lifts his art far above the level of a mere cross-section of everyday events and lends to it its imperishable greatness.

What Daumier began as draftsman and painter, others carried on and developed further. In the dark period after the Napoleonic wars up to the outbreak of the Revolution of July the relation of art to the immediate social occurrences of life had almost been lost. Daumier had reestablished it by making himself the herald of an art out of which spoke the thought and feeling of the people. These endeavors in art were powerfully advanced by the development of the labor movement in Europe. A new time threw its shadow ahead. Labor, which had been so long despised and whose representatives had been regarded as inferior helots, won a new esteem. The working masses began to understand that their creative activity lay at the foundation of all social existence. The spirit of socialism was aroused. And in every country it laid the intellectual foundation for a new community of the future. The people, who had to toil in sweaty slavery, who built palaces and drove shafts deep into the earth to drag forth its treasures; the people, who daily spread life's table for their masters and dragged out their own days in poverty and want, matured gradually to a new understanding and began to strain at the chains that had been put on them.

The Revolution of 1848 proved how deeply this spirit had taken root; not even the blood of the June massacre could drown it out. Full of promise and drunk with hope the call of the International rang later through the lands, seeking to weld together the disinherited of society into a world-encompassing alliance of labor. No longer was the sweat of the poor to feed parasites; the earth was to become once more a home for man; and the fruits of labor, food for all. It was not crumbs from the tables of the rich that they wanted, but justice, and bread and freedom for everyone. Labor was no longer to be the scullion of society, the poor Lazarus who made a show of his suffering before the doors of the rich to soften their hearts. A great yearning surged through the world of the damned. The ideal of a better future had shaken up their deadened souls and filled them with enthusiasm. Now they stretched their hands beyond the boundaries of states, for they felt how everywhere the same need gnawed at their lives, the same hopes burned in their hearts. And so they formed the great Union of Militant Labor out of which a new society was to issue.

Art, too, was seized by this spirit. Depict what *is*, became the watchword of realism. The artist was no longer to be compelled to represent only the "beautiful," which was borrowed from other worlds and was often only a sugar-coated lie. So the world of labor appeared on canvas, men in tattered garments with hard faces in which care had carved its runes. And men discovered with astonishment that even in this world there dwells hidden beauty that they had not perceived before.

François Millet was one of the first apostles of the new evangel of productive labor. Although in his whole nature utterly unpolitical he recognized, nevertheless, the social significance of labor in its deepest sense. Himself a peasant, the man of the furrows had a special place in his heart, for he loved the soil, loved everything that bore its signs and breathed out the fragrance of new-plowed fields. Millet's peasants are no figures of the imagination. In his art there is no place for the pastoral romanticism of fantastic visionaries for whom the products of the imagination must supplant the realities of life. What he presented is hard, unvarnished reality: the man of the soil here has his say, and straightforwardly and eloquently he testifies of the content of his existence. Millet painted his knurled and calloused hands, his bent back, his weather-beaten, bony face; he showed him in his intimate native union with the soil that he tilled and made fruitful with his sweat. These are not the peasants whom we know from Auerbach's village tales, who often produce the impression that they have just had their hair curled and been dressed in their Sunday best to make them fit for the parlor; no, Millet's peasants are genuine. And still there hangs over everything that he produced an air of quiet solemnity which is not artificially conceived but arises from the subject itself. It is the deep breathing of the earth, which keeps time with the eternal rhythm of labor and calls to life in the soul of the beholder that strange vibration which comes close to understanding the unison of all growth. Pictures like *The Gleaners, The Man with the Hoe, The Shepherdess,* or *The Angelus* are monumental in the straightforward greatness of their expression.

It had no easy position, this new art. How they attacked Gustave Courbet, the friend of Proudhon, the "supporter of every revolution," as he called himself, when he dared to "profane the principle of beauty" by putting proletarians on canvas in their work-clothes and proclaiming a new art which no longer borrowed from the classic prototypes of a dead past but drew its material and its inspiration from the modern life that roared about the artist on every side. Works like *The Stonebreakers, The Burial in Ornane, The Man with the Pipe,* whose artistic qualities we cannot sufficiently admire today, were scorned by the academicians and appraised as evidence of a horrible aberration of taste. Yet the realism of Courbet was no more than an attempt to see men and the world in a new light, in which he touched on matters which none before him had perceived. This is shown by his splendid landscapes, their palpable pregnancy and superabundance of life, like a hymn to the principle of fertility.

What inner beauty can be discovered in the world of labor no one has shown better than Constantin Meunier, who was such a fanatical worshiper of the antique beauty of form. Still, amid the reeking chimneys, the pit-mouth structures and the smelting furnaces of the Borinage he felt the hurried pulse-beat of that realm of steel which breathes with iron lungs and moves its mighty limbs in time with the machines. There came to him, too, the knowledge that he belonged to his time and that his art must strike root in it. His yearning for the forms of the antique blended with the powerful impressions that the artist received in the heart of Belgian industry. So he created those mighty figures of labor, which are permeated with yearning for a new world and despite all the hardships of their harsh existence look the present in the eye confident of victory. What strength lives in these figures that swing pickaxes in the bowels of the earth, pour melted steel illumined by a magic glory, stride across dark fields and scatter fertile seeds, or bear great burdens on their sturdy shoulders. Weighty path-breakers of a new time are these, heralds of a new beginning which no power on earth can check. There is an antique greatness in these figures, who advance with firm steps to meet the red dawn of a new day. And just as powerful is the effect of the cyclopean realm in which they walk and strengthen their desire.

In every country there arose exemplars and interpreters of this new art, in whose works the need of the times came to life and struggled to expression. In their productions are mirrored the discord of our social order, its double standard of morals, its heartless egoism, its lack of genuine humanity, the whole moral corrosion of a time that had set up Mammon as Lord of the Earth. And yet another emotion lived in these works: the thunderous hymn of world-encircling labor and the feverish glow of revolutionary popular movements, the timorous longing for a new community of true freedom and justice. A long line of names appears before our eyes, artists from every country ruled by masters, united by the invisible bonds of inner experience and—each in his own way—cooperating in the work of social reconstruction. Charles de Grouxand and A. Th. Steinlen, Leon Frédéric and Antoine Wiertz, Segantini and Luce, Charles Hermanns and E. Laermans, Félicien Rops and Vincent van Gogh, G. F. Watts and Käthe Kollwitz, Franz Masereel, Heinrich Zille, Georg Grosz, Diego Rivera and countless others—they all have their roots in the great social phenomena of their time, and their art has as good as no relation at all to the accident of their national descent.

This applies, however, not only to those artists in whose works a more or less clear social attack finds expression, but to all. Every artist is in the end only a member of a great cultural unity which, along with his personal endowments, determines his work; and in this nationality plays an entirely subordinate role. In art also one recognizes the same universal phenomena that are revealed in every other field of human work; here, too, mutual invigoration within the same culture circle, of which the nation is only a fragment, plays a decisive role. Let us remember the words of Anselm Feuerbach, who was certainly no man of revolutionary trend. "Men have been pleased to represent me as preeminently a German artist. I solemnly protest against this designation, for that which I am I owe in part to myself, in part to the Frenchmen of 1848 and to the old Italians."

It is further significant that this allegedly so German artist was during his lifetime altogether proscribed in Germany itself, and so thoroughly that he was even denied to have any talent as a painter. The nation as such, therefore, not only produces no artists, it lacks all the preconceptions that make it possible to appreciate properly a work of art. The "voice of the blood" was never yet in a position to discover the "race-related features" in a work of art, otherwise the number of the artists who have been so terribly misunderstood, despised and slandered by their contemporaries in their own nation would not be so large.

Let us just keep in mind what a strong influence the various trends in art have exercised over the work of individual artists; from it their nationality has been quite powerless to free them. The different tendencies in art have their source not in the nation, but in the time and the social conditions of the time. Classicism and romanticism, expressionism and impressionism, cubism and futurism are time-phenomena on which the nation has no influence. The close relation between artists who belong, not to the same nation, but to the same school of art is recognizable at the first glance; between two descendants of the same nation, however, of whom one is an adherent of classicism, while the other follows the path of cubism or futurism, there is—so far as concerns their art—no point of contact whatever. This holds good for all arts and also for literature. Between Zola and the adherents of naturalism in other countries there exists an unmistakable kinship; but between Zola and De Villier or De Nerval, although they are all Frenchmen; between Huysmans and Maeterlinck, although they are both Belgians; between Poe and Mark Twain, although they are both Americans; there yawns a wide abyss. All the talk about the "national core" which allegedly lies at the basis of every work of art lacks any deep foundation and is nothing more than a wish-concept.

No, art is not national, any more than science or any other sphere of our intellectual and material life. Let it be granted that climate and external surroundings have a certain influence upon the spiritual status of men, and consequently upon the artist; but this frequently occurs in the same country and within the same nation. That from it there can be deduced no law of nationality is shown by the fact that every northern people that has moved to the south and settled there, like the Normans in Sicily or the Goths in Spain, has not only forgotten its ancient speech in the new homeland, but has also adapted itself to the new surroundings in its emotional life. The national standard, if it could be enforced, would condemn all art to dreary imitation, and take from it just that which alone makes it art—its inner inspiration. What is usually called the "national" is as a rule only the clinging to the past, the despotism of tradition. Even the traditional may be beautiful and may inspire the artist to create; but it must not become the sole compass of life and crush everything new under the weight of a dead past. Where men try to awaken the past to new life, as is happening today so grotesquely in Germany, life becomes dreary and stale, a mere caricature of what has been. For there is no bridge that leads back to the past. Just as a grown man, despite all his longing, can never return to the years of his childhood, but must go on and finish his course of life, so also a people cannot recall to being the history of its past. Every cultural product is universal, most of all, art. It was none other than Hanns Heinz Ewers, who now basks in Adolf Hitler's grace, who gave this truth expression in the words:

> Whole worlds separate the man of culture in Germany from his fellow countrymen, whom he sees every day on the street; but a mere nothing, just a trivial bit of water, separates him from the man of culture in America. Heine felt this and cast it in the teeth of the Frankfurters. Edgar Allan Poe uttered it even more clearly. But most of the artists and scholars and educated men of every people have had so little understanding of it that even to our day Horace's fine *Odi profanum* has been incorrectly interpreted! The artist who wishes to create for "his people" is striving after something impossible and often neglects in doing this something attainable and even higher: to create for the whole world. *Above* the Germans, above Britons and Frenchmen stands a higher nation: the nation of culture; to create for it is the only task worthy of an artist.[5]

Art and culture stand above the nation, above the state. Just as no true artist creates only for a particular people, so art as such can never be stretched on the Procrustean bed of the nation. It will rather, as the finest interpreter of social life, contribute to the preparation for a higher social culture which will overthrow state and nation to open for humankind the portals of a new community which is the goal of their desires.

[5] *Edgar Allan Poe.* Berlin and Leipzig, 1905, p. 39.

Chapter 12

THE NATIONAL STATE AND THE COLLAPSE OF THE OLD COMMUNITY.
THE ERA OF REVOLUTION A RESULT OF LOST SOCIAL EQUILIBRIUM. HIS-
TORICAL CONNECTIONS AS CULTURAL PHENOMENA. THE WEAKENING
OF SOCIAL CONSCIOUSNESS AND PERSONAL INDEPENDENCE. THE FATAL-
ISTIC CHARACTER OF OUR THINKING AND OF THE BELIEF IN THE DE-
TERMINISM OF SOCIAL EVENTS. THE GIANT STATE AND ECONOMIC MO-
NOPOLY AS SCOURGES OF MANKIND. MAN AND MACHINE. INTERNA-
TIONAL ECONOMIC CHAOS. TECHNOCRATIC SCHEMES. THE SOCIAL QUES-
TION A PROBLEM OF CONSUMPTION. IS STATE CAPITALISM A SOLUTION?
INTERNATIONALIZATION OF REGIONS SUPPLYING RAW MATERIAL.
WORLD ECONOMY, NOT WORLD EXPLOITATION. WHAT THE STATE
COSTS US. THE MATERIAL LOSSES OF THE WORLD WAR. THE MADNESS
OF THE TIMES. OVERCOMING THE STATE AND THE NATION BY THE
NEW COMMUNITY.

AFTER the decline of the old city culture and the period of federalism
in Europe the real purpose of social existence was gradually forgotten.
Society is today no longer the natural relation of man to man which finds
expression in community of intellectual and material interests. With the
appearance of the national state all social activity gradually becomes an
instrument to serve the special ends of organizations for political power;
no longer to serve the interests of the community but the wishes and
necessities of privileged classes and castes in the state. Society thus loses
its intrinsic stability and becomes subject to periodic convulsions, arising
from conscious or unconscious efforts to restore the lost coherence.

Louis Blanc traces the germ of the French Revolution back to the
age of the Reformation. In fact, with the Reformation begins a new
chapter of European history which has not to this day reached a definite
end. It has rightly been called the "Era of Revolution," a designation
justified by the fact that all the peoples of the continent were equally
seized and influenced by it. In his enlightening essay, *Die Revolution,*
Gustav Landauer sought to distinguish the various stages of this epoch
and to give them a definite sequence. He refers to one of them thus:

The real Reformation with its intellectual and social changes, its secularizations and state-making, the Peasant War, the English Revolution, the Thirty Years' War, the American War of Independence, [important] less on account of its actual occurrences than of its intellectual processes and ideas, by which it exerted the strongest influence on what now follows: the great French Revolution.

Like Proudhon and, after him, Bakunin, Pi y Margall and Kropotkin, so also Landauer saw in all the revolts and revolutions which from 1789 up to this day have periodically set the various countries in Europe aflame only the working out of the same revolutionary process. This realization confirmed his conviction that the Era of Revolution is not past, but that we are still in the midst of a process of tremendous social change the end of which cannot yet be foreseen. The compelling logic of this point of view is undeniable. One who accepts it cannot help regarding the latest events of the period, the World War, the social movements of the time, the revolutions in Central Europe and especially in Russia, the changes in the capitalistic economic order, and all the social and political changes in Europe since the War, as separate manifestations of the same great revolutionary process. For four hundred years it has again and again stirred up the whole social life of the European peoples, its remote effects are today clearly observable even in other parts of the earth.

The process will not end until a real adjustment is made between the personal objectives of the individual and the general social conditions of life; a sort of synthesis of personal freedom with social justice by the communal action of all—such as shall again give content to society and lay the foundation for a new community. External compulsion will no longer be needed, because this community will have found its inner balance through guarding the interests of all, and will leave no room for the struggle for political and economic power. Only then can the Era of Revolution end, giving way to a social culture in which a new phase of the evolution of mankind will find expression.

Only when we interpret history in this spirit do we arrive at a proper recognition of the common features which in any particular epoch reveal themselves in similar movements in all countries of the same cultural circle. In every great period in history there is primarily noticeable the kind of thinking which springs from the social conditions of the age and which reacts upon these to alter them. In comparison with the general problems which occupy the thoughts of men in any particular period the so-called "national ambitions" (to which, moreover, men have to be artificially trained), have scarcely any significance. They only serve to cloud men's vision of the real cultural processes and even for a longer or shorter time to hinder these in their natural development. Only in their inner connections do the historical events of an epoch become under-

standable to us; and an artificially created national ideology, whose
proponents seek to see every country and every people only in that light
which best serves their separate purposes, can lead to no conclusions about
those connections. For, finally, the whole national history of a people
is always merely the history of a particular state, never the history of its
culture, which always bears the imprint of the period. Our division of
European folk life into the history of individual nations may be necessitated by the existence of modern state organizations, but it is not therefore the less misleading. Such divisions merely create artificial frontiers
which in reality do not exist and which frequently distort the whole
aspect of a period so completely that the beholder misses all its inter-
relations.

Let us for a moment take into account what profound and decisive
influences particular social phenomena of a universal scope have had on
the general character of whole epochs. The spread of Christianity has left
its unmistakable imprint on the whole intellectual life of the European
peoples. Similarly, modern capitalism has during the last two hundred
years fundamentally changed all social institutions, and not alone material
conditions; it has also given an unmistakable special character to all the
intellectual effort of this period. Of the powerful influence of particular
conceptions of life and the universe on the thought of the peoples belonging to the European-American cultural circle we have already spoken.

Is not the present crisis in the whole capitalistic world the most conclusive proof of the inner connections of the epoch which are equally
effective in all countries? Let us not delude ourselves: This is no purely
economic crisis; it is the crisis of present-day society, the crisis of modern
thought, which urges to a reconstruction of our whole mental and spiritual
life, not merely to an adjustment of our economy. It is the beginning of
the great Twilight of the Gods. Out of the whirling chaos of old and
new ideas there will gradually evolve a new enlightenment which will
change the whole intellectual field of view of men and reveal to them
in a new light the essential relation between man and society. For a great
revolution of the spirit is needed to change men's relations to the things
of material life and to inspire them to action in a new direction.

First of all we must learn to face things directly, to be no longer
content to view the phenomena of social life through the spectacles of
philosophic hypothesis or to explain them by any kind of artificially
constructed historical concept. The theory of evolution which at one time
fundamentally revolutionized and transformed the whole thought of our
cultural circle has today become largely a hindrance to our action. We
have busied ourselves too long and too exclusively with the causes and
transitions of social phenomena until the phenomena themselves have
become strange to us and of secondary importance—secondary in the

sense that the immediate effect of things demands from us greater interest than do the causes from which they sprang. We have proved ourselves for many decades to be clever analysts of capitalistic society, but we have lost meanwhile the capacity to renew social life and to disclose to mankind new horizons for its activity. Our thought has lost the ethical content which has its roots in the communal spirit and is too closely tied to purely technical adjustments. We have even gone so far as actually to regard ethical considerations as a weakness, and have persuaded ourselves that they have no influence on the social behavior of men. What this leads to we see today with frightful clarity.

With many the theory of evolution assumes the form of a fatalistic conception of social development, leading them to regard even the most revolting phenomena of the age as the result of unalterable evolutionary processes in which man cannot arbitrarily interfere. This belief in the inevitability and determinism of all events must estrange men from their natural sense of right and wrong and blunt their understanding of the ethical significance of events.[1] We play today with the dangerous thought that the ubiquitously intruding fascism is a necessary final phase of capitalism, which at last prepares the way for Socialism.[2] By such thoughts we not only cripple all resistance to arbitrary and brutal force, but we also justify indirectly the perpetrators of these abominations by regarding them as the executors of historical necessity, whose deeds lie, so to speak, beyond good and evil. It matters little whether this is done consciously

[1] Just one instance out of many of how this works out: When in 1899 the Conservative government of England made war on the South African Boer republics and after a long, murderous struggle finally annexed them, everybody knew that this robber raid was only to secure the undisturbed possession of the Transvaal gold mines. Wilhelm Liebknecht, however, at that time, next to August Bebel, the most noted leader of the German Socialist party and editor of *Vorwärts*, attempted to condone the deed by explaining to his readers that here was an instance of political necessity which had to be faced. For, just as in economic evolution there is the tendency for capital to concentrate in fewer hands and for the small capitalist to be swallowed by the large, so likewise in political evolution it is inevitable that the small states should be absorbed by the great. With such explanations, based at best on pure assumption, we becloud men's perception of the monstrosity of the events themselves and make them insensitive to all the dictates of humanity.

[2] Shortly before Hitler's accession to power this view was so widespread among the adherents of the Communist Party in Germany that the editors of the *Rote Fahne* felt is necessary to take a stand against this dangerous trend, although this view was only the logical consequence of the tactics which the German Communists had pursued from year to year. The fact that Hitler was able to seize power without any resistance from the Socialist and Communist workers is the best illustration of that fatalistic way of thinking that crippled the will of the masses and plunged Germany into the abyss. They had played long with the idea of the inevitability of the dictatorship and at last the dictatorship was here—only it had come from a different direction from what they had expected.

or unconsciously. In reality the brutal acts of violent men and the monstrous crimes now being perpetrated in Germany—and everywhere where fascism has attained a foothold without arousing the slightest protest from the so-called "democratic" governments—have nothing to do with social evolution. We are here dealing simply with the mania for power of small minorities which have known how to exploit a given situation to their own profit.

Having grown accustomed to regard all the defects of present-day society as results of the capitalist economic order, men have forgotten that by such attempts at explanation the facts themselves are not changed. So completely have they forgotten this that even those parties which professedly work towards a complete change of present conditions know of nothing better to do than to settle down in the existing order, and by their methods they have given it new strength. This failure of the socialist parties has destroyed many hopes and made the masses despair of socialism, which they hold responsible for the defeat of the socialist organizations; just as men today hold the social concept of liberalism responsible for the failure of the liberal parties. In reality, it only proves that a movement which looks toward a complete transformation and renewal of social life will never come nearer this goal, may even be compelled to swing farther and farther from its initial purpose, if it attempts to gain a foothold in the old institutions of the present governmental order so that it may in its turn control the political machine. For the machine, because of the way it is built, can work only in a given direction, no matter who pulls its levers. Neither the objectives of socialism nor the aspirations of liberalism have thus far been realized: either their realization has not been seriously attempted or it has again and again been led by the influence of certain forces into wrong channels. And yet the whole evolution of our economic and political conditions shows us today more clearly than ever how right those efforts were and what a dangerous abyss we approached when we trusted to following the "path of evolution" instead of setting ourselves in time to ward off that approaching danger which today threatens us on every side.

One fact must have become clear today to all men seeking fuller enlightenment: The present Giant State and modern economic monopoly have grown into terrible scourges of mankind and lead with ever increasing speed toward a condition which must inevitably end in the most brutal barbarism. It is the madness of this system that to its supporters the machine has become, so to speak, a symbol, and has led them to make all human activity conform to the soulless operation of an apparatus. This happens today everywhere: in economics, in politics, in public education, in law and in all other spheres. The living spirit has thus been shut in the cage of dead ideas, and men have been led to believe that all life is nothing more than an automatic, jerky motion of the moving chain of events. Only from such a mental state could come that heartless egoism which strides over corpses to satisfy its greed and that unchecked power lust which plays with the fate of millions as if they were dead rows of figures and not creatures of flesh and blood. This condition is also the cause of the slavish submission which brings its victims to accept every degradation of their human dignity in dull indifference and without resistance.

The monstrosities of the capitalist system have now assumed a character which must open the eyes of the blindest. The capitalist world contains today millions of unemployed who, together with their families equal the population of a great state. And while these people exist in a gruesome condition of permanent misery, frequently not knowing how to satisfy life's most elementary needs, in many countries there are being destroyed at the government's instigation enormous quantities of commodities because the purchasing power of the masses is too small.[3] If our age could still differentiate between right and wrong, this despicable contempt of all humanity would arouse the social consciousness of men and compel them to take action against such horrors. But we merely register the facts and in most cases do not even sense the cruel meaning of the great human tragedy daily enacted before our eyes.

When the first indications of the present economic crisis were observable in Europe a search for new ways and means was not even considered. Men merely tried to "lower the costs of production" by a thorough "rationalization of industry" without giving the slightest thought to what inevitable consequences such a dangerous experiment would have for the working population. In Germany, even the trade unions supported this disastrous plan of the great industrialists in its entirety by trying to persuade the workers that only thus could the crisis be ended. And the workers at first believed it—until they felt on their own bodies that they had been deceived and plunged into still deeper misery. Then it was again shown how little regard the powerful capitalists have for human

[3] In America four million bales of cotton are being destroyed by order of the authorities by leaving every third row in the plantations unpicked. In Canada they are burning enormous stores of wheat for which there is no market. Brazil destroyed in October, 1932, over 102 million sacks of coffee, and in Argentina they are burning dried meat. In Alaska 400,000 cases of salmon were destroyed, and in New York the authorities had to halt the pollution of streams where fishes were dying from the great quantities of dumped milk. In Australia over a million sheep were killed and buried to prevent "over-production." Great catches of herring were returned to the sea because no buyers appeared. Even in so poverty-stricken a land as Germany great stores of cucumbers and other vegetables rot every year, or are used as manure, because no customers can be found for them. And this is but a short extract from a long list. Its mute accusation cannot easily be misunderstood.

personality. Man was sacrificed without compunction to technique, degraded into a machine, changed into a nonentity, a "productive force" deprived of all human traits, in order that the productive process might function with the least possible friction and without internal obstruction.

Yet it is shown today ever more clearly that this road leads to no better future for man, that the "rationalization" always results in the failure of all its advance estimates. Professor Felix Krueger, director of the Institute for Psychology in Leipzig, declared some years ago that the much lauded Taylor system and the rationalization of industry emanated from a laboratory psychology, the economic failures of which are becoming constantly more apparent. By all experience it is now proved the natural motion sustained by the implicit rhythm of work is less tiring than a forcibly imposed task; for man's action has its origin in the soul, which cannot be chained to any definite scheme or schedule. This has been confirmed over and over again; but for all that it is still believed that the crisis can be overcome in the field of production. The newly arisen "Technocratic School" in America has, with the support of exhaustively inclusive data based on strict scientific observation, proved that our ability to produce is in fact almost unlimited, and that even the great productive capacity of modern industry is in no way proportionate to our technical ability, since a complete application of all our technical achievements would immediately result in a catastrophe.[4]

That by a considerable reduction of the working time a means could be found of limiting the present economic crisis and even of guiding industry back into comparatively normal courses has already been stated, but it would be self-deception to believe that thereby the great problem of the age would be solved. The modern economic problem is less a matter of production than of consumption. It was this fact which Robert Owen adduced in refutation of Adam Smith; and in it the whole economic significance of socialism exhausts itself. That the men of science and technology have opened limitless possibilities to production is not disputed by anyone and needs no special proof. But under our present system every achievement of technology becomes a weapon of capitalism against the people and results in the very opposite of that which it was intended to accomplish. Every technical advance has made men's work heavier and more oppressive and has more and more undermined their economic security. The most important problem of modern economics is not continually to increase production and make it more profitable by new inventions and "better working methods," but to see to it that the achieve-

---

[4] Howard Scott and his 350 scientific collaborators are therefore of the opinion that this imminent catastrophe can only be averted by entrusting the technical men with the direction of industry and radically cutting the hours of work to sixteen per week.

ments of technical ability and the fruits of labor are made equally available to all members of society.

Under the present system, which has made the profit of individuals and not the satisfaction of the needs of all the cardinal points of economics, this is completely excluded. The development of private economy into monopoly economy has made this task still more difficult, for it has put into the hands of single economic organizations a power far transcending the limits of economics and has delivered society completely to the power-lust and ruthless exploitation of modern trustocracy.[5] What influence the kings of high finance and the great industrial concerns have on the politics of the state is too well known to need further elucidation.[6]

Nor does state capitalism, so much discussed today, offer a way out from the spiritual and material distress of the age. On the contrary, it would change the world more completely into a penitentiary and smother any feeling of freedom at its birth, as it is now doing in Russia. If, in spite of this, there are "socialists" who today think they see in state

[5] Coined word: German, *Trustokratie*—*Translator.*

[6] With what hair-raising callousness we are everywhere ready today to sacrifice the lives of millions of men to the economic interests of small minorities is proved by the cable message which the former ambassador in London, Mr. Walter Hines Page, sent on March 5, 1917, to President Wilson (which was followed a month later by America's declaration of war against Germany).

After Page had explained to the President the critical financial status of France and England and had pointed out that this must result in a complete cessation of transatlantic trade, he goes on to say:

"The result of such a stoppage would be a panic in the United States. . . . The world will therefore be divided into two hemispheres, one of them, our own, will have the gold and the commodities: the other, Great Britain and Europe, will need these commodities, but it will have no money with which to pay for them. Moreover, it will have practically no commodities of its own to exchange for them. The financial and commercial result will be almost as bad for the U.S. as for Europe. We shall soon reach this condition unless we take quick action to prevent it. Great Britain and France must have a credit in the U.S. which will be large enough to prevent the collapse of world trade and the whole financial structure of Europe. If the U.S. declares war against Germany, the greatest help which we could give Britain and its allies would be such credit. If we should adopt this policy, an excellent plan would be for our government to make a large investment in a Franco-British loan. Another plan would be to guarantee such a loan. A great advantage would be that all the money would be kept in the United States. We could keep on with our trade and increase it, till the war ends, and after the war Europe would purchase food and enormous supplies of materials with which to reëquip her peace industries. We would thus reap the profit of an uninterrupted and perhaps an enlarging trade over a number of years, and we should hold their securities in payment. On the other hand, if we keep nearly all the gold and Europe cannot pay for reëstablishing its economic life, there may be a world-wide panic for an indefinite period. Of course we cannot extend such a credit unless we go to war with Germany." (Burton J. Hendrick: *The Life and Letters of Walter H. Page*, p. 270.)

capitalism a higher type of economy than we now have, this only proves that they have no clear conception of the essence of either socialism or economics. Capitalistically considered, that is, regarding man as existing for production and not production for man, state capitalism may indeed represent a "higher form of economics"; socialistically considered, such a conception is the cruelest sacrilege against the spirit of socialism and of freedom. But even viewed from a purely economic standpoint, every increase of compulsion on man's industrial activity—and this lies at the foundation of state capitalism—is tantamount to a reduction of his productive ability. Slave labor has never furthered economy, for compulsion robs labor of its psychic incentive and its consciousness of creative action. When slavery was most prevalent in Rome the productivity of the soil constantly decreased, leading finally to a general catastrophe. The same thing was experienced in the time of the feudal system. The more unbearable the forms of serfdom became in European countries, the more meager were the results of labor, the more impoverished the land became. We need to free labor from the fetters of dependence, not to forge the fetters more firmly.

A fundamental change of the present economic system which shall have in view a genuine solution of the problem can be achieved only by abolition of all the monopolies and economic privileges which today profit only small minorities in society and enable those elect ones to impose their brutal interest-economics on the great masses of the people. Only by a fundamental reorganization of labor on the basis of fellowship, serving no other purpose than the satisfaction of the needs of all instead of increasing the profits of individuals as today, can the present economic crisis be overcome and the way cleared for a higher social culture. It is needful to free man from exploitation by man and to secure to him the fruits of his labor. Only thus will it be possible to make each new achievement of technology serviceable to all and prevent that which should be a blessing to all from becoming a curse to most.

Just as minorities within a real folk community cannot be permitted to monopolize vitally important raw materials or means of production for their special interests, so likewise a people, or a nation as a whole, cannot be allowed to create monopolies at the expense of other human groups and subject these to economic exploitation. The whole tendency of capitalism, especially since it entered upon the imperialistic phase of its evolution, is so hopelessly antagonistic to the people and so exceedingly destructive of social welfare because its supporters strive by every means to bring all natural wealth under the control of their monopolies, and to forge on men the fetters of economic dependence. This is always done in the name of the nation, and every party justifies its highwayman policies by appealing to the "national interests," thus concealing their real purposes.

What we seek is not world exploitation but a world economy in which every group of people shall find its natural place and enjoy equal rights with all others. Hence, internationalization of natural resources and territory affording raw materials is one of the most important prerequisites for the existence of a socialistic order of society based on libertarian principles. By mutual treaties and reciprocal covenants the use of all natural treasures must be made available to all human groups if new monopolies are not to arise in the social body, and consequently a new division into classes and a new economic enslavement. We need to call into being a new human community having its roots in equality of economic conditions and uniting all members of the great cultural community by new ties of mutual interest, disregarding the frontiers of the present states. On the basis of the present social system there is no redemption from the slavery of our age, but only a deeper submersion into a state of gruesome misery and horrors without end. Human society must overthrow capitalism unless it wants to perish.

Just as capitalism became more and more dangerous in proportion as economic forces became more strongly concentrated in the hands of its leaders, giving them a power which makes them masters over the life and death of whole peoples, so also the frightful evils of modern state organization become more and more clearly apparent with the growth of the state and the constant enlargement of its powers. The modern Giant State, which has developed *pari passu* with the capitalistic economic system, has today grown into a constant menace to the very existence of society. Not only has this monstrous machine become the greatest obstacle to men's struggle for freedom, forcing with its arms of steel all social life into the prescribed patterns; the maintenance of the machine itself consumes by far the largest part of the state's revenues and deprives intellectual culture more and more of the material basis for its further development.

National defense alone, meaning the standing armies, the armament expenditures and whatever else comes under the head of war and militarism, today consumes in every state 50 to 70 percent of its revenues, which must be raised by taxes and tariffs. In an excellent little essay based on reliable sources and exact calculations Lehmann-Russbüldt, one of the most outspoken opponents of modern investment in armament, says:

> If we figure an approximate yearly fifty thousand million marks for the war budget, one half is on account of the consequences of the World War and the other half for preparation for a new war. This amounts to about one hundred and forty million marks daily. That is the annual budget of a

great city which is daily swallowed by the militaristic Moloch without any productive return. Even in little neutral Switzerland, not involved in the World War, the war budget amounts to 50 percent of the state's income. In the Soviet Union the margin is below 50 percent principally only because the war debts were repudiated. But even in the Soviet Union the war budget is larger than the expenditures for education and culture. This is practically the case in all countries—only not, for example, in Andorra, Costa Rica, and Iceland.[7]

Russbüldt calculated that the cost of educating a man up to his six-teenth year, that is, to the time when his productive ability begins, runs from at least eight thousand reichsmarks up to about fifteen thousand, depending on whether are added the expenditures by the community and the state to the cost of food and clothing in the parental home. But it cost one hundred thousand marks to kill a man in war, of which one-half went to the armament industry; a clear profit to them of fifty thousand reichsmarks.

The material losses of the World War are so fantastic that the totals no longer mean anything to the human mind. We realize that these astronomical figures mean something extraordinary, but that it about all; for there is finally a limit to human comprehension. An understanding of the monstrous sum which these dead figures represent can be given to men only by a sort of graphic presentation.[8]

Whoever, in view of this enormous mass of factual material, still believes that the state, with its hosts armed to the teeth, its armies of bureaucrats, its secret diplomacy and its countless institutions designed to cripple the human spirit, serves to protect humanity is beyond help. In

[7] Otto Lehmann-Russbüldt, *Der Krieg als Geschäft* ("War as a Business"). Berlin, 1933. These data have been materially changed since then, for the armament race has made the ratios still more unfavorable and surrendered to militarism a yet larger share of the state's income. The Soviet Union now spends yearly for military purposes $12,000,000,000. (*The Nation*, N. Y., Feb. 27, 1937.)

[8] This task was undertaken by a member of the U.S. Congress, Victor L. Berger, five years after the war. The task was fairly easy for him, as he had at his disposal in Washington a great mass of material for his calculations. Berger showed that with the fabulous sums the war had swallowed, every family in the United States, in Canada, Australia, Great Britain, France, Belgium, Germany and Russia could have been given a house worth twenty-five hundred dollars with furnishings worth a thousand dollars, and with each such house five acres of land at one hundred dollars an acre, and at that the sum was by no means exhausted: Enough was left to furnish each town of more than twenty thousand inhabitants in the countries mentioned with a public library and a hospital of the value of five million dollars, and besides that a university worth ten millions. But even then this enormous capital had not been fully used up. The rest of the sum invested at 5 percent would have paid the wages of an army of one hundred and twenty-five thousand teachers and one hundred and twenty-five thousand nurses, and still enough would have remained to buy all the physical property in France and Belgium.

reality the existence of the modern state is a constant menace to peace, an ever present incentive to organized mass murder and the destruction of all cultural achievements. Outside of this costly "protection" which the state affords its citizens it creates nothing positive, does not enrich human culture a pennyworth; but at once puts all new cultural achievements in the service of destruction, so that they become, not a blessing to the people, but a curse.

The history of the state is the history of human oppression and intellectual disfranchisement. It is the story of the unlimited lust for power of small minorities which could be satisfied only by the enslavement and exploitation of the people. The deeper the state with its countless agencies penetrates into the sphere of activity of social life, the more its leaders succeed in changing men into mindless automatons of their will, the more inevitably will the world become a vast prison in which at last there will be no breath of freedom. The conditions in Italy, Hungary, Poland, Austria, Russia and Germany speak too eloquent a language for us to be longer deceived about the inevitable consequences of such an "evolution." That along this pathway there lies no rosy future for men is clear to all who have eyes to see and ears to hear. What is today arising on the social horizon of Europe and the world is the dictatorship of darkness which believes that the whole of society can be geared to the wheels of a machine whose steady drive smothers everything organic and elevates the soullessness of mechanics to a principle. Let us not deceive ourselves: *It is not the form of the state, it is the state itself which creates the evil and continually nourishes and fosters it.* The more the government crowds out the social element in human life or forces it under its rule, the more rapidly society dissolves into its separate parts; which then lose all inner connection and either rush thoughtlessly into idiotic collisions over conflicting interests or drift helplessly with the stream, not caring whither they are borne.

The further this state of things progresses the harder it will be to gather men again into a new social community and to persuade them to a renewal of social life. The delusive belief in a dictatorship which is today spreading over Europe like a pestilence is only the ripe fruit of an unthinking belief in the state, which has for decades been implanted in men. Not the *government of men* but the *administration of things* is the great problem set for our age, and it can never be solved within the frame of the present state organization. It is not so much *how* we are governed, but *that* we are governed at all; for this is a mark of our immaturity and prevents us from taking our affairs into our own hands. We purchase the "protection" of the state with our freedom even to stay alive and do not realize that it is this "protection" which makes a hell of our life, while only freedom can endow it with dignity and strength.

There are today only too many who have recognized the evils of dictatorship as such, but who comfort themselves with the fatalistic belief that it is indispensable as a transition stage, provided, that is, that we have in mind the so-called "proletarian dictatorship," which, we are told, is to lead to socialism. Were not the perils by which the young communist state in Russia was threatened on every side a moral justification for the dictatorship? And must one not concede that the dictatorship would yield place to a condition of greater freedom as soon as these perils were overcome and the "proletarian state" had been consolidated internally?

Since then almost twenty years have gone by in that country. And Russia is today the strongest military state in Europe and is bound to France and other states by a strong alliance for mutual security. The Bolshevist state has not only been recognized by all the other powers, it is also represented today in all the bodies of international diplomacy and is exposed to no greater dangers from without than is every other great power in Europe. But the internal political conditions in Russia have not changed; they have grown worse from year to year and have made any hope for the future a mockery. With every year the number of the political victims has become greater. Among them are to be found thousands who for the last fifteen years have been dragged from prison to prison, or have been put to death, not because they have rebelled against the existing system with weapons in their hands, but merely because they were unable to accept the doctrines prescribed by the state and were of a different opinion from the ruling powers as to the solution of the social problem.

This situation cannot be explained by the pressure of external conditions, as so many have naïvely persuaded themselves. It is the logical result of an out and out anti-libertarian attitude which has not the slightest understanding or sympathy for the rights and convictions of men. It is the logic of the totalitarian state, which concedes to the individual only so much justification for his existence as makes him of service to the political machine. A system which could stigmatize freedom as a "bourgeois prejudice" could only lead to such an outcome. In its course it had to raise to a fundamental principle of state the suppression of all free expression of opinion and to make the scaffold and the jail the cornerstone of its existence. More than that: it had to proceed further along this disastrous course than any reactionary system of the past. Its leaders did not content themselves with rendering their revolutionary and socialistic opponents harmless, with dragging them before the bar or burying them alive; they also denied to their victims sincerity of opinion and purity of character, and shrank from no means of picturing them to the world as scoundrels and purchased tools of reaction.

The men and women who sat in the prisons of tsarist Russia were regarded by the liberty-loving world as martyrs to their opinions. Even the prison wardens of tsarism did not have the effrontery to attack their integrity or to question their sincerity. The victims of the proletarian dictatorship, however, were shamelessly besmirched and slandered by their oppressors and held up to the world as the scum of society. And hundreds of thousands of blind fanatics in every country, with their poor brains tuned only to the rhythm of the Moscow waltz, having lost all capacity to think for themselves, or perhaps never having possessed it, babble back without thinking whatever the Russian autocrats have dictated to them.

We have here to do with a reaction that goes deeper and is more disastrous in its consequences than any political reaction of the past. For the reaction of today is not embodied in special systems of government that have grown out of the methods of violence employed by small minorities. The reaction of today is the blind faith of broad masses which proclaims as unconditionally good even the most shameful violation of human rights so long as it is perpetrated by one particular side, and condemns uncritically whatever is damned by that side as false and heretical. Belief in the political infallibility of the dictator today replaces the belief in the religious infallibility of the Catholic pope and leads morally to the same results. It is possible to struggle against the force of reactionary ideas as long as one can appeal to reason and to human experience. Against the blind fanaticism of unthinking parrots who condemn any honest conviction in advance, all reason is powerless. Hitler, Mussolini and Stalin are merely the symbols of this blind faith which ruthlessly condemns everything that opposes its power.

The disgraceful judicial farces over the so-called "Trotzkyists" in Moscow are a bloody illustration of this. Everyone who has even a trace of independent judgment must recognize that the genuine tragedy in these judicial farces has been enacted behind the scenes of the court trial. The oldest and most outstanding leaders of a party, all trusted friends of the dead Lenin, compete with one another before the court in gruesome self-accusation such as has never before been witnessed in a political trial. Each seeks to outdo the others in his depiction of his own unworthiness so as to appear before the world as the despicable tool of fascism; all, however, with astounding unanimity point to Trotzky as the actual instigator of their alleged crimes.

No movement is secure against individual traitors in its ranks. But to believe that the great majority of the most prominent leaders of a movement found themselves prepared for the betrayal of everything that they had formerly preached—for that one must be more than blind. And if, after all, this horrible accusation was based on facts? Then so much the worse. What judgment can one pass on a movement whose oldest and most prominent leaders, all of whom had at some time occupied the highest positions that the party had in its gift, were secretly in the service of reaction? And if the great majority of the old leaders were traitors, who is to guarantee that the three or four of the old guard who are left alive are made of better stuff? Here, too, that law manifests itself that lies at the foundation of every dictatorship: the dictator can know no peace until he has rid himself of all inconvenient competitors. That same implicit logic that forced Robespierre to deliver his friends of yesterday to the headsman, that same logic that impelled Hitler on the bloody night of June 30, 1934, to clear his closest comrades out of his way, that same logic it was that just today drove Stalin to rid himself of the so-called "Trotzkyists" because he was afraid they might become dangerous to his power. For every dictator the dead opponent is the safest opponent.

After all, the same fate had overtaken these victims as they had so often dealt out to their opponents of other factions when they were still in power. They were minds of the same mind and blood of the same blood, inspired by the same obsession for power as their headsmen, treading every law of humanity under foot to maintain their own power. They have been robbed not only of their lives but of their honor, and the odium of treason has been heaped upon their names. But Trotzky too, who in 1924 had the workers and sailors of Kronstadt slaughtered—fourteen thousand men, women and children—was not content with drowning in blood the protest of those pioneers of the Russian Revolution; he and his assistants did not hesitate to denounce their victims to the world as counter-revolutionaries and allies of tsarism. Today he has to endure being represented to the world by his former friends as the ally of Hitler and the tool of fascism. That is the Nemesis of history.

From the same fatalistic conception which believes that it is impossible to dispense with dictatorship as a necessary transition stage to better social conditions, arises also the dangerous belief, which today finds ever wider and wider acceptance, that in the end the world can only choose between communism and fascism, because there is no other practicable way out. Such a view of the situation only proves that its holders are not yet at all clear about the real nature of fascism and communism and have not yet grasped that both grew on the same tree. It must, of course, not be forgotten that "communism" is to be taken here as merely a name for the present Russian system of government, which is as far removed from the original meaning of communism as a social system of economic equality as is every other system of government.

That the original motives of the Bolshevist dictatorship in Russia were different from those of the fascist dictatorship in Italy and Germany is not disputed. But once it was brought into being, dictatorship in Russia, just as in the fascist states, led to the same immediate results; indeed, the similarity of the two systems becomes progressively more apparent. The fact is that the whole internal development of Bolshevism in Russia and the social reconstruction in the fascist countries have reached a stage where, so far as the actual tendencies are concerned, no conflict can any longer be recognized between the two systems. Today we deal only with secondary differences, which can be distinguished also between the fascism of Germany and that of Italy, and which find their explanation in the peculiar conditions in the different countries.

Under Stalin's dictatorship Russia has developed in greater measure into a totalitarian state than has Germany or Italy. The arbitrary and brutal suppression of every other faction and of all freedom of opinion, the reduction of every sphere of public life to the iron control of the state, the omnipotence of an unrestrained and unscrupulous police system which interferes in the most intimate affairs of human beings and supervises every breath of the individual, the unexampled disregard for human life which shrinks from no means of clearing disagreeable elements out of the way—this and much more has taken on in Bolshevist Russia the same scope as in the countries of Hitler and Mussolini. Even the original international tendency of the Bolshevist movement, which could once have been regarded as the essential mark of distinction between Russian state communism and the extreme nationalistic aims of fascism, has completely disappeared under Stalin's régime to give place to a strictly nationalistic education of Russian youth. This youth, it is true, still sings the "Internationale" on ceremonial occasions, but it is no less firmly bound with iron chains to the interests of the national state than is the fascist youth of Germany and Italy.

On the other hand fascism in Germany, and still more definitely in Italy, is turning more and more into the road to state capitalism. The nationalization of all the financial institutions in Italy, the step by step subjection of all foreign trade to the control of the state, the nationalization of heavy industry already announced by Mussolini, and much else, show ever more clearly the tendency toward a development of state capitalism after the Russian pattern, a phenomenon that is causing no little brain-racking for the big capitalist accomplices of fascism. Similar phenomena are today appearing with increasing frequency in Germany. In reality these tendencies are only the logical result of the idea of the totalitarian state, which can never rest content until it has brought every field of social life equally into its service.

Fascism and "communism" are therefore not to be evaluated as the opposition of two different conceptions of the nature of society, they are merely two different forms of the same effort and operate to the same end. And this is not changed in the least by the declaration of war against communism that Hitler has proclaimed with such passion, for every person of insight recognizes clearly that this is just a propagandist trick to scare the bourgeois world out of its wits. Even the ruthless brutality that characterizes the new autocrats in Bolshevist Russia as well as those in the fascist states finds its explanation in the fact that they are all upstarts: the parvenu of power is no whit better than the parvenu of wealth.

That fascism and communism, or better, Stalinism, could ever have been regarded as opposed to one another is explained chiefly by the pitiful behavior of the so-called "democratic" states, which in their defensive struggle against the flood of fascism more and more appropriate its methods, and so are swept inevitably further and further into the current of fascist tendencies. Here is being repeated on a large scale the situation which helped Hitler to his victory in Germany. In their efforts to put a check on the "greater evil" by means of a lesser one the republican parties in Germany kept restricting constitutional rights and privileges more and more until at last there was hardly anything left of the so-called "constitutional" state. In fact, Bruening's government, which enjoyed the full support of the Social Democratic party, governed at last entirely by decree, having eliminated the legislative bodies. Thus, the antagonism between democracy and fascism gradually faded away until at last Hitler emerged as the joyful heir of the German Republic.

But the democratic countries have learned nothing from this example and are now traveling with fatalistic submissiveness along the same path. This is today especially evident in their pitiful behavior with regard to the frightful occurrences in Spain. A conspiracy of power-loving officers rose against a democratic government elected by the people and with the help of foreign mercenaries and under the direction of Hitler and Mussolini let loose a murderous war against their own people that is laying waste the whole country and has already cost hundreds of thousands of human lives. And while an entire people with heroic determination prepares to defend itself against this bloody violation of its rights and liberties and puts up against this handful of conscienceless adventurers such a struggle as the world has never before witnessed, the "democracies" of Europe have known nothing better to do in opposition to this base violation of every human right than to entrench themselves behind a ridiculous neutrality pact—when everyone knew in advance that neither Hitler nor Mussolini would respect it. By this masterpiece of diplomacy a liberty-loving people that is risking the lives of its sons and daughters in defense of its rights, and the cowardly hangmen who threaten to drown these rights in a bath of blood, are treated as equal combatants and put morally on the same footing. Can one wonder, then, that democracy today has no attractions to oppose to fascism?

For months now the world has looked on calmly while the capital of a country is exposed to all the horrors of war, and defenseless women and children are mowed down by fascist barbarians. And nowhere does there rise a word of protest to call a halt to these horrors. Bourgeois democracy has grown senile and has lost all sympathy for the rights it once used to defend. It is this blunting of its morals, this lack of ethical ideals, that cripples its wings and forces it to borrow the methods of the enemy that is threatening to devour it. Centralization of government has broken its spirit and crippled its initiative. That is the reason why many think today that they must choose between fascism and "communism."

If today there still is a choice, it is not that between fascism and "communism," but the choice between despotism and freedom, between brutal compulsion and free agreement, between the exploitation of human beings and cooperative industry for the benefit of all.

Fourier, Proudhon, Pi y Margall and others believed that the nineteenth century would begin the dissolution of the Great State and prepare the way for an epoch of Federations of Free Leagues and Municipalities which, in their opinion, would open for the people of Europe a new period of their history. They were mistaken as to the time, but their point of view is still correct, for governmental centralization has assumed a scope which must fill even the least suspicious with secret dread of the future—in Europe and in the world at large. Only a federalistic social organization, supported by the common interest of all and based on the free agreement of all human groups, can free us from the curse of the political machine which feeds on the sweat and blood of the people.

Federalism is organic collaboration of all social forces towards a common goal on the basis of covenants freely arrived at. Federalism is not disintegration of creative activity, not chaotic running hither and thither; it is the united work and effort of all members for the freedom and welfare of all. It is unity of action, sprung from inner conviction, which finds expression in the vital solidarity of all. It is the voluntary spirit, working from within outward, which does not exhaust itself in mindless imitation of prescribed patterns permitting no personal initiative. Monopoly of power must disappear, together with monopoly of property, that men may be eased of the weight which rests like a mountain on their souls and cripples the wings of the spirit.

Liberation of economics from capitalism! Liberation of society from the state! Under this sign the social struggles of the near future will take place, smoothing the way for a new era of freedom, justice and solidarity. Every movement which strikes capitalism in the core of its being and seeks to free economics from the tyranny of monopoly; every initiative which opposes the state's effective action and aims at the elimination of force from the life of society, is a step nearer to freedom and the coming of a new age. Everything which steers towards the opposite goal

—under whatever name—strengthens consciously or unconsciously the forces of that political, social and economic reaction which today raises its head more threateningly than ever before.

And with the state will disappear also the nation—which is only the state-folk—in order that the concept of humanity may take on a new meaning. This will reveal itself in its every part, and from it the rich manifoldness of life will for the first time create a whole.

The sense of dependence on a higher power, that source of all religious and political bondage which ever chains man to the past and blocks the path to a brighter future, will yield place to an enlightenment which makes man himself the master of his fate. Here also Nietzsche's saying holds true: "Not where you come from will from now on redound to your honor, but whither you are going! Your will and your foot, which tries always to outrun you—that shall be your new honor."

Epilogue

AFTER MANY YEARS of preliminary research, often interrupted by other activities, this book was completed shortly before the seizure of power by the Nazis. This is why its publication in Germany became impossible although all the technical preparations for its printing had already been made. The first Spanish edition (in three volumes) was gotten out in Barcelona, in 1936-1937, by the publishing house *Tierra y Libertad*. The first English edition came out in 1937 (Covici-Friede, New York). A Dutch edition, in three volumes, appeared in Amsterdam in 1939. The second Spanish edition was published in 1942 by *Ediciones Imán* in Buenos Aires. Yiddish, Portuguese and Swedish editions are in preparation at present in Buenos Aires, Sao Paulo and Stockholm, respectively.

In this book I have tried to present an outline of the most important causes of the general decline of our civilization; causes which, ever since the Franco-Prussian war of 1870-1871, became more and more apparent, and which a few years after the publication of this book, led to the monstrous catastrophe of World War II. Many things that had been predicted in this volume have later come to be literally true. That prognosis to be sure, was not so difficult to make, for everybody who attempted to penetrate into the causes of the great decline was bound to reach similar conclusions. All of which points quite obviously to the ways and means which alone are capable today of bringing about a gradual recovery and of steering the general development along lines which may render possible a fruitful and peaceful collaboration of the various national groups. It is up to mankind whether it is going to take to heart the lessons of this greatest of all social catastrophes and whether it is determined, by mending its ways, to open up the possibilities for a better future, or whether it is determined to continue the old game of secret diplomacy, military and political alliances and unbridled power politics which can lead only to new catastrophies, resulting finally in the total destruction of our civilization.

Nor will it be easy to make a new start, and an undertaking of this kind will require the work of several generations. Nobody can expect the frightful chaos left in the wake of a world war to be suddenly followed by a millennium healing all wounds with one stroke and presenting mankind without a struggle, with a world of freedom and justice. A catastrophe of such enormous dimensions cannot be overcome in a few years. The ruin-covered wilderness which we have inherited cannot be cleaned up and cultivated overnight. The demoralizing effects caused by the barbarity of the Nazis and by the war itself, cannot be removed at one stroke.

However, it will be of decisive importance what road we will take, and it will depend upon us whether this road will be a new rise or merely another wrong turn. In the course of history the human race has hardly ever been so urgently confronted by the task of taking its fate into its own hands. Compared with this general task all other questions, including that of what is to become of Germany, pale into utter insignificance, because a new Germany can evolve only in a new Europe and in a new world. Even the complete destruction of Germany and the decimation of her population would be of no avail so long as the premises of the old power politics remain intact and the real causes responsible for the bloody decline of our civilization are not eliminated. A mere change in the power relationships will never succeed in eradicating the evil. One does not remove a danger by shifting it to another place. The same causes always produce the same effects. According to circumstances these effects may assume different forms, but these differences do not touch the core of the evil which always leads to the same consequences.

The belief that the problem could be solved through an alliance of three or five dominant powers likewise denotes a complete misconception of the facts. Even under the most favorable circumstances such an alliance could solve only some definite tasks; but it could not conjure away the danger that threatens us, nor does it offer any protection against new catastrophes affecting the life of the human race. It can force the small nations to accept, temporarily and against their will, certain forms of life, as long as this benefits the big powers; but it will fall to pieces as soon as the internal political and economic contradictions among the dominant powers become more accentuated, leading once more to chaos.

This can be seen even today, when the whole world is still bleeding from a thousand wounds, and millions of human beings are literally starving and being compelled to live under the most appalling circumstances. Instead of concentrating all their efforts upon healing those wounds and upon saving millions from certain death or incurable physical and mental degeneration, by facilitating the reconstruction of the countries destroyed and devastated by the war and by bringing about speedily more or less bearable conditions which could bring about a further development—the dominant powers, in resuming their power politics, are preventing the accomplishment of this all-important task and are sowing the seeds of new dissensions which will inevitably result in disaster.

Right from the start it has become obvious that there are great conflicts between America, England and Russia; the three countries which were called upon to secure a lasting peace. These conflicts are daily becoming more and more difficult to solve. They will not be removed even if an attempt is made to reconcile them through all kinds of superficial compromises. As things now stand these contradictions will remain in existence until an open break becomes inevitable. And if the peoples do not steal a march on their governments, they will again be faced by an accomplished fact, with the atom bomb possibly putting an end to everything. One can hardly expect the heads of the various governments to mend their ways; hence no other end can be foreseen as a result of such suicidal tactics, unless the peoples themselves see the light at last.

By a peculiar irony of history it is precisely Russia, the "red-fatherland of the proletariat," the "land of socialist reality," as it was frequently called, which in its unlimited expansionist ambitions greatly surpasses the imperialism of the western powers. Its insatiable claims are continually conjuring up new dangers unless a stop is put to them in time. Russia, the biggest country of the world, which covers one-sixth of the surface of our planet, has already succeeded—partly due to her secret pact concluded with Hitler in 1939, and partly due to her military operations—in achieving an increase in territory and population, unequaled by any other country. According to a report published in the *New York Times* of March 14, 1946, this increase is distributed as follows:

Territories	Square Miles	Population
Lithuania	24,058	3,029,000
Latvia	20,056	1,950,000
Estonia	18,353	1,120,000
Eastern Poland	68,290	10,150,000
Bessarabia & Bukovina	19,360	3,748,000
District of Moldavia	13,124	2,200,000
Carpatho-Ukraine	4,922	800,000
Eastern Prussia	3,500	400,000
Finnish Karelia	16,173	470,000
Petsamo, Finland	4,087	4,000
Tannu-Tuve (Central Asia)	65,000	64,000
South Sakhalin	14,075	415,000
Kuril Islands	3,949	4,500
Total:	273,947	24,355,500

To this are to be added the following countries of Eastern Europe: Poland, Rumania, Bulgaria, Yugoslavia and to a large extent also Hungary and Czechoslovakia, which have now been brought completely within the orbit of Russia's sphere of influence and are used by her as an instrument of her further expansions towards the South and West. Not to speak of Russia's claims upon Iran, certain parts of Turkey and the former Italian colony of Libya. We are omitting any mention of Russia's ambitions in the Far East because the confusion prevailing there does not permit, for the time being, the formation of a clear picture. The fact that a country which covers such vast expanses is continually pressing new claims for further expansions of territory, should demonstrate to everybody capable of independent thinking that such a course can lead only to another catastrophe, and that it is certainly not apt to give the world the peace which it needs so badly.

It has been repeatedly pointed out in this book that ever since the formation of the big European national states every one of these new powers at first attempted to do away with the local liberties and federative ties which had sprung up from the very life of those nations. This was done by means of violent interference and centralization of all authority, and, after this aim had been attained, they proceeded to extend the influence thus secured upon neighboring countries and to force them to submit to the interests of their foreign policy. Power politics does not know any other limits but those set by a stronger power or those which it cannot overcome at one blow. But the urge to achieve political and economic hegemony does not permit any dominant power to call a halt, and its effects are all the more pernicious the better it has succeeded in enslaving its own people. The degree of despotism in any country has always been the best measure for the danger with which it kept threatening other countries. The entire history of the dominant European powers has for centuries been an almost uninterrupted struggle for hegemony on the Continent; a struggle which always meant a temporary success for the stronger power, until sooner or later new power combinations or other circumstances set limits to their ambitions. However, the same attempts were always soon taken up by another dominant state—with the same sinister results leading to ever new disasters.

This struggle for hegemony is at the root of the ever spreading political centralization which has been continually striving to throttle all local rights and liberties and to reduce the entire life of a people to certain definite norms, because this was most useful to the domestic and foreign ambitions of its rulers. The inevitable result of these senseless efforts in the direction of unintelligent power politics was the same in practically all cases: after its champions had succeeded, by all means of continuous threats and open warfare, to subject other peoples to their will, they themselves eventually became the victims of their insatiable hunger for power. The fact that until now England has constituted an exception to this general rule, is to be explained on one hand by the circumstance that after the defeat of royal absolutism the liberties attained could never be completely cancelled even during the most reactionary periods of her history; and also because her political representatives have until now been the only ones who have learned something from history. This was fully realized by Peter Kropotkin when in his speech delivered on January 7, 1918, to the *League of Federalists* in Moscow, he stated:

"The British Empire supplies us with a drastic lesson. Both the federalist and the centralist methods were tried by it, and the results are quite obvious. Due to the influence of the Liberal Party upon the English people, the British colonies, Canada, Australia and South Africa obtained their full liberty which found its expression not merely in the autonomous management of their own affairs but in a completely independent political administration, with their own legislative bodies, their own finances, their own trade agreements and their own armies. As a result these colonies flourished economically, and they were always ready, whenever England was in trouble, to offer her their assistance at the cost of the greatest sacrifices, as if she were an older sister or mother. The same spirit could also be noticed in the small autonomous islands of Jersey, Guernsey and Man, which enjoy such an independence with regard to their domestic affairs that they are still recognizing the Norman laws in matters of landed property, and that—as far as their relations with other governments are concerned—they do not permit the application of the customs duties on foreign goods which are binding upon England. An autonomy of this kind which is so close to independence, and the federal ties resulting from it, have thus proved to be the most secure foundations of a spiritual unity.—On the other hand, what a contrast in Ireland where in the course of the entire nineteenth century the strong hand of Dublin Castle, that is the administration of a Governor General, had to take the place of a legislative body and of the domestic organization of the country. . . . Centralism is a curse which affects not only autocratic regimes, it has also brought about the ruin of the French and German colonies, at a time when British colonies nearby could flourish and prosper, because they enjoy a broad autonomy and are now gradually developing into a federation of peoples."

Instead of taking to heart these precious lessons of history and going to the root of the real causes of the greatest catastrophe that has ever befallen the human race, it would seem that even the Western countries, for all their long traditions of liberal intellectual trends which played a prominent part during the greatest epochs of their history, are now veering more and more toward the same views which had given rise to the idea of the total state. Not to speak of Russia, because under the so-called proletarian dictatorship it has developed into a full-fledged totalitarian state whose institutions were frequently accepted as a model by victorious Fascism.

These ideas, which today are spreading rapidly, have also given rise to the naive and dangerous belief that armed conflicts could be eliminated in the future by placing the entire world under the police control of a few dominant powers to which all small countries are subjected for better or for worse. The entire situation becomes all the more hopeless due to the fact that, under Russia's pressure, the other powers were forced to consent to the principle that all decisions have to be adopted unanimously by the three or five dominant states, and that even the best proposal could be thwarted if one of these powers made use of its veto. Any important decision can be easily sabotaged by this method.

The effects of such a situation were illustrated during the first sessions of the *Council of the United Nations,* at which it was impossible to engage in any serious deliberations so that, time and again, it became necessary to postpone the discussion of the most important questions upon which the fate of millions of people depends today. There is possibly a saving grace in the fact that this critical situation has become apparent right at the start, for it might open the eyes of many people and show them that such arrangements are a mockery of the most elementary principles of democracy and that no good results could ever be achieved that way. For by following that course the *Council of the United Nations* which had held out such great hopes, can become merely the scene of conflict of a few dominant powers, at which the smaller countries would have hardly anything to say. Granted even that they are permitted to submit their grievances to the Council, the decision will always depend upon a few powers, even though it may not be prevented by a veto; with the result that the smaller nations are delivered to the tender mercies of the Big Three or the Big Five, without being able to raise an effective protest. The best they can do is not to give offence and by compliance buy the favor of that dominant power whose claims in a given situation would be most dangerous to them. This, however, leaves untouched the real foundations of power politics and consequently also the results and the dangers inevitably bound up with such a situation.

Freedom from Fear was one of the great postulates of the *Atlantic Charter;* it has not been mentioned for quite some time. Today this postulate, like all the other freedoms which had been emphasized in the past, sounds almost like a deliberate mockery. For indeed, where is the small country which in the face of the present situation, would show enough courage to complain and to risk all the trouble which a dominant power can cause a smaller nation? In most of the cases the small country will simply be intimidated and accept an obvious injustice. To most of the small countries such a course may seem more advantageous than the privilege of being used as a guinea pig in the contest among the dominant powers. As things stand now it becomes more and more obvious that a lasting peace among the peoples within the narrow boundaries of the present national states is not feasible at all; even if for the time being nobody actually intends to provoke a new war. A real solution of this most important of all questions is not possible so long as the *interests of all* have to yield to the *special interests* of individual national states. To win time it will be necessary to make all kinds of temporary concessions, until one of the dominant powers feels strong enough to risk an armed conflict, unless for some reason or other the other powers are ready to yield without a struggle.

Even total disarmament, the prospect of which was so often held out in the past and which in view of the present situation should be the first prerequisite of a real policy of peace, has lost all meaning after Stalin, in his speech of February 9, 1946, had openly declared that the strengthening and consolidation of the Red Army were the most important task for the purpose of securing Russia's frontiers, and that perhaps another three or more five-year-plans were necessary for the attainment of that aim. Which, in plain language, means that Russia's further industrialization is to be adopted not for the purpose of peace and welfare of the Russian people, but to anticipate all the contingencies of a new war.

This language is not new. These are the very arguments which Bismarck used after the war of 1870-1871 in order to justify the militarization of the new Reich, and which Hitler repeated later for the purpose of securing Germany against the alleged aggressive intentions of her hostile neighbours. It is the same language which has always been used by every despot for the purpose of disguising his own thirst for conquest. Bismarck's *armed peace,* as they called it at that time, eventually led to the militarization of all of Europe and laid the foundation for that fateful international competition in armaments which later on unloosed the red deluge of the First World War. No man with any claim of political sense will dare to assert seriously that in the case of Russia things would take another course. It is the same old struggle for hegemony in Europe and today in Asia as well—except that the roles have been changed and that the Kremlin dictatorship has taken over the inheritance of the Hohenzollern and Hitler.

So far Stalin has obtained more from the past war than any Russian Tsar could ever have hoped for; and as in matters of foreign policy the appetite comes with eating and increases with every mouthful, it is impossible, for the time being, to foresee the further intentions of Russian imperialism whose game is greatly facilitated by the fact that in every country it has at its disposal a fanatical and organized following which does not demur at being used as a tool of Russia's foreign policy, while Hitler had a hard time in recruiting his Quislings.

There is now in existence an entire school of intellectuals many of whom pretend to be Liberals—what is in a name?—who attempt to justify the claims of the Bolshevist autocracy by asserting that today Stalin is fulfilling a historical mission in Europe and in Asia, and that by breaking up the great landed estates in the territories of the Russian sphere of influence, he is creating the possibilities for a new social development, which would preclude the reestablishment of the status quo created by western imperialism. And to render this strange opinion palatable they are pointing to the role played by Napoleon and his armies, which spread the ideas of the Great Revolution throughout Europe, breaking the foundations of absolutist regimes and of feudal institutions.

Those who use this language are devoid of all judgment concerning historical facts. The French Revolution was actually the harbinger of a new epoch. It dealt a mortal blow to royal absolutism and broke to pieces its economic and social institutions. In the *Declaration of the Rights of Man* it laid the foundations for a new humanity and for a new historical development in Europe, just as Jefferson had done in the *Declaration of Independence*. Even though the ideas and the postulates of these two great documents have only partly been carried out, they have nevertheless stimulated the best hopes of all nations and have had a lasting influence upon the entire subsequent history, an influence which has opened up new vistas to the human race and has not disappeared up to the present day. Nor can it be denied that the soldiers of the French armies, who had grown up in the turbulent days of the Great Revolution, carried its spirit into all countries striking blows at royal absolutism from which it could never recover. Not even Napoleon, who had risen from the revolution, and who later was to sin against it so grievously, was able to stop the dissemination of revolutionary ideas in Europe. These ideas penetrated even Russia where they led to the uprising of the Decembrists who wanted to rid their country of its autocracy and its feudal ties in order to substitute for them a free federation of Russian peoples.

The French Revolution, with its after-effects in Europe, was actually the beginning of a new period in the history of the European nations; it put an end to the old regime of royal absolutism and paved the paths for the future. Even all the subsequent mass movements which went beyond the economic aims of liberalism and political democracy and were bent upon driving absolutism out of its last fortress, the economic life of present society, were the direct result of those great intellectual trends, which in all countries had been released by the Great Revolution and which have not run their course as yet.

However, those who attempt to compare the great and imperishable results of this outstanding event of modern history and its intellectual effects upon the social development of Europe, with the aims of Bolshevist imperialism and of its foreign policy, are altogether unable to judge historical events; for they make no distinction between things which could be compared only in a negative sense, but are otherwise as different as day and night. Such analogies are not merely misleading; they also constitute a direct threat to any intellectual and social progress, for they advocate the indorsement of things which are an impediment to any healthy development, and, which under false pretenses, are making peoples willing to accept a new reactionary form of social life whose tendencies are deeply rooted in the absolutist ideas of the past centuries.

What has been developed in Russia for more than a quarter of a century, is a *new absolutism* whose internal and external forms greatly surpass anything that had been achieved by the power politics of old time absolutisms. All the political and social rights and liberties obtained as a result of the French Revolution and its after-effects upon the rest of Europe, including the inviolability of the individual and the right to express one's opinion, have altogether ceased to exist in the Russia of today and in the countries which are in her sphere of influence. The entire press and the printed word in general, the radio, in short all organs of public expression, are subject to a triple censorship, so that practically no opinion may be expressed but that of the government which, consequently, is not subject to any criticism. Of the events occurring in other countries the Russian people learn only what its government believes it advisable for them to know. Even at the time of the tsarist regime the country was never so hermetically sealed, so secluded from all foreign countries as it is today. In a country which can claim the sad distinction of having the most unscrupulous and most despotic police dictatorship, even most elementary personal security is out of question. Only he is secure who unconditionally submits to the men who hold power, provided no unfortunate accident attracts upon him the suspicion of an all-powerful spy system. The ruthless and cruel extermination of all other political trends, and the brutal slaughter of most of the old leaders of the Bolshevist Party under the most revolting circumstances, are the best evidence that this statement is not exaggerated.

To be sure, there are people who are ready to put up with all these undeniable aspects of an unrestricted political absolutism because they believe, or pretend to believe, that the new economic order of the Russian state is amply making up for these features. In their opinion that new economic order is likely to further the development of a socialist economy in other countries as well. This blind faith is based upon a complete misconception of all actual facts. That which today is proclaimed in Russia as a socialist economy has as little in common with the real principles of socialism as has the autocracy of the Kremlin with the struggle of the French Revolution against absolutism. That which today is called by this name in Russia—and unthinking people abroad are repeating it mechanically—is in reality only the last word of modern monopoly capitalism which uses the economic dictatorship of the trusts and cartels for the purpose of eliminating any undesirable competition and of reducing the entire economic life to certain definite norms. The last link of such a development is not socialism but state capitalism with all of its inevitable accompaniments of a new economic feudalism and a new serfdom; and that is the system which today is actually operating in Russia.

The French Revolution had removed the old compulsory ties with which royal absolutism and its twin brother, feudalism, had for centuries kept the peoples in fetters. This is its imperishable merit and the great historical importance of its immediate results. But the Bolshevist dictatorship has restored the old bureaucracy and the feudal ties which had ceased to exist even in Tsarist Russia, and has developed them to their utmost extreme. If it were true that socialism could be achieved only at the price of the complete destruction of personal liberty, individual initiative and independent thinking, then preference would have to be given to the private capitalist system for all its inevitable defects and shortcomings. This truth should be spoken out frankly. Those who deny it can only contribute to subjecting mankind to a new and still more abject slavery.

If the Russian example taught us anything it is only the fact that Socialism without political, social and spiritual freedom is inconceivable, and must inevitably lead to unlimited despotism, uninfluenced in its crass callousness by any ethical restraints. This was clearly recognized by Proudhon, when, almost one hundred years ago, he said that an alliance of Socialism with Absolutism would produce the worst tyranny of all times.

The old belief that dictatorship is only a necessary transition and that the abolition of private capital in industry and agriculture would automatically bring about the liberation of humanity from all reactionary ties of the past, has been so thoroughly discredited, that in the face of reality it has lost all meaning. No power is willing to abdicate voluntarily, and the greater its strength, the less it is inclined to do so. In this respect Proudhon again hit the nail on the head when he pointed out that every provisional government wants to become permanent. This is a trend which has always been the substance of every power organization, a fact which cannot be glossed over with empty verbiage. An all-powerful bureaucracy with its insatiable desire for exerting its tutelage and inescapable network of mechanical rules and regulations for all aspects of private and public life, is a much greater danger to general cultural and social progress than any other form of tyranny, even if private property of the means of production no longer exists, and particularly if the whole economy is subject to the rigid control of a totalitarian state.

In expressing this truism, confirmed by bitter experience, I by no means intend to make the slightest concession to or excuse for the imperialist aspirations of the Western powers, as clearly appears from the contents of this book. The power politics of the national states, and particularly of the dominant powers, with their secret diplomacy, their political and military alliances, their colonial policy and their methods of economic pressure, which in the past so often hampered, if not totally thwarted the social development of smaller nations, added to the perpetual intrigues of high finance and the international armament cartels, has continuously subjected the political and economic life of the peoples to increasingly intolerable periodical convulsions, establishing war danger as a permanent condition. No one who learned his lesson from the two world cataclysms can deny that this problem must be solved if we wish to create a new relationship among the peoples, a relationship in which peaceful conciliation of all interests might be possible. Only those stricken with incurable blindness will fail to recognize that the continuation of imperialist power politics and the old game of hegemonies must in the age of the atom bomb and the prodigious development of modern war technique lead inevitably to the end of all human civilization.

But even considering all these dangers and fully recognizing their importance, it is obvious that the abandonment of the old ways will only be possible where the spiritual and social conditions for a complete transformation of the people are present. Only in countries where the free expression of opinion still exists, and the thoughts and actions of men are not yet entirely subject to the tutelage of the state, is it possible to influence public opinion and to make it recognize these facts. In contemporary Russia, as in any totalitarian state, these important premises are lacking entirely. But wherever free exchange of opinions between peoples is prevented artificially, mutual understanding is impossible due to the absence of their first conditions for advantageous co-operation.

The great task facing us today is not a problem of a few large states, but co-ordinated co-operation of *all* national groups on equal conditions and equal rights. Such a federation is, however, only possible if it is no longer influenced by separate national interests, but sets forth as its aim the furthering of *general* interests, and guarantees to every member of the federation the same right for its aspirations for political, economic and social development. Only a *real federation* of European peoples is today still able to bridge the hostile rivalries between European national groups, fostered and encouraged by a narrow-minded nationalism, detrimental to all civilization. *A European federation is the first condition and the only basis for a future world federation, which can never be attained without an organic union of European peoples.*

It is very significant that up to now it happens to be Russia which most energetically opposes such a solution. Having established a new military and political power sphere in the eastern countries of Europe, extending already far into the central section of the continent, Russia greatly contributes to increase the internal cleavage of Europe, which for many centuries has been the perpetual cause of all hostilities.

Europe is, by its geographical situation, no separate continent like Africa, America or Australia, but a peninsula of the great Asiatic mainland from which it is not separated by any natural frontier. Therefore we are beginning to consider the enormous mass of land stretching from the Pacific to the Atlantic as a geographical unit, and we designate it as Eurasia. What made Europe in our imagination a separate continent were not geographical but political and social reasons. The tribes and peoples which in prehistoric times immigrated from Asia and Africa to Europe, gradually developed into separate peoples and later into nations after undergoing innumerable racial mixtures. In the course of time a common civilization established such close spiritual bonds that the history of no European nationality can be understood without the knowledge of the history of the other peoples. Thus developed a general European civilization, which later spread to North- and South America, to Australia and to parts of Africa. In the East of Europe the development of this civilization was for centuries affected by Mongol influences, while in the South strong Arabic and other influences prevailed. In general, however, this culture or civilization attained more or less uniform characteristics, with many variations and local shades, which are in many respects very different from the various forms of Asiatic civilizations. Among European peoples, however, the great affinity of a common civilization was never destroyed despite subsequent national antagonisms.

This can be ascribed to various historical causes, all of which tended to bring about the same results. The great expansion of the Roman empire over all Europe known at that time had a decisive influence on the cultural structure of the European continent and its various islands and archipelagos. This influence is still to be traced in the legislation of most European nations, and in many other fields. The spiritual heritage of Greece, Asia Minor and North Africa gradually amalgamated in Rome into a civilization formed by many different ingredients, and the continuous conquests of the Romans brought it about that their spiritual and material achievements were introduced wherever they went. To accomplish this was not very difficult since the sparse population of Europe at that time largely consisted of tribes whose primitive conditions of life could not offer any serious obstacle to Rome's civilizational influence, which gradually absorbed the conquered peoples. Though the later innumerable invasions by the so-called barbarians at the time of the great migrations of peoples seriously imperiled and affected Roman culture and civilization, it was inevitable that due to the continuous contact with the Roman world these tribes and peoples became gradually imbued with the Roman spirit.

A still greater influence on the spiritual and cultural development of Europe was exerted by the spread of Christianity in the form given it by the Catholic Church, which penetrated even into regions which were never invaded by the Roman legions. The Church not only took over the mode of Roman Caesarism, formulating its ideas for its own purpose, but it also inherited the widely ramified civilization concentrated for centuries in Rome, which it now was able to use extensively for the power aspirations of the Church. What the Roman State accomplished in the realm of political centralization and with the juridical conceptions resulting therefrom the Church continued in its own manner, by directing the thinking of Europeans into new paths for the purpose of enticing it into the fine meshes of theological dogmas. Its agents were no longer the pro-consuls and procurators of the Roman Empire but priests and monks who served the same cause, penetrating into the most distant regions. This new power proved to be stronger than the power of the Caesars, based merely on military superiority, while the power of the Church was built on psychological influences, which reconciled men with their lot in this world, and convinced them that their fate depended on the will of a higher power, whose benevolence could only be attained through the mediation of the Church. Thus, in the course of centuries, developed Europe's Christian civilization which, producing among the peoples of the continent an undeniable similarity of aspirations, brought them nearer to each other in their thoughts and actions.

This great community of faith, not limited by political frontiers, brought it about that in later periods, when currents and movements opposing the power of the Church and of secular rulers appeared, these new aspirations were also inspired by related or similar ideas. The same spiritual premises produced everywhere the same germs of thinking and led with surprising uniformity to similar results. The differences which appeared were merely differences of degree, caused by local conditions, but the essential relationship could not be denied. Though European culture is one of the most complicated products ever created by men, the spiritual oneness of its nature cannot be mistaken in any period of its history. Every important event recorded in any European country was always reflected more or less strongly in all other countries, and this made the innermost concatenations of the events even more intelligible.

All great currents of thought, which temporarily or permanently influenced the ideas and sentiments of the peoples of the continent, were

European and not *national* phenomena. Even the conception of national-ism itself is no exception, since it developed everywhere at a definite period in Europe's history from the same motives and premises. Every manifesta-tion in the realm of religious or philosophical thinking, any new inter-pretation concerning the significance of political and social modes of life, any important change in the domain of economic possibilities, every new esthetic conception in the field of art and literature, every advance in science, every new phase in the understanding of natural phenomena, all large popular movements, the rise and decline of revolutionary or reac-tionary trends of thought—all these were reflected in the whole cultural orbit to which we belong, and from which we cannot escape. The external proceedings of these manifestations are not identical everywhere, and, due to local differences, often assume different coloration, but their innermost core remained the same and can be easily recognized as such by any keen observer.

Nobody with any discernment will question the existence of active connections in the life of the peoples of our cultural orbit. It is therefore not necessary to create the spiritual premises for a federated Europe, because every nation has these conditions already: time and again they have been emphasized by the best and most unprejudiced minds of all nations. What separates us today are mainly political and economic differ-ences, which for centuries have been artificially promoted and nurtured by stupid pernicious influences of nationalist inspirations and greed for power, which have now become our nemesis.

Every national state, as soon as the growth of its population has enabled it to become a dominant power, has always attempted to hamper the economic development of other nations by establishing special spheres of power and interest, and in this process the weaker nations naturally became the first victims. This trend is one of the most important character-istics of any power politics, and if smaller states, due to their numerically inferior population, do not act in the same way, their alleged virtuous behavior is, as Bakunin once remarked, due mainly to their impotence. But whenever they succeed in gaining more influence and power due to the acquisition of more territory, they invariably follow the example of the dominant powers, as was clearly illustrated by the more or less recent history of Poland, Rumania and Serbia.

For centuries the system of princely absolutism, by its stupid rules and regulations extending to all branches of industrial activity and commercial relations had obstructed artificially the natural progressive evolution of Europe's economy. In a similar way the national state, in the century of capitalism, became, due to its continuous interference in the economic life of the peoples, the eternal source of periodical convulsions of Europe's economic and political equilibrium. In most cases these disturbances wound up in open warfare, with the sole result, that the vicious circle had to begin all over again with the same consequences as heretofore. Import and export duties, high tariffs, special favors or subsidies to certain branches of industry and agriculture at the expense of the general public, the uninterrupted struggle for markets and sources of raw materials, the relentless exploitation of colonial peoples, the practice of dumping and the development of large trusts and cartels favored by the governments, and innumerable other political and economic methods of pressure combined to cut up and to dismember the common economic sphere. Thus the foundation was laid for an unbridled policy of plunder which in its selfish obstinacy does not consider itself bound by any ethical considerations, with brute force as the point of departure for all aspirations.

But as no power can maintain itself by sheer force alone, it is always compelled to justify its ambitions by a certain ideology to disguise its real character. Thus nationalism was evolved into a political religion, for the purpose of replacing individual conceptions of right and wrong by the notion about right as preached by the national state, such as expressed in the sentence: "my country, right or wrong." The accident of the place of birth became the basis and starting point of national education, and human beings became mere vessels of the nation which for the ethical consciousness of right and wrong substituted empty formulas denying the validity of general human considerations. National egoism became the center of political thinking, which determined all relations with other peoples and declared its own nation to be the salt of the earth. It is therefore not astonishing if from the spiritual sterility of nationalist muddleheadedness grew out such rubbish as the idea of the German "master race" (Herrenvolk) or of the Nordic super-race. The mere belief of being the salt of the earth is the seed of that arrogance which looks down upon all other nations. The consequences follow almost automatically, because it is in the nature of all power politics that its protagonists should not be just as well satisfied with the mere belief in their own superiority, but should always be inclined to make the others feel that imagined superiority.

Under these circumstances it was unavoidable that open and undeclared warfare should become a permanent condition of our public life. For though the essential sameness of our cultural orbit tended towards a federal association of the European peoples, the representatives of power politics and nationalism always knew how to find ways and means to prevent such a solution and to impede any peaceful settlement among the various national groups. Where this was bound to lead to was demonstrated by the devastation of whole countries, the barbarous destruction of old seats of culture, the cruel slaughter of millions of people in the flower of their youth, and the indescribable misery of other millions forcefully driven from their native soil, disasters of an immensity never before witnessed in the world. Whoever, despite this terrible relapse into the most brutal barbarism, has not learned his lesson and does not do everything he can to help the people in attaining a life worthy of human beings and to protect future generations from these dangers which today have ruined a whole world, deserves indeed no better lot.

If the advocates of nationalism were at all able to recognize their mistakes, the history of the last hundred years should have convinced them that all their aspirations and ambitions are based on gross misjudgments of political and social facts. Particularly in the case of smaller nations such ambitions are nothing but empty bubbles. Of what value, indeed, is the dream of national sovereignty and so-called national independence in a century of boundless power politics of the dominant nations, which always attempt to include the smaller states in their spheres of power, and to use them as vassals serving their interests? Most of the smaller nationalities which, favored by a temporary shifting of power relations in Europe, obtained their imagined national independence, did no better than jumping from the frying pan into the fire. Their political sovereignty gave them hardly any protection against the ambitions of powerful nations, and made their situation often even more unbearable. National unification may well have benefited that social stratum which includes their new statesmen and professional politicians; but for the masses of the people the general situation has hardly improved.

Indeed who would maintain that the situation of the Polish people was more enviable under the rule of Pilsudski and the "colonels," than under the rule of Russia, Prussia or Austria? Who would claim that Hungary enjoyed greater freedom under Horthy than under the Hapsburg dynasty? Did national sovereignty of Yugoslavia and other Balkan states give their peoples more freedom and greater extension of their rights and liberties? In most cases the very opposite occurred, and quite often rule by compatriots have proved worse than the foreign yoke. However, there are people who cannot be convinced by the most obvious facts. One hundred years ago Heinrich Heine said that the Germans prefered to be lashed with their own whip rather than with a foreign one. But whoever is satisfied with so little should not be surprised if the whip never ceases to belabor his back.

Today the same thing is happening again, except that the roles are reversed. The same *sovereign states*, just mentioned, are now altogether under the influence of the Russian sphere of power. They not only lost their national sovereignty, they also lost the few rights and liberties they enjoyed before. Not only the political situation but the economic conditions as well have become worse for most of these peoples since their *national liberation*. World War I had created nine new sovereign states. All these countries which formerly belonged to larger economic unities, were compelled to create an economy of their own, a task in which none of them really succeeded, with the exception of Czechoslovakia. The latter succeeded only due to the great riches of its subsoil.

But neither did the peoples of Europe's dominant powers really find in their national unification the protection and security, which they had been promised. Due to the shortsighted power politics of their national governments, they were continuously being saddled with new taxes and contributions, which were not only absorbing more and more of the total national income, but were exposing them permanently to the danger of new wars, the logical result of their power politics.

The fate of Germany and Japan, and the terrific injuries inflicted during World War II on all peoples, large and small, should at last convince anyone who has the honest desire to find a way out of the labyrinth of errors, of what little value is national sovereignty which does not give real security to any people and exposes its very existence to ever recurring catastrophes, which permanently impede all peaceful development. The political and social independence of national groups will always remain a Utopia, as long as the economic premises are absent and the wholesome and peaceful co-existence of the peoples is being obstructed by the intrigues and ambitions of power hungry politicians and nationalist megalomaniacs.

A federated Europe with a unified economy, from which no people is excluded by artificial barriers, is, therefore, after the bitter experiences of the past, the only way which can lead us from the ruinous conditions of the past into a brighter future. It will open up new channels for a real reorganization and a rebirth of humanity and make an end of all power politics. This will also make it possible to achieve further changes and improvements for the general organism of our social life and to abolish economic exploitation of individuals and of peoples. As long as labor is considered a mere commodity, to be exchanged for any other merchandise, and the great ethical significance of all human creation is shamefully disregarded, the organization of national economy will continue to bestow upon a small upper crust all the advantages in which the masses at large will not be permitted to participate. Only co-operative collaboration, subject neither to the arbitrary power of monopolistic groups nor to that of a state bureaucracy, will make the production of economic assets equally accessible to all and secure to all members of the various human groups a worth while existence, without limiting their freedom.

The latest achievements of scientific research prove convincingly that such an aim is no longer a Utopian dream, but on the contrary, it has become an undeniable necessity, if we are to avoid the destruction of our civilization and of the human race as well. It is up to all of us whether the atomic bomb which today has become the nightmare of our times, be the doom of human life, or whether the technical utilization of atomic power for the purpose of peace and general prosperity, will be the beginning of a new epoch in our history. Everything depends on our choice.

A federation of European peoples, or at least a beginning towards this end, is the first condition for the creation of a world federation, which will also secure the so-called colonial peoples the same rights for the pursuit of happiness. It will not be easy to achieve this aim, but a beginning must be made if we are not to be plunged again into an abyss. *And this beginning must be made by the peoples themselves.* For this purpose we need a new understanding and the strong will for a rebirth of humanity. And today more than ever the words of the French historian Edgar Quinet apply to the situation:

"The peoples will not rise to greater heights before they have fully realized the depth of their decline."

RUDOLF ROCKER

Crompond, N. Y., May, 1946

BIBLIOGRAPHY

BIBLIOGRAPHY [1]

Adams, John: *Defence of the Constitution and Government of the United States*, 1787.

Adler, Georg: *Geschichte des Sozialismus und Kommunismus von Plato bis zur Gegenwart*, 1899.

Andrews, Stephen Pearl: *The Science of Society*, 1851.

Aristotle: *Politics*.

Arnould, Arthur: *L'état et la révolution*, 1877.

Aulard, A.: *La société des Jacobins*, 1889.

Baird, C. W.: *History of the Rise of the Huguenots*, 1880.

Bakunin, Michael [2]: *Féderalisme, socialisme et antithéologisme*. M. Nettlau, 1895.

———— *Lettres à un Français sur la crise actuelle*, 1870.

———— *L'empire knouto-germanique et la révolution sociale*, 1871.

———— *La théologie politique de Mazzini et l'Internationale*, 1871.

———— *God and the State* (the only English translation of Bakunin's works by Benjamin Tucker), 1883.

Balabanova, A.: *Wesen und Werdegang des italienischen Fascismus*, 1931.

Barker, E.: *The Political Thought of Plato and Aristotle*, 1906.

Barthélemy, C.: *L'esprit de Joseph de Maistre*, 1859.

Bauer, Otto: *Die Nationalitätenfrage und die Sozialdemokratie*, 1907.

Beard, Charles A.: *Economic Origins of Jeffersonian Democracy*, 1915.

Beer, Max: *Allgemeine Geschichte des Sozialismus und der sozialen Kämpfe*, 1929.

Bentham, Jeremy: *Introduction to the Principles of Morals and Legislation*, 1789.

Berens, L. H.: *The Digger Movement in the Days of the Commonwealth: as Revealed in the Writings of Gerrard Winstanley, the Digger, Mystic, Rationalist, Communist and Social Reformer*, 1906.

Berger, M.: *Görres als politischer Publizist*, 1921.

Berkman, Alexander: *The Bolshevist Myth*, 1925.

Bernstein, E.: *Die Voraussetzungen des Sozialismus und die Aufgaben der Sozialdemokratie*, 1899.

———— *Zur Geschichte und Theorie des Sozialismus*, 1900.

———— *Die deutsche Revolution*, 1921.

Bismarck, Otto von: *Gedanken und Erinnerungen*, 1898.

Bisset, Andrew: *Omitted Chapters of the History of England*, 1864.

[1] Most of the works already quoted in the text or in footnotes are not mentioned here.

[2] Editions of Bakunin's works have been published in French (*Oeuvres de M. Bakounine*, 1896-1914, 7 vol.); German (*Michael Bakunins Gesammelte Werke*, 1923-25, 3 vol.); and in Spanish (*Obras completas de Miguel Bakunin*). The Spanish edition contains also his Russian work, "*Etatism and Anarchy*," which had not been translated before into any other European language.

Blanc, Louis: *Histoire de dix ans: 1830-40*, 1841.
———— *Histoire de la révolution française*, 1847-1862.
———— *Histoire de la révolution de 1848*, 1870-80.

Blanqui, August: *Critique sociale*, 1885.

Boétie, Etienne de: *De la servitude volontaire*, 1577.

Bonald, Louis: *Récherches philosophiques sur les premier objects de connaissance morales*, 1818.

Bonaparte, Louis: *Idées napoléoniennes*, 1839.

Borghi, Armando: *L'Italia: Era due Crispi*, 1924.
———— *Mussolini Red and Black*, 1935.

Bourne, H. R. Fox: *The Life of John Locke*, 1876.

Brun, Charles: *Le Régionalisme*, 1911.

Buckle, Th. H.: *History of Civilization in England*, 1885.

Buonarroti, Ph. M.: *Conspiration pour l'égalité, dite de Babeuf*, 1828.

Burdach, K.: *Reformation, Renaissance, Humanismus*, 1918.

Burke, Edmund: *A Vindication of Natural Society*, 1756.
———— *Reflections on the Revolution in France*, 1790.
———— *A Letter to a Noble Lord*, 1796.
———— *Thoughts on a Regicide Peace*, 1796.

Burkhardt, Jakob: *Die Kultur der Renaissance*, 1860.
———— *Die Geschichte der Renaissance*, 1867.
———— *Griechische Kulturgeschichte*, 1898-1900.

Campbell, Douglas: *The Puritan in Holland, England and America*, 1892.

Carlyle, Thomas: *On Heroes, Hero-Worship and the Heroic in History*, 1846.
———— *Letters and Speeches of Oliver Cromwell*, 1845.

Chamberlain, H. St.: *Die Grundlagen des 19. Jahrhunderts*, 1899.

Chaptal, Jean A. Claude de: *De l'industrie française*, 1829.

Chateaubriand, F. René: *Génie du christianisme*, 1802.

Chelčicky, Peter: *Das Netz des Glaubens*. German translation from the old Czech original by Carl Vogl, 1925.

Classen, J.: *Franz von Baaders Gedanken über Staat und Gesellschaft*, 1890.

Clausewitz, Carl von: *Vom Kriege*, 1880, 4th ed.

Clément Mme.: *Histoire de Colbert et son administration*, 1892, 3rd ed.

Coerderoy, E.: *De la révolution dans l'homme et dans la société*, 1852.

Condorcet, M. J.: *Esquisse d'un tableau historique de progrès de l'esprit humain*, 1823, 4th ed.

Considérant Victor: *Destinée sociale*, 1837-1844.
———— *Principes du socialisme: Manifeste de la démocratie du XIXme siècle*, 1844.
———— *Le socialisme devant le vieux monde*, 1848, 2nd ed.

Conway, M. D.: *The Life of Thomas Paine*, 1892.

Cornelissen, Ch.: *La evolución de la sociedad moderna*, 1934.

Costa, Joaquin: *Colectivismo agrario en España: Doctrina y hechos*, 1898.

Cunow, Heinrich: *Die soziale Verfassung des Inkareiches*, 1895.
———— *Die Marxsche Geschichts-Gesellschafts- und Staatstheorie*, 1920-21.

Curtius, Ernst: *Die Jonier vor der jonischen Wanderung*, 1855
————— *Geschichte Griechenlands*, 1857-67.

Dalling, Lord: *The Life of Lord Palmerston*, 1870.

De Greef, G.: *L'evolution des croyances et des doctrines politiques*, 1895.

Dehio, Georg: *Geschichte der deutschen Kunst*, 1919-24.

De Man, Hendrik: *Zur Psychologie des Sozialismus*, 1927.
————— *Sozialismus und National-Fascismus*, 1931.

Dhorme, P.: *La religion Assyro-Babylonienne*, 1910.

Diderot, Denis: *Oeuvres complètes*, 1829.

Diercks, Gustav: *Geschichte Spaniens*, 1895.

Dragomanow, M.: *Michael Bakunins sozialpolitischer Briefwechsel mit A. Herzen und N. P. Ogarew*, 1895.
————— *La Pologne historique et la démocratie moscovite*, 1881.

Emerson, Ralph Waldo: *Essays: Second Series*, 1844.
————— *Representative Men*, 1850.
————— *Journals of Ralph Waldo Emerson*, 1909-14.

Engels, Friedrich: *Herrn Eugen Dührings Umwälzung der Wissenschaft*, 1877.
————— *Der Ursprung der Familie, des Privateigentums und des Staates*, 1884.
————— *Ludwig Feuerbach und der Ausgang der klassisch-deutschen Philosophie*, 1888.

Engländer, S.: *The Abolition of the State*, 1873.

Ewald, A. C.: *Life and Times of Algernon Sidney*, 1873.

Fabbri, Luce: *Camisas negras*, 1935.

Fabbri, Luigi: *Carlo Pisacane*, 1904.
————— *Dittatura e rivoluzione*, 1921.

Ferrari, G.: *La filosofia della rivoluzione*, 1851.
————— *La federazione republicane*, 1851.

Feuerbach, L.: *Das Wesen des Christentums*, 1841.
————— *Das Wesen der Religion*, 1845.

Fourier, Charles: *Traité de l'association domestique-agricole*, 1822-23.
————— *Le nouveau monde industriel et sociétaire*, 1830.

Frantz, Constantin: *Kritik aller Parteien*, 1862.
————— *Das neue Deutschland*, 1871.
————— *Der Föderalismus*, 1879.

Friedländer, L.: *Darstellungen aus der Sittengeschichte Roms*, 1869.

Galton, Sir Francis: *Hereditary Genius, Its Laws and Consequences*, 1869.

Garrido, Fernando: *Historia de las asociaciones obreras en Europa*, 1864.
————— *La España contemporanea*, 1865.
————— *Historia del reinado del último Borbón en España*, 1869.
————— *La revolución en la hacienda del estado, de la provincia y del municipio*, 1870.

Geffroy, Gustave: *L'enfermé*, 1897.

Gentz, Friedrich von: *Über den Ursprung und Charakter des Krieges gegen die französische Revolution*, 1801.

Gibbon, Edward: *The Decline and Fall of the Roman Empire*, 1776-88. (Bury edition, 1896-1900.)

Gille, Paul: *Esquisse d'une philosophie de la dignité humaine*, 1924.

Gobineau, Arthur de: *Essai sur l'inégalité des races humaines*, 1853-55.

Godwin, William: *An Enquiry Concerning Political Justice and Its Influence Upon General Virtue and Happiness*, 1793.

Goldman, Emma: *My Disillusionment in Russia*, 1923.

Görres, Joseph: *Teutschland und die Revolution*, 1819.
―――― *Die Heilige Allianz und die Völker auf dem Kongress zu Verona*, 1822.

Grote, George: *History of Greece*, 1846-56.

Guillaume, James: *L'Internationale: Documents et souvenirs*, 1905-10.
―――― *Karl Marx: Pangermaniste*, 1915.

Gumplówicz, L.: *Der Rassenkampf: Soziologische Untersuchungen*, 1883.
―――― *Die soziologische Staatsidee*, 1892.
―――― *Soziologie und Politik*, 1892.

Gurlitt, C.: *Geschichte des Barockstils, des Rokoko und des Klassizismus*, 1886-89.

Guyau, Jean-Marie: *Esquisse d'une morale sans obligation ni sanction*, 1885.
―――― *L'irreligion de l'avenir: Etude sociologique*, 1887.

Harper, R. F.: *The Code of Hammurabi, King of Babylonia*, 1904.

Haym, Rudolf: *Hegel und seine Zeit*, 1857.
―――― *Herder nach seinem Leben und seinen Werken*, 1880-85.

Hegel, Karl: *Geschichte der Städteverfassung in Italien*, 1847.
―――― *Die Entwicklung des deutschen Städtewesens*, 1898.
―――― *Städte und Gilden der germanischen Völker im Mittelalter*, 1891.

Hegel, W. G.: *Vorlesungen über die Philosophie der Geschichte*; 1832.

Herder, J. G.: *Ideen zur Philosophie der Geschichte der Menschheit*, 1784-91.
―――― *Briefe zur Beförderung der Humanität*, 1794.

Hess, Moses: *Rom und Jerusalem*, 1862.

Hinojosa, Eduardo: *El origin del régimen municipal en Castilla y Leon*, 1919.

Hitler, Adolf: *Mein Kampf*, 1925-27.

Hobbes, Thomas: *Leviathan*, 1655.

Hodde, L. de la: *Histoire des sociétés secrètes*, 1867.

Hooker, Richard: *The Laws of Ecclesiastical Polity*, 1593-94; new edition, 1907.

Humboldt, Wilhelm von: *Ideen zu einem Versuch die Grenzen der Wirksamkeit des Staates zu bestimmen*, 1792. (First published in 1851 after the death of the author.)

Jefferson, Thomas: *Memoirs and Correspondence*, 1829.

Joli, H.: *Ignace de Loyola*, 1899.

Kautsky, Karl: *Nationalität und Internationalität*, 1908.
―――― *Der Weg zur Macht*, 1909.
―――― *Die Befreiung der Nationen*, 1918.
―――― *Die Diktatur des Proletariats*, 1918.
―――― *Terrorismus und Kommunismus*, 1920.
―――― *Materialistische Geschichtsauffassung*, 1927.

Kegan, Paul C.: *William Godwin, His Friends and Contemporaries*, 1876.

Kowalewski, M.: *Die ökonomische Entwicklung Europas bis zum Beginn der kapitalistischen Wirtschaftsform*, 1901-05.
―――― *La France économique et sociale à la veille de la révolution*, 1908.

Kropotkin, Peter: *The State: Its Role in History*, 1898.
———— *Fields, Factories and Workshops*, 1899.
———— *Mutual Aid: A Factor of Evolution*, 1902.
———— *The Great French Revolution*, 1909.
———— *La science moderne et l'anarchie*, 1913.
———— *The Modern State*, 1912.
———— *Ethics: Origin and Development*, 1924.
Kulczycki, L.: *Geschichte der revolutionären Bewegung in Russland*, 1910.
Labriola, Antonio: *Saggi della concezione materialistica della storia*, 1902.
Landauer, Gustav: *Die Revolution*, 1907.
———— *Briefe aus der französischen Revolution*, 1919.
Lange, Albert: *Geschichte des Materialismus und Kritik seiner Bedeutung*, 1866.
Laski, H. J. H.: *Grammar of Politics*, 1925.
Lassalle, F.: *Die Philosophie Fichtes und die Bedeutung des deutschen Volksgeistes*, 1862.
———— *Über Verfassungswesen*, 1862.
———— *Der italienische Krieg und die Aufgabe Preussens*, 1859.
Lazare, Bernard: *Anti-Semitism: Its History and Causes*, 1903.
Lecky, E. H.: *History of European Morals*, 1869.
———— *History of Rationalism in Europe*, 1869.
———— *Democracy and Liberty*, 1896.
Lefrançais, G.: *La Commune et la révolution*, 1896.
Lehmann-Russbueldt, O.: *Die blutige Internationale der Rüstungsindustrie*, 1929.
———— *Der Krieg als Geschäft*, 1932.
Lenéru, M.: *Saint Just*, 1922.
Lenin, N.: *The State and Revolution*, 1917.
———— *The Proletarian Revolution and Kautsky, the Renegade*, 1920.
———— *Will the Bolsheviks Maintain Power?* 1922.
Leseine, V.: *L'influence de Hegel sur Marx*, 1907.
Lessing, G. E.: *Die Erziehung des Menschengeschlechtes*, 1780.
———— *Ernst und Falk*, 1778-80.
———— *Soldaten und Mönche*, 1780.
Letourneau, Ch.: *L'evolution de l'ésclavage dans les diverses races humaines*, 1892.
———— *L'evolution religieuse dans les diverses races humaines*, 1892.
Leverdays, E.: *Les assemblies parlantes: Critique du gouvernement représentatif*, 1883.
Lissagaray, P. O.: *History of the Commune of 1871*, 1898.
Locke, John: *Essay Concerning Human Understanding*, 1690.
———— *Letters on Toleration*, 1682-90.
———— *Treatise on Civil Government*, 1690.
Luce, Siméon: *Histoire de la Jacquerie*, 1895.
Luchaire, A.: *Innocent III, la croisade des Albigeois*, 1905.
Lundin, A. G.: *Influence of J. Bentham on English Democratic Development*, 1920.
Luschan, Felix: *Völker Rassen und Sprachen*, 1922.
Luxemburg, Rosa: *Die russische Revolution*, 1922.
Machiavelli, N.: *The Prince*, 1532. Burd ed., 1891.
Macpherson, J.: *Church History*, 1888.

Maistre, Joseph de: *Du Pape*, 1817.
———— *Soirées de St. Petersburg*, 1821.
Marat, J. P.: *The Chains of Slavery*, 1774.
Marlyn, Carlos: *Wendell Phillips the Agitator*, 1890.
Marx, Karl: *Zur Kritik der politischen Oekonomie*, 1859.
———— *Das Kapital*, 1867. Vol. I.
Marx and Engels: *Die heilige Familie oder Kritik zur kritischen Kritik gegen Bruno Bauer und Konsorten*, 1845.
———— *Das kommunistische Manifest*, 1847.
———— *Briefwechsel zwischen K. Marx und F. Engels*, 1913.
Masaryk, Th. G.: *Die philosophischen und soziologischen Grundlagen des Marxismus*, 1899.
———— *The Spirit of Russia*, 1919.
Masters, Edgar Lee: *Lincoln the Man*, 1931.
Mathiez, A.: *Études robespierristes*, 1897 and 1918.
———— *Les Origines des cultes révolutionaires*, 1904.
Mauthner, Fritz: *Beiträge zu einer Kritik der Sprache*, 1901-02.
———— *Die Sprache*, 1906.
———— *Der Atheismus und seine Geschichte im Abendlande*, 1921-23.
Meaux, Alfred: *Les luttes religieuses en France au XVIme siècle*, 1879.
Mehring, Franz: *Die Geschichte der deutschen Sozialdemokratie*, 1897.
———— *Karl Marx: Geschichte seines Lebens*, 1918.
Melegari, Dora: *La giovine Italia e Giuseppe Mazzini*, 1906.
Merriam, C. Edward: *A History of American Political Theories*, 1903
Merx, O.: *Thomas Münzer und Heinrich Pfeiffer*, 1889.
Meyer, Gustav: *Friedrich Engels*, 1920. Vol. I.
———— *Bismarck and Lassalle*, 1930.
Michels, Robert: *Political Parties*, 1915.
———— *Sozialismus und Fascismus in Italien*, 1925.
Mill, John Stuart: *Essay on Liberty*, 1859.
———— *Considerations on Representative Government*, 1861.
Mommsen, Th.: *Römische Geschichte*, 1854-56.
Montesquieu, Ch. L.: *Lettres persanes*, 1721.
———— *L'esprit des lois*, 1748.
Mosley, Oswald: *The Greater Britain*, 1934.
Mühlenbeck, E.: *Étude sur les origines de la Saint-Alliance*, 1885.
Müller, Max: *Science of Thought*, 1887.
Muñoz, Romero: *Colección de fueros municipales y cartas pueblas*, 1881
Mussolini, Benito: *My Autobiography*, 1928.
Muther, Richard: *Geschichte der Malerei*, 1909.
Myers, G.: *History of Canadian Wealth*, 1914.
Nearing, Scott: *Oil and the Germs of War*, 1916.
Nearing, Scott and J. Freeman: *Dollar Diplomacy*, 1925.
Nettlau, Max: *Michael Bakunin: Eine Biographie*, 1896-1900.
———— *Der Vorfrühling der Anarchie*, 1925.

Nettlau, Max: *Miguel Bakunin, la Internacional y la Alianza en España*, 1925.
——— *Der Anarchismus von Proudhon zu Kropotkin*, 1927.
——— *Bakunin e l'Internazionale in Italia dal 1864 al 1872*, 1928.
——— *Documentos ineditos sobre la Internacional y la Alianza en España*, 1930.
——— *Anarchisten und Sozial-Revolutionäre*, 1931.
——— *Errico Malatesta: Das Leben eines Anarchisten*, 1922.
——— *Eliseo Reclus: La vida de un sabio justo y rebelde*, 1929.
——— *Bibliographie de l'anarchie*, 1897.

Newbold, Walton J. T.: *How Europe Armed for War*, 1916.

Nieuwenhuis, Domela F.: *Le socialisme en danger*, 1897.

Nomad, Max: *Rebels and Renegades*, 1932.

Nordau, Max: *The Interpretation of History*, 1910.

Olveira, J. P.: *Historia de la civilización Ibérica*, 1894.

Onken, W.: *Die Staatslehre des Aristoteles*, 1870.

Oppenheimer, Franz: *Moderne Geschichtsphilosophie*, 1909.
——— *Die soziale Frage und der Sozialismus*, 1912.
——— *System der Soziologie*, 1922-29.

Orsi, P.: *Cavour and the Making of Modern Italy*, 1926, new ed.

Paine, Thomas: *Common Sense*, 1776.
——— *The Rights of Man*, 1792.
——— *The Age of Reason*, 1794-1807.

Pater, W. H.: *Studies in the History of the Renaissance*, 1873.

Pellarin, Ch.: *Charles Fourier: sa vie et sa théorie*, 1872.

Pero, Mejia: *Comunidades de Castilla.*

Pi y Margall, Francisco: *La reacción y la revolución*, 1854.
——— *Las nacionalidades*, 1876.
——— *La federación*, 1880.

Pilsudski, Joseph: *The Memories of a Polish Revolutionary and Soldier*, 1931.

Piron, G.: *Les doctrines économiques en France depuis 1870*, 1925.

Pisacane, Carlo: *La rivoluzione*, 1860.

Plato: *The State.*

Pohlenz, M.: *Staatsgedanke und Staatslehre der Griechen*, 1923.

Prescott, W.: *History of the Conquest of Mexico*, 1843.
——— *The Conquest of Peru*, 1846.

Price, Richard: *Observations on the Nature of Civil Liberty and the Justice and Policy of the War With America*, 1776.

Proudhon, J. P.: *De la création de l'ordre dans l'humanité, ou principes d'organisation politique*, 1848.
——— *Idée générale de la révolution aux XIXme siècle*, 1851.
——— *Philosophie du progrès*, 1853.
——— *De la justice dans la révolution et dans l'eglise*, 1858.
——— *La guerre et la paix*, 1861.
——— *La féderation et l'unité en Italie*, 1862.
——— *Du principe féderatif et la nécessité de reconstituer le parti de la révolution*, 1863.
——— *Nouvelles observations sur l'unité italienne*, 1865.

Proudhon, J. P.: *De la capacité politique des classes ouvrières*, 1865.
———— *Correspondance de P. J. Proudhon*, 1875.

Quinet, Edgar: *Les révolutions d'Italie*, 1848-52.
———— *La révolution*, 1865.
———— *L'esprit nouveau*, 1870-74.

Ranke, Leopold: *Deutsche Geschichte im Zeitalter der Reformation*, 1839-47.
———— *Die römischen Päpste, ihre Kirche und ihr Staat im 16. und 17. Jahrhundert*, 1834-36.

Reclus, Elie: *Les primitifs*, 1903.

Reclus, Elisée: *L'homme et la terre*, 1905-08.
———— *L'evolution, la révolution et l'idéal anarchique*, 1897.

Riley, I. Woodbridge: *American Philosophy: The Early Schools*, 1907.

Rittingshausen, M.: *Die direkte Gesetzgebung durch das Volk*, 1868.

Robinet, J. B.: *Danton, homme d'état*, 1889.

Rogers, J. E. Thorold: *A History of Agriculture and Prices in England*, 1866-1902.
———— *Six Centuries of Work and Wages*, 1884.
———— *Economic Interpretation of History*, 1888.

Rosenberg, Alfred: *Der Mythus des 20. Jahrhunderts*, 1930.

Rosselli, N.: *Mazzini e Bakunin*, 1927.

Rostovtzieff, M. I.: *Social and Economic History of Rome*, 1926.

Rousseau, J. J.: *The Social Contract*, 1762.

Russell, Bertrand: *Roads to Freedom*, 1920.

Russell, C. E.: *Story of Wendell Phillips: Soldier of the Common Good*, 1914.

Sachs, Emanie: *The Terrible Siren*, 1928.

Sacken, E. von: *Katechismus der Baustile*, 1907.

St. Augustine: *The Confessions of St. Augustine.*
———— *Der Gottesstaat.*

Saint-Simon, Henri de: *Réorganisation de la société europeènne*, 1814.
———— *Du système industriel*, 1821.
———— *Le nouveau christianisme*, 1825.

Salvemini, G.: *The History of the Fascist Dictatorship in Italy*, 1927.

Sandoval, P.: *Historia del emperador Carlos V*, 1614, new ed., 1864.

Sayce, A. H.: *Religions of Ancient Egypt and Babylonia*, 1902.

Schubert-Soldern, Victor: *Die Borgia und ihre Zeit*, 1902.

Schulemann, G.: *Die Geschichte der Dalailamas*, 1911.

Schuster, F. M.: *Native American Anarchism*, 1932.

Sidney, Algernon: *Discourses Concerning Government*, 1763.

Simpson, F. M.: *A History of Architectural Development*, 1905-11.

Sismondi, J. Ch.: *Histoire des républiques italiennes du moyen âge*, 1817.
———— *Histoire de la renaissance et de la liberté en Italie*, 1832.

Smith, Adam: *The Theory of Moral Sentiments*, 1759.
———— *Enquiry into the Nature and Causes of the Wealth of Nations*, 1776.

Sorel, Albert: *L'Europe et la révolution française*, 1903-05.

Sorel, George: *Réflexions sur la violence*, 1909.
——— *La décomposition du marxisme*, 1908.
——— *Les illusions du progrès*, 1911, new ed.
Spencer, Herbert: *Social Statics: or the Conditions Essential to Human Happiness Specified and the First of Them Developed*, 1851.
——— *The Individual versus the State*, 1884.
Spengler, Oswald: *Der Untergang des Abendlandes*, 1918-22.
Spirito, Ugo: *Capitalismo e corporatismo*, 1933.
Spooner, Lysander: *Natural Law or the Science of Justice*, 1882.
Sprading, Ch. T.: *Liberty and the Great Libertarians*, 1913.
——— *Freedom and Its Fundamentals*, 1923.
Stalin, Joseph: *About the Opposition*, 1928.
Steinthal, H.: *Der Ursprung der Sprache im Zusammenhang mit den letzten Fragen alles Wissens*, 1851.
Stirner, Max: *Der Einzige und sein Eigentum*, 1845.
——— *Die Geschichte der Reaktion*, 1852.
Strasser, Vera: *Psychologie der Zusammenhänge und Begebenheiten*, 1921.
Strobel, H.: *The German Revolution and After*, 1922.
Suetonius: *The Lives of the Twelve Caesars*, 1931.
Tagore, Rabindranath: *Nationalism*, 1917.
Taine, H.: *Origines de la France contemporaine*, 1875-93.
——— *La philosophie de l'art*, 1881.
Tchernoff, J.: *Le parti républiquain au coup d' état et sous le second empire*, 1906.
Thierry, Augustin: *Considérations sur l'histoire de France*, 1827.
——— *Recueil des monuments inédits de l'histoire de Tier Etat*, 1850-70.
Thoreau, D. H.: *On the Duty of Civil Disobedience* (first published under the title: *Resistance to Civil Government*), 1849.
——— *Life Without Principle*, 1863.
Tivaroni, C.: *Storia critica del risorgimento italiano*, 1892-94.
Tocqueville, A.: *De la démocratie en Amerique*, 1839-40.
Tolstoy, Leo: *A Short Exposition of the Gospels*, 1890.
——— *Church and State, and Other Essays*, 1991.
——— *The Slavery of our Time*, 1900.
——— *War*, 1892.
Toulmin-Smith: *English Guilds*, 1870.
——— *Local Self-Government*, 1851.
Traumann, Rudolf: *Die Monarchomachen*, 1895.
Trotsky, Leon: *Defence of Terrorism*, 1920.
——— *Dictatorship versus Democracy*, 1922.
——— *Lenin*, 1925.
——— *The Permanent Revolution*, 1931.
Tucker, Benjamin R.: *Instead of a Book*, 1893.
Ular, Alexander: *Die Politik*, 1906.
——— *L'empire chinois-russe*, 1904.
Urales, F.: *La evolución de la filosofía en España*, 1909.
Vera y González, E.: *Pi y Margall y la política contemporanea*, 1886.

Vogl, Carl: *Peter Chelčicky, ein Prophet an der Wende der Zeiten*, 1922.

Voltaire: *Traité sur la tolérance*, 1763.

Waddell, L. A.: *The Buddhism of Tibet*, 1895.

Wagner, Richard: *Kunst und Revolution*, 1849.

———— *Das Kunstwerk der Zukunft*, 1850.

Warren, Josiah: *True Civilization: A Subject of Vital and Serious Interest to All People, but Most Immediately to the Men and Women of Labor and Sorrow*, 1863.

Watson, John: *Comte, Mill and Spencer*, 1895.

Wellers, E.: *Die Freiheitsbestrebungen der Deutschem im 18. und 19. Jahrhundert dargestellt in Zeugnissen ihrer Literatur*, 1847.

Whipple, Leon: *The Story of Civil Liberty in the United States*, 1927.

Wilda, W. C.: *Das Gildenwesen im Mittelalter*, 1831.

Wilde, Oscar: *The Soul of Man Under Socialism*, 1891.

Young, Arthur: *Travels in France During the Years 1787, 1788, 1789, 1794.*

Zancada, P.: *El obrero en España*, 1902.

Zimmermann, W.: *Allgemeine Geschichte des grossen deutschen Bauernkrieges*, 1856, 2nd ed.

INDEX

INDEX